HERMETICA

THE ANCIENT GREEK AND
LATIN WRITINGS WHICH
CONTAIN RELIGIOUS OR
PHILOSOPHIC TEACHINGS
ASCRIBED TO

HERMES TRISMEGISTUS

SHAMBHALA PUBLICATIONS, INC.
Horticultural Hall
300 Massachusetts Avenue
Boston, Massachusetts 02115
www.shambhala.com

Printed in the United States of America

Distributed in the United States by Random House, Inc.,
and in Canada by Random House of Canada Ltd

LIBRARY OF CONGRESS CATALOGING-IN-PUBLICATION DATA

Main entry under title:
Hermetica : the ancient Greek and Latin writings which contain religious or
    philosophic teachings ascribed to Hermes Trismegistus.
    Greek and Latin, with English translation.
    Bibliography: p.
    Includes index.
    ISBN 0-87773-339-2 (pbk.)
    ISBN 1-57062-631-6 (pbk.)
    1. Hermetism—Early works to 1800. I. Hermes, Trismegistus.
    II. Scott, Walter, 1855–1925. III. Corpus Hermeticum. English & Greek.
    BF1600.H474   1985   85-8198
    299′.93
    BVG 01

HERMETICA

THE ANCIENT GREEK AND LATIN
WRITINGS WHICH CONTAIN RELIGIOUS
OR PHILOSOPHIC TEACHINGS ASCRIBED TO

HERMES TRISMEGISTUS

EDITED

WITH ENGLISH TRANSLATION AND NOTES

BY

WALTER SCOTT

VOLUME II

Notes on the Corpus Hermeticum

SHAMBHALA
BOSTON 1985

HERMETICA

✤

Plan of the Work

VOL. I. Introduction, Texts
and Translation.

VOLS. II & III. Commentary.

VOL. IV. Testimonia, Appen-
dices and Indices.

CORPVS HERMETICVM

LIBELLVS I

Contents

(i) THE REVELATION. §§ 1–26.

The man who speaks was visited in his sleep by the supreme
Mind, who taught him as follows.

The beginning of things. In the beginning was God (who is
pictured as a boundless expanse of light), and God alone. Then,
formless matter (pictured as a cloud of darkness) came into being.
The formless matter first assumed form by changing into a watery
substance. And from God came forth a Word (hypostatized, and
called son of God), who worked upon the watery substance.
§§ 4–6.

In God are included innumerable Powers; and the Intelligible
World,—the archetype of the Sensible World,—is made up of these
Powers of God. §§ 7–8 a.

Formation of the Sensible World. The watery substance, by the
operation of the Word, was differentiated into (1) fire, which rose
aloft; (2) air, which occupied the region next below the fire; and
(3) gross matter (earth and water intermixed), which remained
below. §§ 8 b, 5 b. (Later on, earth and water were separated,
§ 11 b.)

The making of living beings. The supreme Mind (i. e. God) gave
birth to a second Mind, called 'the Demiurgus', whose station is
the highest sphere of the region of fire; and the Demiurgus made
out of fire and air the seven Planets, whose function is to govern
the sublunar world. Acting in conjunction with the Word (who
now quitted the grosser elements below, and flew up to the region
of fire), the Demiurgus set the Planets circling in their several
spheres.. §§ 9–11 a.

Then, at the bidding of the Demiurgus, the earth and the water
brought forth the irrational animals. § 11 b.

The origin of man. The supreme Mind (i. e. God) gave birth to
(incorporeal) Man, a Being like to God himself. This Man at first
took up his abode in the highest sphere of heaven, beside his brother
the Demiurgus. Thence he descended to the planetary region;

and from each of the seven Planets he received something of its special character. He then looked down from the lowest sphere of heaven into the world of gross matter, the abode of corporeal Nature. He saw in the material things of the world below the reflected image of his own God-derived beauty; and attracted by it, he descended into the region of gross matter, and took corporeal Nature to him as his bride; and the two were joined in one (i. e. the human soul was incarnated). §§ 12–14.

Hence it is that men, though incorporeal and immortal in respect of their true being, are yet in part corporeal and mortal. § 15.

Corporeal Nature, married to the incorporeal Man, brought forth seven Men, who bore the several characters of the seven Planets. Each of these seven Men was (like ourselves) composed of (1) a gross body, made of earth and water; (2) a vital spirit, made of fire and air; and (3) an incorporeal soul and mind.

The seven Men were bisexual (as were the beasts also); and in that state they dwelt on earth until the end of the first age. §§ 16, 17.

Then, each of the seven bisexual Men (as well as each of the bisexual beasts) was divided into two separate beings, the one male, and the other female. God bade the seven couples breed; and from them is descended the existing race of men and women. § 18 a.

The conditions of man's life on earth. If men yield to carnal desire, and love the body, they fall under the power of death; but if they identify themselves with that in them which is incorporeal, they are immortal, and attain to the Good (i. e. to union with God). §§ 18 b, 19.

The men who fail thus to 'recognize themselves' deserve the death which they incur, ⟨because they are guilty of the sin of loving the body;⟩ for the body is composed of matter, and matter is the source of all evil. But those who 'recognize themselves' attain to the Good, because the incorporeal self which they recognize is of one substance with God, and in virtue of it they are sons of God. §§ 20, 21.

But a man cannot 'recognize himself' unless he has Mind in him. Mind enters into men that are good and pure; and its presence in them makes them devote themselves to loving worship of God, and excludes the evil promptings of the bodily senses. But when

men are wicked, Mind abandons them, and its place is taken by the
Avenging Daemon, who tortures them with the fires of evil passion.
§§ 22, 23.

The ascent of the disembodied soul. At death, the gross body is
resolved into earth and water ; the ⟨vital spirit⟩, with the bodily
senses ⟨of which it was the organ⟩, is reabsorbed into ⟨the atmo-
sphere⟩; and stripped of these integuments, the man rises above
the sublunar world, and enters the region of the heavens. As he
mounts upward through the planetary spheres, he gives back to each
planet in succession the evil passion which had come to him from
that planet ; and thus cleansed from all corruption, he takes up his
abode for a time in the highest sphere of heaven. Lastly, he quits
the material universe, and enters the incorporeal world above it,
where dwell the Powers of God ; and himself becoming one among
these Powers, he ' comes to be in God '. §§ 24-26 a.

(ii) THE THANKSGIVING. §§ 30–32.

The man woke from his sleep, full of joy at the revelation that
had been vouchsafed to him, and gave thanks to God in a hymn
of praise.

(iii) THE PREACHING. §§ 27–29.

Then, in obedience to the injunction of his divine visitant (§ 26 b),
he proceeded to make known to his fellow men what had been
made known to him, and teach them how they might be saved.
'Shake off your drunken sleep,' he said ; ' repent; cease to give
yourselves up to death ; accept immortal life.' And some mocked ;
but others besought him to teach them, and he taught them.

The theology of *Corp.* I may be summarized as follows. There
is a supreme God, who is described as ' Mind ' (νοῦς), and as ' Life
and Light '. The supreme God has three sons, viz. the Logos, the
Demiurgus-Nous, and the Anthropos. The Logos and the Demiurgus-
Nous are God's agents in the making of the world. The Logos
operates in the first stage of the *cosmopoiia*, viz. the separation of
the elements. The Demiurgus-Nous operates in the later stage,
viz. the making of living beings (other than man); it is he that
makes the heavenly bodies (immortal ζῷα), and causes the lower
elements to bring forth the mortal and irrational ζῷα. But the Logos
and the Demiurgus-Nous are ' of one substance ', and ultimately

coalesce into one. Anthropos, the third son of God, is a personification of the incorporeal part of man, which has issued from God,
and is destined to go back into God.

Side by side with the conception of the three Sons of God stands
that of the 'Powers' (δυνάμεις) of God. According to this second
conception, God contains or is made up of innumerable Powers;
and individual human souls, if they are true to themselves, will
ultimately become Powers of God, and take their place as such
among his other Powers. It would be possible to bring these two
conceptions into connexion, by saying that the three Sons of God
are his three highest Powers; but the author himself has not thus
connected them. (Perhaps however the δύναμις μεγίστη which is
spoken of in § 5 b may be identified with the Demiurgus-Nous.)

Corp. I is the only *Hermeticum* in which the notion of a transcendental Person named Anthropos presents itself. But a more
or less similar use of the name Anthropos occurs repeatedly in
Christian Gnostic writings.

There can be little doubt that Ἄνθρωπος, thus employed as a
person-name, first came into use as a translation of the Hebrew
name Adam, which means 'man'. Even among Jews who were
uninfluenced by Greek philosophy, there was a tendency to magnify
Adam into something more than a mere man. Some of their
Rabbis said that Adam was bisexual; that his body was at first of
such huge bulk that it filled the world from end to end; and that,
before his fall, he was in possession of the 'heavenly radiance' or
'glory', and shone with such brightness that he obscured the sun.[1]
But an Adam more closely resembling the Anthropos of *Corp.* I
is to be found in Philo, *De opif. mundi* 23. 69—29. 88. Philo there
explains that the 'man' whose making is described in *Gen.* I. 26
(ποιήσωμεν ἄνθρωπον κατ᾽ εἰκόνα ἡμετέραν κ.τ.λ.) is not an individual
man, but the ἰδέα of man (in the Platonic sense of ἰδέα) or the γένος
man. *De opif. mundi* 24. 76 : πάνυ δὲ καλῶς, τὸ γένος ἄνθρωπον
εἰπών, διέκρινε τὰ εἴδη, φήσας ἄρρεν τε καὶ θῆλυ δεδημιουργῆσθαι,
μήπω τῶν ἐν μέρει μορφὴν λαβόντων, ἐπειδὴ τὰ προσεχέστατα τῶν

---

[1] See Bousset *Hauptprobleme der Gnosis*, 1907, p. 198, where references to the
Talmud are given. In Kap. IV ('Der Urmensch') of that book, Bousset has
brought together much material that is valuable as bearing on the origin and
history of the Anthropos-doctrine ; but I find myself unable to agree with some of
his conclusions. Bousset has dealt with the same subject more briefly in his
Religion des Judentums im Neutest. Zeitalter, 1906, pp. 404-407.

LIBELLVS I 5

εἰδῶν ἐνυπάρχει τῷ γένει, καὶ ὥσπερ ἐν κατόπτρῳ διαφαίνεται τοῖς ὀξὺ καθορᾶν δυναμένοις.¹ Afterwards, commenting on *Gen.* 2. 7 (ἔπλασεν ὁ θεὸς τὸν ἄνθρωπον χοῦν ἀπὸ τῆς γῆς κ.τ.λ.), he says that the man whose making is described in this latter passage is the individual man Adam, the ancestor of all individual men of later generations. *Ib.* 46. 134: διαφορὰ παμμεγέθης ἐστὶ τοῦ τε νῦν πλασθέντος ἀνθρώπου καὶ τοῦ κατὰ τὴν εἰκόνα θεοῦ γεγονότος πρότερον· ὁ μὲν γὰρ διαπλασθεὶς αἰσθητὸς ἤδη, μετέχων ποιότητος, ἐκ σώματος καὶ ψυχῆς συνεστώς, ἀνὴρ ἢ γυνή, φύσει θνητός· ὁ δὲ κατὰ τὴν εἰκόνα (i. e. the 'man' spoken of in *Gen.* 1. 26) ἰδέα τις ἢ γένος ἢ σφραγίς,² νοητός, ἀσώματος, οὔτ' ἄρρεν οὔτε θῆλυ, ἄφθαρτος φύσει.³ The Anthropos of *Corp.* I corresponds to the ἄνθρωπος of *Gen.* 1. 26 as interpreted by Philo, inasmuch as he is a personification of the ἰδέα or γένος of humanity; but he also corresponds to the ἄνθρωπος of *Gen.* 2. 7 as interpreted by Philo, inasmuch as he is the ancestor of the human race.⁴ The author of *Corp.* I must have got his conception of Anthropos from Jewish thinkers whose speculations were closely connected with those of Philo. His Anthropos is not the Adam of Genesis, but a transcendental Adam evolved by philosophic Jews out of a combination of *data* supplied by *Genesis* with the Platonic conception of the ἰδέα ἀνθρώπου or αὐτοάνθρωπος.⁵

¹ Philo also says that ὁ κατ' εἰκόνα θεοῦ ἄνθρωπος is the human νοῦς. *Ib.* 23. 69 : τὴν δὲ ἐμφέρειαν (i. e. the likeness of man to God, implied in the words κατ' εἰκόνα) μηδεὶς εἰκαζέτω σώματος χαρακτῆρι· ... ἡ δὲ εἰκὼν λέλεκται κατὰ τὸν τῆς ψυχῆς ἡγεμόνα νοῦν· πρὸς γὰρ ἕνα τὸν τῶν ὅλων ἐκεῖνον ὡς ἂν ἀρχέτυπον ὁ ἐν ἑκάστῳ τῶν κατὰ μέρος ἀπεικονίσθη. It is not clear how this is to be reconciled with the statement that the 'man' in question is the ἰδέα of man, or the γένος man.
² σφραγίς here means the one seal by which many similar impressions are stamped,—the 'type'.
³ Bousset *Rel. des Jud.* p. 405 (see also *Hauptprobleme der Gnosis*, p. 195) says 'Philo hat nun diese Ausführungen nicht aus Gen. 1 u. 2 herausgesponnen, sondern sie an diesen Bericht herangebracht. ... Wir haben auch gar keinen Grund, hier eine Anleihe Philos bei der hellenischen Philosophie anzunehmen, wo so mannigfache und bedeutende Parallelen auf einen Einfluss vom Orient her schliessen lassen '. (One of the Oriental parallels to which he refers is that of the Persian 'Urmensch' Gayomarth.) But I think that Bousset is here mistaken. It seems to me that Philo's Adam (and likewise the Anthropos of *Corp.* I) can be adequately accounted for as a result of the interpretation of *Genesis* by Jews acquainted with Greek philosophy, and that there is no need to assume Persian or other Oriental influence.
⁴ Irenaeus 1. 18. 2 says that some of the followers of the Gnostic Marcus ἄλλον θέλουσι τὸν κατ' εἰκόνα καὶ ὁμοίωσιν Θεοῦ γεγονότα ἀρσενόθηλυν ἄνθρωπον, καὶ τοῦτον εἶναι τὸν πνευματικόν· ἄλλον δὲ τὸν ἐκ τῆς γῆς πλασθέντα. This explanation of *Gen.* 1. 26 and 2. 7 closely resembles that of Philo, who says *inter alia* that ὁ κατ' εἰκόνα θεοῦ ἄνθρωπος is the human νοῦς (= the πνευματικὸς ἄνθρωπος of the followers of Marcus, and the οὐσιώδης ἄνθρωπος of *Corp.* I. 15).
⁵ Cf. Plotinus 6. 7. 6 : ὁ ἐν νῷ ἄνθρωπος (ἔχει ἐν μιμήσει (?)) τὸν πρὸ πάντων τῶν ἀνθρώπων ἄνθρωπον (= the 'idea' of man). But it is possible that the figure

Sources. The doctrine of *Corp.* I is fundamentally Platonic. The Platonic contrast between νοῦς and αἴσθησις, νοητά and αἰσθητά, things incorporeal and things corporeal, presents itself throughout; and the passage about the νοητὸς κόσμος (§§ 7, 8 a) implies acceptance of the Platonic theory of ideal παραδείγματα. The writer speaks as a Platonist in his description of the twofold nature of man (§ 15); and he is an adherent of Platonism in his conviction that the human soul has descended from a higher world, and is destined to return to the higher world whence it came.

In his account of the differentiation of the sexes (§ 18), he has been influenced by Plato's *Symposium*; and reminiscences of particular passages in Plato's writings may be recognized, with more or less probability, in § 12, οὗ ἠγάσθη ὡς ἰδίου τόκου κ.τ.λ. (Pl. *Tim.* 37 c): § 21, οὐ πάντες γὰρ ἄνθρωποι νοῦν ἔχουσιν; κ.τ.λ. (Pl. *Tim.* 51 E): § 19, ἐκ πλάνης ἔρωτος (Pl. *Phaedr.* 238 B). The term τὸ ἀγαθόν, as used in §§ 19, 26 a, is of Platonic origin.

In distinguishing a first νοῦς and a second νοῦς, and assigning the name δημιουργός to the second, the writer is in agreement with certain Platonists of the Roman Empire, and especially with Numenius.

On the other hand, he ignores the Platonic doctrine of *metensomatosis* or reincarnation; and while he is in accord with the Platonists in regarding ὕλη as the source of evil, he appears to reject the Platonic view that ὕλη is without beginning (§ 4).

A trace of Aristotelian influence may perhaps be seen in what is said in § 11 a concerning the eternity of circular motion.

In his physics, the writer's position resembles that of the Stoics. His account of the separation of the four cosmic elements (§ 5 b) agrees with Stoic descriptions of the *diacosmesis*; and the separated elements are disposed by him, as by the Stoics, in a series of concentric spheres (region of fire, divided into the sphere of the fixed stars and the seven planetary spheres; atmosphere; water and earth). The main lines of this system of cosmology had been laid down by Plato and Aristotle; but it was by the Stoics that it was formulated

employed by Plato in *Rep.* 9. 588 C D also contributed. It is there said that the human soul is made up of three things joined together, viz. (1) a many-headed beast (τὸ ἐπιθυμητικόν), (2) a lion (τὸ θυμοειδές), and (3) an ἄνθρωπος (τὸ λογιστικόν). Cf. Iambl. *Protrept.* 5: τὸν ἐν ἡμῖν θεῖον ἄνθρωπον τοῦ πολυκεφάλου θρέμματος ἐγκρατῆ ποιητέον. This 'divine ἄνθρωπος in us' is the οὐσιώδης ἄνθρωπος of *Corp.* 1. 15.

On the Jewish side, the conception of the Anthropos may have been influenced by speculations based on the passage about 'one like unto a son of man' in Daniel 7. 13, and on the use of 'the son of man' as an appellation of the Messiah in Jewish apocalyptic writings (Enoch &c.).

and popularized in the very shape in which we find it in this document. And as we know that Platonism was affected by Stoic influence from the first century B. c. onward, it is probable that the writer's immediate teachers were Platonists of the syncretic school which came into being at that time. Among the terms and conceptions of Stoic origin which occur in *Corp.* I may be noted κατωφερής, § 4 &c.: εἱμαρμένη, § 15 &c.: πνεῦμα (material), in the two senses *air* (§ 9) and *vital spirit* (§ 17): πρόνοια, § 19. In identifying εἱμαρμένη with the influence of the heavenly bodies (§ 9 *fin.*), the writer is in accord with the Stoics of the Roman Empire rather than with Chrysippus.

So far, the doctrine of *Corp.* I may be described as that of a Stoicizing Platonist. But with this Hellenic doctrine are combined ingredients of Jewish origin.[1] From the 'watery substance' onward, the *cosmogonia* of § 8 b ff. is constructed on the same plan as that of *Genesis* ; and verbal reminiscences of *Genesis* may be seen in § 5 b *fin.*, τὸν ⟨ἐπάνω τοῦ ὕδατος ?⟩ ἐπιφερόμενον πνευματικὸν λόγον (*Gen.* 1. 2): § 11 b, ἐξήνεγκεν ⟨ἡ γῆ⟩ ζῷα τετράποδα κ.τ.λ. (Gen. 1. 24 f.): § 12, τὴν τοῦ πατρὸς εἰκόνα ἔχων (*Gen.* 1. 26 f.): § 17, ὁ δὲ ἄνθρωπος ... ἐγένετο εἰς ψυχὴν καὶ νοῦν (*Gen.* 2. 7): § 18, αὐξάνεσθε ... καὶ πληθύνεσθε (*Gen.* 9. 17 and 1. 22, 28). The notion of the splitting of bisexual beings may have been connected in the writer's mind with *Gen.* 2. 21–24, as well as with Pl. *Sympos.* The 'end of the first period', and the following 'speech of God' (§ 18), correspond to the Deluge and the speech of God to Noah in *Gen.* 9. 16 ff. ; and the marriage of 'Man' and 'Nature' in § 14 corresponds to the story of Adam and Eve in *Gen.* 2.

But among the Jewish ingredients of the doctrine of *Corp.* I are included things which could not have been suggested by a mere reading of the text of *Genesis* ; viz. the conception of the δυνάμεις of God, that of the Logos, and that of the transcendental Anthropos. These conceptions must have originated in a school of Jewish thinkers who had brought to bear on the study of their sacred books a knowledge of Greek philosophy.

Now in every one of the points that I have spoken of, the writer's position closely resembles that of Philo Judaeus. Philo also taught a form of Platonism modified by an intermixture of Stoic conceptions,

---

[1] The fact that the contents of *Corp.* I are partly derived from Jewish sources is recognized in a *scholion* on *Corp.* I. 18, which is ascribed to Psellus. See Psellus in *Testim.*

and so interpreted the narrative of *Genesis* as to bring it into accordance with this Hellenic doctrine. The conceptions of the λόγος and the δυνάμεις of God which we find in *Corp.* I are similar to those which we find in Philo; and the Anthropos of *Corp.* I is in the main identical with the Adam of *Gen.* 1 and 2 as explained by Philo. The writer of *Corp.* I cannot have been himself a member of the Jewish community; for there is no trace in this document of that submission to the Jewish Law, and that interest in the Jewish nation, which are conspicuous in Philo's writings. We must conclude then that he was a man of Gentile race and Hellenic education, who had accepted the teachings either of Philo himself, or of Jews of the same school as Philo. How much of his Platonism was transmitted to him by these same Jewish teachers, and how much of it he had learnt directly from Pagan authorities, it is impossible to say.

This would suffice to account for the main body of doctrine in *Corp.* I. But there are certain notions which seem to have been derived from other sources. In his use of the terms *light* and *darkness*, the author may possibly have been influenced by the teaching of the Zoroastrians. His description of the descent and ascent of the soul through the planetary spheres (§§ 13 a and 25) may have been suggested by the similar doctrine of the Mithraists.

The name Poimandres appears to be of Egyptian origin; but apart from this, there is little to indicate that the writer was influenced by the indigenous religion of Egypt. It is possible however that his application of the term ἀρσενόθηλυς to God, and his use of ζωή with reference to God, may have been derived from Egyptian sources.

In reading *Corp.* I, we are here and there reminded of passages in the New Testament; e. g. in the phrase ζωὴ καὶ φῶς (cf. *Ev. Joh.*), and the words παρέδωκας αὐτῷ τὴν πᾶσαν ἐξουσίαν, § 32 (cf. *Ev. Matth.* 28. 18). There are also things in which *Corp.* I resembles the writings of some of the Christian Gnostics; e. g. the description of the descent and ascent of the human soul; the notion of the δημιουργός as a subordinate Being who resides in the highest sphere of heaven; the conception of the Anthropos; and the use of the terms ἡ αὐθεντία and ἡ ὀγδοαδικὴ φύσις. But these resemblances are not to be taken as proofs of borrowing on either side; they rather indicate the use of common sources. The Christian Gnostics, like the author of *Corp.* I, derived a part of their doctrine from a Platonism modified by Stoic influence, and another part of it from Jewish speculations; and so far as their sources were the same, they spoke in similar language. But if the author of *Corp*. I had read the writings of Christian Gnostics, we might expect to find in this document some traces of the Christian element of Gnosticism also. The most distinctive characteristic of Christian doctrine, as compared with that of other religions of the time, was the conception of a 'Saviour', i. e. a divine Person who has descended from a higher world to rescue human souls from their fallen condition;[1] and of this conception, which is prominent in the systems of the Christian Gnostics as well as in that of the Catholic Christians, not the slightest trace appears in *Corp*. I. If the writer has been in any way influenced by his Christian neighbours, it is not in his doctrine that this influence is to be recognized, but rather in his view of his own function as a teacher. He regards himself as one on whom is laid the task of calling mankind to repentance, and ' teaching them how they may be saved '; and it is not impossible that in this respect the author of *Corp*. I was following the example set by the preachers of the Christian Gospel.

Relations of Libellus I to other Hermetica. The author of *Corp*. I seeks to make known to all mankind the truth which has been revealed to him. In this respect, his attitude is very different from that of the Hermetists in general, who depict the teacher as speaking in private to one or two select pupils, and in some instances, expressly bidding his disciples keep secret what they learn from him. (See *Corp*. XIII *fin.*; *Ascl. Lat.* 1 b ; Stob. *Exc.* XI. 4, 5.) The writer of *Ascl. Lat.* I does indeed (in c. 12 b) protest against the φθόνος of those who would debar men from the *gnosis*; but even there, no public preaching is suggested ; and apart from *Corp*. I, the only *Hermeticum* in which the teacher offers himself as a guide to men at large is *Corp*. VII. That document is a fragment of a missionary sermon of precisely the same kind as that of which the heads are given in *Corp*. I. 27 f.; and *Corp*. VII so closely resembles *Corp*. I in thought and diction, that it seems probable that both were written by the same person.

The writer of *Corp*. XIII refers to *Corp*. I as a document known

---

[1] Analogies to the Christian notion of a 'Saviour' may, no doubt, be discovered here and there in other religions of the Roman Empire. For instance, such an analogy may be seen in the *Kore Kosmu*, where we are told that Isis and Osiris came down from heaven to earth to civilize mankind. But in the main, the distinction holds good. The gods of the Pagan mystery-cults might be called 'saviours', but were not held to have 'come down' in the same sense as the Christian Saviour.

to him and his readers. In his time, it was already assumed that the unnamed prophet who speaks in *Corp.* I is Hermes Trismegistus.

The words of *Corp.* XVI. 16 (ταύτην δὲ τὴν διοίκησιν Ἑρμῆς εἱμαρμένην ἐκάλεσεν) look like a reference to *Corp.* I. 9 (ἡ διοίκησις αὐτῶν εἱμαρμένη καλεῖται); and if it is so, the writer of *Corp.* XVI also must have read *Corp.* I, and identified the man who speaks in it with Hermes. But this cannot be considered certain; for it is possible that both authors got the phrase from some document unknown to us. The words ἔρως . . . ὁ πλανώμενος καὶ πλανῶν in *Corp.* XVI. 16 resemble ἐκ πλάνης ἔρωτος in *Corp.* I. 19; but this resemblance counts for little, as the expression may have been suggested to both writers independently by the language of Pl. *Phaedrus* 238 B.

The *cosmogonia* of *Corp.* III resembles that of *Corp.* I, both alike being based on *Genesis*; and the phrase αὐξάνεσθαι ἐν αὐξήσει καὶ πληθύνεσθαι ἐν πλήθει, which occurs in both, must have been either borrowed by one of the two writers from the other, or taken by both from a common Jewish source. But on the other hand, these two documents differ widely in doctrine. The writer of *Corp.* III holds that men cease to exist at death; the writer of *Corp.* I asserts with the strongest emphasis the immortality of human souls. The Hellenic element in *Corp.* III is Stoic, and not Platonic; the Hellenic element in *Corp.* I is mainly Platonic. It is in the Jewish ingredient that the resemblance consists; but even in this, there is a difference; for the Jewish element in *Corp.* III appears to be derived immediately from the text of *Genesis* (or, in the case of the phrase αὐξάνεσθαι κ.τ.λ., from a paraphrase of *Genesis*), whereas the Jewish element in *Corp.* I includes conceptions evolved from *Genesis* by speculation closely related to that of Philo. It may be considered certain then that *Corp.* I and *Corp.* III were not written by the same man; and notwithstanding the points of resemblance, it is doubtful whether either of these two documents was known to the writer of the other.

Ascl. Lat. I. 7 ('homo duplex est, et eius una pars . . . οὐσιώδης', &c.) closely resembles *Corp.* I. 15; and the interpolated passage *Corp.* X. 19 b-22 a has much in common with *Corp.* I. 22 f. But in these cases also, it is impossible to say whether the similarity is due to direct borrowing, or to the use of common sources.

We may conclude then that *Corp.* I was certainly known to the

writer of *Corp.* XIII, and may or may not have been known to the
writers of *Corp.* XVI, *Corp.* III, *Ascl. Lat.* I, and *Corp.* X. 19 b–22 a.
But there is nothing to suggest that it was known to any of the
Hermetic writers except these; and on the whole, *Corp.* I (together
with *Corp.* VII, which may be regarded as an appendage to it) stands
apart from the main body of Hermetic literature. In his open
proclamation of the truth to all who are willing to hear it, this
author differs from the Hermetists in general (including the writer of
Corp. XIII). The name Poimandres occurs nowhere else in the
extant *Hermetica*, except in the passage in *Corp.* XIII where it is
mentioned in connexion with *Corp.* I; the conception of the
transcendental Anthropos does not occur in any of the other documents; and that of the hypostatized Logos is hardly to be found
elsewhere in the Hermetic writings, except in a few sentences quoted
by Cyril. There is reason to think that *Corp.* I and *Corp.* VII were
not originally attributed to Hermes; and it seems probable that
they were written in complete independence of the Hermetic
tradition; that their author was an Alexandrian Platonist who had
come under the influence of Jewish teachers; and that it was not
until most of our *Hermetica* were already in existence, that these two
documents passed into the hands of a Hermetist, and were ascribed
by him to the legendary founder of his religion.

Date. The fact that an extract from *Corp.* I (viz. the *eulogia*,
§§ 31, 32) occurs in a Papyrus of the third century A. D. makes it
certain that this Libellus was written before the end of that century.
The intermixture of Stoic conceptions with its Platonism makes it
certain that it was not written before the first century B. C. Its close
connexion with Philo makes it almost certain that it was not written
until after the Christian era; and the importance attributed to the
influence of the planets points in the same direction. The affinity
of *Corp.* I with the teaching of Numenius (who wrote between 150
and 200 A. D., and is the earliest Pagan Platonist that is known to
have been influenced by Jewish speculation) suggests the second
century A. D. rather than the first; and its resemblances to the
writings of the Christian Gnostics also tell in favour of the second
century. As the writer of *Corp.* XIII refers to *Corp.* I as a known
document, and attributes it to Hermes, it must have been in existence
for some considerable time when *Corp.* XIII was written. There is
reason to think that all our *Hermetica* (or at any rate almost all of

them) were written before A. D. 300;[1] and if *Corp.* XIII is to be dated before A. D. 300, the date of *Corp.* I must be placed a good deal earlier. It is probable then that *Corp.* I was written between A. D. 100 and 200.

Title. The superscription Ἑρμοῦ τρισμεγίστου was probably not written by the author of *Corp.* I. In § 1, the speaker says that Poimandres 'called him by his name'; why is the name not given there? And it is again withheld in §§ 20, 21, where Poimandres says ὦ οὗτος. If the author had meant his readers to understand that the man who tells the story is Hermes Trismegistus, he would have written λέγειν ᾿Ω Ἑρμῆ κ.τ.λ. in place of καλεῖν μου τὸ ὄνομα in § 1, and ὦ Ἑρμῆ in place of ὦ οὗτος in § 20 f. In the text of the document, the writer refrains from naming the man whose vision and preaching he describes; hence it seems to follow that he must have refrained from naming him in the title also, and consequently, that Ἑρμοῦ τρισμεγίστου is a later addition.

If the author had intended to put the narrative into the mouth of a well-known personage, he would have named that personage. On the other hand, if he was speaking in his own person, and narrating what he had himself experienced, his withholding of the name can be more easily accounted for; he may have shrunk from obtruding himself, and felt that it was his message alone, and not his name, that mattered. There is therefore reason to think that the ἐγώ of this document is the author himself, and that *Corp.* I is in substance an autobiography, though the man who speaks has compressed the story of his life into the space of a single night of vision and a single day of preaching. We know from his own words that he was one who set forth to convert mankind, and teach men how they might be saved. In the first three centuries of the Christian era there were many men who took that task upon them. But no other record of him has come down to us; and there is nothing to tell us what success he met with in his enterprise, or how far his influence spread.[2]

§ 1. μετεωρισθείσης μὲν (μοι MSS.) τῆς διανοίας σφόδρα, ⟨⟨ὕπνῳ⟩⟩ ⟨δὲ⟩ κατασχεθεισῶν μου τῶν σωματικῶν αἰσθήσεων. It is necessary to insert ὕπνῳ here; for as the prophet afterwards assumes it to be known that he was asleep when the revelation came to him (§ 30, ὁ τοῦ σώματος

---

[1] A good many of them, if not all, were known to Lactantius, about A. D. 310.
[2] Except *Corp.* XIII, from which it may be inferred that at some later time there was a small fraternity in which *Corp.* I was regarded as a sacred book.

ὕπνος κ.τ.λ.), he must have said so in the first section. In sleep the bodily senses are suppressed, and the mind is for that reason free to rise to loftier heights than in waking life. Cf. Pindar, fr. 131, speaking of prophetic dreams: τὸ γάρ (*sc.* the soul) ἐστι μόνον | ἐκ θεῶν· εὕδει δὲ πρασσόντων μελέων, ἀτὰρ εὐδόντεσσιν ἐν πολλοῖς ὀνείροις | δείκνυσι τερπνῶν ἐφέρποισαν χαλεπῶν τε κρίσιν. Aristotle, fr. 12: ὅταν . . . ἐν τῷ ὑπνοῦν καθ' ἑαυτὴν γένηται ἡ ψυχή, τότε τὴν ἰδίαν ἀπολαβοῦσα φύσιν προμαντεύεταί τε καὶ προαγορεύει τὰ μέλλοντα. Cic. *Div.* 1. 115 : ' viget enim animus in somnis, liberque est sensibus et omni impeditione curarum, iacente et mortuo paene corpore'. Philo *Quis rer. div. heres* 51. 257, Wendland III, p. 59 : ὕπνος γὰρ νοῦ ἐγρήγορσίς ἐστιν αἰσθήσεως· καὶ γὰρ ἐγρήγορσις διανοίας αἰσθήσεως ἀπραξία.

⟨οὐ μέντοι⟩ καθάπερ ⟨τ⟩οἷ⟨ς⟩ [[ὕπνῳ]] βεβαρημένοι⟨ς⟩ ἐκ κόρου τροφῆς ἢ ἐκ κόπου σώματος. Cf. Aristot. Περὶ ὕπνου 456 b : μάλιστα γίνονται ὕπνοι ἀπὸ τῆς τροφῆς· . . . ἔτι δ' ἐκ κόπων ἐνίων. But the prophet cannot have said that his condition was like that of one who has fallen asleep after a heavy meal. A man gorged with food would be in no fit state to receive a divine revelation. See Pl. *Rep.* 9. 571 C–572 A. Cic. *Div.* 1. 60 f. : in our dreams, 'onusti cibo et vino perturbata et confusa cernimus'. *Ib.* 115 : '(Animus in somnis) omnia quae in natura rerum sunt videt, si modo temperatis escis modicisque potionibus ita est affectus ut sopito corpore ipse vigilet. Haec somniantis est divinatio'. Maximus Tyrius 10. 1, p. 111 Hobein : ἐνύπνιον γάρ τι ἐστὶν ἀτεχνῶς οὑτοσὶ ὁ δεῦρο βίος, καθ' ὃν ἡ ψυχή, κατορωρυγμένη ἐν σώματι, ὑπὸ κόρου καὶ πλησμονῆς μόγις πως ὀνειρώττει τὰ ὄντα. ἔρχονται δὲ ταῖς μὲν τῶν πολλῶν ψυχαῖς ὄνειροι δι' ἐλεφαντίνων πυλῶν (Hom. *Od.* 19. 562 ff.)· εἰ δέ που τίς ἐστι καθαρὰ ψυχὴ καὶ νηφάλιος, καὶ ὀλίγα ὑπὸ τοῦ δεῦρο κάρου καὶ τῆς πλησμονῆς ἐπιταραττομένη, εἰκός που ταύτῃ . . . ἀπαντᾶν ὀνείρατα σαφῆ . . . καὶ ἐγγύτατα τῷ ἀληθεῖ. It is possible that the words καθάπερ . . . ἐκ κόπου σώματος have been inserted by a later hand ; but if they were written by the author, he must have meant to say that the sleep in which the vision came was *not* like that which results from bodily repletion or fatigue. I have therefore inserted οὐ μέντοι.

Fulgentius quotes the words ἐκ κόρου τροφῆς ἢ ἐκ κόπου σώματος, but appears to have read κούφου in place of κόπου. The passage occurs in a chapter entitled *Fabula de novem Musis*, and runs thus : 'Septima (Musa appellata est) Terpsicore, id est delectans ⌜instructionem⌝ (-tione ?). Unde et Hermes in Opimandrae libro ait " eccurutrofes et cufusomatos ", id est, absque instructione escae et vacuo corpore. Ergo post inventionem[1] oportet te etiam discernere ac diiudicare quod ⌜invenies⌝ (inveneris?).' Thus he quotes the phrase merely to illustrate the meaning of the second half of the name Terpsicore. He identifies this -*core* (i. e. -*chore* misspelt) with κόρος, and translates κόρος by *instructio*. But what does he mean by *instructio*? The context seems to show that he means 'digestion'. He takes κόρος τροφῆς to signify 'digestion of food' in the literal sense ; and Terpsicore is she who 'delights[2] in digestion' in a metaphorical sense, i. e. finds pleasure in the *discretio* and *diiudicatio* of the material supplied by *inventio*.

He seems to have felt the difficulty involved in making the prophet say that he was like one who has just eaten a heavy meal, and to have tried to evade it by writing '*absque* instructione escae' as his translation of ἐκ κόρου τροφῆς. But ἐκ cannot mean *absque*.

ἔδοξά τινα ὑπερμεγέθη μέτρῳ ἀπεριορίστῳ ⟨ἐν⟩τυγχάνοντα κ.τ.λ. The prophet does not describe the appearance of his visitant, and does not even say here that he saw him, but only that he was aware of a vast and undefined presence, and heard a voice. Indeed the words μέτρῳ ἀπεριορίστῳ imply that there was no definite form or shape to be seen. Cf. § 4 *init.*, ὁρῶ θέαν ἀόριστον, viz. the boundless light by which God, or the divine, Mind, is symbolized. ὑπερμεγέθη μέτρῳ ἀπεριορίστῳ is a clumsy phrase; and it may be suspected that the author wrote τινα μέτρῳ ἀπεριόριστον, and that ὑπερμεγέθη is a gloss.

Τί βούλει ἀκοῦσαι καὶ θεάσασθαι, καὶ νοήσας μαθεῖν καὶ γνῶναι ; The writer has in mind the distinction between αἴσθησις and νόησις. The pupil must first hear (the teacher's words) and see (the vision presented to him), and then exert his thought to apprehend the meaning of what he has heard and seen (νοήσας μαθεῖν καὶ γνῶναι).

§ 2. Ἐγὼ μέν, φησίν, εἰμι ὁ Ποιμάνδρης, ὁ τῆς αὐθεντίας νοῦς. The name Poimandres is employed in *Corp*. I as a designation of the divine νοῦς. It occurs again in *Corp*. XIII. 15. It is once used by the alchemist Zosimus 3. 51. 8 [3] (A. D. 300–350?) : τῶν φυσικῶν τῆς ὕλης κατάπτυσον, καὶ καταδραμοῦσα ἐπὶ τὸν ⌜Ποιμένανδρα⌝[4] (*Corp*. I) καὶ βαπτισθεῖσα τῷ κρατῆρι (*Corp*. IV) ἀνάδραμε ἐπὶ τὸ γένος τὸ σόν. And Fulgentius (*c*. A. D. 500), quoting *Corp*. I. 1, says : 'Hermes in

---

[1] The preceding Muse in his list is she who presides over *inventio*.
[2] I assume *delectans* to be used as the participle of *delector*, regarded as a deponent verb.
[3] Zosimus ii. 8 in *Testim*.
[4] Read Ποιμάνδρην.

Opimandrae¹ libro ait' &c. These are, as far as I know, the only occurrences of the name elsewhere in ancient literature; and in each of these three passages, the writer is referring to *Corp.* I. The name Poimandres has been commonly supposed to be a Greek word derived from ποιμήν and ἀνήρ, and meaning 'shepherd of men'.² It is possible that the author of *Corp.* XIII took the name to mean this; for in § 19 he writes λόγον γὰρ τὸν ⌜σὸν⌝ (ἐμὸν?) ποιμαίνει (ποιμαίνεις σὺ?) ὁ νοῦς, and this phrase may have been suggested to him by the name Ποιμάνδρης. The man who wrote our text of Zosimus certainly took it to mean 'shepherd of men', and consequently altered Ποιμάνδρην into Ποιμένανδρα. But there is not the slightest reason to suppose that the author of *Corp.* I was thinking of a shepherd when he used the name. There is not a word about sheep or shepherding in the document; the prophet does not depict his divine instructor in the guise of a shepherd, and indeed ascribes to him no definite shape or appearance of any sort, but merely says that he was 'very big'. Moreover, a Greek word derived from ποιμήν and ἀνήρ could not take the form ποιμάνδρης. The nearest approach to it that could occur in Greek is ποίμανδρος,³ which might be a shortened form of ποιμένανδρος.

¹ *Opimandrae* is the genitive of Opimandres, i. e. ὁ Ποιμάνδρης taken as a single word.
² Reitzenstein, *Poim.* pp. 11 ff., starting from the mistaken assumption that the Poimandres of *Corp.* I is a shepherd, tries to establish a connexion between *Corp.* I and the *Shepherd* of Hermas. But his argument is not convincing. Hermas, in one of his visions, is visited by a person in the garb of a shepherd; the prophet who speaks in *Corp.* I is visited by a Being who is *not* said to be like a shepherd. Between the contents of the two visions there is not the slightest similarity. Reitzenstein, *ib.* p. 8 and p. 214 f., speaks of a 'Poimandres community', and says that this community possessed 'a sacred writing, *the Sayings of Poimandres*'. But I have failed to find any evidence for the existence either of any such writing, or of any community named after Poimandres. The passages (*Corp.* XIII. 15 and Zosimus, *l. c.*) which he adduces in support of his statement are to be otherwise explained.
³ The mythical founder of Tanagra in Boeotia was named Ποίμανδρος (Paus. 9. 20. 1). Plutarch, *Quaest. Gr.* 37, p. 299, names the founder of Tanagra Ποίμανδρος, and the town which he fortified, Ποιμανδρία. Strabo 9. 2. 10, p. 404: ἡ Ποιμανδρὶς δ' ἐστιν ἡ αὐτὴ τῇ Ταναγρικῇ. Lycophron 326, speaking of the sacrifice of Iphigenia at Aulis (near Tanagra), calls her Ποιμανδρίαν στεφηφόρον βοῦν. (Schol. *ad loc.*: Ποιμανδρία δὲ πόλις Βοιωτίας, ἥτις καὶ Τάναγρα καλεῖται.) There was at Tanagra a cult of Hermes Kriophoros; and at his festival, a youth walked round the city, carrying a lamb on his shoulder (Paus. 9. 22. 2). The name Poimandros may have been in some way connected with this cult; it may have been an epithet of Hermes Kriophoros, or the name of a local deity or hero who was identified with Hermes in later times. But the resemblance between Ποιμάνδρης, the name of an Egyptian impersonation of the divine νοῦς, and Ποίμανδρος, the name of a Boeotian city-founder, must be merely accidental. At most, it is conceivable that the Egyptian name may have been somewhat altered to assimilate it to the Greek name,—supposing that the name of the legendary founder of

As the name Poimandres is not Greek, and as it first occurs in *Corp.* I, which was presumably written in Egypt, it is most likely of Egyptian origin. F. Granger (*The Poimandres of Hermes Trismegistus, J. H. Stud.* vol. v, no. 191, p. 400) suggested that it is a transliteration of the Egyptian *p̣ mtr*, which means 'the witness'. The pronunciation of the term thus written in Egyptian may be inferred from its Coptic equivalent, which, according to Granger, is *p̣ᵐⁿᵉtre*. (Erman, *Aeg. Glossar*, gives ⲙⲛ̄ⲧⲣⲉ as the Coptic form of the Egyptian *mtr*, 'a witness'.) As far as the form of the name is concerned, this explanation seems fairly satisfactory; but it is difficult to account for the substitution of the diphthong οι for the faint vowel-sound of the Coptic article. As to the meaning, it might be said that Poimandres, the divine νοῦς, is the 'witness' by whom the truth is made known to the prophet; and we might compare *Corp.* XII. i. 8, where Hermes, speaking of the Agathos Daimon, says that ἐκεῖνος μόνος, ὡς πρωτόγονος θεός, τὰ πάντα κατιδών, θείους ἀληθῶς λόγους ἐφθέγξατο (which implies that the Agathos Daimon is the 'witness').[1]

Granger's explanation of the name might be accepted, if a better one could not be found. But Mr. F. Ll. Griffith, who has kindly allowed me to consult him on this question among others in which knowledge of the Egyptian language is involved, proposes another derivation, which seems preferable; namely, that Ποιμάνδρης is the Coptic ⲡ-ⲉⲓⲙⲉ-ⲛ-ⲣⲏ, 'the knowledge of the Sun-god'. (He tells me that ⲣⲏ, 'the sun', is usually preceded by the article ⲡ, but that the omission of the article is not unparalleled in late times, and that ⲣⲏ without the article would have a more learned and solemn appearance than the ordinary ⲡ-ⲣⲏ.)

As to the form of the transliteration, there seems to be nothing against this. The δ would almost necessarily be inserted by Greeks for euphony; and the representation of the vowel-sounds of ⲉⲓⲙⲉ

Tanagra chanced to be known to the Greek-speaking Egyptian who first spoke of Poimandres.—The word ποιμάνωρ occurs in Aesch. *Pers.* 241.

[1] Analogous uses of the words μάρτυς and μαρτυρία in the New Testament might be adduced. *Rom.* 8. 16: αὐτὸ τὸ πνεῦμα (the θεῖος νοῦς of the Hermetists) συμμαρτυρεῖ τῷ πνεύματι ἡμῶν ὅτι ἐσμὲν τέκνα θεοῦ. (Poimandres 'bears witness to' the same truth in *Corp.* I.) *Apoc. Joh.* 1. 5 : Jesus Christ, ὁ μάρτυς ὁ πιστός. *Ib.* 3. 14. *Ev. Joh.* 5. 31 *sqq.* and 8. 18. *Ep. Joh.* 1. 5. 6 *sqq.*: τὸ πνεῦμά ἐστιν τὸ μαρτυροῦν. . . . καὶ αὕτη ἐστὶν ἡ μαρτυρία, ὅτι ζωὴν αἰώνιον ἔδωκεν ὁ θεὸς ἡμῖν. (That is also the μαρτυρία of Poimandres in *Corp.* I.)
The words μαρτυρία and αὐθεντία occur together in *Const. Apost.* 5. 7. 30 : λαβόντες ἐντολὴν .. μαθητεῦσαι πάντα τὰ ἔθνη καὶ βαπτίσαι εἰς τὸν αὐτοῦ θάνατον ἐπὶ αὐθεντίᾳ τοῦ θεοῦ τῶν ὅλων . . . καὶ μαρτυρίᾳ τοῦ πνεύματος.

by οι and α may perhaps have been suggested by association with the verb ποιμαίνειν. The meaning given to the name by this derivation would suit the context. The Coptic word ειμε means 'knowledge' or 'perception'; it corresponds to the verb ʿmj, 'to know', given as late Egyptian in Erman's *Aeg. Glossar.* If we assume that it is here used as an equivalent for the Greek νοῦς, *Poimandres* would mean 'the νοῦς of the Sun-god'; and seeing that not only in Egypt, but in the Roman empire at large, the Sun was very generally regarded as the supreme God, or an 'image' or symbol of the supreme God, this name might very well be taken to signify that which the writer of *Corp.* I says it denotes, namely, ὁ τῆς αὐθεντίας νοῦς, 'the Mind of the Sovereign Power' (i. e. of the supreme God).

The word αὐθέντης commonly meant (1) a man who does or has done something (e. g. has committed a murder) with his own hand; (2) one who acts by his own authority, and not in subordination to another. In the latter sense, it is equivalent to αὐτοκράτωρ; and hence αὐθεντία may be used to signify the 'supreme authority' or 'sovereignty' of God. It was thus employed by Cerinthus (Hippol. *Ref. haer.* 7. 33, repeated *ib.* 10. 21): Κ. ἔλεγεν οὐχ ὑπὸ τοῦ πρώτου θεοῦ γεγονέναι τὸν κόσμον, ἀλλ᾽ ὑπὸ δυνάμεως τινὸς κεχωρισμένης τῆς ὑπὲρ πάντα ἐξουσίας, καὶ ἀγνοούσης τὸν ὑπὲρ πάντα θεόν. . . . καὶ μετὰ τὸ βάπτισμα κατελθεῖν εἰς (τὸν Ἰησοῦν) ἐκ τῆς ὑπὲρ τὰ ὅλα αὐθεντίας τὸν Χριστόν. In that passage, ἡ ὑπὲρ τὰ ὅλα αὐθεντία is equivalent to ἡ ὑπὲρ πάντα ἐξουσία and ὁ ὑπὲρ πάντα θεός. Similarly Satornilus (Hippol. *ib.* 7. 28): τὸν ἄνθρωπον δὲ ἀγγέλων εἶναι ποίημα, ἄνωθεν ἀπὸ τῆς αὐθεντίας φωτεινῆς εἰκόνος ἐπιφανείσης· and afterwards, οἰκτείρασα αὐτὸν ἡ ἄνω δύναμις ἔπεμψε σπινθῆρα ζωῆς. (ἡ αὐθεντία is there equivalent to ἡ ἄνω δύναμις.) Epiphanius, *Haer.* 38, says of a sect of Gnostics, οὗτοι φασὶ τὸν Κάιν ἐκ τῆς ἰσχυροτέρας δυνάμεως ὑπάρχειν καὶ τῆς ἄνωθεν αὐθεντίας. In the Latin translation of Irenaeus (1. 31. 1), ἐκ τῆς ἄνωθεν αὐθεντίας is rendered by *a superiore principalitate.*[1]

---

[1] αὐθεντία might also be used in the sense of 'authenticity' or 'genuineness'. Since αὐθέντης might signify 'one who has written or signed a document with his own hand', αὐθεντικός came to mean 'written or signed by the man himself', and thence 'authentic', 'genuine', or 'true'. E. g. in a magic papyrus (Dieterich *Abraxas*, p. 178) the magician says to his god (οἶδα) σου τὸ ἀληθινὸν [ὄνομα] καὶ αὐθεντικὸν ὄνομα. And αὐθέντης seems to have been sometimes used as a substitute for αὐθεντικός in this sense. *Pistis Sophia* c. 126 (C. Schmidt, p. 207): 'Der erster Archon, . . . der mit seinem authentischen (αὐθεντικός) Namen *Enchthonin* genannt wird.' *Ib.*, of the third Archon, 'Ein Hundesgesicht ist sein authentisches

The divine νοῦς assumes a personal form as Poimandres, and in that form speaks to the prophet. But is this νοῦς identical with the supreme God himself, or is it distinguished from the supreme God, and regarded as a Power which emanates from him,—the first and highest of his δυνάμεις? On this question, the language of the writer appears to vary. On the one hand, Poimandres repeatedly speaks of God (ὁ θεός) in the third person, as a being distinct from himself (§ 8 b, ἐκ βουλῆς θεοῦ. § 10, ὁ τοῦ θεοῦ λόγος. § 12, ὁ πατήρ. § 18, ἐκ βουλῆς θεοῦ. Ib., ὁ θεὸς εἶπεν. § 21, ὁ τοῦ θεοῦ λόγος. § 22, παραγίνομαι ἐγὼ ὁ νοῦς . . . καὶ τὸν πατέρα ἱλάσκονται. § 26 a, ὑμνεῖ τὸν πατέρα. . . . ὑμνουσῶν τὸν θεόν. . . . ἀνέρχονται πρὸς τὸν πατέρα. . . . ἐν θεῷ γίνονται. § 26 b, ὑπὸ θεοῦ σωθῇ). But the force of this argument is diminished by the fact that in § 9 init., (where the MSS. give ὁ δὲ νοῦς ὁ θεός, but the true reading is probably ὁ δὲ νοῦς ὁ πρῶτος,) Poimandres speaks of the supreme νοῦς also in the third person, though the νοῦς there spoken of cannot be other than ὁ τῆς αὐθεντίας νοῦς, i. e. Poimandres himself. And on the other hand, the divine νοῦς is expressly identified with the supreme God in the words ἐγώ, νοῦς, ὁ πρῶτος (ὁ σὸς MSS.) θεός § 6, and ὁ πάντων πατήρ [[ὁ]] νοῦς in § 12.[1] It seems therefore that in the theology of Corp. I ὁ τῆς αὐθεντίας νοῦς (also called ὁ νοῦς ὁ πρῶτος, ὁ πάντων πατήρ, and ὁ θεός) is the supreme Being; but the writer makes Poimandres, in the course of his teaching, use the forms of speech which are commonly employed by men, and speak of the supreme Being in the third person, although Poimandres is that very Being.

(αὐθέντης) Gesicht.' Ib. c. 127 : 'Der Drache der äusseren Finsterniss hat zwölf authentische (αὐθέντεις) Namen.' (On the other hand, αὐθέντης appears to mean 'supreme' or 'sovereign' in Pistis Sophia c. 91 : 'Wer das absolute (αὐθέντης) Mysterium des ersten Mysteriums des Unaussprechlichen empfangen hat.' Ib. c. 97 : 'das zwölfte Mysterium . . ., d. h. das absolute (αὐθέντης) Mysterium.') Orac. Sib. 7. 69 (Christian) : ὃς πρὶν καὶ γαίης τε καὶ οὐρανοῦ ἀστερόεντος | αὐθέντης ⌜γένετο⌝ (γεγένητο Alexandre) λόγος πατρί. (αὐθέντης there appears to mean γνήσιος.) The word αὐθεντία might therefore mean 'authenticity' or 'genuineness'; but it cannot very well have that meaning in the phrase ὁ τῆς αὐθεντίας νοῦς.

[1] Starting from the assumption that the νοῦς is a person distinct from ὁ θεός, I thought at first of altering these two passages in which they are identified, by cutting out ἐγώ, νοῦς in § 6, and νοῦς after ὁ πάντων πατήρ in § 12. But I now see that these alterations of the text would not get rid of the identification; for it is clear that the being who is called ὁ πάντων πατήρ in § 12 is the same being who is called ὁ νοῦς ὁ πρῶτος in § 9. The νοῦς δημιουργός, who is son of ὁ νοῦς ὁ πρῶτος, is spoken of in § 13 as 'brother' of Anthropos, who is son of ὁ πάντων πατήρ; from which it follows that the two phrases (ὁ νοῦς ὁ πρῶτος and ὁ πάντων πατήρ) denote the same person.
The words ὁ Ποιμάνδρης ἐμίγη ταῖς δυνάμεσιν in § 26 b might be reconciled with either of the two views.

[[οἶδα ὃ βούλει, καὶ σύνειμί σοι πανταχοῦ.]] If we retain the words οἶδα ὃ βούλει where they stand in the MSS., they serve no apparent purpose, and bring into undue prominence the inconsistency inevitably involved in making an omniscient Being ask for information. If we place them after φησὶν ἐμοὶ πάλιν, they follow naturally on the prophet's answer to the question which Poimandres has asked. Reading ⟨ὃς⟩ καὶ σύνειμί σοι πανταχοῦ, we may take these words as an explanation of οἶδα. The divine νοῦς knows all that is in man's heart, being always present there (if not in all men, at least in the ἔννους ἄνθρωπος, § 21 sq.); though it is only at rare moments that a man is so fully conscious of its presence as the prophet was in his vision.

§ 3. Μαθεῖν θέλω τὰ ὄντα καὶ νοῆσαι τὴν τούτων φύσιν, καὶ γνῶναι τὸν θεόν. I. e. 'I wish (1) to understand the Kosmos, and (2) to know the supracosmic God'. Cf. Corp. XI. ii init. : σύ μοι περὶ τούτου (sc. τοῦ παντὸς καὶ τοῦ θεοῦ) διασάφησον.

§ 4. οὕτως εἰπόντος (τοῦτο εἰπὼν MSS.), ἠλλάγη ⟨⟨εὐθέως πάντα μοι⟩⟩ τῇ ἰδέᾳ καὶ [[ ]] ἤνοικτο ῥοπῇ. In the text of the MSS., the subject of ἠλλάγη is Poimandres. But as no 'form' has hitherto been ascribed to Poimandres, it could hardly be said here that he 'changed in form'. Besides, if he 'changed in form', we ought to be told what new form he assumed; but nothing is said about that. (It is true that the expanse of light which the prophet now sees is meant to symbolize the divine Mind, and Poimandres is that Mind; but the prophet does not know what the light means until he is told its meaning in § 6.) On the other hand, we are told in the following sentence that πάντα (i. e. the visible world) changed into a boundless expanse of light; the subject of ἠλλάγη must therefore have been πάντα, and not Poimandres, who remains, as before, an undefined presence.

φῶς [δὲ] πάντα γεγενημένα. The material world disappears, and there is nothing but φῶς ἀόριστον. The prophet has been transported in his vision to the time before the creation of the world, when Mind or God alone existed; and God is pictured as light diffused through boundless space.

καὶ μετ' ὀλίγον, σκότος κατωφερὲς ἦν ἐν μέρει ⟨τινὶ⟩ γεγενημένον. This is the first beginning of the Kosmos. In a certain part of the expanse of light (i. e. at the place where the Kosmos is subsequently to come into being), there appears a cloud of darkness. This darkness is ἄμορφος ὕλη, the raw material out of which the visible universe

C 2

is to be made. It is called κατωφερές, which is an epithet applied by the Stoics to the grosser and heavier elements, earth and water. This, if the writer thought the matter out clearly, ought to mean that the σκότος (like the 'watery substance' into which it presently changes) tended to gravitate towards a central point, viz. the centre of the future Kosmos. The author rejects the Platonic doctrine that ὕλη is without beginning, and has existed side by side with God from all eternity; but whether it was brought into existence by God's will, or came into being of itself, he does not tell us.

He is in agreement with the Platonists in holding ὕλη to be the source of evil; and he symbolizes its evil influence by picturing it as σκότος φοβερόν τε καὶ στυγνόν, in contrast to the φῶς ἤπιόν τε καὶ ἱλαρόν which stands for God. But the symbolical representation of the good God by light, and the evil ὕλη by darkness, must have been suggested to him by some tradition independent of Platonism. In Greek speculation, an early form of this notion appears in the system of Parmenides, who, in his account of the 'world of illusion', said that the first things were fire and earth, 'or rather, light and darkness'.[1] But the identification of the good principle with light, and the evil principle with darkness, was especially characteristic of the Zoroastrians; and a Zoroastrian conception may very well have been transmitted to the author of *Corp.* I. Hippol. *Ref. haer.* 1. 2. 12 (Diels *Doxogr.* p. 557): Διόδωρος δὲ ὁ Ἐρετριεὺς (unknown) καὶ Ἀριστόξενος ὁ μουσικός (*c.* 300 B. C.) φασι πρὸς Ζαράταν τὸν Χαλδαῖον (i. e. Zoroaster) ἐληλυθέναι Πυθαγόραν· τὸν δὲ ἐκθέσθαι αὐτῷ δύο εἶναι ἀπ᾽ ἀρχῆς τοῖς οὖσιν αἴτια, πατέρα καὶ μητέρα· καὶ πατέρα μὲν φῶς, μητέρα δὲ σκότος· τοῦ δὲ φωτὸς μέρη θερμὸν ξηρὸν κοῦφον ταχύ, τοῦ δὲ σκότους ψυχρὸν ὑγρὸν βαρὺ[2] βραδύ· ἐκ δὲ τούτων πάντα τὸν κόσμον συνεστάναι, ἐκ θηλείας καὶ ἄρρενος. . . . περὶ δὲ τῶν ἐκ γῆς καὶ ⌐κόσμου⌐ (perhaps οὐρανοῦ) γινομένων τάδε φασὶ λέγειν τὸν Ζαράταν· δύο δαίμονας εἶναι, τὸν μὲν οὐράνιον, τὸν δὲ χθόνιον·[3] καὶ τὸν μὲν χθόνιον ⌐ἀνιέναι τὴν

---

[1] Simplicius *in phys.* f. 6. vv. 14-18, following Theophrastus (Diels *Doxogr.* p. 477): οἱ μὲν δύο (τὰς ἀρχὰς ἔθεντο), ὡς Παρμενίδης ἐν τοῖς πρὸς δόξαν πῦρ καὶ γῆν, ἢ μᾶλλον φῶς καὶ σκότος. Parmenides *fr.* 8. 56 ff. Diels: τῇ μὲν φλογὸς αἰθέριον πῦρ, | ἤπιον ὄν, μέγ᾽ ἐλαφρόν, ἑωυτῷ πάντοσε τωὐτόν, | τῷ δ᾽ ἑτέρῳ μὴ τωὐτόν· ἀτὰρ κἀκεῖνο κατ᾽ αὐτὸ | τἀντία νύκτ᾽ ἀδαῆ, πυκινὸν δέμας ἐμβριθές τε. *Ib. fr.* 9: αὐτὰρ ἐπειδὴ πάντα φάος καὶ νὺξ ὀνόμασται, . . . πᾶν πλέον ἐστὶν ὁμοῦ φάεος καὶ νυκτὸς ἀφάντου, | ἴσων ἀμφοτέρων. Plut. *adv. Col.* 1114 B: Parmenides, στοιχεῖα μιγνὺς τὸ λαμπρὸν καὶ σκοτεινόν, ἐκ τούτων τὰ φαινόμενα πάντα καὶ διὰ τούτων ἀποτελεῖ. (The conjecture ἤπιον for ἤδιον in *Corp.* I is supported by the phrase πῦρ ἤπιον ὄν in Parmenides.)

[2] Cf. σκότος κατωφερές in *Corp.* I. 4.

[3] I. e. the Power of Light and the Power of Darkness.

γένεσιν ἐκ τῆς γῆς εἶναι δὲ ὕδωρ⁷,¹ τὸν δὲ οὐράνιον ⟨καταπέμπειν?⟩ πῦρ μετέχον [τοῦ] ἀέρος.² The 'Pythagorean' doctrine here spoken of is clearly connected with that of Parmenides.

Aristoxenus or his authority presumably found this doctrine taught by some Pythagorean, and having noted its resemblance to what he had heard of the Zoroastrian cosmology, inferred that Pythagoras had learnt it from Zoroaster. Cf. Eudemus (*c.* 300 B. C.) in Damascius *De princ.* p. 382 Kopp (Mullach, *Fr. ph. Gr.* III, p. 288 f.) : Μάγοι δὲ καὶ πᾶν τὸ Ἄρειον γένος . . . οἱ μὲν Τόπον, οἱ δὲ Χρόνον καλοῦσι [τὸ νοητὸν ἅπαν καὶ] τὸ ἡνωμένον, ἐξ οὗ διακριθῆναι ἢ θεὸν ἀγαθὸν καὶ δαίμονα κακόν, ἢ φῶς καὶ σκότος πρὸ τούτων, ὡς ἐνίους λέγειν. οὗτοι δ' οὖν καὶ αὐτοὶ³ μετὰ τὴν ἀδιάκριτον φύσιν ⸢διακρινομένην⸣ ποιοῦσι τὴν διττὴν συστοιχὴν τῶν κρειττόνων⁷·⁴ ⟨καὶ⟩ τῆς μὲν ἡγεῖσθαι τὸν Ὡρομάσδην, τῆς δὲ τὸν Ἀρειμάνιον.

The two principles of the Zoroastrians were adopted by Mani. Epiphanius *Haer.* 66. 14 gives the opening words of Mani's work on the 'Mysteries' as follows : ἦν θεὸς καὶ ὕλη, φῶς καὶ σκότος, ἀγαθὸν καὶ κακόν, τοῖς πᾶσιν ἄκρως ἐναντία. Alex. Lycopol. *Contra Manichaei opiniones* 2 (Brinkmann) : ἀρχὰς ἐτίθετο θεὸν καὶ ὕλην, εἶναι δὲ τὸν μὲν θεὸν ἀγαθόν, τὴν δὲ ὕλην κακόν. . . . τὸ δὲ λαμπρὸν καὶ τὸ φῶς καὶ τὸ ἄνω, πάντα ταῦτα σὺν τῷ θεῷ εἶναι, τὸ ἀμυδρὸν δὲ καὶ τὸ σκότος καὶ τὸ κάτω σὺν τῇ ὕλῃ. As the use of the terms 'light' and 'darkness' in *Corp.* I closely resembles Mani's use of them, it seems probable that it was derived from the same source, i. e. from the Zoroastrians.

Plotinus repeatedly describes ὕλη as 'darkness'; e. g. 1. 8. 4 : (ἡ ψυχὴ) σκότον ὁρᾷ, καὶ ἔχει ἤδη ὕλην. Plot. 4. 3. 9 (on the formation of body by soul) : ἐπ' ἄκροις τοῖς ἐσχάτοις τοῦ πυρὸς (= φωτός) σκότος ἐγένετο· ὅπερ ἰδοῦσα ἡ ψυχή, ἐπείπερ ὑπέστη (τὸ σκότος), ἐμόρφωσεν αὐτό.

¹ The sense required is ἀνιέναι ⟨εἰς⟩ τὴν γένεσιν γῆν καὶ ὕδωρ (or γῆν μετέχουσαν ὕδατος).
² 'Fire which partakes of air' is what the Stoics called *pneuma*. The gross substance of the human or animal body consists of earth and water from below ; the *pneuma*, which is the vehicle of life, consists of fire and air from above.
³ I. e. this second school of 'Magi'.
⁴ The text is corrupt here ; but the general meaning is clear. There are two φύσεις ('substances'), viz. light and darkness, and in connexion with them, two συστοιχίαι (series) of deities ; the series of good deities is headed by Ormazd, and the series of evil deities by Ahriman.
In identifying the good God with light and the evil ὕλη with darkness, the writer of *Corp.* I agrees with the second of the two schools of Magi spoken of by Eudemus ; but he differs from them in putting light at the beginning, and making the darkness come into being later, instead of positing an 'undiscriminated substance' out of which both light and darkness came by differentiation.

ⁿσκολιῶς πεπειραμένον⌐ [ὡς εἰκάσαι με].¹ ὡς εἰκάσαι με is probably
a misplaced doublet of ὡς εἰκάσαι a few lines below.   πεπειραμένον
might possibly be a corruption of ἐπαίρομενον (the darkness being
pictured as consisting of wreaths of smoke curling upward); but
ἐπαιρόμενον would be hardly consistent with κατωφερές above.

εἶδον (εἰδότα MSS., ἰδόντα B²) μεταβαλλόμενον τὸ σκότος εἰς ὑγράν
τινα φύσιν ἀφάτως τεταραγμένην.   εἰδότα may be a conflation of two
readings, εἶδον and εἶτα.   The ὑγρὰ φύσις corresponds to the watery
chaos which occurs in the Babylonian cosmogony, in *Genesis* 1, and
in the Stoic *diacosmesis*.²   Cf. *Corp.* III. 1 b, ἦν γὰρ σκότος [[   ]] ἐν
ἀβύσσῳ, καὶ ὕδωρ ⟨⟨ἄπειρον⟩⟩, and see notes *ad loc.*   The writer of
Corp. I, instead of putting the watery chaos at the beginning, as the
Babylonians and the author of *Gen.* 1 did, has prefixed a description
of its origin.   But from the watery chaos onward, his cosmogony is
constructed on the same lines as that of *Gen.* 1.

καὶ καπνὸν ἀποδιδοῦσαν ὡς ἀπὸ πυρός.   It seems strange to say that
smoke 'as from fire' is given off by a 'watery substance'.   But the
statement may be accounted for, if we take it to be the writer's
interpretation of the phrase in *Gen.* 1, καὶ σκότος ἐπάνω τῆς ἀβύσσου.
The darkness which 'was upon the face of' the watery substance
when this substance had already come into being must be something
different from that darkness which had changed into the watery
substance itself; and the writer takes it to be a sort of murky smoke
rising from the surface of the watery mass.

Mani (Alex. Lycopol. 3) said that ὕλη, when all 'light' or divine
substance has been extracted from it, becomes a πῦρ καυστικὸν μέν,
σκοτῶδες δὲ καὶ ἀφεγγές, νυκτὶ προσόμοιον.   It is possible that some
similar statement, derived from a Zoroastrian source, may have been
in the writer's mind.

καί τινα ἦχον ⌐ἀποτελοῦσαν⌐ ἀνεκλάλητον γοώδη.   ἦχον ἀποτελεῖν,

---

¹ Reitzenstein writes σκολιῶς ἐσπειραμένον, ὡς εἰκάσαι με (δρακόντι), and compares
Hippol. *Ref. haer.* 5. 9 (doctrine of the Naassenes): Νάας δέ ἐστιν ὁ ὄφις. . . . εἶναι
δὲ τὸν ὄφιν λέγουσιν οὗτοι τὴν ὑγρὰν οὐσίαν, καθάπερ καὶ Θαλῆς ὁ Μιλήσιος· καὶ μηδὲν
δύνασθαι τῶν ὄντων ὅλως, ἀθανάτων ἢ θνητῶν, . . . συνεστάναι χωρὶς αὐτοῦ· ὑποκεῖσθαι
δὲ αὐτῷ τὰ πάντα. . . . καὶ εἶναι αὐτὸν ἀγαθόν, ὥστε τὸ κάλλος καὶ τὴν ὡραιότητα
ἐπιδιδόναι πᾶσι τοῖς οὖσι.   But there is little resemblance between the snake of the
Naassenes, which is the source of all good, and the 'grim and terrible darkness' of
Corp. I, which stands for ἄμορφος ὕλη, and is the source of all evil.   It is true that
a 'dragon of darkness', regarded as an evil power, occurs in other writings of the
period; but a mention of it would be inappropriate here.   The σκότος of *Corp.* I is
at this stage formless; as yet, it has not even assumed its first form, that of 'watery
substance'.
² It might also be compared to the Egyptian *Nu*: but the cosmogony of *Corp.* I
is more nearly related to that of *Genesis* than to that of the Egyptians.

'to accomplish a noise', is hardly Greek; and there is probably some corruption. We should have expected ἤκουσα, to correspond to εἶδον above; and perhaps the author may have written something like ἦχον ἀφιείσης ἤκουσα.

No 'noise' is mentioned in this connexion in *Genesis*; but in descriptions of the 'last things' in Judaeo-Christian Apocalypses, (some of the details of which, according to Gunkel, *Schöpfung und Chaos*, are derived from traditional descriptions of the 'first things',) we hear of 'the roaring of the sea' (Luke 21. 25: ἐν ἀπορίᾳ ἤχους θαλάσσης καὶ σάλου).

[εἶτα] βοὴ ⟨γὰρ⟩ ἐξ αὐτῆς ἀσύναρθρος ἐξεπέμπετο. The writer contrasts the 'inarticulate roar' of the watery chaos with the λόγος which issued from 'the Light', i. e. from God. λόγος means primarily 'speech', i. e. significant utterance; and the author, though he hypostatizes the λόγος, still continues to regard it as the 'spoken word' of God. The words φωνὴν φωτός must have been applied to the λόγος, and not, as in the MSS., to the 'inarticulate roar'.

§ 5 a. λόγος ἅγιος ἐπέβη τῇ ⟨ὑγρᾷ⟩ φύσει. This corresponds to πνεῦμα θεοῦ ἐπεφέρετο ἐπάνω τοῦ ὕδατος in *Gen.* I. 2 ; but it also corresponds to εἶπεν ὁ θεός in *Gen.* I. 3 &c. The writer identifies the 'spirit of God' which 'moved upon the face of the waters' with 'the word of God' by which the world was made. Cf. § 5 b, διὰ τὸν ... ἐπιφερόμενον πνευματικὸν λόγον. Herm. *Fragm.* 27 : ὁ γὰρ λόγος αὐτοῦ ... ἔγκυον τὸ ὕδωρ ἐποίησεν. (The ὕδωρ there spoken of is the ὑγρὰ φύσις of *Corp.* I.)

§ 5 b. [[καὶ πῦρ ἄκρατον ... πνευματικὸν λόγον.]] This passage evidently belongs to the account of the origin of the elements, which is introduced by the question in § 8 b *init.* (τὰ στοιχεῖα τῆς φύσεως πόθεν ὑπέστη ;). It must have followed, and not preceded, the description of the νοητὸς κόσμος in §§ 7, 8 a.

§ 6. [[εἰς ἀκοὴν]] ὁ δὲ Ποιμάνδρης ⟨⟨εἰς ἀκοὴν⟩⟩ ἐμοὶ ... φησί. εἰς ἀκοήν is meaningless where it stands in the MSS. If we place it after Ποιμάνδρης, it serves to mark the distinction between what the prophet *saw* in his vision and what he *heard* Poimandres say.

Τὸ φῶς ἐκεῖνο, ἔφη, ἐγώ, νοῦς, ὁ πρῶτος θεός (ὁ σὸς θεός MSS.). There is no reason why the supreme Mind should say 'I am *thy* God '; and σός is probably a corruption of ἄος or α'ος, an abbreviation for πρῶτος. See *Corp.* III *init.* An instance of πρῶτος written in the form α'ος occurs in *Catal. codd. astrol. Graec.* II, p. 39.

ὁ δὲ ἐκ [νοὸς] φωτ[εῖν]ὸς λόγος υἱὸς θεοῦ. The thing to be explained by Poimandres is the thing which the prophet has just perceived in his vision, viz. 'the Word which came forth from the light'; this therefore ought to be the subject of the proposition. The prophet saw the light, but did not see Mind, and did not perceive that the Word came forth 'from Mind'; ἐκ νοός therefore can hardly be right. And the epithet φωτεινός is not suitable; we have been told that the Word came forth from the light, but not that the Word itself was 'bright' or 'shining'; it was a thing heard, not a thing seen. If we write ὁ δὲ ἐκ φωτὸς λόγος, all difficulties are removed. (We may suppose that νοός is an accidentally misplaced doublet of the preceding νοῦς, and that φωτός, which had been rendered meaningless by the insertion of νοός before it, was altered into φωτεινός to make sense.) Poimandres explains to the prophet (1) that the light which he saw is God, and (2) that the Word which came forth from the light is son of God.

The λόγος is here hypostatized, as in Philo *passim*; and the conception of 'the Word of God' as a person, and a 'son of God', must have been adopted by the writer of *Corp.* I from Jewish speculations similar to those of Philo.[1] On the Jewish hypostatization of God's λόγος, see Bousset, *Rel. des Judentums*, p. 399; Schürer, *Gesch. des jüd. Volkes* III, p. 708 ff.; Zeller, *Phil. der Griechen* III, Abth. ii (1903), pp. 418–434. Philo's notion of the divine Logos was based partly on the Mosaic account of the creation,[2] and partly on the Stoic[3] use of the word λόγος to describe the God who pervades the Kosmos and operates in it.[4] Philo's Logos may be regarded as the Stoic God

---

[1] Celsus (Origen *c. Cels.* 2. 31) represented a Jew as saying to the Christians εἴ γε ὁ λόγος ἐστὶν ὑμῖν υἱὸς τοῦ θεοῦ, καὶ ἡμεῖς ἐπαινοῦμεν. To this Origen replies that he has never heard a Jew admit τὸ λόγον εἶναι τὸν υἱὸν τοῦ θεοῦ. But the Jew Philo repeatedly asserts, if not precisely this, at least τὸ τὸν λόγον εἶναι υἱὸν θεοῦ. E. g. Philo *De agric.* 12. 51, Wendland II, p. 105: ὁ ποιμὴν καὶ βασιλεὺς θεός governs all things in the universe, προστησάμενος τὸν ὀρθὸν αὐτοῦ λόγον καὶ πρωτόγονον υἱόν, ὃς τὴν ἐπιμέλειαν τῆς ἱερᾶς ταύτης ἀγέλης οἷά τις μεγάλου βασιλέως ὕπαρχος διαδέξεται. See also *De conf. ling.* 28. 146, Wendland II, p. 257, τὸν πρωτόγονον αὐτοῦ λόγον κ.τ.λ.

[2] 'By the word of the Lord were the heavens made.' Philo *Legg. alleg.* 3. 31. 96, Cohn I, p. 134: ὁ λόγος αὐτοῦ . . ., ᾧ καθάπερ ὀργάνῳ προσχρησάμενος ἐκοσμοποίει. *De cherubim* 35. 127, Cohn I, p. 200: εὑρήσεις γὰρ αἴτιον μὲν (τοῦ κόσμου) τὸν θεόν, ὑφ' οὗ γέγονεν, ὕλην δὲ τὰ τέσσαρα στοιχεῖα, ἐξ ὧν συνεκράθη, ὄργανον δὲ λόγον θεοῦ, δι' οὗ κατεσκευάσθη. In *Corp.* I, it is in connexion with the making of the world that the Logos is spoken of.

[3] The Stoics found (or thought they found) this use of the word in Heraclitus.

[4] It has been thought by some that the influence of certain analogous doctrines taught by Egyptian priests also contributed more or less to the development of Philo's theory of the Logos. (Specimens of such Egyptian doctrines are given by Reitzenstein, *Poimandres*, p. 59 ff., and Moret, *Mystères Égyptiens*, 1913, pp. 108–139.) This is not quite impossible; but I do not think it can be held to have been

dematerialized, with a supracosmic God (the God of Platonism) set up above him. His distinction between God and the Logos is an instance of the distinction between a 'first God' and a 'second God' which presents itself in various forms in the teachings of the syncretic Platonists of the Roman empire; and this distinction, wherever it occurs in their writings, seems to have resulted from a combination of Platonic and Stoic conceptions. The transcendent God of Platonism being debarred from contact with matter, a second God was needed to operate in the world; and the immanent God of Stoicism was at hand to supply the need. The Platonists therefore adopted the God of the Stoics, but made him subordinate to their own transcendent God; and Philo, influenced in part by the Stoic use of the word λόγος, and in part by its use in the LXX to signify the 'word' or *fiat* by which God made the world (and the 'word of the Lord' by which He spoke to the prophets), gave the name Logos to the subordinate God of his system.

God's λόγος is already imagined as a person distinct from God in *Sap. Sal.* (time of Augustus?) 18. 15, in a description of the slaying of the first-born of Egypt : ὁ παντοδύναμός σου λόγος ἀπ᾿ οὐρανῶν ἐκ θρόνων βασιλείων ἀπότομος πολεμιστὴς εἰς μέσον τῆς ὀλεθρίας ἥλατο γῆς, ξίφος ὀξὺ τὴν ἀνυπόκριτον ἐπιταγήν σου φέρων,¹ καὶ στὰς ἐπλήρωσεν τὰ πάντα θανάτου· καὶ οὐρανοῦ μὲν ἥπτετο, βεβήκει δ᾿ ἐπὶ γῆς.² But this is an isolated instance ; and Schürer says 'as it seems, Philo was the first to posit such an intermediate being between God and the world under the name of Logos'.³

Οὕτω γνῶθι, τὸ ἐν σοὶ βλέπων [ ]· ⟨ἐπεὶ καὶ ἐν σοὶ ὁ⟩ λόγος υἱός, ὁ δὲ νοῦς πατήρ.—(Οὕτω γνῶθι· τὸ ἐν σοὶ βλέπον καὶ ἀκοῦον (*al.* βλέπων καὶ ἀκούων) λόγος κυρίου, ὁ δὲ νοῦς πατὴρ θεός MSS.). This sentence is meaningless in the MSS. Its restoration is doubtful; but with the alterations which I have made, we get a satisfactory sense. 'What

---

proved. At any rate, the *chief* sources of the Philonian Logos-doctrine, if not the only sources, were Jewish and Stoic; and it can be sufficiently accounted for as an outcome of Judaeo-Stoic speculation, without assuming any part of it to have been derived from the indigenous religion of Egypt.

¹ The λόγος is here said to 'bear the command of God' as a thing distinct from himself; he cannot therefore be merely a figurative personification of that command, but must be regarded as an actual person.

² Cf. *Ps.* 107. 20, ἀπέστειλεν τὸν λόγον αὐτοῦ καὶ ἰάσατο αὐτούς, where the language makes it at least possible for a reader to regard the λόγος as a person. Origen (*c. Cels.* 2. 31) quotes that verse in support of the Christian doctrine of the λόγος.

³ Zeller (III, Abth. ii, p. 430) agrees in the main with Schürer on this point, though he speaks somewhat more guardedly.

26 CORPVS HERMETICVM

do you mean', the prophet asks, 'by saying that the divine λόγος is *son* of the divine νοῦς?' Poimandres answers: 'The relation between the divine λόγος and the divine νοῦς is analogous to the relation between the human λόγος and the human νοῦς. Your λόγος (speech) may be called *son* of your νοῦς (mind or thought), because it issues from your νοῦς, and is inseparably connected with it; and in the same sense, the divine λόγος may be called *son* of the divine νοῦς.' Cf. Philo *De cher.* 2. 7, Cohn I, p. 171 (quoted by Clem. *Strom.* 5. 8; see Cohn I, p. lx): the name Abram was changed to Abraham, which means "πατὴρ ἐκλεκτὸς ἤχους". ἠχεῖ μὲν γὰρ ὁ γεγωνὸς λόγος, πατὴρ δὲ τούτου ὁ νοῦς, ἐξειλεγμένος δὲ ὁ τοῦ σπουδαίου νοῦς. Clem. *Strom.* 4. 162: ὅθεν καὶ διδάσκαλος ⌜μόνος ὁ μόνος ὑψίστου ἄγνου⌝ πατρός (διδάσκαλος μόνος ὁ λόγος, υἱὸς τοῦ νοῦ πατρός Schwartz), ὁ παιδεύων τὸν ἄνθρωπον.

Compare the Christian *Hermippus* (Kroll and Viereck) 1. 13. 97: ὅθεν (*sc.* from the combination of νοῦς, λόγος, and ψυχὴ καὶ πνεῦμα in ourselves) ἡμεῖς ὁρμώμενοι, καὶ ἐπὶ θεοῦ τρεῖς ὑποστάσεις κατανοήσαντες σέβομεν, καὶ τὸ τῆς ζωαρχικῆς τριάδος ἀνεκαλύφθη μυστήριον· ὁ γὰρ νοῦς ἐν ἡμῖν, τοῦτ' ἐν ἐκείνοις πατήρ· ὁ δὲ λόγος, υἱός· ὁ δὲ ψυχὴ καὶ πνεῦμα, καὶ παρ' αὐτοῖς ἄχραντον καὶ ζωοποιόν ἐστι πνεῦμα. Cf. also a document Περὶ πατρὸς καὶ υἱοῦ, probably written by Sarapion, bishop of Thmuis in Egypt, about A. D. 350 (Wobbermin, *Texte und Unters. N. F.* II. 3 b, p. 22): πῶς οὖν "ἀεὶ πατὴρ" καὶ "ἀεὶ υἱὸς" νοῆσαι ἄμεινον; πατήρ εἰμι τοῦ λόγου τοῦ ἐμοῦ, καὶ ὅτε βούλομαι τὸν λόγον μου προφέρω, καὶ εἰς ἑτέρας ἀκοὰς φθάνων ὁ λόγος ὁ ἐμὸς οὐ διῃρέθη ἀπ' ἐμοῦ. ⟨And so it is in the case of the Father and the Son;⟩ θέλημα γὰρ πατρός ἐστιν ὁ λόγος αὐτοῦ. πανταχοῦ οὖν διακονῶν τῷ πατρί, οὐ διαιρεῖται ἀπ' αὐτοῦ. *Ib.* p. 23: ἡνίκα ὁ λόγος ἐν τῷ νοὶ ἠρεμεῖ, τότε σιγή ἐστιν· ὅτε δὲ βούλεται ὁ νοῦς φωτίσαι τὰ πάντα, ὁ λόγος προέρχεται πρὸς φωτισμὸν τοῦ παντός. For the explanation of divine things by a reference to what the pupil knows about himself, cf. *Corp.* XI. ii. 19 *init.*, where the teacher says to the pupil τοῦτο νόησον ἀπὸ σεαυτοῦ. *Ib.* 12 a: τί μέγα τῷ θεῷ ... ποιεῖν, σοῦ τοσαῦτα ποιοῦντος; *Ib.* 14 a: ἰδὲ τί σοὶ ἐγγίνεται.

The text of *Corp.* I was presumably altered by a Christian, who failed to understand that the writer was here speaking of *man's* λόγος and *man's* νοῦς, and consequently introduced an irrelevant mention of 'the Word of the Lord' and 'God the Father'.

§ 7. εἰπὼν τοσαῦτα (εἰπόντος ταῦτα MSS.). 'He spoke (only) so much'; i. e. at this point he ceased to speak, and proceeded to influence me in a different way.

ἐπὶ πλείονα χρόνον ἀντώπησέ μοι. He 'gazed straight into my eyes'. Here Poimandres is for the first time spoken of as if he were visible in human form, and we are told that the prophet 'trembled at his appearance (ἰδέα)'. But even now, no definite human shape is described. What is meant is that the divine visitant imposes his influence on the prophet, as one man might influence and, so to speak, hypnotize another by a long and earnest gaze. Thus influenced, the prophet's νοῦς is raised to a higher potency, and enabled to see the vision of the νοητὸς κόσμος.

θεωρῶ ἐν τῷ νοΐ μου τὸ φῶς ἐν δυνάμεσιν ἀναριθμήτοις ὄν, καὶ κόσμον ἀπεριόριστον γεγενημένον. The writer has adopted from the Platonists (or from some Platonizing Jew of the same school as Philo) the conception of a νοητὸς κόσμος. This 'intelligible world' is the παράδειγμα in God's mind, after the model of which the 'sensible world' is organized. Cf. Philo De conf. ling. 34. 171 f., Wendland II, p. 262 : εἰς ὧν ὁ θεὸς ἀμυθήτους περὶ αὐτὸν ἔχει δυνάμεις. . . . διὰ τούτων τῶν δυνάμεων ὁ ἀσώματος καὶ νοητὸς ἐπάγη κόσμος, τὸ τοῦ φαινομένου τοῦδε ἀρχέτυπον, ἰδέαις ἀοράτοις συσταθείς, ὥσπερ οὗτος σώμασιν ὁρατοῖς. The παράδειγμα must be in existence before the organization of the sensible world begins, and is therefore rightly mentioned at this point. Compare Philo De opif. mundi 4. 16—10. 36, where the 'first day' of creation in Genesis is explained as meaning the creation of the νοητὸς κόσμος.[1]

The prophet now sees that the 'Light' is not uniform and homogeneous, as it at first appeared to him to be. It is an organized whole consisting of innumerable δυνάμεις, and may therefore be called a κόσμος; but it is not περιόριστος, as is the αἰσθητὸς κόσμος. The δυνάμεις of which it consists are, in one aspect, the Platonic ἰδέαι, i. e. the παραδείγματα of the several parts of the sensible world ; but inasmuch as the ἰδέαι are 'thoughts which God thinks', these same δυνάμεις are, in another aspect, parts of God himself, and the whole which is made up of them is the 'Light' which stands for God. 'God thinks himself' (ἑαυτὸν νοεῖ), as Aristotle said ; and in the view of the writer of Corp. I, as in that of Plotinus, the divine νοῦς and the sum of its νοητά are identical.

Compare the doctrine of the Docetae, in Hippol. Ref. haer. 8. 9 : κεκόσμητο μὲν ⌜ἀνενδεὴς⌝ (ἀνενδεῶς) πᾶσα ἡ νοητὴ φύσις, φῶς δὲ

---

[1] Philo retains the form of the Mosaic narrative, in which the creation is described as a series of events in time, though he is aware that in reality the νοητὸς κόσμος is not in time, and cannot have begun to be.

ἦν ἅπαντα ἐκεῖνα τὰ νοητὰ καὶ αἰώνια, φῶς δὲ οὐκ ἄμορφον οὐδὲ ἀργόν, οὐδὲ οἰονεί τινος ἐπιποιοῦντος δεόμενον· ἀλλὰ ἔχον ἐν ἑαυτῷ... ἀπείρους ἰδέας ζῴων τῶν ἐκεῖ πολυποικίλων, κατέλαμψεν ἄνωθεν εἰς τὸ ὑποκείμενον χάος. τὸ δέ, φωτισθὲν ὁμοῦ καὶ μορφωθὲν ἐκείναις ἄνωθεν ταῖς πολυποικίλοις ἰδέαις, πῆξιν ἔλαβε, καὶ ἀνεδέξατο τὰς ἰδέας τὰς ἄνωθεν ἁπάσας.

[[καὶ περισχέσθαι τὸ πῦρ . . . κρατούμενον.]] This has nothing to do with the νοητὸς κόσμος; it is evidently a misplaced fragment of the account of the formation of the αἰσθητὸς κόσμος, which begins at § 8 b *init.*

ταῦτα δὲ ἐγὼ διενοήθην ὁρῶν διὰ τὸν τοῦ Ποιμάνδρου λόγον. διενοήθην ὁρῶν is equivalent to θεωρῶ ἐν τῷ νοΐ μου above. The 'intelligible world' can be 'seen' only with the eye of the mind. The λόγος ('speech') of Poimandres, which caused the prophet to see it, is the preceding command, νόει τὸ φῶς καὶ γνώριζε τοῦτο. We might rather have expected to be told that he saw it διὰ τὴν τοῦ Ποιμάνδρου ἀντώπησιν. But we may understand that the λόγος and the ἀντώπησις operated together; the command worked like a spell, and its power was supplemented by the gaze.

§ 8 a. Εἶδες ἐν τῷ νῷ τὸ ἀρχέτυπον εἶδος, τὸ προάρχον τῆς ἀρχῆς, τὸ ἀπέραντον (τῆς ἀπεράντου MSS.). The word ἀρχή is to be understood as in *Gen.* I. I, ἐν ἀρχῇ ἐποίησεν ὁ θεὸς τὸν οὐρανὸν καὶ τὴν γῆν. The intelligible world was in existence before God began to make the sensible world out of formless ὕλη. There is no meaning in saying that the 'beginning' of the sensible world was ἀπέραντος; but as an epithet of the νοητὸς κόσμος, the word ἀπέραντος may be understood in the same sense as ἀπεριόριστος above. Simon Magus called the supreme God τὴν μεγάλην δύναμιν, τὴν ἀπέραντον (Hippol. *Ref. haer.* 6. 9).

§ 8 b. ⟨τὰ⟩ στοιχεῖα τῆς φύσεως πόθεν ὑπέστη; . . . Ἐκ βουλῆς θεοῦ, ἥτις [[λαβοῦσα τὸν λόγον]] [καὶ] ἰδοῦσα τὸν καλὸν κόσμον ἐμιμήσατο. The 'physical' (i. e. material) elements are fire, air water, and earth, out of which the αἰσθητὸς κόσμος is constructed. The first stage in its making is the formation of these four elements by differentiation out of the watery chaos. The writer uses the word φύσις to signify the material universe. The καλὸς κόσμος is the νοητὸς κόσμος. The βουλὴ θεοῦ, by which the αἰσθητὸς κόσμος is made after the model of the νοητὸς κόσμος, corresponds to the πρόνοια θεοῦ of the Stoics, and the βούλησις or θέλημα τοῦ θεοῦ spoken of in some of the *Hermetica.* Its function is the same as that of the creative λόγος of God in the writer's Jewish authorities (cf. *Ps.* 32 (33). 6, τῷ λόγῳ τοῦ κυρίου οἱ οὐρανοὶ ἐστερεώθησαν and Philo *Legg. alleg.* 3. 31. 96, quoted above); but having adopted the terms λόγος and βουλή from different sources, the author of *Corp.* I does not himself identify them. He here personifies the βουλὴ θεοῦ for the moment; but the personification is hardly more than a literary figure, and God's βουλή does not take part as a person in the mythical events which follow, as the λόγος does.

It is difficult to find any meaning in the statement that God's βουλή ' took ' or ' received ' the λόγος; and it seems best to assume that in the original text the phrase λαβοῦσα τὸν λόγον was applied to the ὑγρὰ φύσις, and was intended to refer back to λόγος ἅγιος ἐπέβη τῇ ⟨ὑγρᾷ⟩ φύσει in § 5 a. The λόγος 'took its stand upon' the watery substance; and the watery substance, having thus ' received the λόγος ', was developed into an ordered world. Compare § 11 b, οὐ γὰρ ἔτι εἶχε τὸν λόγον (ἡ φύσις).

ἐκοσμοποιήθη, διακριθέντων ἐξ αὐτῆς τῶν στοιχείων, ἐξ ὧν καὶ τὸ γέννημα τῶν ἐμψύχων.—(κοσμοποιηθεῖσα διὰ τῶν ἑαυτῆς στοιχείων καὶ γεννημάτων ψυχῶν MSS.). The traditional text is mere nonsense; and I have rewritten it so as to express what I suppose to have been the author's meaning. It is to be presumed that he here spoke of the two stages of the κοσμοποιία, viz. (1) the separation of the elements, and (2) the production of living creatures from the separated elements. The second of these two stages is the process described in § 11 b.

§ **5 b.** **καὶ ⟨γὰρ⟩ πῦρ . . . κρέμασθαι αὐτὸν ἀπ' αὐτοῦ.** This passage, misplaced in the MSS., corresponds to the account of the separation of the elements in *Corp.* III 2 a (ἀπεχωρίσθη τὰ ἐλαφρὰ κ.τ.λ.). Both writers alike have substituted for the Mosaic description of the separation of ' the waters above the firmament ' from ' the waters below the firmament ' a description of the separation of the elements which is based on the Stoic physics.

κοῦφον δὲ ἦν καὶ ὀξύ, δραστικόν τε. Cf. *Hermippus* (Kroll and Viereck) 1. 6. 37 : τὸ μὲν (πῦρ) λίαν δραστικόν, ὀξύ τε καὶ κοῦφον ὂν καὶ λεπτομερές.

ἀναβαίνων [τοσοῦτον] (ἀναβαίνοντος αὐτοῦ MSS.) **μέχρι τοῦ πυρός.** If τοσοῦτον is the right reading, it must mean ' only so far '; the air rose till it reached the fire above, but no farther. But as this meaning is sufficiently expressed by μέχρι τοῦ πυρός, it is probable that τοσοῦτον has been added by a later hand.

ὡς δοκεῖν κρέμασθαι αὐτὸν ἀπ' αὐτοῦ. In the parallel passage, *Corp.* III. 2 a, ἀνακρέμασθαι occurs ; but it is differently employed. In *Corp.* III, the fire is 'suspended aloft', and rests upon the air below it ; in *Corp.* I, the air 'appears to be suspended from the fire', being situated immediately below the fire.

⟨⟨καὶ περιεσχέθη (περισχέσθαι MSS.) τὸ πῦρ δυνάμει μεγίστῃ, καὶ στάσιν ἔσχε (ἐσχηκέναι MSS.) κρατούμενον.⟩⟩ These words were probably suggested by the mention of a στερέωμα in connexion with the separation of the waters in *Genesis*. The meaning seems to be that the fire was (so to speak) solidified in the form of a firmly fixed sphere. The 'mighty Power' which operated as God's agent in the fixing of the 'firmament' is probably the δημιουργὸς νοῦς spoken of in § 9, who resides in the outermost sphere of heaven (or in the space immediately beyond it?), 'encompassing' that sphere, and holding it in place. But as we have not yet been told of the existence of the δημιουργὸς νοῦς, the writer cannot at this stage mention him by his proper name, and therefore merely refers to him vaguely as a δύναμις μεγίστη.

γῆ δὲ καὶ ὕδωρ ἔμενε καθ' ἑαυτὰ συμμεμιγμένα. Fire and air having been separated out from the 'watery substance' of the primal chaos, what remained of it was a mixture of earth and water. Cf. Philo *De opif. mundi* 11. 38, Cohn I, p. 11 : after the making of the firmament, ἐπειδὴ τὸ σύμπαν ὕδωρ εἰς ἅπασαν τὴν γῆν ἀνεκέχυτο καὶ διὰ πάντων αὐτῆς ἐπεφοιτήκει τῶν μερῶν, οἷα σπογγίας ἀναπεπωκυίας ἰκμάδα, ὡς εἶναι τέλμα[τα] καὶ βαθὺν πηλόν, ἀμφοτέρων τῶν στοιχείων ἀναδεδευμένων καὶ συγκεχυμένων τρόπον φυράματος εἰς μίαν ἀδιάκριτον καὶ ἄμορφον φύσιν κ.τ.λ. In Philo, as in *Genesis* and in *Corp.* III, the separation of earth and water follows immediately ; but in *Corp.* I, it does not take place (or at any rate is not mentioned in our text) until a later stage ; see § 11 b.

κινούμενα δὲ ἦν διὰ τὸν ⟨ἐπάνω⟩ ⟨⟨τοῦ ὕδατος⟩⟩ ἐπιφερόμενον πνευματικὸν λόγον. It seems certain that the word ἐπιφερόμενον was suggested by *Gen.* 1. 2, LXX (καὶ πνεῦμα θεοῦ ἐπεφέρετο ἐπάνω τοῦ ὕδατος) ; and as τοῦ ὕδατος makes confusion where it stands in the MSS., the simplest remedy is to transpose it to this place, and insert ἐπάνω before it. The ὕδωρ here spoken of must be the mass of mingled (or, more strictly speaking, still undifferentiated) earth and water ; and this inaccurate use of the word ὕδατος can be most easily accounted for by assuming that the phrase was taken over unaltered from the Greek *Genesis*. The meaning must be that

the λόγος, which, before the separation of the elements, 'took its
stand upon' the undifferentiated 'watery substance', now hovers
close above that portion of the watery substance which still remains
below in the form of undifferentiated earth and water. It afterwards
quits that position and flies up to heaven (§ 10). For the epithet
πνευματικός, cf. *Ps.* 32 (33). 6, where τῷ πνεύματι τοῦ στόματος αὐτοῦ
stands in parallelism with τῷ λόγῳ τοῦ κυρίου. The author must
have meant that the λόγος consists of πνεῦμα, i. e. gaseous substance, and 'moves' the watery mass below it, as the wind puts
the surface of the sea in motion. From the Stoic point of view,
there is no inconsistency in holding that the λόγος is a gaseous
substance, and at the same time a living person.

§ 9. ὁ δὲ νοῦς ὁ πρῶτος (νοῦς ὁ θεός MSS.), [[ἀρρενόθηλυς ὤν]],
⟨ὁ⟩ ζωὴ καὶ φῶς ὑπάρχων. ὁ πρῶτος is wanted, to stand in contrast
to ἕτερον νοῦν below. Most likely πρῶτος was written ᾱος, as before
(see § 6), and ᾱος was corrupted into θ̄ς, i. e. θεός. Similarly below,
where the MSS. give νοῦν δημιουργόν, ὃς θεὸς . . . ὤν, it is probable
that θεὸς is a corruption of βος, i. e. δεύτερος.

The phrase ἀρρενόθηλυς ὤν is out of place ; it must have been
intended to go with and explain ἀπεκύησεν, which is properly used
of the mother, and not of the father. For the description of the
supreme God as ἀρρενόθηλυς, compare *Ascl. Lat.* III. 20 b, 21.

The phrase ζωὴ καὶ φῶς is repeatedly used in *Corp.* I as a known
name or description of God. Compare the use of the words ζωή
and φῶς in the Fourth Gospel.[1] The use of φῶς to denote God
may have been partly due to Zoroastrian influence ; and that of
ζωή may possibly have been derived from phrases used in Egyptian
cults. (See prefatory note on *Corp.* XI. i.)

ἀπεκύησε⟨ν⟩ [λόγῳ]. The word λόγῳ is meaningless here. Perhaps
Reitzenstein is right in striking it out ; but how did it come to be
inserted ? Sense might be made in another way, by writing ⟨πρὸς
τῷ⟩ λόγῳ, 'in addition to the Word'. We were told before that
the Logos is son of God ; we are now told that God has another
son also.

ἕτερον νοῦν δημιουργόν. The writer distinguishes a first νοῦς, who is
the supreme God, and a second νοῦς, who is the immediate 'Maker'
of the contents of the material universe. In this he agrees with
Numenius. See Numen. *ap.* Euseb. *Praep. ev.* 11. 18, quoted in

---

[1] And in the Old Testament ; e. g. *Ps.* 35 (36). 10 : παρὰ σοὶ πηγὴ ζωῆς, ἐν τῷ φωτί
σου ὀψόμεθα φῶς.

prefatory note on *Corp.* II. Cf. *Oracula Chaldaica* (*c.* A. D. 200 ?), Kroll, p. 14 : πάντα γὰρ ἐξετέλεσσε πατήρ, καὶ νῷ παρέδωκε | δευτέρῳ, ὃν πρῶτον κληΐζετε πᾶν γένος ἀνδρῶν. In the Christian Gnostic systems also, the Demiurgus was distinguished from the supreme God ; and in most of them, he was enthroned (as in *Corp.* I) in or immediately above the highest sphere of the material heavens.[1] But most of the Christian Gnostics insisted on the inferiority of the Demiurgus to the supreme God more strongly than the author of *Corp.* I does, and separated the one from the other by a larger interval ; and some of them regarded the Demiurgus as a positively evil power.

The Demiurgus-Nous of *Corp.* I begins his work only when the four elements have already been separated ; his function is to make the ζῷα, both ἀθάνατα (the heavenly bodies) and θνητά, with the exception of man, who is of different origin. The making of plants, which is placed before the making of the heavenly bodies in *Gen.* 1, and is coupled with the making of mortal ζῷα in *Corp.* III, is omitted in *Corp.* I.

The conception of the Demiurgus-Nous, which the writer of *Corp.* I has adopted from the Platonists of his time, corresponds to the Judaeo-Stoic conception of the λόγος ; and one or the other is in reality superfluous. The author however sought to include both of them side by side in his system ; and finding in *Gen.* 1 a mention of ' the spirit of God moving on the face of the waters ', he identified the λόγος with this ' spirit of God ', and accordingly assigned to the λόγος the preliminary work of separating the elements, while he reserved for the Demiurgus-Nous the function of making ζῷα. But he is conscious of their fundamental identity, and shows it by saying in § 10 that the λόγος, after the completion of his task in the lower world, flew up to heaven, and ' was united with the Demiurgus-Nous ; for he was of one substance with him '. From that point onward, the two are one.

ἐδημιούργησε⟨ν ἐκ⟩ ⟨⟨πυρὸς καὶ πνεύματος⟩⟩ διοικητ⟨ορ⟩άς τινας ἑπτά. From the reference to this passage in § 16 (τῶν ἑπτὰ . . . οὓς ἔφην σοι ἐκ πυρὸς καὶ πνεύματος ⟨γεγονέναι⟩), it may be inferred that the words ἐκ πυρὸς καὶ πνεύματος originally stood where I have placed them. The ' seven Governors ' are the planets. The Stoics said that the moon consists of a mixture of fire and air, and the

---

[1] The Demiurgus-Nous corresponds in some respects to the supreme God of the Stoics ; and the Stoics located their supreme God in the highest sphere of heaven.

other six planets, of fire alone.[1] But the author of *Corp*. I says that all seven are made of 'fire and *pneuma*'; and this presumably means that they are all alike made of fire and *air* in combination. The Stoic πνεῦμα was commonly regarded as a mixture of fire and air; but when the word πνεῦμα is so used as to exclude an intermixture of fire, it must be taken to mean air. πνεῦμα means the element air in Pl. *Phileb*. 29 A. Cf. Hippol. *Ref. haer.* 4. 43 (quoted in note on § 17 below) and *Corp*. III. 2 a. This paragraph corresponds to *Gen*. 1. 14–19 ('God said, Let there be lights in the firmament ... to rule over the day and over the night' &c.), and to *Corp*. III. 2 b (διηρθρώθη ⟨ἡ πυρίνη οὐσία⟩ σὺν τοῖς ἐν αὐτῇ θεοῖς κ.τ.λ.).

ἡ διοίκησις αὐτῶν εἱμαρμένη καλεῖται. The notion that Heimarmene is brought to bear on things below by the movements of the heavenly bodies occurs repeatedly in the *Hermetica*. Cf. *Corp*. XVI. 16 : ταύτην δὲ τὴν διοίκησιν (*sc*. the administration of the sublunar world by the planets, through the agency of their subordinates the daemons) Ἑρμῆς εἱμαρμένην ἐκάλεσεν. Herm. *ap*. Stob. *Exc*. XII. 2 : ὅπλον γὰρ εἱμαρμένης οἱ ἀστέρες κ.τ.λ. *Corp*. III. 4 : πρὸς μοῖραν δρομήματος ⟨ἐγ⟩κυκλίων θεῶν. The writer of *Corp*. I says nothing about the fixed stars, and takes into account the influence of the planets alone.

εἱμαρμένη is a Stoic term. The identification of Heimarmene with the operation of the heavenly bodies is characteristic rather of the later Stoicism.

§ 10. ἐπήδησεν εὐθὺς ἐκ τῶν κατωφερῶν στοιχείων ⟨⟨τῆς φύσεως⟩⟩ [τοῦ θεοῦ] ὁ τοῦ θεοῦ λόγος εἰς τὸ καθαρὸν [[τῆς φύσεως]] δημιούργημα. τὰ κατωφερῆ στοιχεῖα (a Stoic term) signifies the two heavy elements, earth and water. τοῦ θεοῦ has been duplicated by error, and τῆς φύσεως has been transposed. Cf. § 8 b : τὰ στοιχεῖα τῆς φύσεως πόθεν ὑπέστη ; The καθαρὸν δημιούργημα is the material heaven, which has just been organized by the Demiurgus-Nous. It is καθαρόν, because free from any intermixture of the grosser elements. The heavens apparently consist of fire alone, though their inhabitants, the planets, are made of a mixture of fire and air.

---

[1] Chrysippus, in Arius Didymus, Diels *Doxogr*. p. 458 : διὰ ⟨τῶν τεττάρων στοιχείων⟩ τινὸς ἢ τινῶν ἢ καὶ πάντων τὰ λοιπὰ συνέστηκε· διὰ μὲν τῶν τεττάρων, ὡς ... τὰ ἐπὶ γῆς πάντα συγκρίματα· διὰ δυοῖν δέ, ὡς ἡ σελήνη διὰ πυρὸς καὶ ἀέρος συνέστηκε· δι' ἑνὸς δέ, ὡς ὁ ἥλιος· ... ὁ γὰρ ἥλιος πῦρ ἐστιν εἰλικρινές.

34   CORPVS HERMETICVM

ὁμοούσιος γὰρ ἦν. The word ὁμοούσιος was in use before it was brought into prominence by the disputes with which the Council of Nicaea was concerned. Plotinus 4. 7. 10: διὰ συγγένειαν καὶ τὸ ὁμοούσιον. It occurs repeatedly in Gnostic documents quoted by Hippol. *Ref. haer.* (A. D. 220–230), e. g. 5. 17.

The Logos and the Demiurgus-Nous are 'of one substance'; but is that substance material or immaterial? If the author had· been asked that question, he might have been puzzled how to answer it. The phrase τὸν πνευματικὸν λόγον in § 5 b *fin.* seems to imply that the Logos is material; and in stirring the watery mass, it operates like a wind. But on the other hand, the Demiurgus-Nous is presumably of the same substance as his parent the supreme Nous, who is ζωὴ καὶ φῶς; and though φῶς in the literal sense is a material thing, the ζωὴ καὶ φῶς of this document is clearly not αἰσθητόν, but νοητόν. The truth is that the author has not completely succeeded in harmonizing the Stoic and Platonic conceptions which he has adopted. When speaking of λόγος, he speaks as a Stoic, and therefore as one who assumes all things to be material; when speaking of νοῦς, he speaks as a Platonist, and regards Mind as incorporeal.

§ 11 a. ὁ δὲ δημιουργὸς νοῦς σὺν τῷ λόγῳ, [ὁ] περιίσχων τοὺς κύκλους καὶ δινῶν ῥοίζῳ, ἔστρεψε τὰ ἑαυτοῦ δημιουργήματα. The δημιουργήματα of the Demiurgus-Nous are the planets (and presumably the fixed stars also, though the latter have not been expressly mentioned). He 'encompasses' the spheres in which the planets are fixed; for his abode is in (or immediately beyond) the outermost sphere. On the arrival of the Logos, who henceforward 'is united with him' and co-operates with him, he sets in motion the planets which he has fashioned, and makes them move in circular orbits. The mention of the λόγος in this connexion is perhaps intended to suggest that the movements of the heavenly bodies are 'rational'.

εἴασε στρέφεσθαι ἀπ' ἀρχῆς ἀορίστου εἰς ἀπέραντον τέλος· ἄρχεται γὰρ οὗ λήγει ἡ [δὲ] τούτων περιφορά. The movement is circular, and therefore everlasting; for a circle has no terminal point. Cf. *Ascl. Lat.* III. 40 b: 'sic est enim rotundita⟨ti⟩s volubilis ratio, ut ita sibi coartata sint cuncta, ut initium quod sit volubilitatis ignores.' The phrase ἄρχεται οὗ λήγει is not quite accurate; for there is no point at which the movement 'ceases'. But the writer's meaning is that any point in the orbit may be considered the end of a circuit, but that, if thus regarded, it must at the same time be regarded as the beginning of a fresh circuit.

The words ἀπ' ἀρχῆς ἀορίστου seem to imply that the movement of the heavenly bodies is not only without end, but also without beginning; yet we have just been told that it *has* had a beginning. Perhaps what is here said about circular movement was taken over unaltered from an Aristotelian source, in which the movement of the heavens was assumed to be without beginning, as well as without end.

11 b. ⟨ἡ δὲ φύσις⟩, καθὼς ἠθέλησεν ὁ νοῦς, ἐκ τῶν κατωφερῶν στοιχείων ζῷα ἤνεγκεν ἄλογα. This paragraph corresponds to *Gen.* I. 20–25, and to *Corp.* III. 3 a. Having described the making of the heavenly bodies (τὰ ἀθάνατα ζῷα), the writer proceeds to describe the making of τὰ θνητὰ ζῷα.

The subject of the sentence has been lost; but the context makes it almost certain that it was ἡ φύσις. 'Nature' (i. e. either the force which operates in the sublunar world, or the sublunar world itself, regarded as a living agent,) brought forth animals 'according to the will of νοῦς'. The νοῦς here spoken of must be the Demiurgus-Nous, since in § 12 *init.* (ὁ δὲ πάντων πατὴρ νοῦς κ.τ.λ.) the supreme Nous is contrasted with it; and as ὁ νοῦς without qualification is ambiguous, it may be suspected that some qualifying word (δημιουργός or δεύτερος) has been lost before νοῦς. The Demiurgus-Nous, being stationed in the highest heaven, does not directly act in his own person in the sublunar world; but he gives orders to φύσις, and by her his will is executed. Thus the words ⟨ἡ φύσις⟩, καθὼς ἠθέλησεν ὁ ⟨δημιουργὸς⟩ νοῦς, ἐκ τῶν κατωφερῶν στοιχείων ζῷα ἤνεγκεν κ.τ.λ. correspond to 'God said, Let the earth bring forth' &c. in *Gen.* I, and to ἀνῆκε δὲ ἕκαστος θεὸς (i. e. each of the lower elements) τὸ προσταχθὲν αὐτῷ κ.τ.λ. in *Corp.* III. In the κατωφερῆ στοιχεῖα air is here included as well as water and earth; all three are 'downward-tending' as compared with fire.

ἄλογα· οὐ γὰρ ἔτι εἶχε (sc. ἡ φύσις) τὸν λόγον. The Logos has quitted the sublunar world. His departure has left the sublunar world devoid of 'reason'; and the animals which φύσις produces there are consequently 'irrational'. The word λόγος here means 'the faculty of reason', by the absence of which beasts are distinguished from men. In §§ 5 a and 6, it rather meant God's 'speech', i. e. his creative *fiat*; but the writer may have been hardly conscious that he was using it in different senses. The ἄλογα ζῷα are 'the animals which have not reason'; but they are also 'the animals which cannot talk'.

διεκεχώριστο (διακεχώρισται MSS.) δὲ ἀπ' ἀλλήλων ἥ τε γῆ καὶ τὸ ὕδωρ. As we were told in § 5 b that earth and water 'remained intermingled', it was necessary for the writer to mention their separation at the point where he speaks of the different kinds of animals which earth and water respectively produced, if he had not mentioned it before. But in this position, the clause interrupts the narrative of the *zoogonia* by an awkward parenthesis; and it is possible that it has been misplaced, and ought to stand earlier. With the substitution of διεχωρίσθη for διακεχώρισται, it might be put at the beginning of § 11 b, before ἡ δὲ φύσις κ.τ.λ. [καθὼς ἠθέλησεν ὁ νοῦς.] As there is no apparent reason for repeating these words here, I take them to be a misplaced doublet of καθὼς ... νοῦς above.

καὶ ἐξήνεγκεν ⟨ἡ γῆ⟩ [ἀπ' αὐτῆς ἃ εἶχε] ζῷα τετράποδα ⟨καὶ⟩ ἑρπετά, θηρία ἄγρια καὶ ἥμερα. I can make nothing of the words ἀπ' αὐτῆς ἃ εἶχε. (Is ἃ εἶχε a corruption of ἀνῆκε, an alternative for ἐξήνεγκεν?) The rest of the sentence closely resembles *Gen.* 1. 24 f. : καὶ εἶπεν ὁ θεός Ἐξαγαγέτω ἡ γῆ ... τετράποδα καὶ ἑρπετὰ καὶ θηρία τῆς γῆς κατὰ γένος. ... καὶ ἐποίησεν ὁ θεὸς τὰ θηρία ... καὶ τὰ κτήνη ... καὶ πάντα τὰ ἑρπετά. (Cf. *Gen.* 1. 12 : καὶ ἐξήνεγκεν ἡ γῆ βοτάνην κ.τ.λ.)

With the making of the irrational animals, the *demiurgia* in the narrower sense of the word is completed ; and it only remains to explain the origin of man. The genesis of man is the climax in which the whole process of creation culminates, just as in *Gen.* 1 and in *Corp.* III. In his account of the origin of man, the writer is still influenced by the Jewish *Genesis* ; but this part of his doctrine, though partly based on that of *Genesis*, has been developed into something which differs widely from it.

§ 12. ὁ δὲ πάντων πατὴρ [[ὁ]] νοῦς, ⟨⟨ὃ⟩⟩ ὢν ζωὴ καὶ φῶς, ἀπεκύησεν ἄνθρωπον αὐτῷ ⟨ὅμ⟩οιον (ἴσον MSS.). The rest of the ζῷα, both ἀθάνατα and θνητά, were made by the 'second God', the Demiurgus-Nous. But man is of a different and higher origin. He is no mere product of nature ; he is son of the supreme God, and peer of the second God. And though he has fallen from his high estate, and is now sunk in matter, he has before him the prospect of returning to his true home above, and resuming his lost glory.

In the myth which here begins, the human race is represented by a person named Anthropos, who is the archetype and the ancestor of mankind.

The author cannot have said that Man, even before his fall, was 'equal' (ἴσος) to the supreme God. There cannot be two supreme Gods; and it is evident from the contents of *Corp.* I as a whole that the Anthropos is *not* equal to 'the Father of all'. The right word is ὅμοιον :[1] cf. *Gen.* i. 26, ποιήσωμεν ἄνθρωπον κατ' εἰκόνα ἡμετέραν καὶ καθ' ὁμοίωσιν.

The word ὅμοιον may have lost its first two letters and been changed into ἴσον by mere accident ; or a Christian reader may have bethought him of the doctrine that God the Son is 'equal to the Father as touching his Godhead', and tried to introduce it here by substituting ἴσον for ὅμοιον,—though very inappropriately, as the Anthropos of *Corp.* I has little resemblance to the Second Person of the Christian Trinity.

The Anthropos of *Corp.* I is 'like his Father' in this respect among others, that he is ἀρρενόθηλυς. (§ 15.) It would be possible for one who held this doctrine to find support for it in *Gen.* i. 27 : ἐποίησεν ὁ θεὸς τὸν ἄνθρωπον· κατ' εἰκόνα θεοῦ ἐποίησεν αὐτόν· ἄρσεν καὶ θῆλυ ἐποίησεν αὐτούς. If a reader could persuade himself that αὐτούς is here equivalent to αὐτόν, he might take these words to mean that the first ἄνθρωπος was ἀρσενόθηλυς, like God who made him. Cf. Sir Thomas Browne, ed. Wilkin, vol. ii, p. 469 : 'Plato, and some of the Rabbins, . . . conceived the first man an hermaphrodite ; and Marcus Leo, the learned Jew, in some sense hath allowed it ; affirming that Adam, in one *suppositum*, contained both male and female.[2] And therefore, when it is said in the text, that "God created man in his own image, in the image of God created he him, male and female created he them" : applying the singular and plural unto Adam, it might denote that in one substance and in himself he included both sexes, which was after divided, and the female called woman.'

οὗ ἠγάσθη (ἠράσθη MSS.) ὡς ἰδίου τόκου· περικαλλὴς γὰρ ⟨ἦν⟩, τὴν τοῦ πατρὸς εἰκόνα ἔχων. A father is not 'enamoured of' his son; and ἠράσθη is undoubtedly a corruption of ἠγάσθη. (Cf. ἠγάσθησαν in § 13 a.) It is only in the relation between Ἄνθρωπος and Φύσις (§ 14) that ἔρως is brought into action in the writer's mythical narrative. The language of this passage is partly borrowed from Pl. *Tim.* 37 c : ὡς δὲ κινηθὲν αὐτὸ (*sc.* τὸν κόσμον) καὶ ζῶν ἐνόησε . . . ὁ γεννήσας πατήρ,

---

[1] If we were to retain ἴσον, it would be necessary to substitute for αὐτῷ some term denoting the *second* God. But that would involve a larger alteration of the text.

[2] For the statement that 'the first man was bisexual', Bousset, *Hauptprobleme der Gnosis*, p. 198, refers to *Bereshith Rabba* cap. 8 on *Gen.* i. 26 ; *Bamidbar R.* cap. 14 ; and *Berachoth* 61 a.

ἠγάσθη τε καὶ εὐφρανθεὶς κ.τ.λ. But in the *Timaeus*, the son in whom the father 'takes delight' is the Kosmos.[1] In *Corp*. I, the son spoken of is Man; but the writer has transferred to the relation between God and Man the terms used by Plato to describe the relation between God and the Kosmos. And there is another difference. In the *Timaeus*, the son (viz. the αἰσθητὸς κόσμος) is made in the likeness, not of the Father, but of the νοητὸς κόσμος; but in *Corp*. I, the son (viz. Man) 'bears the image' of the Father himself. The words τὴν τοῦ πατρὸς εἰκόνα ἔχων were doubtless suggested by κατ' εἰκόνα θεοῦ in *Gen*. I. 26 f.

The same sentence of the *Timaeus* is imitated in *Ascl. Lat.* I. 8 : ἠγάσθη τε καὶ πάνυ ἐφίλησεν ὡς ἴδιον τόκον. (The son is there the Kosmos, as in Pl. *Tim*.) Another reminiscence of the Platonic passage occurs in Basilides, Hippol. *Ref. haer*. 7. 23 : the Demiurgus (not the supreme God) ἠξίωσε μὴ εἶναι μόνος, ἀλλὰ ἐποίησεν ἑαυτῷ καὶ ἐγέννησεν ἐκ τῶν ὑποκειμένων υἱὸν ἑαυτοῦ πολὺ κρείττονα καὶ σοφώτερον. ... ἰδὼν οὖν τὸν υἱὸν ἐθαύμασε καὶ ἠγάπησε καὶ κατεπλάγη· τοιοῦτον γάρ τι κάλλος ἐφαίνετο υἱοῦ τῷ μεγάλῳ ἄρχοντι.

καὶ παρέδωκεν αὐτῷ πάντα τὰ δημιουργήματα.—(καὶ παρέδωκε τὰ ἑαυτοῦ πάντα δημιουργήματα MSS.) The reading τὰ ἑαυτοῦ ... δημιουργήματα, 'the things which he himself (*sc*. the supreme God) had made', cannot be right; for it is not the supreme God, but the second God, that is called ὁ δημιουργός in *Corp*. I.

As to the statement that God delivered over to Man 'all things that had been made', see note on ἔχων πᾶσαν ἐξουσίαν in § 14.

§ 13 a. ⟨ὁ δέ,⟩ ⟨⟨γενόμενος ἐν τῇ δημιουργικῇ σφαίρᾳ,⟩⟩ ⟨⟨κατενόησε τοῦ ἀδελφοῦ τὰ δημιουργήματα⟩⟩ ⟨⟨τοῦ ἐπικειμένου ἐπὶ τοῦ πυρός⟩⟩. [καὶ] κατανοήσας δὲ κ.τ.λ. This paragraph is in great confusion. I have rewritten it freely, by way of an attempt to make it express what the author presumably meant; but there is little hope of restoring his actual words. We should expect to be told where Anthropos was, before we are told what he did; I have therefore placed γενόμενος ἐν τῇ δημιουργικῇ σφαίρᾳ at the beginning. And κατενόησε κ.τ.λ. ought to precede κατανοήσας δὲ κ.τ.λ. The 'demiurgic sphere' is the sphere in which the Demiurgus-Nous resides, i. e. the highest sphere of heaven; and it is there that Anthropos also took up his abode when he first came into being. The 'brother' of Anthropos is the Demiurgus-Nous, both of them being sons of the supreme Nous; and ὁ ἐπικεί-

[1] A similar thought is expressed in *Gen*. I. 31 : ἴδεν ὁ θεὸς τὰ πάντα ὅσα ἐποίησεν, καὶ ἰδοὺ καλὰ λίαν.

μενος ἐπὶ τοῦ πυρός, 'he who is set over the region of fire (i. e. the heavens)', must also be the Demiurgus-Nous, who, as we were told before, 'encompasses' the region of fire, and has made and governs the inhabitants of that region, viz. the planets. The word κατανοῆσαι, which follows τοῦ ἐπικειμένου ἐπὶ τοῦ πυρός where that phrase stands in the MSS., may perhaps be a miswriting of κατανοήσας, which follows τοῦ ἐπικειμένου ἐπὶ τοῦ πυρός at the place to which I have transposed it.

κατανοήσας δὲ τὴν τοῦ δημιουργοῦ κτίσιν ἐν τῷ πυρί (πατρί MSS.), ἠβουλήθη καὶ αὐτὸς δημιουργεῖν. 'The creation of the Demiurgus-Nous in the region of fire' is the making of the planets. Anthropos observes that the Demiurgus-Nous has made immortal ζῷα in the heavens; and he seeks to emulate his brother, and produce a race of ζῷα on his own account. He executes this design by generating mankind.[1] The design must have been innocent in itself; for it was permitted (συνεχωρήθη) by the supreme God. But it was executed amiss. Perhaps we are meant to understand that Anthropos, being ἀρσενόθηλυς, might and should have produced a race of living beings from himself alone. His descendants would then have been free from the contamination of ὕλη; they would have been, like their parent, incorporeal,—soul without body, or νοῦς without αἴσθησις; and as such, they would have been immortal. But he was misled by ἔρως, and fell into the error of uniting himself with φύσις. Hence his descendants have in them the 'darkness and death' which comes from their mother, φύσις (that is to say, from ὕλη), as well as the 'life and light' which comes to them from their father, the Anthropos. They are 'double'; and though immortal in respect of one part of their twofold nature, they are mortal in respect of the other part. This is our prophet's version of the Mosaic story of 'the fall of man'.

⟨. . .⟩ ⟨⟨πᾶσαν ἐνέργειαν ἐν ἑαυτῷ ἔχοντα τῶν διοικητόρων⟩⟩ οἱ δὲ ἠγάσθησαν αὐτοῦ. I have placed the words πᾶσαν . . . διοικητόρων here, because they are clearly out of place where they stand in the MSS., and when transposed to this position, they serve to supply the needed antecedent to οἱ δέ, which undoubtedly means the planets. But something has been lost before them. In the

---

[1] This appears to be the writer's meaning; for we are not told that Anthropos 'made' anything except his own descendants; and indeed, there was nothing else left for him to make. The verb γεννᾶν is frequently used as an equivalent for ποιεῖν or δημιουργεῖν (e. g. in Pl. *Tim. passim*); and here δημιουργεῖν seems to mean *generare*. Cf. *Corp.* II. 17 a : πατρὸς γὰρ τὸ ποιεῖν.

missing passage, the writer must have said that Anthropos descended
from the 'demiurgic sphere', and associated with the planets in the
lower spheres of heaven.

ἕκαστος δὲ μετεδίδου τῆς ἰδίας φύσεως (τάξεως MSS.). τάξεως is
meaningless; and from the words μεταλαβὼν τῆς αὐτῶν φύσεως in
the following sentence, it may be inferred that the author here wrote
φύσεως, or something equivalent to it. Cf. ἔχοντος γὰρ αὐτοῦ . . .
τῶν ἑπτὰ τὴν φύσιν in § 16.

This statement is explained by § 25, in which we are told that
the human soul, in the course of its ascent to God, renders up to
each of the planets one of the evil πάθη which cleaved to it during
its residence on earth.   The process spoken of in § 13 a must be the
reverse of this; and the things which Anthropos receives from the
planets in the course of his descent must be the same things which
the soul gives back to the planets in the course of its ascent, viz.
the evil πάθη.   The planets are ἐμπαθεῖς;[1] and in his association
with the planets, Anthropos receives from each of them the special
kind of πάθος which belongs to it.   This is the first stage in the
process of his degradation or corruption, and the cause of the
disastrous event which follows.

§ 13 b. καταμαθὼν τὴν τούτων οὐσίαν.   What is the point of saying
that Anthropos 'learnt the being' of the planets?   Perhaps it is
implied that he now came to know (and experience) the evil πάθη
which are inherent in the substance of the planets, whereas hitherto
he had known good alone.   If so, we might compare 'the tree of
the knowledge of good and evil' in *Gen.* 2.

ἠβουλήθη ἀναρρῆξαι τὴν περιφέρειαν τῶν κύκλων.   The fiery firmament has been fashioned by the Demiurgus-Nous into a series of
concentric spheres,—the sphere of the fixed stars, and the seven
spheres of the planets; and as Anthropos has had dealings with all
the planets in succession, we must suppose him to have arrived at
the lowest of the celestial spheres, that of the moon.   The lunar
sphere is the barrier between the heavens and the sublunar world;
and he now seeks to break through this barrier, and enter into
communication with what lies below it.   We are not told that *this*

---

[1] This corresponds with the writer's view that the planets are made of intermingled fire and air, and not of unmixed fire.   The doctrine that an intermixture
of air in the (material) soul goes along with an intermixture of πάθη in the
character was taught by Posidonius.   Perhaps it is implied that in the planetary
region Anthropos assumes a body made of πῦρ καὶ πνεῦμα, like the bodies of the
planets.

design was approved by God; and it seems to be at this point that the overt error or sin of Anthropos begins.

§ 14. [ὁ τοῦ τῶν θνητῶν κόσμου καὶ τῶν ἀλόγων ζῴων ἔχων πᾶσαν ἐξουσίαν.] This is probably a reminiscence of *Gen.* i. 26–28 : ἀρχέτωσαν (οἱ ἄνθρωποι) τῶν ἰχθύων τῆς θαλάσσης καὶ τῶν πετείνων τοῦ οὐρανοῦ καὶ τῶν κτηνῶν καὶ πάσης τῆς γῆς καὶ πάντων τῶν ἑρπετῶν τῶν ἑρπόντων ἐπὶ τῆς γῆς. . . . καὶ κατακυριεύσατε αὐτῆς, καὶ ἄρχετε κ.τ.λ. Here, the dominion of man over τὰ ἐπίγεια alone is spoken of, as in *Gen.* i. But elsewhere, the author says that God has given man dominion or authority over τὰ οὐράνια also. § 12 *fin.* : παρέδωκεν αὐτῷ πάντα τὰ δημιουργήματα. § 15 : πάντων τὴν ἐξουσίαν ἔχων. § 32 *fin.* : παρέδωκας αὐτῷ τὴν πᾶσαν ἐξουσίαν. Cf. *Ascl. Lat.* I. 6 a : 'omnia illi licent' (= πάντων ἐξουσίαν ἔχει). The true man (i. e. the νοῦς in man, or the man who has got *gnosis*) is superior to the whole material universe; or in other words, he is 'above Heimarmene'.

These phrases resemble *Matth.* 28. 18 : ἐδόθη μοι πᾶσα ἐξουσία ἐν οὐρανῷ καὶ ἐπὶ γῆς.[1] But there is no reason to think that the author of *Corp.* I borrowed from the First Gospel, or *vice versa*; the truth is rather that each of the two writers independently adopted a current phrase. The words are differently applied; in *Corp.* I the ἐξουσία is given to Man (and, by implication, to every 'illuminated' man), but in *Ev. Matth.* it is given to Jesus.

It might perhaps be possible to retain the words ὁ τοῦ τῶν θνητῶν κ.τ.λ. where they stand in § 14, if we wrote ὡς in place of ὁ; but they are hardly to the point in this connexion, and it seems more likely that they have been shifted from some other position.

διὰ τῆς ἁρμονίας παρέκυψεν, ἀναρρήξας τὸ κύτος (κράτος MSS.). For κύτος in the sense of 'the cosmic sphere', cf. Pap. mag. Par. i. 1119 : χαῖρε τὸ πνεῦμα τὸ διῆκον ἀπὸ οὐρανοῦ ἐπὶ γῆν, καὶ ἀπὸ γῆς τῆς ἐν μέσῳ κύτ⟨ε⟩ι τοῦ κόσμου ἄχρι τῶν περάτων τῆς ἀβύσσου (i. e. of space). *Ib.* 2828 (to the Moon-goddess): ἡ πολυχώρητον ⌐κόσμον νυκτὸς⌐ (*lege* κόσμου κύτος) ἀμφιέπουσα.

Anthropos broke a hole in the lowest sphere of heaven, and looked down through the opening. The ἁρμονία is the structure of the heavens. The writer seems to have adopted the Pythagorean phrase

[1] Moffatt, *Theology of the Gospels*, p. 156, says 'the phrase in *Matth.* 28. 18, "All ἐξουσία is given to me in heaven and on earth", is an echo of the Danielic prediction that "there was given to him (i. e. the Son of Man) dominion and glory and a kingdom"'.

'the harmony of the spheres'; but he employs it in an altered sense. He is thinking, not of music, but rather of carpentry; the heavens are compared to the framework of a roof or dome fitted together by a builder.

καὶ ἔδειξε τῇ κατωφερεῖ φύσει (τὴν κατωφερῆ φύσιν MSS.) τὴν καλὴν τοῦ θεοῦ μορφήν. The writer uses φύσις in the sense of the material universe as a whole, or the sum of the four στοιχεῖα ; and accordingly, ἡ κατωφερὴς φύσις means τὰ κατωφερῆ στοιχεῖα, i. e. earth and water, or (if we include air also under τὰ κατωφερῆ στοιχεῖα, as in § 11 b,) the sublunar world. But in the writer's myth or allegory, this φύσις is personified, and is pictured in the form of a woman. The καλὴ τοῦ θεοῦ μορφή is the 'likeness of God' borne by the Anthropos.

The imagery of this paragraph was probably suggested, in part at least, by the story of the fall of Adam. ('The woman gave me of the tree, and I did eat'; and 'in the day that thou eatest thereof thou shalt surely die'.) As the conception of Anthropos in *Corp.* I has been developed out of the Adam of *Genesis*, it may very well be that the part played by Φύσις in the fall of Anthropos is the writer's version of the part played by Eve in the fall of Adam. It is true that in the Mosaic narrative itself the temptation to which Adam yielded is not said to be that of sexual desire ; but in interpretations of the story which were commonly accepted by Jews and Christians at the time when *Corp.* I was written, the sexual motive was brought to the front, and the sin of Adam was held to consist in giving way to sexual impulse.[1] Philo (*De opif. mundi* 56. 157 ff.) explains the Mosaic story as an allegory, in which Adam stands for νοῦς, Eve for αἴσθησις, and the serpent for ἡδονή;[2] and thus interpreted, it has much in common with the account of the relation between Ἄνθρωπος and Φύσις in *Corp.* I. But Pagan myths of the marriage of Heaven and Earth under various names (Uranos and Gaia, Zeus and Hera, &c.) may also have been in the writer's mind.

The descent of the incorporeal Anthropos into the world of gross

---

[1] Cf. Mani, whose doctrine is given as follows in Milman, *Hist. Christ.* II, p. 266 : ' Eve's beauty was the fatal tree of Paradise, for which Adam was content to fall. It was by this union that the sensual or concupiscent soul triumphed over the pure and divine spirit (*De mor. Manichaeor.* c. 19, *Acta Archelai* c. 10) ; and it was by marriage, by sexual union, that the darkening race was propagated.'

[2] *De opif. mundi* 59. 165 : ἐν ἡμῖν γὰρ ἀνδρὸς μὲν ἔχει λόγον ὁ νοῦς, γυναικὸς δ' αἴσθησις· ἡδονὴ δὲ προτέραις ἐντυγχάνει καὶ ἐνομιλεῖ ταῖς αἰσθήσεσι, δι' ὧν καὶ τὸν ἡγεμόνα νοῦν φενακίζει· ... ὁ δ' αὐτίκα δελεασθεὶς ὑπήκοος ἀνθ' ἡγεμόνος, καὶ δοῦλος ἀντὶ δεσπότου, καὶ ἀντὶ πολίτου φυγάς, καὶ θνητὸς ἀντ' ἀθανάτου γίνεται. Compare with this *Corp.* I. 15, where the result of the marriage of Ἄνθρωπος with Φύσις is described in similar words : ἀθάνατος γὰρ ὢν ... τὰ θνητὰ πάσχει κ.τ.λ.

matter is comparable to the descent of Sophia (regarded as a symbol or prototype of the human soul) in some of the Gnostic systems.[1] But though the thing signified is the same or similar, the symbolism is for the most part different; and that of *Corp.* I is more closely connected with *Genesis.*

ἐμειδίασεν ἔρωτι ⟨⟨ἀκορέστῳ⟩⟩ ⟨⟨τοῦ ἀνθρώπου⟩⟩, [ἄτε] τῆς καλλίστης μορφῆς [[τοῦ ἀνθρώπου]] τὸ εἶδος ἐν τῷ ὕδατι ⟨ἀναδ⟩ιδοῦσα, καὶ τὸ σκίασμα ἐπὶ τῆς γῆς. ἀκόρεστος is not a suitable epithet for κάλλος, but may very well be applied to ἔρως. The false reading ἰδοῦσα perverts the meaning of the sentence. The author cannot have said that Φύσις sees and falls in love with the reflection of the divine form in earth and water,—i. e. in herself. What she sees is Anthropos (the εἰκών of the supreme God) looking down on her through the hole which he has broken in the sky. She 'smiles with passionate desire for him'; and her smile takes the form of a reflection or shadow of his beauty on the surface of land and sea. He sees this borrowed beauty of φύσις,—a reflection of his own beauty,—and Narcissus-like, he loves it.[2] It is perhaps implied that the beauty of material things is not inherent in the things themselves, but is projected into them by the man who contemplates them.[3]

ἐφίλησε, καὶ ἠβουλήθη αὐτοῦ οἰκεῖν. The word ἐφίλησε does not signify the passionate desire expressed by ἔρωτι ἀκορέστῳ; it is not until Anthropos has actually descended into the lower world that he is said to be overcome by ἔρως. Hitherto, he has only looked down from above; he now descends into the world of gross matter, and takes up his abode there.

ἅμα δὲ τῇ βουλῇ (or perhaps βουλή⟨σει⟩) ἐγένετο ἐνέργεια. 'No sooner purposed than done.' In the case of the incorporeal Anthropos, as in that of the supreme God himself, to purpose or to will is to accomplish. Cf. *Ascl. Lat.* I. 8: 'voluntas etenim dei ipsa est summa perfectio, utpote cum voluisse et perfecisse uno eodemque temporis puncto conpleat.'

---

[1] Compare especially the 'Barbelognostics' in Irenaeus 1. 29. 4: 'Emissum dicunt Spiritum sanctum, quem et Sophiam et Prunicum vocant. Hunc igitur, videntem reliqua omnia coniugationem habentia, se autem sine coniugatione, quaesisse cui adunaretur; et quum non inVeniret, . . . prospiciebat ad inferiores partes, putans hic invenire coniugem.'

[2] Cf. Plotinus 4. 3. 12: ἀνθρώπων δὲ ψυχαί, εἴδωλα αὐτῶν ἰδοῦσαι οἷον Διονύσου ἐν κατόπτρῳ (an Orphic term), ἐκεῖ (i. e. κάτω) ἐγένοντο, ἄνωθεν ὁρμηθεῖσαι.

[3] Cf. B. Croce, *Aesthetic*, Eng. tr. 1909, pp. 159–162: 'The beautiful is not a physical fact; it does not belong to things, but to the activity of man, to spiritual energy. . . . As regards natural beauty, man is like the mythical Narcissus at the fountain.'

ᾤκησε τὴν ἄλογον ⌐μορφήν⌐. The author cannot have written μορφήν, but may have written οὐσίαν or ὕλην. At any rate, his meaning must have been that Anthropos is henceforward domiciled in the sublunar world (which, as we were told in § 11 b, is ἄλογος,) and is 'clasped in the embrace of Φύσις and intermingled with her'; that is to say, the human soul is now incarnated. If the writer still adheres to his notion of an individual person named Anthropos, we must suppose him to imagine the hitherto incorporeal Anthropos as henceforward living on earth in bodily shape, a bisexual Adam. But it is difficult to picture his mode of existence after his incarnation. Where and how did he live? And what became of him? Did he die in course of time, as other men die? As the writer leaves these questions unanswered, it is to be presumed that he did not put them to himself. At this stage, the imagery of his myth is already fading away; and when he speaks of the incarnation of Anthropos, his meaning is, not that the hero of his story began an earthly life at a certain moment, but that all human souls are thus incarnated. The Anthropos here ceases to be imagined as a particular person with a life-history of his own, and his name becomes merely a name for any or every man; Ἄνθρωπος passes away into ἄνθρωπος.

ἡ δὲ φύσις λαβοῦσα τὸν ἐρώμενον περιεπλάκη. Cf. the doctrine attributed to Ammonius Saccas in Nemesius *De nat. hom.* c. 3, p. 135 Matth. (Zeller *Phil. der Gr.* III. Abth. ii (1903), p. 507): τῇ σχέσει καὶ τῇ πρός τι ῥοπῇ καὶ διαθέσει δεδέσθαι φαμὲν ὑπὸ τοῦ σώματος τὴν ψυχήν, ὡς λέγομεν ὑπὸ τῆς ἐρωμένης (δεδέσθαι) τὸν ἐραστήν. As Ammonius Saccas left nothing in writing, Nemesius must have got this from some writer of the school of Plotinus.

§ 15. καὶ διὰ τοῦτο . . . κρατεῖται. In this paragraph, the meaning of the myth, or the lesson to be learnt from it, is clearly set forth. We men are descended on one side from the incorporeal Anthropos, who is son of the supreme God, and whose substance is 'Life and Light'; and on the other side, from corporeal Φύσις, whose substance is ὕλη, which is connected with darkness and death. We are therefore of twofold nature. In respect of one part (the οὐσιώδης ἄνθρωπος in us), we are exalted above all that is material; in respect of the other part, we are subject to material things, and therefore to Heimarmene, the power by which material things are governed. The higher part is the true self; and before our incarnation, we were wholly of that higher nature. The lower part is an accretion which has resulted from the descent of the soul into the world of gross matter. And

there lies before us the alternative of salvation or perdition, 'life' or
'death', according as in our earthly life the one part or the other gets
the upper hand.

This is the Platonic doctrine of the nature of man; and the writer's
statement of it would have been accepted, in the main at least, by
every Platonist of his time. Cf. *Ascl. Lat.* I. 7 b : 'solum enim
animal homo duplex est; et eius una pars simplex, quae, ut Graeci
aiunt, οὐσιώδης, quam vocamus divinae similitudinis formam &c.'
ὑπεράνω ⟨γὰρ⟩ [οὖν] ὧν τῆς ἁρμονίας, [ἐναρμόνιος] ⟨εἱμαρμένης⟩ γέγονε
δοῦλος. Elsewhere in this document, ἁρμονία means 'the structure of
the heavens'. ἐναρμόνιος should therefore mean either 'residing in
the heavens', or 'having the heavens inside him'; but neither of
these meanings suits the context. Moreover, δοῦλος requires a
genitive. It is therefore probable that ἐναρμόνιος is a corruption of
εἱμαρμένης.

ἀρρενόθηλυς δὲ ὢν ἐξ ἀρρενοθήλεος ὄν⟨τος τοῦ⟩ πατρός, καὶ ἄυπνος ἀπὸ
ἀύπνου, ⟨ὑπ' ἔρωτος καὶ λήθης⟩ κρατεῖται. God is bisexual. In *Ascl.
Lat.* III. 20 b., where the same epithet is applied to him, the thoughts
which it conveys are that God generates the universe from himself
alone, and that human procreation is an antitype of God's generative
activity. But in *Corp.* I, the word connotes rather absence of sexual
differentiation, and consequently, freedom from sexual passion. Cf.
Gospel acc. to the Egyptians, Clem. Alex. *Strom.* 3. 13. 92 (see also
Clem. ad Cor. 2. 12. 2) : death shall cease ὅταν τὸ τῆς αἰσχύνης ἔνδυμα
πατήσητε, καὶ ὅταν γένηται τὰ δύο ἕν, καὶ τὸ ἄρρεν μετὰ τῆς θηλείας
οὔτε ἄρρεν οὔτε θῆλυ. The Naassene 'Attis-document', Hippol. *Ref.
haer.* 5. 7 : ἀπεκόπη γάρ, φησίν, ὁ Ἄττις (who in that document is identified with Anthropos or the 'Son of Anthropos'), τουτέστιν ἀπὸ τῶν
χοϊκῶν τῆς κτίσεως κάτωθεν μερῶν, καὶ ἐπὶ τὴν αἰωνίαν ἄνω μετελήλυθεν
οὐσίαν, ὅπου, φησίν, οὐκ ἔστιν οὔτε θῆλυ οὔτε ἄρσεν,[1] ἀλλὰ καινὴ κτίσις,
καινὸς ἄνθρωπος, ὅς ἐστιν ἀρσενόθηλυς.

The οὐσιώδης ἄνθρωπος (i. e. man in respect of his incorporeal and
immortal part) is, like God, 'bisexual', in the sense that he is neither
male nor female, and therefore not liable to ἔρως (sexual desire); he
is as the angels of heaven, who οὔτε γαμοῦσιν οὔτε γαμίζονται (Mark 12.
25). It is only the lower and earthly part of man that is concerned
with sexual intercourse. The author of *Corp.* I, since he makes ἔρως
the cause of death, must have held marriage to be evil. In this

---

[1] Cf. *Ep. Gal.* 3. 28 : Χριστὸν ἐνεδύσασθε· οὐκ ἔνι ... ἄρσεν καὶ θῆλυ· πάντες γὰρ
ὑμεῖς εἷς ἐστὲ ἐν Χριστῷ Ἰησοῦ.

respect he is at the opposite extreme from the author of *Ascl. Lat.* III, who regards sexual intercourse as a 'sacrament'. God is also ἄυπνος; i. e. his νόησις is not intermittent, as is that of men. 'Our birth is but a sleep and a forgetting'; and man's earthly life as a whole is often described as a sleep. Cf. *Corp.* X. 5, where it is said that in this life even those who are able to catch glimpses of the beatific vision κατακοιμίζονται πολλάκις ὑπὸ τοῦ σώματος. ⟨ὑπ' ἔρωτος καὶ λήθης⟩ κρατεῖται. The author must have said what it is that 'holds' or 'masters' men; and he must have used two distinct terms, one with reference to ἀρρενόθηλυς, and the other with reference to ἄυπνος. The first of the two must certainly have been ἔρως; the second may very likely have been λήθη. But ὑπ' ἔρωτος καὶ μέθης would also be possible; cf. μέθη καὶ ὕπνῳ in § 27. Drunkenness is associated with sleep in *Corp.* VII also.

§ 16. καὶ αὐτὸς γὰρ ἐρῶ τοῦ λόγου. 'I too am mastered by ἔρως; I have a passionate desire to hear what yet remains to be told.' The verb ἐρῶ was suggested by the preceding mention of ἔρως. The prophet perceives that his divine teacher is now on the verge of revealing to him the origin of the human race; and he is eager to learn the truth concerning this matter above all.

τοῦτο ἔστι τὸ [[ ]] μυστήριον ⟨τὸ⟩ μέχρι τῆσδε τῆς ἡμέρας ⟪κεκρυμμένον⟫. 'This' appears to be the doctrine which Poimandres immediately proceeds to set forth, i. e. that which is contained in §§ 16 and 17. It is a doctrine which 'has been kept secret until this day'; this must mean that it has never been taught before. The rest of the teaching of *Corp.* I is matter of tradition, restated and no doubt modified by the author, but not originated by him. But the doctrine of 'the seven Anthropoi' was his own invention; as it seemed to him, it had come to him from God by direct revelation; and it had been revealed to none before him.

μυστήριον here means 'a holy truth which has not been made known till now'. This is the sense in which the word is commonly used by Paul; see Armitage Robinson, *Ep. to the Ephesians*, p. 234 ff., 'on the meaning of μυστήριον in the New Testament'. (Compare especially *Ephes.* 3. 3–5.) There is no suggestion that the truth in question ought to be kept secret by the man to whom it is revealed; on the contrary, the prophet holds that he has a mission to proclaim to all mankind what has been revealed to him.

ἡ φύσις . . . ἀπεκύησεν ἑπτὰ ἀνθρώπους πρὸς τὰς φύσεις τῶν ἑπτὰ διοικητόρων, ἀρρενοθήλεας καὶ μεταρσίους. These seven Anthropoi are the issue of the marriage described above; their father is the first Anthropos, and their mother is Φύσις. They must therefore have in them something of the nature of either parent. It is implied that they have inherited 'Life and Light' from their father, and the dark and deadly influence of ὕλη from their mother. But they have inherited from their father something else as well, viz. the 'natures' or distinctive characters of the seven planets, which, as we were told in § 13 a, he received into himself during his sojourn in the heavens; and it may be inferred from § 25 that these planetary 'natures' are seven evil πάθη.

It is not clear how the seven kinds of πάθη which mankind inherit through the seven Anthropoi from the first Anthropos are to be distinguished from the evil influences of ὕλη which they inherit from Φύσις. It would seem that either without the other would suffice to account for the moral evil which exists in men. The truth is that the author has included in his system two different accounts of the origin of moral evil,—one, which attributes it to the influence of ὕλη, and has been taken over by him from the Platonists, and another, which attributes it to the influence of the planets, and is in part an innovation of his own,—and has left them standing side by side but unconnected.

We are evidently meant to understand that each of the seven Anthropoi bears the special character of one of the seven planets. One of them is characterized by the deceitfulness which comes from the planet Mercury, another by the lust which comes from the planet Venus, and so on. And as these seven Anthropoi are the ancestors of the human race, the writer's meaning must be that there are seven distinct classes or types of men, each of which is specially influenced by one of the seven planets, and shows an evil disposition derived from that planet. The men governed by the planet Mercury are deceitful, and the men governed by the planet Venus are lustful. The notion that the character of the individual man is determined by the influence of the heavenly bodies (or by Heimarmene, using the heavenly bodies as her instruments,) was commonly accepted in the writer's time; and it was held by many that a man's disposition depends on the planet which was dominant at the moment of his birth. (Our language still retains a vestige of this astrological doctrine, in the use of the words 'jovial', 'mercurial', and 'saturnine'.) The author of Corp. I has adopted this belief from the society around him. According to his view, Heimarmene, i.e. the influence of the heavenly bodies as a whole, is split up into seven distinct influences, corresponding to the seven planets; and mankind is divided into seven classes, each of which is specially subject to one of these seven planetary influences. When a man is 'illuminated', or has attained to *gnosis*, he is no longer subject to the baleful influence of his planet, and the 'ruling passion' derived from that planet is suppressed in him. But the many are 'slaves of Heimarmene', whose dominion manifests itself in the working of evil passions, and takes seven different forms, according as the man is subject to one or other of the seven planets through which Heimarmene operates on the world below.

The innovation introduced by the author of *Corp.* I consists in this, that he describes the planetary influence not as brought to bear directly on each individual man at his birth, or throughout his life, but as an inheritance which has descended to him from one of a group of seven primal Anthropoi, who in their turn had inherited it from their father, the first Anthropos. He tells us that the doctrine of the seven Anthropoi is a novelty; it had been 'hidden' till the day when the divine Nous revealed it to him. But though the notion as worked out by him and incorporated in his system is no doubt original, we may presume that it was suggested to him by some mythological tradition, and that he had in mind some well-known group of seven gods or superhuman persons, who might be used to serve his purpose. Perhaps the simplest hypothesis would be that he was thinking of the seven Greek deities after whom the planets were named.[1] The euhemeristic theories prevalent in his time had changed these θεοί into ἄνθρωποι, who were supposed to have lived at a remote time in the past; and it would be an easy step to represent the seven ἄνθρωποι named Kronos, Zeus, &c. as the 'supermen' from whom the human race is descended. But there were other groups of seven superhuman beings, more or less closely connected with the seven planets;[2] and

[1] Apollo and Artemis might stand for the sun and the moon.
[2] E. g. the seven Archangels of the Jews. In the *Mithrasliturgie* edited by Dieterich, the supreme God, who resides at the North Pole, is attended by a group of seven youths and a group of seven maidens; these two groups appear to be the stars of the Great Bear and the stars of the Little Bear respectively, but their number might cause them to be associated with the seven planets also. If the two groups were fused into one, we should have a group of seven bisexual beings.

According to the Orphic tradition, there were fourteen Titans, seven male and seven female (Proclus *in Pl. Tim.* 5. 295 D, Abel *Orphica fr.* 95 : τίκτει γὰρ ἡ Γῆ, λαθοῦσα τὸν Οὐρανόν, ὥς φησιν ὁ θεολόγος, " ἑπτὰ μὲν εὐειδεῖς κούρας, . . . ἑπτὰ δὲ παῖδας ἄνακτας") ; and the lower or earthly part of man was derived from the Titans. So far, the seven bisexual Anthropoi of *Corp.* I correspond to the seven pairs of Orphic Titans. There does not seem to have been any connexion between

as the writer has not given names to his Anthropoi, we have no means
of knowing what particular form of mythological reminiscence sug-
gested the conception to him. In the text of the MSS., the seven Anthropoi are said to be μετάρ-
σιοι, i. e. 'up aloft', or 'raised high in air'. The word would be
applicable, for instance, to the Platonic daemons, whose abode is the
atmosphere. But as the seven Anthropoi have bodies composed of
gross matter, it necessarily follows that they live upon the surface of
the earth, like ordinary men, from whom they differ only in the fact
that they are bisexual. The word μεταρσίους therefore seems inappropriate. If it is to be retained, we must take it to mean ' standing
erect ', as opposed to the beasts. Cf. Philo *De opif. mundi* 51. 147,
Cohn I, p. 51 : ᾗ δὲ (ὁ ἄνθρωπος) μετέωρον ⟨καὶ?⟩ ἀπὸ γῆς ἀνώφοιτον
ἐξῆρται τὸ σῶμα (i. e. stands erect), λέγοιτ' ἂν ἐνδίκως ἀεροπόρον εἶναι.

μὴ ἔκτρεχε. ' Do not digress.' 'The prophet thought he was about
to be told the origin of the existing race of men and women. That
is what he is eager to hear ; and when Poimandres interposes the
doctrine of the seven Anthropoi, which appears to him to be less
directly connected with his own interests, he can hardly restrain his
impatience.

§ 17. ⟨⟨ἐξήνεγκεν ἡ φύσις τὰ σώματα·⟩⟩ . . . ὁ δὲ ἄνθρωπος . . . ἐγένετο
εἰς ψυχὴν καὶ νοῦν, The composition of the seven Anthropoi is here
described. They consist, like ourselves, of a material part and an
immaterial part.[1] The material part, in their case as in ours, is a
body composed of the material elements ; and it comes to them
from their mother Φύσις, who is a personification of the material
elements. The immaterial part, in their case as in ours, is ψυχή and
νοῦς; and it comes to them from their father, the first Anthropos.
For the word ἐξήνεγκεν, cf. ἐξήνεγκεν ⟨ἡ γῆ⟩ ζῷα τετράποδα κ.τ.λ. in § 11 b.
Φύσις ' brought forth ' the seven Anthropoi, as Gaia brought forth the
Titans and the Giants; and if the author formed in his own mind
any definite picture of their birth, he probably thought of them as

---

the Orphic Titans and the planets; but this may be one of the innovations made
by the author of *Corp.* I.
   It is possible that the writer found support for his doctrine of the seven Anthropoi
in *Gen.* 6. 4: οἱ δὲ γίγαντες ἦσαν ἐπὶ τῆς γῆς ἐν ταῖς ἡμέραις ἐκείναις· . . . ἐκεῖνοι
ἦσαν οἱ γίγαντες οἱ ἀπ' αἰῶνος, οἱ ἄνθρωποι οἱ ὀνομαστοί. In the Hellenistic period,
the γίγαντες of Greek mythology were often confused with the Titans.
   [1] The material part corresponds to the χοῦς ἀπὸ τῆς γῆς in *Gen.* 2. 7 : the
immaterial part corresponds to the πνοὴ ζωῆς in the same passage. The phrase
ὁ δὲ ἄνθρωπος ἐγένετο εἰς ψυχὴν καὶ νοῦν was probably suggested by ἐγένετο ὁ
ἄνθρωπος εἰς ψυχὴν ζῶσαν in *Gen.* 2. 7.

springing up out of the earth like plants.   It was thus that, according
to a notion widely spread among the Greeks, the first men had come
into being.   Something of the sort is implied in the phrase ἄνδρες
γηγενεῖς addressed to mankind in § 27.

θηλυκὴ γὰρ ἦν ⟨ἡ γῆ⟩, καὶ ⟨τὸ⟩ ὕδωρ ὀχευτικόν.   The visible and
tangible body (as opposed to the invisible and intangible, but still
material, *pneuma* or 'vital spirit') is composed of the two grosser
elements, earth and water.   In the combination of earth and water,
earth is relatively passive, and water is relatively active ; and this
distinction is expressed by calling the earth ' female ', and the water
' male '.   The Stoics more commonly called fire and air together
δραστικά (= ὀχευτικά), and earth and water together παθητικά
(= θηλυκά).   Nemesius *De nat. hom.* c. 5, p. 126 : the Stoics say
τῶν στοιχείων τὰ μὲν εἶναι δραστικά, τὰ δὲ παθητικά· δραστικὰ μὲν ἀέρα
καὶ πῦρ, παθητικὰ δὲ γῆν καὶ ὕδωρ.   But a closer parallel occurs in
Hippol. *Ref. haer.* 4. 43.   Hippolytus there gives a doctrine which
he calls 'Egyptian'; it is rather the doctrine of some Stoicizing
Pythagorean, but its author perhaps assumed that Pythagoras had
learnt it in Egypt.   According to this doctrine, fire and πνεῦμα (air)
are τὸ ἀγαθοποιόν τε καὶ ἀνωφερὲς καὶ ἀρσενικόν· earth and water are
τὸ κατωφερὲς θηλυκόν τε καὶ κακοποιόν.   καὶ αὐτὰ δὲ πάλιν τὰ ἄνω δύο
στοιχεῖα ἑαυτοῖς συγκρινόμενα ἔχουσιν ἐν ἑαυτοῖς τὸ ἄρρεν καὶ τὸ θῆλυ
πρὸς εὐκαρπίαν καὶ αὔξησιν τῶν ὅλων· καὶ τὸ μὲν πῦρ ἄρρεν ἐστί, τὸ δὲ
πνεῦμα θῆλυ.   καὶ πάλιν τὸ ὕδωρ ἄρρεν ἐστίν, ἡ δὲ γῆ θῆλυ.   καὶ οὕτως
ἀπ' ἀρχῆς συνεβίωσε τὸ πῦρ τῷ πνεύματι, τῇ δὲ γῇ τὸ ὕδωρ· ὥσπερ γὰρ
δύναμις τοῦ πνεύματός ἐστι τὸ πῦρ, οὕτως καὶ τῆς γῆς τὸ ὕδωρ.

[τὸ δὲ ἐκ πυρὸς πέπειρον.]   'That part of them which was made of
fire was ripe.'   This is nonsense ; and the words must have been
inserted through some error.

ἐκ δὲ αἰθέρος τὸ πνεῦμα ἔλαβον (ἔλαβε MSS.).   The πνεῦμα is here
the 'vital spirit' of a man, which belongs to the material part of him,
and is sharply distinguished from the immaterial ψυχή and νοῦς. Cf.
Corp. X. 13 ff., where the πνεῦμα is called the 'vehicle' (ὄχημα) or
'vesture' (ἔνδυμα) of the ψυχή.   The 'vital spirit' was commonly
thought to consist of the two finer elements, fire and air ; and this
was presumably the view held by the author of *Corp.* I.   It is
possible that αἰθέρος is a corruption of ἀέρος ⟨καὶ πυρός⟩; but if we
retain αἰθέρος, we must say that αἰθήρ here means 'fire and air', or
'air saturated with fire'.   The pure bright air of the upper atmosphere was sometimes called αἰθήρ, as for instance in Pseudo-Pl.

Epinomis. In the *Oracula Chaldaica* (Kroll, p. 35, Procl. *in Tim.* 154 e), αἴθρη is used as a synonym of ἀήρ; the Demiurgus is there said to have made the Kosmos ἐκ πυρὸς ἐξ ὕδατος καὶ γῆς καὶ παντρόφου αἴθρης.

⟨. . .⟩ πρὸς τὸ εἶδος τοῦ ἀνθρώπου. In the missing words, the author must have spoken of the incorporeal part, in contrast to τὰ σώματα above. The incorporeal part of each of the seven Anthropoi was derived from the first Anthropos, and resembled the first Anthropos as he was before his incarnation.

ὁ δὲ ἄνθρωπος ἐκ ζωῆς καὶ φωτὸς ἐγένετο εἰς ψυχὴν καὶ νοῦν. The first Anthropos, before his descent into the world of matter, consisted wholly of the substance of the supreme God, which is ' Life and Light '. He transmitted this incorporeal substance to his seven sons; and in them, the ' Life ' became ψυχή, and the ' Light ' became νοῦς.

Every part of their being has now been accounted for. Each of the seven was composed, as we ourselves are, of (1) a gross body, consisting of earth and water, (2) a *pneuma*, consisting of fire and air, and (3) a ψυχή and a νοῦς, consisting of the incorporeal substance of God. But they still differed from us, their descendants, in that they were bisexual. The making of men and women is completed by the differentiation of the sexes, which follows in the next paragraph.

μέχρι περιόδου τέλους. The state of things which has just been described remained unaltered until the end of one ' age ', and the beginning of another.

Hesiod's list of the five ' ages ' (γένη), beginning with the age of gold, and ending with the present age of iron, was known to every Greek schoolboy. In Hellenistic times, the notion of a series of ages into which the world's history is divided was modified by association with the astral and Stoic doctrine of *apocatastasis*, according to which things run in cycles, and at the end of each period, all things are made new. A division of history into successive ages (γενεαί) was adopted by Hellenistic Jews, and occurs repeatedly in the Jewish *Sibylline Oracles*; and the mention of a series of ages in Virg. *Ecl.* 4 ('magnus ab integro saeclorum nascitur ordo') was probably suggested in part by Jewish *Sibyllina*. To a Jew, the most obvious instance of 'the end of a period' and the beginning of another would be the Deluge;[1] and the author of

[1] Compare the narrative of the Flood in the Jewish *Orac. Sib.* 1. 125 ff., and

Corp. I was probably thinking of the Mosaic narrative of the Flood. In *Genesis*, the Giants, to whom the seven Anthropoi correspond in some respects, are said to have dwelt upon the earth in the period which the Flood ended, and are spoken of immediately before the story of the Flood is told.

§ 18. πάντα γὰρ τὰ ζῷα, ἀρρενοθήλεα ὄντα, διελύετο ἅμα τῷ ἀνθρώπῳ.

We here learn, what we were not told before, that not only the seven Anthropoi, but also the birds, beasts, and fishes, the production of which was described in § 11 b, were bisexual until the end of the first age, and therefore did not begin to breed until the beginning of the second age. The bisexuality of the first Anthropos (from which that of his sons, the seven Anthropoi, follows) might, as has already been pointed out, be found in *Gen.* 1. 27 by a reader disposed thus to interpret the words; and similarly, it would be possible to interpret the phrase δύο δύο, ἄρσεν καὶ θῆλυ, which occurs repeatedly in the Mosaic narrative of the Flood, as meaning that down to that time the beasts also were bisexual, or in other words, that each individual among them was a still undivided pair.

The notion that men and women were brought into existence by splitting bisexual beings into two parts was doubtless suggested by the speech of Aristophanes in Pl. *Sympos.* 189–193. But a reader of *Genesis* might find support for it in *Gen.* 2. 21–24, where we are told that God ἔλαβεν μίαν τῶν πλευρῶν (τοῦ 'Αδάμ) . . . καὶ ᾠκοδόμησεν . . . τὴν πλευρὰν . . . εἰς γυναῖκα. . . . ἕνεκεν τούτου . . . ἔσονται οἱ δύο εἰς σάρκα μίαν. This amounts to saying that God divided the man into two parts, and made one of the two parts into a woman; and the resemblance might be made closer by taking μίαν τῶν πλευρῶν to mean 'one of his two sides' instead of 'one of his ribs'.[1]

ὁ δὲ θεὸς εὐθὺς εἶπεν ἁγίῳ λόγῳ· Αὐξάνεσθε ἐν αὐξήσει καὶ πληθύνεσθε ἐν πλήθει πάντα τὰ κτίσματα καὶ δημιουργήματα. This corresponds to the words spoken by God in *Gen.* 8. 15 ff. : καὶ εἶπεν Κύριος ὁ θεὸς τῷ Νῶε λέγων Ἔξελθε ἐκ τῆς κιβωτοῦ, σὺ καὶ ἡ γυνή σου κ.τ.λ., καὶ πάντα τὰ

especially ll. 283 ff. : when Noah and his family came forth from the Ark, ἔνθ' αὖτις βιότοιο νέη ἀνέτειλε γενέθλη | χρυσείη πρώτη, ἥτις πέλεθ' ἑκτη, ἀρίστη | ἐξότε πρωτόπλαστος ἀνὴρ γένετ'. In describing the Flood, the Sibyl speaks as an eye-witness ; she was the wife of one of Noah's sons, and was herself one of the passengers in the Ark.

[1] Reitzenstein (*Poim.* p. 110) refers to *Bereshith Rabba* (transl. Wünsche, p. 30), where a certain Rabbi is said to have taught that 'the first man, when he was first made, had two faces ; but God sawed him into two halves, and formed out of him two backs, which were turned in opposite directions'.

LIBELLVS I: §§ 17, 18 53

θηρία ὅσα ἐστὶν μετὰ σοῦ . . . καὶ αὐξάνεσθε καὶ πληθύνεσθε ἐπὶ τῆς γῆς.¹ In *Genesis*, the command 'increase and multiply' is addressed to fishes, birds, and men at the time of their first creation also (*Gen.* 1. 22 and 28); but the writer of *Corp.* I, having assumed that men and beasts alike were originally bisexual, and incapable of breeding, necessarily defers this injunction until the beginning of the second age, and makes it follow on the separation of the sexes.

There can be no doubt that the phrase αὐξάνεσθε καὶ πληθύνεσθε came to him from *Genesis*. But he has altered it by inserting ἐν αὐξήσει and ἐν πλήθει. (Cf. *Corp.* III. 3 b : εἰς τὸ αὐξάνεσθαι ἐν αὐξήσει καὶ πληθύνεσθαι ἐν πλήθει.) This form of words is a Hebraism ; but the Hebrew idiom of which it is a rendering is not employed in the command 'increase and multiply' as given in *Genesis*. We must therefore suppose that the writer's more immediate authority was not *Genesis* itself, but some document based on a Semitic original in which the words of *Genesis* were paraphrased or expanded.

καὶ ἀναγνωρισάτω ὁ ἔννους ⟨ἄνθρωπος⟩ ἑαυτὸν ὄντα ἀθάνατον, καὶ τὸν αἴτιον τοῦ θανάτου ἔρωτα [καὶ πάντα τὰ] ὄντα. It seems probable that πάντα τά came from πάντα τὰ κτίσματα above, and καί was inserted to make sense of it.

The writer makes God supplement the command 'increase and multiply' by a statement of the conditions under which men may escape death and attain to immortality. This might be called his version of God's διαθήκη with man ; it takes the place of the διαθήκη in *Gen.* 9. 11 ff. (οὐκ ἀποθανεῖται πᾶσα σὰρξ ἔτι ἀπὸ τοῦ ὕδατος τοῦ κατακλυσμοῦ κ.τ.λ.). But he may have had in mind also the speech of God in Pl. *Tim.* 42 A, addressed to the souls about to be incarnated : ὁπότε δὴ σώμασιν ἐμφυτευθεῖεν . . ., πρῶτον μὲν αἴσθησιν ἀναγκαῖον εἴη . . . πᾶσιν . . . ξύμφυτον γίγνεσθαι, δεύτερον δὲ ἡδονῇ καὶ λύπῃ μεμιγμένον ἔρωτα . . . καὶ ὁ μὲν εὖ τὸν προσήκοντα χρόνον βιούς, πάλιν εἰς τὴν τοῦ ξυννόμου πορευθεὶς οἴκησιν ἄστρου, βίον εὐδαίμονα καὶ συνήθη ἔξοι. (The 'immortality' spoken of in *Corp.* I corresponds to the 'happy life' promised in Pl. *Tim.*)

Man is distinguished from the beasts by the fact that he is (at least potentially) ἔννους ; and νοῦς is immortal. If he recognizes the

¹ Compare the version of this speech of God which is given in *Orac. Sib.* I. 267 ff. : οὐρανόθι πρὸ | θεσπεσίη μεγάλοιο θεοῦ πάλιν ἴαχε φωνὴ | τοῖον ἔπος· " Νῶε, πεφυλαγμένε πιστὲ δίκαιε, | θαρσαλέως ἔξελθε σὺν υἱέσι καί τε δάμαρτι | καὶ νύμφαις τρισσαῖς, καὶ πλήσατε γαῖαν ἅπασαν | αὐξόμενοι πληθυνόμενοι, τὰ δίκαια νέμοντες | ἀλλήλοις, γενεαῖς γενεῶν, ἄχρις εἰς κρίσιν ἥξει | πᾶν γένος ⌜ἀνθρώπων⌝ (ἀνθρώπειον ?), ἐπεὶ κρίσις ἔσσετ' ἅπασιν."

immortal νοῦς in him as his true self,[1] or identifies himself with it, he has overcome ἔρως, and is freed from the power of death. If on the other hand he ignores the νοῦς in him, and yields to ἔρως, he is a mere mortal creature, like the beasts. The θάνατος from which man may escape cannot be the dissolution of the body ; for to this all men alike are liable. It is rather the condition of a soul wholly immersed in matter, and enslaved by the πάθη to which matter gives rise. The life of a man in whom the bodily affections have the upper hand is not life, but death. (Cf. Corp. VII 2 b, where the body is called ὁ ζῶν θάνατος κ.τ.λ.) What will become of such a man when his present life on earth is ended, the writer of Corp. I does not expressly tell us ; but from § 24 it may be inferred that he will be resolved into the elements of which he was composed, and will cease to exist as an individual.[2] νοῦς only is immortal; and in the man who fails to ' recognize ' his true self, there is no νοῦς to survive.

' The cause of death is ἔρως.' It was through yielding to ἔρως that the first Anthropos was incarnated, and so fell under the dominion of death ; and it is through yielding to ἔρως that men deprive themselves of immortality. ἔρως is (or is inseparably connected with) love of the body (§ 19) ; and he who would be immortal must 'hate his body' (Corp. IV. 6 b).

⟨ὁ δὲ ἀναγνωρίσας ἑαυτὸν εἰς τὸ ἀγαθὸν χωρεῖ.⟩ We are told in § 21 init. that these words (or something like them) occurred in ' God's speech' ; they must therefore be inserted here. This clause of God's speech is paraphrased in § 19, in the words ὁ ἀναγνωρίσας ἑαυτὸν ἐλήλυθεν εἰς τὸ ὑπερούσιον ἀγαθόν, and is commented on in § 21.

§ 19. ἡ πρόνοια διὰ τῆς εἱμαρμένης καὶ ἁρμονίας τὰς μίξεις ἐποιήσατο, καὶ τὰς γενέσεις κατέστησε. God's πρόνοια is momentarily personified here, as God's βουλή was in § 8 b. εἱμαρμένης and ἁρμονίας are probably alternative readings ; either might stand, but hardly both together. It would, however, be possible to write διὰ τῆς ἁρμονίας καθ' εἱμαρμένην . . . τὰς γενέσεις κατέστησε. The births are determined by ' the structure of the heavens ', i. e. by the influences of the heavenly bodies ; and the heavenly bodies are the instruments by means of which Heimarmene works.

---

[1] For ὁ ἀναγνωρίσας ἑαυτόν, cf. Philo Migr. Abr. 3. 13, Wendl. II, p. 271 : ἐπειδὰν γοῦν ὁ νοῦς ἄρξηται γνωρίζειν ἑαυτὸν καὶ τοῖς νοητοῖς ἐνομιλεῖν θεωρήμασιν, ἅπαν τὸ κλινόμενον τῆς ψυχῆς πρὸς τὸ αἰσθητὸν εἶδος ἀπώσεται· . . . συνοικεῖν γὰρ ἀμήχανον τὸν ἀσωμάτων καὶ ἀφθάρτων ἔρωτι κατεσχημένον τῷ πρὸς τὰ αἰσθητὰ καὶ θνητὰ ῥέποντι.

[2] It is to be noted that there is no mention of metensomatosis or reincarnation in Corp. I.

ὁ ἀναγνωρίσας ἑαυτὸν ἐλήλυθεν εἰς τὸ ὑπερούσιον (περιούσιον MSS.)
ἀγαθόν. The text from this point to the end of § 23 is a commentary
on the preceding 'speech of God'.

No satisfactory sense can be got out of περιούσιον; but τὸ ὑπερούσιον ἀγαθόν may be taken to mean 'the supracosmic Good', and this
would serve as a synonym for ἀθανασία. (Cf. τοῦτο ἔστι τὸ ἀγαθόν in
§ 26 a fin.). Platonists said that the Good or God is 'above οὐσία';
the phrase was suggested to them by Pl. Rep. 6. 509 B (ἔτι ἐπέκεινα
τῆς οὐσίας). But the writer of Corp. I probably meant that the good
to which ὁ ἀναγνωρίσας ἑαυτόν attains is above οὐσία in the Stoic sense
of that word, i. e. above all 'material substance'; it is incorporeal.
The tense of ἐλήλυθεν is significant. He who has recognized his
true self has already entered into immortality. Though in the body,
he is no longer of the body; he belongs to another and a higher
world.

ὁ δὲ ἀγαπήσας [[τὸ]] ἐκ πλάνης ἔρωτος ⟨⟨τὸ⟩⟩ σῶμα. For the phrase ἐκ
πλάνης ἔρωτος, cf. Corp. XVI. 16 as emended : ὁ λόγον οὐκ ἔχων ἔρως
..., ὁ πλανώμενος καὶ πλανῶν. See Pl. Phaedr. 238 B.

§ 20. ὅτι προκατάρχεται . . . τὸ σῶμα συνέστηκεν. Death results
from the body ; and man is mortal so far as he is identified with his
body. It must be so, because the body, being material, is derived
from the 'grim darkness' spoken of in § 4. That 'darkness' is the
substance of death, as the 'light' there spoken of is the substance of
life.

This might serve as an answer to the question 'why are men subject to death?' But it is not an answer to the question which is here
asked, viz. 'why do men deserve the death to which they are subjected?'
If they deserve it (ἄξιοί εἰσι τοῦ θ.), that must be because of some sin
which they have committed. The sin of which death is the penalty
was described in mythical language as that of the first Anthropos, who
yielded to ἔρως, and wilfully entered into union with matter ; and it
might be said that all men who 'love the body' sink themselves in
matter by their own choice, and so repeat his sin in their own persons.
Something like this must have been the author's meaning ; and we
must assume that some words describing the sin of which death is the
penalty have been lost after τὸ σῶμα συνέστηκεν.

§ 21. ὁ ἀναγνωρίσας (ἐνόησας MSS.) ἑαυτὸν εἰς ⟨τὸ⟩ ἀγαθὸν χωρεῖ (εἰς
αὑτὸν χωρεῖ MSS.). The paraphrase of these words in § 19 makes it
almost certain that the author wrote τὸ ἀγαθόν here, and probable that
he wrote ὁ ἀναγνωρίσας.

ἐξ οὗ γέγονεν ὁ ἄνθρωπος. ὁ ἄνθρωπος is here the true self, i. e. the incorporeal part of man (which is derived from the first Anthropos), as opposed to the body. ' The Good ' is ' Light and Life ', the substance of God ; the true man is of that substance, and is reabsorbed into it.

Εὖ φῄς [λαλῶν ⟨ὅτι⟩ φῶς . . . ἄνθρωπος]. The words φῶς . . . ἄνθρωπος are a mere repetition of the preceding sentence. This explanation of the meaning of εὖ φῄς is correct, but superfluous ; and it was probably added by a later hand.

οὐ πάντες γὰρ ἄνθρωποι νοῦν ἔχουσιν ; Cf. Pl. Tim. 51 E : νοῦ δὲ (μετέχειν φατέον) θεούς, ἀνθρώπων δὲ γένος βραχύ τι. Corp. IV. 3. Ascl. Lat. I. 7 a and III. 18 b.

§ 22. παραγίνομαι ἐγὼ ὁ νοῦς τοῖς ὁσίοις κ.τ.λ. The νοῦς of the individual man is consubstantial with the divine νοῦς.

With §§ 22, 23 (παραγίνομαι ἐγώ . . . πῦρ ἐπὶ πλεῖον αὐξάνει) compare Corp. X. 19 b–22 a. That passage is an addition to Corp. X by a different hand ; and its writer may perhaps have read Corp. I. But he uses the word νοῦς differently ; he distinguishes two kinds of νοῦς, viz. a good νοῦς which enters into the godly man, and a bad νοῦς which enters into the ungodly man. The good νοῦς and the bad νοῦς of Corp. X. 19 b–22 a correspond respectively to the νοῦς and the τιμωρὸς δαίμων of Corp. I.

The τιμωρὸς δαίμων is here spoken of as a well-known personage. The Jews knew him under various names (Satan &c.). Platonists more commonly spoke of τιμωροὶ δαίμονες in the plural ; cf. Lydus de mens. 4. 32 (a fragment of the Λόγος τέλειος, connected with Ascl. Lat. III. 33 b) : τοὺς μὲν τιμωροὺς τῶν δαιμόνων, ἐν αὐτῇ τῇ ὕλῃ παρόντας, τιμωρεῖσθαι τὸ ἀνθρώπειον κατ' ἀξίαν.

§ 23. τὴν ὀξύτητα τοῦ πυρὸς προσβάλλων. The ' fire ' is metaphorical ; it is the fire of evil passion. The same metaphor is employed in Corp. X. 20 (ποῖον πῦρ τοσαύτην φλόγα ἔχει ὅσην ἡ ἀσέβεια ; The impious soul cries out καίομαι, φλέγομαι). The verb πυροῦσθαι is used in Greek poetry in the sense ' to be inflamed with passion ', and especially ' to burn with love ' ; but the description of evil passion in Corp. I and Corp. X. 20 as a fire by which the wicked are tortured in this life was probably suggested by accounts of a fiery hell in which sinners are punished after death. The notion of a penal hell-fire existed among the Zoroastrians from early times, and was current among the Jews at the time when Corp. I was written ; it occurs, for instance, in the Jewish Sibyllina.

καὶ μᾶλλον ἐπὶ τὰς ἀνομίας αὐτὸν ὁπλίζει, ἵνα τύχῃ μείζονος τιμωρίας.
When a man has once fallen into the fundamental sin of 'loving the
body', he already deserves punishment; and 'the avenging daemon'
punishes him by driving him into acts of crime, and thereby causing
him to incur the penalties which follow on such acts. Cf. *Corp.* XII.
i. 5–7, where it is similarly said that the wicked are punished by
being forced to commit crimes. But the function of making them
commit crimes is there assigned, not to 'the avenging daemon', but
to Heimarmene.

οὐ παύεται ⟨⟨σκοτομαχῶν⟩⟩. The words ἀκορέστως σκοτομαχῶν are
manifestly wrong where they stand in the MSS.; and I have disposed
of σκοτομαχῶν by inserting it here. The man is struggling in the
dark, and therefore at random, and to no good purpose. He has not
the 'light' of νοῦς to direct his efforts.

ἐπ' ὀρέξεις ἀπλέτους ⟨. . .⟩, τὴν ἐπιθυμίαν ἔχων ἀκόρεστον. The
reading of the MSS., ἐπ' ὀρέξεις ἀπλέτους τὴν ἐπιθυμίαν ἔχων, could
only be translated 'aiming his desire at boundless appetites'; but
that is a strange phrase. The object towards which ἐπιθυμία is
directed is not ὄρεξις, but ἡδονή. It is possible that the author wrote
ἐφ' ἡδονὰς ἀπλέτους, and that ὀρέξεις has come from τὰς ὀρέξεις written
as an alternative for τὴν ἐπιθυμίαν. Cf. *Corp.* XII. i. 4, where ἐπιθυμία,
ὄρεξις, and ἡδονή occur together.

§ 24. ἔτι δέ μοι εἰπὲ ⟨περὶ⟩ τῆς ἀνόδου τῆς γινομένης. So far, the
author has been speaking of man's life on earth. He now goes on
to describe the ascent of the disembodied soul to the world above.

⟨⟨πῶς εἰς ζωὴν χωρήσω.⟩⟩ These words, which are evidently out of
place in § 21, fit in satisfactorily here, and supply a reason for the
use of the second person (εἶχες, παραδίδως) in what follows.

Πρῶτον μὲν ἐν τῇ ἀναλύσει τοῦ σώματος τοῦ ὑλικοῦ παραδίδως[ιν] αὐτὸ
τὸ σῶμα εἰς ἀλλοίωσιν. This is awkwardly expressed; and it may be
suspected that the author wrote something like πρῶτον μὲν ἐν τῇ
ἀλλοίωσει ('when the time comes for you to be changed',—a
euphemism for 'at your death',—) παραδίδως αὐτὸ τὸ σῶμα ⟨τῇ φύσει
(i. e. to the force that works in earth and water)⟩ εἰς ἀνάλυσιν ('for
dissolution').

καὶ τὸ ⌜ἦθος⌝ τῷ ⌜δαίμονι⌝ . . . παραδίδως. If we retain ἦθος, it must
be taken to mean the sum of the πάθη. But we are told in § 25
that the man afterwards renders up his evil πάθη or vicious tendencies
to the planets from which they were derived; and if he has already
parted with his ἦθος before he reaches the heavens, how can he still

have these πάθη in him when he comes to the planets? It is evident then that something is wrong.

Now it appears from § 17 that the parts of which a man is composed are (1) the gross body, made of earth and water; (2) the πνεῦμα, made of fire and air; and (3) the ψυχή and νοῦς, made of 'Life and Light'. These several parts ought now to be disposed of in succession. We are first told what becomes of the gross body (τὸ σῶμα). It is 'delivered up' while the man is still on earth, and it is there resolved into the mass of earth and water whence it came. We should expect to be next told what becomes of the πνεῦμα; and as the πνεῦμα is of gaseous substance, and the man apparently does not part with it till after he has quitted earth and water, and has already parted with it when he reaches the planetary spheres (i. e. the region of fire), it seems probable that the author here wrote τὸ πνεῦμα τῷ ἀέρι παραδίδως, or something to that effect. We may suppose that a Christian reader was puzzled by the word πνεῦμα (which in his usage meant, not the material 'vital spirit', but the highest and divinest part of man), and tried to improve the sense by altering the text, and writing 'you deliver up your (vicious) character to the Devil'.

ἀνενέργητον. The work of the πνεῦμα as a part of the individual man is ended.

καὶ αἱ αἰσθήσεις τοῦ σώματος εἰς τὰς ἑαυτῶν πηγὰς ἐπανέρχονται. The writer regards the bodily senses as parts of the material πνεῦμα which permeates the body. This is the Stoic view. Iambl. De an., Stob. I. 49. 33, vol. i, p. 368 W.: πνεύματα γὰρ ἀπὸ τοῦ ἡγεμονικοῦ φασιν (οἱ Στωικοὶ) διατείνειν ἄλλα κατ' ἄλλα, τὰ μὲν εἰς ὀφθαλμούς, τὰ δὲ εἰς ὦτα, τὰ δὲ εἰς ἄλλα αἰσθητήρια. Aetius, Diels Doxogr. p. 410: according to the Stoics, ἀπὸ τοῦ ἡγεμονικοῦ ἑπτὰ μέρη ἐστὶ τῆς ψυχῆς ἐκπεφυκότα καὶ ἐκτεινόμενα εἰς τὸ σῶμα καθάπερ αἱ ἀπὸ τοῦ πολύποδος πλεκτάναι· τῶν δὲ ἑπτὰ μερῶν τῆς ψυχῆς πέντε μέν εἰσι τὰ αἰσθητήρια, ὅρασις ὄσφρησις ἀκοὴ γεῦσις καὶ ἁφή. ὧν ἡ μὲν ὅρασις ἐστὶ πνεῦμα διατεῖνον ἀπὸ ἡγεμονικοῦ μέχρις ὀφθαλμῶν, ἀκοὴ δὲ κ.τ.λ. (The Stoics held the ψυχή to be a material thing, and called it πνεῦμα πὼς ἔχον; so that the ψυχή spoken of in that passage corresponds to the πνεῦμα spoken of in Corp. I.) Compare the doctrine of τὸ φανταστικὸν πνεῦμα which is expounded by Synesius in his De insomniis; e. g. 1289 c (Migne): τὸ φανταστικὸν πνεῦμα κοινότατόν ἐστιν αἰσθητήριον, καὶ σῶμα πρῶτον ψυχῆς. See note on ἡ αἴσθησις σῶμα in Herm. ap. Stob. Exc. III. 21.

μέρη ⟨τοῦ κόσμου⟩ γινόμεναι, καὶ πάλιν συνιστάμεναι εἰς [τὰς] ⟨ἑτέρας⟩

ἐνεργείας. The αἰσθήσεις, being parts of the πνεῦμα of the individual man, go back into the mass of cosmic πνεῦμα whence they came, i. e. into the atmosphere. But in course of time, the same 'pneumatic' matter enters into other organisms, and in them, again assumes the function of sense-perception. Cf. Iambl. *De an.*, Stob. I. 49. 43, vol. i, p. 384 W. : ἤτοι γὰρ λύεται ἑκάστη δύναμις ἄλογος (τῆς ψυχῆς) εἰς τὴν ὅλην ζωὴν τοῦ παντός, ἀφ' ἧς ἀπεμερίσθη· ἢ καὶ ὅτι μάλιστα μένει ἀμετάβλητος, ὥσπερ ἡγεῖται Πορφύριος· ἢ καὶ χωρισθεῖσα ἀπὸ τῆς διανοίας ἡ ὅλη ἄλογος ζωὴ μένει καὶ αὐτὴ διασωζομένη ἐν τῷ κόσμῳ, ὥσπερ οἱ παλαιότατοι τῶν ἱερέων ἀποφαίνονται. The ἄλογοι δυνάμεις are, or include, the αἰσθήσεις ; and the writer of *Corp.* I apparently holds the first of the three views spoken of by Iamblichus. (As to the third of these views, see *Corp.* X. 16.) Proclus *in Pl. Tim.* p. 311 : of the Platonists, οἱ μέν, τὴν λογικὴν ψυχὴν μόνην ἀθάνατον ἀπολείποντες, φθείρουσι τήν τε ἄλογον ζωὴν σύμπασαν καὶ τὸ πνευματικὸν ὄχημα τῆς ψυχῆς, κατὰ τὴν εἰς γένεσιν ῥοπὴν τῆς ψυχῆς τὴν ὑπόστασιν διδόντες αὐτοῖς, μόνον τε νοῦν ἀθάνατον διατηροῦντες . . ., τοὺς Ἀττικοὺς λέγω καὶ Ἀλβίνους καὶ τοιούτους τινάς·[1] οἱ δὲ . . ., ὥσπερ οἱ περὶ Πορφύριον, . . . παραιτοῦνται μὲν τὴν καλουμένην φθορὰν κατασκεδαννύναι τοῦ τε ὀχήματος καὶ τῆς ἀλόγου ψυχῆς, ἀναστοιχειοῦσθαι δὲ αὐτά φασι καὶ ἀναλύεσθαί τινα τρόπον εἰς τὰς σφαίρας,[2] ἀφ' ὧν τὴν σύνθεσιν ἔλαχε· φυράματα δὲ εἶναι ταῦτα ἐκ τῶν οὐρανίων σφαιρῶν, καὶ κατιοῦσαν αὐτὰ συλλέγειν τὴν ψυχήν· ὥστε καὶ εἶναι ταῦτα καὶ μὴ εἶναι, αὐτὰ δὲ ἕκαστα μηκέτι εἶναι, μηδὲ διαμένειν τὴν ἰδιότητα αὐτῶν.[3] καὶ δοκοῦσιν ἕπεσθαι τοῖς λογίοις (*Oracula Chaldaica*), ἐν τῇ καθόδῳ τὴν ψυχὴν λέγουσι συλλέγειν αὐτό, λαμβάνουσαν " αἴθρης μέρος ἠελίου τε σελήνης τε καὶ ὅσα ἠέρι συνέχονται ".

---

[1] I. e. the Platonists Atticus and Albinus (second century A. D.) said that at a man's death his 'irrational part' (the αἰσθητικόν and παθητικόν) perishes completely, and his νοῦς alone continues to exist.
[2] Cf. *Corp.* I. 25. The ὄχημα τῆς ψυχῆς spoken of by Proclus corresponds to the πνεῦμα ('vital spirit') spoken of in *Corp.* I. 17 and 24 ; the ἄλογος ζωή or ἄλογος ψυχή spoken of by Proclus corresponds both to the αἰσθήσεις spoken of in *Corp.* I. 24 (and there regarded as parts of the πνεῦμα), and to the planetary πάθη spoken of in *Corp.* I. 25.
[3] I. e. at death the man's αἰσθητικόν ceases to exist as an individual and separate thing ; but in another sense it continues to exist, being absorbed into the cosmic mass. This agrees closely with the doctrine of *Corp.* I. 24.
Proclus here ascribes to Porphyry the first of the three views distinguished by Iamblichus in the passage quoted above ; Iamblichus, on the other hand, ascribes to Porphyry the second of those three views. Porphyry himself ('Αφορμαὶ πρὸς τὰ νοητά 29) says ἐξελθούσῃ (τῇ ψυχῇ) τοῦ στερεοῦ σώματος τὸ πνεῦμα συνομαρτεῖ, ὃ ἐκ τῶν σφαιρῶν συνελέξατο· and this seems to show that Iamblichus is right in what he says about him. But perhaps Porphyry spoke differently in different writings.

[καὶ ὁ θυμὸς καὶ ἡ ἐπιθυμία εἰς τὴν ἄλογον φύσιν χωρεῖ.] This statement implies that the man gets rid of θυμός and ἐπιθυμία while he is still in the sublunar region. But in the following section we are told that, when he quits that region and enters the heavens, he still has in him certain evil πάθη, which might be collectively described as θυμός and ἐπιθυμία; and one of these πάθη is actually called ἡ ἐπιθυμητικὴ ἀπατή. The author can hardly have been guilty of so manifest an inconsistency; and it is most likely that the words καὶ ὁ θυμὸς . . . χωρεῖ were inserted by some one else,—possibly by the same person who altered πνεῦμα into ἦθος above.

Even when these words have been struck out, a difficulty still remains; for a man who has got rid of his αἰσθήσεις could hardly continue to be liable to the πάθη enumerated in connexion with the planets. But the inconsistency of making the man retain the πάθη after he has got rid of the αἰσθήσεις is less obvious than that of making him retain the πάθη after he has got rid of θυμός and ἐπιθυμία, and the writer may have failed to notice it.

§ 25. τῇ πρώτῃ ζώνῃ δίδωσι . . . καὶ τῇ ἑβδόμῃ τὸ ἐνεδρεῦον ψεῦδος. We were told in § 13 a that the first Anthropos, in the course of his descent into the lower world, took into himself the distinctive qualities (φύσεις) of the several planets. All individual men have inherited these qualities from their ancestor the first Anthropos; and we are now told that the disembodied soul, in the course of its ascent to the higher world, renders them back to the planets to which they severally belong, and so gets rid of them. In his list of the planetary influences, the writer has adopted astrological notions which were current in his time. The αὐξητικὴ καὶ μειωτικὴ ἐνέργεια (i. e. the operation of what Aristotle called the θρεπτικὴ ψυχή, or τὸ θρεπτικὸν τῆς ψυχῆς μόριον,) comes from the Moon; fraud, from Mercury; lust, from Venus; pride, from the Sun; audacity, from Mars; covetousness, from Jupiter; and deceitfulness, from Saturn. (The distinction between ἡ μηχανὴ τῶν κακῶν δόλων, which is attributed to Mercury, and τὸ ἐνεδρεῦον ψεῦδος, which is attributed to Saturn, perhaps consists in a difference of motive. The 'Mercurial' man deceives others with a view to his own gain; the 'Saturnine' man deceives others out of malice, and his object is to do them mischief.)

The influence of the moon, as here described, is neither good nor bad,—except in so far as change in itself is bad, as compared with the immutability of the higher world; but the influences of the six other planets are assumed to be morally bad. In regarding the planets as maleficent powers, the author agrees with some of the Christian Gnostics.

A list of the planetary influences is given in the verses which Stobaeus (*Exc.* XXIX) ascribes to 'Hermes' : δάκρυ μέν ἐστι Κρόνος, Ζεὺς ⟨δ'⟩ ἡ γένεσις, λόγος Ἑρμῆς, | θυμὸς Ἄρης, Μήνη δ' ἄρ' ὕπνος, Κυθέρεια δ' ὄρεξις. The writer of those verses agrees with *Corp.* I in attributing ὄρεξις to Venus, and in calling Mars θρασύς, but differs as to the characteristics of the other planets. Cf. Firmicus Maternus *Math.* 1. 22 : 'si Saturnus facit cautos graves tardos avaros ac tacitos, Iuppiter maturos bonos benignos ac modestos, Mars crudeles perfidos ac feroces, Sol religiosos nobiles ac superbos, Venus luxuriosos venustos et honesto gratiae splendore fulgentes, Mercurius astutos callidos et concitati animi mobilitalibus turbulentos, Luna acutos splendidos elegantes et popularis splendoris gratia praevalentes.'

As to the notion that the soul receives certain things from the planets in the course of its descent, and renders them back to the planets in the course of its ascent, see Wendland, *Hellen.-Röm. Kultur*, pp. 165–171, and Dieterich, *Mithrasliturgie*, p. 180 ff. This notion, (in which the Stoic conception of the structure of the universe, as popularized by Posidonius, is presupposed,) seems to have been adopted by the Mithraists of the Roman Empire, and symbolically represented in their ritual.[1] It was probably from the Mithraists that it passed to certain Gnostics, who substituted names of angels for those of the seven planet-gods (Orig. *c. Cels.* 6. 22–31) ; and it may very well have been transmitted from the Mithraists to the author of *Corp.* I also.

The notion was accepted by some of the later Platonists ; cf. Porph. *Aphormai* 29, quoted above. Arnobius *Adv. nat.* 2. 16 speaks of certain Platonists who say that 'dum ad corpora labimur et properamus humana, ex mundanis circulis sequuntur nos causae quibus

---

[1] We hear of a κλῖμαξ ἑπτάπυλος (i. e. a staircase barred by seven successive gates) in connexion with the subterranean sanctuaries of the Mithraists. Celsus, in Orig. *c. Cels.* 6. 22 : αἰνίττεται ταῦτα (viz. the descent and ascent of the soul) καὶ ὁ Περσῶν λόγος, καὶ ἡ τοῦ Μίθρου τελετὴ παρ' αὐτοῖς ἐστιν. ἔστι γάρ τι ἐν αὐτῇ σύμβολον τῶν δύο τῶν ἐν οὐρανῷ περιόδων, τῆς τε ἀπλανοῦς καὶ τῆς εἰς τοὺς πλάνητας αὖ ⌜γεγενημένης⌝ (*al.* νενεμημένης), καὶ τῆς δι' αὐτῶν τῆς ψυχῆς διεξόδου. τοιόνδε τὸ σύμβολον· κλῖμαξ ⌜ὑψίπυλος⌝ (ἑπτάπυλος Boherel), ἐπὶ δ' αὐτῇ πύλη ὀγδόη. . . . τὴν πρώτην (πύλην) τίθενται Κρόνου . . .· ἑβδόμην ἡλίου. (The order in which the planets are arranged is that of the days of the week reversed.) The details of the Mithraic ritual (τελετή) spoken of by Celsus are unknown ; did the worshippers enact the descent of the soul to earth by passing down the staircase into the cave, and the ascent of the soul, by going up the staircase from the cave to the open air above? Cf. Porphyry *De antro nymph.* 6, quoted in note on *Corp.* VIII. 3.

62 CORPVS HERMETICVM

mali simus'. *Ib.* 2. 28, arguing against that doctrine, Arnobius asks
how embodied souls can know 'quas ex quibus circulis qualitates,
dum in haec loca labuntur, attraxerint'. Macrobius *Somn.* 1. 12. 68 :
'de zodiaco et lacteo (i. e. from the outermost sphere, the *ogdoas* of
Corp. I,) ad subiectas sphaeras anima delapsa, dum per illas labitur,
in singulis singulos motus quos in exercitio est habitura producit, in
Saturni (sphaera) ratiocinationem et intelligentiam, in Iovis vim
agendi, in Martis animositatem, in Solis sentiendi opinandique
naturam, desiderii vero motum in Veneris, pronuntiandi et interpre-
tandi quae sentiat in orbe Mercurii, naturam vero plantandi et
augendi corpora ingressu globi lunaris exercet'. Servius *ad Virg.*
Aen. 11. 51 : 'dicunt physici, quum nasci coeperimus, sortimur a sole
spiritum, a luna corpus, a Venere cupiditatem, a Saturno humorem,
quae omnia singulis reddere videntur extincti.' Serv. *ad V. Aen.* 6.
714 : 'mathematici fingunt quod singulorum numinum potestatibus
corpus et anima connexa sint, quia quum descendunt animae, trahunt
secum torporem Saturni, Martis iracundiam, Veneris libidinem,
Mercurii lucri cupiditatem, Iovis regni desiderium.' Cf. Porphyry
as reported by Proclus *in Pl. Tim.* p. 311, quoted above in note on
§ 24.

A somewhat less close resemblance to the doctrine of *Corp.* I. 24
and 25 may be seen in what Basilides says about the death and
ascension of Jesus (Hippol. *Ref. haer.* 7. 27) : γέγονε δὲ ταῦτα, φησίν,
ἵνα ἀπαρχὴ τῆς φυλοκρινήσεως γένηται τῶν συγκεχυμένων ὁ Ἰησοῦς. . . .
ἀναγκαῖον ἦν τὰ συγκεχυμένα φυλοκρινηθῆναι διὰ τῆς τοῦ Ἰησοῦ διαιρέσεως.
ἔπαθεν οὖν τοῦτο ὅπερ ἦν αὐτοῦ σωματικὸν μέρος, ὃ ἦν τῆς ἀμορφίας,[1] καὶ
ἀπεκατέστη εἰς τὴν ἀμορφίαν· ἀνέστη δὲ τοῦτο ὅπερ ἦν ψυχικὸν αὐτοῦ
μέρος, ὅπερ ἦν τῆς ἑβδομάδος,[2] καὶ ἀπεκατέστη εἰς τὴν ἑβδομάδα· ἀνή-
στη[σε] δὲ τοῦτο ὅπερ ἦν τῆς ἀκρωρείας οἰκεῖον τοῦ μεγάλου ἄρχοντος,[3] καὶ
ἔμεινε παρὰ τὸν ἄρχοντα τὸν μέγαν ⌐ἀνήνεγκε⌐ (ἀνηνέχθη) δὲ μέχρις ἄνω
τοῦτο ὅπερ ἦν τοῦ μεθορίου πνεύματος, καὶ ἔμεινεν ἐν τῷ μεθορίῳ πνεύματι.[4]
ἀπεκαθάρθη δὲ ἡ υἱότης ἡ τρίτη[5] δι' αὐτοῦ, . . . καὶ ἀνῆλθε πρὸς τὴν

[1] I. e. of gross matter.
[2] The *hebdomas* is the region of the seven planetary spheres.
[3] 'The ἀκρώρεια of the great Archon' is the sphere of the fixed stars, the abode
of the Demiurgus.
[4] I. e. at the boundary between the material world and the immaterial world, the
latter being thought of as filling the space outside the Kosmos.
[5] The τρίτη υἱότης is the divine element which had been intermixed with matter
in the lower world. (Is it merely a coincidence that the Anthropos of *Corp.* I is
third son of the supreme God ?)

μακαρίαν νιότητα,¹ διὰ πάντων τούτων διελθοῦσα. ... τῆς οὖν φυλοκρινήσεως ἀπαρχὴ γέγονεν ὁ Ἰησοῦς· ... τούτῳ γὰρ τῷ τρόπῳ φησὶν ὅλην τὴν νιότητα τὴν καταλελειμμένην εἰς τὴν ἀμορφίαν ... δεῖν φυλοκρινηθῆναι, ᾧ τρόπῳ καὶ ὁ Ἰησοῦς πεφυλοκρίνηται. The last sentence implies that in the case of every man a like 'separation of things of diverse nature' is destined to take place. Basilides has adopted and applied to Jesus a doctrine which in certain Pagan schools was taught concerning men in general. Compare the doctrine of a Gnostic sect in Irenaeus 1. 30. 12 : 'descendisse autem eum (*sc.* Christum) per septem caelos, assimilatum (esse) ⸢filiis⸣ (τοῖς ἄρχουσιν?) eorum dicunt, et sensim eorum evacuasse virtutem.'

§ 26 a. γυμνωθεὶς ἀπὸ τῶν τῆς ἁρμονίας ἐνεργημάτων. The τῆς ἁρμονίας ἐνεργήματα are the planetary πάθη which have just been enumerated. As to γυμνωθείς, cf. Plotinus 1. 6. 7 : ἀναβατέον οὖν πάλιν ἐπὶ τὸ ἀγαθόν. ... τεύξις δὲ αὐτοῦ ἀναβαίνουσι πρὸς τὸ ἄνω, καὶ ἐπιστραφεῖσι, καὶ ἀποδυομένοις ἃ καταβαίνοντες ἠμφιέσμεθα· οἷον ἐπὶ τὰ ἅγια τῶν ἱερῶν τοῖς ἀνιοῦσι καθάρσεις τε καὶ ἱματίων ἀποθέσεις τῶν πρίν, καὶ τὸ γυμνοῖς ἀνιέναι· ἕως ἄν τις ⸢παρελθὼν⸣ (ἀποβαλὼν?) πᾶν ὅσον ἀλλότριον τοῦ θεοῦ, αὐτῷ μόνῳ αὐτὸ μόνον ἴδῃ κ.τ.λ. I do not know what particular ritual Plotinus had in mind. Did the Mithraists thus strip themselves when they were ascending their κλῖμαξ ἑπτάπυλος?

γίνεται ἐπὶ τὴν ὀγδοαδικὴν (ὀγδοατικὴν MSS.) φύσιν. 'The substance of the *ogdoas*' is the eighth and outermost sphere, that of the fixed stars. This is the δημιουργικὴ σφαῖρα spoken of in § 13 a, i. e. the seat of the Demiurgus-Nous ; and it was there that Anthropos was situated before his descent through the region of the planets. It is the sphere to which the ὀγδόη πύλη of the Mithraists corresponded (Orig. *c. Cels.* 6. 22, quoted above). Cf. Clem. Alex. *Strom.* 4. 161 : εἴτε ἑπτὰ οὐρανοὶ οὕς τινες ἀριθμοῦσι κατ᾽ ἐπανάβασιν, εἴτε καὶ ἡ ἀπλανὴς χώρα ἡ πλησιάζουσα τῷ νοητῷ κόσμῳ ὀγδοὰς λέγοιτο. The word ὀγδοάς is frequently used in this sense in the writings of the Christian Gnostics ; e.g. Basilides, Hippol. *Ref. haer.* 7. 27 : ἔστιν ὁ κόσμος διῃρημένος εἰς (1) ὀγδοάδα (the sphere of the fixed stars), ἥτις ἐστὶν ἡ κεφαλὴ τοῦ παντὸς κόσμου, ... καὶ εἰς (2) ἑβδομάδα (the region of the seven planets),² ἥτις ἐστὶν ⸢ἡ κεφαλὴ τῆς ἑβδομάδος ὁ δημιουργὸς τῶν

---

¹ The μακαρία νιότης is that 'Sonship' which ἅμα τῷ γενέσθαι τοῦ σπέρματος τὴν πρώτην καταβολὴν ... ἀνῆλθε καὶ ἀνέδραμε κάτωθεν ἄνω, and has ever since remained above, in union with God.
² Cf. Irenaeus 1. 30. 9 : the Ophites 'sanctam hebdomadam septem stellas quas dicunt planetas esse volunt'.
Hippolytus, *Ref. haer.* 7. 26, apparently reports Basilides as saying that there

ὑποκειμένων⌉,¹ καὶ εἰς (3) τοῦτο τὸ διάστημα τὸ καθ' ἡμᾶς (the sublunar world), ὅπου ἐστὶν ἡ ἀμορφία. The Valentinians used the word ὀγδοάς in two different senses. Their 'first ὀγδοάς' was the group of the eight highest Aeons. But they also used ὀγδοάς as Basilides used it, in the sense of 'the eighth sphere', i. e. the sphere of the fixed stars, which is above the planetary *hebdomas*. E. g. the Valentinian Theodotus, Clem. Alex. *fragm.* 63 : ἡ μὲν οὖν τῶν πνευματικῶν ἀνάπαυσις . . . ἐν ὀγδοάδι . . . παρὰ τῇ μητρί (Sophia), ⌈ἔχοντα⌉ (*lege* ἐχόντων) τὰς ψυχὰς [τὰ] ἐνδύματα ² ἄχρι συντελείας· ³ αἱ δὲ ἄλλαι πισταὶ ψυχαὶ παρὰ τῷ δημιουργῷ.⁴ περὶ δὲ τὴν συντέλειαν ἀναχωροῦσι καὶ αὗται εἰς ὀγδοάδα. . . . τὸ δὲ ἐντεῦθεν, ἀποθέμενα τὰ πνευματικὰ (nom.) τὰς ψυχὰς κ.τ.λ. enter into the *pleroma* (which is above the material Kosmos), καὶ πρὸς τὴν τοῦ ⌈πνεύματος⌉ ὄψιν ἔρχονται, αἰῶνες νοεροὶ γενόμενα. (This passage has much in common with the description of the ascent of the soul in *Corp.* I.) *Ib.* 80 : ὃν γεννᾷ ἡ μήτηρ, εἰς θάνατον ἄγεται καὶ εἰς κόσμον· ὃν δὲ ἀναγεννᾷ Χριστός, εἰς ζωὴν μετατίθεται εἰς ὀγδοάδα (i. e. into the 'eighth sphere', which is above the seat of the Valentinian Demiurgus, and beyond the reach of the planetary πάθη).⁵

are 365 οὐρανοί in the *hebdomas*. His words are these : ἐπεὶ οὖν καὶ τὰ ἐν τῇ ἐβδομάδι πάντα πεφώτιστο . . .·—κτίσεις γάρ εἰσι ⌈κατ' αὐτὰ τὰ διαστήματα καὶ κατ' αὐτοὺς⌉ (*lege* κατὰ τοῦτο τὸ διάστημα, sc. in the planetary region) ἄπειροι καὶ ἀρχαὶ καὶ δυνάμεις καὶ ἐξουσίαι, . . . ἔνθα καὶ τριακοσίους ἑξήκοντα πέντε οὐρανοὺς φάσκουσι, καὶ τὸν μέγαν ἄρχοντα αὐτῶν εἶναι τὸν Ἀβρασάξ . . .·—ἀλλ' ἐπεί, φησί, ταῦθ' οὕτως ἐγένετο, ἔδει λοιπὸν καὶ τὴν ἀμορφίαν ⟨τὴν⟩ καθ' ἡμᾶς (i. e. the sublunar world) φωτισθῆναι. If this statement is to be accepted, the meaning may perhaps have been, not that there is a series of 365 concentric spheres, but that there are 365 different *aspects* of the heavens, corresponding to the 365 days of the year. Each of these aspects of the heavens—or in other words, each of the days of the year—is presided over by a different Power (a χρονοκράτωρ, as Egyptian astrologers would have said) ; and all these 365 Powers together are subject to 'the great Archon' Abrasax, who is lord of the whole region of the planets. Cf. Irenaeus I. 24. 7 : 'trecentorum (possibly *trecentas*?) autem sexaginta quinque caelorum locales positiones distribuunt (Basilidiani), similiter ut mathematici : illorum (sc. *mathematicorum*, "astrologers") enim theoremata accipientes, in suum characterem doctrinae transtulerunt : esse autem principem illorum Ἀβραξᾶς (εἶναι δὲ τὸν ἄρχοντα αὐτῶν φησιν Ἀβρασάξ Theodoret), et propter hoc cccⅬxv numeros habere in se.' The letters of the name Ἀβρασάξ or Ἀβράξας, taken as numbers, make up the number 365 when added together. (It was noted that the letters of the name Μείθρας also make up the number 365 ; Jerome *in Amos* lib. I.)

¹ Perhaps ἡ κεφαλὴ [ ] τῶν ὑποκειμένων.
² The πνευματικόν is the highest part of the man ; the ψυχή is a lower part, and is regarded as a 'vesture' or 'integument' of the πνευματικόν.
³ I. e. until the final consummation of all things.
⁴ I. e. in the planetary *hebdomas*, which is the seat of the Demiurgus in the Valentinian system.
⁵ Basilides sometimes used ὀγδοάς and ἐβδομάς as personal names, signifying respectively 'the Power that resides in the eighth sphere' and 'the Power that resides in the seven planetary spheres'; e. g. Hippol. *Ref. haer.* 7. 25 : ἦν . . .

τὴν ἰδίαν δύναμιν ἔχων. The man has at this stage recovered the powers proper to his true nature, which he had lost through his descent into gross matter. ὑμνεῖ σὺν τοῖς ⟨ἐκεῖ⟩ οὖσι τὸν πατέρα. Those who are 'there' (i. e. in the sphere of the fixed stars) are (1) the star-gods, and (2) other human souls, which have previously mounted to that sphere. The notion that human souls of the highest order, after their release from the body, take up their abode in the sphere of the fixed stars, can be traced back (perhaps through Posidonius) to Heraclides Ponticus.[1] See Cic. *Somn. Scip.*; and cf. *Corp.* X. 7 *fin.*: αὕτη (viz. residence among the astral gods) ψυχῆς ἡ τελειοτάτη δόξα. The author of *Corp.* I has adopted this notion; but he regards an abode in this region, not as the highest to which the soul can attain, but as a stage on the way to something yet higher.

ἀκούει καὶ τῶν δυνάμεων, ὑπὲρ τὴν ὀγδοαδικὴν φύσιν οὐσῶν, φωνῇ τινι ἰδίᾳ ὑμνουσῶν τὸν θεόν. As to the hymns sung by the δυνάμεις, cf. Valentinus, Hippol. *Ref. haer.* 6. 31 *fin.*: ἀνέδραμεν . . . ὁ Χριστὸς καὶ τὸ Ἅγιον Πνεῦμα πρὸς τὸν Νοῦν καὶ τὴν Ἀλήθειαν ἐντὸς τοῦ ὅρου (i. e. into the *pleroma* with which extracosmic space is filled), ⌈ἡ⌉ (ἵν᾽ ᾖ) μετὰ τῶν ἄλλων αἰώνων δοξάζων τὸν Πατέρα. For φωνῇ τινι ἰδίᾳ, cf. ταῖς γλώσσαις . . . τῶν ἀγγέλων in 1 *Cor.* 13. 1. *Testament of Job* (Reitzenstein *Poim.* p. 57): the first of Job's three daughters ἀπεφθέγξατο τοὺς ἀγγελικοὺς ὕμνους ἐν ἀγγελικῇ φωνῇ, καὶ ὕμνον ἀνέμελπε τῷ θεῷ κατὰ τὴν ἀγγελικὴν ὑμνολογίαν· the second

βασιλεὺς καὶ κύριος ὡς ἐδόκει τῶν ὅλων ὁ μέγας ἄρχων, ἡ Ὀγδοάς· ἦν δὲ καὶ τούτου τοῦ διαστήματος βασιλεὺς καὶ κύριος ἡ Ἑβδομάς. And in the same way, the Valentinians, holding the eighth sphere to be the abode of Achamoth-Sophia, and the planetary *hebdomas* to be the abode of her son the Demiurgus, sometimes called Sophia herself Ὀγδοάς, and the Demiurgus Ἑβδομάς. Irenaeus 1. 5. 3: (τὴν Ἀχαμώθ) καὶ Ὀγδοάδα καλοῦσι καὶ Σοφίαν . . . · ἔχειν δὲ τὸν τῆς μεσότητος τόπον αὐτήν, καὶ εἶναι ὑπεράνω μὲν τοῦ δημιουργοῦ, ὑποκάτω δὲ τοῦ πληρώματος μέχρι συντελείας. *Ib.* 1. 5. 2: Ἑβδομάδα καλοῦσιν αὐτόν (*sc.* τὸν δημιουργόν), τὴν δὲ μητέρα τὴν Ἀχαμὼθ Ὀγδοάδα, ἀποσώζουσαν τὸν ἀριθμὸν ⌈τοῦ⌉ (τῆς) ἀρχεγόνου καὶ πρώτης τοῦ πληρώματος ὀγδοάδος. (The latter passage shows that the Valentinians, having adopted from their predecessors their use of ὀγδοάς in the sense of 'the eighth sphere', sought to connect this with their other use of it in the sense of 'the first eight Aeons'.)

A similar use of Ὀγδοάς as a person-name occurs in a magic papyrus (Pap. Leyd. W. 139. 45 Leemann: Reitzenstein *Poim.*, p. 54): τὸ κύριον ὄνομα, ὅ ἐστιν Ὀγδοὰς ὄνομα, ὁ τὰ πάντα ἐπιτάσσων καὶ διοικῶν· τούτῳ γὰρ ὑπετάγησαν ἄγγελοι, ἀρχάγγελοι, δαίμονες, δαιμόνισσαι, καὶ πάντα τὰ ὑπὸ τὴν κτίσιν. *Ib.* 141. 5: χρήσῃ τῷ μεγάλῳ ὀνόματι, ὅ ἐστιν Ὀγδοὰς ὄνομα, ὁ τὰ πάντα διοικῶν τὰ κατὰ τὴν φύσιν. This Being, who 'governs all things created', and 'administers all things in the material universe', corresponds to the 'great Archon' or Demiurgus who resides in 'the eighth sphere' in the system of Basilides.

[1] A suggestion of something like it occurs in Pl. *Tim.* 42 B: εἰς τὴν τοῦ ξυννόμου πορευθεὶς οἴκησιν ἄστρου, βίον εὐδαίμονα καὶ συνήθη ἕξοι.

2806·2   F

sang hymns in 'the language (διάλεκτος) of the Archontes'; and the third, in 'the language of the Cherubim'.

We were told in § 7 that the 'Light' which stands for God is subdivided into innumerable δυνάμεις. That is, the supreme God is pictured as a Being made up of innumerable 'Powers', which fill the boundless space outside the Kosmos. In § 26 a, these 'Powers' are regarded as persons. The Catholic Christians spoke of three divine 'Persons'; the Valentinians, of thirty. The author of *Corp.* I recognizes innumerable Persons in a somewhat similar sense; and he holds that individual human souls may be added to the number of them (δυνάμεις καὶ αὐτοὶ γενόμενοι ἐν θεῷ γίνονται). His conception of the δυνάμεις of God resembles that of Philo. (See Bousset, *Rel. des Judentums*, Kap. XVIII; and Zeller, *Phil. der Gr.* III, Abth. 2 (1903), pp. 407–418.) Philo speaks much of God's δυνάμεις. He repeatedly says that the two chief δυνάμεις of God are ἡ ποιητικὴ δύναμις (also called ἡ εὐεργέτις δύναμις and ἡ τοῦ θεοῦ ἀγαθότης), and ἡ βασιλικὴ δύναμις (also called ἀρχή, ἐξουσία, ἡγεμονία, τὸ κράτος, ἡ ἡγεμονικὴ καὶ δεσποτικὴ ἐξουσία, and ἡ κολαστήριος δύναμις). In *De fuga et invent.* 18. 94 ff., Wendland III, p. 130, he adds three others, the operation of which is limited to God's dealings with erring men, viz. ἡ ἵλεως δύναμις (by which God pardons repentant sinners), ἡ προστακτική (by which God gives commands to men), and ἡ ἀπαγορευτική (by which God issues prohibitions); and he there says that these five δυνάμεις are subordinate to the θεῖος λόγος, which is the first and chief δύναμις, and the ἡνίοχος τῶν δυνάμεων. Cf. *De cherubim* 9. 27, Cohn I, p. 176: κατὰ τὸν ἕνα ὄντως ὄντα θεὸν δύο τὰς ἀνωτάτω εἶναι καὶ πρώτας δυνάμεις ἀγαθότητα καὶ ἐξουσίαν, . . . τρίτον δὲ συνάγοντα ἀμφοῖν μέσον εἶναι λόγον, λόγῳ γὰρ καὶ ἄρχοντα καὶ ἀγαθὸν εἶναι τὸν θεόν. In other passages, he says that the two chief δυνάμεις of God are ἡ ποιητική and ἡ βασιλική, and does not mention the λόγος in connexion with them. Elsewhere, he says that the δυνάμεις of God are unlimited in number;[1] and he identifies them (1) with the Platonic ἰδέαι, (2) with the (σπερματικοὶ) λόγοι of the Stoics, and (3) with the 'angels' of the Jews and the 'daemons' of the Platonists. At times, a δύναμις of God means to Philo merely a mode or department of God's action. But at other times, he conceives the δυνάμεις as persons distinct from God; he speaks of them as God's δορυφόροι,

[1] *De conf. ling.* 34. 171, Wendland II, p. 262: εἷς ὢν ὁ θεὸς ἀμυθήτους περὶ αὐτὸν ἔχει δυνάμεις, ἀρωγοὺς καὶ σωτηρίους τοῦ γενομένου πάσας.

and even calls them ψυχαί (*De conf. ling. l.c.*). See also Philo *Legat. ad Caium* 1. 6, Cohn VI, p. 156.

Philo's hypostatization of the δυνάμεις is an instance of a mode of thought which was common among the Jews of his time. There are traces in the New Testament of a tendency to hypostatize the δύναμις θεοῦ; e. g. 1 *Cor.* 1. 24 : Χριστὸν θεοῦ δύναμιν καὶ θεοῦ σοφίαν. Luke 1. 35 : δύναμις Ὑψίστου ἐπισκιάσει σοι (where δύναμις Ὑψίστου stands in parallelism with πνεῦμα ἅγιον). Luke 22. 69 : ἔσται ὁ υἱὸς τοῦ ἀνθρώπου καθήμενος ἐκ δεξιῶν τῆς δυνάμεως τοῦ θεοῦ. In *Ep. Eph.* 1. 21 (ὑπεράνω πάσης ἀρχῆς καὶ ἐξουσίας καὶ δυνάμεως καὶ κυριότητος), the δυνάμεις are persons. Simon Magus called himself ἡ μεγάλη δύναμις,[1] probably meaning thereby that in him the divine νοῦς or λόγος had 'become flesh'. Simon, as reported by Hippolytus, spoke also of subordinate δυνάμεις, which he distinguished from 'the great Power' (ἡ μεγάλη δύναμις, ἡ ἀπέραντος). The term δύναμις was similarly used by some of the Christian Gnostics, e. g. by Satornilus.[2]

καὶ τότε τάξει ἀνέρχονται πρὸς τὸν πατέρα. The souls 'ascend to the Father'; i. e. they quit the material Kosmos, and enter the incorporeal world, which is filled with the presence of God ; or, as some of the Gnostics would have expressed it, they enter the *pleroma*. And they enter it in due order or succession (τάξει), as each of them in turn becomes fit for this supreme exaltation.

[θεωθῆναι]. If we retain this word, we must take it as equivalent to ἐν θεῷ γενέσθαι in the sense explained above. But the sentence reads better without it ; and it seems most likely that it has been added by a later hand.

§ 26 b. καθοδηγὸς γίνῃ τοῖς ἀξίοις. The prophet is to preach to all mankind ; but it is only 'the worthy' among his hearers that will accept him as their guide.

ὁ Ποιμάνδρης ἐμίγη ταῖς δυνάμεσιν. The divine Mind, which has assumed a quasi-corporeal form for the purpose of communicating with the prophet, returns to the incorporeal world, and resumes its

---

[1] *Acts* 8. 10: ᾧ προσεῖχον πάντες . . . λέγοντες Οὗτός ἐστιν ἡ Δύναμις τοῦ θεοῦ ἡ καλουμένη Μεγάλη. Irenaeus 1. 23. 2 : 'esse se (dixit Simon) sublimissimam virtutem (i. e. δύναμιν), hoc est eum qui sit super omnia Pater.' Hippol. *Ref. haeres.* 6. 19 : ἑαυτὸν δὲ λέγων τὴν ὑπὲρ πάντα δύναμιν εἶναι.
[2] Hippol. *Ref. haeres.* 7. 28 : Satornilus said ἕνα πατέρα ἄγνωστον τοῖς πᾶσιν ὑπάρχειν, τὸν ποιήσαντα ἀγγέλους, ἀρχαγγέλους, δυνάμεις, ἐξουσίας. Epiphan. *Haer.* 23 : Satornilus said τὸν σωτῆρα ἀπεστάλθαι ἀπὸ Πατρὸς κατὰ τὴν γνώμην τῶν δυνάμεων.

functions as the supreme Being in whom all the δυνάμεις are comprehended.

§§ 27-29. [[ἐγὼ δὲ εὐχαριστήσας . . . τὴν ἰδίαν κοίτην.]] This passage is out of place. § 30, in which the prophet describes his state of mind on waking at the conclusion of his vision, must have been meant to follow immediately after the account of the vision itself ; and his hymn of thanksgiving (§ 31 f.), which follows rightly on § 30, must have preceded § 27, the opening words of which (ἐγὼ δὲ εὐχαριστήσας κ.τ.λ.) refer back to it. When the text is thus rearranged, the order is perfectly satisfactory. The prophet first speaks of his own reception of the revelation (§§ 30-32), and then proceeds to describe how he preached to others the *gnosis* which had been revealed to him ; and he brings his narrative to a fitting close, by making his hearers go to bed at the end of the day thus spent, § 29 *fin.* (Compare the conclusion of the First Book of the *Iliad.*) It is possible that the order of the paragraphs was deliberately changed by some one who intended the *libellus* to be read as a 'lesson' at a meeting of worshippers, and considered that it would serve this liturgical purpose better if the hymn (in which the congregation might join) were placed at the end.

§ 30. τὴν εὐεργεσίαν τοῦ Ποιμάνδρου ἀνεγραψάμην εἰς ἐμαυτόν. The more usual construction would be εὐεργέτην τὸν Π. ἀνεγραψάμην, ' I registered his name on the tablet of my memory as that of a benefactor'. Cf. Pl. *Gorg.* 506 C : εὐεργέτης παρ᾽ ἐμοὶ ἀναγεγράψει.

πληρωθεὶς ὧν ἤθελον. These words refer back to § 3, μαθεῖν θέλω τὰ ὄντα . . . καὶ γνῶναι τὸν θεόν.

ἡ τοῦ λόγου ἀφορία (ἐκφορὰ MSS.) γέννημα[τα] ⌜ἀγαθῶν⌝. The phrase ἡ τοῦ λόγου ⌜ἐκφορά⌝ is parallel to the preceding σιωπή ; it is therefore evident that ἐκφορά (' utterance') is wrong. In his sleep, the prophet uttered no words ; he was only dreaming that he spoke. ἀφορία gives the sense required, and suits well with the following γέννημα and the preceding ἐγκύμων. The word ἀγαθῶν can hardly be right, because γέννημα[τα] ἀγαθῶν too closely resembles ἐγκύμων τοῦ ἀγαθοῦ. We might get a good antithesis to λόγου (' speech') by writing ἁγίων ⟨νοημάτων⟩, ' holy thoughts'.

λαβόντι ἀπὸ τοῦ Ποιμάνδρου, τουτέστι τοῦ τῆς αὐθεντίας (νοός, τὸν . . .) λόγον.—(λαβόντι ἀπὸ τοῦ νοός μου, τουτέστι τοῦ Ποιμάνδρου τοῦ τῆς αὐθεντίας λόγου MSS.) With the correction τὸν τῆς αὐθεντίας λόγον for τοῦ τῆς αὐθεντίας λόγου, and the omission of μου, the reading of the MSS. would be intelligible, if we take αὐθεντία to mean ' the absolute truth', though not if we take it to mean 'the sovereignty'. But it seems more probable that Poimandres was here again called ὁ τῆς αὐθεντίας νοῦς, as in § 2.

§§ 31, 32. ἅγιος ὁ θεὸς ... τὴν πᾶσαν ἐξουσίαν. This hymn occurs in a collection of Christian prayers, Berlin Papyrus 9794. (*Berl. Klass. Texte*, Heft VI, *Altchristliche Texte*. See Reitzenstein and Wendland, 'Zwei angeblich christliche Gebete', *Nachrichten von der k. Gesellschaft der Wissensch.*, *Göttingen*, *Philol.-hist. Klasse*, 1910, Heft 4, p. 324 ff.) We are told that the Papyrus was written in the third century. There is no doubt that the hymn was composed to form part of *Corp.* I, and was borrowed thence by the Christian compiler of the collection of prayers in the Papyrus; for some of the phrases in it were clearly suggested by passages in *Corp.* I (e.g. ζωὴν καὶ φῶς, and παρέδωκας αὐτῷ τὴν πᾶσαν ἐξουσίαν). It must have been extracted from the Pagan *Poimandres*-document by some Christian who considered it suitable for use in his own worship. The Christian who adopted it added a doxology at the end, and probably inserted the words τὸ γὰρ πνεῦμά μου ⟨. . .⟩ τῷ θείῳ πνεύματι.

§ 31. ἅγιος (ὁ θεός, ὁ ὑποδ)είξας μοι [ἀπὸ τοῦ ν̣ι̣ος] ζωὴν καὶ φ(ῶς). This clause is omitted in *codd. Corp.*; but as the words ὁ ὑποδείξας μοι ζωὴν καὶ φῶς were evidently written with reference to what has gone before in *Corpus* I, it is to be presumed that it originally belonged to that document,[1] and was taken thence, with the rest of the hymn, by the compiler of *Pap.*

For ἀπὸ τοῦ ν̣ι̣ος, Reitzenstein writes ἀπὸ τοῦ Νοός. But this is hardly intelligible. If διά were written in place of ἀπό, the meaning might be διὰ τοῦ Ποιμάνδρου; and if Poimandres could be regarded as a person distinct from the supreme God, it might very well be said that God has revealed 'Life and Light' to the prophet through the agency of Poimandres. But we have seen reason to think that the writer's view is rather that Poimandres, ὁ τῆς αὐθεντίας νοῦς, is identical with the supreme God; and if so, this explanation cannot be accepted. It seems best therefore to assume that ἀπὸ τοῦ νοός has been wrongly inserted here. It may possibly be a misplaced doublet of the words ἀπὸ τοῦ νοός which occur in the text of the MSS. a few lines above.

ἅγιος ὁ θεός, ὁ πατὴρ τῶν ὅλων *codd. Corp.*—ἅγιος ὁ θεὸς κ(αὶ πατὴρ τῶ)ν ὅλων [ἅγιος εἶ] (ὁ πρὸ) ἀρχῆ(ς ὤν) *Pap.* As given in *codd. Corp.*, the first clause of this triplet is too short to match the second and the

---

[1] It ought therefore to have been printed in the text.

third ; it is therefore probable that it originally included the phrase of which ἀρχη, preserved in *Pap.*, is a remnant. The Berlin editors of *Pap.* write ὁ ἀπ' ἀρχῆς ὤν; but perhaps ὁ πρὸ ἀρχῆς ὤν is preferable. Cf. § 8 a : τὸ ἀρχέτυπον εἶδος, τὸ προάρχον τῆς ἀρχῆς. In the vision described in § 4, the 'light' which stands for God is in existence before the first rudiment of the future Kosmos comes into being.

οὗ ἡ βουλὴ τελεῖται ἀπὸ τῶν ⌜ἰδίων⌝ δυνάμεων. ἀπό is here, as often in post-classical writings, used in the sense of ὑπό with a passive verb. For βουλή, cf. ἐκ βουλῆς θεοῦ in § 8 b. The δυνάμεις are the 'Powers of God' which were spoken of in § 7 and § 26 a sq. The epithet ἰδίων can hardly be right ; there is no need to emphasize the fact that the δυνάμεις are Powers of God, and not of some one else. It would be possible to write ⟨ἀ⟩ιδίων ; but though the Powers are, no doubt, 'everlasting' or 'eternal', there would be little point in saying so here. Perhaps the author wrote εἰδικῶν, 'individual' or 'several'. (For this meaning of εἰδικός, see note on *Ascl. Lat.* I. 2 b *fin.*) The personified δυνάμεις correspond, in one aspect, to the 'departmental gods' of Pagan theologies. Each individual among them has some special function of his own in the administration of the universe; and by discharging their several functions, they collectively fulfil the all-comprehensive βουλή of God.

ὃς γνωσθῆναι βούλεται. Cf. *Corp.* X. 15 a : θέλει γνωρίζεσθαι. *Corp.* VII. 2 a : ἀφορῶντες τῇ καρδίᾳ εἰς τὸν ⟨οὕτως⟩ ὁραθῆναι θέλοντα. God's will that men should know him is a part of his universal βουλή.

ὁ λόγῳ συστησάμενος τὰ ὄντα. λόγος here means God's *fiat*, and is no more hypostatized than in *Ps.* 32 (33) 6, τῷ λόγῳ τοῦ κυρίου οἱ οὐρανοὶ ἐστερεώθησαν. But it is nevertheless possible that the phrase was suggested by what was said about the hypostatized λόγος of God in § 5 a.

ἅγιος εἶ, ὃν ἡ φύσις οὐκ ἠμαύρωσεν·
ἅγιος εἶ, οὗ πᾶσα φύσις εἰκὼν ἔφυ.

So *Pap.*; in *codd. Corp.* the two clauses are interchanged. The order of *Pap.* seems preferable. In the first clause, the verb is ἐμαύρωσεν (no doubt a miswriting of ἠμαύρωσεν) in *Pap.*, but ἐμόρφωσεν in *codd. Corp.* If we accept ἐμόρφωσεν, we must take φύσις to mean here the power which imposes forms on matter. God is not included in the sphere of operation of this power ; for God, being incorporeal, has no μορφή. But this conception of μορφή, and of φύσις as the imposer of μορφαί, does not occur elsewhere in *Corp.* I ; and ἠμαύρωσεν seems the better reading, as being in accordance with the notion of φῶς and σκότος which is prominent throughout the document. 'God is light, and in him is no darkness at all' (*Ep. Joh.* 1. 1. 5). Man also, in respect of his true being, is unmixed light; but in his case, the light has been obscured through his marriage with φύσις, that is, through his descent into the world of matter, and incarnation in a material body. God, on the other hand, remains on high, apart from all that is material, and unaffected by the darkening influence of ὕλη.

οὗ πᾶσα φύσις εἰκὼν ἔφυ. ἡ πᾶσα φύσις is the material universe ; and the material universe is an 'image' of God. Cf. *Ascl. Lat.* I. 10 : 'dei, cuius sunt imagines duae mundus et homo'. *Corp.* VIII. 2 : ὁ κατ᾽ εἰκόνα αὐτοῦ ὑπ᾽ αὐτοῦ γενόμενος (*sc.* ὁ κόσμος).

The three clauses of this triplet deal with the relation between God and the Kosmos. The material world has been made by God ; but God is not affected by the evil influence of the ὕλη of which it is made ; and whatever good there is in it is a copy or reflection of the Good which is in God.

ὁ πάσης δυναστείας (δυνάστεως *Pap.* : δυνάμεως *codd. Corp.*) **ἰσχυρό-τερος.** δυνάστεως is probably a conflation of two readings, δυναστείας and δυνάμεως. As δυνάμεων was used a few lines above in a sense not applicable here, δυναστείας is the more likely reading.

δέξαι λογικὰς θυσίας ἁγνάς. Cf. *Corp.* XIII. 18 : δέξαι . . . λογικὴν θυσίαν. *Ib.* 21 : πέμπω λογικὰς θυσίας. A λογικὴ θυσία is an act of worship which consists in verbal adoration, as opposed to a material offering. Tertullian *On Prayer*, 27 : ' most excellent is every custom which . . . helps us to bring to God, as our best victim, a well-enriched prayer ; for this is the spiritual victim which has abolished the former sacrifices '. The epithet ἁγνάς implies that such worship alone is acceptable to God, and that θυσίαι in the literal sense (i. e. material offerings, and especially bloody sacrifices) are ' impure '. See *Ascl. Lat.* 41 a. But perhaps ἁγνὰς ought to be bracketed.

ἀπὸ ψυχῆς καὶ καρδίας πρὸς σὲ ἀνατεταμένης. Cf. *Ascl. Lat.* 41 b : ψυχῇ πάσῃ καὶ καρδίᾳ πρὸς σὲ ἀνατεταμένῃ.

σιωπῇ φωνούμενε. Cf. *Corp.* X. 5 : ἡ γὰρ γνῶσις αὐτοῦ βαθεῖα σιωπή ἐστι.

§ 32. αἰτουμένῳ τὸ μὴ σφαλῆναι. Cf. *Ascl. Lat.* 41 b : θέλησον ἡμᾶς διατηρηθῆναι . . . καὶ μήποτε σφαλῆναι τοῦ τοιούτου βίου.

τῆς γνώσεως τῆς κατ᾽ οὐσίαν ἡμῶν *codd. Corp.*—τῆς γνώσεως τῆς κατὰ ⌈υφος⌉ (ὕψος?) ἡμῶν αὐτῶν *Pap.* The reading of *codd. Corp.* might be understood to mean either ' the *gnosis* which corresponds to our true and incorporeal being (i. e. to the νοῦς in us)', or 'such (imperfect) *gnosis* as (earthly) beings like us are capable of acquiring'. The former explanation perhaps agrees better with the tone of the context. But the phrase τῆς κατ' οὐσίαν ἡμῶν, taken in either sense, seems irrelevant here; we should rather have expected the speaker to say 'the *gnosis* to which I have attained'. The reading of *Pap.* is meaningless; with the emendation ὕψος ('our exalted station') in place of νφος, the phrase might perhaps be taken as equivalent to τῆς κατ' οὐσίαν ἡμῶν in the first of the two senses explained above. But I am inclined to think that both texts are corrupt here. Possibly the true reading may be τῆς κατ⟨ὰ τὴν ἐξ⟩ουσίαν ἡμῶν (the ἐξουσία which God has given to man).

καὶ ἐνδυνάμωσόν με, ⟨ἵνα⟩ [καὶ] τῆς χάριτος ταύτης ⟨τυχὼν⟩ φωτίσω τοὺς ἐν ἀγνοίᾳ τοῦ γένους μου. 'This boon' means the revelation which the prophet has received. He prays that supernatural power may be given him, in order that he may be enabled to illuminate others as he himself has been illuminated, and so obey the injunction of Poimandres (§ 26 b : οὐχ ὡς πάντα παραλαβὼν καθοδηγὸς γίνῃ κ.τ.λ.). —τοὺς τοῦ γένους μου means 'my fellow-men'; cf. καθοδηγὸς ἐγενόμην τοῦ γένους in § 29.

[τὸ γὰρ πνεῦμά μου τῷ θείῳ πνεύματι] *Pap.* : om. codd. *Corp.* These words are meaningless as they stand in *Pap.* Reitzenstein inserts συμπνεῖ after μου, and takes the meaning to be ' my spirit is in accord with the divine spirit'. But this can hardly have been written by the author of the hymn. We have found πνεῦμα used in this document in two different senses, viz. (1) 'the element air' (§§ 9, 16), and (2) the 'vital spirit' of the individual man (§ 17). But both these uses of the word belong to the same *stratum* of Greek thought, and are connected with the Stoic system; in both of them alike, the πνεῦμα is a material thing of gaseous substance. If we retain the words of *Pap.*, we must say that the author has here used πνεῦμα in an entirely different sense, to signify the divine Mind, and the highest and incorporeal part of man. But he elsewhere uses the Platonic term νοῦς to express this conception; and it is difficult to see why he should here use πνεῦμα as a substitute for νοῦς. On the other hand, πνεῦμα was habitually thus used by the Christians, from Paul onward. Hence it may be inferred that these words were inserted by a Christian, and presumably by the Christian who adopted this Pagan hymn for use in his own worship, and included it in the collection of Christian prayers contained in the Papyrus.

If this clause was added by a Christian, it is possible that the missing verb is συμμαρτυρεῖ. Cf. *Ep. Rom.* 8. 16: αὐτὸ τὸ πνεῦμα συνμαρτυρεῖ τῷ πνεύματι ἡμῶν ὅτι ἐσμὲν τέκνα θεοῦ. A Christian reader of the Hermetic prayer might very well be reminded of that text by the words υἱοὺς δὲ σοῦ and πιστεύω καὶ μαρτυρῶ, which precede and follow the interpolation.

⟨. . .⟩ διὸ πιστεύω καὶ μαρτυρῶ ⟨ὅτι⟩ εἰς ζωὴν καὶ φῶς χωρῶ. The prophet 'believes' this himself, and 'bears witness to it' in his preaching to others. But διό is meaningless, and there is no clear connexion of thought with what precedes. It may perhaps have been because he felt the need of something to which διό could refer, that the Christian interpolator inserted before it the words τὸ γὰρ πνεῦμα κ.τ.λ. But I am inclined to suspect that in the earliest form of *Corp.* I the greater part of this hymn or prayer was absent, and that the prophet's *eulogia* originally ran as follows: ἅγιος ὁ θεός, ὁ ὑποδείξας μοι ζωὴν καὶ φῶς· [ ] διὸ πιστεύω καὶ μαρτυρῶ ὅτι εἰς ζωὴν καὶ φῶς χωρῶ. εὐλόγητος εἶ, πάτερ· ὁ σὸς (υἱὸς?) συναγιάζειν σοι βούλεται, καθὼς παρέδωκας αὐτῷ τὴν πᾶσαν ἐξουσίαν. 'God has set before me the promise of Life and Light; therefore, I believe and testify that I enter into Life and Light.' We may suppose that some one afterwards expanded this short *eulogia* by inserting the three ἅγιος-triplets, and the petitions which follow them; whence it resulted that διό was separated from the clause to which it originally referred. But if so, the addition had already been made when the document came into the hands of the Christian compiler of the collection of prayers in the Papyrus, and must therefore have been made in or before the third century A. D.

ὁ σὸς ἄνθρωπος συναγιάζειν σοι βούλεται. 'Thy man' is the higher and incorporeal part of the man, i. e. the νοῦς in him, which is derived from the first Anthropos, and in virtue of which he is a son of God. But perhaps the author may have written ὁ σὸς υἱός, which would suit better with the preceding πάτερ. The phrase ὁ σὸς ἄνθρωπος is borrowed from *Corp.* I in *Corp.* XIII. 20 (ὁ σὸς ἄνθρωπος ταῦτα βοᾷ); but the text of *Corp.* I may have already been altered when it was read by the writer of *Corp.* XIII.

συναγιάζειν σοι must mean 'to be holy as thou art holy', with reference to ἅγιος ὁ θεός above. But ἁγιάζειν usually means 'to make holy', and we should rather have expected συναγιάζεσθαι.

παρέδωκας αὐτῷ τὴν πᾶσαν ἐξουσίαν. Cf. πάντων τὴν ἐξουσίαν ἔχων in § 15, and ἔχοντες ἐξουσίαν τῆς ἀθανασίας μεταλαβεῖν in § 28. Man, as son of God, is αὐτεξούσιος; he is no slave of Heimarmene, but is free to unite himself with God, if he will; and the man who speaks *does* will to do so (βούλεται). Cf. *Ev. Joh.* i. 12 : ὅσοι δὲ ἔλαβον αὐτόν, ἔδωκεν αὐτοῖς ἐξουσίαν τέκνα θεοῦ γενέσθαι.

§ 27. Ὦ λαοί, ἄνδρες γηγενεῖς, κ.τ.λ. *Corp.* VII is an expansion of this missionary sermon.

Men, in respect of their lower nature, are 'sons of earth' (γηγενεῖς). As long as they remain unilluminated, the earthly nature which they inherit from φύσις, the mother of their race, is predominant, and 'Man, the son of God', is dormant in them.

μέθη '... ἑαυτοὺς ἐκδεδωκότες. Cf. Pl. *Phaedo* 79 c : ἡ ψυχή, ὅταν μὲν τῷ σώματι προσχρῆται εἰς τὸ σκοπεῖν τι..., τότε μὲν... πλανᾶται καὶ ταράττεται καὶ ἰλιγγιᾷ ὥσπερ μεθύουσα.

§ 28. οἱ συνοδεύσαντες τῇ πλάνῃ καὶ συγκοινωνήσαντες τῇ ἀγνοίᾳ. 'Error' and 'Ignorance' are here personified by a figure of speech.

§ 29. ἔσπειρα ⟨ἐν⟩ αὐτοῖς τοὺς τῆς σοφίας λόγους, καὶ ἐτράφη[σαν] ⟨τὸ σπαρὲν⟩ ἐκ τοῦ ἀμβροσίου ὕδατος. The notion of 'the water of immortality' occurs in many different regions. We meet with it in Babylonian myths. Cf. the ὕδωρ ζῶν spoken of in *Ev. Joh.* 4. 10–14 and 7. 37 f. The Orphici spoke of 'the fount of Mnemosyne', in contrast to 'the fount of Lethe'. But as the writer of *Corp.* I has just spoken of sowing seed, he must have gone on to speak, not of water which men drink, but of water with which the seed is watered. If then we retain ἐτράφησαν, we must understand οἱ λόγοι as its subject. But a reader would more naturally take the subject of ἐτράφησαν to be the men to whom ἐν αὐτοῖς refers ; and as this cannot be what the author meant, it is more likely that he wrote ἐτράφη τὸ σπαρέν, or something of the sort. The thought partly resembles that of Paul in I *Cor.* 3. 6 : ἐγὼ ἐφύτευσα, Ἀπολλὼς ἐπότισεν, ἀλλὰ ὁ θεὸς ηὔξανεν. The preacher sows the seed of wisdom ; but it is God that supplies the water which makes the seed grow.

ὅλοις (ὅλης MSS.) ἐκέλευσα αὐτοῖς εὐχαριστεῖν τῷ θεῷ. καὶ ἀναπληρώσαντες τὴν εὐχαριστίαν κ.τ.λ. εὐχαριστία here means a liturgical thanksgiving. This is not far from the sense in which the word was used in the early Christian Church, whence our word 'Eucharist'. Cf. Justin *Apol.* I. 13. I : τὸν δημιουργὸν τοῦδε τοῦ παντὸς ... λόγῳ εὐχῆς καὶ εὐχαριστίας ... αἰνοῦντες. *Ib.* I. 65. 3 : ἔπειτα προσφέρεται τῷ προεστῶτι τῶν ἀδελφῶν ἄρτος καὶ ποτήριον ὕδατος καὶ κράματος, καὶ οὗτος λαβὼν αἶνον καὶ δόξαν τῷ πατρὶ τῶν ὅλων ... ἀναπέμπει, καὶ εὐχαριστίαν ὑπὲρ τοῦ κατηξιῶσθαι τούτων παρ' αὐτοῦ ἐπὶ πολὺ ποιεῖται· οὗ συντελέσαντος τὰς εὐχὰς καὶ τὴν εὐχαριστίαν πᾶς ὁ παρὼν λαὸς ἐπευφημεῖ λέγων Ἀμήν.

LIBELLVS II

In the MSS. of the *Corpus Hermeticum*, the text of *Libellus II* begins at the words ἢ θεός in § 4 b. The part of the text which precedes these words has been preserved by Stobaeus.[1] It is possible that, in the original document, the passage given by Stobaeus was preceded by some introductory sentences; but there is no reason to think that any considerable part of the dialogue is missing.

In the *Corpus*, this piece is entitled Ἑρμοῦ πρὸς Τὰτ λόγος καθολικός. But this cannot have been the title of a dialogue in which the pupil addressed by Hermes is Asclepius; and there can be no doubt that the right explanation is that which is given by Reitzenstein (*Poimandres*, p. 193). The *libellus* which originally stood second in the *Corpus* bore the title Ἑρμοῦ πρὸς Τὰτ λόγ. καθ. In a MS. from which all our MSS. are derived, this title chanced to come at the bottom of a page, and several following leaves were torn out and lost. In these lost leaves were contained both the whole of the *libellus* to which the title Ἑρμοῦ πρὸς Τὰτ λόγ. καθ. belonged, and the title and beginning of the next *libellus* (our Libellus II), which originally stood third.[2] Thus the title of the lost second *libellus* came to be immediately followed by the words ἢ θεός κ.τ.λ. of our Libellus II, and was consequently taken to be the title of the *libellus* beginning with those words.

It appears from the headings of Stobaeus's three extracts from this document that it was known to him, not as one of the pieces of our *Corpus*, but as one of a collection of 'Discourses of Hermes to Asclepius'.

Corp. II is described in the concluding words as an *introduction* to a course of philosophy (προγνωσία τις τῆς πάντων φύσεως); hence it may be inferred that its writer intended it to be the first of a progressive series of discourses of Hermes.

Contents of Libellus II.

That which encompasses the Kosmos, and within which the movement of the Kosmos takes place, must be something incorporeal; consequently, it must be either identical with God, or closely connected

---

[1] This passage was restored to its place at the beginning of *Corp.* II by Patrizzi, who was the first to see that Stobaeus's extract had been taken from this document.
[2] Assuming that only one *libellus* has been lost. But it is of course possible that the missing leaves contained two or more *libelli*.

with God (§§ 1-4 a). But it is not identical with God; therefore, it must be something closely connected with God (§§ 4 b-6 a). It must also be motionless (§ 6 b).—But is it not void? No, for there is no such thing as void (§§ 10, 11).—

That by which the Kosmos as a whole, and all bodies within the Kosmos, are moved, is something incorporeal (viz. soul) which is within the body moved (§§ 8 b, 9). And this thing also is motionless (§ 6 b).

The incorporeal thing which encompasses the Kosmos is Nous (§ 12 a). But there is something above Nous, viz. the Good, which is the source of Nous and Aletheia (§ 12 b).

What then is God? God is distinct from and above Nous; he is the cause of the existence of Nous and Aletheia, and of all else (§ 13). God is identical with the Good; and no other being than God can properly be called good (§§ 14-16).

(A passage concerning the movement of the heavenly bodies, §§ 6 b-8 a, and a passage in which the duty of procreation is asserted, § 17 a, seem to have been subsequently added.)

The argument starts with certain propositions concerning movement (κίνησις); but the treatment of this topic is merely preliminary to the account of God which is given in §§ 12-16; and it is in these latter sections that the substance of the προγνωσία imparted in this dialogue is to be found. The doctrine set forth may be shortly stated thus; 'God is above and distinct from Nous; he is the source from which Nous issues, and is identical with τὸ ἀγαθόν'.

In the first part of the dialogue (§§ 1-11), the argument is confused by the intermixture of statements concerning τὸ κινοῦν (= τὸ ὑφ' οὗ κινεῖται τὸ κινούμενον) with others concerning τὸ ἐν ᾧ κινεῖται. How far the author is responsible for this confusion, and how far it has been caused by subsequent dislocation of portions of the text, it is difficult to guess; but the Hermetist's meaning would certainly have been more clearly expressed if the two topics (that of τὸ ἐν ᾧ and that of τὸ ὑφ' οὗ) had been kept separate.

The sources of Libellus II.

The doctrine is mainly Platonic. The conception of τὸ ἀσώματον is derived from Plato; and the source of the view that God is ἀνουσίαστος (§ 4 b), and of the statement that νοῦς and ἀλήθεια are 'rays' emitted by τὸ ἀγαθόν (§ 12 b), is to be found in Pl. Rep. 6. 508 E ff. In his identification of God with τὸ ἀγαθόν, and in his account of the relation between God and Nous, the writer is in agreement with many Platonists of the Roman Empire; and in the latter, he must have drawn from the same Platonic sources as the Christian Gnostics who spoke of Nous as an emanation from the Propator. The doctrine that ψυχή is ἀκίνητος (§ 6 b, τὸ κινοῦν ἔστηκεν) is not Platonic, but Aristotelian. The discussion of τὸ κενόν (§§ 10, 11) presupposes the Stoic doctrine of extracosmic κενόν, against which it is directed. The use of the word τόπος as a name for the extracosmic Nous is probably of Jewish origin. There is nothing distinctively Egyptian in this dialogue; and there is no trace of Christian influence.

Date.

This *libellus* must necessarily have been written later than the revival of Platonism which took place in the first century B. C.; but how much later, it is difficult to guess. From the word προγνωσία in § 17 b, it may perhaps be inferred that it was one of the earlier of the series of *Hermes to Asclepius* dialogues, the latest of which seem to have been written shortly before A. D. 300. (See notes on the dates of *Ascl. Lat.* III and *Corp.* IX.) It could hardly be said that any date between A. D. 1 and 250 is impossible; but the affinity of the doctrine of Nous in *Corp.* II to that of Platonists such as Numenius (A. D. 150–200), and to that of Valentinus and other Christian Gnostics, affords some ground for conjecturing that it was written between A. D. 100 and 250.

I append here, for comparison with *Corp.* II and with other *Hermetica*, the fragments of Numenius in which he speaks of 'the first God' and 'the second God'.

Euseb. *Pr. ev.* 11. 18. 1–24:

ὁ δὲ Νουμήνιος, τὰ Πλάτωνος πρεσβεύων, ἐν τοῖς Περὶ τἀγαθοῦ τάδε καὶ αὐτὸς περὶ τοῦ δευτέρου αἰτίου[1] λέγων διερμηνεύει·

1. " τὸν μέλλοντα δὲ συνήσειν θεοῦ πέρι πρώτου καὶ δευτέρου χρὴ πρότερον διελέσθαι ἕκαστα ἐν τάξει καὶ ἐν εὐθημοσύνῃ τινί. ... 3. ὁ θεὸς ὁ μὲν πρῶτος, ἐν ἑαυτῷ ὤν, ἐστὶν ἁπλοῦς, διὰ τὸ ἑαυτῷ συγγινόμενος διόλου μή ποτε εἶναι διαιρετός· ὁ θεὸς μέντοι ὁ δεύτερος ⌜καὶ τρίτος⌝[2] ἐστὶν εἷς, συμφερόμενος δὲ τῇ ὕλῃ, δυάδι οὔσῃ, ἑνοῖ μὲν αὐτήν, σχίζεται δὲ ὑπ' αὐτῆς, ἐπιθυμητικὸν ἦθος[3] ἐχούσης καὶ ῥεούσης. 4. τῷ οὖν μὴ εἶναι πρὸς τῷ

---

[1] I. e. the second God.
[2] In place of καὶ τρίτος (which is meaningless), something like καθ' ἑαυτὸν μέν, or (as below) πρὸς ἑαυτῷ μὲν ὤν, is needed.
[3] ἦθος Dindorf : εἶδος Mullach.

νοητῷ,—ἦν γὰρ ἂν πρὸς ἑαυτῷ,—διὰ τὸ ⟨εἰς ?⟩ τὴν ὕλην βλέπειν, ταύτης ἐπιμελούμενος ἀπερίοπτος ἑαυτοῦ γίνεται. 5. καὶ ἅπτεται τοῦ αἰσθητοῦ καὶ περιέπει, ἀνάγει τε ἔτι εἰς τὸ ἴδιον ἦθος, ⌜ἀπορεξόμενος⌝¹ τῆς ὕλης."

6. καὶ μεθ' ἕτερά φησι·

"καὶ γὰρ οὔ τι² δημιουργεῖν ⌜ἐστι χρεὼν⌝³ τὸν πρῶτον· καὶ τοῦ δημιουργοῦντος δὲ [περὶ πατρὸς καὶ υἱοῦ]⁴ χρὴ [εἶναι] νομίζεσθαι⁵ πατέρα τὸν πρῶτον θεόν. 7. εἰ μὲν οὖν περὶ τοῦ δημιουργοῦ⁶ ζητοῖμεν, φάσκοντες ⌜δεῖν τὸν πρότερον ὑπάρξαντα οὕτως ἂν ποιεῖν ἔχειν διαφερόντως⌝,⁷ οἰκεία ἡ πρόσοδος αὕτη γεγονυῖα ἂν εἴη τοῦ λόγου· εἰ δὲ περὶ τοῦ δημιουργοῦ μή ἐστιν ὁ λόγος, ζητοῦμεν δὲ περὶ τοῦ πρώτου, ἀφοσιοῦμαί τε τὰ λεχθέντα, καὶ ἔστω μὲν ἐκεῖνα ἄρρητα, μέτειμι δὲ ἑλεῖν τὸν λόγον ἑτέρωθεν θηράσας. 8. πρὸ μέντοι τοῦ λόγου τῆς ἁλώσεως, διομολογησώμεθα ἡμῖν αὐτοῖς ὁμολογίαν οὐκ ἀμφισβητήσιμον ἀκοῦσαι, τὸν μὲν πρῶτον θεὸν ἀργὸν εἶναι ἔργων ξυμπάντων, καὶ βασιλέα,⁸ τὸν δημιουργικὸν δὲ θεὸν ἡγεμονεῖν, δι' οὐρανοῦ ἰόντα. 9. διὰ δὲ τούτου καὶ ⌜ὁ στόλος ἡμῖν⌝⁹ ἐστι, κάτω τοῦ νοῦ πεμπομένου ἐν διεξόδῳ πᾶσι τοῖς ⟨αὐτοῦ? sc. τοῦ νοῦ⟩ κοινωνῆσαι συντεταγμένοις. 10. βλέποντος μὲν οὖν καὶ ἐπεστραμμένου πρὸς ἡμῶν ἕκαστον τοῦ θεοῦ,¹⁰ συμβαίνει ζῆν τε καὶ βιώσκεσθαι τότε τὰ σώματα, ⌜κηδεύοντα⌝¹¹ τοῦ θεοῦ τοῖς ἀκροβολισμοῖς·¹² μεταστρέφοντος δὲ εἰς τὴν ἑαυτοῦ περιωπὴν τοῦ θεοῦ,¹³ ταῦτα μὲν ἀποσβέννυσθαι, τὸν δὲ νοῦν ζῆν, βίου ἐπαυρόμενον εὐδαίμονος."¹⁴

¹ ἀπορεξόμενος MSS. : ἐπορεξάμενος Dindorf : ἀπορεγόμενος Mullach. Possibly ἐπορεγομένης τῆς ὕλης? (Cf. ἐπιθυμητικὸν ἦθος ἐχούσης above.)

² οὔ τι Mullach, Gifford : οὔτε MSS.

³ Perhaps ἐστι χρεὼν ⟨εἰπεῖν⟩? 'We ought not to say that the first God δημιουργεῖ.'

⁴ περὶ πατρὸς καὶ υἱοῦ is doubtless a marginal note inserted in the text by error.

⁵ χρὴ εἶναι νομίζεσθαι MSS., Dindorf : χρὴ νομίζειν Mullach.

⁶ δημιουργοῦ Mullach : δημιουργικοῦ Dindorf.

⁷ Possibly, εἰ μὲν οὖν περὶ τοῦ δημ. ζητοῦντες φάσκοιμεν δεῖν ⟨αὐ⟩τόν, πρότερον ὑπάρξαντα ⟨ἀγαθόν⟩, οὕτω ⟨π⟩ἂν⟨τα⟩ ποιεῖν ⟨ὥστε⟩ ἔχειν διαφερόντως (= ὥστε πάντα εὖ ἔχειν). Cf. Pl. Tim. 29 E, ἀγαθὸς ἦν κ.τ.λ. That is Plato's πρόσοδος τοῦ λόγου in the Timaeus.

⁸ The first God is a king or emperor, who sits untroubled in his palace ; the second God is a viceroy or subordinate ruler (ἡγεμών), who goes forth into the world to execute the king's will. Perhaps we ought to read κατὰ βασιλέα, 'in the manner of a king'.

⁹ Perhaps, ὁ ⟨τοῦ ἐν⟩ ἡμῖν ⟨νοῦ⟩ στόλος, 'the sending forth to us of the νοῦς that is in us'. At any rate, that must be what is meant.

¹⁰ Sc. the second God.

¹¹ κηδεύοντα MSS. : κηδευόμενα Viger : κηδεύοντος Dindorf.

¹² τοῖς ἀκροβολισμοῖς (sc. τοῦ φωτός) = ταῖς ἀκτῖσι, the radiations of his influence. Some of the Hermetists would have said ταῖς ἐνεργείαις.

¹³ A reminiscence of Pl. Politicus 272 E : τοῦ παντὸς ὁ κυβερνήτης, οἷον πηδαλίων οἴακος ἀφέμενος, εἰς τὴν αὑτοῦ περιωπὴν ἀπέστη. The phrase τὴν ἑαυτοῦ περιωπήν is here equivalent to τὸ ἑαυτὸν νοεῖν.

¹⁴ As long as the Demiurgus (i. e. the divine νοῦς operating in the sensible world) directs his attention to a man, he infuses life into that man's body, and the man continues to live embodied upon earth ; but when the Demiurgus averts his

11. ταῦτα μὲν ὁ Νουμήνιος· σὺ δέ γε παράθες αὐτοῖς τὰ ἀπὸ τῆς τοῦ Δαβὶδ προφητείας (Ps. 103 (104) 24 and 27–30). ...

13. πάλιν δ' αὖ ... ὁ Νουμήνιος ἐπάκουσον οἷα περὶ τοῦ δευτέρου αἰτίου θεολογεῖ·

14. "ὥσπερ δὲ πάλιν λόγος ἐστὶ γεωργῷ πρὸς τὸν ¹ φυτεύοντα ἀναφερόμενος, τὸν αὐτὸν λόγον μάλιστά ⌐ἐστιν⌐¹² ὁ πρῶτος θεὸς πρὸς τὸν δημιουργόν. ὁ μὲν ⌐γε ὤν⌐¹³ σπέρμα πάσης ψυχῆς σπείρει εἰς τὰ μεταλαγχάνοντα αὐτοῦ χρήματα σύμπαντα· ὁ ⌐νομοθέτης⌐¹⁴ δὲ φυτεύει καὶ διανέμει καὶ μεταφυτεύει εἰς ἡμᾶς ἑκάστους τὰ ἐκεῖθεν προκαταβεβλημένα." ⁵

15. καὶ ἑξῆς δὲ πάλιν περὶ τοῦ πῶς ἀπὸ τοῦ πρώτου αἰτίου τὸ δεύτερον ὑπέστη ⁶ τοιάδε φησίν·

"ὁπόσα δὲ δοθέντα μέτεισι πρὸς τὸν λαμβάνοντα, ἀπελθόντα ἐκ τοῦ δεδωκότος,—⟨οἷα δὴ⟩⁷ θεραπεία,⁸ χρήματα, νόμισμα κοῖλον, ἐπίσημον,⁹—

attention from the man, then the man's body dies (ταῦτα μὲν ἀποσβέννυσθαι), but the νοῦς that was in him,—the νοῦς which is his true self,—lives on, and enjoys a life of bliss (being re-united with the divine νοῦς, from which it was parted during the man's life on earth). The divine νοῦς ἑαυτὸν νοεῖ; and the disembodied soul, being made one with the divine νοῦς, shares in that beatific contemplation.

¹ τὸν Viger : τὰ MSS.
² μάλιστά ἐστιν MSS. : μάλιστα ἔχει Viger.
³ Mullach translates 'Nam primus quidem, quum omnis animae semen sit', &c.; that is, he makes σπέρμα nominative, and takes ὢν σπέρμα to mean 'being seed'. But that is impossible; a sower does not sow himself, and is not the seed which he sows. σπέρμα must be accusative, and object of σπείρει. One might conjecture ὁ μὲν γὰρ ἓν σπέρμα πάσης ψυχῆς σπείρει εἰς τὰ μεταλαγχάνοντα αὐτῆς χρήματα σύμπαντα. 'The first God sows one seed (or one sowing) of all soul (or life), to serve for all things together that partake of soul.' (εἰς is not quite satisfactory; but perhaps a word or two that would have made the meaning clearer may have been lost before εἰς.)
Cf. Basilides ap. Hippol. Ref. haer. 7. 21 (quoted in note on Corp. IX. 6) : (ὁ θεὸς) καταβαλόμενος . . . σπέρμα τι ἕν, ἔχον πᾶσαν ἐν ἑαυτῷ τὴν τοῦ κόσμου πανσπερμίαν, κ.τ.λ.
⁴ Numenius cannot have called the second God 'the lawgiver'. The sense wanted could be got by striking out νομοθέτης; but how did the word get in? Perhaps we ought to read ποιητής.
⁵ Perhaps τὸ ἐκεῖ προκαταβεβλημένον, viz. the σπέρμα spoken of above. (καταβεβλημένον is equivalent to ἐσπαρμένον.)
I suppose the γεωργός is the owner of the garden, or head-gardener, and the φυτεύων is the labourer who works under his direction. The head-gardener sows a single sowing (of some kind of vegetable) in the seed-bed, once for all; the labourer plants out the seedlings, and attends to them one by one.
This extract is obscure; but perhaps it may be taken to mean that the first God emits from himself, in the νοητὸς κόσμος, by one timeless operation, one undivided world-soul (one mass of soul-stuff, as it were); and the second God, working in the αἰσθητὸς κόσμος, implants portions of this one soul in all individual organisms, and transfers portions of it from one organism to another.
⁶ I. e. how the second God came into existence by issuing from the first God.
⁷ οἷα δὴ add. Viger.
⁸ θεραπεία, 'service', i. e. slaves.
⁹ νόμισμα ἐπίσημον is coined money; but what is νόμισμα κοῖλον? Perhaps we ought to read ⟨ἀργύριον⟩ κοῖλον, ἐπίσημον, 'silver plate and coin', and strike out νόμισμα as a gloss.

ταυτὶ μὲν οὖν ἐστι θνητὰ καὶ ἀνθρώπινα· τὰ δὲ θεῖά ἐστιν οἷα μεταδοθέντα
[ἐνθένδ' ἐκεῖθι γεγενημένα] ἐνθένδε τε οὐκ ἀπελήλυθε, κακεῖθι γενόμενα τὸν
μὲν ¹ ὤνησε, τὸν δ' ² οὐκ ἔβλαψε [[καὶ προσώνησε τῇ περὶ ὧν ἠπίστατο
ἀναμνήσει]].³ 16. ἔστι δὲ τοῦτο τὸ καλὸν χρῆμα ἐπιστήμη ἡ καλή, ἧς
ὤνατο μὲν ὁ λαβών, οὐκ ἀπολείπεται δ' αὐτῆς ὁ δεδωκώς, ⟨⟨καὶ προσώνατο ⁴
τῇ περὶ ὧν ἠπίστατο ἀναμνήσει⟩⟩. οἷον ἂν ἴδοις ἐξαφθέντα ἀφ' ἑτέρου
λύχνου λύχνον, φῶς ἔχοντα ὃ μὴ τὸν πρότερον ἀφείλατο, ἀλλὰ τῆς ἐν αὐτῷ
ὕλης πρὸς τὸ ἐκείνου πῦρ ἐξαφθείσης. 17. τοιοῦτόν τι ⁵ χρῆμά ἐστι τὸ
τῆς ἐπιστήμης, ἣ δοθεῖσα καὶ ληφθεῖσα παραμένει μὲν τῷ δεδωκότι,
σύνεστι δὲ τῷ λαβόντι ἡ αὐτή. 18. τούτου δὲ τὸ αἴτιον, ὦ ξένε,⁶ οὐδέν
ἐστιν ἀνθρώπινον, ἀλλ' ὅτι ⁷ ἕξις τε καὶ οὐσία ἡ ἔχουσα τὴν ἐπιστήμην ⁸ ἡ
αὐτή ἐστι παρά τε τῷ δεδωκότι θεῷ καὶ παρὰ τῷ εἰληφότι ἐμοὶ καὶ σοί.
19. διὸ καὶ ὁ Πλάτων ⁹ τὴν σοφίαν ὑπὸ Προμηθέως ἐλθεῖν εἰς ἀνθρώπους
μετὰ φανοτάτου τινὸς πυρὸς ἔφη." ¹⁰

20. καὶ πάλιν ὑποβὰς ἑξῆς φησιν·

"εἰσὶ δ' οὗτοι βίοι ὁ μὲν πρώτου, ὁ δὲ δευτέρου θεοῦ.¹¹ δηλονότι ὁ
μὲν πρῶτος θεός ἐστιν ¹² ἑστώς, ὁ δὲ δεύτερος ἔμπαλίν ἐστι κινούμενος.
ὁ μὲν οὖν πρῶτος περὶ τὰ νοητά, ὁ δὲ δεύτερος περὶ τά ⟨τε⟩ νοητὰ καὶ ⟨τὰ⟩

¹ *Sc.* the recipient.　　　　² *Sc.* the giver.
³ The words καὶ ... ἀναμνήσει unduly anticipate the following sentence ; the
reader has not yet been told that the thing spoken of is ἐπιστήμη. I have therefore
transposed this clause to § 16. (It may have been added by a reader, but must in
any case have been meant to stand where I have put it.)
⁴ The teacher, when he imparts knowledge to his pupil, gets a benefit by recalling
to mind what he already knows.
I have altered προσώνησε into προσώνατο, as ὤνατο occurs in the same sentence ;
but ὠν⟨ήσ⟩ατο and προσωνήσατο would do equally well.
⁵ τοιοῦτόν τι *scripsi* : τοιοῦτον τὸ MSS.
⁶ ὦ ξένε seems to show that the book from which this and the adjacent extracts
were taken was a dialogue.
⁷ I. e. τούτου τὸ αἴτιόν ἐστιν ὅτι κ.τ.λ.
⁸ The ἕξις καὶ οὐσία ἡ ἔχουσα τὴν ἐπιστήμην is νοῦς. The νοῦς in you and me is
one with the divine νοῦς.
⁹ This refers to Pl. *Phileb.* 16 C : θεῶν μὲν εἰς ἀνθρώπους δόσις . . . ποθὲν ἐκ θεῶν
ἐρρίφη διά τινος Προμηθέως ἅμα φανοτάτῳ τινὶ πυρί.
¹⁰ In this extract nothing is said about the first God and the second God ; yet
Eusebius says (§ 15 *init.*) that Numenius was here speaking περὶ τοῦ πῶς ἀπὸ τοῦ
πρώτου αἰτίου τὸ δεύτερον ὑπέστη. If Eusebius is right in this, we must suppose
that Numenius went on to say that, as a teacher loses nothing when he imparts
knowledge to a pupil, and as the gods lost nothing when 'fire' (i. e. the light of
wisdom) was conveyed from them to men by Prometheus, so the first God loses
nothing of his own being when he puts forth from him the second God.
¹¹ The distinction might be expressed by saying that the βίος of the first God is
αἰώνιος (in the Platonic sense of αἰών), and that of the second God is (partly at
least) ἐν χρόνῳ.
¹² θεός ἐστιν Viger : θεὸς ἔσται MSS. The same tense must have been used in this
and the following clause ; but it would be possible to write ἔσται in both places,
meaning ' it follows that it is so '.—δηλόνοτι . . . κινούμενος may perhaps be a
marginal note.

αἰσθητά. 21. μὴ θαυμάσῃς δ᾿ εἰ τοῦτ᾿ ἔφην· πολὺ γὰρ ἔτι θαυμαστό-
τερον ἀκούσῃ. ἀντὶ γὰρ τῆς προσούσης τῷ δευτέρῳ κινήσεως, τὴν
προσοῦσαν τῷ πρώτῳ στάσιν φημὶ εἶναι κίνησιν σύμφυτον,¹ ἀφ᾿ ἧς ἥ
τε τάξις τοῦ κόσμου καὶ ἡ μονὴ ἡ ἀίδιος ² καὶ ἡ σωτηρία ἀναχεῖται εἰς
τὰ ὅλα."

22. ἐπὶ τούτοις καὶ ἐν τῷ ἕκτῳ³ προστίθησι ταῦτα·

"ἐπειδὴ ᾔδει ὁ Πλάτων παρὰ τοῖς ἀνθρώποις τὸν μὲν δημιουργὸν
γινωσκόμενον μόνον, τὸν μέντοι πρῶτον νοῦν,⁴ ὅστις καλεῖται αὐτὸ ὄν,⁵
παντάπασιν ἀγνοούμενον παρ᾿ αὐτοῖς, διὰ τοῦτο οὕτως εἶπεν, ὥσπερ ἂν ⟨εἴ⟩
τις [οὕτω] λέγοι,⁶ 23. 'ὦ ἄνθρωποι, ὃν τοπάζετε ὑμεῖς νοῦν οὐκ ἔστι
πρῶτος, ἀλλὰ ἕτερος πρὸ τούτου νοῦς πρεσβύτερος καὶ θειότερος.'"⁷

24. καὶ μεθ᾿ ἕτερα ἐπιλέγει·

"κυβερνήτης μέν που ἐν μέσῳ πελάγει φορούμενος, ὑπὲρ πηδαλίων ὑψίζυγος, τοῖς οἴαξι διθύνει τὴν ναῦν ἐφεζόμενος· ὄμματα δ᾿
αὐτοῦ καὶ νοῦς εὐθὺ τοῦ αἰθέρος ξυντέταται πρὸς τὰ μετάρσια, καὶ ἡ
ὁδὸς αὐτῷ ἄνω δι᾿ οὐρανοῦ ⌜ἄπεισι⌝,⁸ πλέοντι κάτω κατὰ τὴν θάλατ-
ταν. οὕτω καὶ ὁ δημιουργὸς τὴν ὕλην, τοῦ μήτε διακροῦσαι⁹ μήτε
ἀποπλαγχθῆναι ¹⁰ αὐτήν, ⟨τῇ?⟩ ἁρμονίᾳ ξυνδησάμενος,¹¹ αὐτὸς μὲν ὑπὲρ

---

¹ σύμφυτον probably means 'corresponding to his (unique) nature' (and therefore differing from all other κίνησις). The first God is ἑστώς; but his στάσις must not be taken to mean inertness or inactivity. The first God works as an efficient cause, and produces effects in the Kosmos; and his στάσις is in that sense a κίνησις. The unvarying order (τάξις) and everlasting duration (μονὴ ἡ ἀίδιος and σωτηρία) of the Kosmos are effects caused by the στάσις of the first God.

² μονὴ ἡ ἀίδιος Mullach, Gifford : μονὴ ἀίδιος Dindorf.

³ I. e. this extract is taken from Book VI of Numenius Περὶ τἀγαθοῦ.

⁴ Numenius uses the term ὁ πρῶτος νοῦς as a synonym of ὁ πρῶτος θεός; and he uses the terms ὁ δεύτερος νοῦς and ὁ δημιουργός as synonyms of ὁ δεύτερος θεός. He here says that ὁ πρῶτος νοῦς, i. e. the first God, is αὐτὸ ὄν; and in other passages he identifies him with τὸ ἀγαθόν. He does not say (as Plotinus did later on, and as the author of *Corp. Herm.* II does) that the first God, called τὸ ἀγαθόν (or τὸ ἕν), is ἐπέκεινα νοῦ καὶ οὐσίας, i. e. distinct from and above νοῦς and τὸ ὄντως ὄν.

⁵ αὐτὸ ὄν Dindorf : αὐτόν Mullach.

⁶ ὥσπερ ἂν τις οὕτω λέγοι MSS. : ὥσπερ ἂν εἴ τις οὕτω λέγοι Mullach : οὕτω seclusi.

⁷ Cf. *Oracula Chaldaica* (Kroll, p. 14) : πάντα γὰρ ἐξετέλεσσε πατήρ (i. e. the first νοῦς), καὶ νῷ παρέδωκε | δευτέρῳ, ὃν πρῶτον κλῄζετε πᾶν γένος ἀνδρῶν ('whom ye, O mankind, (wrongly) call first').

To what passage of Plato is Numenius here referring ? Probably Pl. *Ep.* 2. 312 E, περὶ τὸν πάντων βασιλέα κ.τ.λ.

⁸ Some such verb as δείκνυται or φαίνεται would make sense. (φ)αινεται might possibly be corrupted into απεισι.

⁹ διακροῦσαι MSS. : διακρουσθῆναι Mullach. Perhaps διακρού⟨ασθ⟩αι, 'to evade' or 'escape from control'.

¹⁰ ἀποπλεχθῆναι MSS. : ἀποπλαγχθῆναι Dindorf : περιπλανηθῆναι Mullach.

¹¹ For the notion that the Demiurgus 'bound ὕλη together, lest it should wander away', cf. *Corp. Herm.* VIII. 3, where we are told that God fashioned the sphere of heaven out of a part of ὕλη, and enclosed the rest of ὕλη within this sphere, ἵνα μὴ ἡ ὕλη, τῆς (τοῦ παντὸς σώματος) συστάσεως θελήσασα ἀποστῆναι, διαλυθῇ εἰς τὴν

ταύτης¹ ἴδρυται, οἷον ὑπὲρ νεώς ἐπὶ θαλάττης τῆς ὕλης,² τὴν ἁρμονίαν δὲ ἰθύνει, ταῖς ἰδέαις οἰακίζων,³ βλέπει τε, ἀντὶ τοῦ οὐρανοῦ, εἰς τὸν ἄνω θεόν, προσαγόμενον αὐτοῦ τὰ ὄμματα·⁴ λαμβάνει δὲ τὸ μὲν κριτικὸν ἀπὸ τῆς θεωρίας, τὸ δ' ὁρμητικὸν ἀπὸ τῆς ἐφέσεως."⁵

Euseb. *Pr. ev.* 11. 22. 1–10:

πάλιν δὲ καὶ ὁ Νουμήνιος ἐν τοῖς Περὶ τἀγαθοῦ, τὴν τοῦ Πλάτωνος διάνοιαν ἑρμηνεύων, τοῦτον διέξεισι τὸν τρόπον.⁶

1. "τὰ μὲν οὖν σώματα λαβεῖν⁷ ἡμῖν ἔξεστι, σημαινομένοις· ἔκ τε ὁμοίων, ἀπό τε τῶν ἐν τοῖς παρακειμένοις γνωρισμάτων ἐνόντων.⁸ τἀγαθὸν δὲ οὐδενὸς ἐκ παρακειμένου, οὐδ' οὖν⁹ ἀπὸ ὁμοίου [αἰσθητοῦ] ἐστι λαβεῖν μηχανὴ [τις] οὐδεμία· ἀλλὰ δεήσει,—οἷον εἴ τις ἐπὶ σκοπῇ καθήμενος ναῦν ἁλιάδα βραχεῖάν τινα τούτων τῶν ἐπακτρίδων τῶν ⌜μόνων⌝, μίαν, μόνην,

ἑαυτῆς ἀταξίαν.   But what does Numenius mean by ἁρμονία? If the thought is similar to that in *Corp.* VIII, it would seem that ἁρμονία (or rather, perhaps, (τῇ) ἁρμονίᾳ) ξυνδησάμενος must mean 'having bound ὕλη together by means of the framework or structure of the heavens', the word ἁρμονία being used in the same sense as in *Corp. Herm.* I. In the phrase τὴν ἁρμονίαν δὲ ἰθύνει below, τὴν ἁρμονίαν appears to mean τὸν κόσμον.

¹ ταύτης probably means τῆς ὕλης.   Perhaps, ὑπὲρ ταύτης ἴδρυται, οἷον ἐπὶ νεὼς ὑπὲρ θαλάττης [τῆς ὕλης].

² The steersman is the Demiurgus, i. e. the second God; the ship which he steers is the Kosmos; the sky at which he gazes, and by which he directs the ship's course, is the first God (that is to say, τὸ ἀγαθόν); and the sea on which the ship is sailing is ὕλη.   In this last point, the simile does not seem to work out rightly; for the Kosmos is made of ὕλη, but a ship is not made of sea.   Numenius probably meant that ὕλη is like the sea in respect of its ἄτακτος κίνησις, but was unable to make this comparison consistent with the rest of the simile.

³ The Demiurgus 'steers' (i. e. guides or directs the world-process) ' by means of the archetypal forms ', which are the thoughts or purposes of the first God, and which the Demiurgus 'sees' in contemplating the first God.

⁴ The first God ' attracts the eyes ' of the Demiurgus.

⁵ τὸ κριτικόν is that in him which discerns or apprehends truth; and this he gets ἀπὸ τῆς θεωρίας, 'from his contemplation (of the first God, that is, of the Good)'. τὸ ὁρμητικόν is that in him which impels him to action; and this he gets ἀπὸ τῆς ἐφέσεως, 'from his desire (for the first God or the Good)'.   The word θεωρία may perhaps convey the meaning required without any supplement; but a genitive (τοῦ ἄνω θεοῦ, or τοῦ ἀγαθοῦ) seems to be needed with τῆς ἐφέσεως, and may very likely have been written there, and omitted by error.

⁶ This extract (taken from Book I of Numen. Περὶ τἀγαθοῦ) appears to be the beginning of a passage in which Numenius dealt with the question how knowledge of the Good is to be got.   Later on in the same work (see § 3 below) he demonstrated that the Good is identical with the first God.

⁷ λαβεῖν = καταλαβεῖν, *to apprehend* or *get a true notion of* a thing.

⁸ We can get knowledge of a corporeal thing, or learn to understand it, (1) ἐξ ὁμοίων, i. e. by noting its resemblance to things already known to us, and thence inferring that it has qualities like theirs; and (2) ἀπὸ παρακειμένων, i. e. by noting and drawing inferences from its relations to things adjacent to it.   But in neither of these ways can we get knowledge of the Good; for there is nothing that is like the Good, and nothing that is adjacent to it.   The Good is μόνον, ἔρημον; it abides in solitude, far removed from all things perceptible by sense; and only when we have withdrawn ourselves from all things perceptible by sense can we draw near to it.

⁹ οὐδ' οὖν Mullach: οὐδ' αὖ Dindorf.

ἔρημον, μετακυμίοις¹ ἐχομένην, ὀξὺ δεδορκὼς μιᾷ βολῇ κατεῖδε⟨ν⟩ [τὴν ναῦν],²—οὕτω δή τινά, ἀπελθόντα πόρρω τῶν αἰσθητῶν, ὁμιλῆσαι τῷ ἀγαθῷ μόνῳ μόνον, ἔνθα μήτε τις ἄνθρωπος μήτε τι ζῷον ἕτερον, μηδὲ σῶμα μέγα μηδὲ σμικρόν, ἀλλά τις ἄφατος καὶ ἀδιήγητος ἀτέχνως ἐρημία θεσπέσιος, ἔνθα τοῦ ἀγαθοῦ ἤθη ⟨. . .⟩ διατριβαί τε καὶ ἀγλαΐαι,³ αὐτὸ δὲ ἐν εἰρήνῃ, ἐν εὐμενείᾳ, τὸ ἤρεμον, ⌐τὸ ἡγεμονικόν,⌐⁴ ἵλεων, ἐποχούμενον ἐπὶ τῇ οὐσίᾳ. 2. εἰ δέ τις, πρὸς τοῖς αἰσθητοῖς λιπαρῶν, τὸ ἀγαθὸν ⟨τούτοις⟩⁵ ἐφιπτάμενον φαντάζεται, κἄπειτα τρυφῶν οἴοιτο τῷ ἀγαθῷ ἐντετυχηκέναι, τοῦ παντὸς ἁμαρτάνει. τῷ γὰρ ὄντι οὐ ῥᾳδίας, θείας δὲ πρὸς αὐτὸ δεῖ μεθόδου· καί ἐστι κράτιστον, τῶν αἰσθητῶν ἀμελήσαντι, νεανιευσαμένῳ πρὸς τὰ μαθήματα,⁶ τοὺς ἀριθμοὺς θεασαμένῳ, οὕτως ἐκμελετῆσαι μάθημα, τί ἐστι τὸ ⌐ὄν⌐."⁷

3. ταῦτα μὲν ἐν τῷ πρώτῳ.

ἐν δὲ τῷ πέμπτῳ⁸ ταῦτά φησιν·

"εἰ δ' ἐστὶ μὲν νοητὸν ἡ οὐσία καὶ ἡ ἰδέα, ταύτης δ' ὡμολόγηται πρεσβύτερον καὶ αἴτιον εἶναι ὁ ⟨πρῶτος⟩⁹ νοῦς, αὐτὸς οὗτος μόνος εὕρηται ὢν τὸ ἀγαθόν.¹⁰ καὶ γὰρ [εἰ]¹¹ ὁ μὲν δημιουργὸς θεός¹² ἐστι γενέσεως ἀρχή,¹³ τὸ

---

¹ μετακυμίοις Dindorf : μετακυμίαις Mullach. The boat is almost hidden in the trough of the sea, or is visible only at intervals, when it emerges from the trough.

² The simile of the fishing-boat seen far out at sea is meant to illustrate the ἐρημία of the Good (there is nothing ' adjacent to it '), and also to suggest that the Good is barely visible even to the keenest (mental) eye.

³ ' In that solitude are the haunts and pastimes and festivities of the Good ; but the Good itself dwells in peace ', &c. That can hardly be right. The mention of διατριβαί and ἀγλαΐαι of the Good seems incongruous with the context ; and with what is ' the Good itself' contrasted ? It seems probable that there is a lacuna after ἤθη, and that the words διατριβαί τε καὶ ἀγλαΐαι are part of a clause in which was described the bliss enjoyed by the man who seeks the Good and finds his way to it (ὁμιλεῖ τῷ ἀγαθῷ μόνῳ μόνος, as was said above). On this hypothesis, it is possible to account for ἐν εὐμενείᾳ (' goodwill ' or ' favour ') and ἵλεων (' gracious '), which imply a relation between the Good and man, and would be inexplicable if nothing were said about man in the context.

⁴ τὸ ἡγεμονικόν is inappropriate here ; and τὸ ἡγεμον- may be a doublet of τὸ ἤρεμον. Perhaps, [τὸ] ἤρεμον, [τὸ ἡγεμονικόν,] ἵλεως (or ἱλαρῶς?) ἐποχούμενον τῇ οὐσίᾳ. (For ἱλαρῶς, cf. Corp. Herm. I. 4, where God is pictured as φῶς ἤπιόν τε καὶ ἱλαρόν.)

⁵ τούτοις addidi. The Good is not to be found in the world of sense.

⁶ νεανιευσαμένῳ πρὸς τὰ μαθήματα secludendum ? This and τοὺς ἀριθμοὺς θεασαμένῳ appear to be alternatives ; either might stand, but hardly both together ; and the fact that μάθημα follows closely makes it preferable to cut out the first.

⁷ τὸ ὄν Dindorf : τὸ ἕν Mullach. Possibly τὸ ⟨ἀσώματ⟩ον, or τὸ ⟨νοητ⟩όν ? It was as an ἀφορμή πρὸς τὰ νοητά that the study of mathematics was valued by the Platonists.

⁸ Book V of Numen. Περὶ τἀγαθοῦ.

⁹ πρῶτος addidi. Either ὁ πρῶτος νοῦς, or the equivalent term ὁ πρῶτος θεός, is needed here.

¹⁰ On this point Plotinus differed from Numenius. According to Plotinus, τὸ ἀγαθόν is the first God, but is distinct from νοῦς, and ἐπέκεινα νοῦ.

¹¹ εἰ seclusi. ¹² I. e. the second νοῦς.

¹³ ἀρχή Mullach : ἀρκεῖ Dindorf.—γενέσεως means τῶν γιγνομένων ; οὐσίας means τῶν ὄντως ὄντων.

⟨δὲ⟩¹ ἀγαθὸν οὐσίας ἐϲτὶν² ἀρχή. ἀνάλογον δὲ τούτῳ³ μὲν ὁ δημιουργὸς θεός, ὧν αὐτοῦ μιμητής, τῇ δὲ οὐσίᾳ ἡ γένεσις, εἰκὼν αὐτῆς οϒϲΑ⁴ καὶ μίμημα. 4. εἰ ΓΑΡ⁵ ὁ δημιουργὸς ὁ τῆς γενέσεώς ἐστιν ἀγαθός, ἢ που ἔσται [καὶ] ὁ τῆς οὐσίας δημιουργὸς⁶ αὐτοάγαθον, σύμφυτο⟨ς ὢ⟩ν⁷ τῇ οὐσίᾳ. ὁ γὰρ δεύτερος διττὸς ὢν ⌈αὐτοποιεῖ τήν τε ἰδέαν ἑαυτοῦ καὶ τὸν κόσμον, δημιουργὸς ὤν· ἔπειτα θεωρητικὸς ὅλως⌉.⁸ 5. συλλελογισμένων δ' ἡμῶν ὀνόματα τεττάρων πραγμάτων, τέτταρα ἔστω ταῦτα· ὁ μὲν πρῶτος θεός, αὐτοάγαθον· ὁ δὲ τούτου μιμητὴς δημιουργός, ἀγαθός· ἡ δ' οὐσία, μία μὲν ἡ τοῦ πρώτου, ἑτέρα δὲ ἡ τοῦ δευτέρου. ⌈ἧς⌉⁹ μίμημα ὁ [καλὸς] κόσμος,¹⁰ κεκαλλωπισμένος μετουσίᾳ τοῦ καλοῦ."

6. καὶ ἐν τῷ ἕκτῳ¹¹ δὲ ἐπιλέγει·

" μετέχει δὲ αὐτοῦ¹² τὰ μετίσχοντα ἐν ἄλλῳ μὲν οὐδενί, ἐν δὲ μόνῳ τῷ

¹ δὲ *addidi*. ² ἐστὶν Mullach, Gifford : εἶναι MSS.
³ *Sc.* τῷ ἀγαθῷ (neuter), or in other words, τῷ πρώτῳ θεῷ. The meaning is that the second God is to the first God (who is τὸ ἀγαθόν) as the world of τὰ γιγνόμενα is to the world of τὰ ὄντως ὄντα.
⁴ εἰκὼν αὐτῆς ἐστι MSS. : εἰκὼν αὐτῆς οὖσα Mullach, Gifford : εἰκὼν γὰρ αὐτῆς ἐστι Dindorf.
⁵ εἰ γὰρ Mullach, Gifford : εἴπερ MSS.
⁶ I. e. the first God, who is here (by exception) called a δημιουργός, as being maker of τὰ ὄντως ὄντα. Elsewhere, the word δημιουργός is used by Numenius only to denote the second God, maker of τὰ γιγνόμενα.
⁷ σύμφυτος ὢν *scripsi* : σύμφυτον MSS. The first God is ' of one nature with' τὰ ὄντως ὄντα which are made by him.
⁸ *Sic* Dindorf : ὁ γὰρ δεύτερος, διττὸς ὢν αὐτός, ποιεῖ τήν τε κ.τ.λ. Mullach. Perhaps : ὁ γὰρ δεύτερος, διττὸς ὢν αὐτός, ποιεῖ τήν τε οϒϲίαν ἑαυτοῦ καὶ ⟨τὴν γένεσιν⟩, τοϒ κόσμοϒ δημιουργὸς ὤν· ἐπεὶ[τα] θεωρητικὸς ὅλως (ὁ πρῶτος). For διττὸς ὤν, cf. Numen. above (Eus. 11. 18. 3 *sq.* and 10), where we are told that the second God both 'looks toward himself' and 'looks toward ὕλη '. The second God is both θεωρητικός and πρακτικός; the first God is θεωρητικὸς ὅλως.
I can see no sense in ποιεῖ τὴν ἰδέαν ἑαυτοῦ; what could ' the ἰδέα of the second God' mean? In § 9 below, τὸ ἀγαθόν is called τοῦ δημιουργοῦ ἰδέα, i. e. the archetype of which the Demiurgus is a copy ; but it would be absurd to say that the Demiurgus makes that. I conjecture τὴν οὐσίαν ἑαυτοῦ, the (corporeal) substance which the second God employs in making the material world,—that is to say, the cosmic elements collectively (οὐσία in the Stoic sense). This would agree with what is said below, οὐσία μία μὲν ἡ τοῦ πρώτου (θεοῦ), ἑτέρα δὲ ἡ τοῦ δευτέρου. The elements, being permanent relatively to τὰ γιγνόμενα καὶ ἀπολλύμενα which are made of them, may be called ὄντα (οὐσία in one sense) ; but the archetypal ἰδέαι are ὄντως ὄντα (οὐσία in another and a higher sense).
The Demiurgus first makes the elements (τὴν οὐσίαν ἑαυτοῦ), and then makes the Kosmos and the organisms in it (τὴν γένεσιν) out of the elements. And that is just what Plato's Demiurgus does in the *Timaeus*.
⁹ We ought to read here ⟨τ⟩ῆς ⟨δὲ τοῦ πρώτου οὐσίας⟩ μίμημα ὁ κόσμος, or something to that effect. The Kosmos is a μίμημα of τὰ ὄντως ὄντα (= the archetypal ἰδέαι).
¹⁰ Perhaps : ὁ ⟨κόσμος.⟩ καλὸς ⟨δὲ ὁ⟩ κόσμος, κ.τ.λ.
¹¹ Book VI of Numen. Περὶ τἀγαθοῦ.
¹² αὐτοῦ probably stands for τοῦ πρώτου θεοῦ. It might be taken to stand for τοῦ ἀγαθοῦ ; but as Numenius writes καὶ τῆς ⟨τοῦ⟩ ἀγαθοῦ συμβάσεως in the following sentence, he was probably speaking of the first God here.

φρονεῖν.¹ ταύτῃ² ἄρα καὶ τῆς ⟨τοῦ⟩ ἀγαθοῦ συμβάσεως ὀνίναιτ᾽ ἄν, ἄλλως δ᾽ οὔ. καὶ μὲν δὴ ⌜τὸ φρονεῖν τοῦτο δεῖν⌝³ συντετύχηκε μόνῳ τῷ πρώτῳ. ὑφ᾽ οὗ οὖν τὰ ἄλλα ἀποχραίνεται⁴ καὶ ἀγαθοῦται, ἐὰν τοῦτο ἐκείνῳ μόνον μόνῳ προσῇ, ἀβελτέρας ἂν εἴη ψυχῆς ἔτι ἀμφιλογεῖν.⁵ 7. εἰ γὰρ ἀγαθός ἐστιν ὁ δεύτερος οὐ παρ᾽ ἑαυτοῦ, παρὰ δὲ τοῦ πρώτου, πῶς οἷόν τε, ὑφ᾽ οὗ μετουσίας ἐστὶν οὗτος ἀγαθός, μὴ ⟨τὸ⟩⁶ ἀγαθὸν ⟨εἶναι⟩,⁷ ἄλλως τε κἂν τύχῃ αὐτοῦ ὡς ⟨τοῦ⟩ ἀγαθοῦ⁸ μεταλαχὼν ὁ δεύτερος; 8. οὕτω τοι ὁ Πλάτων ἐκ συλλογισμοῦ τῷ ὀξὺ βλέποντι ἀπέδωκε τὸ ἀγαθὸν ὅτι ἐστὶν ἕν ⟨...⟩."⁹

9. καὶ πάλιν ἐξῆς φησι·

"ταῦτα δὲ οὕτως ἔχοντα ⌜ἔθη μὲν⌝¹⁰ ὁ Πλάτων ἄλλῃ καὶ ἄλλῃ χωρίσας. ἰδίᾳ μὲν γὰρ τὸν κυκλικὸν ⟨λόγον⟩¹¹ ἐπὶ τοῦ δημιουργοῦ ἐγράψατο ἐν Τιμαίῳ, εἰπὼν 'ἀγαθὸς ἦν'.¹² ἐν δὲ τῇ Πολιτείᾳ¹³ τὸ ἀγαθὸν εἶπεν 'ἀγαθοῦ ἰδέαν', ὡς δὴ τοῦ δημιουργοῦ ἰδέαν οὖσαν τὸ ἀγαθόν, ὅστις¹⁴ πέφανται ἡμῖν ἀγαθὸς μετουσίᾳ τοῦ πρώτου [τε καὶ μόνου].¹⁵ 10. ὥσπερ

---

¹ φρονεῖν is equivalent to νοεῖν. Things (including men) partake of the first God if and so far as they partake of νοῦς, or have some νοῦς in them.

² Sc. τῷ φρονεῖν. By that alone can things 'associate' or 'be in agreement' (συμβαίνειν) with the Good.

³ δεῖν (al. δὲ) MSS.: δεόντως Mullach: δὴ Dindorf: γε Gifford. But the corruption probably extends beyond this one word. It could hardly be said that τὸ φρονεῖν συντετύχηκε ('occurs together'?) with the first God alone. I have thought of proposing καὶ μὲν δὴ τῷ φρονεῖν τούτῳ (ἰ)δεῖν συντετύχηκε(ν ἡμῖν) μόνῳ τὸν πρῶτον. 'It is by this φρονεῖν (i. e. by using our νοῦς), and by this alone, that it has befallen us to see the first God' (i. e. that we have had the happiness to see him).

⁴ ἀποχραίνεται, if sound, must be taken to mean 'receive colour by transference from something'. Perhaps ὑποχραίνεται, which might mean 'are tinged with colour', would be better.

⁵ 'If then that from which the other things take their colour, and by which the other things are rendered good,—if that, and that alone, appertains to the first God, and to him alone, it would be foolish to doubt about this any longer.' That is to say, 'If that is so, the proposition which I have been discussing is indisputably true.' That which is here said to be certainly true must be the statement that the first God is identical with the Good; and a statement to that effect must have been made by Numenius in the passage which preceded this extract.

⁶ τὸ addidi.   ⁷ εἶναι add. Viger.

⁸ Ought we to read here ὡς ⟨τοῦ⟩ ἀγαθοῦ, or ὡς ἀγαθός? With either reading, this last clause (ἄλλως τε κἂν κ.τ.λ.) seems to add nothing fresh to what has already been said.

⁹ Perhaps, ὅτι ἐστὶν ἐν ⟨τῷ πρώτῳ θεῷ⟩ or something equivalent: 'that the Good is one with the first God'.

¹⁰ ἔθη μὲν MSS.: ἔθηκεν Dindorf: ἤδη ἐστὶ μὲν Mullach. Perhaps, ᾔδει μὲν ὁ Πλ., ἄλλῃ ⟨δὲ⟩ καὶ ἄλλῃ ⟨ἐ⟩χώρισεν.

¹¹ 'Vel addenda vox λόγον, vel certe supplenda' Viger. κυκλικός means in circulation, in common use, current or popular.

¹² Pl. Tim. 29 E.   ¹³ Pl. Rep. 6. 507 sqq.

¹⁴ ὅστις Mullach, Gifford: ὅτι Dindorf.

¹⁵ Sc. θεοῦ or νοῦ. It is possible to call the first God μόνος, meaning that he dwells ἐν μονότητι or ἐρημίᾳ; but it is confusing to do so in a sentence in which a second God is spoken of together with him; and for that reason it seems best to bracket τε καὶ μόνου.

γὰρ ἄνθρωποι μὲν λέγονται τυπωθέντες ὑπὸ τῆς ἀνθρώπου ἰδέας, βόες δ᾿ ὑπὸ τῆς βοός, ἵπποι δ᾿ ὑπὸ τῆς ἵππου ἰδέας, οὕτω καὶ εἰκότως ὁ δημιουργὸς ⟨ἀγαθὸς λέγεται, τυπωθεὶς ὑπὸ τῆς τοῦ ἀγαθοῦ ἰδέας⟩.[1] εἰ δέ[2] ἐστι μετουσίᾳ τοῦ πρώτου [[ἀγαθοῦ]][3] ἀγαθὸς ⟨ὁ δημιουργός⟩,[4] ἰδέα ⟨⟨ἀγαθοῦ⟩⟩ ἂν εἴη ὁ πρῶτος νοῦς, ὢν αὐτοάγαθον."

Proclus *In Tim.* 93 A (commenting on Pl. *Tim.* 28 c, τὸν μὲν οὖν ποιητὴν καὶ πατέρα τοῦδε τοῦ παντός κ.τ.λ.) :

Νουμήνιος μὲν γάρ, τρεῖς ἀνυμνήσας θεούς, πατέρα μὲν καλεῖ τὸν πρῶτον, ποιητὴν δὲ τὸν δεύτερον, ποίημα δὲ τὸν τρίτον. ὁ γὰρ κόσμος κατ᾿ αὐτὸν ὁ τρίτος ἐστὶ θεός·[5] ὥστε ὁ κατ᾿ αὐτὸν δημιουργὸς διττός, ὅ τε πρῶτος θεὸς καὶ ὁ δεύτερος,[6] τὸ δὲ δημιουργούμενον ὁ τρίτος. ἄμεινον γὰρ τοῦτο λέγειν, ἢ ὡς ἐκεῖνός φησιν τραγῳδῶν, πάππον, ἔγγονον, ἀπόγονον.[7]

Proclus *In Tim.* 268 A (commenting on Pl. *Tim.* 39 E, ᾗπερ οὖν νοῦς ἐνούσας ἰδέας τῷ ὃ ἔστι ζῷον, οἷαί τε ἔνεισι καὶ ὅσαι, καθορᾷ, τοιαύτας καὶ τοσαύτας διενοήθη δεῖν καὶ τόδε σχεῖν) :

Νουμήνιος δὲ τὸν μὲν πρῶτον (*sc.* νοῦν⟩ κατὰ τὸ ὃ ἔστι ζῷον τάττει,[8] καί φησιν ἐν προσχρήσει τοῦ δευτέρου νοεῖν· τὸν δὲ δεύτερον κατὰ τὸν νοῦν, καὶ τοῦτον αὖ ἐν προσχρήσει τοῦ τρίτου δημιουργεῖν· τὸν δὲ τρίτον

---

[1] I have added ἀγαθὸς . . . ἰδέας, which must, if not expressed, be understood, to make sense of the argument.

[2] εἰ δέ *scripsi* : εἴπερ MSS.

[3] ἀγαθοῦ *hinc transposui.* We must understand θεοῦ or νοῦ with τοῦ πρώτου, as before.

[4] ὁ δημιουργός *addidi.*

[5] When Numenius spoke of a 'third God' in addition to the first and second, he meant thereby the Kosmos, regarded as a living being, body and soul together,—the ζῷον that is called θεὸς αἰσθητός in Pl. *Tim. fin.*

[6] I. e. Numenius divided the one Demiurgus of Pl. *Tim.* into two distinct Gods, whom he called 'the first God' and 'the second God'. That agrees with Euseb. 11. 22. 4, where Numenius calls the second God ὁ τῆς γενέσεως δημιουργός, and the first God ὁ τῆς οὐσίας δημιουργός; but in the rest of the extracts in Euseb., Numenius uses the word δημιουργός only to denote the second God (= second νοῦς), and adds a first God (= first νοῦς, = τὸ ἀγαθόν,) distinct from and above the δημιουργός.

[7] ἔγγονος, *grandson* ; ἀπόγονος, *descendant.* This must mean that Numenius called the first God 'grandfather' of the Kosmos, and that he called the Kosmos 'grandson' and 'descendant' of the first God. It is implied that he called the second God son of the first God, and the Kosmos son of the second God (as in Pl. *Tim.* the Kosmos is called son of the Demiurgus).

[8] This obscure passage may perhaps be interpreted as follows : 'Numenius takes the first νοῦς (of his own system, who is τὸ ἀγαθόν,) to correspond to (i. e. to be signified by) Plato's τὸ ὃ ἔστι ζῷον (the ideal archetype of the αἰσθητὸς κόσμος) ; and he takes the second νοῦς (of his own system, who is the Demiurgus,) to correspond to Plato's νοῦς.' The first νοῦς νοεῖ (and does nothing else ; ἑαυτὸν and τὰς ἐν ἑαυτῷ ἰδέας νοεῖ) ; the second νοῦς contemplates (καθορᾷ) the first νοῦς and the ἰδέαι which ' are in ' the first νοῦς (that is to say, the thoughts which the first νοῦς thinks), and δημιουργεῖ after the pattern of those ἰδέαι. That, it would seem, is what Numenius took Plato's sentence to mean. But I do not know what can be meant by ἐν προσχρήσει τοῦ δευτέρου ('making use of the second νοῦς in addition' ?) and ἐν προσχρήσει τοῦ τρίτου.

κατὰ τὸν (al. τὸ) διανοούμενον.¹—ταῦτα² δὲ (says Proclus) ὅτι μὲν ἔχει τινὰς καθ᾿ ἑαυτὰ διαφοράς, πρόδηλον· οὐχ οὕτω δὲ διῄρηται νῦν ὑπὸ τοῦ Πλάτωνος ὥστε ἕτερον μὲν εἶναι τὸν νοοῦντα νοῦν, ἕτερον δὲ τὸν διανοούμενον.³

Corp. II, §§ 1–6 a. Πᾶν τὸ κινούμενον ... ὡς ἐνέργεια χωρητική. In 1–4 a, the writer shows that ὁ τόπος (i. e. τὸ ἐν ᾧ κινεῖται ὁ κόσμος) is (1) μέγας, and (2) ἀσώματος. From the proposition that ὁ τόπος is ἀσώματος, he proceeds in the following paragraph (4 b–6 a) to draw the inference that ὁ τόπος is θεῖόν τι. Then follows a digression ; but in § 12 a he resumes the argument at the point at which he left it in § 6 a, and announces that ὁ τόπος is νοῦς. That is the proposition for which §§ 1–6 a are intended to prepare the way.

In § 1, certain general statements are made concerning κίνησις ; in §§ 2–4 a, these statements are applied to the case of the Kosmos.

§ 1. ['Ἰσχυρότερον ἄρα τὸ κινοῦν τοῦ κινουμένου.—'Ἰσχυρότερον γάρ.—] This mention of τὸ κινοῦν is evidently out of place. The preceding and following sentences are concerned, not with τὸ κινοῦν, but with τὸ ἐν ᾧ κινεῖται ; and the latter alone is under consideration down to the end of § 6 a. Moreover, ἄρα is meaningless, as the proposition cannot be inferred from anything that has preceded it.

The statement may perhaps have been transposed to this place from some other part of the dialogue. It would be more appropriate in connexion with §§ 8 b, 9, where τὸ κινοῦν is discussed. It cannot be fitted into the extant text at that point ; but it may possibly be a remnant of a lost passage which preceded § 8 b.

§ 2. πεπλήρωται γάρ. The Kosmos is wholly filled with bodies ; it contains no void. Cf. *Ascl. Lat.* III. 33 a : 'omnia enim mundi sunt membra plenissima ... corporibus.'

Σῶμα δὲ ὁ κόσμος ;—Σῶμα.—Καὶ κινούμενον ;—Μάλιστα. These words

---

¹ If my interpretation of τάττει κατά is right, this clause must mean 'Numenius takes the third (God of his system, who is the αἰσθητὸς κόσμος) to correspond to τὸ διανοούμενον (implied in Plato's word διενοήθη)', i. e. the thing which is thought out in detail, planned, or designed by the Demiurgus.

διανοούμενον must here be passive in meaning ; though, in ἕτερον δὲ τὸν διανοούμενον below, the word is in the middle voice, and active in meaning. The ambiguity might be avoided by writing here κατὰ τὸ δημιουργούμενον in place of κατὰ τὸ διανοούμενον.

² ταῦτα means, I suppose, τὸ νοεῖν and τὸ δημιουργεῖν. There is a difference between these two functions of the divine νοῦς ; but that, says Proclus, is not a sufficient reason for saying that there are two distinct νόες.

³ Numenius said that there are two νόες, one of whom νοεῖ, and the other διανοεῖται (*med.*) and δημιουργεῖ ; and he thought that this was what Plato meant. But Proclus says that Numenius was mistaken in thus interpreting what Plato wrote.

are awkwardly placed; the argument would run more smoothly if they were cut out. Perhaps they ought to stand at the beginning of § 2. The original text may have been something like this : ⟨⟨Σῶμα δὲ οὗτος ὁ κόσμος;—Σῶμα.—Καὶ κινούμενον;—Μάλιστα.—⟩⟩ Μέγας δὲ ὁ κόσμος . . .;—Οὕτως ἔχει.—[[ ]] Πηλίκον οὖν δεῖ τὸν τόπον εἶναι κ.τ.λ.

§ 3. Πηλίκον . . . καὶ ποταπὸν τὴν φύσιν ; The second of these two questions anticipates Ποταπῆς δὲ φύσεως below. The answer to the first question is Παμμέγεθές τι χρῆμα. The answer to the second is Ἀσώματον.

τῆς φορᾶς τὴν συνέχειαν. The movement of which the writer is chiefly thinking is the circular movement of the outermost sphere of heaven. This sphere must have room to move freely; if it were closely enveloped and pressed upon by some (corporeal) thing outside it, its movement would be checked.

§ 4 a. Ἀσώματος οὖν ὁ τόπος. This proposition is ostensibly inferred from the axiom laid down in § 1, ἐναντίαν ἔχειν φύσιν ἀνάγκη τὸ ἐν ᾧ κινεῖται τῇ τοῦ κινουμένου. But that axiom, in the sense in which it is used to draw this inference, is manifestly untrue ; for we are perpetually seeing instances of a body moving in another body, i. e. in a thing which is not ' of opposite nature ' in respect of corporeality. As a logical demonstration then, the argument is invalid. But the Hermetist assumes that all existing bodies are included in the spherical body which he calls the Kosmos (πεπλήρωται ὁ κόσμος πάντων ὅσα ἔστι σωμάτων) ; and on that assumption, whatever is outside the Kosmos must be incorporeal, though not for the reason he gives.

§ 4 b. τὸ δὲ ἀσώματον ἢ θεῖόν ἐστιν ἢ ὁ θεός. The conception of τὸ ἀσώματον was first clearly defined by Plato,[1] who asserted the existence of an incorporeal world of νοητά, distinct and separate from the corporeal world of αἰσθητά. To a Platonist, τὸ ἀσώματον means primarily, if not solely, τὸ νοητόν ; and τὸ νοητόν is ἢ θεῖον ἢ ὁ θεός. See Herm. ap. Stob. Exc. VIII. We are there told that there are in man three kinds of ἀσώματα ; the first of the three kinds is ἐξ αὐτῆς τῆς πρώτης καὶ νοητῆς οὐσίας, and appears to be identical with νοῦς.

The real existence of things incorporeal, which the Platonists asserted, was denied by the Stoics. Hence Platonists and Stoics, while agreeing that all bodies are included in the Kosmos, differed

---

[1] The word ἀσώματος occurs only five times in Plato's Dialogues (Phaedo 85 E, Soph. 246 B, 247 C, Polit. 286 A, Phileb. 64 B). But the conception which the later Platonists used this word to express is present throughout a large part of his writings, though he more commonly expresses it by means of other terms (ἀόρατος, ἀειδής, νοητός, &c.).

in their answers to the question 'what is there outside the Kosmos?'
The Stoics said that outside the Kosmos there is 'infinite void'
(κενὸν ἄπειρον). Now according to the genuine Platonic doctrine,
terms of spatial extension are inapplicable to the incorporeal, and the
νοητά cannot be located in space, either inside the Kosmos or outside
it; and men who held this doctrine might have been expected to say,
like the Stoics, that there is nothing outside the Kosmos except empty
space. But many Platonists found it difficult to maintain their conception of the incorporeal consistently. They were inclined to take
the symbolical language of Plato's myths in a literal sense; and they
could not refrain from imagining that the incorporeal νοητά (or in
other words, ὁ θεός and τὰ θεῖα) are situated in the boundless space
outside the Kosmos. Cf. Ascl. Lat. III. 33 a as emended: 'nec
istud enim quod dicitur extra mundum, si tamen est aliquid, inane
esse credo, sic adeo plenum (οὔτω γε πλῆρες ὄν) intellegibilium rerum,
id est divinitati suae similium.'

But the writer of Corp. II is not content with saying that τὰ θεῖα are
situated ἐν τῷ ἐκτὸς τοῦ κόσμου τόπῳ, or that they fill the extracosmic
space with their presence; he asserts that this τόπος is θεῖόν τι; and
we learn from § 12 a that the θεῖον of which he is thinking, and with
which he identifies the extracosmic τόπος, is the divine νοῦς. His
meaning is, that τὸ ἐν ᾧ κινεῖται ὁ κόσμος is Nous; or in other words,
that the space outside the Kosmos (that space which the Stoics held
to be void) is filled with Nous. But he expresses this view in an
unusual way. He uses the word τόπος in an altered sense, and
employs it to denote, not the extracosmic space itself, but that
incorporeal substance with which he holds the extracosmic space to
be filled, namely, the divine Nous. (Cf. Corp. V. 10 b as emended:
σὺ γὰρ ὁ τόπος τῶν ὄντων· οὐ τόπος ἐστὶν ἄλλος οὐδεὶς παρὰ σέ, πάντα δὲ
ἐν σοί.) Thus used, τόπος bears a meaning not far removed from that
of αἰών in Corp. XI. i. 2: ὁ οὖν αἰὼν ἐν τῷ θεῷ, ὁ δὲ κόσμος ἐν τῷ αἰῶνι.
. . . καὶ ὁ μὲν αἰὼν ἕστηκε περὶ τὸν θεόν, ὁ δὲ κόσμος κινεῖται ἐν τῷ αἰῶνι.
Cf. Ascl. Lat. III. 30 init.: 'in ipsa vitali aeternitate locus est
mundi'; that is to say, aeternitas (αἰών) is τὸ περιέχον, within which
the Kosmos is located.[1]

This peculiar use of the word τόπος must have been suggested to
the Hermetist by its employment as a name of God, or of a god, by

---

[1] Iamblichus (Simplic. Categ. 92 a; see Zeller III. ii, p. 764) said that the word
τόπος is applicable to things incorporeal as well as to things corporeal, and that
the supreme Deity may be called the τόπος in which all things are contained.

some of his contemporaries. There are traces of such a use of the word 'Place' among the Persians. Eudemus *ap.* Damasc. *De princip.* (quoted in note on *Corp.* I. 4) : Μάγοι δὲ καὶ πᾶν τὸ Ἄρειον γένος . . . οἱ μὲν Τόπον οἱ δὲ Χρόνον καλοῦσι τὸ νοητὸν ἅπαν καὶ τὸ ἡνωμένον, κ.τ.λ. It appears from this that, about 300 B. C., some of the Zoroastrians called the primal Being, from whom both the Good God and the Bad God emanated, by a name which Greeks translated by Τόπος. This primal Being is Zerwan, the Persian god of time, who was worshipped by the Mithraists of the Roman empire under the names Αἰών and Κρόνος ; [1] and it is possible that, among his other appellations, that of Τόπος may have been still used by some of his worshippers in Egypt under Roman rule.

But it is of more importance that God was frequently called 'Place' by *Jews* of that period. R. Eisler, *Weltenmantel und Himmelzelt*, p. 471, n. 3, and 744, gives numerous references to passages in the Talmud, in which the word *māqōm* (place) is thus used ; e. g. 'The Holy One is the place of the world (i. e. ὁ τόπος ἐν ᾧ περιέχεται ὁ κόσμος); the world is not the place of the Holy One.' [2] 'The ancient teachers applied the name *māqōm* to God, because he produces all, determines all, and bounds all. . . . God pervades the world ; he is the space which supports it, the extension which upholds it.' [3] And Philo uses the word τόπος in the same way. E. g. *De somn.* I. 11. 62, Wendland III, p. 218 : τριχῶς δὲ ἐπινοεῖται τόπος, ἅπαξ μὲν χώρα ὑπὸ σώματος πεπληρωμένη, κατὰ δεύτερον δὲ τρόπον ὁ θεῖος λόγος, ὃν ἐκπεπλήρωκεν ὅλον δι' ὅλων ἀσωμάτοις δυνάμεσιν ὁ θεός. . . . κατὰ δὲ τρίτον σημαινόμενον αὐτὸς ὁ θεὸς καλεῖται τόπος, τῷ περιέχειν μὲν τὰ ὅλα, περιέχεσθαι δὲ πρὸς μηδενὸς ἁπλῶς, καὶ τῷ καταφυγὴν τῶν συμπάντων αὐτὸν εἶναι, καὶ ἐπειδήπερ αὐτός ἐστι χώρα ἑαυτοῦ, κεχωρηκὼς ἑαυτὸν καὶ ἐμφερόμενος μόνῳ ἑαυτῷ. ἐγὼ μὲν οὖν οὔκ εἰμι τόπος, ἀλλ' ἐν τόπῳ, καὶ ἕκαστον τῶν ὄντων ὁμοίως· τὸ γὰρ περιεχόμενον διαφέρει τοῦ περιέχοντος· τὸ δὲ θεῖον, ὑπ' οὐδενὸς περιεχόμενον, ἀναγκαίως ἐστὶν αὐτὸ τόπος ἑαυτοῦ.

---

[1] Cumont, *Mystères de Mithra*, 1902, p. 90 : 'Au sommet de la hiérarchie divine et à l'origine des choses, la théologie mithriaque, héritière de celle des mages zervanistes, plaçait le Temps infini. On l'appelait parfois Αἰών ou *Saeculum*, Κρόνος ou *Saturnus*, mais ces désignations étaient conventionnelles et contingentes, car il était regardé comme ineffable, comme sans nom aussi bien que sans sexe et sans passions.'

[2] Abelson, *The immanence of God in Rabb. lit.*, p. 109, says that statements to this effect are ' to be found *passim* in Rabbinic literature '; he quotes *Genesis Rabba* 68. 9 as an instance.

[3] Bousset, *Rel. des Judentums*, p. 363, says that the use of the word 'place' as a name of God is frequent in the *Mishna*, but that there is scarcely a trace of it in Jewish literature before the first century A. D.

Cf. Philo *De Cherubim* 14. 49, Cohn I, p. 182 : God is ἀσωμάτων
ἰδεῶν ἀσώματος χώρα. *De fuga et invent.* 14. 75, Wendland III,
p. 125 : τόπον γὰρ καλεῖ νῦν (*Exod.* 21. 13) οὐ χώραν ἐκπεπληρωμένην
ὑπὸ σώματος, ἀλλὰ δι' ὑπονοιῶν αὐτὸν τὸν θεόν, ἐπειδὴ περιέχων οὐ περιέχεται, καὶ ὅτι καταφυγὴ τῶν ὅλων ἐστί. A similar use of τόπος occurs
in the writings of some of the Christian Gnostics, who doubtless
adopted it from the Jews. Hippolytus *Ref. haeres.* 6. 32 says of the
Demiurgus of the Valentinians, (i. e. the inferior deity who was the
maker of the material Kosmos, and was identified with the God of
the Jews,) καλεῖται δὲ καὶ τόπος[1] ὑπ' αὐτῶν, καὶ ἑβδομάς, καὶ παλαιὸς τῶν
ἡμερῶν. Cf. the Valentinian Theodotus in Clem. Alex. *Exc.* § 34 :
κατελείφθησαν δὲ αἱ ἀριστεραὶ (δυνάμεις) ὑπὸ τοῦ τόπου (i. e. τοῦ
δημιουργοῦ) μορφωθῆναι. τῆς μητρὸς οὖν (sc. τῆς Σοφίας) . . . εἰσελ-
θούσης εἰς τὸ πλήρωμα, τότε ὁ τόπος (i. e. ὁ δημιουργὸς) τὴν ἐξουσίαν τῆς
μητρὸς καὶ τὴν τάξιν ἀπολήψεται ἣν νῦν ἔχει ἡ μήτηρ. *Ib.* § 38 : ποταμὸς
ἐκπορεύεται πυρὸς ὑποκάτω τοῦ θρόνου τοῦ τόπου, καὶ ῥεῖ εἰς τὸ κενὸν τοῦ
ἐκτισμένου· . . . καὶ αὐτὸς δὲ ὁ τόπος πυρινός ἐστι. (Hippol. 6. 32 says
that the Valentinian Demiurgus is πυρώδης.) . . . καὶ ὁ Ἰησοῦς παρα-
κληθεὶς συνεκαθέσθη τῷ τόπῳ, . . . ἵνα τὸν τόπον ἡμερώσῃ. The word
τόπος is similarly used in one of the Gnostic documents published by
C. Schmidt (*Koptisch-gnostische Schriften* I, p. 344) : 'They praise
him, saying ". . . thou art Father in the Fathers, and thou art God
in the Gods, and thou art Lord in the Lords, and thou art Place
(τόπος) in the Places (τόποι)."' *Ib.* p. 335 : 'This is the first Father
of the All. . . . This is the αὐτοφυὴς and αὐτογέννητος τόπος.' *Ib.* :
'(Out of him?) has arisen the second τόπος, who will be named
δημιουργὸς and Father and λόγος and πηγὴ and νοῦς.' Compare also
the words addressed to God by Arnobius, *Adv. nat.* 1. 31 : 'Prima
enim tu causa es, locus rerum ac spatium, fundamentum cunctorum
quaecumque sunt.'

The writer of *Corp.* II identifies the τόπος ἐν ᾧ περιέχεται ὁ κόσμος,
not with the supreme God himself, but with the divine Nous, which,
as he tells us in § 12 b sq., issues from and is subordinate to the
supreme God. Thus the meaning which he assigns to the word τόπος
resembles the second of the three meanings assigned to it by Philo,
viz. that of ὁ θεῖος λόγος. There can be little doubt that the Hermetist, in thus using the word, was directly or indirectly influenced
by some Jewish authority.

---

[1] This is the reading of the MS. Duncker and Schneidewin insert μεσότητος
after τόπος ; but there is no good reason for doing so.

τὸ δὲ θεῖον λέγω νῦν οὐ τὸ γεννητόν, ἀλλὰ τὸ ἀγέννητον. The author may have written γενητόν, ἀγένητον ; the forms γενητός and γεννητός seem to be used without distinction of meaning in the *Hermetica* and other writings of the time.

The adjective θεῖος might be applied, not only to τὰ ἀγέννητα (that is, τὰ ὄντως ὄντα, things eternal and unchanging), but also to γεννητά (that is, things belonging to the world of time and change) ; e. g. the heavenly bodies might be described as θεῖα σώματα, and the Kosmos itself might be called θεῖος. The writer therefore warns us that the term θεῖον is here used in its stricter and higher sense, and must be understood as connoting ἀγεννησία. That with which the space outside the Kosmos is filled is perhaps not ὁ θεός, but only θεῖόν τι; but if so, it must at any rate be ἀγέννητον.

ἐὰν μὲν οὖν ᾖ θεῖον, οὐσιωδές ἐστιν· ἐὰν δὲ ᾖ ⟨ὁ⟩ θεός, καὶ ἀνουσίαστον γίνεται ⟨καὶ ἀνόητον ?⟩. γίνεται does not here mean ' it becomes (something which it was not before)'; for God cannot change. The meaning is 'we must infer (from its identity with God) that it is ἀνουσίαστον'. That which is θεῖον (in the stricter sense explained above) is οὐσιῶδες ; i. e. it is of the nature of τὸ ὄντως ὄν, as opposed to τὰ γιγνόμενα. But ὁ θεός is ἀνουσίαστος ; that is to say, he is not οὐσιώδης, but is exalted above οὐσία. This statement is derived from the passage about the ἰδέα τοῦ ἀγαθοῦ in Pl. *Rep.* 6. 508 E ff., and especially from the words οὐκ οὐσίας ὄντος τοῦ ἀγαθοῦ, ἀλλ᾽ ἔτι ἐπέκεινα τῆς οὐσίας πρεσβείᾳ καὶ δυνάμει ὑπερέχοντος. The writer of *Corp.* II identifies τὸ ἀγαθόν with God (see §§ 14–16); and he here applies to God what Plato said about τὸ ἀγαθόν. The thought that the supreme God is above οὐσία, or prior to οὐσία, was familiar to the later Platonists ; and the adjectives ὑπερούσιος and προούσιος were employed by them to express it. But I have not met with the word ἀνουσίαστος in this sense elsewhere.[1] Does it mean ' not *to be deemed* οὐσία'? Or ought we to read ἀνούσιον?

Plato *l. c.* couples οὐσία with γνῶσις (or ἐπιστήμη), the mental process by which οὐσία is known, and exalts τὸ ἀγαθόν above both

---

[1] The word ἀνουσίαστος occurs in the heading of a magic charm, *Pap. mag. Par.* i. 2441 (Wünsch, *Aus einem gr. Zauberpapyrus*, Leitzmann *Kleine Texte* 84, p. 4) : Ἀγωγή, . . . ἄγουσα ἀσχέτους, καὶ ἀνουσιάστους, μονοημέρους. That is to say, ' This charm will draw people to you so that nothing can hold them back ; it will draw them to you within a single day, even though they are not worked on by means of an οὐσία '. The word οὐσία, as there used, is a technical term of Graeco-Egyptian magic ; it means a *material thing* employed by a sorcerer in the working of his spell, and especially a thing taken from the body of the person who is to be worked on,—for instance, a lock of hair, or a scrap of worn clothing.

alike, saying that it is distinct from both, and is the cause or source of both.[1] If then the Hermetist had that passage or some paraphrase of it in his mind, he would be likely to couple with ἀνουσίαστον some adjective signifying a corresponding negation of knowledge or thought. And as the following sentences apparently deal with the question whether, or in what sense, God is νοητός, there is a strong probability that the original reading was καὶ ἀνουσίαστον γίνεται ⟨καὶ ἀνόητον⟩. (Compare § 13 : ὁ οὖν θεὸς οὐ νοῦς ἐστιν, αἴτιος δὲ τοῦ ⟨νοῦν⟩ εἶναι.) By inserting καὶ ἀνόητον, we make a connexion with what follows, and at the same time give a meaning to the otherwise otiose καί which stands before ἀνουσίαστον. God is καὶ ἀνουσίαστος (or ἀνούσιος) καὶ ἀνόητος· that is to say, he is above οὐσία, and he is also above νόησις.[2] But the statement that God is ἀνόητος is ambiguous. It might mean either that God οὐ νοεῖ, or that God οὐ νοεῖται; it might be taken to imply either that he is something other and higher than νοῦς, or that he cannot be apprehended by human thought. Some explanation of its meaning is therefore needed; and the following sentences were probably intended to explain it.

§§ 5–6 a. ἄλλως δὲ . . . ἐνέργεια χωρητική. This passage is almost hopelessly corrupt; but the author's meaning may perhaps be guessed. I assume that he here said that ὁ θεός is νοητός in one sense, and ὁ τόπος is νοητός in another sense, and that he thence inferred that ὁ τόπος is something other than ὁ θεός; and I have rewritten the Greek accordingly.

§ 5. νοητὸς γὰρ πρώτως (πρῶτος MSS.) ὁ θεός ἐστιν ⟨ἑαυτῷ, ὁ δὲ τόπος⟩ ἡμῖν, οὐχ ἑαυτῷ. According to the MSS., the Hermetist says that God οὐχ ἑαυτῷ νοητός ἐστι; which is equivalent to denying that God ἑαυτὸν νοεῖ. Aristotle said that God ἑαυτὸν νοεῖ;[3] and that statement was commonly accepted by Platonists.[4] On the other hand, Plotinus says that τὸ ἓν (the Supreme, which is beyond or prior to νοῦς and τὸ ὄν) οὐ νοεῖ.[5] If then the author of Corp. II

---

[1] τοῖς γιγνωσκομένοις τοίνυν μὴ μόνον τὸ γιγνώσκεσθαι φάναι ὑπὸ τοῦ ἀγαθοῦ παρεῖναι, ἀλλὰ καὶ τὸ εἶναί τε καὶ τὴν οὐσίαν ὑπ' ἐκείνου αὐτοῖς προσεῖναι.

[2] Hippol. Ref. haeres. 7. 21 says that Basilides placed at the head of his system an οὐκ ὢν θεός, who ἀνοήτως . . . κόσμον ἠθέλησε ποιῆσαι, κ.τ.λ. This is equivalent to saying that God is ἀνούσιος and ἀνόητος. The passage of Basilides in which it occurs is an extreme and intentionally paradoxical statement of the Platonic doctrine that God is ἐπέκεινα τῆς οὐσίας.

[3] Ar. Metaph. 12. 9, 1074 b 33. See Zeller Aristotle I, p. 398.

[4] Cf. Abammonis responsum 8. 3 (Testim.), where it is said to be taught by 'Hermes' (that is, by some Egyptian Platonist) that 'the first νοῦς' is νοῦς ἑαυτὸν νοῶν καὶ τὰς νοήσεις εἰς ἑαυτὸν ἐπιστρέφων.

[5] See Plotinus 5. 6, περὶ τοῦ τὸ ἐπέκεινα τοῦ ὄντος μὴ νοεῖν. 5. 6. 2 : τὸ ἐπέκεινα

meant by ὁ θεός what Plotinus meant by τὸ ἕν, and agreed with Plotinus on this point, it would be possible for him to say that ὁ θεὸς οὐχ ἑαυτὸν νοεῖ, and is not ἑαυτῷ νοητός. But it seems more likely that he agreed with Numenius, who said (Euseb. *Pr. ev.* 11. 18. 3 sq.) that the first God (also called by him the first νοῦς) ἑαυτῷ συγγίνεται διόλου, and that the second God (also called by him the second νοῦς) is not πρὸς ἑαυτῷ, but τῆς ὕλης ἐπιμελούμενος ἀπερίοπτος ἑαυτοῦ γίνεται. This implies that, according to Numenius, the first God ἑαυτὸν νοεῖ, and the second God, so far at least as he is concerned with the material world, οὐχ ἑαυτὸν νοεῖ. If we assume that the θεός of *Corp.* II corresponds to the first God or first νοῦς of Numenius, and that the τόπος of *Corp.* II corresponds to the second God or second νοῦς of Numenius, a sense that agrees with that assumption can be got by writing νοητὸς ... ὁ θεός ἐστιν ⟨ἑαυτῷ, ὁ δὲ τόπος⟩ ἡμῖν, οὐχ ἑαυτῷ.

If the meaningless πρῶτος of the MSS. is a miswriting of πρώτως, 'primarily', this word implies that ὁ θεός is not *only* νοητὸς ἑαυτῷ, but is also, in some sense, νοητὸς ἡμῖν. A Platonist might say either that God is νοητὸς ἡμῖν or that God is not νοητὸς ἡμῖν. (Men are capable of apprehending God; yet no man can apprehend God adequately.)

If the word νοητός is taken merely as opposed to αἰσθητός, and equivalent to ἀσώματος, in that sense at least God is νοητός; and the unconnected scrap ⟨οὐ γὰρ ?⟩ αἰσθήσει ὑποπίπτει ὁ θεός may be a part of a statement to that effect. The other phrases in § 5 which I have bracketed, [ἄλλο τι ὢν τοῦ νοουμένου] and [διὰ τοῦτο ἡμῖν νοεῖται], may perhaps be remnants of a marginal note on the paragraph.

§ 6 a. εἰ δὲ νοητὸς ὁ τόπος οὐχ ⟨ὡς⟩ ὁ θεός, [ ] ἀλλ' ὡς ἐνέργεια χωρητική, ⟨⟨ἄλλο τί ἐστι⟩⟩ ⟨τοῦ θεοῦ ὁ τόπος⟩. The question whether ὁ τόπος is ὁ θεός, or is θεῖόν τι but not ὁ θεός, which was raised at the beginning of the paragraph, must surely have been answered before the writer quitted the subject. We know from §§ 12 a–13 what his answer would be, viz. that this τόπος is θεῖόν τι, but is not ὁ θεός. I have therefore added here the words ἄλλο τί ἐστι τοῦ θεοῦ ὁ τόπος.

ἐνέργεια must be taken to mean ἐνέργεια θεοῦ. (See note on *Corp.* X. 1 b.) The τόπος-νοῦς is not God himself, but a certain manifesta-

τοῦ πρώτως νοοῦντος οὐκ ἂν ἔτι νοοῖ. ... πρὸς μὲν τὸν νοῦν νοητὸς ἔσται, καθ' ἑαυτὸν δὲ οὔτε νοοῦν οὔτε νοητὸν κυρίως ἔσται. Plot. 6. 9. 6: οὐδὲ νόησις (ἐστι τῷ ἑνί), ἵνα μὴ ἑτερότης (ᾖ). ... τί γὰρ καὶ νοήσει; ἢ ἑαυτόν; ... ἐν δὲ ὄν, συνὸν ἑαυτῷ, οὐ δεῖται νοήσεως ἑαυτοῦ.

tion of God's activity. This ἐνέργεια is hypostatized, and is regarded as a 'second God'.

§§ 6 b–8 a. πᾶν δὲ τὸ κινούμενον ... καὶ ὑπὸ στάσεως κινεῖται.   It seems impossible to make sense of this paragraph; it has probably been ruined by unintelligent interpolation.   It begins with the assertion that everything which is moved is moved (1) *in* something stationary, and (2) *by* something stationary; and it ends with the same assertion repeated in different words.   But the instances which seem intended to illustrate these two propositions, or one or other of the two, have no discoverable connexion with either.

§ 6 b. πᾶν δὲ τὸ κινούμενον οὐκ ἐν κινουμένῳ κινεῖται, ἀλλ' ἐν ἑστῶτι.   Taken in their obvious sense, the words οὐκ ἐν κινουμένῳ κινεῖται are manifestly false; there are plenty of κινούμενα which are contained in other κινούμενα.   But the writer probably meant that there must be a ἑστός outside the outermost κινούμενον, and intended to suggest the inference that τὸ τὸν κόσμον περιέχον (i. e. the τόπος-νοῦς) is motionless.   Bodies alone are subject to movement; the divine Nous by which the Kosmos is encompassed is ἀσώματος, and partakes of the eternal stability and changelessness of the supreme God.

καὶ τὸ κινοῦν δὲ ἕστηκεν. We learn from § 8 b sq. that τὸ κινοῦν is ψυχή, or something analogous to ψυχή, and that it resides within the body which it moves.   The Kosmos as a whole, or the outermost sphere of the Kosmos, is moved by a world-soul; individual organisms within the Kosmos are moved by their several ψυχαί.   In what relation the soul (τὸ κινοῦν) residing in the Kosmos stands to the τόπος-νοῦς (τὸ ἐν ᾧ κινεῖται) which occupies the space outside the Kosmos, we are not informed; but it may perhaps be inferred from § 12 a (or rather, from a conjectural restoration of § 12 a,) that the cosmic soul and the individual souls owe their power of originating movement to the 'light' with which the τόπος-νοῦς irradiates them, that is to say, to the life which the divine Nous infuses into them.[1]

We are here told that τὸ κινοῦν (i. e. ψυχή) is itself motionless. This is a point on which the Aristotelians differed from the Platonists. Aetius, Diels *Doxogr*. p. 392: Πλάτων ἀεικίνητον μὲν τὴν ψυχήν ... Ἀριστοτέλης ἀκίνητον τὴν ψυχήν, πάσης κινήσεως προηγουμένην. On this question, the writer of *Corp*. II sides with the Aristotelians, and

---

[1] Here again, we may compare Numenius (Euseb. *Pr. ev*. 11. 18. 10): βλέποντος μὲν οὖν καὶ ἐπεστραμμένου πρὸς ἡμῶν ἕκαστον τοῦ θεοῦ (i. e. the 'second God') συμβαίνει ζῆν τε καὶ βιώσκεσθαι τότε τὰ σώματα, κ.τ.λ.

against the Platonists, who said that the soul is 'self-moving'. See
Pl. *Phaedr.* 245 C D, and *Legg.* X. 894 ff.[1]

Πῶς οὖν . . . τὰ ἐνθάδε ⟨κινοῦντα⟩ συγκινεῖται τοῖς κινουμένοις; Ought
we to read τὰ ἐνθάδε ⟨κινοῦντα⟩ συγκινεῖται τοῖς κινουμένοις (codd. Corp.),
or τὰ ἐνθάδε ⟨κινούμενα⟩ συγκινεῖται τοῖς κινοῦσιν (codd. Stob.)? In
either case, Hermes and Asclepius seem to be here speaking of τὸ
κινοῦν, and not of τὸ ἐν ᾧ κινεῖται. And it appears from the words
κινεῖσθαι ὑπὸ τῆς ἀπλάνους σφαίρας that the sphere of the fixed stars
is discussed as an instance of τὸ κινοῦν, and not as an instance of τὸ
ἐν ᾧ κινεῖται. Yet that sphere is certainly not τὸ κινοῦν in the sense
in which this term is explained in §§ 8 b, 9 ; it is not the incorporeal
soul of the planet-spheres. Besides, we have just been told that τὸ
κινοῦν (as well as τὸ ἐν ᾧ κινεῖται) is motionless; and the sphere of
the fixed stars is not motionless. What then has the instance of the
spheres to do with the subject under discussion? I cannot answer
that question; and I can only conjecture that the passage about the
spheres was inserted by some one who did not understand the
meaning of the dialogue.

We can dimly discern through the fog of words that the writer of
this passage is seeking to show that, in the movement of the spheres,
there is something which stands fast. And he seems to have thought
that, by showing this, he would confirm the preceding statement
(πᾶν τὸ κινούμενον ἐν ἑστῶτι κινεῖται, καὶ τὸ κινοῦν δὲ ἔστηκεν,) or one
of the two parts of that statement. But what is it that stands fast?
Certainly neither the sphere of the fixed stars, nor any of the planet-
spheres. The movement of a planet (or of the sphere to which the
planet was supposed to be affixed) could be described in two different
ways. The simpler way of describing it was to say that the fixed
stars travel daily round the earth, and the sun, for instance, also
travels daily round the earth in the same direction, but not quite so
fast. The other way of describing it was to say that the sun is
carried daily round the earth with the fixed stars, but has also an
independent and slower movement of its own in the opposite
direction,[2] and that the visible movement of the sun is a compound
of these two different movements. The writer, since he speaks of

---

[1] The notion that τὸ κινοῦν is ψυχή occurs in a *Cosmopoiia* (second century A. D. ?)
made use of by a sorcerer in a magic Papyrus edited by Dieterich, *Abraxas*, p. 184:
when the Creator 'laughed' for the seventh time, ἐγένετο ψυχή. ὁ δὲ θεὸς ἔφη
" πάντα κινήσεις ". . . . τοῦτ' εἰπόντος τοῦ θεοῦ πάντα ἐκινήθη.

[2] Thus Cleomedes, *De motu corp. cael.* 1. 3. 16, compares the movement of the
planets to that of ants creeping on a potter's wheel in the opposite direction to that
in which the wheel is revolving.

ἀντικίνησις, must have conceived the movement of the planets in the latter way. But where is the στάσις to be found? The result of the composition of the sun's two different movements is, not that it stands still, but that it moves from East to West a little less swiftly than it would if it had only that movement which belongs to it in common with the fixed stars. Neither the fixed stars nor the planets are stationary. The only things in the material universe which could with any show of reason be said to stand fast are, firstly, the common axis [1] of the revolving spheres, or some point in that axis (e. g. one of the Poles in which it terminates, or the centre of the earth), and secondly, the globular earth, massed round the central point of the whole system. And as the writer does not mention the earth, but does mention the North Pole, round which he says the Bears revolve (κίνησιν τὴν περὶ τὸ αὐτό), we must conclude that the thing to which he ascribes στάσις is the Pole.[2] But if so, his point of view is entirely different from that of the writer of the rest of the dialogue, who ascribes στάσις only to ἀσώματα, viz. (1) the τόπος-νοῦς (τὸ ἐν ᾧ κινεῖται τὸ κινούμενον) outside the Kosmos, and (2) ψυχὴ (τὸ κινοῦν) within the Kosmos.

But there is a further difficulty. The writer seems to assert that the στάσις of which he speaks is caused by the ἐναντιότης of the two movements, viz. the movement of the ἀπλανὴς σφαῖρα in the one direction, and the movement of the planet-spheres in the other direction (ἡ γὰρ ἀντιτυπία στάσις φορᾶς). But what could be meant by saying that the Pole is kept fixed in its place by the combined effect

[1] The obliquity of the orbits of the planets is not mentioned in this passage, and seems to be left out of account.

[2] In the Mithraic cult, the North Pole seems to have been of great importance. In the *Mithrasliturgie* edited by Dieterich (pp. 12–14 and 69–78), the North Pole is the abode of the μέγιστος θεός (*sc.* Mithras), to whom Helios, the ruler of the planet-region, is subordinated. This 'greatest God' holds in his right hand μόσχου ὦμον χρύσεον, ὅς ἐστιν ἄρκτος ἡ κινοῦσα καὶ ἀντιστρέφουσα τὸν οὐρανόν· and he is attended by a group of seven gods, who are called οἱ πολοκράτορες τοῦ οὐρανοῦ, . . . οἱ κνωδακοφύλακες, . . . οἱ στρέφοντες ὑπὸ ἐν κέλευσμα τὸν περιδίνητον τοῦ κύκλου ἄξονα τοῦ οὐρανοῦ, and who, no doubt, represent the seven stars of one of the two Bears. (There is a corresponding group of seven maidens, who presumably stand for the seven stars of the other Bear.) It might therefore be conjectured that the passage concerning the movements of the stars was inserted in *Corp.* II by some one who was influenced by Mithraism, and who was thus led to locate the 'static' νοῦς by which the moving universe is governed at the North Pole, instead of in extracosmic space, where the author of *Corp.* II places it.

Cf. Proclus *In Eucl.* (Friedlein), p. 90, l. 11 : ἄλλοι δὲ ἀπορρητότεροι λόγοι καὶ τὸν δημιουργὸν ἐφεστάναι τῷ κόσμῳ λέγουσι τοῖς πόλοις ἐποχούμενον, καὶ δι᾽ ἔρωτος θείου τὸ πᾶν ἐπιστρέφοντα πρὸς ἑαυτόν. The word ἀπορρητότεροι seems to imply that this doctrine was taught in connexion with some mystery-cult, which may perhaps have been that of Mithras.

of these two opposite movements? To this question I can give no answer.

The instance of the man swimming against a current (§ 8 a) appears to be given as an illustration of the principle that the combined effect of two contrary movements is to produce stability or immobility. But if so, the instance is absurdly inappropriate.[1] In the case of the swimmer there is nothing analogous to the Pole; he could only be compared to one of the planets, borne from East to West together with the fixed stars, but at the same time moving from West to East with an independent movement of its own. But this comparison also breaks down. It is assumed that the swimmer is stationary (ἡ ἀντιτυπία ... στάσις γίνεται τῷ ἀνθρώπῳ); and if so, the velocity with which he swims must be equal to the velocity of the contrary current. But the velocity of the planet's independent movement is not equal to that of the contrary movement of the fixed stars; and the planet is not stationary.

τὰς γὰρ σφαίρας ἔφης τὰς πλανωμένας κινεῖσθαι ὑπὸ τῆς ἀπλανοῦς σφαίρας. The connexion of thought would be made clearer if this were followed by something like καίτοι συγκινεῖται ταῖς πλανωμέναις ἡ ἀπλανής. It is to this latter proposition (implied, if not expressed,) that Hermes replies Οὐκ ἔστιν αὕτη συγκίνησις.

The word ἔφης must be meant to refer to some earlier discourse of Hermes to Asclepius. Yet the doctrine taught in this dialogue is described in the concluding sentence as προγνωσία τις, i. e. as the *beginning* of a course of instruction.

ἡ δὲ ἐναντίωσις ⟨⟨τῆς κινήσεως⟩⟩ τὴν ἀντέρεισιν [[ ]] ἔχει ἑστῶσαν. τὴν ἀντέρεισιν appears to be used in the sense of τὸ ἀντερεῖδον, the 'fulcrum', i. e. the common axis of the spheres which revolve in opposite directions.

§ 7. [περὶ δὲ τὸ αὐτὸ στρεφομένας.] This must be cut out; for Hermes would not go on to ask 'what sort of movement' (Κίνησιν ποίαν) if he had just answered that question himself.

κίνησίς ἐστιν ὑπὸ στάσεως κατεχομένη. Here it seems clear that the στάσις spoken of is that of τὸ περὶ ὃ κινοῦνται αἱ ἄρκτοι, i. e. that of the Pole. But where, in this instance, is the ἐναντιότης κινήσεως, to which στάσις was said to be due? Does the writer regard the movements of the two Bears, circling in the same direction, but on opposite sides of the Pole, as two 'opposite' movements?

---

[1] Galen, *De musc. motu* I. 7 f., K. vol. iv, p. 400 (Arnim, *Stoic. vet. fr.* II, p. 148), employs the instance of the swimmer in a rational way, to illustrate the case of a body held at rest by two equal and opposite pressures or tensions.

κωλύει τὸ ὑπὲρ αὐτό. It appears from the context that this must be intended to mean 'prevents them from diverging from their circular orbits'; but it is difficult to see how that sense can be got out of the words.

§§ 8 b–9. ἡ οὖν κίνησις κ.τ.λ. Here we have a discussion of τὸ κινοῦν, which down to this point has only been mentioned incidentally. But the fresh topic is introduced with strange abruptness ; and it is probable that the beginning of the paragraph about τὸ κινοῦν has been lost.

§ 8 b. οὐχ ὑπὸ τῶν κατεκτὸς τοῦ σώματος συμβαίνει γίνεσθαι, ἀλλ' ὑπὸ τῶν ἐντὸς εἰς τὸ κατεκτός, ἤτοι ψυχῆς [ἢ πνεύματος] ἢ ἄλλου τινὸς ἀσωμάτου. The Kosmos is not moved by something which pushes it from without, but by its ψυχή, which impels it from within. And the same may be said of every individual man and animal. (The writer is here thinking of spontaneous movement only, and leaves out of account the case of a man or animal pushed, dragged, or carried by another man or animal.) The ψυχή is incorporeal, but at the same time is regarded as residing 'within' the body of the man or animal. The phrase εἰς τὸ κατεκτός, which is bracketed by Wachsmuth, may be allowed to stand. A living organism is moved 'from within outwards', and not 'from without inwards'; that is, the movement is originated by the soul, which is within the body, and passes thence to the bodily organs, and to material things outside the body.

I have bracketed ἢ πνεύματος. If these words are retained, πνεῦμα is classed among the ἀσώματα. But the incorporeal πνεῦμα spoken of by orthodox and Gnostic Christians (a Semitic equivalent for the Platonic νοῦς) occurs rarely, if at all, in the *Hermetica*. When the Hermetists speak of πνεῦμα, they commonly use the word in the Stoic sense, and mean by it a gaseous substance (σῶμα, not ἀσώματον), which they regard as the corporeal vehicle or envelope of the incorporeal soul. The words ἢ πνεύματος may have been inserted by some one who was in the habit of using πνεῦμα as the Christians used it.

But if πνεῦμα is excluded, how are we to understand ἤτοι ψυχῆς ἢ ἄλλου τινὸς ἀσωμάτου? What other incorporeal thing besides ψυχή can be included under the head of τὸ κινοῦν by which living bodies are moved? Possibly φύσις? Or ἐνέργειαι, in the sense in which that term is used in some of the *Hermes to Ammon* documents?

σῶμα γὰρ ἔμψυχον οὐ(χ ὑπὸ σώματος) κινεῖ⟨ται⟩· ἀλλ' οὐδὲ τὸ σύνολον σῶμα. By this restoration, the sense unquestionably required is clearly expressed. It would be possible to interpret in the same sense

the reading of codd. Corp. (σῶμα γὰρ σῶμα ἔμψυχον οὐ κινεῖ κ.τ.λ.);
but no intelligent writer would use a form of words so ambiguous.

§ 9. ὁρᾷς γοῦν καταβαρυνομένην τὴν ψυχήν, ὅταν μόνη δύο σώματα φέρῃ.
The soul 'carries' the body. Hence, when a man carries a burden,
his soul has to carry both his body and the burden; and it feels
oppressed, because an extra burden is added to its usual load.

(ὥστε) καὶ [ὅτι μὲν] ἐν τίνι κινεῖται τὰ κινούμενα, καὶ ὑπὸ τίνος, δῆλον.
The reading of the MSS. (καὶ ὅτι μὲν ἔν τινι . . . καὶ ὑπό τινος δῆλον) is
a mere repetition of the first sentence of the dialogue, Πᾶν τὸ κινούμενον . . . οὐκ ἔν τινι κινεῖται καὶ ὑπό τινος; Neither Hermes nor Asclepius
could have any reason for repeating at this stage the truism with
which the argument started. But if we write the interrogative τίνι,
τίνος, in place of the indefinite pronoun, the reference back to the
opening of the dialogue becomes intelligible. Hermes points out
that he has now answered the two questions which were there raised;
he has explained both ' in what τὰ κινούμενα are moved ' (§§ 1–6 a),
and ' by what they are moved ' (§§ 8 b, 9).

§§ 10–11. Ἐν κενῷ . . . μεστά ἐστιν. Asclepius here interposes an
objection. Does not all movement presuppose a κενόν? If bodies
were packed against one another without intervening void, would not
movement be impossible? And if so, must not the space outside the
Kosmos be void, to render the movement of the Kosmos possible?
How then can that space be ' full ' of θεῖόν τι, as Hermes asserts?

An argument similar to that on which Asclepius's objection is based
was commonly used by those who asserted the existence of void.
Cf. Ar. *Phys.* 4. 6. 213 b: (λέγουσιν οἱ φάσκοντες κενὸν εἶναι) ὅτι
κίνησις ἡ κατὰ τόπον οὐκ ἂν εἴη (εἰ μὴ εἴη κενόν)· τὸ γὰρ πλῆρες ἀδύνατον
εἶναι δέξασθαί τι. But those who argued thus meant that a body
cannot move unless there is a void space *into* which it may move.
Asclepius goes further, and suggests that the outer sphere of the
Kosmos could not revolve if there were not a void space *within*
which it revolves. We might express his thought by saying that the
movement would be stopped by friction. Cf. § 3, ἵνα . . . μὴ θλιβό-
μενον τὸ κινούμενον ὑπὸ τῆς στενότητος ἐπίσχῃ τὴν κίνησιν, where Hermes
himself seemed to assume the same principle.

The objection might have been better placed at the close of
Hermes' explanation of τὸ ἐν ᾧ κινεῖται, to which it refers, i. e. immediately after § 6 a; but it is not unreasonable that Asclepius
should refrain from mentioning his doubt until both the subjects under
discussion (τὸ κινοῦν as well as τὸ ἐν ᾧ κινεῖται) have been dealt with·

With this passage on τὸ κενόν should be compared *Ascl. Lat.* III.
33 a *sq.*, which closely resembles it. . The Stoic doctrine, according to
which τὸ ἐκτὸς τοῦ κόσμου is κενὸν ἄπειρον, is presupposed ; the writer's
object is to declare and justify his rejection of that doctrine. He
points out that the apparently void spaces *within* the Kosmos are not
really void, but are filled with some corporeal substance, such as air.
Within the Kosmos then, there is no void; and, since bodies
certainly move within the Kosmos, Asclepius's notion that there cannot
be movement unless the moving body has void space juxtaposed to
it is thus shown to be untenable. It is true that this argument does
not directly bear on the question whether void space exists *outside*
the Kosmos ; but the reasoning by which Asclepius was led to think
that there *must* be void space outside the Kosmos is shown to be
invalid.

Since κενόν can mean nothing else than ' space which is not occupied by something corporeal ', the question whether the extracosmic
space is κενόν or is ' filled' with something incorporeal is in reality
futile. That which is ἀσώματον in the proper sense of the word is
not extended in space, and cannot ' fill' space or be situated in space.
But the Hermetist tacitly assumes that the ἀσώματον of which he is
speaking, viz. the divine Nous, is σωματικόν to this extent at least,
that it is capable of occupying space ; and the word κενόν appears to
him to be inapplicable to the space which is ' filled' with that ἀσώματον. He probably pictured the divine Nous to himself as a thing
which pervades extracosmic space in the form of an impalpable
vapour, or a diffused light.

§ 10. μόνον δὲ τὸ μὴ ὄν κενόν ἐστι. This is a reminiscence of the
language of Democritus, who called the empty space between the
atoms τὸ μὴ ὄν, though at the same time he said that it exists no less
truly than τὸ ὄν, i. e. the atoms. Ar. *Metaph.* 1. 4. 985 b 4 : Λεύκιπ-
πος δὲ καὶ . . . Δημόκριτος στοιχεῖα μὲν τὸ πλῆρες καὶ τὸ κενὸν εἶναί φασι,
λέγοντες τὸ μὲν ὄν, τὸ δὲ μὴ ὄν.

⟨⟨τὸ γὰρ ὑπάρχον⟩⟩ . . . εἰ μὴ μεστὸν τῆς ὑπάρξεως ἦν. The text of
the *Corpus* and that of Stobaeus have been differently corrupted ;
I have tried to make sense of the passage by combining the indications of both. The argument appears to amount to this ; ' τὸ
ὑπάρχον cannot be void ; but τὸ ὄν is ὑπάρχον ; therefore, τὸ ὄν cannot
be void.' The writer feels that the term τὸ ὑπάρχον connotes absence
of void more evidently than the synonymous term τὸ ὄν. The word
ξένον in codd. Corp. is doubtless a corruption of κενόν.

§ 11. οὐ διὰ πάντων διήκει τῶν ὄντων, καὶ πάντα διῆκον πληροῖ; The writer speaks of air in nearly the same words in which the Stoics spoke of the cosmic πνεῦμα (a mixture of fire and air). Cf Alex. Aphrod., p. 223. 25 Bruns: the Stoics say τὸ πᾶν ἡνῶσθαί τε καὶ συνέχεσθαι πνεύματός τινος διὰ παντὸς διήκοντος αὐτοῦ. But the Stoics, in accordance with their doctrine of κρᾶσις δι' ὅλων,[1] held that πνεῦμα is present in every part of sublunar space, even in those parts of it which are occupied by other bodies. The Hermetist does not adopt this view with respect to air; for he proceeds to say that air is excluded from those parts of space which are occupied by other bodies. His meaning therefore must be merely that all interstices between other bodies are filled with air.

σῶμα δὲ οὐκ ἐκ τῶν τεσσάρων σωμάτων κεκραμένον συνέστηκε; No portion of any one of the four elements actually presents itself unmixed with the other three. (Cf. *Corp.* IX. 7 : πάντα δέ ἐστι σύνθετα.) That which we commonly call 'air', for instance, is really a mixture of all four elements, but a mixture in which the element air preponderates. It is not the element air then, but the mixed body commonly called air, that occupies all apparently empty spaces in the Kosmos.

It may be doubted whether the writer would have denied that elemental fire exists unmixed in the heavens; but he is not here thinking of the heavens.

ὑπάρξεως (ὑπάρξει codd. Stob. : ὑπάρχει codd. Corp.) γὰρ μεστά ἐστιν [ἀέρος καὶ πνεύματος]. The meaning of πνεῦμα here must be different from its meaning in [ἢ πνεύματος], § 8 b ; for the thing here spoken of is σῶμα, and the thing spoken of in 8 b is ἀσώματον. But καὶ πνεύματος at least ought certainly to be cut out; for in the argument which this sentence ends, air alone, and not πνεῦμα, is spoken of. I think however that it is best to cut out ἀέρος also; for we have to account for the readings ὑπάρχει γάρ and ὑπάρχει γὰρ καί of the MSS. ; and this can best be done by assuming that the author wrote ὑπάρξεως γὰρ μεστά ἐστιν, 'for they are full of something which exists', viz. air. (Cf. εἰ μὴ μεστὸν τῆς ὑπάρξεως ἦν in § 10.) When ὑπάρξεως had been corrupted, some one inserted ἀέρος καὶ πνεύματος to make sense. Perhaps the interpolator borrowed these words from the Greek original of *Ascl. Lat.* III. 33 c : 'spiritu tamen et aere vacuum esse non possit.'

---

[1] Plut. *Comm. not.* 37. 1077 e : the Stoics say σῶμα χωρεῖν διὰ σώματος, κενὸν μηδετέρου περιέχοντος, ἀλλὰ τοῦ πλήρους εἰς τὸ πλῆρες ἐνδυομένου. They held that it is possible for the same portion of space to be occupied simultaneously by two or more different bodies. See Arnim, *Sto. vet.* II, p. 151 ff.

§ 12 a. Τὸν οὖν τόπον . . . τί εἴπομεν; It is clear that εἴπομεν (codd. Stob.) and not εἴπωμεν (codd. Corp.) is the right reading. Having dealt with τὸ κινοῦν, and disposed of the objection about τὸ κενόν, Hermes resumes the discussion of τὸ ἐν ᾧ κινεῖται at the point at which he left it at the end of § 6 a; and he begins by reminding Asclepius of one of the conclusions there arrived at, viz. that the τόπος in question is ἀσώματος.

Τὸ οὖν ἀσώματον ⟨τοῦτο⟩. It seems necessary to insert τοῦτο; for besides the extracosmic νοῦς here spoken of, there is at least one other kind of ἀσώματον, viz. the intracosmic ψυχή by which the Kosmos and the bodies contained in it are moved (§§ 8 b, 9).

Νοῦς ὅλος. Ought we to write νοῦς ὅλος, ἐξ ὅλου ἑαυτὸν ἐμπεριέχων? Or νοῦς, ὅλος ἐξ ὅλου ἑαυτὸν ἐμπ.? The MSS. of *Corp.* give νοῦς, λόγος, ἐξ ὅλου κ.τ.λ.; but λόγος must be a corruption of ὅλος.

ἑαυτὸν ἐμπεριέχων. This means that the τόπος-νοῦς by which the Kosmos is encompassed is not itself encompassed by anything else, or that there is nothing else outside it. The Hermetist might have said that this Nous ὑπὸ τοῦ θεοῦ ἐμπεριέχεται· but his view appears to be that, though the divine Nous is located in space, the supreme God, whom he distinguishes from it, is not in space. Yet a different view seems to be implied in what is said below about the μέγεθος of τὸ ἀγαθόν.

ἐλεύθερος σωματικῆς πλάνης.—(ἐλεύθερος σώματος πάντος, ἀπλανής MSS.) It is superfluous to tell us that an ἀσώματον is ἐλεύθερον σώματος παντός. I have therefore altered ἀπλανής into πλάνης, and taken this to be the genitive dependent on ἐλεύθερος. The unmeaning σώματι καί which follows ἀπαθής in codd. Corp. may have resulted from a misplacement of σωματικῆς; and παντός may have come from πλάνης by duplication.

χωρητικὸς συμπάντων καὶ σωτήριος τῶν ὄντων. The divine Nous (*qua* τόπος) 'contains all things' (cf. ὡς ἐνέργεια χωρητική in § 6 a). And it 'preserves all things'; i. e. it is (in subordination to the supreme God) the agent by whom the universe and all things in it are maintained in existence. In this respect it corresponds to the second and demiurgic God of Numenius, though the writer of *Corp.* II does not use the word δημιουργός in describing it.

⟨ἀφ' οὗ (?) τὸ⟩ ⟨⟨τῆς ψυχῆς⟩⟩ ⟨φῶς⟩. Some explanation of the relation between the extracosmic νοῦς and the intracosmic ψυχή is wanted; and the words τῆς ψυχῆς, which occur in the MSS. at the end of § 12 b, probably formed part of such an explanation. The writer might be expected to say that the divine Nous (τὸ ἐν ᾧ κινεῖται ὁ κόσμος) is that by which the soul (τὸ κινοῦν, including both the cosmic soul and the souls of individual men) is 'illuminated' or vitalized.

The text of 12 a b is badly damaged, and my attempted restoration of it is open to much doubt; but it seems probable that the description of νοῦς ended at the end of 12 a, and that the thing spoken of in 12 b was τὸ ἀγαθόν.

§ 12 b. ⟨⟨Τί οὖν φῇς⟩⟩ ⟨⟨τὸ ἀγαθόν⟩⟩ ;—⟨⟨Τὸ ἀρχέτυπον φῶς⟩⟩, οὗ ὥσπερ ἀκτῖνές εἰσι(ν) [[ ]] ⟨ὅ τε νοῦς καὶ⟩ ἡ ἀλήθεια. This passage is manifestly based on the discussion of 'the idea of the Good' in Pl. Rep. 508 E ff., where Plato's Socrates compares the Good to the sun.

In the traditional text, τὸ ἀγαθόν is called one of the ἀκτῖνες of something else. But as the writer holds that τὸ ἀγαθόν is identical with the supreme God, and is the primary source of all things, he cannot have called it an ἀκτίς emitted by something else. The words τὸ ἀγαθόν therefore must be out of place. The author's meaning must have been that certain things are ὥσπερ ἀκτῖνες τοῦ ἀγαθοῦ, i. e. that these things are emitted by τὸ ἀγαθόν as rays are emitted by the sun.

But what are these 'rays' or radiations of the Good? One of them is ἡ ἀλήθεια. But as ἀκτῖνές εἰσι is in the plural, at least one other 'ray' must have been mentioned. Now Plato l. c. speaks of ἀλήθεια as a thing produced or emitted by τὸ ἀγαθόν; and he repeatedly couples with it another thing, viz. ἐπιστήμη or γνῶσις,[1] which, he says, is also produced or emitted by τὸ ἀγαθόν. The leading thought of that passage would be correctly expressed by saying that ἐπιστήμη (or its synonym γνῶσις) and ἀλήθεια are ὥσπερ ἀκτῖνες τοῦ ἀγαθοῦ. Hence it may be inferred that the other 'ray' which the Hermetist coupled with ἀλήθεια was either ἐπιστήμη, or something closely connected with ἐπιστήμη; and as the topic under discussion in this part of the dialogue is the relation between νοῦς and τὸ ἀγαθόν (= ὁ θεός), there is strong reason to conclude that he wrote οὗ ὥσπερ ἀκτῖνές εἰσιν ⟨ὅ τε νοῦς καὶ⟩ ἡ ἀλήθεια.[2] That the

---

[1] Pl. Rep. 508 E ff.: αἰτίαν δ' ἐπιστήμης οὖσαν καὶ ἀληθείας (τὴν τοῦ ἀγαθοῦ ἰδέαν) . . . . οὕτω δὲ καλῶν ἀμφοτέρων ὄντων, γνώσεώς τε καὶ ἀληθείας . . . ἀγαθοειδῆ μὲν νομίζειν ταῦτ' ἀμφότερα (viz. ἐπιστήμην καὶ ἀλήθειαν) ὀρθόν, ἀγαθὸν δὲ ἡγεῖσθαι ὁπότερον αὐτῶν οὐκ ὀρθόν . . . . ἐπιστήμην μὲν καὶ ἀλήθειαν παρέχει (τὸ ἀγαθόν). The word ἀλήθεια is here used by Plato in the sense of 'reality' rather than 'truth'; and a few lines further on, the phrase τὸ εἶναί τε καὶ τὴν οὐσίαν (τῶν γιγνωσκομένων) is substituted for it as an equivalent.

[2] The combination νοῦν καὶ ἀλήθειαν occurs in Pl. Rep. 6. 490 B: μιγεὶς τῷ ὄντι ὄντως, γεννήσας νοῦν καὶ ἀλήθειαν, . . . οὕτω λήγοι ὠδῖνος.

Platonists of the second century A. D. were accustomed thus to couple together νοῦς and ἀλήθεια, is proved by the use made of these terms by the Gnostic Valentinus, who gave the names Νοῦς and Ἀλήθεια to the first pair of Aeons put forth by the supreme God.[1] It may be added that the Hermetist would have no reason for mentioning ἀλήθεια here, unless he spoke of it as the correlate (or in the language of Valentinus, the σύζυγος) of νοῦς, with which he is more especially concerned.   For the series τὸ ἀγαθόν, νοῦς, ψυχή, cf. Plotinus 5. 1. 8 : αἴτιον μὲν τὸν νοῦν (λέγει ὁ Πλάτων)· δημιουργὸς γὰρ ὁ νοῦς αὐτῷ· τοῦτον δέ φησι τὴν ψυχὴν ποιεῖν . . . τοῦ δὲ αἰτίου, νοῦ ὄντος, πατέρα φησὶ τἀγαθόν, [καὶ] τὸ ἐπέκεινα νοῦ καὶ ἐπέκεινα οὐσίας· . . . ὥστε Πλάτωνα εἰδέναι ἐκ μὲν τἀγαθοῦ τὸν νοῦν, ἐκ δὲ τοῦ νοῦ τὴν ψυχήν.

The ἀρχέτυπον φῶς of which the Hermetist speaks must, I think, be τὸ ἀγαθόν itself.   The statement that τὸ ἀγαθόν is 'the archetypal light' corresponds to Plato's statement that ἡ ἰδέα τοῦ ἀγαθοῦ is the sun of the intelligible world.   The phrase implies that there is another φῶς which is an εἰκών of the archetype ; and this other and subordinate φῶς may be the 'light' which the extracosmic νοῦς gives forth, and by which the intracosmic ψυχή is irradiated.   Cf. Philo *De somn.* 1. 13. 75, vol. iii, p. 223 Wendland : ὁ θεὸς φῶς ἐστι, . . . καὶ οὐ μόνον φῶς, ἀλλὰ καὶ παντὸς ἑτέρου φωτὸς ἀρχέτυπον, μᾶλλον δὲ παντὸς ἀρχετύπου πρεσβύτερον καὶ ἀνώτερον.   Plotinus 5. 1. 6 *sq.* and 5. 3. 12, quoted in note on *Corp.* XII i. 1.

§ 13. Ὁ οὖν θεὸς τί ἐστιν ;—Ὁ μηδέτερον (μηδὲ ἕν MSS.) τούτων ὑπάρχων, ὧν δὲ καὶ ⟨⟨τούτοις⟩⟩ τοῦ εἶναι [[ ]] αἴτιος, καὶ πᾶσι κ.τ.λ.   Of the things to which τούτοις refers, ἀλήθεια is certainly one ; and if my explanation of the passage is right, the other is νοῦς.   (We are told below that ὁ θεὸς οὐ νοῦς ἐστιν, αἴτιος δὲ τοῦ ⟨νοῦν⟩ εἶναι.)   The writer has just said that νοῦς and ἀλήθεια are 'rays' emitted by τὸ ἀγαθόν ; he now says that the cause of their existence is God, who (as he tells us in § 15 f.) is identical with τὸ ἀγαθόν.

πάντα δέ ἐστι τὰ ⟨γινόμενα⟩ ἐκ τῶν ὄντων γινόμενα, οὐκ (οὐχὶ μὴ MSS.) ἐκ τῶν μὴ ὄντων.   The writer apparently holds that the Kosmos is without beginning, and denies creation *ex nihilo*.   God is the supreme cause of all things, inasmuch as he is the source of Nous, by whom the Kosmos is maintained in being (νοῦς is σωτήριος τῶν

---

[1] Cf. Irenaeus 2. 12. 2 : according to the doctrine of Valentinus, *unum et idem fiet Nus et Alethia, semper adhaerentes invicem.*   This part of the Valentinian system must have been derived from Pl. *Rep.* l. c.

ὄντων, § 12 a); but God's agent Nous makes each thing, not out of nothing, but out of something else which existed before it.

τὰ γὰρ μὴ ὄντα οὐ φύσιν ἔχει τοῦ δύνασθαι γενέσθαι ⟨τι⟩. That which is not cannot become anything, or turn into anything. This is merely another way of saying that ἐκ τῶν μὴ ὄντων οὐ δύναται γενέσθαι τι.

[τοῦ μηδέποτ' εἶναι.] These words have, no doubt, come by duplication from the following τοῦ μὴ εἶναί ποτε. Things which now exist cannot at any time pass out of existence; they can only change into something else. Cf. *Corp.* VIII, Ότι οὐδὲν τῶν ὄντων ἀπόλλυται. The words Τί οὖν φής cannot have been intended to stand here; I have found a possible place for them above, in § 12 b.

ὁ οὖν θεὸς οὐ νοῦς ἐστιν, αἴτιος δὲ τοῦ ⟨νοῦν⟩ εἶναι. Cf. *Abammonis Resp.* 8. 1 ff., where the Egyptian priest Abammon answers the question τί τὸ πρῶτον αἴτιον ἡγοῦνται εἶναι Αἰγύπτιοι, πότερον νοῦν ἢ ὑπὲρ νοῦν. The doctrine that the supreme God is ὑπὲρ νοῦν and αἴτιος τοῦ νοῦν εἶναι was current among the Platonists of the Roman empire, and was adopted from them by Valentinus and other Gnostics. Ps.-Archytas (first century A.D. ?), Stob. 1. 41. 2, vol. i, p. 280 W.: τὸ δὲ τοιοῦτον (*sc.* the *principium* which imposes form on formless matter) οὐ νόον μόνον εἶμεν δεῖ, ἀλλὰ καὶ νόω τι κρέσσον· νόω δὲ κρέσσον ἐστὶν ὅπερ ὀνομάζομεν θεόν. Irenaeus 1. 24. 3: 'Basilides . . . ostendens Nun . . . ab innato natum Patre.'

[οὐδὲ πνεῦμα . . .] [οὐδὲ φῶς, αἴτιος δὲ τοῦ φῶς εἶναι.] The mention of πνεῦμα may be ascribed to the same interpolator who inserted πνεῦμα in § 8 b. If we take φῶς to mean τὸ τῆς ψυχῆς φῶς, 'the light by which the soul is illuminated', i. e. the secondary and derivative φῶς spoken of in § 12 a, the words οὐδὲ φῶς, αἴτιος δὲ τοῦ φῶς εἶναι might be regarded as another way of saying that God (= τὸ ἀγαθόν) is τὸ ἀρχέτυπον φῶς. But as the matter under consideration is the relation between God and Nous, it is more likely that the paragraph ended with a statement of that relation, and that the words concerning φῶς were added by another hand.

§ 14. τὸν θεὸν δυσὶ ταύταις ταῖς προσηγορίαις σέβεσθαι δεῖ. What are the 'two appellations'? The writer of § 17 a must have taken them to be τὸ ἀγαθόν and ὁ πατήρ. 'The Good' has been spoken of already; but the word πατήρ does not occur until § 17 a, and the reader could not be expected to supply it out of his own head in § 14. If the two names meant by the author of § 14 were 'the Good' and 'the Father', some words in which his meaning was explained (e. g. τῇ τοῦ ἀγαθοῦ καὶ τῇ τοῦ πατρός, in apposition to ταύταις ταῖς προσηγορίαις,) must have fallen out. But it is more probable that the two names of which he is speaking are those which he has already been employing, viz. ὁ θεός and τὸ ἀγαθόν, and that § 17 a, in which the second of the two names is taken to be ὁ πατήρ, was subsequently added by some one else. In § 15, we are told that it is impious to call God by any other name except 'the Good'. This shows that the two names which the author recognized were ὁ θεός and τὸ ἀγαθόν; and the writer of § 17 a, in calling God 'the Father', is guilty of the very impiety which is denounced in § 15.

In *Corp.* X, the phrase ὁ θεὸς καὶ πατήρ, ⟨ὁ⟩ καὶ τὸ ἀγαθόν, occurs repeatedly as a name of God; but in that document the words ὁ καὶ τὸ ἀγαθόν have probably been inserted by a later hand.

οὔτε γὰρ τῶν ἄλλων ... τις δύναται ... ἀγαθὸς εἶναι ἢ μόνος ὁ θεός. *Corp.* VI is an expansion of this thought. Compare Mark 10. 18, Luke 18. 19: Τί με λέγεις ἀγαθόν; οὐδεὶς ἀγαθὸς εἰ μὴ εἷς ὁ θεός. Matt. 19. 17: τί με ἐρωτᾷς περὶ τοῦ ἀγαθοῦ; εἷς ἐστιν ὁ ἀγαθός. The saying must have been widely current, and there is no reason to suppose that the Hermetist derived it from the Gospels. It might be suggested to a Platonist by the discussion of the ode of Simonides in Pl. *Protag.* 341 E.

§ 15. τοσοῦτον γάρ ἐστι τοῦ ἀγαθοῦ τὸ μέγεθος. Here the Good (i.e. God) is described as extended in space. We are told that neither body nor soul is spacious enough to contain it, and that it is coextensive with the whole sum of things corporeal and incorporeal; that is to say, it extends through all space, both cosmic and extra-cosmic. But perhaps the Hermetist meant these statements to be understood metaphorically, and not literally.

§ 16. τετιμημένοι τῇ τοῦ θεοῦ προσηγορίᾳ. We honour the sub-ordinate gods by applying to them an appellation which properly belongs to the supreme God alone, i.e. by calling them ἀγαθοί.

The same phrase occurs in the prayer or hymn at the end of *Ascl. Lat.*: ἄφραστον ὄνομα, τετιμημένον τῇ τοῦ θεοῦ προσηγορίᾳ, ... καὶ εὐλογούμενον τῇ τοῦ πατρός. But in that passage, the words are used in a different sense, and it is the supreme Deity himself that is there said to be 'honoured by the appellation θεός'. It would seem that the writer of *Ascl. Lat.* 41 b read the phrase in *Corp.* II (which is probably the earlier of the two documents), but either misunderstood it, or intentionally employed it in a different way.

[καὶ ἓν γένος ἀμφοτέρων, ἐξ οὗ τὰ γένη πάντα.] γένος is a strange word to use with reference to God; and when two things are said to 'have the same γένος', or belong to the same γένος, it is implied that they are specifically different, rather than that they are identical, which is the point on which the writer is here insisting.

[ὁ γὰρ θεὸς ἀγαθός ἐστιν, ὡς ἅπαντα διδοὺς καὶ μηδὲν λαμβάνων.]—(ὁ γὰρ ἀγαθὸς ἅπαντά ἐστι διδοὺς καὶ μηδὲν λαμβάνων MSS.) Cf. Corp. V. 10 b : πάντα δίδως καὶ οὐδὲν λαμβάνεις. Corp. X. 3 : τῷ μηδὲν λαμβάνοντι. Corp. IX. 9 : οὐκ ἔξωθεν αὐτὰ προσλαμβάνων, ἔξω δὲ ἐπιδιδούς.

The reading of the MSS. is certainly wrong; for in an independent statement the negative would be οὐδέν, not μηδέν.[1] But even in the form into which I have altered it, the sentence is out of place here; for at this stage the writer is asserting, not that God is ἀγαθός, but that God is τὸ ἀγαθόν. If the words ὁ γὰρ . . . μηδὲν λαμβάνων occurred at all in the original text, they probably followed ἢ μόνος ὁ θεός in § 14.

[ὁ οὖν θεὸς πάντα δίδωσι καὶ οὐδὲν λαμβάνει.] ὁ οὖν θεός is a duplication of the first three words of the following sentence; and πάντα δίδωσι καὶ οὐδὲν λαμβάνει is an alternative for ἅπαντά ἐστι διδοὺς καὶ μηδὲν λαμβάνων.

ὁ οὖν θεὸς ⟨τὸ⟩ ἀγαθόν, καὶ τὸ ἀγαθὸν ὁ θεός. Cf. Philo De special. leg. 2. 53 (De septen. 5), Cohn V, p. 99 : μόνος γὰρ (ὁ θεὸς) εὐδαίμων καὶ μακάριος, παντὸς μὲν ἀμέτοχος κακοῦ, πλήρης δ' ἀγαθῶν τελείων, μᾶλλον δ', εἰ χρὴ τἀληθὲς εἰπεῖν, αὐτὸς ὢν τὸ ἀγαθόν,[2] ὃς οὐρανῷ καὶ γῇ τὰ κατὰ μέρος ὤμβρησεν ἀγαθά. Proclus on Pl. Tim. 28 says that the Platonist Atticus (A. D. 160–180) identified the Demiurgus with 'the Good' (τὸν δημιουργὸν εἰς ταὐτὸν ἄγει τἀγαθῷ).

The statement that 'God is the Good, and the Good is God' forms a fitting conclusion to the dialogue; and there can be little doubt that in the original text these words were immediately followed by τοσαῦτα . . . λελέχθω κ.τ.λ. (§ 17 b). The topic of procreation, which is introduced in § 17 a, has no connexion with the preceding argument, though the person who appended that section contrived to produce a superficial appearance of continuity by referring to the mention of two προσηγορίαι of God in § 14.

---

[1] It would be possible to avoid this difficulty without inserting θεός, by writing ὁ γὰρ ἀγαθός ἐστιν ὁ ἅπαντα διδοὺς καὶ μηδὲν λαμβάνων.
[2] But in Opif. mund. 2. 8, Cohn I, p. 3, Philo says that God (who is there called ὁ τῶν ὅλων νοῦς) is κρείττων ἢ αὐτὸ τὸ ἀγαθὸν καὶ αὐτὸ τὸ καλόν.

§ **17 a.** πατρὸς γὰρ τὸ ποιεῖν. ποιεῖν is here used in the sense 'to beget', as in the compound παιδοποιεῖν.

σπουδὴ . . . εὐσεβεστάτη . . . ἐστιν ἡ παιδοποιία. The thought that human procreation is an imitation of the creative energy of God, which is implied in this passage, is more fully expressed in *Corp.* XI ii. 14 a, and in *Ascl. Lat.* III. 20 b *sq.* The view that the begetting of offspring is incumbent on man as a sacred duty is implied in *Ascl. Lat.* III. 20 b *sq.*, but is more directly asserted in *Corp.* II. 17 a. The writer must have found in his environment some special reason for insisting on it. In saying that to die childless is 'a great misfortune', he is in accord with a sentiment which was strongly rooted among Greeks, Jews, and Egyptians alike ; and he finds religious support for it in his doctrine of 'God the Father'. But in his time, there were many who preferred to remain childless, some from a wish to avoid trouble, expense, and anxiety, and others, (especially Pythagoreans, Platonists, and Christians,) on account of the *contemptus mundi*, and hatred of the body, to which their beliefs gave support. The first of these two motives finds frequent expression in literature, from the time of Euripides downward; see for instance the passages collected in Stobaeus 4. 22. 28 *sqq.* Hense, Ὅτι οὐκ ἀγαθὸν τὸ γαμεῖν, and *ib.* 4. 24. 16 *sqq.*, Ὅτι ἀσύμφορον τὸ ἔχειν τέκνα. Augustus found that the tendency to 'race-suicide' was becoming a grave public danger, and enacted laws to check it. The same sort of inducements to prefer a celibate life which were felt in Italy in the time of Augustus were no doubt also felt in Egypt some generations later; and as the writer of *Corp.* II. 17 a bids his readers μὴ συνησθῆναι, 'not to rejoice with' a childless man (as with one who is fortunate), it may be inferred that he is arguing chiefly against those who thought childlessness the more comfortable state. On the other hand, the writer of *Ascl. Lat.* III was probably thinking rather of Christian ascetics who abstained from procreation on religious grounds.

δίκην οὗτος δίδωσι μετὰ θάνατον τοῖς δαίμοσιν. The notion that the agents by whom sin is punished after death are daemons occurs in Plato's myths. See *Ascl. Lat.* III. 28. The writer of *Corp.* II. 17 a holds that the punishment inflicted by the daemons, in some cases at least, takes the form of a penal reincarnation ; on this, cf. *Corp.* X. 8 a. Plutarch, in his 'Vision of Thespesius', *De sera numinis vindicta* 567 F, describes the daemon-torturers reshaping guilty souls to fit them for reincarnation in the bodies to which they are condemned.

σῶμα . . . μήτε ἀνδρὸς μήτε γυναικὸς φύσιν ἔχον. This means a body

other than human. Those who refuse to discharge the function incumbent on them as ἄνδρες or γυναῖκες will be punished by reincarnation in beast-bodies.

[[ὅπερ ἐστὶ κατηραμένον ὑπὸ τοῦ ἡλίου.]] What is it that is 'cursed
by the Sun'?[1] According to the reading of the MSS., the thing
which is 'cursed' is σῶμα οὔτε ἀνδρὸς οὔτε γυναικὸς φύσιν ἔχον. A de-
formed or defective human body might be said to be 'accursed', but
hardly the normal body of a beast. It seems more likely that the
clause has been misplaced, and ought to stand after ἄτεκνόν τινα ἐξ
ἀνθρώπων ἀπαλλαγῆναι; it is childlessness that is the accursed thing.

But why does the writer add ὑπὸ τοῦ ἡλίου? Perhaps the Sun-god,
being himself the cosmic source of life and growth, might be thought
to look with displeasure on those who refuse to co-operate with him
by begetting children. The phrase may have been in use as
a traditional formula in some solar cult.

LIBELLVS III

The text of *Corp.* III, as given in the MSS., is so corrupt as to be
almost wholly meaningless; and I have altered it with a free hand.
It is not likely that the conjecturally emended text which is here
printed is precisely what the author wrote; but I think it probable
that, in the main at least, it correctly represents his meaning.

There is no necessity to take this little piece to be an extract from
a longer treatise; it appears to be a complete whole in itself, and it
is rounded off by a recurrence, in the concluding words, to the same
thought with which it began. It is the concentrated essence of some
unknown Egyptian's reflections on the universe.

The author of *Corp.* III had read the first chapter of *Genesis*. It
is impossible to doubt this, when we compare the corresponding
passages in detail.

Genesis i (LXX).	*Corp.* III.
1. ἐν ἀρχῇ ἐποίησεν ὁ θεὸς τὸν οὐρανὸν καὶ τὴν γῆν.	1 a. ἀρχὴ τῶν ὄντων ὁ θεός.

---

[1] '*Under* the sun' would rather be ὑπὸ τὸν ἥλιον. (Cf. *Eccl. passim*, e. g. 2. 18:
σύμπαντα μόχθον μου ὃν ἐγὼ κοπιῶ ὑπὸ τὸν ἥλιον.) It would be possible to write
ὑπὸ τὸν ἥλιον, and (perhaps assuming a lacuna before ὑπό) to take this as meaning
'during life on earth', as opposed to μετὰ θάνατον; but there is no need to reject
the phrase 'cursed by the Sun'. Cf. καταραθέντα ὑπὸ τοῦ ἡλίου, in a passage
quoted from Hermes by the alchemist Olympiodorus (*Testim.*, Zosimus *Adden-
dum* (c)).

2. ἡ δὲ γῆ ἦν ἀόρατος καὶ ἀκατασκεύαστος,

καὶ σκότος ἐπάνω τῆς ἀβύσσου·

καὶ πνεῦμα θεοῦ ἐπεφέρετο ἐπάνω
τοῦ ὕδατος.
3. καὶ εἶπεν ὁ θεός Γενηθήτω φῶς·
καὶ ἐγένετο φῶς. . . .
7. καὶ ἐποίησεν ὁ θεὸς τὸ στε-
ρέωμα· καὶ διεχώρισεν ὁ θεὸς ἀνὰ
μέσον τοῦ ὕδατος ὃ ἦν ὑποκάτω τοῦ
στερεώματος, καὶ ἀνὰ μέσον τοῦ
ὕδατος τοῦ ἐπάνω τοῦ στερεώματος.
8. καὶ ἐκάλεσεν ὁ θεὸς τὸ στερέωμα
οὐρανόν. . . . 9. καὶ συνήχθη τὸ
ὕδωρ τὸ ὑποκάτω τοῦ οὐρανοῦ εἰς
τὰς συναγωγὰς αὐτῶν, καὶ ὤφθη ἡ
ξηρά. 10. καὶ ἐκάλεσεν ὁ θεὸς τὴν
ξηρὰν γῆν . . .
11. καὶ εἶπεν ὁ θεός Βλαστησάτω
ἡ γῆ βοτάνην χόρτου, σπεῖρον
σπέρμα κατὰ γένος καὶ καθ᾽ ὁμοιότητα, καὶ ξύλον κάρπιμον ποιοῦν
καρπόν, οὗ τὸ σπέρμα αὐτοῦ ἐν
αὐτῷ κατὰ γένος εἰς ὁμοιότητα ἐπὶ
τῆς γῆς· καὶ ἐγένετο οὕτως. 12.
καὶ ἐξήνεγκεν ἡ γῆ βοτάνην χόρτου. . . .
14. καὶ εἶπεν ὁ θεός Γενηθήτωσαν
φωστῆρες ἐν τῷ στερεώματι τοῦ οὐρανοῦ εἰς φαῦσιν τῆς γῆς, καὶ ἄρχειν
τῆς ἡμέρας καὶ τῆς νυκτός, . . . καὶ
ἔστωσαν εἰς σημεῖα . . . 15. καὶ
ἐγένετο οὕτως. . . .
20. καὶ εἶπεν ὁ θεός Ἐξαγαγέτω
τὰ ὕδατα ἑρπετὰ ψυχῶν ζωσῶν καὶ
πετεινὰ . . .· καὶ ἐγένετο οὕτως. 21.
καὶ ἐποίησεν ὁ θεὸς τὰ κήτη τὰ μεγάλα καὶ πᾶσαν ψυχὴν ζῴων ἑρπε-

2 a (differently placed) : ἀδιορίστων δὲ ὄντων ἁπάντων καὶ ἀκατασκευάστων.
1 b. ἦν γὰρ σκότος ἄπειρον ἐν
ἀβύσσῳ,
καὶ ὕδωρ, καὶ πνεῦμα λεπτὸν νοερόν, δυνάμει θείᾳ ⟨. . .⟩ον τὰ ἐν χάει.
ἀνείθη δὴ φῶς ἅγιον.

⟨. . .⟩ στοιχεῖα καὶ θεοὶ πάντες. . . .
2 a. ἀποδιωρίσθη τὰ ἐλαφρὰ εἰς
ὕψος, καὶ τὰ βαρέα ἐθεμελιώθη ὑφ᾽
ὑγρᾷ ἄμμῳ. . . . ἀνακρεμασθέντων
πνεύματι ὀχεῖσθαι.
(1 b. καὶ ἐπάγη ὑπ᾽ ἄμμῳ ἐξ
ὑγρᾶς οὐσίας.)

3 a (differently placed) : καὶ
πᾶσα σπορὰ ἔνσπορος. καὶ (ἐγένετο) χόρτος καὶ ἄνθους παντὸς
χλοή· τὸ σπέρμα τῆς παλιγγενεσίας
ἐν ἑαυτοῖς.
(1 b. ⌈καταδιαιροῦσι⌉ φύσεως ἐν-
σπόρου.)

2 b. καὶ ὤφθη ὁ οὐρανὸς ἐν κύκλοις ἑπτά, καὶ θεοὶ [ταῖς] ἐν ἄστρων
ἰδέαις ὀπτανόμενοι σὺν τοῖς αὐτῶν
σημείοις ἅπασι. καὶ διηρθρώθη σὺν
τοῖς ἐν αὐτῇ θεοῖς.
3 a. ἄνηκε δὲ ἕκαστος θεὸς διὰ
τῆς ἰδίας δυνάμεως τὸ προσταχθὲν
αὐτῷ· καὶ ἐγένετο . . . ἔνυδρα καὶ
πτηνά.

τῶν, ἃ ἐξήγαγεν τὰ ὕδατα κατὰ γένη
αὐτῶν, καὶ πᾶν πετεινὸν πτερωτὸν
κατὰ γένος. . . .

22. καὶ ηὐλόγησεν αὐτὰ (*sc.* the   (See § 3 b below.)
fishes and the birds) ὁ θεὸς λέγων
Αὐξάνεσθε καὶ πληθύνεσθε. . . .

24. καὶ εἶπεν ὁ θεὸς Ἐξαγαγέτω   (Differently placed): καὶ ἐγέ-
ἡ γῆ ψυχὴν ζῶσαν κατὰ γένος, τε-   νετο θηρία τετράποδα καὶ ἑρπετά.
τράποδα καὶ ἑρπετὰ καὶ θηρία τῆς
γῆς κατὰ γένος· καὶ ἐγένετο οὕτως.
. . .

26. Ποιήσωμεν ἄνθρωπον . . .·   3 b. . . . γενέσεις τῶν ἀνθρώπων,
καὶ ἀρχέτωσαν τῶν ἰχθύων τῆς θα-   εἰς . . . πάντων τῶν ὑπ' οὐρανὸν δε-
λάσσης καὶ τῶν πετεινῶν τοῦ οὐρα-   σπότειαν, . . .
νοῦ καὶ τῶν κτηνῶν καὶ πάσης
τῆς γῆς. . . .

28. καὶ ηὐλόγησεν αὐτοὺς ὁ θεὸς   εἰς τὸ αὐξάνεσθαι ἐν αὐξήσει καὶ
λέγων Αὐξάνεσθε καὶ πληθύνεσθε,   πληθύνεσθαι ἐν πλήθει.
καὶ πληρώσατε τὴν γῆν καὶ κατα-
κυριεύσατε αὐτῆς.

It is evident then that the writer of *Corp.* III knew the Mosaic
account of the creation. But he also knew the Stoic cosmology;
and in this document, he has tried to harmonize the one with the
other, and so to 'reconcile *Genesis* with science'.

We have fragments of another cosmogony, which appears to have
been likewise derived in part from *Genesis* and in part from Stoic
science, but was said by its author to be based on writings of Thoth,
whom the Greeks called Hermes Trismegistus,—namely, the cosmogony of Sanchuniathon, as reported by Philo Byblius; [1] and it seems
worth while to compare this with *Corp.* III. Philo Bybl. is quoted
as follows by Eusebius, *Pr. ev.* i. 10. 1 (33 b) sqq.[2]

"Τὴν τῶν ὅλων ἀρχὴν ὑποτίθεται (ὁ Σαγχουνιάθων) ἀέρα ζοφώδη καὶ
πνευματώδη, ἢ πνοὴν ἀέρος ζοφώδους,[3] καὶ χάος θολερὸν ἐρεβῶδες,[4] (ὃ

---

[1] Date of Philo Byblius, *c.* A. D. 64–140 (Christ *Gesch. Gr. Litt.*). He may
have written this book about A. D. 100–120.

[2] The text here given is based on that of Gifford's edition, 1903.

[3] ἀὴρ πνευματώδης and πνοὴ ἀέρος appear to be two alternative translations of a
Semitic term corresponding to the 'spirit of God' in *Genesis* 1. 2, and the πνεῦμα
λεπτὸν νοερόν in *Corp.* III. In what follows, this same thing is called simply τὸ
πνεῦμα. The epithet ζοφώδης corresponds to the 'darkness upon the face of the
deep' in *Genesis*.

[4] The χάος θολερὸν ἐρεβῶδες, which is coupled with the πνεῦμα, and is the other

καλεῖται) ⟨⟨μῶτ· τοῦτό τινές φασιν ἰλύν, οἱ δὲ ὑδατώδους μίξεως σῆψιν.⟩⟩[1] ταῦτα δὲ[2] εἶναι ἄπειρα, καὶ διὰ πολὺν αἰῶνα μὴ ἔχειν πέρας.[3] ὅτε δέ, φησίν, ἠράσθη ⟨τοῦ μῶτ⟩ τὸ·πνεῦμα, τῶν ⟨ἀ⟩ιδίων ἀρχῶν [[καὶ]] ἐγένετο σύγκρασις.[4] ⟨⟨καὶ⟩⟩ ἡ ⟨συμ⟩πλοκὴ ἐκείνη ἐκλήθη πόθος.[5] αὕτη δὲ ἀρχὴ

of the two primal things, corresponds to *tehōm* ('the deep') and 'the waters' in *Genesis*, and to ἄβυσσος, ὕδωρ, and τὰ ἐν χάει in *Corp*. III.

[1] I have inserted here the words μῶτ . . . σῆψιν, which are evidently misplaced where they occur below in the text of Eusebius. They must have been meant to apply to the 'turbid chaos' or formless watery mass; and it is to be presumed that μωτ is a Semitic word, of which Philo Byblius, as before, gives two alternative explanations, viz. ἰλύς ('mud '), and ὑδατώδους μίξεως σῆψις ('a fermenting watery mixture'). A word meaning 'the waters' (Heb. *mayim*) would serve the purpose. I find it stated that the Semitic word for water occurs in the form *mōi* in Aramaic; and it is possible that μωτ is a miswriting for μωι. Cf. Assyrian *mū*, pl. *mē*. (The Egyptian for water is *mw*, Coptic ⲙⲟⲟⲩ; but the immediate source of Philo Bybl. must have been Semitic, and not Egyptian.)

In Damascius's account of the Babylonian cosmogony, *De princip.* (Kopp) c. 125, p. 384 (Gunkel, *Schöpfung und Chaos*, p. 17), there is a Being named Μωυμῖς, son of Ἀπασῶν and Ταυθέ (i. e. *Apsū* and *Tiāmat*,—'Αβυσσος and *Tehōm*) ; and *mummu* (' die tosende Wassertiefe', Delitzsch,) is sometimes used in Babylonian documents as the name of the messenger of Apsū (Langdon, *The Babylonian Epic of Creation*, 1923, p. 72). But Mr. Langdon (*ib.*) also says that ' *Mummu* is an ordinary word for "form", which was personified as creative reason, and inherent in the first principle, water'. Is there any connexion between this *Mummu*—Μωυμῖς and the μωτ of Philo Bybl.?

It has occurred to me that μωτ might possibly be *tehōm* written backwards. A Greek might conceivably make this mistake in transcribing a Semitic word written from right to left; but this is hardly probable.

The origin of the word μῶτ is doubtful, but we are not left in doubt as to its meaning in this passage; for the writer himself tells us that it may here be taken to mean ἰλύς. For our present purpose then, μῶτ means ' mud '.

[2] Viz. the πνεῦμα and the χάος θολερόν (also called μῶτ).

[3] πέρας is here used in its Pythagorean sense, as an equivalent of εἶδος or μορφή. (Cf. Philo *Special. leg.* I. 329, Cohn V, p. 79: ἀπείρου (= ἀμόρφου) καὶ πεφυρμένης ὕλης.) For a long time, the two primal things (the πνεῦμα and the μῶτ) continued to be unformed or unordered. This clause corresponds to ' the earth (i. e. all that existed in the beginning) was waste and void (*tohu wa bohu*) ' in *Genesis*, and to ἀδιορίστων ὄντων ἁπάντων καὶ ἀκατασκευάστων in *Corp*. III. The epithet ἄπειρον occurs in *Corp*. III. I b, and in the original text of that passage, was probably applied to ὕδωρ, i. e. the formless watery mass.

[4] In Eusebius, the reading is ἠράσθη τὸ πνεῦμα τῶν ἰδίων ἀρχῶν. But that is nonsense. The πνεῦμα is itself one of the two ἀρχαί, and has no ' ἀρχαί of its own ' of which it might become enamoured. The writer must have meant that there were two ἀίδιοι ἀρχαί (i. e. two things without beginning), viz. the *pneuma* and the *watery mass*, and that at a certain time the former became enamoured of the latter, and the two (which had hitherto been separate) consequently came to be inter-mingled. This is his interpretation of the phrase in the Hebrew *Genesis*, 'the spirit of God was brooding upon the face of the waters '. His πνεῦμα corresponds to ' the spirit of God '; his μῶτ corresponds to ' the waters ' ; and the Hebrew word which our translators render by ' was brooding ' is taken by him to mean ἠράσθη.

[5] πόθος or ἔρως occurs at the beginning of many cosmogonies, from Hesiod downward. Some of these were no doubt known to the writer; and by his interpretation of the Hebrew text, he has contrived to find this same πόθος in the first chapter of *Genesis* also.

Compare the 'Sidonian' cosmogony reported by Eudemus (Damascius *De princ.* p. 382 Kopp: Mullach *Fr. Ph. Gr.* III, p. 289): Σιδώνιοι . . . περὶ πάντων Χρόνον

κτίσεως ἀπάντων· [αὐτὸ δὲ οὐκ ἐγίνωσκε τὴν αὐτοῦ κτίσιν·]¹ καὶ ἐκ τῆς
[αὐ]τοῦ ⟨μὼτ⟩ συμπλοκῆς ⟨καὶ⟩ τοῦ πνεύματος ἐγένετο [[μώτ· τοῦτό τινές
φασιν ἰλύν, οἱ δὲ ὑδατώδους μίξεως σῆψιν]]·[καὶ ἐκ ταύτης ἐγένετο] πᾶσα
σπορὰ κτίσεως.² καὶ ⟨αὕτη⟩ γένεσις τῶν ὅλων. [[ἦν δέ τινα ζῷα οὐκ
ἔχοντα αἴσθησιν.]] [[ἐξ ὧν ἐγένετο ζῷα νοερά, καὶ ἐκλήθη ζωφασημίν,
τοῦτ' ἔστιν οὐρανοῦ κατόπται.]]³ καὶ ἀνεπλάσθη ⟨τὸ⟩ ⟨⟨μὼτ⟩⟩ ὁμοίως ᾠοῦ

ὑποτίθενται καὶ Πόθον καὶ Ὁμίχλην· Πόθου δὲ καὶ Ὁμίχλης μιγέντων ὡς δυεῖν ἀρχαῖν
Ἀέρα γενέσθαι καὶ Αὔραν, . . . πάλιν δὲ ἐκ τούτων ἀμφοῖν Ὦτον γεννηθῆναι. There
is some confusion here; πόθος ought to be the name of the συμπλοκή itself, as in
Sanchuniathon, or of the Power which presides over the συμπλοκή, and not the
name of one of the two who are joined in marriage. Perhaps we ought to read
Χρόνου δέ in place of Πόθου δέ. It is probable that Χρόνος is Κρόνος, i.e. the
Phoenician god El. There are two ἀρχαί; but they have little resemblance to the
two ἀρχαί of Sanchuniathon. Is Ὦτος the same as the μώτ of Sanchuniathon? If
so, it is differently dealt with, and is made a son of Ἀήρ and Αὔρα (two different
forms of πνεῦμα), instead of being married to πνεῦμα.

Damascius ib. mentions also a cosmogony of the Phoenician Mochus, in which
the two ἀρχαί are Αἰθήρ and Ἀήρ. These correspond to the Ἀήρ and Αὔρα of the
'Sidonian' cosmogony; and they probably mean either 'the upper air' and 'the
lower air' (cf. the αἰθήρ and ἀήρ of the *Epinomis*), or 'bright air' and 'dark air'.

These two Phoenician cosmogonies do not show any such resemblance to that of
the Hebrew *Genesis* as is apparent in the cosmogony of Sanchuniathon.

¹ The words αὐτὸ . . . κτίσιν are unintelligible, and have presumably been
inserted by error. If we read αὐτὸς δὲ . . . τὴν αὐτοῦ κτίσιν, we might take them to
be a note appended by a Christian, and suggested by the mention of κτίσις in the
preceding clause : 'The deluded heathen who wrote this did not know how he
himself had been created.'

² With the alterations which I have made, we get an intelligible sentence. 'This
(namely, the intermixture of the two primal things, *pneuma* and *mōt*,) was the
beginning of the creation of all things ; and from the marriage of *mōt* and *pneuma*
came forth all the brood of things created.' [καὶ ἐκ ταύτης ἐγένετο] is a doublet of
καὶ ἐκ τῆς . . . συμπλοκῆς . . . ἐγένετο above.

³ It is clear that the words ἦν δέ τινα . . . οὐρανοῦ κατόπται have been wrongly
inserted here. It would be absurd to talk about ζῷα at a stage when the production
of ζῷα cannot yet have taken place, and when even the cosmic sphere has not yet been
shaped. (Its shaping is first spoken of in the following sentence.) It is to be
presumed that these misplaced fragments have come from the paragraph which
followed the κοσμογονία of Sanchuniathon, and which Eusebius calls his ζῳογονία.

I suppose the strange phrase ζῷα οὐκ ἔχοντα αἴσθησιν (which, in the terminology
of the Greek schools, would be self-contradictory,) is a translation of some Semitic
equivalent of the term ἄλογα ζῷα, and means the beasts ; and the 'animals which
possess intelligence and contemplate heaven' must be the human race. Cf. εἰς
κατοπτείαν οὐρανοῦ in *Corp.* III. 3 b, where 'the contemplation of heaven' is
mentioned as one of the functions of man, or one of the purposes for which he has
been made. It is a thought which very commonly occurs in Hellenistic writings,
that men, in contrast to the beasts, have been so constructed as to stand erect, in
order that they may look up to heaven. See note on *Corp.* XII ii. 20 a.

The clause about men can hardly have been intended to follow immediately
after the clause about beasts; for if it were, ἐξ ὧν would refer to the beasts, and it
would be implied that the writer held men to be descended from beasts, which is
not likely. More probably, we have here two separate fragments, and ἐξ ὧν (if
rightly read) refers to something which has been lost.

ζωφασημίν is Semitic. The words of which it is a transliteration are those which
in Hebrew would take the form *tsōpheh*, 'one who watches', and *hash-shāmayim*,
'heaven'. Philo Byblius is therefore right in saying that it means οὐρανοῦ κατόπται.
He has here retained a phrase of the Semitic original, and added his translation of

σχήματι,¹ ⟨. . .⟩.² καὶ ἐξέλαμψε⟨ν⟩ [[μῶτ]] ἥλιός τε καὶ σελήνη, ἀστέρες τε καὶ ἄστρα μεγάλα."³

τοιαύτη μὲν (says Eusebius) αὐτῶν ἡ κοσμογονία, ἄντικρυς ἀθεότητα εἰσάγουσα· ἴδωμεν δὲ ἑξῆς ὡς καὶ τὴν ζῳογονίαν⁴ ὑποστῆναι λέγει. φησὶν οὖν (ὁ Σαγχουνιάθων)· "[[καὶ τοῦ ἀέρος διαυγασθέντος⁵ διὰ ⟨τὴν τοῦ ἡλίου⟩ πύρωσιν⁶ καὶ τῆς θαλάσσης καὶ τῆς γῆς, ἐγένετο πνεύματα καὶ νέφη καὶ

it. (Perhaps Philo may have written ζωφὲ ἁ(σ)σημίν, which would agree more closely with the Hebrew.)

It is evident from this and other indications that Philo Byblius is telling the truth when he says that his work is a translation of a Semitic text. He did not then invent the so-called 'writings of Sanchuniathon' out of his own head, as has sometimes been supposed ; he had them before him, written in Phoenician, or some cognate language, and translated them out of that language into Greek. But the Semitic original which he translated must have been of recent date. As the *cosmogonia* with which it began was constructed, like that of *Corp.* III, by blending data supplied by *Genesis* I with conceptions derived from Stoic physics, it cannot have been written before the third century B. C.; and it is most likely that it was written either after the Christian era, or not long before it.

¹ Something 'was moulded into an egg-like (i. e. spherical) form'. The subject of ἀνεπλάσθη has been lost. It must have been τὸ μῶτ ; and I have accordingly transposed μῶτ to this place from the following sentence, where it interrupts the sense. The mass of unformed matter, under the influence of the *pneuma* by which it was now permeated, was moulded into the shape of a spherical Kosmos.

The world-egg occurs in Egyptian and Orphic cosmogonies, but not, as far as I know, in Babylonian documents.

² A passage describing the separation of the four elements, and corresponding to *Corp.* III. 2 a, must have occurred here; but it has been lost. Something of the sort is presupposed in what follows (ἐπειδὴ διεκρίθη κ.τ.λ.).

³ This sentence corresponds to *Corp.* III. 2 b.

⁴ A *zoogonia* must mean an account of the origin of beasts and men, such as is given in *Corp.* III. 3 a *sq.* Eusebius here says that he is going to give the *zoogonia* of Sanchuniathon ; and at the end of the paragraph which these words introduce, he says that he has given it (τοιαύτη αὐτοῖς καὶ ἡ ζῳογονία). Yet he does nothing of the sort. It is true that the disconnected fragment with which this paragraph ends (καὶ ἐκινήθη . . . ἄρρεν καὶ θῆλυ) may very well have occurred in a *zoogonia.* But in the rest of the paragraph, not a word is said about the origin of beasts and men. It deals with an entirely different topic ; it is an explanation of the origin of thunderstorms. And the subject of thunderstorms is apparently introduced for the purpose of explaining how men (τὰ νοερὰ ζῷα), assumed to be already living on the earth, came to imagine a thunder-god, and to worship this imaginary being. The *zoogonia* then has disappeared, all except three detached scraps, two of which (viz. ἦν δέ τινα ζῷα οὐκ ἔχοντα αἴσθησιν and ἐξ ὧν . . . οὐρανοῦ κατόπται) have got into wrong places ; and a theory of thunderstorms has been substituted for it. This explanation of thunderstorms probably occurred later on in the Sanchuniathon-document, and has been transposed to this place through some blunder. It is based on the Stoic physics ; and the writer's object is to show that the phenomena of thunderstorms, which men mistakenly attribute to the action of a personal god, result from the operation of physical laws. The passage shows the same atheistic tendency as the other extracts from 'Sanchuniathon', in which it is asserted that the gods of the traditional mythologies are not gods, but men who lived a long time ago.

⁵ διαυγάσαντος Euseb.

⁶ The πύρωσις is the heat and light of the sun (cf. διὰ τὴν τοῦ ἡλίου πύρωσιν below). There may have been a preceding mention of φῶς (as in *Genesis* and *Corp.* III) at the beginning of the lost passage on the separation of the elements ; but it is also possible that the writer of the Sanchuniathon-document deliberately

οὐρανίων ὑδάτων μέγισται καταφοραὶ καὶ χύσεις· καὶ ⟨γὰρ⟩ ἐπειδὴ διεκρίθη ⟨τὰ στοιχεῖα⟩¹ καὶ ⟨εἰς⟩ τοὺ⟨ς⟩ ἰδίου⟨ς⟩ τόπου⟨ς⟩ διεχωρίσθη, [διὰ τὴν τοῦ ἡλίου πύρωσιν]² [καὶ] πάλιν συνήντησε πάντα ἐν ἀέρι τάδε τοῖσδε, καὶ συνέρραξαν, βρονταί τε ἀπετελέσθησαν καὶ ἀστραπαί. καὶ πρὸς τὸν πάταγον τῶν βροντῶν τὰ προγεγραμμένα νοερὰ ζῷα ⌈ἐγρηγόρησεν⌉,³ καὶ πρὸς τὸν ἦχον ἐπτύρη· ⟨. . .⟩.⁴]] καὶ ἐκινήθη ἔν τε γῇ καὶ θαλάσσῃ ἄρρεν καὶ θῆλυ."

τοιαύτη αὐτοῖς (says Eusebius) καὶ ἡ ζῳογονία. τούτοις ἑξῆς ὁ αὐτὸς συγγραφεὺς (sc. Philo Bybl.) ἐπιφέρει λέγων· "ταῦθ' ηὑρέθη ἐν τῇ κοσμογονίᾳ γεγραμμένα Τααύτου καὶ τοῖς ἐκείνου ὑπομνήμασιν,⁵ ἔκ τε στοχασμῶν

diverged from *Genesis* in this respect, because, like modern readers, he found it difficult to understand how there could be light before the sun had come into existence.

¹ When the Kosmos was first formed, the elements were separated, and arranged in distinct strata; but 'after their separation' (i. e. in the world as we know it), portions of them are continually quitting the regions originally assigned to them; fire, in the form of light and heat, descends from above, and watery exhalations rise from below. These detached portions of the higher and lower elements come into contact with one another in the atmosphere, and their conflict produces storms. This theory of storms resembles the meteorology of Posidonius.

² This is probably a doublet of διὰ ⟨τὴν τοῦ ἡλίου⟩ πύρωσιν above.

³ ἐγρηγόρησεν must be either a misreading or an inexact translation of some Semitic verb. Something like 'were startled' is wanted, to correspond to ἐπτύρη ('were scared').

⁴ ('and they thought there must be a God who thunders, and they began to worship him.') Cf. Sext. Emp. 9. 24: εἰσι δὲ οἱ ἀπὸ τῶν γιγνομένων κατὰ τὸν κόσμον παραδόξων ὑπονοήσαντες εἰς ἔννοιαν ἡμᾶς ἐληλυθέναι θεῶν· ἀφ' ἧς φαίνεται εἶναι δόξης καὶ ὁ Δημόκριτος· ὁρῶντες γάρ, φησί, τὰ ἐν τοῖς μετεώροις παθήματα οἱ παλαιοὶ τῶν ἀνθρώπων, καθάπερ βροντὰς καὶ ἀστραπὰς κεραυνούς τε καὶ ἄστρων συνόδους ἡλίου τε καὶ σελήνης ἐκλείψεις, ἐδειματοῦντο, θεοὺς οἰόμενοι τούτων αἰτίους εἶναι. Similarly Critias, in his account of the origin of religion (Diels *Vorsokr.* p. 621), mentions, *inter alia*, ἀστραπὰς . . . δεινὰ δὲ κτυπήματα βροντῆς.

⁵ Cf. Philo Bybl. in Euseb. *ib.* 1. 9. 24: ὁ Σαγχουνιάθων . . . τὰ ἐξ ἀρχῆς, ἀφ' οὗ τὰ πάντα συνέστη, παρὰ πάντων εἰδέναι ποθῶν, πολὺ φροντιστικῶς ἐξεμάστευσε τὰ Τααύτου, εἰδὼς ὅτι τῶν ὑφ' ἡλίῳ γεγονότων πρῶτός ἐστι [[Τάαυτος ὁ]] τῶν γραμμάτων τὴν εὕρεσιν ἐπινοήσας καὶ τῆς τῶν ὑπομνημάτων γραφῆς κατάρξας ⟨⟨ὁ Τάαυτος⟩⟩, [[καὶ ἀπὸ τοῦδε ὥσπερ κρηπῖδα βαλόμενος τοῦ λόγου]]—ὃν Αἰγύπτιοι μὲν ἐκάλεσαν Θωύθ, Ἀλεξανδρεῖς δὲ Θώθ, Ἑρμῆν δὲ Ἕλληνες μετέφρασαν,—⟨⟨καὶ ἀπὸ τοῦδε ὥσπερ κρηπῖδα βαλόμενος τοῦ λόγου⟩⟩. (This sentence, as given in the MSS., is intolerably clumsy and confused; I have made the meaning clear by transposing Τάαυτος and καὶ ἀπὸ . . . τοῦ λόγου.)

'Taautos' is the Egyptian Thoth; and in the text above, Philo Byblius says that Sanchuniathon constructed his *cosmogonia* out of material which he found in the writings of Thoth, and supplemented by his own reflections. Philo Bybl. must have read a statement to that effect in the Sanchuniathon-document. This might be thought to indicate that the author of that document had access to some of the Greek *Hermetica*; and in that case, *Corp.* III itself might possibly have been known to him. But it is more likely that his statement that he had read and made use of writings of Thoth was a mere figment. He certainly had no scruple about inventing authorities; for in another passage (Porphyr. *ap.* Euseb. *ib.* 1. 9. 21), when he was speaking about his sources for early Hebrew history, he mentioned, as one of the most important of them, certain memoirs written by ''Ἱερόμβαλος (Jerubbaal), priest of the god Ἰευώ (Jahwe)'. He must have got the name Jerubbaal (which is the other name of Gideon, the Hebrew ' Judge ',) out of the

καὶ τεκμηρίων ὧν ἑώρακεν αὐτοῦ (sc. τοῦ Σαγχουνιάθωνος) ἡ διάνοια καὶ
ηὗρε καὶ ἡμῖν ἐφώτισεν."

If we compare the *cosmogonia* of 'Sanchuniathon' with *Corp*. III,
we find that in their theology the two writers are at opposite poles.
The author of *Corp*. III makes it his object to assert the supremacy
of God over φύσις. The author of the Sanchuniathon-document, on
the other hand, is content with φύσις, and sees no need of a God.
As Eusebius expresses it, ἄντικρυς ἀθεότητα εἰσάγει· 'his doctrine is
sheer atheism'. He recognizes no deity at all ;—except indeed that
he so far personifies his two physical ἀρχαί, the μώτ and the πνεῦμα,
i. e. the primal 'mud' and the primal 'gas', as to say that one of
them fell in love with the other ;[1] and even that, perhaps, is not
much more than a figure of speech.

But in other respects, there are close resemblances between the
two documents. Both writers agree in saying that (leaving God out
of account) the two things which existed in the beginning, and out of
which the universe has been evolved, were 'mud' and 'gas' ; and
the two cosmogonies seem to have been arranged in the same order,
and constructed on similar lines, though this is less apparent, owing
to the loss of parts of the Sanchuniathon-document. Both writers
were acquainted with the Stoic physics ; and both of them had read
the first chapter of *Genesis*. The author of *Corp*. III had read that
chapter in the Greek translation of the LXX, and the other writer
probably in the Hebrew text. There is no reason to suppose that
either of them borrowed from the other ; but both these cosmogonies
were constructed out of the same or similar materials.

Corp. III shows hardly a trace of Platonism ;[2] and its writer
definitely rejects the Platonic doctrine of the survival of the individual
soul. It contains nothing distinctively Egyptian ; and there is not

Book of Judges, and invented the historical writings of that ancient chief. (It may
be remarked in passing that a man who had read the *Book of Judges* must almost
necessarily have read the first chapter of *Genesis*, and had its contents in mind
when he was composing a cosmogony.) He would not hesitate then, if it suited
his purpose, to invent cosmogonic writings of Thoth, who must have been known
to him by report as an ancient Egyptian sage, believed to have been the earliest of
all writers upon earth, and the author of the sacred books which the Egyptian
priests had in their keeping. And he may very likely have assumed that Moses,
whose *Book of Genesis* was one of the sources which he really used, had derived his
cosmogonic knowledge from earlier writings of Thoth.

[1] Compare the statement that the two light elements, fire and air, are 'male',
and the two heavy elements, earth and water, are 'female' (Hippol. *Ref. haer.* 4. 43,
quoted in note on *Corp.* I. 17).

[2] See note on πᾶσαν ἐνσαρκοῖ ψυχήν in § 3 b.

the slightest sign of Christian influence. The document may be shortly described as Judaeo-Stoic.

I can find no clear indication of date in *Corp*. III. It might conceivably have been written at any time after the translation of *Genesis* into Greek, and the rise of Stoicism, in the third century B. C., and before the date of the latest of our Hermetic writings, which is probably not far from A. D. 300. If we could be sure that the heading in which it is ascribed to Hermes Trismegistus was written by the author of the document, that might be a reason for presuming that it was not very far separated in time from the other *Hermetica*, most of which were written almost certainly after the Christian era, and probably not before the second century at the earliest. But there is nothing in the document itself to connect it with Hermes; and it is quite possible that it was written in complete independence of the Hermetic tradition, and that the superscription which attributes it to Hermes was added at some later time, when it had passed into the hands of a Hermetist. It differs markedly in character and style from most of the other *Hermetica*. It shows traces of a connexion with *Corp*. I, which contains a similar *cosmogonia*, and presents similar evidence of acquaintance with the early chapters of *Genesis*. But *Corp*. I also differs widely from the bulk of the *Hermetica*; and in all the rest of the Hermetic literature, signs of Jewish influence are few and faint.[1]

But though it is conceivable that *Corp*. III may have been written in the third or second century B.C., so early a date is hardly probable. It seems reasonable to consider that attempts to amalgamate the Mosaic account of the creation with the Stoic cosmology are not likely to have been made until both had been long and widely known; and the prominence given to astral influences in the system of *Corp*. III connects it with the later rather than the earlier Stoicism. The resemblance between this document and the *cosmogonia* of Sanchuniathon makes it likely that both belong to the same period; and I am inclined to conjecture that both of them were written in the first century A. D.

Title. ⟨ὅτι⟩ πρῶτος ἀπάντων (δόξα πάντων MSS.) ὁ θεός. The δόξα of God, i. e. his 'glory', was frequently spoken of by Jews (see Bousset, *Rel. des Judentums*, pp. 362 and 398); but I can find no

---

[1] The peculiar use of ὁ τόπος in *Corp*. II is probably of Jewish origin; and some of the Hermetic fragments quoted by Cyril show knowledge of the first chapter of *Genesis*.

meaning in the statement that God is the δόξα of things. God might be called ἀρχὴ πάντων, or πηγὴ πάντων, or ῥίζα πάντων; but it is difficult to see how any of these words could be corrupted into δόξα. It seems more probable that the author wrote πρῶτος ἀπάντων. (Cf. *Corp.* VIII. 2 *init.*: πρῶτος γὰρ πάντων . . . ὁ δημιουργὸς τῶν ὅλων θεός.) The word πρῶτος may have been written in the abbreviated form ᾱος (see *Corp.* I. 6). If we assume that the second word was ἀπάντων, that gives an α to follow; and the letters ΑΟΣΑ might easily be read as ΔΟΞΑ.

The MSS. give the words ⌈δόξα⌉ πάντων ὁ θεός . . . καὶ φύσις θεία as the beginning of the discourse. But it is more likely that these words were written as a heading, with ὅτι before them, and that the discourse itself began with the sentence which follows (ἀρχὴ τῶν ὄντων ὁ θεός κ.τ.λ.). This accounts for the repetition of ὁ θεός, which would otherwise be purposeless.

καὶ ⟨ἡ⟩ φύσις θεία. The writer both begins and ends by asserting that 'nature is divine', that is to say, that the force by which all cosmic processes are carried on issues from God, and is directed by God's sovereign will. He must therefore have had in mind some persons who denied that doctrine. His position is that of the Stoics, who employed the word φύσις, among other terms, to describe God's working in the universe. The contrary view was held in its extreme form by the Epicureans. But the Aristotelians also were inclined to minimize the action of the Divine in the sublunar world, and to speak of φύσις as a power distinct from God and working independently of him; and some people, for that reason, denounced them as little better than Epicureans.[1] The Aristotelian Strato (who was called ὁ φυσικός) went so far as to 'renounce the idea of God as a being separate and distinct from the world as a whole, and content himself with φύσις', which he regarded as 'a necessary force operating without consciousness and reflection' (Zeller, *Aristotle*, Eng. tr. II, p. 455). And the position of the sceptical Academics was similar. E. g. in Cic. *Nat. deor.* 3. 27, the Academic speaker says 'At enim (quaeritur) unde animum arripuerimus, si nullus fuerit

---

[1] E. g. the Platonist Atticus (*c.* A. D. 170), in Euseb. *Pr. ev.* 15. 5. 7: ὁ μὲν Πλάτων εἰς θεὸν καὶ ἐκ θεοῦ πάντα ἀνάπτει· but Aristotle, like Epicūrus, denies that the world is governed by God. "τί οὖν ;" φήσαι τις ἄν· "ἐν ταὐτῷ τάττεις Ἀριστοτέλην καὶ Ἐπίκουρον ;" πάνυ μὲν οὖν, ὥς γε πρὸς τὸ προκείμενον· . . . κατ' ἴσον γὰρ παρ' ἀμφοτέροις τὸ ἐκ θεῶν ἀμελὲς εἰς τοὺς ἀνθρώπους. . . . Epicurus banishes the gods to a place outside the Kosmos; but Aristotle, ὑπ' αὐτὴν τὴν ὄψιν τῶν θεῶν τὰ ἀνθρώπινα πράγματα ὑποθείς, εἴασεν ἀτημέλητα καὶ ἀφρόντιστα, φύσει τινὶ καὶ οὐ θεοῦ λογισμῷ διοικούμενα.

in mundo. . . . Naturae ista sunt, . . . omnia cientis et agitantis
motibus et mutationibus suis. . . . Illa vero ⌐cohaeret et permanet⌐
(cohaerent et permanent *edd.*) naturae viribus, non deorum '. *Ib.* 2.
81, the Stoic speaker contrasts the two views: ' alii naturam esse
censent vim quandam sine ratione cientem motus in corporibus
necessarios ; alii autem (*sc.* the Stoics) vim participem rationis atque
ordinis, (i. e. 'divine',) . . . cuius sollertiam . . . nemo opifex con-
sequi possit imitando.' Lactant. *Div. inst.* 2. 8. 23 (criticizing the
Academic speaker in Cic. *Nat. deor.*): 'melius igitur Seneca . . . ,
qui vidit nihil aliud esse naturam quam deum. . . . Cum igitur ortum
rerum tribuis naturae ac detrahis deo, (you are in error).'

1 a. ἀρχὴ τῶν ὄντων ὁ θεός, καὶ νοῦ, καὶ φύσεως, καὶ ὕλης (καὶ νοῦς
καὶ φύσις καὶ ὕλη MSS.). φύσις is the force which works on ὕλη ;
and the external world consists of ὕλη and φύσις in combination.
νοῦς, I suppose, is here the human mind, in contrast to the external
world ; cf. ' quaeritur unde animum arripuerimus ' in Cic. *Nat. deor.*,
quoted above.

If I have restored the words rightly, the writer says that God is
the source (or maker) of ὕλη. Cf. *Abammonis Resp.* (*Testim.*) 8. 3 :
ὕλην δὲ παρήγαγεν ὁ θεός, κ.τ.λ. The statement that God is ἀρχὴ
ὕλης contradicts the Platonic doctrine that ὕλη is without beginning,
and exists independently of God ; but it agrees with the doctrine
taught (in later times at least) by the Jews, and adopted from
them by the Christians, that God made the world *ex nihilo*, and
not out of pre-existent ὕλη. Origen, *De princip.* 2. 9. 1, says that
God τοσαύτην ὕλην κατεσκεύασεν, ὅσην ἠδύνατο κατακοσμῆσαι. Lactantius, *Div. inst.* 1. 5. 9 and 2. 8. 8 ff., says that God first made
materia (ὕλη), and then made all things out of it. The question
whether ὕλη is or is not ἀγέννητος and σύγχρονος τῷ θεῷ (coeval
with God) is discussed at some length in Methodius Περὶ τοῦ
αὐτεξουσίου.

σοφία(ς) εἰς δεῖξιν ⟨ποιήσας πάντ⟩α. Cf. *Corp.* XIV. 3 : the Maker
of the universe is μόνος ὄντως σοφὸς τὰ πάντα. The word σοφία was
used by Jews especially, but sometimes by Stoics also, in connexion
with God's making of the world.

For the thought, cf. Methodius Περὶ τοῦ αὐτεξουσίου 22. 3 (see
prefatory note on *Ascl. Lat.* II) : φημὶ τοιγαροῦν πολλὰς ὑποθέσεις
ὑπάρχειν τῷ θεῷ καθ' ἃς δημιουργεῖν αὐτὸν ἔδει· πρῶτον μὲν ⟨τὴν⟩ τῆς
τέχνης ἐπιστήμην, ἣν ἀργεῖν [μὲν] οὐκ ἐχρῆν. . . . ὥσπερ γὰρ εἴ τις ἐπιστήμην ἔχων ἢ μουσικῆς ἢ αὖ πάλιν ἰατρικῆς ἢ τεκτονικῆς, εἰς ὅσον τοῦ

ἔργου μὴ ἔχεται μηδὲ δι' αὐτοῦ τὴν ἐπιστήμην δείκνυσιν, μάτην ⟨τὴν⟩ τέχνην ἔχειν δοκεῖ, μήτε αὐτὸς ἀπολαύων ὧν ἐπίσταται, μήτε ἑτέροις γνῶσιν παρέχων τούτων τῶν ἔργων, καὶ τὸ ἐντεῦθεν ὅμοιος τῷ μηδὲ τὴν ἀρχὴν ἐπισταμένῳ γίγνεται, μὴ οὔσης τῆς τέχνης ἐνεργοῦς· ἑκάστῃ γὰρ τῶν τεχνῶν διὰ τῆς ἐνεργείας τὴν δεῖξιν λαμβάνει καί, ὡς λόγον εἰπεῖν, τὴν τοῦ εἶναι σύστασιν.

καὶ τοῦ θεοῦ ἐνέργεια ἡ φύσις, κατ' ἀνάγκην καὶ τέλος καὶ ἀνανέωσιν (ἐνεργοῦσα).—(τὸ θεῖον καὶ ἡ φύσις καὶ ἐνέργεια καὶ ἀνάγκη καὶ τέλος καὶ ἀνανέωσις MSS.) It is difficult to see what could be meant by ἐνέργεια coupled with φύσις and ἀνάγκη, and placed between them. It is true that the word ἐνέργειαι is sometimes used in the sense of αἱ τοῦ θεοῦ ἐνέργειαι, 'God's workings' (see *Corp.* X. 1 b and 22 b); but there would be no reason here for inserting ἐνέργεια in that sense. It seems more likely that ἐνέργεια has been shifted, and that what the author said is that ἡ φύσις is τοῦ θεοῦ ἐνέργεια. Cf. *Corp.* XI. i. 5 *init.*: εἴτε ἀνάγκην, εἴτε πρόνοιαν, εἴτε φύσιν, εἴτε ἄλλο τι οἴεται . . . τις, τοῦτο ἐστιν ὁ θεὸς ἐνεργῶν. See also *Ascl. Lat.* III. 39 (Lydus).

The word ἀνάγκη is here a synonym for εἱμαρμένη; and in the view of the writer of *Corp.* III, 'necessity' or 'destiny' is brought to bear on things below by the movements of the heavenly bodies. (See § 4.) τέλος, coupled with ἀνανέωσις, must mean τελευτή, i. e. extinction. τέλος and ἀνανέωσις together (the 'extinction' and 'renewal' of sublunar things) are wrought by φύσις, the action of which is determined by the movements of the heavenly bodies; and these movements are themselves determined by God's will. φύσις is therefore θεία.

1 b. ἦν γὰρ σκότος [[ἄπειρον]] ἐν ἀβύσσῳ, καὶ ὕδωρ ⟨⟨ἄπειρον⟩⟩, καὶ πνεῦμα λεπτὸν κ.τ.λ. Some epithet of ὕδωρ is wanted, to match the epithets applied to πνεῦμα; and the sentence is improved by shifting ἄπειρον.

The author evidently had in mind the similar words in *Gen.* 1 (σκότος ἐπάνω τοῦ ἀβύσσου LXX). It would be easy to bring the text into still closer agreement with *Genesis* by writing ἐπ' ἀβύσσῳ in place of ἐν ἀβύσσῳ.

καὶ πνεῦμα λεπτὸν νοερόν, δυνάμει θείᾳ (. . . .)ον τὰ ἐν χάει. The writer has taken over from *Genesis* the πνεῦμα θεοῦ which 'moved upon the face of the waters' (ἐπεφέρετο ἐπάνω τοῦ ὕδατος LXX); but he identifies it with the πνεῦμα of the Stoics, i. e. the gaseous substance (a mixture of air and fire) which pervades and animates the Kosmos. This substance is λεπτόν ('rare'), as compared with the denser mass of τὰ ἐν χάει; and it is νοερόν, i. e. living, conscious, and intelligent.

A participle agreeing with πνεῦμα, and governing τὰ ἐν χάει, has been lost. The Stoic word διῆκον ('pervading' or 'permeating') may be conjectured ; but the LXX would rather suggest ἐπιφερόμενον τοῖς ἐν χάει.

⟨⟨ἀδιορίστων δὲ ὄντων ἁπάντων καὶ ἀκατασκευάστων.⟩⟩ These words are out of place in the MSS. ; they must have preceded the description of the *demiurgia*, which begins with the emission of light (ἀνείθη δὴ φῶς ἅγιον). The word ἀκατασκευάστων shows that the writer's source was the LXX, and not the Hebrew *Genesis*. In the LXX, the corresponding words are ἡ δὲ γῆ ἦν ἀόρατος καὶ ἀκατασκεύαστος ; and it is very unlikely that two persons would independently hit on ἀκατασκεύαστος as a translation of the Hebrew *bohu*.

[[καὶ ἐπάγη ὑπ' ἄμμῳ ἐξ ὑγρᾶς οὐσίας]]. The author cannot have said that *the light* 'was solidified out of watery substance'; light is not a solid body. These words doubtless belong to the following passage about the elements (§ 2 a), and describe the formation of the solid earth by separation out of the hitherto undifferentiated mud or slime.

⟨καὶ ἐγένετο τὰ⟩ στοιχεῖα [καὶ θεοὶ πάντες]. The results which followed on the emission of light are first shortly summed up in these words, and then more fully described in § 2 a. The θεοί recognized by the author of *Corp.* III are the heavenly bodies (§§ 2 b, 3 b, and 4), and the cosmic elements (§ 3 a *init.*). But to couple θεοί in the sense of cosmic elements with στοιχεῖα would be to say the same thing twice over ; and a mention of the heavenly bodies at this stage would be premature. It seems best therefore to assume that καὶ θεοὶ πάντες has been added by a later hand.

§ 2 a. ἀπεχωρίσθη (ἀποδιωρίσθη MSS.) τὰ ἐλαφρὰ εἰς ὕψος κ.τ.λ. This passage corresponds to the dividing of 'the waters under the firmament' from 'the waters above the firmament' in *Genesis*. In the Stoic physics, which the writer of *Corp.* III had adopted, there were no 'waters above the firmament'; he therefore took the 'waters' here spoken of in *Genesis* to stand for matter in general. He substituted the lighter elements (τὰ ἀνωφερῆ, fire and air,) for 'the waters above the firmament', and the heavier elements (τὰ κατωφερῆ, water and earth,) for 'the waters under the firmament', and proceeded to describe the separation of the four elements, in accordance with Stoic doctrine. The text is badly damaged, but his meaning seems to have been as follows. In the beginning, there were two distinct things, viz. ὕδωρ ἄπειρον and πνεῦμα λεπτόν. The

former was not exactly water, but the substance out of which earth
and water were subsequently differentiated ; and similarly, the πνεῦμα
was not air or fire, but the substance out of which fire and air were
subsequently differentiated. We might call the one 'mud', and the
other 'gas'. The 'gas' was living and intelligent (νοερόν); the
'mud' was presumably inert and lifeless.¹ When light appeared,
the separation of the elements took place. The 'gas' (τὰ ἐλαφρὰ)
rose, and was differentiated into two distinct elements, fire and air ;
and the fire rose above the air. (This seems to be the meaning of
ἀνακρεμασθέντος ⟨τοῦ πυρὸς τῷ⟩ πνεύματι ὀχεῖσθαι.) The 'mud' (τὰ
βαρέα) sank, and was differentiated into two distinct elements, water
and earth ; and the earth settled down, partly in the form of sand ²
at the bottom of the sea, and partly in the form of dry land. (Compare what is said about the separation of the elements in *Corp.* I. 5 b.)
The Stoics described the *diacosmesis* as follows. Zeno, in Arius
Didymus, Diels *Doxogr.* p. 469 : τοιαύτην δὲ δεήσει εἶναι ἐν περιόδῳ
τὴν τοῦ ὅλου διακόσμησιν ἐκ τῆς οὐσίας· ὅταν ἐκ πυρὸς τροπὴ εἰς ὕδωρ δι'
ἀέρος γένηται, τὸ μέν τι ὑφίστασθαι καὶ γῆν συνίστασθαι, [καὶ] ἐκ τοῦ
λοίπου δὲ τὸ μὲν διαμένειν ὕδωρ, ἐκ δὲ τοῦ ἀτμιζομένου ἀέρα γίνεσθαι, ἔκ
τινος δὲ τοῦ ἀέρος πῦρ ἐξάπτειν.³ Cleanthes (*ib.* p. 470) : ἐκφλογι-
σθέντος τοῦ παντός, συνίζειν τὸ μέσον αὐτοῦ πρῶτον, εἶτα τὰ ἐχόμενα
ἀποσβέννυσθαι δι' ὅλου. τοῦ δὲ παντὸς ἐξυγρανθέντος ⌈τὸ ἔσχατον τοῦ
πυρὸς ἀντιτυπήσαντος αὐτῷ τοῦ μέσου⌉⁴ τρέπεσθαι πάλιν εἰς τοὐναντίον,
εἶθ' οὕτω τρεπόμενον ἄνω φησὶν αὔξεσθαι, καὶ ἄρχεσθαι διακοσμεῖν τὸ
ὅλον. Chrysippus, in Plut. *Sto. repugn.* 41, p. 1053 : ἡ δὲ πυρὸς μεταβολή ἐστι τοιαύτη· δι' ἀέρος εἰς ὕδωρ τρέπεται· κἀκ τούτου γῆς ὑφιστα-
μένης ἀὴρ ἀναθυμιᾶται· λεπτυνομένου δὲ τοῦ ἀέρος ὁ αἰθὴρ περιχεῖται

---

¹ As the participle preceding τὰ ἐν χάει has been lost, we are left in doubt how
the writer conceived the original relation between these two substances. He may
have said that the 'gas' was above (ἐπεφέρετο ἐπάνω LXX), and the 'mud' below.
But the words ἀπεχωρίσθη τὰ ἐλαφρὰ εἰς ὕψος are more easily explained if we
assume him to have said that the 'gas' *permeated* the 'mud' (διῆκον). In the latter
case, we must suppose that the two substances were distinct in character, but were
contained in the same space.

² 'Sand' is mentioned in connexion with God's creative action in *Jer.* 5. 22 : τὸν
τάξαντα ἄμμον ὅριον τῇ θαλάσσῃ, . . . καὶ ἠχήσουσιν τὰ κύματα αὐτῆς καὶ οὐχ
ὑπερβήσεται αὐτό. But the ἄμμος of *Corp.* III seems to be the 'foundation' on
which the water rests, i. e. the sandy sea-bottom, and not the sandy shore.

³ Perhaps ἐξάπτεσθαι.

⁴ 'The probable meaning is, that the last remains of the original fire begin a
motion in the opposite direction' (Zeller). Perhaps : τὸ δὲ πᾶν ἐξυγρανθέν, τοῦ
ἐσχάτου τοῦ πυρὸς ἀντιτυπήσαντος αὐτῷ τοῦ μέσου ⟨λειφθέντος⟩, (i. e. 'when the last
of the fire, which has remained in the midst of it, reacts upon it',) τρέπεσθαι πάλιν
εἰς τοὐναντίον· εἶθ' οὕτω τρεπομένου (sc. τοῦ παντός), ἄνω φησὶν αὔξεσθαι ⟨τὸ πῦρ⟩
κ.τ.λ.

κύκλῳ. Chrysipp. in Plut. *ib.* : διόλου μὲν γὰρ ὢν ὁ κόσμος πυρώδης, εὐθὺς καὶ ψυχή ἐστιν ἑαυτοῦ καὶ ἡγεμονικόν·[1] ὅτε δέ, μεταβαλὼν εἰς τὸ ὑγρὸν καὶ τὴν ἐναπολειφθεῖσαν ψυχήν,[2] τρόπον τινὰ εἰς σῶμα καὶ ψυχὴν μετέβαλεν, ὥστε συνεστάναι ἐκ τούτων, ἄλλον τινὰ ἔσχε λόγον. Diog. Laert. 7. 135–137: ἕν τε εἶναι θεὸν καὶ νοῦν καὶ εἱμαρμένην καὶ Δία, πολλαῖς τε ἑτέραις ὀνομασίαις[3] προσονομάζεσθαι. κατ' ἀρχὰς μὲν οὖν καθ' αὑτὸν ὄντα,[4] τρέπειν τὴν πᾶσαν οὐσίαν δι' ἀέρος εἰς ὕδωρ.[5] καὶ ὥσπερ ἐν τῇ γονῇ τὸ σπέρμα[6] περιέχεται, οὕτω καὶ τοῦτον, σπερματικὸν λόγον ὄντα τοῦ κόσμου, τοιόνδε ὑπολιπέσθαι ἐν τῷ ὑγρῷ,[7] εὐεργὸν αὑτῷ ποιοῦντα τὴν ὕλην πρὸς τὴν τῶν ἑξῆς γένεσιν. εἶτα ἀπογεννᾶν πρῶτον τὰ τέσσαρα στοιχεῖα, πῦρ, ὕδωρ, ἀέρα, γῆν. . . . ἀνωτάτω μὲν οὖν εἶναι τὸ πῦρ, ὃ δὴ αἰθέρα καλεῖσθαι, ἐν ᾧ πρώτην τὴν τῶν ἀπλανῶν σφαῖραν γεννᾶσθαι, εἶτα τὴν τῶν πλανωμένων· μεθ' ἣν τὸν ἀέρα· εἶτα τὸ ὕδωρ· ὑποστάθμην δὲ πάντων τὴν γῆν, μέσην ἁπάντων οὖσαν. *Ib.* 142 : γίνεσθαι δὲ τὸν κόσμον, ὅταν ἐκ πυρὸς ἡ οὐσία τραπῇ δι' ἀέρος εἰς ὑγρότητα, εἶτα τὸ παχυμερὲς αὐτοῦ συστὰν ἀποτελεσθῇ γῆ, τὸ δὲ λεπτομερὲς ἐξαραιώθη,[8] καὶ τοῦτ' ἐπὶ πλέον λεπτυνθὲν πῦρ ἀπογεννήσῃ. Clem. Alex. *Strom.* 5. 14. 105 : λέγει[9] ὅτι πῦρ ὑπὸ τοῦ διοικοῦντος λόγου καὶ θεοῦ τὰ σύμπαντα δι' ἀέρος εἰς ὑγρόν, ⌈τὸ ὡς⌉[10] σπέρμα τῆς διακοσμήσεως . . . · ἐκ δὲ τούτου αὖθις γίνεται γῆ καὶ οὐρανὸς καὶ τὰ ἐμπεριεχόμενα. Dio Chrysost.[11] 36. 55, 452 M. :[12] (at the completion of the *ecpyrosis*), λειφθεὶς δὴ μόνος ὁ νοῦς (i. e. the νοερὸν πῦρ, which is God,) . . . οὐδενὸς ἐν αὐτῷ πυκνοῦ λειφθέντος, ἀλλὰ πάσης ἐπικρατούσης μανότητος, . . . τὴν καθαρωτάτην λαβὼν αὐγῆς[13] ἀκηράτου φύσιν, εὐθὺς ἐπόθησε τὸν ἐξ ἀρχῆς βίον.[14] ἔρωτα δὴ λαβὼν . . . ὥρμησεν ἐπὶ τὸ γεννᾶν καὶ διανέμειν ἕκαστα, καὶ δημιουργεῖν

---

[1] I. e. at the completion of the *ecpyrosis*, the world is all soul (= νοερὸν πῦρ).

[2] I. e. when it has changed into a watery mass permeated by a fiery soul (or living πνεῦμα).

[3] Among these many names were φύσις and ἀνάγκη.

[4] At the beginning of each *diacosmesis* there is nothing but fire, and this fire is God.

[5] The fire changes into water, having first become air at an intermediate stage of the process.

[6] Perhaps rather τὸ πνεῦμα, the 'vital spirit' of the individual in its most rudimentary form. Cf. καθάπερ ἐν γονῇ πνεῦμα in Dio Chrysost., quoted below.

[7] I. e. at this stage there exist (1) a watery mass, and (2) God, in the form of νοερὸν πνεῦμα, permeating the mass.

[8] *Al.* ἐξαερωθῇ : 'fortasse ἐξαραιωθὲν ⟨ἀέρα⟩ κᾆτ' ἐπὶ πλέον' Arnim.

[9] *Sc.* Heraclitus (as interpreted by the Stoics).

[10] Perhaps ἔχον ἐν ἑαυτῷ τό.

[11] Dio calls the doctrine which he is here expounding 'Zoroastrian'; but it is mainly, if not wholly, Stoic.

[12] The text here given is based on that of Dindorf, 1857.

[13] αὐγῆς edd. : αὐτὸς codd.

[14] I. e. desired to return to the state of things before the *ecpyrosis*.

τὸν ὄντα νῦν κόσμον .... ἀστράψας¹ δὲ ⌜ὅλον⌝ οὐκ ἄτακτον οὐδὲ ῥυπαρὰν
ἀστραπὴν ...², ἀλλὰ καθαρὰν καὶ ἀμιγῆ παντὸς σκοτεινοῦ, μετέβαλε
ῥᾳδίως ἅμα τῇ νοήσει. μνησθεὶς δὲ ... γενέσεως, ἐπράυνε καὶ ἀνῆκεν
αὑτόν, καὶ πολὺ τοῦ φωτὸς ἀποσβέσας, εἰς ἀέρα πυρώδη³ τρέπεται ⌜πυρὸς
ἠπίου⌝.⁴ μιχθεὶς δὲ τότε "Ηρᾳ⁵ ... ἀφίησι τὴν πᾶσαν αὖ τοῦ παντὸς
γονήν. ... ὑγρὰν δὲ ποιήσας τὴν ὅλην οὐσίαν, [ἐν σπέρμα τοῦ παντός,]⁶
αὐτὸς ἐν τούτῳ διαθέων, καθάπερ ἐν γονῇ πνεῦμα τὸ πλάττον καὶ δημιουργοῦν, [[τότε δὴ μάλιστα ... οὐκ ἀπὸ τρόπου (see below)]] τὰ λοιπὰ ἤδη
ῥᾳδίως πλάττει καὶ τυποῖ, λείαν καὶ μαλακὴν αὐτῷ περιχέας τὴν οὐσίαν
καὶ πᾶσαν εἴκουσαν εὐπετῶς, ⟨⟨τότε δὴ μάλιστα προσεοικὼς τῇ τῶν ἄλλων
συστάσει ζῴων, καθ' ὅσον ἐκ ψυχῆς καὶ σώματος συνεστάναι λέγοιτ' ἂν
οὐκ ἀπὸ τρόπου.⟩⟩⁷ ἐργασάμενος δὲ καὶ τελεώσας ἀπέδειξεν ἐξ ἀρχῆς τὸν
ὄντα κόσμον κ.τ.λ.

According to the Stoic doctrine then, the first stage of the *diacosmesis* consists in the transmutation of the greater part of the universal
fire ('through air') into water; and when this first process has been
completed, the universe is a mass of water, having latent within
it, and diffused throughout it, living and intelligent fire or *pneuma*.
Then follows a second and distinct stage, in which the latent *pneuma*
works on the watery substance through which it is diffused, and
differentiates it into the four cosmic elements.

The writer of *Corp.* III ignores the Stoic doctrine of a periodically
recurrent *ecpyrosis* and *diacosmesis*, and speaks only of a *genesis* of the
Kosmos which took place once for all. He also ignores the first
stage of the *diacosmesis* as described by the Stoics, i.e. the transmutation of the universal fire (all but a hidden remnant) into water. But
the state of things which he assumes to have existed 'in the beginning'

---

¹ I. e. the *demiurgia* or *diacosmesis* began with a flash of light. No such flash
of light occurs in the Stoic *cosmogonia*; this detail then may have been borrowed
by Dio from some oriental source. It is possible even that it may have been
transmitted to him from *Genesis*, in which the creation begins with 'Let there be
light'.
² Not such lightning as we see in storms.
³ 'Fiery air' is πνεῦμα.
⁴ Something like ἐκ πυρὸς ἀμιγοῦς is wanted here.
⁵ 'Hera' means air. This allegorical interpretation of the marriage of Zeus and
Hera was borrowed by Dio from Chrysippus; see Arnim *Sto. vet. fr.* II, p. 314.
⁶ The words ἐν ... παντός break the connexion here, and look like a misplaced
explanation of τὴν πᾶσαν τοῦ παντὸς γονήν.
⁷ I have inserted here the words τότε δὴ ... ἀπὸ τρόπου, which it seems necessary
to remove from the place where they stand in the traditional text. It is only when
God (the πῦρ νοερόν) has fashioned for himself a body composed of gross matter
(αὑτῷ περιχέας τὴν οὐσίαν), that he can be compared to a ζῷον consisting of ψυχή
and σῶμα. For this comparison, cf. Chrysippus, quoted above.

is identical with that which, according to the Stoics, followed on the transmutation of fire into water; and from that point onward, his cosmogony agrees with theirs.

If the founders of Stoicism had invented their system *de novo*, they would have had no motive for interposing a watery chaos between the primal fire and the differentiated elements of the present world; and the more obvious course would have been to say that air, water, and earth were formed from fire by successive condensations.[1] But the conception of a waste of waters out of which the ordered universe has been developed was a piece of earlier tradition which they retained; and there can be little doubt that this tradition was of Babylonian origin. The notion must have arisen in a country where the land was yearly seen emerging from the floods at the end of the rainy season (Gunkel, *Schöpfung und Chaos*, p. 15); and Babylonia is such a country. Long before the time of Zeno the first Stoic, there were ways of communication by which Babylonian notions might be transmitted to Greek thinkers; and the theory of Thales, who held water to be the ἀρχή of all things, may perhaps have been derived from that region. But Zeno's successors, if not Zeno himself, may also have read the writings of Berosus, by which the Babylonian cosmology was more directly and more fully made known to the Greeks. Berosus said that 'in the beginning all was darkness and water'; and after giving a summary of the Babylonian creation-myth, he explained its meaning thus: 'this tale is an allegorical description of natural occurrences. The All was once fluid; . . . but the god Bel . . . divided the darkness in the midst, and so separated earth and heaven from one another, and therewith established the order of the universe.' (Gunkel, *Schöpfung und Chaos*, pp. 17–19.) The account of the beginning of things which is given in the first chapter of *Genesis* was no doubt ultimately derived, in part at least, from the same Babylonian sources; but the two parted streams of tradition had been flowing in separate channels for many centuries, when they were brought together again by the writer of *Corp*. III.

§ 2 b. διηρθρώθη ⟨ἡ πυρίνη οὐσία⟩ σὺν τοῖς ἐν αὐτῇ θεοῖς. αὐτῇ refers to the lost subject of διηρθρώθη, and shows that it must have been feminine. I have inserted ἡ πυρίνη οὐσία; but it would be equally possible to write ἡ πυρίνη φύσις.

---

[1] This is what Chrysippus did say, when he was speaking, not of the first formation of the world, but of that transmutation of the elements which is perpetually going on in the world in which we live. (Arius Didymus, Diels *Doxogr*. p. 458.)

καὶ θεοὶ . . . σὺν τοῖς αὐτῶν σημείοις ἅπασι. These θεοί are the stars.
The writer has taken over the word σημεῖα from the LXX (ἔστωσαν
εἰς σημεῖα, 'let them be for signs'); but he uses it in a different
sense. It here means 'constellations'.

καὶ περιειλίχθη τὸ αἰθέριον κυκλίῳ δρομήματι.—(καὶ περιελήγη (so A)
τὸ περικύκλιον ἀέρι κυκλίῳ δρομήματι MSS.) I have cut out περικύκλιον, which I take to be a doublet of ⌈ἀέρι⌉ κυκλίῳ.

πνεύματι θείῳ ὀχούμενον. Cf. πνεύματι ὀχεῖσθαι above. The revolving
fiery heaven 'rides on' or 'is vehicled upon' the air, which is situated
immediately below it. The writer here applies to the air, as an
element distinct from fire, the same word, πνεῦμα, which he previously
applied to the undifferentiated 'gas'. (For πνεῦμα in the sense of
air, cf. Corp. I. 9.) The air is called θεῖον, as the 'gas' was called
νοερόν before. It is itself a god, as are the other three elements;
and it is God's instrument, by means of which the life he gives is
conveyed into all terrestrial creatures.

§ 3 a. ἀνῆκε δὲ ἕκαστος θεὸς . . . τὸ προσταχθὲν αὐτῷ κ.τ.λ. The
'gods' here spoken of are the several elements. At God's bidding,
the earth produced quadrupeds and reptiles; the water, fishes; the
air, birds; and the earth again, plants. (As to the fire, we have
already been told that the heavenly bodies were formed from it.)
In this paragraph, the writer follows Genesis closely. But he was
dissatisfied with the strange order of events in Genesis, according to
which the plants were created before the heavenly bodies; he therefore shifted the production of plants, and coupled it with the
production of animals.

[καὶ πᾶσα σπορὰ ἔνσπορος]. I take this phrase to be a misplacement of something connected with τὸ σπέρμα τῆς παλιγγενεσίας ἐν
ἑαυτοῖς in the following line. The words are corrupt; but ἔνσπορος
must have been intended to convey the same meaning as the phrase
in Genesis, οὗ τὸ σπέρμα αὐτοῦ ἐν αὐτῷ, 'whose seed is in itself'. In
Genesis, it is the plants alone that are said to 'have seed in them
after their kinds'; but perhaps the writer of Corp. III meant the
phrase to apply to animals and plants together.

§ 3 b. ⟨. . .⟩ τε γενέσεις τῶν ἀνθρώπων. An account of the making
of man, the event in which the whole process of creation culminated,
must necessarily have occurred here; but it has been lost. In the
words γενέσεις τῶν ἀνθρώπων κ.τ.λ., the writer is speaking of the pro-
pagation of the human race, and assumes that at least a first pair of
human beings is already in existence.

[εἰς ἔργων θείων γνῶσιν . . . ἀγαθῶν ἐπίγνωσιν]. This appears to be a doublet of εἰς κατοπτείαν . . . εἴς τε σημεῖα ἀγαθῶν below. Compare the following phrases :—

εἰς ἔργων θείων γνῶσιν   εἰς κατοπτείαν . . . ἔργων θείων
καὶ φύσεως ἐνεργοῦσαν μαρτυρίαν   καὶ φύσεως ἐνεργείας
καὶ ἀγαθῶν ἐπίγνωσιν   εἴς τε σημεῖα ἀγαθῶν

The two passages cannot have been intended to stand together in the same paragraph ; one of them must have been written as an alternative or substitute for the other. The first of the two contains the significant words καὶ (εἰς) πάντων τῶν ὑπ᾽ οὐρανὸν δεσποτείαν, which correspond to the passage in *Genesis*, ἀρχέτωσαν . . . πάσης τῆς γῆς κ.τ.λ. It seems probable that this phrase originally stood in the second passage also, and followed εἰς κατοπτείαν οὐρανοῦ there. When κατοπτεία οὐρανοῦ and πάντων τῶν ὑπ᾽ οὐρανὸν δεσποτεία are brought together, the combination resembles the description of man's twofold function in *Ascl. Lat.* I. 8 : 'et mirari atque adorare caelestia, et [in]colere atque gubernare terrena.'

[καὶ πλῆθος ἀνθρώπων]. These words are meaningless here. Perhaps (εἰς) πλῆθος ἀνθρώπων may have been written as an explanation of ἐν πλήθει below.

εἰς τὸ αὐξάνεσθαι ἐν αὐξήσει καὶ πληθύνεσθαι ἐν πλήθει. This is evidently derived from αὐξάνεσθε καὶ πληθύνεσθε in *Gen.* I. 22 and 28.[1] But how are we to account for the addition of ἐν αὐξήσει and ἐν πλήθει ? This construction is a Hebraism ; but the Hebrew idiom which it represents[2] is not employed in the phrase 'increase and multiply' in *Gen.* I. On the other hand, the very same form of words occurs in *Corp.* I. 18, where we are told that God said to men and beasts αὐξάνεσθε ἐν αὐξήσει καὶ πληθύνεσθε ἐν πλήθει. This looks as if the writer of one of these two documents had borrowed from the other. But it is possible to account for the facts without assuming that either the writer of *Corp.* I or the writer of *Corp.* III had read what the other wrote, if we suppose that both of them alike got the phrase, not indeed from *Genesis* directly, but from some document based on a Semitic paraphrase of *Genesis*, in which the verbs 'increase' and 'multiply' were thus emphasized.

---

[1] Cf. *Gen.* 8. 17 (after the flood): αὐξάνεσθε καὶ πληθύνεσθε ἐπὶ τῆς γῆς. *Gen.* 9. 7 : αὐξάνεσθε καὶ πληθύνεσθε, καὶ πληρώσατε τὴν γῆν καὶ πληθύνεσθε ἐπὶ τῆς γῆς. *Gen.* 17. 20 (of Ishmael) : αὐξανῶ αὐτὸν καὶ πληθυνῶ αὐτὸν σφόδρα. *Gen.* 35. 11 (to Jacob) : αὐξάνου καὶ πληθύνου. *Gen.* 48. 4 (to Jacob): ἐγώ σε αὐξανῶ καὶ πληθυνῶ. *Exod.* 1. 7 : the children of Israel ηὐξήθησαν καὶ ἐπληθύνθησαν.

[2] This Hebrew idiom is differently rendered in *Gen.* 16. 10 (to Hagar) and *Gen.* 22. 17 (to Abraham) : πληθύνων πληθυνῶ τὸ σπέρμα σου.

πᾶσαν ἐνσαρκ(ο)ῖ (ἐν σαρκὶ MSS.) ψυχὴν διὰ δρομήματος θεῶν ἐγκυκλίων. A verb is needed ; and as the writer is here speaking, not of the first creation of man, but of the births which take place in successive generations, the present is the right tense. I have therefore written ἐνσαρκοῖ. In incarnating human souls, God uses the revolutions of the stars as his instrument ; that is, human births are determined by astral influences. (See *Ascl. Lat.* III. 35.) The verb ἐνσαρκοῦν may perhaps have been adopted from some Platonist, as it would more naturally be employed by a person who believed in the pre-existence of the soul ; but it does not necessarily imply this belief. Man is ἔμψυχος, i. e. he consists of a body with a soul inside it ; and the soul may be said to be 'put into the body', though its individual existence begins at the moment of birth. It is clear from what follows that the writer did not himself admit the existence of un-embodied souls.

παρασκευάσας (τερασπορίας MSS.) εἰς κατοπτ(ε)ίαν οὐρανοῦ κ.τ.λ. The strange word τερασπορίας ('sowing of portents'?) is unquestionably due to corruption. It seems clear that some participle must have stood here ; and παρασκευάσας suits the context well. By writing ἐνσαρκοῖ for ἐν σαρκί, and παρασκευάσας for τερασπορίας, the chaos of words in this section can be reduced to grammatical order.

[καὶ δρομήματος οὐρανίων θεῶν.] This is probably a misplaced doublet of διὰ δρομήματος θεῶν ἐγκυκλίων.

⟨⟨εἰς γνῶσιν θείας δυνάμεως⟩⟩ [ἔργων θείων] καὶ φύσεως ἐνεργείας ⟨⟨μαρτυρίαν⟩⟩. The words ἔργων θείων, which occur above in the doublet of this passage, were probably written here as an alternative for θείας δυνάμεως. The balance of the phrases is improved by inserting μαρτυρίαν, which occurs in the doublet. Compare with this clause the description of 'the purpose for which man was made' in *Corp.* IV. 2 as emended : θεατὴς γὰρ τῶν ἔργων τοῦ θεοῦ ὁ ἄνθρωπος· καὶ ⟨ἐπὶ τοῦτο ἐγένετο, τὸ τὸν κόσμον⟩ θαυμάσαι, καὶ γνωρίσαι τὸν ποιήσαντα.

εἴς τε σημείωσιν (σημεῖα MSS.) ἀγαθῶν. By writing σημείωσιν in place of σημεῖα, we get a phrase nearly equivalent to the words ἀγαθῶν ἐπίγνωσιν in the doublet above. σημειοῦσθαι means either 'to mark or note a thing', or 'to infer a thing from indications'.

μοίρας ⌜ὀχλουμένης⌝ γνῶναι ἀγαθῶν καὶ φαύλων. This is an explanation of σημείωσιν ἀγαθῶν. The meaning must be 'to learn to distinguish good things from bad things'. μοῖρα ('a division') may mean 'a class', regarded as divided or distinguished from another class ; and the sense required may be got either by cutting out

ὀχλουμένης, or by writing μοίρας κεχωρισμένας γνῶναι. Cf. Pl. *Phileb.*
54 C : ἐν τῇ τοῦ ἀγαθοῦ μοίρᾳ ἐκεῖνό ἐστι. . . . εἰς ἄλλην ἢ τὴν τοῦ
ἀγαθοῦ μοῖραν (τὴν ἡδονὴν) τιθέντες.

As the author of *Corp.* III had certainly read the first chapter of
Genesis, it is probable that he had read the second and third chapters
also ; and this phrase may have been suggested to him by 'the tree
of the knowledge of good and evil' in *Gen.* 2. But if so, he must
have deliberately rejected the teaching of that passage in one respect.
The God of *Gen.* 2 f. seeks to debar man from 'the knowledge of
good and evil'. The God of the Platonists and Stoics is devoid of
φθόνος, and intends man to acquire that knowledge ; and in this
matter, the writer of *Corp.* III sides with the Platonists and Stoics.

πᾶσαν [ἀγαθῶν] δαιδαλουργίαν εὑρεῖν. ἀγαθῶν is awkward ; and as
the word has occurred twice just before, it is most likely that it has
been repeated here by error. The thought expressed by πᾶσαν
δαιδαλουργίαν εὑρεῖν resembles that of Soph. *Ant.* 332 ff. (πολλὰ τὰ
δεινά, κοὐδὲν ἀνθρώπου δεινότερον πέλει κ.τ.λ.).

§ 4. βιῶσαί τε καὶ ἀφανισθῆναι (σοφισθῆναι MSS.) πρὸς μοῖραν
δρομήματος (ἐγ)κυκλίων θεῶν. μοῖρα here means the 'lot' or 'destiny'
assigned to each man by the revolutions of the starry heavens. Not
only the man's birth, but the course and end of his life also, are
determined by the movements of the stars. The writer does not
add that men, by observing the stars, can discover beforehand what
is destined for them. If this were added, the view expressed would
amount to a belief in astrology.

Each individual man, at the termination of his life on earth,
'disappears' (ἀφανίζεται), and 'undergoes dissolution' (ἀναλύεται εἰς
(τὰ στοιχεῖα?)). Not only is there no mention of a survival of the
individual soul after the dissolution of the body, but the contrary
is clearly implied. Nothing of a man continues to exist after his
death, except his 'name' (i. e. the memory of him in the minds of
living men) ; and even that, in most cases, fades away in a little while.

μεγάλα ἀπομνημονεύματα τεχνουργημάτων ἐπὶ τῆς γῆς καταλιπόντες.
Perhaps the writer was thinking of the old kings who built the
pyramids. But ἀπομνημονεύματα τεχνουργημάτων might be taken to
include the works of the poet and the statesman as well as those
of the builder ; for ποιητική and πολιτική also are τέχναι. Cf. Hor. *Od.*
3. 30 : 'exegi monumentum aere perennius : . . . non omnis moriar.'

πᾶσαν γένεσιν ἐμψύχου σαρκὸς καὶ καρποῦ σπορᾶς (διαδέξεται φθορά).
Men, beasts, and plants alike (must perish). The end of the sentence

is lost; but its meaning can be inferred with certainty from the context. Perhaps the author's thought might be better expressed by writing ⟨ὥσπερ⟩ καὶ καρποῦ σπορᾶς. 'All flesh is grass.' οἵη περ φύλλων γενεή, τοίη δὲ καὶ ἀνδρῶν.

[καὶ πάσας (πάσης MSS.) τεχνουργίας]. If we retain these words, we must take them in connexion with ἀπομνημονεύματα τεχνουργημάτων, and the thought suggested would be this : 'not only do men perish, but their works perish also; and though the names of great men may be preserved through long ages by the memorials they have left behind them, yet even the greatest will be forgotten in the end.' But the phrase is awkwardly interposed, and hardly suits the context ; it cannot be said of the works of human art that they are 'renewed by the operation of the stars', in the sense in which this is said of human and animal births and vegetable growths.

ἀνανεωθήσεται [ἀνάγκη] [καὶ ἀνανεώσει] θεῶν [καὶ φύσεως] ⟨ἐγ⟩κυκλίων ἐναριθμίῳ (κύκλου ἐναριθμίου MSS.) δρομήματι. The reading is very uncertain ; but this, or something like it, must have been the meaning. ἀνανεώσει may have come by duplication from ἀνανεωθήσεται ; and ἀνάγκη καὶ φύσει may have been inserted as an explanatory note on θεῶν . . . δρομήματι. Sense might be made in another way, by shifting φύσεως, and writing ἀνάνεωθήσεται ἀνάγκῃ φύσεως, καὶ θεῶν ἐγκυκλίων ἐναριθμίῳ δρομήματι.

That which decays and passes away is 'renewed', but only by substitution. The individual perishes, but the race is immortal. The dead do not live again, but others are born to succeed them. And this unceasing renewal of life on earth is caused by the unvarying movements of the heavenly bodies, through the operation of which fresh births are continually taking place. The force by which the renewal is effected may be called φύσις; but φύσις is dependent on the movements of the stars, and therefore on the sovereign power of God, by whom the stars themselves were made and set in motion.

It is to be noted that, in the first part of the text, the lacunae which we have found it necessary to assume occur at nearly equal intervals. This suggests a suspicion that in the writing from which our MSS. are derived the lacunae came at the ends of the lines. In the appended transcript of the conjecturally restored text, the Greek is divided into lines in accordance with this hypothesis,[1] The

[1] One or more lines, in which the making of man was described, have probably been lost between l. 13 and l. 14.

numbers of the letters in the first eight lines, not counting the
lacunae at the ends, are 59, 67, 67, 65, 67, 70, 26, 64; and adding the
letters of my conjectural supplements, we get the numbers 64,
78, 76, 69, 79, 80, 38, 76. In the first line, which contains the
title, the letters may have been more widely spaced; and this might
account for their smaller number (59 without the supplement, 64
with it). At the end of the fourth line, the missing word may have
been longer; if, for instance, we wrote ⟨ἐπιφερόμεν⟩ον τοῖς in place
of ⟨διῆκ⟩ον τά, we should have a line of 75 letters instead of 69.
We must suppose that a large part of the seventh line has been
lost in some other way; but seven of the eight lacunae might be
accounted for by assuming that the Greek was written in lines of
75–80 letters, and that a piece at one side of the column was torn
off. Lines of this length [1] are exceptional; but even longer lines
occur in some of the Oxyrhynchus papyri; and a document of this
kind, which may have been scribbled down by some sort of Pagan
hermit in a hut at the edge of the desert, would not necessarily
be written according to the rules commonly observed in libraries
and bookshops.

The probability that the Greek was written in lines of 75–80
letters is somewhat increased by the positions of the lacunae in the
last section. In the restoration of that part of the document
especially, there is much uncertainty; but in the conjectural text
of § 4 we find lacunae again occurring at nearly equal intervals;
and these intervals are of about the same length as before. If we
place the lacunae at the beginning of the lines, the last four lines
yield the numbers $x+63$, $9+70$ ($=79$), $15+70$ ($=85$),[2] $10+66$
($=76$); and these numbers look as if they were in some way
connected with those of the first eight lines. Assuming that the
Greek was divided into lines as here shown, and that it was written
on the face of a detached piece of papyrus, the two groups of
lacunae may have been caused by the destruction of two opposite
corners of the leaf. But if we suppose that it was written partly

[1] In this transcript, all the words are written out in full; but it must be
remembered that in the archetype the lines may have been somewhat shortened by
the use of abbreviations.

[2] The total number of letters (85) in l. 22 is rather too large; but the excess is
due to the fact that my conjectural supplement (διαδέξεται φθορά) extends to 15
letters, whereas the supplements of the line before and the line after contain
respectively 9 and 10 letters only. If we wrote, for instance, πᾶσαν γένεσιν . . .
(αἱρήσει φθορά), or πᾶσα γένεσις . . . (ὑπείξει φθορᾷ) (12 letters), l. 22 would be
reduced to 82 letters; if we wrote πᾶσα γένεσις . . . (φθαρήσεται) (10 letters), the
total would be 80.

on the face of the leaf and partly on the back, and that the writing on the back began at l. 20, both groups of lacunae may have been caused by the destruction of one corner.

1. Ἑρμοῦ τοῦ τρισμεγίστου λόγος ἱερός. ⟨Ὅτι⟩ πρῶτος ἁπάντων ὁ θεός, καὶ θεῖον ⟨τὸ πᾶν⟩,

2. καὶ ἡ φύσις θεία. Ἀρχὴ τῶν ὄντων ὁ θεός, καὶ νοῦ καὶ φύσεως καὶ ὕλης, σοφίας εἰς δεῖξιν ⟨ποιήσας πάντ⟩

3. α, πάντων ὢν ἀρχή· καὶ τοῦ θεοῦ ἐνέργεια ἡ φύσις, κατ᾽ ἀνάγκην καὶ τέλος καὶ ἀναγκώσιν ⟨ἐνεργοῦσα⟩.

4. ἦν γὰρ σκότος ἐν ἀβύσσῳ, καὶ ὕδωρ ἄπειρον, καὶ πνεῦμα λεπτὸν νοερόν, δυνάμει θείᾳ ⟨διῆκ·?⟩

5. ον τὰ ἐν χάει. ἀδιορίστων δὲ ὄντων ἁπάντων καὶ ἀκατασκευάστων, ἀνείθη δὴ φῶς ἅγιον ⟨καὶ ἐγένετο τὰ⟩

6. στοιχεῖα. τῶν γὰρ ὅλων διορισθέντων, ἀπεχωρίσθη τὰ ἐλαφρὰ εἰς ὕψος, ἀνακρεμασθέντος ⟨τοῦ πυρὸς τῷ⟩

7. πνεύματι ὀχεῖσθαι, καὶ τὰ βαρέα ⟨κατηνέχθη⟩ . . . . ⟨. . . καὶ⟩

8. ἐθεμελιώθη ὑφ᾽ ὑγρᾷ οὐσίᾳ ἄμμος, καὶ ἐπάγη ἡ ξηρὰ ἐξ ὑγρᾶς οὐσίας. καὶ διηρθρώθη ⟨ἡ πυρίνη οὐσία⟩

9. σὺν τοῖς ἐν αὐτῇ θεοῖς· καὶ ὤφθη ὁ οὐρανὸς ἐν κύκλοις ἑπτά, καὶ θεοὶ ἐν ἄστρων ἰδέαις ὀπτανόμενοι σὺν

10. τοῖς αὐτῶν σημείοις ἅπασι· καὶ περιειλίχθη τὸ αἰθέριον κύκλῳ δρομήματι, πνεύματι θείῳ ὀχούμενον.

11. ἀνῆκε δὲ ἕκαστος θεὸς διὰ τῆς ἰδίας δυνάμεως τὸ προσταχθὲν αὐτῷ· καὶ ἐγένετο θηρία τετράποδα καὶ

12. ἑρπετὰ καὶ ἔνυδρα καὶ πτηνά, καὶ χόρτος καὶ ἄνθους παντὸς χλόη, κατὰ διαίρεσιν φύσεων ἔσπορα,

13. τὸ σπέρμα τῆς παλιγγενεσίας ἐν ἑαυτοῖς σπερμογονοῦντα. ⟨. . .⟩

14. . . . . ⟨. . .⟩ γενέσεις τῶν ἀνθρώπων, ἐκέλευσέ τε

15. αὐξάνεσθαι ἐν αὐξήσει καὶ πληθύνεσθαι ἐν πλήθει. καὶ πᾶσαν ἔνσαρκον ψυχὴν διὰ δρομήματος

16. θεῶν ἐγκυκλίων, παρασκευάσας εἰς κατοπτείαν οὐρανοῦ, καὶ πάντων τῶν ὑπ᾽ οὐρανὸν δεσποτείαν,

17. καὶ εἰς γνῶσιν θείας δυνάμεως, καὶ φύσεως ἐνεργείας μαρτυρίαν, εἴς τε σημείωσιν ἀγαθῶν, μοίρας

18. διαγνῶναι ἀγαθῶν καὶ φαύλων, καὶ πᾶσαν δαιδαλουργίαν εὑρεῖν. ὑπάρχει τε αὐτοῖς βιῶσαί τε καὶ

19. ἀφανισθῆναι πρὸς μοῖραν δρομήματος ἐγκυκλίων θεῶν, καὶ ἀναλυθῆναι εἰς ⟨τὰ στοιχεῖα. καὶ οἱ

20. μὲν ὀνομαστοὶ⟩ ἔσονται, μεγάλα ὑπομνημονεύματα τεχνουργημάτων ἐπὶ τῆς γῆς καταλιπόντες·

21. ⟨τῶν δὲ πολλ⟩ ῶν τὰ ὀνόματα ὁ χρόνος ἀμαυρώσει. καὶ πᾶσαν γένεσιν ἐμψύχου σαρκὸς καὶ καρποῦ σπορᾶς

22. ⟨διαδέξεται φθορά?⟩· τὰ δὲ ἐλαττούμενα ἀνανεωθήσεται θεῶν ἐγκυκλίων ἐναριθμίῳ δρομήματι. τοῦ γὰρ θεοῦ

23. ⟨ἐκκρέματα⟩· ἡ πᾶσα κοσμικὴ σύγκρασις, φύσει ἀνανεουμένη· ἐν γὰρ τῷ θεῷ καὶ ἡ φύσις καθέστηκεν.

LIBELLVS IV

Contents

⟨God is incorporeal ;⟩ and that which is incorporeal is ĭmperceptible by sense. God is prior to all corporeal things, and has made them all.   § 1 b.

Having made the Kosmos, God sent man down to earth. And man was made for this purpose, that he might admire the Kosmos, and learn to know its Maker.   § 2.

God has ordained that those men only shall have mind who seek it by their own free choice. The men without mind give heed only to corporeal things, and ignore all that is higher. But those who have sought and received the gift of mind rise above earthly things, and see the Good ; and thenceforward they scorn all that is corporeal, and press on towards God.   · §§ 3–6 a.

If you would receive the gift of mind, you must begin by hating the body. You are free to choose either things corporeal and mortal, or things incorporeal and divine ; but you cannot have the one without rejecting the other. Those who choose the incorporeal win glory by their choice ; those who choose the corporeal exist to no good purpose, and are a mere encumbrance in God's world. God is blameless ; if we suffer evil, it is because we ourselves have chosen the evil.   §§ 6 b–8 a.

We have to rise above all that is corporeal, and make our way up to the Good. And to do this, we must put forth all our strength. It is not easy ; for the things that attract us here below are visible, and the Good is invisible.   §§ 8 b, 9.

. . . (*A lacuna of unknown length.*) . . .

God is the source whence all things have their being. He is to things as the arithmetical unit is to the numbers derived from it ; that is to say, he contains all things, and is contained by none ; he generates all things, and is generated by none ; he is perfect, and all things else are imperfect.   §§ 10, 11 a.

If you meditate on God, you will find yourself led upward ; for when a man has once caught sight of things divine, they draw him to them.   § 11 b.

Sources. The doctrine of *Corp.* IV is wholly Platonic. The contrast between 'things corporeal' and 'things incorporeal' which runs through the document is the Platonic contrast between αἰσθητά and νοητά; and the exhortation to 'hate the body' is in accordance with a side of Plato's teaching which is prominent in the *Phaedo*. The Platonic doctrine that human souls existed in a higher world before their incarnation is taken for granted (§ 2, κατέπεμψε; § 9, ἐπὶ τὰ παλαιὰ καὶ ἀρχαῖα ἀνακάμπτειν); and the doctrine that some souls return to that higher world after death is alluded to in § 4 (πιστεύουσα ὅτι ἀνελεύσῃ); though the state of disembodied souls is not directly dealt with. The comparison of God to the μονάς was doubtless suggested by a theory of numbers which was adopted by Plato's immediate successors, and must have been known to all Platonists. The term τὸ ἀγαθόν is employed in its Platonic sense, § 8 b. Reminiscences of the *Timaeus* occur in the account of the *demiurgia*, §§ 1 b, 2. The influence of particular passages in Plato's dialogues is to be recognized in the assertion of man's freedom of choice, §§ 6 b, 8 a (Pl. *Rep.* 10. 617 E); in the mention of φθόνος, § 3 (Pl. *Phaedrus* 247 A?); and probably in the mention of the loadstone, § 11 b (Pl. *Ion* 533 D).

The allegory of the *crater* may possibly have been suggested by Christian invitations to baptism; but this is a doubtful point. The words οὐ χερσὶν ἀλλὰ λόγῳ in § 1 a may have been inserted by a Christian.

Date. On the hypothesis of Christian influence in § 4, a late date must be assumed; for such familiarity with a Christian rite as this implies would hardly have been possible for a Pagan writer before the latter part of the third century. Setting that hypothesis aside, I can find no indication of date in *Corp.* IV except its general resemblance to other *Hermetica*, from which we may infer that it was probably written in the second or third century A. D.

Title. The title ὁ κρατήρ refers to the allegory in § 4. We have no means of knowing whether this title was given to the dialogue by its author, or subsequently inserted by some one else. The second title, ἡ μονάς, which is applicable only to §§ 10, 11 a, was probably added later.

§ 1 a. ἐπειδὴ τὸν πάντα κ.τ.λ. The text of §§ 1 a, 1 b is in confusion. The beginning of the dialogue is missing; there is no apodosis to the clause which stands first in the MSS. (ἐπειδὴ . . . ἀλλὰ λόγῳ); and there is no satisfactory connexion of thought between the sentence ὥστε οὕτως ὑπολάμβανε . . . τὰ ὄντα and the following sentence, τοῦτο γάρ ἐστι τὸ σῶμα ἐκείνου κ.τ.λ. I have tried to express what I suppose to have been the writer's meaning by re-arranging the sentences. It may be presumed that the passage ὥστε οὕτως ὑπολάμβανε . . . τὰ ὄντα stood at or near the end of a paragraph which dealt with the making of the Kosmos ; and the words ἐπεὶ δὲ τὸν πάντα κόσμον ἐποίησεν ὁ δημιουργός supply a suitable transition from this to the following paragraph, § 2, which deals with the 'sending down' or embodiment of man.

[οὐ χερσὶν ἀλλὰ λόγῳ]. These words would evidently be out of place at the beginning of § 2 ; if therefore we are right in transposing ἐπειδὴ . . . ὁ δημιουργός to that position, it follows that οὐ χερσὶν ἀλλὰ λόγῳ must have been added after the clause had been shifted from its original place.

The λόγος here spoken of is the creative *fiat* of the Demiurgus. It is not hypostatized or personified. The notion that God made the world 'by his word' or 'by the breath ot his mouth' was familiar to the Jews; cf. *Psalm* 33. 6. It appears to have been familiar to the Egyptians also, from a time long before the beginnings of Hebrew literature. Moret, *Rituel en Égypte*, 1902, p. 155 : 'l'idée de la force créatrice du verbe existe déjà nettement dès les textes des pyramides'[1] The thought expressed by the words οὐ χερσὶν ἀλλὰ λόγῳ might therefore have been derived from sources either Jewish or Egyptian. But if these words were added later, it is most likely that they were inserted by a Christian.

§ 1 b. τ⟨οι⟩οῦτο γάρ ἐστι τὸ ⟨ἀ⟩σῶμα⟨τον⟩ [[ἐκείνου]]. If we retain τὸ σῶμα ἐκείνου, the reading of the MSS., we must say that the writer, by a bold paradox, ascribes a 'body' to God, though at the same time he denies that God's 'body' has any of the qualities of other bodies. But the statement that God has a body is not only unparalleled in Hermetic literature,[2] but is also irreconcilable with what is said elsewhere in this document. (See especially § 6 b : δύο γὰρ ὄντων τῶν ὄντων, σώματος καὶ ἀσωμάτου, ἐν οἷς τὸ θνητὸν καὶ τὸ θεῖον.) There can therefore be little doubt that the text is corrupt. It would be possible to write εἶδος in place of σῶμα ; compare the ἰδέα

---

[1] See also Moret, *Mystères égyptiens*, 1913, ch. 2, 'Le mystère du verbe créateur'. But Moret hardly distinguishes with sufficient clearness between the doctrine that God made or makes things by his creative *fiat* (which may be ascribed to the Egyptians without hesitation), and the doctrine of a Logos regarded as a person distinct from the supreme God. (See note on *Corp.* I. 6.) The latter doctrine also may perhaps have existed in Egypt before the Hellenistic period ; but the evidence for its existence seems to be far less conclusive.

[2] See *Corp.* XIV. 7 : τοῦτό ἐστι τοῦ θεοῦ ὥσπερ ⌈σῶμα⌉, ἡ ποίησις.

ἀσώματος of God which is spoken of in *Corp.* XI. ii. 16 b. But it seems most likely that the writer, having asserted that God is ἀσώματος in the lost passage which preceded this sentence, here went on to explain what sort of thing τὸ ἀσώματον is. I have accordingly written τὸ ἀσώματον. The word ἐκείνου may have come from ἐκεῖνος misplaced.

οὔτε γὰρ πῦρ ἐστιν⟨⟨ἐκεῖνος⟩⟩, οὔτε ὕδωρ, οὔτε ἀήρ, οὔτε πνεῦμα. God was identified with fire by Heraclitus ; with water, by Thales ; with air, by Anaximenes and Diogenes of Apollonia ; and with fire or *pneuma* (i. e. heated air) by the Stoics. That which is common to all these theories is the notion that God is corporeal ; and this is the notion against which the Hermetist is contending.

ὡς αὐτοῦ προόντος (ὡς τοῦ παρόντος MSS.). Cf. Herm. *ap.* Stob. *Exc.* XXI. 1 : ἔστι τοίνυν τὸ προὸν ἐπ⟨έκεινα⟩ πάντων τῶν ὄντων κ.τ.λ. In Iren. 1. 1. 1, the term προών is applied to the supreme God of the Valentinians (the Bythos or Propator). In the writings of Plotinus and his successors, τὸ προόν would mean τὸ ἔν, τὸ ἐπέκεινα οὐσίας (καὶ νοῦ) ; but the writer of *Corp.* IV means merely that the existence of God is prior to the existence of the corporeal universe.

ἀγαθὸς γὰρ ὤν, ⌜μόνῳ ἑαυτῷ τοῦτο ἀναθεῖναι⌝ Stob.—ἀγαθὸς ὤν. ⌜μόνῳ γὰρ τούτῳ ἀνατέθεικεν⌝ Corp. As the phrase ἀγαθὸς ὤν is here used in connexion with the *demiurgia*, it was probably suggested by Pl. *Tim.* 29 E : ἀγαθὸς ἦν, . . . · (φθόνου) δ' ἐκτὸς ὢν πάντα ὅτι μάλιστα γενέσθαι ἐβουλήθη παραπλήσια ἑαυτῷ . . .. βουληθεὶς γὰρ ὁ θεὸς ἀγαθὰ μὲν πάντα, φλαῦρον δὲ μηδὲν εἶναι κατὰ δύναμιν, οὕτω δὴ πᾶν ὅσον ἦν ὁρατὸν . . . εἰς τάξιν . . . ἤγαγεν ἐκ τῆς ἀταξίας. And if the writer was thinking of that passage, he may perhaps have written something like ἀγαθὸς γὰρ ὤν, ⟨ἐβουλήθη πάντα⟩ ἀγαθὰ εἶναι. The words μόνῳ ἑαυτῷ τοῦτο (μόνῳ γὰρ τούτῳ codd. Corp.) might be a corruption of μόνος αὐτός ('inasmuch as he, *and he alone*, was good ') ; or they might possibly have come by duplication from μόνου τῇ δὲ αὐτοῦ in the preceding sentence.

§ 2. ἠθέλησε καὶ τὴν γῆν κοσμῆσαι. If my rearrangement of the passage is right, τὴν γῆν is contrasted with τὸν πάντα κόσμον. Having made the Kosmos, God bethought him that something more was needed to complete the order and beauty of the earthly part of it, and supplied what was lacking by peopling the earth with men. The thought is somewhat similar to that of Pl. *Tim.* 41 B, where the Demiurgus, having made the gods, says that mortal creatures have not yet been made ; τούτων δὲ μὴ γενομένων, οὐρανὸς (i. e. the universe) ἀτελὴς ἔσται· τὰ γὰρ ἄπαντ' ἐν αὐτῷ γένη ζῴων οὐκ ἔξει, δεῖ δέ, εἰ μέλλει τέλεος ἱκανῶς εἶναι. Cf. *Kore Kosmu, Exc.* XXIII. 9 : after the first creation, ἡ ⟨τῶν ὑποκειμένων⟩ φύσις ἐτύγχανε στεῖρα, until the gods represented to the supreme God ὅτι δέον ἐστὶ συγκοσμηθῆναι ⟨καὶ⟩ ταῦ)τα· whereupon the supreme God proceeded to make souls. Perhaps the word κοσμῆσαι implies that it is a part of man's function to tend and beautify the earth ; if so, we may compare *Ascl. Lat.* I. 10 : 'curam propriam diligentiae suae (suscipiens homo) efficit ut sit ipse et mundus uterque ornamento sibi.' *Ib.* 8 : 'sine quibus (*sc.* the work of the human arts and crafts) mundum deus noluit esse perfectum.'

κόσμον δὲ θείου σώματος κατέπεμψε τὸν ἄνθρωπον, ⟨εἰκόνα⟩ ζῴου ἀθανάτου ζῷον θνητόν.   There is here a play on the two meanings of the word κόσμος ('universe' and 'ornament'), as in 'ut sit ipse et mundus ornamento sibi' (*Ascl. Lat.*). The θεῖον σῶμα is ἡ γῆ ; the ζῷον ἀθάνατον is the Kosmos, of which man (the microcosm)[1] is an image.   But the combination of the two phrases is somewhat awkward ; and it may be suspected that εἰκόνα ζῴου ἀθανάτου ζῷον θνητόν has been added by a later hand.

The word κατέπεμψε shows that the writer holds the Platonic doctrine that human souls existed ἄνω before they were embodied on earth.   In the *Timaeus*, we are told in mythical language that the souls were made by the Demiurgus, and that when made, they were first placed in the stars, and afterwards sent down to earth. But the writer of *Corp.* IV, as he says nothing about the 'making' of souls, may have held that individual human souls are without beginning.   It is true that he repeatedly says that man γέγονε ('has been made ') for a certain purpose ; but when he uses this expression, he is speaking of man as an earthly organism composed ot body and soul, and not of the unembodied soul.

[[καὶ ὁ μὲν κόσμος . . . τὸν νοῦν.]]   This must have been written to introduce the topic of the distribution of νοῦς, and must therefore have stood at the beginning of § 3.

θεατὴς γὰρ [[ἐγένετο]] τῶν ἔργων τοῦ θεοῦ ὁ ἄνθρωπος. Cf. *Ascl. Lat.* I. 8, where it is said that when God had made the Kosmos, 'esse voluit alium qui illum quem ex se fecerat intueri potuisset', and

---

[1] The saying that man is a μικρὸς κόσμος was attributed to Democritus (Diels *Fr. Vorsokr.* p. 398). In Ar. *Phys.* 252 b 26, a ζῷον of any kind is said to be a μικρὸς κόσμος.

therefore he made man. *Corp*. III 3 b, as emended : παρασκευάσας (τὸν ἄνθρωπον) εἰς κατοπτείαν οὐρανοῦ, . . . καὶ εἰς γνῶσιν θείας δυνάμεως, καὶ φύσεως ἐνεργείας μαρτυρίαν. Iamblichus, *Protrept*. 9, says that Pythagoras, when he was asked what is the purpose οὗ χάριν ἡ φύσις ἡμᾶς ἐγέννησε καὶ ὁ θεός, answered, "τὸ θεάσασθαι τὸν οὐρανόν·" καὶ ἑαυτὸν δὲ θεωρὸν ἔφασκεν εἶναι τῆς φύσεως, καὶ τούτου ἕνεκα παρεληλυθέναι εἰς τὸν βίον.

Something to which γάρ refers, and which connected this sentence with what precedes, must have been lost.

καὶ ⟨ἐπὶ τοῦτο ⟨⟨ἐγένετο⟩⟩, τὸ τὸν κόσμον⟩ θαυμάσαι, καὶ γνωρίσαι τὸν ποιήσαντα.—(καὶ ἐθαύμασε καὶ ἐγνώρισε τὸν ποιήσαντα MSS.) As we are afterwards told that many men do not ' come to know the Maker', the indicatives ἐθαύμασε and ἐγνώρισε, which imply that man in general does so, can hardly be right. In the following sections, the writer speaks of ' the purpose for which man was made' as a thing known to the reader; hence it may be inferred that he somewhere said what that purpose is. And if so, there can be little doubt that he said it at the end of the paragraph about the ' sending down' of man, and in some such words as I have written.

§ 3. τὸν λόγον καὶ τὸν νοῦν. It may be doubted whether λόγος ought here to be translated ' speech' or ' reason'. But in the parallel passage *Corp*. XII i. 12 (δύο ταῦτα τῷ ἀνθρώπῳ ὁ θεὸς . . . ἐχαρίσατο, . . . τόν τε νοῦν καὶ τὸν λόγον κ.τ.λ.), the word clearly means ' speech'.

τὸν δὲ νοῦν οὐκέτι (πᾶσι τοῖς ἀνθρώποις ἐμέρισε). The νοῦς of this dialogue is the higher sort of νοῦς, which only a few men possess; and the lower sort of νοῦς, which goes along with speech, and is possessed by all mankind, is not expressly mentioned. Cf. *Corp*. I. 21 *fin*. : οὐ πάντες γὰρ ἄνθρωποι νοῦν ἔχουσιν; *Ascl. Lat*. I. 7 a : ' non omnes . . . intellegentiam veram adepti sunt.'

ὁ γὰρ φθόνος οὐκ οὐρανόθεν (ἔνθεν MSS.) ἄρχεται. It would be possible to write ἄνωθεν; but ἔνθεν, the reading of the MSS., may very likely have arisen out of οὐνόθεν (i. e. οὐρανόθεν abbreviated).

φθόνος does not ' start from' heaven or ' begin with' heaven; i. e. οὐ πᾶσιν ἐγγίγνεται ἀπὸ τῶν οὐρανίων ἀρχόμενος· it is not present in all beings from God downward. Cf. Pl. *Phaedrus* 247 A : ἕπεται δὲ (τοῖς θεοῖς) ὁ ἀεὶ ἐθέλων τε καὶ δυνάμενος· φθόνος γὰρ ἔξω θείου χόρου ἵσταται. Pl. *Tim*. 29 E : τούτου δὲ (*sc*. φθόνου) ἐκτὸς ὢν (ὁ θεὸς) κ.τ.λ.

ὥσπερ ἆθλον. *Nous,* or the *gnosis* of which *nous* is the organ, is a thing to be striven for. The Hermetists speak of *gnosis* sometimes as a gift bestowed by God's grace, and at other times, as a thing to be sought by human effort. This writer takes the latter view, and insists on man's freedom to choose either the higher life or the lower.

§ 4. κρατῆρα μέγαν . . . κατέπεμψε κ.τ.λ. This passage was known to the alchemist Zosimus; see Zosim. ii. 8 (*Testim.*), βαπτισθεῖσα τῷ κρατῆρι.

Whence did the writer of *Corp.* IV get his notion of 'a great basin filled with νοῦς', in which men's 'hearts' are invited to dip themselves? The figure must have been suggested to him by some sacramental rite with which he was acquainted; but it seems clear that he himself attached no value and ascribed no efficacy to the sacramental rite of which he was thinking, and that he uses it merely as a figure to illustrate his doctrine of νοῦς. To what cult did the rite which he had in mind belong? It is not impossible that his allegory was suggested by the Christian sacrament of baptism, and that the κρατήρ corresponds to the Christian font. The use of the words βαπτίζειν and πιστεύειν, and the mention of a κήρυγμα by which all are invited to undergo the rite, agree well with this hypothesis; and the language of § 4 might have been used by a Christian almost without alteration, except that he would have spoken of πνεῦμα instead of νοῦς. But on the other hand, it seems improbable that a Pagan, writing before the end of the third century, would have been so familiar with the Christian rite of baptism as to base an allegory on it. Did a similar practice of sacramental dipping exist in any Pagan cult which is likely to have been known to the writer of *Corp.* IV? Purifications by sprinkling, washing, or bathing were no doubt in constant use in the indigenous cults of Egypt, and in almost all the other religions of the time.[1] But the rite presupposed in *Corp.* IV. 4 is not a mere ceremonial purification, but an operation of sacramental efficacy, by which the personality of the votary

---

[1] On the Jewish rites of purification by washing or dipping, see Schürer, *Geschichte des Jüdischen Volkes,* 4th ed., II, p. 564 f., and III, pp. 181-185. Proselytes, at their admission to the Jewish community, were cleansed from the pollutions of their Pagan life by a ceremonial ablution. This is spoken of in the exhortation addressed to Pagans in the Jewish *Orac. Sibyl.* 4. 162 ff. (written probably towards the end of the first century A.D.): ἆ μέλεοι μετάθεσθε βροτοὶ τάδε· .. | ἐν ποταμοῖς λούσασθε ὅλον δέμας ἀενάοισιν, | χεῖρας τ' ἐκτανύσαντες ἐς αἰθέρα τῶν πάρος ἔργων | συγγνώμην αἰτεῖσθε. But this Jewish 'baptism' of proselytes (if it is to be called by that name) hardly amounted to a sacrament.

is profoundly transformed; and if a non-Christian 'baptism' in that sense was anywhere in existence, it is most likely to have existed in Syria, or at any rate, to have been of Syrian origin.[1]

We have further to consider from what source the writer of *Corp.* IV can have got the term κρατήρ, which he uses to denote the tank or basin in which the votaries are dipped. In Pl. *Tim.* 41 D, the vessel in which the Demiurgus 'mixed' or 'blended' the substances of which he made the world-soul and the individual souls is called a κρατήρ. Cf. Lucian *Bis accusatus* 34. 834 (a jesting reference to the *Timaeus*): ἐκεῖνα σμικρολογούμενος, εἰ ἀθάνατος ἡ ψυχή, καὶ πόσας κοτύλας ὁ θεός, ὁπότε τὸν κόσμον κατεσκευάζετο, τῆς ἀμιγοῦς καὶ κατὰ ταὐτὰ ἐχούσης οὐσίας ἐνέχεεν ἐς τὸν κρατῆρα ἐν ᾧ τὰ πάντα ἐκεράννυτο.[2] But the κρατήρ of *Corp.* IV, which is a receptacle containing a liquid in which people dip themselves, cannot have been derived from the 'mixing-bowl' or 'crucible' spoken of in the *Timaeus.*

There seem to have been two Orphic poems called Κρατήρ. Servius *ad Aen.* 6. 667 (Abel *Orphica* fr. 159): 'ad (Musaeum Orpheus) primum carmen scripsit quod appellatur Crater.' Joannes Diaconus *ad Hes. Theog.* 617 (Abel *ib.* fr. 164): ἄκουε γὰρ τοῦ Ὀρφέως ἐν τῷ λεγομένῳ Κρατῆρι τάδε σοι λέγοντος· Ἔστιν δὴ πάντων ἀρχὴ Ζεύς, ζῆν γὰρ ἔδωκε κ.τ.λ. Joannes Diaconus *ad Hes. Theog.* 950 (Abel *ib.* fr. 160): μαρτυρεῖ καὶ ἐν τῷ μικροτέρῳ Κρατῆρι (i. e. in the shorter of the two poems which bore that title) ὁ Ὀρφεύς, τάδε λέγων· Ἑρμῆς δ' ἑρμηνεὺς τῶν πάντων κ.τ.λ. The poem from which these extracts were taken seems to have contained a catalogue of gods, with explanations of their names and functions in the Stoic manner. We are not told the meaning of the title Κρατήρ which was given

---

[1] See notes on *Corp.* XIII, and Appendix on Rebirth.

It is no doubt possible that in some of the many Egyptian temple-cults a sacramental rite of dipping in a basin or tank was practised. (There seems to be an allusion to some such rite in the Egyptian *Book of the Dead*, 'Chapter of the going forth by day', Erman's transl. 459 f., quoted by Dieterich *Mithraslit.* p. 195 'My uncleanness is driven away, and the sin which was upon me is cast down. I *have washed myself in those two great ponds which are in Heracleopolis*, in which the offering of men is purified for that great god who dwells there. I go on the way where I *wash my head in the lake of the righteous*.') But the writer of *Corp.* IV speaks of an invitation to all who will to receive this baptism; and that is hardly in accordance with the spirit of the Egyptian religion. In the cults of Egypt, the privilege of sacramental initiation appears to have been almost entirely restricted to the priests.

[2] Arnobius 2. 25 says that the *anima* (*humana*) was spoken of by certain Platonists as *affluens ex crateribus vivis.* This phrase was probably suggested by the passage in the *Timaeus.*

to it; but Joannes Diaconus, in the same connexion, quotes from 'Orpheus' the line Ζεὺς δέ τε πάντων ἐστὶ ⌐θεὸς⌐ (πατὴρ?) πάντων τε κεραστής (A el fr. 161); and it seems probable that this fragment also belongs to ' the smaller *Crater*', and that the poem was so named because it said that Zeus 'mixed all things in a bowl' when he made the Kosmos. (Cf. τὸν κρατῆρα ἐν ᾧ τὰ πάντα ἐκεράννυτο in Lucian.) If so, the κρατήρ of *Corp.* IV can have nothing to do with 'the smaller *Crater*' of Orpheus.

We are also told that in some Orphic poem ' the *crater* of Diony-sus' was spoken of. Proclus *in Tim.* 316 A (Abel *Orph.* p. 216): καὶ 'Ορφεὺς οἶδε μὲν καὶ τὸν τοῦ Διονύσου κρατῆρα, πολλοὺς δὲ καὶ ἄλλους (κρατῆρας) ἱδρύει περὶ τὴν ἡλιακὴν τράπεζαν. Macrobius *Somn. Scip.* 1. 12. 8 identifies the constellation called the *Crater* with 'the *crater* of Dionysus', and says that unembodied souls drink from it, and being thereby intoxicated, are drawn down to earth and embodied there. To Macrobius then, 'the *crater* of Dionysus' meant the vessel which contains the drink of Lethe; and the term may possibly have had the same meaning in the Orphic passage to which Proclus refers. But it is evident that the Hermetist's notion of a bath or font filled with Mind cannot be in any way connected with Macrobius's notion of a drinking-vessel filled with the wine of Lethe.

It might with somewhat more show of reason be conjectured that the legend that Empedocles leapt into the *crater* of Aetna arose through perversion of a saying that he plunged into the κρατήρ of divine fire (i. e. of νοῦς), and so became a god. Diog. Laert. 8. 69: Ἱππόβοτος δέ φησιν ἐξαναστάντα (τὸν 'Εμπεδοκλέα) ὡδευκέναι ὡς ἐπὶ τὴν Αἴτνην, εἶτα παραγενόμενον ἐπὶ τοὺς κρατῆρας τοῦ πυρὸς ἐναλέσθαι καὶ ἀφανισθῆναι, βουλόμενον τὴν περὶ αὐτοῦ φήμην βεβαιῶσαι ὅτι γεγόνοι θεός. (I do not know the date of Hippobotus; but the story was commonly known in the time of Horace, *Ars poet.* 464.) On this hypothesis, the Hermetist's allegory might possibly have been suggested by a conception which originated among the Orphici or Pythagoreans of Sicily and South Italy. But there is no evidence that the word κρατήρ was thus employed by any Pagan school or sect; and perhaps the passage about 'the basin filled with mind' can be most satisfactorily accounted for by assuming that the author of *Corp.* IV, though himself a Pagan, had heard or read a Christian invitation to baptism, and adapted a few sentences of it to his own purpose.

ταῖς τῶν ἀνθρώπων καρδίαις. καρδία here means 'soul'. Cf. § 11 b, τοῖς τῆς καρδίας ὀφθαλμοῖς. The word was not thus used by Plato,[1] nor by philosophic writers in general after Plato's time. On the other hand, it is habitually thus used in the Septuagint and the New Testament. Its employment here might therefore be considered to tell in favour of the hypothesis that the source of this passage was Christian. But the word 'heart' was used in the sense of 'soul' or 'mind' by Egyptians also.

Βάπτισον σεαυτὴν ἡ δυναμένη. ἡ δυναμένη would seem to imply that there are some men who cannot 'dip themselves' in the bath of Mind. But it is difficult to reconcile this with the writer's view that the choice between the higher and the lower life is open to all (§ 6 b: ἡ αἵρεσις θατέρου καταλείπεται τῷ ἐλέσθαι βουλομένῳ). It seems probable therefore that the author wrote, not ἡ δυναμένη, but ἡ βουλομένη.

πιστεύουσα ὅτι ἀνελεύσῃ πρὸς τὸν καταπέμψαντα τὸν κρατῆρα. τὸν κρατῆρα is an awkward repetition of τοῦτον τὸν κρατῆρα close above; and it may be suspected that the true reading is τόν ⟨σε⟩ καταπέμψαντα (cf. κατέπεμψε τὸν ἄνθρωπον in § 2), and that τὸν κρατῆρα has been added by error. In the traditional text, τὸν καταπέμψαντα τὸν κρατῆρα refers to κρατῆρα . . . κατέπεμψε at the beginning of § 4; but I am inclined to think that we ought to read some such word as κατέστησε there in place of κατέπεμψε. The 'sending down' of a 'great tank' from heaven is a process that it is not very easy to picture; and κατέστησε would agree better with the preceding verb ἱδρύσατο.

τέλειοι ἐγένοντο ἄνθρωποι, τὸν νοῦν δεξάμενοι. A man without νοῦς is ἀτελής; it is only when he has received νοῦς that he becomes a complete or fully-developed man. The word τέλειος sometimes carried with it religious associations connected with τελετή and τέλος in the sense of 'initiation'. But in this sentence, the common and popular meaning of τέλειος gives a satisfactory sense, and there is no need to look for any other.[2]

---

[1] Its use in the speech of Alcibiades, Pl. *Sympos.* 218 A (τὴν καρδίαν γὰρ ἢ ψυχὴν ἢ ὅ τι δεῖ αὐτὸ ὀνομάσαι πληγείς τε καὶ δηχθεὶς ὑπὸ τῶν ἐν φιλοσοφίᾳ λόγων) is an isolated instance.

[2] Reitzenstein (*Hellen. Mysterienrel.* p. 165) says that the Hermetist associated the word τέλειοι with τελετή, and meant to imply by it that the men of whom he speaks are 'consecrated' (*geweiht*) by a sacramental rite. But I see no reason to think that any such meaning was intended here.

Reitzenstein *ib.* says 'ein κρατήρ wird bei der Reinigung oder Taufe in den griechischen Mysterien immer verwendet'; but he does not give any authority for

§§ 4, 5. ὅσοι δὲ ἥμαρτον τοῦ κηρύγματος ... γεγονέναι πιστεύοντες. There is evidently something wrong in the long string of participles which this passage contains ; but it is doubtful how the text ought to be corrected. The words τὸν νοῦν μὴ προσειληφότες correspond to τὸν νοῦν δεξάμενοι above ; it therefore seems probable, on the ground of symmetry, that the sentence ended at προσειληφότες. If so, we have to provide a subject and a verb for the sentence which follows. I have provided a subject by inserting καὶ οὗτοι μέν, which seems needed to match ὅσοι δὲ ... μετέσχον, οὗτοι below ; and a verb, by altering ἔχοντες into συνέχονται.

§ 5. [αἱ δὲ αἰσθήσεις τούτων ταῖς τῶν ἀλόγων ζῴων παραπλήσιαι.] The two sorts of men are sufficiently distinguished by the fact that the one sort possesses νοῦς and the other does not ; why should it be said that their αἰσθήσεις also differ ? And if the αἰσθήσεις of the ἄνους ἄνθρωπος are like those of the beasts, in what respect do the αἰσθήσεις of the ἔννους ἄνθρωπος differ from those of the beasts ? We might rather have supposed that, in respect of their αἰσθήσεις, all men are alike. Besides, there is some awkwardness in saying that the ἄνους ἄνθρωπος is like the ἄλογα ζῷα, when we have just been told that he possesses λόγος. It seems best therefore to bracket these words.

ὀργῇ καὶ ἀκρασίᾳ συνέχονται.—(καὶ ἐν θυμῷ καὶ ἐν ὀργῇ τὴν κρᾶσιν ἔχοντες MSS.) There is no meaning in τὴν κρᾶσιν ἔχοντες ; and ἀκρασίᾳ is a probable correction. It may be considered a substitute for ἐπιθυμίᾳ ; and some such word is needed to suit the following phrase ταῖς τῶν σωμάτων ἡδοναῖς καὶ ὀρέξεσι, which has nothing to do with θυμός or ὀργή. The words καὶ· ἐν θυμῷ are probably a variant for καὶ ἐν ὀργῇ. In Corp. XIII. 7 b, ἀκρασία stands third, and ὀργή tenth, in a list of twelve evil passions.

θαυμάζοντες τὰ οὐ θέας ἄξια.—(οὐ θαυμάζοντες οὐ τὰ θέας ἄξια MSS.) The reading of the MSS. seems to have resulted from a mixture of θαυμάζοντες τὰ οὐ θέας ἄξια and οὐ θαυμάζοντες τὰ θέας ἄξια.

§ 6 a. αὕτη ... ἡ τοῦ νοῦ ἐστιν ἐνέργεια, ἐπιστήμης τῶν θείων εὐπορία καὶ τοῦ θεοῦ κατανοήσεως.—(αὕτη ... ἡ τοῦ νοῦ ἐστιν ἐπιστήμη, τῶν θείων ἐντορία, καὶ ἡ τοῦ θεοῦ κατανόησις MSS.) There is no such word as ἐντορία ; and the correction ἐπιστήμης ... εὐπορία is confirmed by τὸν νοῦν ἔχων καὶ τῆς ἐπιστήμης μεταλήψῃ below. The phrase

this statement. At Eleusis, the preliminary purification of the *mystae* by bathing took place, not in a κρατήρ, but in the sea, as is shown by the cry ἅλαδε μύσται. I know of no Greek mysteries in which bathing or dipping was the central or most significant part of the sacramental action, as it is in the Hermetist's allegory.

ἐπιστήμη τῶν θείων καὶ τοῦ θεοῦ κατανόησις is equivalent to γνῶσις; and γνώσεως εὐπορία might very well be said to be the ἐνέργεια of νοῦς. Some such word as ἐνέργεια is wanted here; and there is a superfluous ἐνέργεια at the beginning of § 7, which may possibly have been transposed from § 6 a.

§ 6 b. Κἀγὼ ⟨⟨τοῦ κρατῆρος⟩⟩ βαπτισθῆναι βούλομαι. A mention of the κρατήρ is out of place at the end of § 6 a, as Hermes is there describing the results produced by the possession of νοῦς, and has ceased to talk about the 'basin'. On the other hand, τοῦ κρατῆρος is wanted to supplement βαπτισθῆναι in the words spoken by Tat. A genitive might be used with βαπτίζεσθαι, as with λούεσθαι. Cf. ἐβαπτίσαντο τοῦ νοός in § 4.

ἐὰν μὴ πρῶτον τὸ σῶμα μισήσῃς, . . . σεαυτὸν φιλῆσαι οὐ δύνασαι· φιλήσας δὲ σεαυτόν, νοῦν ἕξεις. Tat's words, 'I wish to be dipped in the basin', mean 'I wish to get νοῦς'; and Hermes replies: 'If you wish to get νοῦς, the way to do so is to hate your body, and love yourself'. τὸ σῶμα means the separate and narrowly limited self of the man who is sunk in matter; and σεαυτόν means 'your true self', i. e. the larger and higher self of the man who has risen above the limitations of the material world. Cf. *Corp.* XI. ii. 21 a: ἐὰν δὲ κατακλείσῃς σου τὴν ψυχὴν ἐν τῷ σώματι κ.τ.λ. On the two meanings of φίλαυτος, see Ar. *Eth. Nic.* 9. 8. The man whom the Hermetist describes as 'loving himself' corresponds to Aristotle's σπουδαῖος, who is ready, if need be, to die for others, and by that very fact, shows himself to be φίλαυτος in the sense that he seeks τὸ καλόν for himself. The Hermetist, however, was probably not thinking of the man who shows his φιλαυτία by unselfish action, but rather of the man who develops that which is best and highest in himself by religious meditation, and in that way seeks and finds his true good.

Πῶς ταῦτα λέγεις; ταῦτα means especially the paradoxical statement 'if you do not first hate your body, you cannot love yourself'.

ἡ αἵρεσις θατέρου καταλείπεται. The writer insists on man's freedom of choice. Cf. Pl. *Rep.* 10. 617 E: οὐχ ὑμᾶς δαίμων λήξεται, ἀλλ' ὑμεῖς δαίμονα αἱρήσεσθε. . . . ἀρετὴ δὲ ἀδέσποτον· ἣν τιμῶν καὶ ἀτιμάζων πλέον καὶ ἔλαττον αὐτῆς ἕκαστος ἕξει. αἰτία ἑλομένου· θεὸς ἀναίτιος. That passage was frequently referred to by later writers [1] as a *locus classicus* on the subject of free will; and

---

[1] See e.g. Porphyry περὶ τοῦ ἐφ' ἡμῖν, Stob. 1. 8. 39, vol. ii, p. 163 W.

the author of *Corp*. IV no doubt had it in mind. Cf. ὁ μὲν θεὸς ἀναίτιος in § 8 a.

οὐ γὰρ ἀμφότερα οἷόν τε καταλαβεῖν.—(οὐ γάρ ἐστιν ἀμφότερα ἐν οἷς τε ἡ ἐξαίρεσις καταλείπεται MSS.) You are free to choose either the one or the other (*sc.* either τὰ θνητά, the illusory goods of the corporeal world, or τὰ θεῖα, the real goods of the incorporeal world), but you cannot have both. This must have been the writer's meaning, though it may be doubted in what words he expressed it. The phrase ἡ ἐξαίρεσις καταλείπεται is a doublet of ἡ αἵρεσις θατέρου καταλείπεται above, and has taken the place of the original ending of the sentence.

τὸ δὲ ἕτερον ἐλαττωθὲν τὴν τοῦ ἑτέρου ἐφανέρωσεν ἐνέργειαν. When the body 'gets the worst of it', and the man ceases to be influenced by the bodily πάθη, then τὸ θεῖον works, and the effects of its working become manifest in him; and the reverse takes place when the body gets the upper hand.

§ 7. ⟨⟨οὐ μόνον⟩⟩ τὸν ἄνθρωπον ἀποσώζουσα, ἀλλὰ καὶ τὴν πρὸς ⟨τὸν⟩ θεὸν εὐσέβειαν ἐπιδεικνῦσα. (ἀποθεῶσαι . . . ἐπιδείκνυσιν MSS.) It would be a strange anticlimax to say that something 'not only changes a man into a god, but also shows that he is pious'. We need two phrases which can stand in contrast with τὸν μὲν ἄνθρωπον ἀπώλεσεν, . . . εἰς ⟨δὲ⟩ τὸν θεὸν ἐπλημμέλησεν· and the opposite of ἀπολέσαι is σῶσαι. It may therefore be presumed that the author wrote ἀποσώζουσα. The choice of the better not only 'brings the man off safe' (from the evils which beset him who 'loves the body'), but also entitles him to claim the merit of piety. If it merely saved him from misery, the αἵρεσις τοῦ κρείττονος might be called σύμφορος, but hardly καλή; but since it also shows him to be εὐσεβής, it is καλλίστη.

οὐδὲν δὲ ⟨ἧττον⟩ εἰς τὸν θεὸν ἐπλημμέλησεν [ἢ τοῦτο μόνον]. What is wanted here, to match the words τὴν πρὸς τὸν θεὸν εὐσέβειαν ἐπιδεικνῦσα above, is a statement to the effect that the choice of the worse shows the man to be δυσσεβής. The meaning required may be obtained by writing οὐδὲν δὲ ἧττον; and we may suppose that, after ἧττον had dropped out, some one tried to restore sense by adding ἢ τοῦτο μόνον. (οὐδὲν ἤ occurs repeatedly in the *Hermetica* in the sense of οὐδὲν ἀλλ' ἤ.)

οὗτοι μόνον πομπεύουσιν ἐν τῷ κόσμῳ. If a man fails to recognize 'for what purpose he has been made' (ἐπὶ τί γέγονεν, § 4), and does not discharge the function which his Maker has assigned to him, he is offending against God. The life of such a man serves no good purpose; it is nothing but an unmeaning show; and his presence in the world is a mere hindrance to those who seek to live as God meant them to live.

The writer speaks of πομπαί with evident dislike. What sort of 'processions' was he thinking of? The πομπαί most frequently seen in the streets of Alexandria and other Egyptian towns must have been religious processions, more or less resembling the πομπή of Isis at Corinth which is described by Apuleius. The Hermetists in general may have taken little interest in the ceremonial of the established cults; but we should hardly have expected one of them to speak of such things with positive contempt. The writer of *Ascl. Lat.* III would certainly not have spoken in this tone about a piece of religious ritual, and would not have said that it has no efficacy (οὐδὲν ἐνεργῆσαι δύναται); but it is possible that the writer of *Corp.* IV was more averse to the usages of the popular religion. At any rate, it is not the religious significance of the πομπή that he is here concerned with; he is thinking of it merely as a train of people passing through the streets; and his point is that the persons who take part in the procession are led passively along (παραγόμενοι), and are not only doing no useful work themselves, but hindering other people from going about their business. To one who wanted only to be left in peace to live the contemplative life, the tumult of a city festival, culminating at the time when the procession was on its way, may well have been a mere annoyance.

The word πομπή is similarly used by the alchemist Zosimus (i. 4 *Testim.*; Reitzenstein *Poim.* p. 102): τοὺς τοιούτους δὲ ἀνθρώπους ὁ Ἑρμῆς ἐν τῷ περὶ φύσεων ἐκάλει ἄνοας, τῆς εἱμαρμένης μόνον¹ ὄντας πομπάς,² κ.τ.λ. *Corp.* IV was certainly known to Zosimus, since he speaks elsewhere of 'dipping oneself in the *Crater*'; but it is not clear whether he is here referring to it, or to some other Hermetic document. In *Corp.* IV, Hermes does not indeed use the word ἄνοες, but he says that men of this sort are devoid of νοῦς, and also speaks of τὰ ἀσώματα. But on the other hand he says nothing about εἱμαρμένη; and if Zosimus is referring to *Corp.* IV, he must himself have introduced the conception of εἱμαρμένη (i. e. the power by which τὰ σωματικά are governed) in giving his interpretation of its contents. Zosimus gives to the document of which

¹ μόνους codd. : μόνον Reitz.
² I. e. led passively along by Heimarmene.

he speaks the title Περὶ φύσεων (possibly Περὶ ⟨τῶν δύο⟩ φύσεων?). This might be taken to mean either 'concerning the two kinds of things' (viz. σώματα and ἀσώματα), or 'concerning the two kinds of men' (viz. ἔννοες and ἄνοες); and understood in either of these senses, it would be a possible title for *Corp.* IV.[1]

Reitzenstein *Poim.* p. 102 says that the simile of the πομπή 'is taken from Greek philosophy'; but I do not know to what philosophic writings he refers. The comparison of a πομπή is used in a different way by Epictetus, *Diss.* 4. 1. 104: οὐχὶ ἐκεῖνός (sc. ὁ θεός) σε εἰσήγαγεν; οὐχ ὡς θνητόν; οὐχ ὡς μετὰ ὀλίγου σαρκιδίου ζήσοντα ἐπὶ γῆς, καὶ θεασόμενον τὴν διοίκησιν αὐτοῦ, καὶ συμπομπεύσοντα αὐτῷ καὶ συνεορτάσοντα πρὸς ὀλίγον; οὐ θέλεις οὖν, ἕως δέδοταί σοι θεασάμενος τὴν πομπὴν καὶ τὴν πανήγυριν, εἶτα, ὅταν σ' ἐξάγῃ, πορεύεσθαι προσκυνήσας καὶ εὐχαριστήσας ὑπὲρ ὧν ἤκουσας καὶ εἶδες; In that passage, the πομπή is a show exhibited to us for our entertainment.—Marcus Aurelius 7. 3 describes human life as πομπῆς κενοσπουδία. This is a somewhat closer parallel; but the word πομπή must have had different associations for a Roman emperor.

§ 8 a. ὁ μὲν θεὸς ἀναίτιος, ἡμεῖς δὲ αἴτιοι τῶν κακῶν, ταῦτα προκρίνοντες τῶν ἀγαθῶν. The germ of this thought is as old as Homer. In *Od.* 1. 32 *sqq.*, Zeus says οἷον δή νυ θεοὺς βροτοὶ αἰτιόωνται. | ἐξ ἡμέων γάρ φασι κάκ' ἔμμεναι· οἱ δὲ καὶ αὐτοὶ | σφῇσιν ἀτασθαλίῃσιν ὑπὲρ μόρον ἄλγε' ἔχουσιν. But there can be little doubt that the source from which the Hermetist got it was Pl. *Rep.* 10. 617 E. Compare also Pl. *Tim.* 42 D, where the Demiurgus explains to the new-made souls the laws under which they are to live; διαθεσμοθετήσας δὲ πάντα αὐτοῖς ταῦτα, ἵνα τῆς ἔπειτα εἴη κακίας ἑκάστων ἀναίτιος, ἔσπειρε κ.τ.λ. *Rep.* 2. 379 C: τῶν δὲ κακῶν ἄλλ' ἄττα δεῖ ζητεῖν τὰ αἴτια, ἀλλ' οὐ τὸν θεόν.

§ 8 b. ⟨. . .⟩ ὁρᾷς . . . πόσα ἡμᾶς δεῖ σώματα . . . διεξελθεῖν. The thought expressed in this passage may be connected with that of the preceding paragraph in this way: 'in order to draw near to God, who is incorporeal, we must reject all that is corporeal; we must therefore rise above the corporeal Kosmos.' But in the traditional text, the connexion is not apparent; it seems necessary therefore to assume a lacuna before ὁρᾷς.

When he says that 'we must pass through many bodies in succession', the writer does not mean that we must be many times

---

[1] In IV. 6 b (δύο γὰρ ὄντων τῶν ὄντων, σώματος καὶ ἀσωμάτου), one might very well read οὐσῶν τῶν φύσεων in place of ὄντων τῶν ὄντων.

incarnated. He is speaking of men who are still living on earth, not of the destiny of the soul after death ; and his meaning is that we must ascend *in thought* to the heavens, and beyond them, to reach 'the incorporeal', which here, as often, is spoken of as if it were situated in extracosmic space. Cf. § 5: πάντα ἐμπεριλαβόντες τῷ ἑαυτῶν νοΐ, . . . τὰ ἐν οὐρανῷ, καὶ εἴ τί ἐστιν ὑπὲρ οὐρανόν. The many 'bodies' which the mind must successively traverse in its upward course are, first, the atmosphere, (or perhaps a lower and a higher stratum of the atmosphere, as in the system of Posidonius), and then, the several subdivisions of the region of fire, namely, the seven planet-spheres, and the sphere of the fixed stars. Compare *Corp.* XI. ii. 19, where the ascent of the ψυχή (i. e. the mind or thought) is similarly described.

καὶ πόσους χοροὺς δαιμόνων [[ ]] καὶ δρόμους ἀστέρων. This is another way of describing the same ascent through successive strata of matter. The daemons are the inhabitants of the atmosphere ; the planets and fixed stars are the inhabitants of the region of fire.

⟨. . . ἀ⟩διάβατον γὰρ τὸ ἀγαθόν, καὶ ἀπέραντον. The region of τὸ ἀσώματον, which is above the highest heaven, and extends beyond it without limit, is filled with the Good. (Cf. § 5, τοσοῦτον ἑαυτοὺς ὑψώσαντες εἶδον τὸ ἀγαθόν.) When you have once entered that region, you will never come to the end of it, or reach its further boundary ; you may continue your ascent for ever, and there will still be more of the Good above you.

Here again, the connexion of the thought with what precedes can be guessed without difficulty ; but the writer must have expressed it, and some words or sentences must therefore have been lost before ἀδιάβατον.

καὶ ἀτελές, αὐτῷ δὲ καὶ ἄναρχον, ἡμῖν δὲ δοκοῦν ἀρχὴν ἔχειν τὴν γνῶσιν. The Good is correlative to God, if not identical with God (see *Corp.* II, *Corp.* VI, and *Corp.* X) ; and 'for itself', or in itself, it is without end and without beginning, even as God is. 'For us' also (ἡμῖν, as opposed to ἑαυτῷ or ἁπλῶς), it is without end ; that is to say, the man who has once attained to it will continue to enjoy the possession of it for ever. But ' for us ' it is not without beginning. The unilluminated man is not aware of its existence. It is only when a man gets *gnosis* that the eternally existent Good presents itself to his consciousness ; and from his point of view, the existence of the Good appears to begin at the moment when he first becomes conscious of it.

§ 9. πάνυ γάρ ἐστι δύσκολον ⟨σκολιόν MSS.⟩. For δύσκολον, cf. Εv.
Marc. 10. 24 : πῶς δύσκολόν ἐστιν εἰς τὴν βασιλείαν τοῦ θεοῦ εἰσελθεῖν.
ἐπὶ τὰ παλαιὰ καὶ ἀρχαῖα ἀνακάμπτειν. The συνήθη καὶ παρόντα are
τὰ σωματικά (Plato's αἰσθητά), to which we have grown accustomed
since our incarnation ; the παλαιὰ καὶ ἀρχαῖα are τὰ ἀσώματα (Plato's
νοητά), i. e. the things of the higher world in which we lived before
we were 'sent down' to earth.

τὰ δὲ ἀφανῆ δυσπιστίαν ποιεῖ. The fact that these things are ἀφανῆ
makes it difficult to believe in their existence. The words ἀφανής
and φανερός are here employed as in *Corp.* V.

φανερώτερα δέ ἐστι τὰ κακά. The κακά are the corporeal things
which seem to us to be goods, but are really evils. Cf. *Corp.* VI.
2 b–4 a and 6.

τὸ δὲ ἀγαθὸν . . . πᾶσιν ἀνόμοιον. This passage is meaningless in
the MSS. ; I have put a meaning into it by transposing ἀδύνατον . . .
φανῆναι, and inserting ὅτι. If the words τὸ δὲ ἀγαθὸν ἀφανὲς τοῖς
φανεροῖς are sound, they must be explained in accordance with the
statement ἀδύνατον γὰρ ἀσώματον σώματι φανῆναι, and τὰ φανερά
must here be taken to mean our bodily organs of sense, which are
themselves perceptible by sense. We cannot see the Good with
our bodily eyes ; for the Good is incorporeal, and that which is
incorporeal cannot be seen by that which is corporeal.

διὰ τοῦτο, ⟨ὅτι⟩ αὐτῷ μέν ἐστιν ὅμοιον, τοῖς δὲ ἄλλοις πᾶσιν ἀνόμοιον.
Cf. § 1 b, as emended : τοιοῦτο γάρ ἐστι τὸ ἀσώματον, οὐχ . . . ὁρατόν,
. . . οὐδὲ ἄλλῳ τινὶ ὅμοιον.[1] It is to be presumed that in § 9, as well as
in § 1 b, the subject is τὸ ἀσώματον. When the writer speaks of
ὅμοιον and ἀνόμοιον, he is thinking of the saying that 'like is known
by like'. (Cf. *Corp.* XI. ii. 20 b : τὸ γὰρ ὅμοιον τῷ ὁμοίῳ νοητόν. Ar.
De an. 1. 2, 404 b 17 : γινώσκεσθαι γὰρ τῷ ὁμοίῳ τὸ ὅμοιον. Philolaus, in Sext. Emp. *Math.* 7. 92 : ὑπὸ τοῦ ὁμοίου τὸ ὅμοιον καταλαμβάνεσθαι πέφυκεν.) That which is ἀσώματον is 'unlike' σῶμα, and
therefore cannot be apprehended by the σωματικαὶ αἰσθήσεις ; but it
can be apprehended by the νοῦς in man, which is itself ἀσώματος ;
for all that is ἀσώματον is αὐτῷ ὅμοιον, or in other words, all ἀσώματα
are ἀλλήλοις ὅμοια.

[αὕτη διαφορὰ . . . πρὸς τὸ ὅμοιον.] I can make nothing of this ;
and it seems best to assume that it is a marginal note.

[1] A similar phrase occurs in a sentence attributed to Philolaus in Philo *De opif.
mundi* 33. 100, Cohn I, p. 34 : ἔστι γὰρ ἡγεμὼν καὶ ἄρχων ἁπάντων θεὸς εἷς, ἀεὶ ὤν,
μόνιμος, ἀκίνητος, αὐτὸς αὐτῷ ὅμοιος, ἕτερος τῶν ἄλλων.

§ 10. ⟨. . .⟩ [[ἡ γὰρ μονὰς . . . καὶ ῥίζα]] κ.τ.λ. The breach of continuity at the beginning of § 10 can be accounted for only by supposing that a connecting passage has been lost.[1]

The text of § 10 is in confusion; and the best way of restoring order seems to be to assume that the writer first said that a certain thing is the ἀρχή of all things, and then illustrated his meaning by the comparison of the arithmetical unit, which is the ἀρχή of all numbers. If so, the words ἡ γὰρ μονάς are out of place at the beginning of the paragraph. Moreover, the pointlessness of the repetition οὖσα ἀρχὴ καὶ ῥίζα . . . ὡς ἂν ῥίζα καὶ ἀρχή shows that there is something wrong in the first sentence. I have therefore removed the words ἡ γὰρ μονάς, πάντων οὖσα ῥίζα καὶ ἀρχή, and inserted them below, where they fit in well. But what is the lost subject for which ἡ μονάς has been substituted? What is it that is here said to be the ἀρχή of all things? It might be τὸ ἀγαθόν, or τὸ θεῖον, or ὁ θεός. But in § 11 b, we read αὕτη σοι . . . ὑπογέγραπται τοῦ θεοῦ εἰκών· and if these words were meant to refer to §§ 10, 11 a, it would seem that the lost subject of § 10 *init.* must be ὁ θεός. Compare *Hermippus* (Kroll and Viereck) 1. 18. 135 : ἡ δὲ μονὰς ἐν μὲν τοῖς ἀριθμοῖς ἀρχὴ καὶ ῥίζα τις ὑπόκειται, ἐν δὲ τοῖς νοητοῖς ὁ θεός, ἀφ' οὗ καθάπερ ἐκ πηγῆς ἐρρύη τὰ ὄντα.

ἐξ οὐδενὸς ἀλλ' ἢ [ἐξ] αὐτῆς. It is difficult to see any definite meaning in the statement that a thing 'has arisen out of itself', or 'has been generated by itself'; but to the Hermetists, and other writers of their time, the phrase appeared to express an important truth. The epithet αὐτογέννητος, 'generated by himself', was frequently applied to God, and seems to have been regarded as equivalent to ἀγέννητος, 'without beginning'. See *Ascl. Lat.* II. 14 b : 'ex se nata sunt'. αὐτογενής occurs in the same sense in Pseudo-Philolaus (Diels *Vorsokr.* p. 249): ἀριθμὸν εἶναι τῆς τῶν κοσμικῶν αἰωνίας διαμονῆς κρατιστεύοισαν καὶ αὐτογενῆ ('unerschaffene' Diels) συνοχήν.

μονάδι οὖν ⟨ἔοικεν ὁ θεός⟩.—(μονὰς οὖν ἀρχή (or ἡ ἀρχή), codd. Corp. : μονὰς οὖσα οὖν ἀρχή codd. Stob.) If my reconstruction of the passage is correct, this is the first mention of the monad; and we must suppose that the writer here wrote something to the effect that 'God (*qua* ἀρχή) is like the monad'.

The use of the μονάς as an εἰκών of the 'uncaused cause' of all things was, no doubt, suggested to the writer by the arithmetical

---

[1] Or else, that 10–11 b is a fragment of another document, and has been appended to *Corp.* IV by error.

speculations of Pythagoreans and Pythagorizing Platonists. But the Hermetist, if I have interpreted him rightly, uses the arithmetical unit merely as an 'image' or illustration, by means of which the learner may be helped to comprehend the nature of the ἀρχὴ πάντων; he does not identify it with the ἀρχὴ πάντων itself. He does not say, as some Platonists did, that the μονάς *is* God, or that God *is* the μονάς, but only that the relation of God to things is *analogous* to the relation of the unit to numbers.

Plato spoke much of τὸ ἕν in contrast to τὰ πολλά; but he did not, in his written dialogues at least, use the word μονάς with any special significance. But Plato's pupils and successors, Speusippus and Xenocrates, adopted from Pythagorean sources a sort of arithmetical theology;[1] and we are told that Xenocrates said that the μονάς is the supreme God. Aetius, Diels *Doxogr.* p. 304 : Ξενοκράτης ... τὴν μονάδα καὶ τὴν δυάδα θεούς, τὴν μὲν ὡς ἄρρενα, πατρὸς ἔχουσαν τάξιν, ἐν οὐρανῷ βασιλεύουσαν, ἥντινα προσαγορεύει καὶ Ζῆνα καὶ περιττὸν καὶ νοῦν, ὅστις ἐστὶν αὐτῷ πρῶτος θεός· τὴν δ' ὡς θήλειαν, μητρὸς θεῶν δίκην, τῆς ὑπὸ τὸν οὐρανὸν λήξεως ἡγουμένην, ἥτις ἐστὶν αὐτῷ ψυχὴ τοῦ παντός. From the time of Xenocrates onward, there are frequent instances of this deification of the number one. 'Pythagoras', in Aetius (*Doxogr.* p. 281): τὴν μονάδα καὶ τὴν ἀόριστον δυάδα (τίθησιν) ἐν ταῖς ἀρχαῖς· σπεύδει δὲ αὐτῷ τῶν ἀρχῶν ἡ μὲν (*sc.* ἡ μονὰς) ἐπὶ τὸ ποιητικὸν αἴτιον καὶ εἰδικόν, ὅπερ ἐστὶ νοῦς, ὁ θεός, ἡ δὲ (*sc.* ἡ ἀόριστος δυὰς) ἐπὶ τὸ παθητικόν τε καὶ ὑλικόν, ὅπερ ἐστὶν ὁ ὁρατὸς κόσμος. ... νοῦς μὲν οὖν ἡ μονάς ἐστιν κ.τ.λ. Aetius, *Doxogr.* p. 302 : Πυθαγόρας τῶν ἀρχῶν τὴν μονάδα θεὸν καὶ τἀγαθόν, ἥτις ἐστὶν ἡ τοῦ ἑνὸς φύσις, αὐτὸς ὁ νοῦς, καὶ τὴν ἀόριστον δυάδα καὶ τὸ κακόν, περὶ ἥν ἐστι τὸ ὑλικὸν πλῆθος. (This passage is evidently corrupt ; perhaps the original text was something like this : Π. ἀρχὰς τὴν μονάδα, ἥτις ἐστὶν ὁ νοῦς καὶ αὐτὸς ὁ θεὸς καὶ τἀγαθόν, καὶ τὴν ἀόριστον δυάδα, περὶ ἥν ἐστι τὸ ὑλικὸν πλῆθος καὶ τὸ κακόν.) Hippol. *Ref. haer.* 1. 2 (Diels *Doxogr.* p. 555): Pythagoras μονάδα μὲν εἶναι ἀπεφήνατο τὸν θεόν. Compare the 'Egyptian' (i. e. Pythagorean) doctrine in Hippol. *ib.* 4. 43 : ἔφασαν τὸν θεὸν εἶναι μονάδα ἀδιαίρετον καὶ αὐτὴν ἑαυτὴν γεννῶσαν, καὶ ἐξ αὐτῆς τὰ πάντα κατεσκευάσθαι. αὐτὴ γάρ, φησίν, ἀγέννητος οὖσα, τοὺς ἑξῆς ἀριθμοὺς γεννᾷ· οἷον ἐφ' ἑαυτὴν ἡ μονὰς ἐπιπροστεθεῖσα γεννᾷ τὴν δυάδα, καὶ ὁμοίως ἐπιπροστιθεμένη γεννᾷ τὴν

---

[1] It appears from Aristotle's reports of Plato's 'unwritten' teaching that Plato himself, in his old age, went some way in this direction; and the metaphysics of his earlier successors contained 'a large admixture of arithmetical mysticism' (Zeller, *Plato*, Eng. tr. p. 565).

τριάδα καὶ τετράδα μέχρι τῆς δεκάδος. Synesius, *Hymn.* 1. 52 (Migne 66.

1589 A): ὁ μέν, αὐτόσσυτος¹ ἀρχά, | ταμίας πατήρ τε ⟨π⟩άντων,² || ἀλό-
χευτος,³ ὑψιθώκων | ὑπὲρ οὐρανοῦ καρήνων, || ἀλύτῳ κύδεϊ γαίων, | θεὸς
ἔμπεδος θαάσσει, || ἐνοτήτων ἑνὰς ἁγνὴ | μονάδων μονάς τε πρώτη, ||
⌐ἁπλοτήτας ἀκροτήτων | ἐνώσασα⌐¹⁴ καὶ τεκοῦσα || ὑπερουσίοις λοχείαις· ⁵||
ὅθεν αὐτὴ προθοροῦσα | ⌐διὰ πρωτόσπορον εἶδος⌐ || μονάς, ἄρρητα χυ-
θεῖσα, | τρικορύμβον ἔσχεν ἀλκάν· ⁶|| ὑπερούσιος δὲ παγὰ | στέφεται καλ-
λεϊ παίδων || ἀπὸ κέντρου τε θορόντων | περὶ κέντρον τε ῥυέντων. Synes.
Hymn. 2. 69: μέγα χαῖρε, ῥίζα κόσμου, | μέγα χαῖρε, κέντρον ὄντων, |
μονὰς ἀμβρότων ἀριθμῶν. *Ib.* 3. 171: παγὰ παγῶν, [ἀρχῶν ἀρχά,] ῥιζῶν
ῥίζα, | μονὰς εἶ μονάδων, ἀριθμῶν ⌐ἀριθμός.⌐¹⁷ *Ib.* 4. 60: μονὰς ὦ μονά-
δων, πάτερ ὦ πατέρων, | ἀρχῶν ἀρχά, παγῶν παγά, κ.τ.λ.

πάντα ἀριθμὸν ἐμπεριέχει, ὑπὸ μηδενὸς ἐμπεριεχομένη. The unit
'contains in itself every number, and is contained in no number'.
In the obvious sense of the words, this is the reverse of the truth;
the number one does not contain the number three, and is contained
in the number three. But the writer probably meant that the unit
contains the other numbers *implicitly*, or *in germ*, i. e. that they can
be developed out of it (by a series of additions), but it cannot be
developed out of them (by the same process).

πάντα ἀριθμὸν γεννᾷ. Cf. *Corp.* XII. ii. 15 a: αἱ δὲ ἑνάδες τὸν ἀριθμὸν
γεννῶσι καὶ αὔξουσι. Pseudo-Plutarch, Stob. 1 (*Prooem.*) 2, vol. i,
p. 16 W.: ἡ μονὰς γονὴ ὑπὸ Τιμαίου τοῦ Λοκροῦ προσαγορεύεται, ὡς
ἄρχουσα τῆς τῶν ἀριθμῶν γενέσεως. Just as we say that 'one and one
make two', the Greeks were accustomed to say that the unit *generates*
(γεννᾷ) the other numbers, meaning by this that each number is
produced by adding a unit to the preceding number ($1 + 1 = 2$,
$2 + 1 = 3$, &c.). It was probably, in part at least, through this use
of the word γεννᾶν, that some of the Pythagoreans and Platonists
were led to hypostatize the arithmetical unit, and ascribe to it
a demiurgic power;⁸ and applying to things in general the principle

---

¹ = αὐτογέννητος.　　　　² ὄντων Migne.　　　　³ = ἀγέννητος.
⁴ Perhaps ἁπλότητος ἀκρότητας γονόωσα.
⁵ Cf. *ib.* 2. 63: σὺ πατήρ, σὺ δ' ἐσσὶ μάτηρ.
⁶ The meaning of this (if it can be said to have a meaning) appears to be that
the supreme God is a μονὰς μονάδων, or προμονάς, from which issues a μονάς which
is also a τριάς (i. e. the Christian Trinity). Cf. Synes. *Hymn.* 3. 210: ὑμνῶ σε,
τριάς· μονὰς εἶ, τριὰς ὤν· τριὰς εἶ, μονὰς ὤν.
⁷ Perhaps ἀριθμῶν ἀρχά.
⁸ The earlier Pythagoreans probably meant by 'the *monas*', not the abstract
arithmetical unit, but a point situated in space; and some of them, in their
cosmogonic speculations, began by positing such a *monas* in the midst of τὸ ἄπειρον,
and ascribing generative or demiurgic activity to it.

which they thought they had discovered in the relations of numbers, they identified 'the Monad' with God, the πάντων γεννητής. But from this confusion of thought the writer of *Corp*. IV seems to have kept himself free.

§ 11 a. [καὶ τὸ μὲν αὐξητὸν ... τὴν μονάδα χωρῆσαι.] This passage is omitted by Stobaeus; and it is probably a note inserted in the Corpus-text by some reader. The words τὸ μὲν αὐξητὸν αὐξάνεται ἀπὸ τῆς μονάδος mean that the numbers are produced from the unit by successive additions. This is merely another way of saying that the unit πάντα ἀριθμὸν γεννᾷ. But when we are told that the numbers 'increase from' the unit, it might be thought to follow that, since they are all *greater* than the unit, any one of them would be more fit than the unit to serve as a symbol of God ; and the writer's object seems to have been to guard against this inference. 'It is true', he says, 'that the number three, for instance, is greater than the unit ; yet it is inferior to the unit ; and its inferiority is shown in this, that it is incapable of containing the unit, whereas the unit can and does contain the number three.' The verb χωρεῖν here is equivalent to ἐμπεριέχειν above.

§ 11 b. αὕτη σοι ... ὑπογέγραπται τοῦ θεοῦ εἰκών. Applying the analogy of the numerical unit to God, we may infer from what has been said about the unit (1) that God πάντα ἐμπεριέχει and ὑπ' οὐδενὸς ἐμπεριέχεται, (2) that God πάντα γεννᾷ and ὑπ' οὐδενὸς γεννᾶται, and (3) that God is τέλειος, ἀδιαίρετος, ἀναύξητος καὶ ἀμείωτος, whereas τὰ ὑπὸ τοῦ θεοῦ γεννώμενα are ἀτελῆ, διαιρετά, αὐξητὰ καὶ μειωτά.

τοῖς τῆς καρδίας ὀφθαλμοῖς. καρδία, as here used, corresponds to the νοῦς of *Corp*. V. 2, τοῖς τοῦ νοῦ ὀφθαλμοῖς.

αὐτή σε ἡ [εἰκὼν] ⟨θέα⟩ ὁδηγήσει. If we read ἡ εἰκών, it must be taken to mean ἡ μονάς, to which the preceding words (αὕτη σοι . . . ὑπογέγραπται τοῦ θεοῦ εἰκών) refer ; and Hermes must be understood to say that the arithmetical unit, or the comparison of God to the arithmetical unit, 'will guide you on your upward way'. But that is hardly satisfactory. A better sense may be got by writing θέα here, and taking it to refer to εἰ θεάσῃ above.

ἔχει γάρ τι ἴδιον ⌈ἡ θέα⌉· τοὺς φθάσαντας θεάσασθαι κατέχει, καὶ ἀνέλκει καθάπερ φασὶν ἡ Μαγνῆτις λίθος τὸν σίδηρον. The subject of ἔχει, κατέχει, and ἀνέλκει, which is the same as the object of θεάσασθαι, can hardly have been ἡ θέα. Something like τὸ θεῖον would serve the purpose.

κατέχεσθαι means 'to be possessed' by a deity. Compare Pl. *Ion*

533 D : ἔστι δὲ τοῦτο τέχνη μὲν οὐκ ὂν παρά σοι, . . . θεία δὲ δύναμις,
ἥ σε κινεῖ, ὥσπερ ἐν τῇ λίθῳ ἣν Εὐριπίδης μὲν Μαγνῆτιν ὠνόμασεν. . . .
πάντες γὰρ οἱ . . . ποιηταὶ . . . ἔνθεοι ὄντες καὶ κατεχόμενοι κ.τ.λ.
As τὸ κατέχεσθαι and ἡ Μαγνῆτις λίθος are spoken of together both
in the *Ion* and in *Corp.* IV, it is probable that the thought was
suggested to the Hermetist by the passage in the *Ion.* For the
comparison of the magnet, cf. Porphyr. *De abst.* 4. 20 : προσπεφυκὼς
τῷ θεῷ μᾶλλον ἢ σίδηρος τῷ μάγνητι.

LIBELLVS V

Contents

God is unseen, and ever-existent.   He brings all things into being ;
but he himself is not brought into being.   Coming into being means
appearing as a thing perceived by sense, and God causes all things
thus to appear ; but he himself does not thus appear ; he is unseen,
or hidden.   § 1 b.

Yet, inasmuch as he causes all things to appear, he can be seen
in all things ; but he can be seen by thought alone, and not with
the bodily eyes.   Seeing the Kosmos with your eyes, you can
apprehend by thought Him of whom the Kosmos is an image.   § 2.

The heavenly bodies observe order in their movements ; and
air, sea, and earth are likewise ordered.   Now where there is order,
there must be one who has established the order ; there must therefore be a Maker and Master of all these.   (It is true that there
are some things which are out of order ; but these things also
are subject to the Master, and will be brought to order by him.)
§§ 3, 4.

If you could see all parts of the Kosmos at one view, you
would see everywhere the hidden God manifested through his
works.   § 5.

You can also see him in all mortal organisms.   For instance,
the structure of the human body shows evident marks of design ;
there must therefore be a Craftsman who made it.   §§ 6–8.

All things then have been made or generated by the one God.
He could not exist if he were not always and everywhere producing
things.   He is all things that now are, and all things that are to be
hereafter.   § 9.

God, though hidden, is yet manifest ; for he is all things. § 10 a.

How can I worship Thee? Thou art everywhere; all things are Thine ; Thou art in all times alike ; Thou art the author of all. I cannot do or say anything by my own power; for I am not other than Thou. There is nothing that Thou art not. §§ 10 b, 11.

Thou art Mind, and Father, and God, and Good. § 11 *fin.*

Sources. The distinction between τὸ ἀφανές and τὸ φανερόν corresponds to the Platonic distinction between τὸ νοητόν and τὸ αἰσθητόν. But the terms ἀφανές and φανερόν are not thus used by Plato; the writer must therefore have got them from some other source; and his use of these terms may possibly be due to Egyptian influence.

In the description of the human body (§ 6), the influence of the *Timaeus* may perhaps be recognized in the list of the internal organs, and especially in the words ὀχετεύσας and σηραγγώσας.

In the argument that the structure of the human body shows design, the writer handles in a cursory and superficial way a topic on which the Stoics were accustomed to dilate ; see e. g. Cic. *Nat. deor.* 2. 134–146 (probably from Posidonius). The remark that the Demiurgus has concealed the unseemly parts of the body may be traced back to Panaetius.

The term φαντασία (§ 1 b) has been adopted either from the Aristotelians or from the Stoics, but probably from the latter.

When the writer of *Corp.* V says that God is the 'maker' and 'father' of all things, he is using the language of the *Timaeus*. But he also says that God 'is' all things. The latter statement, which is hardly consistent with the former, must have been derived from a different source. It might perhaps be accounted for as a development of Stoic theology ; but it may also have been suggested by the diction of hymns used in the worship of the Egyptian gods. The phrases καὶ τὰ ὄντα καὶ τὰ μὴ ὄντα (§ 9), and τὸ γενόμενον, τὸ μὴ γενόμενον (§ 11), as here employed, may perhaps be of Egyptian origin. In the concluding hymn, the worshipper's denial that he is other than God (ὡς ἄλλος ὤν ;) is in accordance with the distinctive character of Egyptian religion.

A sign of Jewish influence may perhaps be seen in the statement that God is the τόπος of all things (§ 10 b) ; and possibly also in the use of ὁ κύριος as a name of God (§ 2).

The document shows no trace of Christian influence.

Date. There is little evidence of date in *Corp.* V, except the intermixture of Stoic conceptions with Platonism, which shows that this document, like the *Hermetica* in general, cannot be earlier than the first century B. C. It appears from the introductory words that it was one of the διεξοδικοὶ λόγοι addressed to Tat ; and these were presumably later than the˜γενικοὶ λόγοι. It may therefore be reasonably conjectured that *Corp.* V was written in the third century A. D.

Title. ὅτι ἀφανὴς ⟨. . . ὁ⟩ θεὸς φανερώτατός ἐστι. In § 1 b, the writer asserts that God is ἀφανής ; in the rest of the document, he asserts that God is φανερώτατος. On the assumption that the heading referred to the contents of § 2 *sqq.* only, sense might be restored by striking out ἀφανής. If it referred to § 1 b also, the meaning required might be got by writing ὅτι ⟨καὶ⟩ ἀφανὴς ⟨ὁ⟩ θεὸς ⟨καὶ⟩ φανερώτατός ἐστι· or ὅτι ⟨καίπερ⟩ ἀφανὴς ⟨ὢν (or εἶναι δοκῶν) ὁ⟩ θεὸς φανερώτατός ἐστι· or ὅτι ⟨πὴ μὲν⟩ ἀφανὴς ⟨ὁ⟩ θεός, ⟨πὴ δὲ⟩ φανερώτατός ἐστι.

§ 1 a. καὶ τόνδε σοι τὸν λόγον, ὦ Τάτ, διεξελεύσομαι. The verb διεξέρχεσθαι corresponds to the substantive διέξοδος ; it is therefore probable that this document was one of the series known as οἱ πρὸς Τὰτ διεξοδικοὶ λόγοι, and that at least one other λόγος preceded it in that series.

ὅπως μὴ ἀμύητος ᾖς τοῦ κρείττονος θεοῦ ὀνόματος. The pupil is to be 'initiated' ; that is, the *gnosis* which this discourse is to reveal to him is spoken of as a μυστήριον. But it is a 'mystery' only in a metaphorical sense. Sacramental ritual, which was the essence of the Greek mystery-cults, is wholly absent ; and the *gnosis* is imparted to the pupil by oral instruction only. The term ἀμύητος may be taken as implying, firstly, that the *gnosis* has hitherto been known only to a few (and possibly, that those to whom it is known ought to reveal it only to the few who are worthy to receive the revelation) ; and secondly, that he to whom it is revealed is thereby brought into communion with the deity concerned,—that is, in this case, with the supreme God. Cf. *Ascl. Lat.* III 19 a, 'tibi . . . divina nudo mysteria' ; and see note on *Corp.* I. 16.

τοῦ κρείττονος θεοῦ ὀνόματος, if that is the right reading,[1] must be the genitive of ὁ κρείττων θεοῦ ὀνόματος, 'He who is mightier than

---

[1] The phrase is obscure ; the author's meaning might be more clearly expressed by writing τοῦ κρείττονος πάντων ὀνομάτων here, and ὁ παντὸς ὀνόματος κρείττων in § 10 a.

the name θεός ', i. e. too great to be rightly called θεός. See § 10 a
and 9 *init.*; and compare *Ascl. Lat.* III. 20 a. The word θεός is
applied to many subordinate beings; it is inadequate to describe
the supreme and all-inclusive Being. The writer subsequently uses
the name θεός (§ 7 *fin.*, § 11 *fin.*), as well as others (ὁ κύριος, ὁ πατήρ,
&c.); but he holds that the supreme Being is, strictly speaking,
either παντώνυμος or ἀνώνυμος (§ 10 a). Cf. *Exc.* VI. 19 : ὁ θεός,
μᾶλλον δὲ τὸ μεῖζόν τι ὂν ⌈τοῦ θεοῦ τὸ ὄνομα⌉.

τὸ δοκοῦν τοῖς πολλοῖς ἀφανές. The ἀφανές of which this writer
speaks is the ἀόρατον or ἀειδές (i. e. νοητόν) of Plato. God is ἀφανής ;
that is, he is not directly apprehensible by the senses. But the
word ἀφανής is not employed in this connexion by Plato ; and it is
possible that the author of *Corp.* V was influenced in his choice
of the term by language used in the Egyptian cults. ' According
to the received explanation in the time of the New Kingdom, the
name of the God *Amen* signifies " The Hidden One " ' (Wiedemann,
Rel. of the Ancient Egyptians, Eng. tr. p. 108). Brugsch, *Rel. und
Myth.* p. 97, quotes from Egyptian documents : ' God is hidden, and
his form is known to no man.' ' No one has searched out his
likeness.' ' He is hidden to gods and men.' ' He is a secret for
his creatures.'

In the system attributed by Hippolytus to Simon Magus, the
terms κρυπτόν [1] and φανερόν were used as ἀφανές and φανερόν are
used in *Corp.* V.   Hippol. *Ref. haer.* 6. 9 : ἔστι δὲ τοῦτο (*sc.* τὸ κρυπτὸν
καὶ τὸ φανερὸν) ὅπερ . . . Πλάτων νοητὸν καὶ αἰσθητὸν (καλεῖ). . . .
καθόλου δὲ [ἐστιν] εἰπεῖν, πάντων τῶν ὄντων, αἰσθητῶν τε καὶ νοητῶν,
ὦν (ὁ Σίμων) κρυφίων καὶ φανερῶν προσαγορεύει, κ.τ.λ.

§ 1 b. πᾶν γὰρ τὸ φαινόμενον γεννητόν· . . . τὸ δὲ ἀφανὲς ἀεὶ ἔστι.
To this writer, τὸ φανῆναι and τὸ γενέσθαι are equivalents. The
things of the sensible world have no substantive existence ; they are
merely φαινόμενα. And they 'appear' only for a time; it is the
' hidden' or ' unseen' alone that 'exists everlastingly'.[2] The thought
is derived from Plato, though the terms used to express it are not
those which Plato commonly employed. As here stated, the
doctrine resembles Berkeley's idealism. In the world of sense, *esse*
is *percipi.* There are no really existent ' external objects'; there
is nothing but perceptions (φαντασίαι), and God, who causes the

---

[1] Cf. ἔκρυψας, *Corp.* V. 11.
[2] Cf. Paul, 2 *Cor.* 4. 18 : μὴ σκοπούντων ἡμῶν τὰ βλεπόμενα, ἀλλὰ τὰ μὴ βλεπό-
μενα· τὰ γὰρ βλεπόμενα πρόσκαιρα, τὰ δὲ μὴ βλεπόμενα αἰώνια.

perceptions.[1] Cf. Herm. *ap.* Stob. *Exc.* II A. 18 : τὸ ψεῦδός (i. e. the sensible world) φημι τῆς ἀληθείας (i. e. τοῦ θεοῦ) ἐνέργημα εἶναι.

αὐτὸς ἀφανὴς ὤν. Here we find the writer speaking no longer of τὸ ἀφανές in the neuter, but of ὁ ἀφανής (θεός) in the masculine. Some words in which the transition from τὸ ἀφανές to ὁ ἀφανής was made have probably been lost.

οὐκ αὐτὸς γεννώμενος ἐν φαντασίᾳ. φαντασία is a technical term of the Aristotelian and Stoic[2] theory of cognition. It signifies the mental image which results from the action of an object on the bodily sense-organs, or the process by which this mental image is produced. Aetius (Diels *Doxogr.* p. 401) gives Chrysippus's definition of φαντασία as follows : φαντασία ... ἐστὶ πάθος ἐν τῇ ψυχῇ γιγνόμενον, ἐνδεικνύμενον ἐν αὐτῷ καὶ τὸ πεποιηκός· οἷον ἐπειδὰν δι᾽ ὄψεως θεωρῶμεν τὸ λευκόν, ἔστι πάθος τὸ ἐγγεγενημένον διὰ τῆς ὁράσεως ἐν τῇ ψυχῇ· καὶ ⟨κατὰ⟩ τοῦτο τὸ πάθος εἰπεῖν ἔχομεν ὅτι ὑπόκειται λευκὸν κινοῦν ἡμᾶς. ... ἡ φαντασία δείκνυσιν ἑαυτὴν καὶ τὸ πεποιηκὸς αὐτήν. Chrysippus took for granted the reality of τὸ πεποιηκός, i. e. the

---

[1] Sir William Jones, writing with reference to the Indian doctrine of *Maya*, says : ' The inextricable difficulties attending the vulgar notion of material substances ... induced many of the wisest among the ancients, and some of the most enlightened among the moderns, to believe that the whole creation was rather an *energy* than a work, by which the Infinite Being, who is present at all times and in all places, exhibits to the minds of His creatures a set of perceptions, like a wonderful picture or piece of music, always varied, yet always uniform ; so that all bodies and their qualities exist, indeed, to every wise and useful purpose, but exist only as far as they are perceived.' (Hargrave Jennings, *The Rosicrucians*, p. 147.)

There was frequent communication by sea between Roman Egypt and India ; and it is not impossible that some Indian notions may have been transmitted to Egyptian Greeks. Numenius, in Book I of his Περὶ τἀγαθοῦ, mentioned the Brahmans (together with the Jews, the Zoroastrians, and the Egyptians) as one of the peoples whose religious rites and philosophic doctrines he would have to adduce and compare with the teachings of Plato and Pythagoras. (The passage is given as follows in Euseb. *Pr. ev.* 9. 7 : δεήσει ... ἐπικαλέσασθαι τὰ ἔθνη τὰ εὐδοκιμοῦντα, προσφερόμενον αὐτῶν τὰς τελετὰς καὶ τὰ δόγματα, τάς τε ⌈ἱδρύσεις συντελουμένας Πλάτωνι ὁμολογουμένως⌉, ὁπόσας Βραχμᾶνες καὶ Ἰουδαῖοι καὶ Μάγοι καὶ Αἰγύπτιοι διέθεντο. Neither ἱδρύσεις nor συντελουμένας makes sense. I am inclined to conjecture that Numenius wrote τάς τε ἱερὰς (βίβλους or γραφὰς) δηλούντα Πλάτωνι ὁμολογούσας, ὁπόσας Βραχμᾶνες ... διέθεντο, ' showing that all the sacred books which the Brahmans &c. composed agree with Plato ', or something to that effect. He had read some of the sacred books of the Jews, and doubtless knew—or thought he knew—something about those of the Zoroastrians and the Egyptians ; and he may have had some information about Indian writings also.) Moreover, both the fictitious visit of Apollonius Tyaneus to India described in Philostr. *Vita Apollon.*, and the historical fact that Plotinus made an attempt to visit India, show that in the third century A.D. Greek thinkers had some inkling of the significance of Indian philosophy. But the doctrine of *Corp.* V can be sufficiently accounted for as a development of Platonism, without assuming Indian influence.

[2] Plato, *Soph.* 264 A, defines a φαντασία as a δόξα which πάρεστί τινι μὴ καθ᾽ αὑτήν, ἀλλὰ δι᾽ αἰσθήσεως, i.e. an opinion which is formed in the mind as the result of an impression on the senses ; but he does not habitually use the word.

external object; but the writer of *Corp.* V here ignores τὸ πεποιηκός, and speaks only of ὁ πάντα φαντασιῶν (i. e. ὁ τὰς φαντασίας ποιῶν, or ὁ τὰ πράγματα γεννῶν ἐν φαντασίᾳ,) namely, God.

ἡ γὰρ φαντασία μόνων τῶν γεννητῶν ἐστιν. τὰ γεννητά are presented to us in φαντασία; indeed, it is only in our φαντασία that they exist; 'for γένεσις is nothing but φαντασία'. But ὁ ἀγέννητος θεός is not presented to us in φαντασία; he is therefore ἀφανής.

§ 2. τὰ δὲ πάντα φαντασιῶν, διὰ πάντων φαίνεται. In the preceding paragraph, the writer has shown that God is ἀφανής; he now proceeds to show that God is φανερός. Cf. *Corp.* XI. ii. 22 a: τίς αὐτοῦ φανερώτερος;

We commonly suppose that our φαντασίαι are caused by external objects, and we say that we see those objects. But in reality, our φαντασίαι are caused by God; it is really God then that we see.[1]

τῷ κυρίῳ καὶ πατρί, [καὶ] ⟨τῷ⟩ μόνῳ καὶ [οὐχ] ἑνὶ ⟨ἀγαθῷ?⟩ [ἀλλ' ἀφ' οὗ ὁ εἶς]. The words οὐχ ἑνὶ ἀλλ' ἀφ' οὗ ὁ εἶς are inconsistent with the rest of the *libellus*. Everywhere else, this writer speaks only of the one God as Demiurgus, and does not recognize a distinct and subordinate Being called ὁ εἶς. It might be conjectured that the words which I have bracketed were written by some Platonist who distinguished a first and a second supracosmic God (corresponding to the ἕν and the νοῦς of Plotinus); but if so, we should have expected him to give the name ὁ εἶς to the first God, not to the second. Possibly ἀλλ' ἀφ' οὗ may be a corruption of ἀγαθῷ, and οὐχ and ὁ εἶς may have been subsequently added to make sense. For τῷ μόνῳ καὶ ἑνὶ ⟨ἀγαθῷ⟩, cf. *Corp.* II. 14: οὔτε γὰρ τῶν ἄλλων . . . τις δύναται . . . ἀγαθὸς εἶναι, ἢ μόνος ὁ θεός. But ὁ εἶς καὶ μόνος might be used (without ἀγαθός) as a name of the supreme God.

ἀκτῖνά σοι κἂν μίαν αὐτοῦ. Cf. *Corp.* XVI. 16: ⟨ὅ⟩τῳ οὖν ἐν τῷ λογικῷ ἀκτὶς ἐπιλάμπει κ.τ.λ. The divine νοῦς is the light by which the 'gnostic' is illuminated; and it is by that light alone that a man can 'see' God.

⟨⟨εἰ δὲ καὶ τὸ ἐν σοὶ . . ., πῶς . . . φανήσεται;⟩⟩ This sentence is clearly out of place at the end of the section, where it stands in the MSS. Here, it suits the context perfectly. The words τὸ ἐν σοί,

---

[1] Cf. Tennyson, *The Higher Pantheism*: 'The sun, the moon, the stars, the seas, the hills and the plains—Are not these, O Soul, the Vision of Him who reigns? . . . And the ear of man cannot hear, and the eye of man cannot see; But if we could see and hear, this Vision—were it not He?'

which are obscure when taken by themselves, are satisfactorily explained by the preceding νόησις . . . ἀφανὴς οὖσα; and διὰ τῶν ὀφθαλμῶν ('with your bodily eyes') prepares the way for the contrasted phrase, τοῖς τοῦ νοῦ ὀφθαλμοῖς, which follows. It may therefore be considered certain that the sentence was intended to stand where I have placed it. For the thought that ἡ ἐν ἡμῖν νόησις is ἀφανής, and is in that respect comparable to God, cf. *Corp.* XI. ii *fin.*: ὁ νοῦς (the human mind) ὁρᾶται ἐν τῷ νοεῖν, ὁ θεὸς ἐν τῷ ποιεῖν.

τὴν εἰκόνα τοῦ θεοῦ: i. e. the sensible Kosmos. Cf. *Ascl. Lat.* I. 10 : 'dei, cuius sunt imagines duae mundus et homo.' You can see τὰ οὐράνια; you can both see and grasp with your hands τὰ θνητά, e. g. a human body.

§§ 3–5. εἰ δὲ θέλεις αὐτὸν ἰδεῖν . . . φαινόμενον δι᾽ ὧν ποιεῖ. Compare *Corp.* XI. ii. 6 b–11, where it is shown by a similar argument that there must be a 'Maker' of the Kosmos. In both passages alike, the τάξις τοῦ παντός is insisted on; but the word ζωή, which is the keynote of *Corp.* XI. ii, is not employed in *Corp.* V. Cf. Methodius Περὶ τοῦ αὐτεξουσίου (Bonwetsch) 2. 3 ff. (a 'Valentinian' speaks) : I observed that the sea is under control, οὐκ ὑπερβαίνουσα τὸν οἰκεῖον τόπον, ὡς ἔπος εἰπεῖν θεῖόν τι πρόσταγμα πεφοβημένη. . . . ἀλλά μοι καὶ περὶ τοῦ ἡλίου ζητεῖν ἐδόκει, . . . ὅτι μηδὲ οὗτος παρέρχεται τὸν οἰκεῖον δρόμον, ἀλλὰ καὶ αὐτός, ὡς ἔνεστιν εἰπεῖν, ἐντολήν τινα φυλάττει κρείττονος. καὶ . . . ἑώρων . . . σελήνην . . ., ὅτι τε καὶ αὐτὴ τηρεῖ τὸν κύκλον τῶν ἡμερῶν. καί μοι ἐδόκει τὸ ἐντεῦθεν ὡς θεία τις ὑπάρχει οἰκονομία καὶ δύναμις κρειττόνων (al. κρείττονος) ἡ συνέχουσα τὰ ὅλα, ἣν καὶ θεὸν δικαίως ἂν εἴποιμεν.

§ 3. [τάξις γὰρ πᾶσα]. This may possibly be a misplaced doublet of πᾶσα γὰρ τάξις in § 4.

ὁ ἥλιος . . . ᾧ πάντες εἴκουσιν οἱ οὐράνιοι θεοὶ ὡσανεὶ βασιλεῖ. Cf. *Corp.* XVI, and *Corp.* XI. ii. 7 as emended : τοῦ ἡλίου, . . . τοῦ . . . πάσης τάξεως ἄρχοντος, καὶ ἡγεμόνος τῶν ἑπτὰ κόσμων.

ἕκαστος τούτων τῶν ἀστέρων ⟨⟨περιώρισται ἀριθμῷ καὶ τόπῳ⟩⟩. The words περιώρισται . . . τόπῳ are evidently out of place where they stand in the MSS.; and something of the sort is needed here to complete the sentence. By ἀριθμῷ must be meant the 'measure' or 'extent' of the planet's orbit. Thus περιώρισται ἀριθμῷ καὶ τόπῳ corresponds to τὸν τ[ρ]όπον καὶ τὸ μέγεθος τοῦ δρόμου ὁρίσας below.

§ 4. ⟨ἡ⟩ ἄρκτος, ⟨⟨ἡ⟩⟩ . . . τὸν πάντα κόσμον συμπεριφέρουσα. The two Bears, as depicted on a celestial globe or planisphere, looked

like two animals walking in the same direction round the Pole (see
e. g. Boll, *Sphaera*, Tafel I) ; and this, no doubt, suggested the notion
that they worked like mill-horses, and made the whole sphere of the
fixed stars revolve, or that one of them did so. Cf. Herm. *ap.* Stob.
Exc. VI. 13 : (τῆς ἄρκτου) ἡ ἐνέργειά ἐστι καθάπερ ἄξονος, . . . περὶ
⟨τὸ⟩ αὐτὸ στρεφομένης, ἐνεργούσης δὲ τὴν ⟨τοῦ⟩ ζῳοφόρου κύκλου
⟨περιφοράν⟩. The Mithraic *Apathanatismos* (Dieterich ' *Mithrasliturgie* ') p. 14 : ἄρκτος ἡ κινοῦσα καὶ ἀντιστρέφουσα τὸν οὐρανόν.

⟨. . .⟩ τίς ὁ τοῦτο κεκτημένος τὸ ὄργανον ; According to the traditional
text, the writer passes abruptly from the highest heaven to sea and
earth. But it is more probable that he mentioned all the four
elements in succession, and that after discussing the heavens (i. e.
the region of fire) he spoke of the air before dealing with the water
and the earth. If so, the ὄργανον is air, regarded as the ' instrument '
by means of which life is conveyed into terrestrial organisms and
maintained in them. Cf. *Ascl. Lat.* III. 19 b *fin.* : ' aer vero
organum est vel machina omnium, per quam omnia fiunt.' The
function here assigned to air corresponds to that which the Stoics
assigned to πνεῦμα, i. e. warmed air. (*Ib.* 17 a : ' spiritu . . .,
qui quasi organum vel machina summi dei voluntati subiectus est.')
A similar function seems to be assigned to φῶς, or illuminated
air, in *Corp.* XI. ii. 7. In *Corp.* X. 18, the ὄργανον is fire.

ἀλλ' οὐκ ἀδέσποτος οὐδὲ αὕτη . . . τὸν μηδέπω αὐτῇ τὴν τάξιν τάξαντα.
Here the writer touches on the problem of evil. The evil in the
world (τὸ ἄμετρον or τὸ ἄτακτον) is ὕλη which the Demiurgus has not
yet brought to order ; it is a survival of the primitive chaos. But
sooner or later, order will be imposed on it ; that is, the evil will be
changed to good. The Hermetist seems to be thinking chiefly of
physical evil ; he holds that ' plagues and earthquakes break not
Heaven's design ', but only show that Heaven's design is still in
process of execution, and has not yet been completely carried out.
But the solution which he suggests might be applied to moral evil
(' a Borgia or a Catiline ') also.

§ 5. ἀέρος τὸ ἀνειμένον. ἀνειμένος means ' free to roam at large '.
The wind ' bloweth where it listeth '.

§ 6. εἰ ⟨δὲ⟩ θέλεις καὶ διὰ τῶν θνητῶν κ.τ.λ. After speaking of τὰ
ἀθάνατα, i. e. the heavenly bodies and the elements, the writer passes
on to τὰ θνητά. The Maker's skill may be seen in the bodies of all
animals,—men and beasts on land, and fishes in the sea. As an
instance, the Hermetist takes the human body, and speaks of its

construction in detail. Some words introducing this special instance
have probably been lost. The topic may have been suggested by
the description of the making of the human body in Pl. *Tim.* 69 ff. ;
but the writer does not, like Plato, discuss the *functions* of the bodily
organs; he contents himself with speaking of their shape.

This is probably the passage to which Lactantius refers in *Div.
inst.* 2. 10. 14 (*Testim.*).

τὴν καλὴν ταύτην καὶ θείαν [τοῦ ἀνθρώπου] εἰκόνα. If we retain τοῦ
ἀνθρώπου, the meaning must be, not 'this image of man', but 'this
image, namely, man'. But the phrase is awkwardly ambiguous;
and it seems best to cut out τοῦ ἀνθρώπου, which may have come
from a repetition of τὸν ἄνθρωπον above.

The human body is a living statue; cf. § 8 *init.*, ἀνδριάντα μὲν ἡ
εἰκόνα.[1] The epithet θείαν may perhaps have been intended to
suggest the thought that man is an image of God; but that thought
is not here fully expressed.

ὁ τὰ νεῦρα ἐκτείνας καὶ δεσμεύσας. The word δεσμεύσας shows that
the writer means by τὰ νεῦρα the 'sinews' or 'tendons', and not the
'nerves'. In Plato (*Tim.* 74 B, D) and Aristotle, νεῦρα means
'sinews'. Erasistratus, about 258 B. C., 'won the highest fame by
his discovery of the function and nature of the nerves' (Puschmann,
Gesch. der Medizin, p. 296). After his time, νεῦρα came to be used
by medical writers in the sense of 'nerves'; but the word continued
to be used also in the earlier sense of 'sinews'.

ὁ ὀχετεύσας τὰς φλέβας. Cf. Pl. *Tim.* 77 C: τὸ σῶμα αὐτὸ ἡμῶν
διωχέτευσαν, τέμνοντες οἷον ἐν κήποις ὀχετούς. . . . καὶ πρῶτον μὲν
ὀχετοὺς κρυφαίους . . . δύο φλέβας ἔτεμον νωτιαίας κ.τ.λ.

[[τίς ὁ τὸν σπλῆνα ἐκτείνας;]] It is not likely that the author
placed an organ of such subordinate importance as the spleen first
among all the internal organs. In Pl. *Tim.* 72 C, the spleen is
mentioned as an appendage of the liver, and we are told that it
serves as a sponge or napkin to cleanse the mirror-like surface of the
liver and keep it bright. I have accordingly placed the mention of
the spleen next after that of the liver.

τὴν καρδίαν πυραμοειδῆ ποιήσας. Ar. *Hist. an.* 496 a 19 : τὸ ἄκρον
(τῆς καρδίας) εἰς ὀξὺ συνῆκται. The Hermetist must have meant
'conical' rather than 'pyramidal'. The word πυραμοειδής means
'conical' in Pseudo-Ar. Περὶ φυτῶν 2. 7, 827 b 11–16.

---

[1] Lactantius *l. c.* contrasts God's work, the making of a living man, with that of
Prometheus, who, he says, merely made lifeless statues.

⟨καὶ⟩ [τίς ὁ] τὰ νεῦρα ⟨αὐτῇ⟩ συνθείς; It has been proposed to substitute some other word for νεῦρα. Flussas conjectured πλευρά; but it would be strange to interpose 'the ribs' or ' sides' between 'the heart' and 'the liver'. The writer mentions in succession all the chief internal organs,—heart, liver, spleen, lungs, and κοιλία (which may be taken to mean stomach and bowels together). In Pl. *Tim.* 70 A ff., the same organs are spoken of, in the order (1) heart, (2) lungs, (3) liver, (4) spleen, (5) abdomen and bowels. As there is no other organ which is likely to have been mentioned here, it is to be presumed that the words τὰ νεῦρα συνθείς, as well as those which precede, have to do with the heart; and I have therefore inserted αὐτῇ. As to the connexion of the νεῦρα with the heart, cf. Aristot. *Hist. an.* 3. 5, 515 a 27: ἡ μὲν ἀρχὴ (τῶν νεύρων) ἐστὶν ἐκ τῆς καρδίας· καὶ γὰρ ἐν αὐτῇ ἡ καρδία ἔχει νεῦρα κ.τ.λ. Ar. *Part. an.* 3. 4, 666 b 13: ἔχει δὲ καὶ νεύρων πλῆθος ἡ καρδία, καὶ τοῦτ' εὐλόγως· ἀπὸ ταύτης γὰρ αἱ κινήσεις. περαίνονται δὲ διὰ τοῦ ἕλκειν καὶ ἀνιέναι· δεῖ οὖν τοιαύτης ὑπηρεσίας καὶ ἰσχύος. The νεῦρα were regarded as the 'strings' by which the limbs are moved (cf. ἀγάλματα νευρό-σπαστα, 'puppets moved by strings'); and it was thought that the heart is the organ which pulls the strings, and that the νεῦρα must therefore be connected with the heart. Cic. *Nat. deor.* 2. 55. 139 (probably from Posidonius): 'huc adde nervos, a quibus artus continentur, . . . qui sicut venae et arteriae a corde ⌐tractae et profectae⌐ (tracti et profecti *edd.*) in corpus omne ducuntur.' J. B. Mayor *ad loc.* says that *nervos* here 'includes no doubt both tendons and nerves properly so called '.

ὁ τὸν πνεύμονα σηραγγώσας. Cf. Pl. *Tim.* 70 C: τὴν τοῦ πλεύμονος ἰδέαν ἐνεφύτευσαν, . . . σήραγγας ἐντὸς ἔχουσαν οἷον σπόγγου κατατετρη-μένας.

ὁ τὰ τιμιώτατα εἰς τὸ φανερὸν ἐκτυπώσας, καὶ τὰ αἰσχρὰ κρύψας. Cf. Cic. *De off.* 1. 35. 126 (from Panaetius): 'natura ... formam nostram reliquamque figuram, in qua esset species honesta, eam posuit in promptu, quae partes autem corporis ad naturae necessitatem datae aspectu essent deformem habiturae ..., eas contexit atque abdidit.' A partly similar thought occurs in 1 *Cor.* 12. 22–24.

§ 7. ποία μήτηρ, ποῖος πατήρ, εἰ μὴ ὁ ἀφανὴς θεός; To the Greeks, the notion of a Mother of all that lives (Mother Earth, ἡ μεγάλη μήτηρ, known under many different names,—Gaia, Rhea, Cybele, &c.,) was as familiar as the notion of a Father of all. In Roman Egypt, the name by which the Mother was best known was Isis.

But perhaps the writer was not thinking of gods and goddesses, but rather of the human parents of the child. The growing embryo is fashioned with consummate skill, and the work of thus fashioning it is certainly not done either by the mother or by the father; it must therefore be done by some one else; and who can that be, if not 'the unseen God'? Cf. Psalm 139. 13–16.

§ 9. τοῦτο αὐτῷ τὸ ἔργον ἐστί, ⟨τὸ⟩ πατέρα εἶναι. Cf. *Corp.* XI. i. 5, as emended: τί δὲ αὐτοῦ ἄλλο ἔργον ἢ τὸ ποιεῖν; XI. ii. 13 b–14 a: τὸ τοῦ θεοῦ ἔργον ἓν ὄν, ἵνα πάντα γίνηται, κ.τ.λ.

τούτου ἐστιν ⟨ἡ⟩ οὐσία τὸ κινεῖν (κύειν MSS.) πάντα καὶ ποιεῖν. The verb κύειν or κυεῖν is used of the mother only, not of the father. The writer of *Ascl. Lat.* III, who asserts that God is ἀρσενόθηλυς, might have said that ὁ θεός both γεννᾷ and κύει; but in *Corp.* V, there is (apart from ποία μήτηρ, ποῖος πατήρ above, which need not be thus understood,) no hint of that doctrine, except in this one word κύειν; and the bisexuality of God can hardly have been tacitly assumed here. There can therefore be little doubt that κύειν is corrupt; and κινεῖν is an obvious emendation. Cf. *Corp.* XI. ii. 17 c: τοῦτο γὰρ ὥσπερ (οὐσία?) ἐστι τοῦ θεοῦ, ⟨τὸ⟩ κινεῖν τὰ πάντα καὶ ζωοποιεῖν. *Corp.* IX. 9: τοῦτο ἔστιν ἡ αἴσθησις καὶ νόησις τοῦ θεοῦ, τὸ τὰ πάντα ἀεὶ κινεῖν.

τοῦτον δεῖ (ἀεὶ MSS.) μὴ εἶναι, εἰ μὴ πάντα ἀεὶ ποιοῦντα. Cf. *Corp.* XI. ii. 12 b: ἀλλ' οὐδὲ δυνατὸν χωρὶς τοῦ ἐκεῖνα ποιεῖν τὸν θεὸν εἶναι, κ.τ.λ. *Ib.* 17 c: οὐδὲ ὁ θεὸς δύναται ⟨εἶναι⟩ μὴ ποιῶν τὸ ἀγαθόν.

τὰ μὲν γὰρ ὄντα ἐφανέρωσε, τὰ δὲ μὴ ὄντα ἔχει ἐν ἑαυτῷ. τὰ μὴ ὄντα are the things which are to be hereafter. They have not yet come into being; but they exist already in God's thought or purpose, and so God may be said to 'contain them in himself'. *Ascl. Lat.* I. 2 a: 'omnia unum esse et unum omnia, utpote quae in creatore fuerint omnia, antequam creasset omnia.' Compare the 'Unknown Gnostic document' in C. Schmidt, *Koptisch-Gnostische Schriften* I, p. 358: 'Thou art the δημιουργός[1] of those things which have not yet manifested themselves; for these Thou alone knowest, we know them not.'

The phrase 'that which is and that which is not' occurs frequently in Egyptian documents (Erman, *Aeg. Grammatik*, p. 192).

§ 10 a. ὀνόματα ἔχει ἅπαντα . . . ὄνομα οὐκ ἔχει. Cf. *Ascl. Lat.* III. 20 a: 'innominem vel potius omninominem.' 'Unknown Gnostic

[1] It is not clear what is meant by δημιουργός here; we might rather have expected 'Thou art the τόπος of', &c.

document,' C. Schmidt, *Kopt.-Gnost. Schriften* I, p. 366 : ' He has no name, and all names belong to Him.'

§ 10 b. τίς οὖν σε εὐλογῆσαι κ.τ.λ.   The *libellus* ends with a hymn addressed to the supreme God. Compare the hymns in *Corp.* I, *Corp.* XIII, and *Ascl. Lat. fin.*

σὺ γὰρ ὁ τόπος τῶν ὄντων· οὐ τόπος ἐστὶν ἄλλος οὐδεὶς παρὰ σέ.—(οὐ γὰρ τρόπος οὐ τόπος ἐστὶ περὶ σέ, οὐδὲ ἄλλο οὐδὲν τῶν ὄντων MSS.) The words οὐ γὰρ τρόπος are meaningless. It is possible that τρόπος has come by duplication from the following τόπος; but it seems more likely that the Hermetist wrote σὺ γὰρ ὁ τόπος, 'thou art the place in which all things are contained'. Compare the τόπος (= νοῦς) of *Corp.* II, and the Jewish parallels there quoted.[1] Thus corrected, the sentence follows suitably on the question ποῦ βλέπων εὐλογήσω σε; It is impossible to choose out any one place, and say that God is there rather than elsewhere ; for God is himself the all-containing ' place '. The words οὐδὲ ἄλλο οὐδὲν τῶν ὄντων are irrelevant ; if they are not wholly spurious, they must be corrupt. The passage cannot be restored with certainty ; but the writer's meaning was probably not far from that which is expressed by my rewriting of the words.

The Egyptians considered it important that the worshipper should face in a particular direction during prayer. Cf. *Ascl. Lat.* 41 a, ' orare . . . in austrum respicientes ' &c.

⟨. . .⟩ πάντα ἀπὸ σοῦ· πάντα δίδως, καὶ οὐδὲν λαμβάνεις. This has nothing to do with the question ' in which direction am I to look ? ' It must therefore be presumed that it followed on another question which has fallen out of the text ; and that question probably was, ' What can I offer to thee ? ' (Cf. *Ascl. Lat.* 41 a, where Hermes rejects the proposal to burn incense.) The writer's object is to show that, in the worship of the supreme God, all rites employed in the cults of subordinate deities are inadequate ; and among those rites, the most important were θυσίαι and ὕμνοι. A satisfactory meaning might therefore be obtained by inserting τίνα δὲ σοὶ πέμψω θυσίαν ; Cf. *Corp.* XIII. 21 : σοὶ . . . πέμπω λογικὰς θυσίας. As to πάντα δίδως καὶ οὐδὲν λαμβάνεις. cf. *Corp.* II. 16 : ὁ οὖν θεὸς πάντα δίδωσι καὶ οὐδὲν λαμβάνει.

§ 11. πότε δέ σε ὑμνήσω ;   Cf. Clem. Alex. *Strom.* 7. 35 : οὔτε ὡρισμένον τόπον οὔτε ἐξαίρετον ἱερόν, οὐδὲ μὴν ἑορτάς τινας καὶ ἡμέρας

---

[1] Ménard quotes an Indian parallel from the *Baghavat-Gita* : ' Tu es . . . le lieu du monde.'

ἀποτεταγμένας, ἀλλὰ τὸν πάντα βίον ὁ γνωστικός, ἐν παντὶ τόπῳ, . . .
τιμᾷ τὸν θεόν, τουτέστιν χάριν ὁμολογεῖ τῆς γνώσεως καὶ τῆς πολιτείας.
. . . τοιοῦτος ὁ πάντη παρεῖναι τὸν θεὸν πεπεισμένος, οὐχὶ δὲ ἐν τόποις
τισὶν ὡρισμένοις κατακεκλεισμένον ὑπολαβών. . . . πάντα τοίνυν τὸν βίον
ἑορτὴν ἄγοντες, πάντη πάντοθεν παρεῖναι τὸν θεὸν πεπεισμένοι, γεωργοῦμεν
αἰνοῦντες, πλέομεν ὑμνοῦντες, κατὰ τὴν ἄλλην πολιτείαν ἐνθέως ἀναστρεφό-
μεθα.

ὑπὲρ ὧν ἐποίησας, ἢ ὑπὲρ ὧν οὐκ ἐποίησας; The things which God
'has not made' are, I suppose, the things which have not yet come
into being, but which are destined to come into being hereafter.
Cf. τὰ ὄντα καὶ τὰ μὴ ὄντα in § 9, and τὸ γενόμενον . . . τὸ μὴ γενόμενον
below.

ὑπὲρ ὧν ἐφανέρωσας, ἢ ὑπὲρ ὧν ἔκρυψας; The things which God
'has hidden' are τὰ ἀφανῆ, i. e. τὰ νοητά.

διὰ τί⟨νος⟩ δὲ καὶ ὑμνήσω σε; διὰ τί (MSS.) is not satisfactory. If
we retain it, the implied answer must be 'there is no reason why
I should adore thee'. The preceding clauses signify that any
adoration limited to particular places and times is inadequate; but
this phrase would mean that all adoration is useless, and the
Hermetist would not say that. A better sense may be got by
writing διὰ τίνος, 'wherewith shall I sing hymns to thee?' The
obvious answer to that question would be διὰ τῆς φωνῆς, or διὰ τοῦ
λόγου. But the Hermetist reflects that man has no power of his
own to speak or act (σὺ εἶ ὃ ἂν λέγω). When a man is said to 'sing
praise to God', it seems to be implied that he has a power of
utterance in himself, as a being distinct from God; but I have no
such power, and when I praise God, it is God that speaks in me
or through me. Cf. *Corp.* XIII. 18–20: ζωὴ καὶ φῶς, ἀφ' ὑμῶν (not
from *me*) χωρεῖ ἡ εὐλογία. . . . ὁ σὸς λόγος δι' ἐμοῦ ὑμνεῖ σε. . . .
ὁ σὸς ἄνθρωπος ταῦτα βοᾷ διὰ . . . τῶν κτισμάτων σου.

ὡς ἐμαυτοῦ ὤν; ὡς ἔχων τι ἴδιον; Cf. Philo *Leg. alleg.* 3. 70. 195,
Cohn I, p. 156: μόνῳ ἁρμόττει θεῷ λέγειν "τὸ ἐμόν", αὐτοῦ γὰρ ὄντως
κτήματα μόνου τὰ πάντα.

ὡς ἄλλος ὤν; σὺ γὰρ εἶ ὃ [ἐ]ὰν ὦ. This is the typical utterance of
mysticism; 'I am Thou, and Thou art I.' In the Greek mystery-
cults, the worshipper sought some kind and degree of union with
the particular deity to whom his worship was addressed; but among
the Greeks, the abolition of the boundary-walls of separate personality
was seldom spoken of in such emphatic and uncompromising terms.
In Egypt, on the other hand, the Pyramid-texts of the VIth Dynasty

(2500 B.C. or earlier) are full of phrases which show that by that time the primitive worshipper's sense of identification with the object of his worship (or at least his assurance that he would, after death, be identified with his god) had already been stereotyped in traditional formulas of unknown antiquity; and the same sort of language persists in Egyptian documents of all periods,[1] down to the time when the magicians of the Roman age borrowed the phrase σὺ ἐγὼ καὶ ἐγὼ σύ[2] from reputable cults to use it for their own sordid purposes. The tone of this hymn is not Greek, but Egyptian.

οὐ γὰρ πάντα εἶ, καὶ ἄλλο οὐδὲν ἔστιν ὃ μὴ σὺ εἶ. Cf. *Martyrium Petri* (Lipsius-Bonnet, *Acta Apost. Apocr.* I, p. 96): σὺ τὸ πᾶν, καὶ τὸ πᾶν ἐν σοί· καὶ τὸ ὂν σύ, καὶ οὐκ ἐστιν ἄλλο ὃ ἔστιν εἰ μὴ μόνος σύ.

νοῦς μὲν ⟨εἶ⟩, νοούμενος, πατὴρ δέ, δημιουργῶν. God is Mind, in that he designs things, and Father, in that he produces or 'manifests' the things which he has designed. We might rather have expected πατὴρ δέ, γεννῶν; but δημιουργεῖν, 'to create', is interchangeable with γεννᾶν.

[ὕλης μὲν . . . νοῦ δέ θεός]. This passage is evidently out of place here. See *Corp.* XII. i. 14 a, where the same statement occurs in a more suitable context.

There is some reason to suspect that the preceding sentence also (νοῦς μὲν εἶ . . . πάντα ποιῶν) has been added by a later hand. It is not closely connected in thought with what comes before it; and it is something of an anticlimax, after the sweeping statement 'Thou art all things', to add that God *makes* things. Perhaps the hymn originally ended thus: σὺ γὰρ πάντα εἶ· [[ ]] σὺ εἶ πᾶν τὸ γενόμενον, σὺ τὸ μὴ γενόμενον, ⟨⟨καὶ ἄλλο οὐδὲν ἔστιν ὃ μὴ σὺ εἶ.⟩⟩

---

[1] Cf. ἕνωσις πρὸς τοὺς θεούς in *Abammonis responsum* (*Testim.*) *passim*.

[2] E.g. *Pap. mag.* Leid. W. 17. 44 sq.: εἰσέλθοις τὸν ἐμὸν νοῦν καὶ τὰς ἐμὰς φρένας εἰς τὸν ἄπαντα χρόνον . . . σὺ γὰρ εἶ ἐγώ, καὶ ἐγὼ σύ. *Pap. mag.* Lond. 122. 37 : σὺ γὰρ ἐγώ, καὶ ἐγὼ σύ· 'thy name is mine, and mine is thine', *etc.* Cf. Ophite *Evangelium Evae* (Reitzenstein *Poim.* p. 242), quoted in note on *Corp.* XI. ii. 21 b: 'I heard a voice as of thunder, which spoke to me and said ἐγὼ σὺ καὶ σὺ ἐγώ,' κ.τ.λ. In that passage, the words are addressed by the god to his worshipper; more often, they are addressed by the worshipper to his god.

LIBELLVS VI

Corp. VI is a discourse on τὸ ἀγαθόν and τὸ καλόν. The point on which the writer insists is that nothing good or beautiful is to be found in the world in which we live. This document is distinguished from most of the other *Hermetica* by its intensely pessimistic tone. The Kosmos is described in it as ' one mass of evil '. Men may indeed attain to *gnosis*; i. e. they may come to know God, and, in knowing God, to know the Beautiful and the Good ; but even for the man who has got *gnosis*, beauty and goodness are unattainable as long as he is in the body ; and of the life after death, the writer does not speak.

The doctrine is Platonic ; and there is no trace of anything distinctively Egyptian, Jewish, or Christian. The conceptions of τὸ ἀγαθόν and τὸ καλόν are derived from Plato, and that of τὸ καλόν more especially from the *Symposium* and the *Phaedrus*. But in his sweeping condemnation of the Kosmos and all things in it, the writer goes beyond Plato,[1] and agrees rather with some of the Neo-Pythagoreans and some of the Christian Gnostics.[2] The document contains no clear indication of date ; but as this sort of *contemptus mundi* was more prevalent in the second and third centuries A. D. than in earlier times, the tone of *Corp.* VI affords some reason for thinking that it ought to be assigned to that period. Two or three verbal agreements with Numenius point towards the same conclusion, as far as any significance can be ascribed to them.

What is the relation between *Corp.* VI and *Corp.* II? The doctrine of *Corp.* VI. 1–4 a concerning τὸ ἀγαθόν resembles that of *Corp.* II. 14–16 ; but it is not quite the same. In *Corp.* II, ' the Good' is completely identified with God ; in *Corp.* VI, 'the Good' (or ' Goodness ') is described as a 'part' of God, a property of God, and a thing inseparably connected with him, but is not absolutely identified with God, except in two phrases which are hardly consistent with their context, and have probably been added by a later hand. Moreover, there is no trace in *Corp.* VI of the doctrine of a supra-

---

[1] Compare and contrast Pl. *Legg.* 10. 906 A : συγκεχωρήκαμεν ἡμῖν αὐτοῖς εἶναι μὲν τὸν οὐρανὸν (i. e. the Kosmos) πολλῶν μεστὸν ἀγαθῶν, εἶναι δὲ καὶ τῶν ἐναντίων, πλειόνων δὲ τῶν μὴ (ἀγαθῶν). In the *Timaeus*, Plato τὸν κόσμον ἐπαινεῖ καὶ θεὸν λέγει εἶναι εὐδαίμονα (Plotinus 4. 8. 1).

[2] The doctrine that ' the Kosmos is evil ' is that against which Plotinus especially protests in his controversy with the Gnostics (*Enn.* 2. 9, Πρὸς τοὺς κακὸν τὸν δημιουργὸν τοῦ κόσμου καὶ τὸν κόσμον κακὸν εἶναι λέγοντας).

cosmic Nous distinct from and subordinate to the supreme God, which is taught in *Corp*. II. For these reasons, it is improbable that *Corp*. VI was written by the same person as *Corp*. II ; but its author may perhaps have known *Corp*. II, and may possibly have intended *Corp*. VI to be read as a sequel to it. (In both II and VI, the pupil is Asclepius.)

The author of *Corp*. X probably had *Corp*. VI before him ; and he seems to have made it his aim to supplement the teaching of *Corp*. VI, and to correct its pessimistic tendency.

Contents

A. §§ 1–4 a : περὶ τοῦ ἀγαθοῦ.

The Good is changeless, free from wants, and exempt from perturbations (or evil passions). But these attributes belong to God alone; therefore the Good (or Goodness) is in God alone. (§§ 1, 2 a.)

The Good is not in the Kosmos, nor in anything contained in it. The Kosmos is good in this one respect, that it is productive, but in no other respect. It is subject to perturbation ; and where there is perturbation, the Good cannot be. (§§ 2 b, 3 a.) The Kosmos is one mass of evil. (§ 4 a.)

The Good is not in man ; for man's material body subjects him to evil passions and delusions. And the worst of all the evils that beset him is the error of thinking evils to be goods. (§§ 3 b, 4 a.)

B. §§ 4 b–6 : περὶ τοῦ καλοῦ καὶ τοῦ ἀγαθοῦ.

The Beautiful ⟨is inseparably connected with the Good (?) ; and⟩ the Beautiful and the Good may be described as the very essence of God. But the Beautiful and the Good (or Beauty and Goodness) are not in the Kosmos, and cannot be seen by the eye. They are parts of God, or properties of God; and man can apprehend them only so far as he can apprehend God. It is by piety alone that we can attain to knowledge of the Beautiful and the Good. (§§ 4 b, 5.)

But no man can be beautiful and good. Men are encompassed by evils; most men think these very evils to be goods; and no man can escape from them. (§ 6.)

§ 1 a. τὸ ἀγαθὸν . . . [ἐν οὐδενί ἐστιν εἰ μὴ ἐν μόνῳ τῷ θεῷ. μᾶλλον δὲ τὸ ἀγαθὸν αὐτός ἐστιν ὁ θεός [ἀεί]. εἰ δὲ οὕτως,] οὐσίαν εἶναι δεῖ κ.τ.λ. The words ἐν οὐδενί . . .. εἰ δὲ οὕτως are an interruption. There can be little doubt that the author began by describing τὸ ἀγαθόν, and then, in § 1 b, proceeded to say that it belongs to God alone. ἐν οὐδενί ἐστιν εἰ μὴ ἐν μόνῳ τῷ θεῷ is merely a repetition of the words of the heading, ὅτι ἐν μόνῳ τῷ θεῷ τὸ ἀγαθόν ἐστιν. The words μᾶλλον δὲ τὸ ἀγαθὸν αὐτός ἐστιν ὁ θεός are perhaps a subsequent addition. Cf. [ἢ αὐτός ἐστιν ὁ θεὸς τὸ ἀγαθόν] in § 3 b *init.* The statement that 'the Good is God himself', or 'God himself is the Good', hardly agrees with the rest of the document. The writer says that the Good is *in* God; but except in these two clauses, it is nowhere said or implied that τὸ ἀγαθόν is *identical with* God; and the language used in other parts of the discourse would be difficult to reconcile with that proposition. See especially § 4 b, where we are told that τὸ καλόν and τὸ ἀγαθόν are 'parts of God', and that God is in love with them. Both μᾶλλον δὲ τὸ ἀγαθὸν αὐτός ἐστιν ὁ θεός in § 1 a, and ἢ αὐτός ἐστιν ὁ θεὸς τὸ ἀγαθόν in § 3 b, may have been inserted by some one who had been reading *Corp.* II, the conclusion of which is ὁ οὖν θεὸς ⟨τὸ⟩ ἀγαθόν, καὶ τὸ ἀγαθὸν ὁ θεός.

The meaningless [ἀεί] may have resulted either from a duplication of εἰ, or from a misplacement of δεῖ.

τὸ ἀγαθὸν . . . οὐσίαν εἶναι (or νοεῖν?) δεῖ πάσης κινήσεως καὶ γενέσεως ἔρημον. οὐσία here means ὄν τι, 'a thing'. It is similarly used in § 2 a, where ἐν τῇ τοιαύτῃ οὐσίᾳ, 'in a thing such as that', is parallel to ἐν οὐδενὶ τῶν ἄλλων, 'in no other thing'. οὐσία is often used by Platonists in the sense of 'eternal and changeless existence' as opposed to γένεσις (whence οὐσιώδης, as employed in *Corp.* I. 15 &c.); but it cannot bear that meaning here; for if it did, the following words πάσης κινήσεως καὶ γενέσεως ἔρημον would be superfluous.

[δὲ οὐδέν ἐστιν]. This may have come from ἐν οὐδενί ἐστιν above.

αὐτὴν δὲ περὶ αὐτὴν στατικὴν ἐνέργειαν ἔχουσαν.—(αὐτῆς· περὶ δὲ αὐτὴν στατικὴν ἐνέργειαν ἔχουσα MSS.) The Good is active, but its activity does not involve movement or change; it is ἑστός. Cf. *Ascl. Lat.* III. 30: 'solus deus stabilis' &c. *Corp.* X. 11: ἡ δὲ νοητὴ στάσις κινεῖ τὴν ὑλικὴν κίνησιν. Numenius *ap.* Euseb. *Pr. ev.* 11. 18. 21: τὴν προσοῦσαν τῷ πρώτῳ (θεῷ) στάσιν φημὶ εἶναι κίνησιν σύμφυτον.

ἀνενδεῆ καὶ ⟨παθῶν⟩ ἀπείρητον (or ἀπείρατον). ἀπείριτον, the reading of the MSS., cannot be right. ἀπείριτος (= ἄπειρος, 'endless',) occurs in Homer and Hesiod, but seldom in later literature; and the statement that τὸ ἀγαθόν is 'endless' would here be irrelevant. The writer is arguing thus : 'τὸ ἀγαθόν has certain properties; these properties are to be found in God, and in God alone; therefore τὸ ἀγαθόν is in God alone.' Now in describing the properties of God, the point on which he dwells is that God is not subject to certain πάθη, viz. ἐπιθυμία, λύπη, ἔρως, ὀργή, ζῆλος; and this would not be to the purpose, unless he had previously said that τὸ ἀγαθόν is free from such πάθη. The passage about God might be summarized by saying that God is ἀνενδεὴς καὶ παθῶν ἀπείρατος; the writer must therefore have previously said that τὸ ἀγαθόν is ἀνενδεὲς καὶ παθῶν ἀπείρατον, or something to that effect. Cf. § 2 a : ὅπου δὲ τὸ ἀγαθόν, οὐδὲ ἓν πάθος.

πᾶν γὰρ τὸ χορηγοῦν ἀγαθὸν [ὅταν] λέγεται (λέγω MSS.). The meaning might be more clearly expressed by writing τὸ ⟨ὁτιοῦν⟩ χορηγοῦν, 'everything which supplies anything at all', and thus emphasizing the opposition to πάντα καὶ ἀεὶ χορηγοῦν below. And [ὅταν] might then be accounted for as having come from ὁτιοῦν misplaced.

The statement 'I call all things good which furnish a supply of anything' is hardly consistent with the author's assertion that the Kosmos is πλήρωμα τῆς κακίας, which implies that he would call nothing in the world good; it is therefore most likely that he wrote, not λέγω, but λέγεται; 'the word ἀγαθόν is commonly thus used.'

§ 1 b. [λύπη γὰρ κακίας μέρος]. Cf. Corp. XIII. 7 b, where λύπη takes a place among the vices or evil passions, side by side with ἀκρασία, ἐπιθυμία, ἀδικία, &c., and χαρά, its opposite, is ranked with ἐγκράτεια, καρτερία, δικαιοσύνη &c. The statement λύπη κακίας μέρος is unobjectionable in itself; but as it is not wanted here, and disturbs the symmetry of the passage, it is most likely a marginal note inserted in the text by error.

οὔτε κρεῖττον αὐτοῦ ἐστιν οὐδέν, ὑφ' οὗ ἀδικηθεὶς πολεμήσει (ὑφ' οὗ πολεμηθήσεται MSS.). The reading of the MSS. ('by which he will have war made on him') does not make sense; for a war might be begun by one who was not 'the stronger'. Nor would sense be restored by writing ὑφ' οὗ ⟨κατα⟩πολεμηθήσεται, 'by which he will be vanquished'; for defeat is not a πάθος in the same sense as ἐπιθυμία, ὀργή, &c. Now the words τὸ ἀδικηθῆναι καὶ διὰ τοῦτο are evidently out of place in the MSS., where they separate σύζυγον from ἐρασθήσεται; and it seems probable that they have arisen out of something originally connected with οὔτε κρεῖττον ... οὐδέν. I have therefore inserted ἀδικηθείς here, and altered πολεμηθήσεται into πολεμήσει to make sense in combination with it. It is true that τὸ πολεμεῖν is not, strictly speaking, a πάθος; but it may be regarded as implying τὸ ἐχθαίρειν, and ἔχθρα is a πάθος. The writer may have had in mind the θεομαχίαι of Greek mythology, which had long been a scandal to pious thinkers.

οὔτε σύζυγόν (perhaps σύζυγός) ἐστιν αὐτῷ, [ ] οὗ ἐρασθήσεται. Compare the system of Valentinus, in which each pair of Aeons consists of a male and a female σύζυγος, i. e. a husband and a wife. On the question whether the supreme God (called Proarche, Propator, and Bythos) had a σύζυγος, the Valentinians differed among themselves. Irenaeus 1. 11. 15: some of the Valentinians (τὸν Βυθὸν) ἄζυγον λέγουσι, μήτε ἄρρενα μήτε θήλειαν . . .· ἄλλοι δὲ ἀρρενόθηλυν αὐτὸν λέγουσιν εἶναι, ἑρμαφροδίτου φύσιν αὐτῷ περιάπτοντες. Σιγὴν δὲ πάλιν ἄλλοι συνευνέτιν αὐτῷ προσάπτουσιν, ἵνα γένηται πρώτη συζυγία. Hippol. *Ref. haer.* 6. 29: οἱ μὲν γὰρ (of the Valentinians) . . . ἄθηλυν καὶ ἄζυγον καὶ μόνον τὸν Πατέρα (i. e. the Propator) νομίζουσιν εἶναι· οἱ δέ, ἀδύνατον νομίζοντες [δύνασθαι] ἐξ ἄρρενος μόνου γένεσιν ὅλως τῶν γεγενημένων γενέσθαι τινός, καὶ τῷ πατρὶ τῶν ὅλων, ἵνα γένηται πατήρ, Σιγὴν ἐξ ἀνάγκης συναριθμοῦσι [τὴν] σύζυγον. In the version of the Valentinian doctrine which is given in Iren. 1. 1. 1, the consort of the Propator is named Ἔννοια, Χάρις, and Σιγή. *Ib.* 1. 12. 1: the Valentinian Ptolemaeus assigned to the Bythos two σύζυγοι, named Ἔννοια and Θέλημα (πρῶτον γὰρ ἐνενοήθη προβαλεῖν, φησίν, εἶτα ἠθέλησε). In the *Pistis Sophia* (C. Schmidt, pp. 2, 14, 24, 138,) χωρισσύζυγοι, 'without consorts', is used as an epithet of a certain class of divine Persons. The writer of *Corp.* VI may perhaps have heard of the Valentinian doctrine of συζυγίαι, and must certainly have met with analogous doctrines.[1]

In § 4 b, we are told that God ἐρᾷ τοῦ καλοῦ καὶ τοῦ ἀγαθοῦ. But as τὸ καλόν and τὸ ἀγαθόν are there called 'parts of God', the statement that God 'is in love with them' does not imply that he has a σύζυγος, i. e. a consort other than himself, but rather corresponds to the doctrine that God is ἀρσενόθηλυς; and the ἔρως there spoken of is not regarded as a πάθος.

οὔτε ἀνήκοον, ᾧ ὀργισθήσεται. The will of God finds complete and instant fulfilment. Cf. *Ascl. Lat.* I. 8: 'placitum enim dei necessitas

---

[1] Arnobius *Adv. nat.* 3. 8 speaks of the attribution of sex to God as a Pagan error rejected by Christians; 'non enim deus mas est, sed nomen eius generis masculini est.'

sequitur, voluntatem comitatur effectus.' But if God is good, he must will only what is good ; and if nothing is disobedient to God's will, it would seem to follow that all things must be good. How then can this view be reconciled with the assertion that the Kosmos is πλήρωμα τῆς κακίας (§ 4 a), and that the highest good to which man can attain is only a smaller share of evil (§ 3 b)? Does the good God will that the Kosmos shall be full of evil, and that men shall be wicked?[1] With this difficulty the writer of *Corp.* VI makes no attempt to deal. Other men of his time tried to reconcile the existence of evil with the goodness of God by asserting that there is something which is 'disobedient' to him, viz. either an intractable ὕλη (see *Ascl. Lat.* II), or an evil God or Daemon. The notion of an evil God at enmity with the good God was adopted[2] by some of the Christian heretics, e. g. in part by Marcion, and more fully by Mani ; (see Bousset, *Hauptprobleme der Gnosis*, pp. 91–119 ;) and a modified form of the same doctrine presents itself in the Satan of the Jews, and in the Christian conception of the Devil, who was commonly held to be 'disobedient to God', and to have power to thwart God's will to some extent in the present world, though destined to be overcome at some future time. Moreover, Jews and Christians were agreed that men can disobey God, and that most men are disobedient to him. On the question whether God is angry with those who disobey him, opinions differed ; Lactantius, for instance, (*De ira dei*) asserts it ; Arnobius (*Adv. nat.* 1. 17 and 23) denies it, adhering to the Platonic view that God is ἀπαθής. The writer of *Ascl. Lat.* III holds that not only the supreme God, but the astral gods also, are ἀπαθεῖς, and that the 'terrestrial gods' alone are subject to anger ; see *Ascl. Lat.* III. 40 a, where it is said that the higher Powers ' nec ira commoventur nec flectuntur gratia '.

§ 2 a. ὥσπερ ⌜γὰρ⌝ οὐδὲν τῶν ⟨κακῶν⟩ κ.τ.λ. If we retain γάρ, it must be taken as referring back to μόνῳ in § 1 b *init.* (μόνῳ τῷ θεῷ). But a more obvious connexion would be got if δέ were written in place of γάρ.

καὶ ἐν τοῖς μικροῖς καὶ ἐν τοῖς μεγάλοις. A similar phrase occurs in Numenius Περὶ τἀγαθοῦ (Euseb. *Pr. ev.* 11. 22. 1, quoted in prefatory

---

[1] Arnobius *Adv. nat.* 2. 54 : 'si cuncta (dei) voluntate conficiuntur, nec citra eius nutum quicquam potest in rebus vel provenire vel cadere, necessario sequitur ut mala etiam cuncta voluntate eius intellegantur enasci.'

[2] In the main, from the Zoroastrians. But suggestions of this doctrine may have been found also in Plato's mention of a κακὴ ψυχή (*Legg.* 10. 896–898), and in the Egyptian conception of Set-Typhon (Plut. *Is. et Os.*).

note on *Corp.* II): μηδὲ σῶμα μέγα μηδὲ σμικρόν, ἀλλά τις ... ἐρημία θεσπέσιος. The phrase πάσης κινήσεως καὶ γενέσεως ἔρημον in *Corp.* VI. 1 a corresponds to Numenius's word ἐρημία.

αὐτῆς τῆς γενέσεως παθητῆς οὔσης. This probably means that all processes of birth and growth result from some sort of ὁρμή (emotional impulse), and therefore imply the presence of πάθος (emotional disturbance). The agent at work in all such processes (the Aristotelian φύσις) is seeking to attain to some end or ' good '. If the end were realized, the process would cease. As long as the process goes on, the end is still unrealized, i. e. the good is not yet present ; and as the cosmic process never ceases, it follows that the good is never present in the Kosmos. If then feeling of any kind is ascribed to the agent in the cosmic process, it must be the feeling of unsatisfied desire ; ('the whole creation groaneth and travaileth in pain together ' ;) and such a feeling is a πάθος.[1] On the other hand, the good, which remains ever unattained in the γένεσις of the Kosmos, is eternally realized in the στάσις of God. God is ἀνενδεής, and has no unsatisfied desire ; if he can be said to ' desire' the good, (ἐρᾷ τοῦ καλοῦ καὶ τοῦ ἀγαθοῦ, § 4 b,) his desire is eternally fulfilled ; for the good which he desires is eternally present in him. Cf. Methodius *Contra Porphyrium*, Bonwetsch, p. 347 : εἴτε γὰρ τὸ ἀγαθὸν θέλει (ὁ θεός), αὐτὸς ὢν τὸ ἀγαθὸν ἐν ἑαυτῷ μένει· εἴτε τὸ καλὸν ὑπάρχει ἐραστὸν αὐτῷ, αὐτὸς ὢν τὸ μόνον καλὸν εἰς ἑαυτὸν βλέπει.

§ 2 a *fin.*, **2 b** *init.* ἀδύνατον ἐν γενέσει ... οὕτω καὶ τοῦ ἀγαθοῦ. Didymus, *De Trinitate* 2. 3 (*Testim.*), quotes this passage ; and in the same paragraph he uses some other phrases borrowed from *Corp.* VI (κατὰ σύγκρισιν δὲ τοῦ κακοῦ τὸ ἀγαθὸν ... τέτακται· τὸ γὰρ μὴ λίαν κακὸν ... ἀγαθὸν ἐνθάδε προσείρηται from VI. 3 b, and ὅπου νύξ, οὐχ ἡμέρα from VI. 2 a).

§ 2 b. μετουσία πάντων ἐστὶν ἐν τῇ ὕλῃ ⟨δια?⟩δεδομένη. By πάντων we must understand πάντων τῶν νοητῶν εἰδῶν. The νοητὰ εἴδη or παραδείγματα are not present in material things ; but material things 'partake of' them. The Kosmos may in this sense 'partake of' τὸ ἀγαθόν ; i. e. ' copies' (εἰκόνες or εἴδωλα) of the Good may appear in it, though the Good itself never enters into it.

τοῦτον τὸν τρόπον ἀγαθὸς ὁ κόσμος. Here the writer makes a reluctant concession to the opinion of the majority of the Hermetists, who held that the Kosmos is in some sense good. Cf. *Corp.* IX. 4 b :

---

[1] Cf. Numenius (Euseb. *Pr. ev.* 11. 18. 3) : ἐπιθυμητικὸν ἦθος ἐχούσης (τῆς ὕλης), καὶ ῥεούσης.

χωρίον γὰρ (τῆς κακίας) ἡ γῆ, οὐχ ὁ κόσμος, ὡς ἔνιοί ποτε ἐροῦσι βλασφημοῦντες. *Ascl. Lat.* III. 25 : 'hic mundus, . . . bonum multiformi imaginum varietate conpositum' &c. *Ib.* 27 a : '(dei) imago mundus, boni ⟨bonus⟩', &c. *Corp.* X. 10 b, as emended : οὐ κακὸς ὁ κόσμος, οὐκέτι δὲ ἀγαθός· ὑλικὸς γάρ, καὶ παθητός.

καθὰ καὶ αὐτὸς πάντα ποιεῖ. God is the supreme Maker of all things; but the Kosmos (the 'second God') is the proximate maker of individual organisms. Thus the procreative energy of the Kosmos is a 'copy' of the creative energy of God; and as the absolute goodness of God is manifested in his creative energy, so the secondary and derivative goodness of the Kosmos is manifested in the operation of the cosmic forces by which living organisms are brought into being.

§ 3 a. [[ἐν δὲ τῷ ἀνθρώπῳ . . . ἐνθάδε τὸ ἀγαθόν]]. The mention of man is out of place here; it interrupts the discussion of the Kosmos, which is continued in what is said in the rest of § 3 a. It is most likely that the writer first disposed of the question whether the Kosmos is good, and then proceeded, in § 3 b, to discuss the question whether man is good. I have therefore transposed the words about man to § 3 b.

[[τὸ δὲ ἐνθάδε . . . ἐλάχιστον.]] ἀδύνατον οὖν . . . τῆς κακίας. If we read these words in the order in which they are given in the MSS., it is not clear what is meant by οὖν. A more satisfactory sense can be got by interchanging the two clauses, and making οὖν refer to καὶ γὰρ παθητός ἐστι καὶ παθητῶν ποιητής.

[κακούμενον γὰρ οὐκέτι ἀγαθὸν μένει· μὴ μεῖναν δέ, κακὸν γίνεται.] The words κακούμενον γὰρ ⟨τὸ ἀγαθὸν⟩ οὐκέτι ἀγαθὸν μένει were probably written as an alternative for κακοῦται γὰρ ἐνθάδε τὸ ἀγαθόν; and μὴ μεῖναν δὲ κακὸν γίνεται is an addition which adds nothing.

§ 3 b. ⟨⟨ἐν δὲ τῷ ἀνθρώπῳ κατὰ σύγκρισιν τοῦ κακοῦ τὸ ἀγαθὸν λέλεκται (κατὰ σύγκρισιν τοῦ ἀγαθοῦ τὸ κακὸν τέτακται MSS.)· τὸ γὰρ μὴ λίαν κακὸν ἐνθάδε [τὸ] ἀγαθὸν⟩⟩ ⟨προσείρηται⟩. When ἐν δὲ τῷ ἀνθρώπῳ is placed here, it stands in contrast with ἐν μόνῳ τῷ θεῷ, and the δέ serves to express this contrast.

The writer's meaning is that the word 'good', when applied to a man, signifies only that he is not so bad as he might be, or as other men are. This may be a reminiscence of Pl. *Protag.* 339 A ff., where Socrates comments on the ode of Simonides, ἄνδρ' ἀγαθὸν μὲν ἀλαθέως γενέσθαι χαλεπόν· . . . θεὸς ἂν μόνος τοῦτ' ἔχοι γέρας. . . . ἔμοιγ' ἐξαρκεῖ ὃς ἂν μὴ κακὸς ᾖ μηδ' ἄγαν ἀπάλαμνος.

It is difficult to make sense of τέτακται; yet it is the word used by Didymus in his borrowing from this passage. If the original reading was λέλεκται, this must have been altered into τέτακται before Didymus wrote, i. e. before A. D. 380–398.

οὐ γὰρ χωρεῖ (*sc.* τὸ ἀγαθὸν, acc.) σῶμα ὑλικόν (nom.). Cf. *Corp*. II. 14 *fin.*: σῶμα γάρ ἐστι καὶ ψυχὴ τόπον οὐκ ἔχοντα χωρῆσαι δυνάμενον τὸ ἀγαθόν.

ἕκαστον τούτων . . . [ἐμ]πεπίστευται ἐνθάδε [τὸ] μέγιστον εἶναι ἀγαθόν. The writer cannot have meant to say that πόνοι καὶ ἀλγηδόνες &c. are believed by men to be great goods. Few men think that pain and grief are goods. The meaning must be that the things which the πάθη impel men to seek (e. g. the satisfaction of vicious or morbid desires) are believed by men to be good, whereas they are really evil; but this meaning is not clearly expressed. The same thought recurs in § 6 : τὸ κακὸν πιστεύσαντα ἀγαθὸν εἶναι κ.τ.λ.

τὸ μᾶλλον ἀνυπέρβλητον κακόν. These words would more naturally be applied to one particular evil; it is strange to say that each of a number of evils is 'an evil not to be surpassed'. Perhaps the phrase has been inserted by a later hand.

[ἡ γαστριμαργία] [ἡ] τῶν κακῶν πάντων χορηγὸς ἡ πλάνη ⟨αὕτη⟩ [ ] ἐστί. There is no occasion to speak of gluttony here. ἡ γαστριμαργία must have been inserted by some ascetic transcriber who misunderstood the text, and thought it necessary to supply a subject for ἀνυπέρβλητον κακόν, or for τῶν κακῶν πάντων χορηγός.

§ 4 a. τῷ εἰς νοῦν μοι βαλόντι . . . ὅτι ἀδύνατόν ἐστιν αὐτὸ ἐν τῷ κόσμῳ εἶναι. The Hermetist thanks God that he has learnt that nothing in this world is good. He is thus secured against 'the greatest evil of all', viz. the error of believing this or that evil thing to be good.

ὁ γὰρ κόσμος πλήρωμά ἐστι τῆς κακίας, ὁ δὲ θεὸς τοῦ ἀγαθοῦ. The meaning of πλήρωμα is well illustrated by Philo *De praem. et poen.* 11. 65, Cohn V, p. 350 : γενομένη δὲ πλήρωμα ἀρετῶν ἥδε ἡ ψυχὴ . . ., οὐδὲν ἐν ἑαυτῇ καταλιποῦσα κενὸν εἰς πάροδον ἄλλων. The Kosmos is completely filled with evil, so that no room is left in it for any good to enter; and God is completely filled with good, so that no room is left in him for any evil to enter.

[ἡ τὸ ἀγαθὸν τοῦ θεοῦ]. The original writer would hardly have said that the Good 'is wholly filled with God', or 'is one mass of God'. These words may be attributed to the same interpolator who inserted [μᾶλλον δὲ τὸ ἀγαθὸν αὐτός ἐστιν ὁ θεός] in § 1, and [ἢ αὐτός ἐστιν ὁ θεὸς τὸ ἀγαθόν] in § 3 b, and probably also [ἢ αὐτὰ τοῦ θεοῦ ἐρᾷ] in § 4 b *fin.*

§ 4 b. ⟨. . .⟩ ⌜αἱ γὰρ ἐξοχαὶ τῶν καλῶν κ.τ.λ.⌝ The writer now proceeds to deal with τὸ καλόν, and to explain its relation to τὸ ἀγαθόν and to God. τὸ καλόν is the object of the Platonic ἔρως; and in this part of *Corp.* VI, the influence of Pl. *Sympos.* and *Phaedrus* may be recognized. The beginning of the paragraph must have been lost; for the γάρ implies some preceding mention of τὸ καλόν. And the first lines of what follows the lacuna (αἱ γὰρ ἐξοχαὶ . . . οὐσίαι ἐκείνου) are hopelessly corrupt.

καὶ καθαρώτεραι καὶ εἰλικρινέσταται (*al.* -τεραι). The author must have written either two superlatives or two comparatives. The same two adjectives occur in connexion with τὸ καλόν in Pl. *Sympos.* 211 D: τί δῆτα, ἔφη, οἰόμεθα, εἴ τῳ γένοιτο αὐτὸ τὸ καλὸν ἰδεῖν εἰλικρινές, καθαρόν, ἄμικτον, κ.τ.λ. The Hermetist presumably had that passage in mind; and perhaps he here said something about the relation between τὰ καλά and αὐτὸ τὸ καλόν.

ἡ οὐσία τοῦ θεοῦ, εἴ γε οὐσίαν ἔχει, τὸ καλόν ἐστι [τὸ δὲ καλὸν] καὶ ⟨τὸ⟩ ἀγαθόν. It would be possible to say τὸ δὲ καλὸν καὶ ἀγαθόν, 'the Beautiful is also good'; but as the writer repeatedly couples τὸ καλόν and τὸ ἀγαθόν together in the following sentences, it is most likely that here also he wrote τὸ καλὸν καὶ τὸ ἀγαθόν.

He asserts, with some hesitation, that τὸ καλόν and τὸ ἀγαθόν are the οὐσία of God. But he does not say that they are absolutely identical with God; his meaning seems to be rather that beauty and goodness are the most essential attributes of God. A few lines below, he calls τὸ καλόν and τὸ ἀγαθόν 'parts' of God.

As to εἴ γε οὐσίαν ἔχει, cf. *Corp.* XII. i *init.*: εἴ γέ τις ἔστιν οὐσία θεοῦ. This reservation was doubtless suggested by the Platonic doctrine that God is ἐπέκεινα τῆς οὐσίας. See *Corp.* II. 4 b.

⟨ὑπὸ δὲ τούτων (or τῷ δὲ τούτων φωτί ?)⟩ οὐδὲν ἔστι καταλάμπεσθαι (καταλαβέσθαι MSS.) τῶν ἐν τῷ κόσμῳ. It would be possible to make sense by writing ⟨τούτων δὲ⟩ οὐδέν ἐστι καταλαβέσθαι (in the sense of καταλαβεῖν) [τῶν] ἐν τῷ κόσμῳ, 'it is impossible to find aught of them in the world'; but it is more likely that the author wrote καταλάμπεσθαι. Plato described τὸ ἀγαθόν as the sun of the intelligible world; and in Pl. *Rep.* 6. 508 D, οὗ καταλάμπει ἀλήθειά τε καὶ τὸ ὄν is parallel to ὧν ὁ ἥλιος καταλάμπει. (Cf. τὸ ἀρχέτυπον φῶς in *Corp.* II. 12 b.) κάλλος is associated with light, and described as 'shining', in Pl. *Phaedrus* 250 D: περὶ δὲ κάλλους, ὥσπερ εἴπομεν, μετ' ἐκείνων τε ἔλαμπεν ὄν, δεῦρό τε ἐλθόντες κατειλήφαμεν αὐτὸ διὰ τῆς ἐναργεστάτης αἰσθήσεως τῶν ἡμετέρων (sc. τῆς ὄψεως) στίλβον ἐναργέστατα.

τὰ δὲ μὴ (ὀφθαλμῷ) ὑποπίπτοντα ⟨ἀληθῆ?⟩, μάλιστα δὲ ἡ τοῦ καλοῦ καὶ τοῦ ἀγαθοῦ ⟨ἰδέα?⟩. ἀληθῆ ('real') is a suitable word to stand in contrast to εἴδωλα and σκιαγραφίαι; cf. Herm. ap. Stob. Exc. II A, περὶ ἀληθείας. The missing word after ἀγαθοῦ is very likely ἰδέα; but it might also be οὐσία or φύσις.

⟨⟨ὁλόκληρα,⟩⟩ ἐρασμιώτατα. Both these adjectives occur in Pl. Phaedrus 250 C, D: (τὴν τελετὴν) ἣν ὠργιάζομεν (in our antenatal bliss) ὁλόκληροι μὲν αὐτοὶ ὄντες καὶ ἀπαθεῖς κακῶν ὅσα ἡμᾶς ἐν ὑστέρῳ χρόνῳ ὑπέμενεν, ὁλόκληρα δὲ καὶ ἁπλᾶ καὶ ἀτρεμῆ καὶ εὐδαίμονα φάσματα μυούμενοί τε καὶ ἐποπτεύοντες ἐν αὐγῇ καθαρᾷ, καθαροὶ ὄντες. . . . νῦν δὲ κάλλος μόνον ταύτην ἔσχε μοῖραν, ὥστ' ἐκφανέστατον εἶναι καὶ ἐρασμιώτατον. The word ὁλόκληρος (integer) may be rendered ' unblemished '. In Phaedr. l. c. ὁλόκληροι is coupled with ἀπαθεῖς κακῶν; in Tim. 44 c, ὁλόκληρος is coupled with ὑγιής, and means 'whole' as opposed to 'sick'. From the context in the Phaedrus, it may perhaps be inferred that the word was in some way associated with the Eleusinian mysteries.

§ 5. τὸ καλὸν καὶ ⟨τὸ⟩ ἀγαθόν, [τὸ ὑπέρλαμπρον] τὸ ⌜ὑπερλαμπόμενον⌝ ὑπὸ τοῦ θεοῦ. τὸ ὑπέρλαμπρον (al. ὑπέρλαμπον) has probably come by duplication from τὸ ὑπερλαμπόμενον. But what can be meant by τὸ ὑπερλαμπόμενον ὑπὸ τοῦ θεοῦ? These words would naturally mean ' which is outshone by God '; but that would not suit the context. Possibly the original reading may have been something like τὸ περιλαμπόμενον ὑπὸ τοῦ θεοῦ ⟨φῶς⟩, ' the light which God sheds round about him '.

ἐκεῖνο τὸ ἀγαθὸν ἀμίμητον. Possibly we ought to read ἀΛΑΛητον in place of ἀΜΙΜητον. Cf. Corp. X. 5 as emended: τὸ κάλλος τοῦ ἀγαθοῦ, ἐκεῖνο τὸ ἄφθαρτον, τὸ ἀλάλητον (ἄληπτον MSS.).

§ 6. τὴν [περὶ] τῆς εὐσεβείας ὁδόν. Compare what is said about ἡ πρὸς ἀλήθειαν ὁδός in Herm. ap. Stob. Exc. II B. 5.

καλὸν καὶ ἀγαθὸν τολμῶσι λέγειν ἄνθρωπον. The writer is thinking of the common use of the term καλὸς κἀγαθός or καλοκἀγαθός in speaking of a man whom one likes and respects.

μηδὲ ὄναρ θεασάμενον εἴ τί ἐστιν ἀγαθόν. This description is not applicable to the writer himself, and those who, like him, have 'trodden the path of piety'; for such men know that the Good exists, and do not mistake the evils of human life on earth for goods. What is here said about 'a man' applies therefore to most men, but not to all men. But even the pious cannot be truly called καλοὶ καὶ ἀγαθοί; for though they are free from the worst errors of their fellows, and know the evils to be evils, they still 'have need of' the evils, and 'cannot live without them'. The writer may perhaps have hoped that the Good, though it is unattainable on earth, will be attainable to the pious after their release from the prison of the body; but in this document, he makes no mention of any such prospect.

τὸ κακὸν πιστεύσαντα ἀγαθὸν εἶναι. Cf. Herm. *ap.* Stob. XI. 2. (19) and (21): ὁ θεὸς ἀγαθός, ὁ ἄνθρωπος κακός. . . . οἱ θεοὶ τὰ ἀγαθὰ αἱροῦνται· ⟨οἱ ἄνθρωποι τὰ κακὰ αἱροῦνται⟩ ὡς ἀγαθά. This was already a current saying in the time of Sophocles. *Antig.* 621: σοφίᾳ γὰρ ἔκ του κλεινὸν ἔπος πέφανται, τὸ κακὸν δοκεῖν ποτ᾽ ἐσθλὸν τῷδ᾽ ἔμμεν, ὅτῳ φρένας θεὸς ἄγει πρὸς ἄταν. But the Hermetist does not, like the wise man quoted by Sophocles, make God the author of the delusion. In § 3 b, he implies that such ἀπάται καὶ δόξαι ἀνόητοι result from the incarnation of the soul in a σῶμα ὑλικόν; but he does not explain how the soul has come to be incarnated.

ἀγωνιζόμενον ἵνα μὴ μόνον ἔχῃ (τὸ κακόν), ἀλλὰ καὶ ἐπαύξῃ. What are the evil things which men mistake for goods, and strive to keep and to increase? They cannot be the πάθη themselves; they must be the things towards which our carnal desires are directed, that is, the material means of life (e. g. food, or the money needed to buy it). These are the things which we 'cannot shun or hate', and 'without which we cannot live'. Cf. Philo *Leg. alleg.* 3. 50. 147, Cohn I, p. 145: ὁ τέλειος σοφὸς ὅλον μὲν τὸν θυμὸν ἰσχύει παραιτήσασθαι καὶ ἀποκόψαι, ὀργῆς κατεξαναστάς, τὴν δὲ κοιλίαν ἐκτεμεῖν ἀδυνατεῖ· τοῖς γὰρ ἀναγκαίοις σιτίοις καὶ ποτοῖς ἡ φύσις βιάζεται χρῆσθαι καὶ τὸν ὀλιγοδεέστατον καὶ καταφρονητικὸν αὐτῶν τῶν ἀναγκαίων, καὶ ἀσιτίαν αὐτῶν μελετῶντα. Porphyry, *De abst.* 3. 27, says that, man's end being τὸ ὁμοιοῦσθαι θεῷ, one would come nearer to realizing that deal if one could abstain, not only from the flesh of animals, but from vegetables also; εἰ δὲ μή, ἀλλ᾽ ἐντεῦθέν γε τὸ τῆς φύσεως ἡμῶν ἐλάττωμα, . . . ὅτι τὸ θεῖον ἀκήρατον καὶ ἐν πᾶσιν ἀβλαβὲς σώζειν οὐ δυνάμεθα· οὐ γὰρ ἐν πᾶσιν ἦμεν ἀπροσδεεῖς. αἰτία δὲ ἡ γένεσις, καὶ τὸ ἐν τῇ πενίᾳ ἡμᾶς γενέσθαι.[1]

---

[1] Cf. Eucken, *Life's Basis and Life's Ideal*, Eng. tr., p. 163: 'From the altitudes occupied by the spiritual life, submission to the impulses and the goods of sense seems to be something mean and base; and yet without these man cannot possibly

LIBELLVS VII

This piece should be read in connexion with *Corp.* I, of which it may be considered an appendage. It is an expansion of the abridged sermon given in *Corp.* I. 27, 28; and the attitude of the preacher is identical in the two documents. He does not, like the teacher depicted in most of the *Hermetica*, merely instruct a few select pupils in privacy; he is a man who feels that he has a mission to convert his fellow men in general, and to lead them to the *gnosis* in which he himself has found salvation. This missionary spirit is peculiar to *Corp.* I and *Corp.* VII, and places them in a different class from the rest of the Hermetic documents. Both of them are ascribed to Hermes Trismegistus in the headings prefixed to them in the MSS.; but there is nothing in the contents of either to confirm this ascription; and it is probable that in the case of both alike, the author himself never thought of putting his words into the mouth of a prehistoric prophet, but meant them to be read as spoken by himself in his own person.

The view that the body is the enemy, which is the one definite lesson taught in *Corp.* VII, is the same that is taught through the myth of the Archanthropos in *Corp.* I. Almost every thought in *Corp.* VII has its parallel in the longer document; and there is nothing in the one which is out of keeping with the contents of the other.` There is therefore strong reason to think that both were written by the same man. Compare the following:—

Corp. VII.	*Corp.* I.
1 a. μεθύοντες, τὸν τῆς ἀγνωσίας ἄκρατον ἐκπιόντες. . . . στῆτε νήψαντες. 2 a. ὅπου οὐδὲ εἷς μεθύει, ἀλλὰ πάντες νήφουσιν.	27. οἱ μέθῃ . . . ἑαυτοὺς ἐκδεδωκότες [[καὶ]] τῇ ἀγνωσίᾳ τοῦ θεοῦ, νήψατε. 30. τῆς ψυχῆς νῆψις.
1 b. ἐνορμίζεσθαι τοῖς τῆς σωτηρίας λιμέσι.	26 b. ὅπως τὸ γένος τῆς ἀνθρωπότητος . . . σωθῇ. 29. διδάσκων πῶς . . . σωθήσονται.
2 a. ζητήσατε χειράγωγον τὸν ὁδηγήσοντα ὑμᾶς ἐπὶ τὰς τῆς γνώσεως θύρας.	26 b. (τί οὐ) καθοδηγὸς γίνῃ τοῖς ἀξίοις; 29. καθοδηγὸς ἐγενόμην τοῦ γένους.

preserve his life. . . . There is something in our life which we cannot dispense with, yet which, from the spiritual point of view, it is an imperative duty to shake off.'

2 a. ἀφορῶντες τῇ καρδίᾳ . . . ·
ὑ γὰρ . . . ὁρατὸς ὀφθαλμοῖς.

2 a. οὐ γάρ ἐστιν ἀκουστός, οὐδὲ
λεκτός.

2 a. τὸ λαμπρὸν φῶς, τὸ καθαρὸν
σκότους.

2 a. τὸν (τῇ καρδίᾳ) ὁραθῆναι
θέλοντα.

2 a. νῷ καὶ καρδίᾳ.

2 b. (τὸ σῶμα,) τὸν σκοτεινὸν
περίβολον, . . . τὸν τῆς φθορᾶς
δεσμόν, τὸν ζῶντα θάνατον, κ.τ.λ.

2 b. τὸν . . . ὧν ἐπιθυμεῖς (?) σοι
φθονοῦντα.

3. τὸ κάλλος τῆς ἀληθείας.

3. μυσαρᾶς ἡδονῆς (τὰ αἰσθητήρια) ἐμπλήσας.

30. (ἐγένετο) ἡ κάμμυσις τῶν
ὀφθαλμῶν ἀληθινὴ ὅρασις.

30. καὶ ἡ σιωπή μου ἐγκύμων
τοῦ ἀγαθοῦ. 31. ἀνεκλάλητε, ἄρρητε, σιωπῇ φωνούμενε.

4. φῶς and σκότος. 6. τὸ φῶς
ἐκεῖνο . . . νοῦς. 9, 12. ὁ δὲ νοῦς
. . . ζωὴ καὶ φῶς. 21. φῶς καὶ
ζωή ἐστιν ὁ θεὸς καὶ πατήρ. 28.
ἀπαλλάγητε τοῦ σκοτεινοῦ. 32. εἰς
ζωὴν καὶ φῶς χωρῶ.

31. γνωσθῆναί βούλεται.

31. ψυχῆς καὶ καρδίας.

15. ὁ ἄνθρωπος θνητὸς μὲν διὰ
τὸ σῶμα. 19. ὁ δὲ ἀγαπήσας . . .
τὸ σῶμα, οὗτος μένει ἐν τῷ σκότει
. . . πάσχων τὰ τοῦ θανάτου. 22.
τὰ προσπίπτοντα ἐνεργήματα τοῦ
σώματος.

30. πληρωθεὶς ὧν ἤθελον ἐξηυφράνθην.

27. τὸ τῆς εὐσεβείας καὶ γνώσεως
κάλλος. 30. ⟨ἐπὶ τὸ πεδίον?⟩ τῆς
ἀληθείας ἦλθον.

22. μυσάττονται τὰς αἰσθήσεις.

I have given reasons for assigning *Corp.* I to the period
A.D. 100–200; *Corp.* VII may therefore be dated between the
same limits.

§ 1 a. Ποῖ φέρεσθε; Men are possessed and carried away by an
evil power, which the preacher compares to that which takes
possession of the drunkard. (Cf. Hor. *Od.* 3. 25. 1 : 'Quo me,
Bacche, rapis tui plenum?') He afterwards compares this same
power to the current which sweeps a boat along. The contrary of
φέρεσθε μεθύοντες is expressed by στῆτε νήψαντες below ; 'make a
firm stand (against the force which has hitherto swept you away); rid
yourselves of this drunkenness.'

μεθύοντες. As Mr. Mead points out, the same metaphor is

employed in one of the *Logia Jesu* (Klostermann, *Apocrypha* II, p. 16): ἔστην ἐν μέσῳ τοῦ κόσμου ... καὶ εὗρον πάντας μεθύοντας, καὶ οὐδένα εὗρον διψῶντα (i. e. νήφοντα?) ἐν αὐτοῖς. καὶ πονεῖ ἡ ψυχή μου ἐπὶ τοῖς υἱοῖς τῶν ἀνθρώπων, ὅτι τυφλοί εἰσιν τῇ καρδίᾳ αὐτῶν καὶ οὐ βλέπουσιν. The latter part of this *Logion* resembles *Corp.* VII. 1 a, ἀναβλέψαντες τοῖς τῆς καρδίας ὀφθαλμοῖς, and 2 a *fin.*, ἀφορῶντες τῇ καρδίᾳ κ.τ.λ. In both documents alike, blindness is associated with drunkenness.

The state of the soul when affected by the body is compared to drunkenness in Pl. *Phaedo* 79 c (the soul πλανᾶται καὶ ταράττεται καὶ ἰλιγγιᾷ ὥσπερ μεθύουσα); and the metaphor occurs in the writings of the later Platonists, e. g. Porphyr. *De abst.* 4. 20 *fin.* : men hate τοὺς ὑπομιμνήσκοντας κἀκ τῆς μέθης ἀνανῆψαι παρακαλοῦντας.

τὸν τῆς ἀγνωσίας ἄκρατον [λόγον] ἐκπιόντες. *Agnosia* (which includes estrangement from God as well as ignorance of God) comprises all that is evil in human life, as its opposite, *gnosis*, comprises all that is good. Cf. *Corp.* X. 8 b: κακία δὲ ψυχῆς ἀγνωσία· ... τοὐναντίον δὲ ἀρετὴ ψυχῆς γνῶσις. *Corp.* XI. ii. 21 b, as emended : ἡ γὰρ τελεία κακία τὸ ἀγνοεῖν τὸν θεόν.

It would be possible to speak of the λόγος of γνῶσις ('the teaching by which *gnosis* is conveyed'); but it is hardly possible to speak of the λόγος of ἀγνωσία ; for ἀγνωσία is not associated with any particular doctrine, and might rather be called ἀλογία. No substantive is needed with ἄκρατον (*sc.* οἶνον); but some reader may have thought that a substantive was wanted, and inserted an unsuitable one.

ἀλλ' ἤδη αὐτὸν καὶ ἐμεῖτε. Is ἐμεῖτε indicative or imperative? Probably indicative. If the writer had meant to say '*vomit forth* the strong drink of ἀγνωσία', i. e. 'rid yourselves of it', he would rather have written ἀλλ' ἤδη αὐτὸν ἐξεμέσατε (ἐξεμεῖν, not ἐμεῖν ; and aorist, as in στῆτε, which follows,—not present). If the verb is indicative, it may be taken to signify the outpouring of foul words and deeds in which the 'drunkenness' of those who have not *gnosis* is manifested. They have reached the last and ugliest extreme of drunkenness ; that is what is meant by ἤδη καί.

τοῖς τῆς καρδίας ὀφθαλμοῖς. Cf. *Corp.* IV. 11 b: τοῖς τῆς καρδίας ὀφθαλμοῖς. *Corp.* V. 2 : τοῖς τοῦ νοῦ ὀφθαλμοῖς.

There is a very close resemblance between the words of *Corp.* VII. 1 a and those used by Eusebius (*Adversus Hieroclem*, printed in Kayser's edition of Philostratus, vol. i, p. 411, § 47) with reference to the fatalistic doctrine which he finds in Philostratus's *Life of*

Apollonius Tyaneus: ἀλλὰ γὰρ πρὸς ταῦτα τῆς ἀληθείας ὁ κῆρυξ ἀναβοήσεται λέγων· Ὦ ἄνθρωποι, θνητὸν καὶ ἐπίκηρον γένος, ποῖ δὴ φέρεσθε, τὸν τῆς ἀγνωσίας ἄκρατον ἐμπιόντες; λήξατε ποτὲ καὶ διανήψατε τῆς μέθης, καὶ διανοίας ὀρθοῖς ὄμμασι τὸ σεμνὸν τῆς ἀληθείας ἐνοπτρίσασθε πρόσωπον. Either Eusebius had read *Corp*. VII, or he and the author of *Corp*. VII got these phrases from a common source.

§ I b. ἡ γὰρ τῆς ἀγνωσίας κακία ἐπικλύζει πᾶσαν τὴν γῆν. ἡ τῆς ἀγνωσίας κακία might mean either 'this evil thing, *agnosia*', or 'the evil which results from *agnosia*'.

The figure or parable which runs through this paragraph is not that of a voyage on the open sea, but that of a journey on the Nile. The river is in high flood (ἐπικλύζει πᾶσαν τὴν γῆν); the current is swift, and makes it difficult for the boat to gain the sheltered landing-place (λιμήν) at which the traveller is aiming. But the steersman takes advantage of an eddy or counter-current (ἀνάρροια), and brings the boat safely in. The traveller lands, and finds a guide, who leads him through the town 'to the door' of the temple which we must suppose to be the goal of his pilgrimage.

καὶ συσσύρει (συμφθείρει MSS.) τὴν ἐν τῷ σώματι κατακεκλεισμένην ψυχήν. The soul of the godless man is 'penned up' in the narrow cell of the body. Cf. *Corp*. XI. ii. 21 a: ἐὰν δὲ κατακλείσῃς σου τὴν ψυχὴν ἐν τῷ σώματι, . . . τί σοι καὶ τῷ θεῷ;

The word κατακεκλεισμένην brings in a metaphor inconsistent with the figure of the river-journey; but that is unobjectionable, because in this phrase the writer is not developing the figure itself, but explaining its application. The fate of 'the soul that is shut up in the body',—that is, the godless soul,—is like that of the traveller who fails to fetch up at the landing-place, and is swept along down stream, away from the sanctuary towards which his journey was, or should have been, directed. But it is difficult to defend the verb συμφθείρει ('corrupts'), which is placed between and closely connected with two phrases referring to the river (ἐπικλύζει πᾶσαν τὴν γῆν and μὴ ἐῶσα ἐνορμίζεσθαι κ.τ.λ.), and yet presents an entirely different picture. We are told that *agnosia*, like the swollen river, 'floods the land, *corrupts* the (godless) soul, and does not suffer it to reach the haven'. This can hardly be right. Besides, there is no apparent reason for using the compound συμφθείρει instead of φθείρει. A satisfactory sense may be got by substituting συσσύρει, 'sweeps along with it'.[1]

[1] For συσσύρει, cf. Numenius *ap*. Euseb. *Pr. ev*. 14. 8. 2: Carneades ἐξηγείρετο

§ 2 a. ζητήσατε χειραγωγόν, τὸν ὁδηγήσοντα ὑμᾶς κ.τ.λ. He who seeks *gnosis* needs some one who has already attained to it to lead him on his way. The preacher probably means it to be understood that he himself is such a guide, and is ready to give his services to all who will accept them.

ἐπὶ τὰς τῆς γνώσεως θύρας. For the moment, *Gnosis* is personified. The preacher represents her as the deity whose temple the traveller in his parable is seeking; and he proceeds to depict her sanctuary, describing it as a place filled with unmixed light, and speaking of the votaries who are gathered there. His use of the plural (πάντες νήφουσι κ.τ.λ.) may perhaps be taken to show that he has in mind a community of γνωστικοί,—comparable to a Jewish synagogue or a Christian *ecclesia*,—of which the convert will become a member.

τὸ λαμπρὸν φῶς, τὸ καθαρὸν σκότους. This phrase shows that in the writer's circle φῶς was a recognized name for God, or for the presence and power of God. (Cf. *Corp.* I *passim*.) The word is used as in the Fourth Gospel. Cf. *Ep. Joh.* I. I. 5: ὁ θεὸς φῶς ἐστιν, καὶ σκοτία οὐκ ἔστιν ἐν αὐτῷ οὐδεμία.

ἀφορῶντες τῇ καρδίᾳ εἰς τὸν ⟨οὕτως⟩ ὁραθῆναι θέλοντα. Cf. *Corp.* I. 31 : (ὁ θεὸς) γνωσθῆναι βούλεται. *Corp.* X. 15 a : (ὁ θεὸς) θέλει γνωρίζεσθαι. It is necessary to insert οὕτως (*sc.* τῇ καρδίᾳ), on account of the following words, οὐ γάρ ἐστιν . . . ὁρατὸς ὀφθαλμοῖς, ἀλλὰ νῷ καὶ καρδίᾳ. If the preacher had merely said that God ὁραθῆναι βούλεται, there would be no meaning in the γάρ.

οὐ γάρ ἐστιν ἀκουστός, οὐδὲ λεκτός. Cf. *Corp.* X. 9: ὁ γὰρ θεὸς . . . οὔτε λέγεται οὔτε ἀκούεται. The teaching of the ' guide ' is, no doubt, needed; yet *gnosis* cannot be conveyed from one man to another by verbal instruction; it must spring up spontaneously in the heart of him who seeks God. See *Corp.* IX *fin*.

§ 2 b. πρῶτον δὲ δεῖ σε περιρρήξασθαι ὃν φορεῖς χιτῶνα. The χιτών is the body; and the preacher denounces it in the most emphatic language. Cf. *Corp.* IV. 6 b: ἐὰν μὴ πρῶτον τὸ σῶμα μισήσῃς κ.τ.λ. This hatred of the body was shared in various degrees by the later Platonists and Pythagoreans in general, and by many of the Catholic Christians, and was carried to extreme lengths by some of the Christian Gnostics, and especially by the Manichaeans. Compare Paul, *Gal.* 5. 17: ἡ γὰρ σὰρξ ἐπιθυμεῖ κατὰ τοῦ πνεύματος,[1]

λάβρος οἷον ποταμὸς ῥοώδης, πάντα καταπιμπλὰς τὰ τῇδε καὶ τἀκεῖθι, καὶ εἰσέπιπτε καὶ συνέσυρε τοὺς ἀκούοντας διὰ θορύβου.

[1] A Hermetist would have said κατὰ τοῦ νοῦ.

τὸ δὲ πνεῦμα κατὰ τῆς σαρκός, . . . ἵνα μὴ ἃ ἐὰν θέλητε ταῦτα ποιῆτε.[1]
Rom. 7. 5–8. 8 : ὅτε γὰρ ἦμεν ἐν τῇ σαρκί, τὰ παθήματα τῶν ἁμαρτιῶν
. . . ἐνηργεῖτο ἐν τοῖς μέλεσιν ἡμῶν εἰς τὸ καρποφορῆσαι τῷ θανάτῳ.
. . . ὁ νόμος πνευματικός ἐστιν·[2] ἐγὼ δὲ σάρκινός εἰμι, πεπραμένος ὑπὸ
τὴν ἁμαρτίαν. . . . οἶδα γὰρ ὅτι οὐκ οἰκεῖ . . . ἐν τῇ σαρκί μου ἀγαθόν.
. . . τίς με ῥύσεται ἐκ τοῦ σώματος τοῦ θανάτου τούτου ; . . . τὸ γὰρ
φρόνημα τῆς σαρκὸς θάνατος . . .· οἱ δὲ ἐν σαρκὶ ὄντες θεῷ ἀρέσαι[3]
οὐ δύνανται. Philo calls the body a παμμίαρον δεσμωτήριον (*De migr.
Abr.* 2. 9, Wendland II, p. 270) ; a εἱρκτή (*Quis rer. div. her.* 14. 68,
Wendl. III, p. 16). Cf. Philo *De migr. Abr.* 3. 16, Wendl. II,
p. 271 : εἰσὶ δ' οἳ μέχρι τῆς τελευτῆς . . . ὥσπερ λάρνακι ἢ σορῷ
. . . (τῷ σώματι) ἐνετάφησαν. *Leg. alleg.* 3. 22. 69, Cohn I, p. 127 :
τὸν γὰρ δερμάτινον ὄγκον ἡμῶν, τὸ σῶμα, . . . πονηρόν τε καὶ ἐπίβουλον
τῆς ψυχῆς οὐκ ἀγνοεῖ, καὶ νεκρὸν καὶ τεθνηκὸς αἰεί· μὴ γὰρ ἄλλο τι
νοήσῃς ἕκαστον ἡμῶν ποιεῖν ἢ νεκροφορεῖν. *Leg. alleg.* 1. 33. 108,
Cohn I, p. 89 : ὡς νῦν μέν, ὅτε ζῶμεν, τεθνηκυίας τῆς ψυχῆς, καὶ ὡς
ἂν ἐν σήματι τῷ σώματι ἐντετυμβευμένης, εἰ δὲ ἀποθάνοιμεν, τῆς ψυχῆς
ζώσης τὸν ἴδιον βίον, καὶ ἀπηλλαγμένης κακοῦ καὶ νεκροῦ συνδέτου τοῦ
σώματος. This sort of language is derived in part from Pl. *Phaedo*
64 ff., and other passages in Plato ; but some of the later Platonists
went far beyond Plato in their hatred of the body.

⟨⟨τὸν σκοτεινὸν περίβολον⟩⟩. The numerous metaphors by which
the body is here described are mutually inconsistent ; but their
inconsistency becomes less obtrusive, and the transitions easier, if
we shift τὸν σκοτεινὸν περίβολον, and place it next after χιτῶνα.
The body is first compared to a garment—χιτών, περίβολος, ὕφασμα,
(στήριγμα ?) ; it is then called a δεσμός, i. e. a thing by which the soul
is bound ; (a garment might act as a δεσμός ;) the mention of φθορά
in combination with δεσμός suggests the three terms which follow,
viz. 'death', 'corpse', and 'tomb' ; and finally, the pernicious thing
is personified as a 'robber' and an 'enemy'.

τὸ τῆς ἀγνωσίας ὕφασμα, τὸ τῆς κακίας ⌜στήριγμα.⌝ How are the
genitives to be understood? ἀγνωσίας ὕφασμα would most naturally
signify 'a web *made of* or *consisting of* ignorance'. But the writer's
meaning must have been that the woven structure of the body
produces or *results in* ignorance. The soul which is wrapped in it
forgets its antenatal *gnosis*, and is sunk in *lethe*.

---

[1] Compare τὸν ὧν ἐφίεσαι μισοῦντα καὶ ὧν ἐπιθυμεῖς σοι φθονοῦντα in *Corp.* VII as emended.
[2] A Hermetist would have spoken of ἡ γνῶσις in place of ὁ νόμος.
[3] A Hermetist would have said θεὸν γνῶναι.

It is a strange mixture of metaphors to say that a piece of woven stuff (ὕφασμα) is a 'prop' of wickedness or evil; and there can be little doubt that στήριγμα is a misreading. Possibly the author may have written τὸν .... στήμονα, 'the *warp* of evil', carrying on the notion expressed by ὕφασμα.

⟨⟨ ⟨τὸν⟩ ἐχθρὸν⟩⟩ τὸν ὧν ἐφίεσαι μισοῦντα καὶ ὧν ἐπιθυμεῖς σου φθονοῦντα. —(τὸν δι' ὧν φιλεῖ μισοῦντα, καὶ δι' ὧν μισεῖ φθονοῦντα MSS.) The reading of the MSS. can only be translated 'who hates the things by means of which he loves, and grudges the things by means of which he hates' (or, 'and grudges by means of the things which he hates'.) But there is no meaning in that. Emended as above, the passage makes good sense. Your enemy the body 'hates the things which you seek after (i. e. τὰ ἀσώματα καὶ θεῖα,—in Paul's language, τὰ πνευματικά), and grudges you the things which you desire.'

A substantive is needed here, to match the words with which the preceding phrases end. If there is no expressed substantive, we are forced to understand ληστήν; and that does not make good sense. A man who robs you is not one who 'hates the things which you seek after'; he is rather one who loves them overmuch. ἐχθρόν is just the word that is wanted; and as an epithet of χιτῶνα in the following sentence, it is clearly out of place. I have therefore transposed it.

§ 3. ἄγχων σε κάτω πρὸς αὐτόν. Cf. *Corp.* X. 24 a : (ψυχὴν) τῷ σώματι προσηρτημένην καὶ ὑπ' αὐτοῦ ἀγχομένην κάτω. *Ascl. Lat.* I. 12 a : 'animam obtorto, ut aiunt, detinet collo.'

τὸ ἐκεῖ μένον (ἐγκείμενον MSS.) ἀγαθόν. If we retain ἐγκείμενον, we must take the words to mean 'the Good which is situated in Reality', or 'situated in the beauty of Reality'. But that is hardly satisfactory. ἐκεῖ μένον, 'abiding in the other and higher world', is better.

τὰ [δοκοῦντα καὶ μὴ] νομιζόμενα αἰσθητήρια ἀναίσθητα ποιῶν. (καὶ μὴ A : ἐμοὶ Q : μοι καὶ Turn.) Both μὴ and μοι are unmeaning; and to say δοκοῦντα καὶ νομιζόμενα would be to say the same thing twice over. Perhaps the readings of the MSS. may have arisen out of δοκοῦντα καὶ μὴ ⟨ὄντα⟩, written as an alternative for νομιζόμενα.

Those who live in subjection to the body cannot see or hear aright; and the eyes and ears of such people do not deserve the name 'organs of sense', which is commonly applied to them. 'O foolish people, and without understanding, which have eyes, and see not; which have ears, and hear not' (Jerem. 5. 21). The preacher here includes under the term αἴσθησις that ' seeing with the heart' which in § 2 a he distinguished from 'seeing with the eyes'; and his meaning is that those who see with the bodily eyes alone, and not 'with the heart', ought to be called blind (ἀναίσθητοι), because they cannot 'see the things they ought to see' (ἃ βλέπειν δεῖ, i. e. τὰ ἀσώματα καὶ θεῖα). It is the eyes and ears of the heart, and not the bodily organs, that are 'stuffed up'.

The piece ends abruptly at the words βλέπειν σε δεῖ, and there is no fitting conclusion. It is probable therefore that only the beginning of the preacher's discourse is given in *Corp.* VII, and the rest of it has been lost.

LIBELLVS VIII

Contents

. . . Nothing dies. The Kosmos is a living and immortal being; and no part of such a being can die. § 1 b.

The Kosmos is the second God. It has been made, and is maintained in being, by the first God. The first God is eternal (i. e. without beginning, as well as without end). The Kosmos is not without beginning, but it is immortal; for it has been made immortal by its Maker, who is eternal. § 2.

God made the Kosmos out of formless or unordered matter, which existed beside him from all eternity. Out of that part of matter which was wholly subject to his will, he fashioned the sphere of heaven; and within this sphere he enclosed the rest of matter. On the matter enclosed within the sphere he imposed manifold forms, so that the cavity (i. e. the sublunar world) was filled with living creatures; and he made the whole structure immortal, so that matter might never revert to its primal disorder. Yet a vestige of that disorder remains in the sublunar world, and manifests itself in the growth and decay of terrestrial organisms. The order of the heavenly bodies is perfect; their movement is cyclic or recurrent, ⟨and accordingly, they are individually immortal.⟩ Terrestrial organisms suffer dissolution; but by this dissolution they are reabsorbed into the cosmic elements, which are immortal. Thus, though the consciousness of each terrestrial being ceases, life never perishes. §§ 3, 4.

Man is made in the image of the Kosmos, and feels himself
a part of it; but he differs from all other terrestrial creatures, in
that God has given him mind. Hence he not only perceives the
corporeal Kosmos, but also apprehends the incorporeal God. And
from the relation of man to God and to the Kosmos, it follows that
man is immortal.

The Kosmos is made by God; and man is made by the Kosmos.
Thus God is the supreme author of all. § 5.

Sources. ' Nothing perishes; there is no death.' That is the thesis
maintained in *Corp.* VIII; and it is likewise maintained in *Corp.*
XII. ii. 15 b–18. Both the writer of VIII and the writer of XII.
ii doubtless had in mind the often-quoted lines of Euripides
Chrysippus, fr. 836 Nauck:[1] χωρεῖ δ' ὀπίσω | τὰ μὲν ἐκ γαίας φύντ'
εἰς γαῖαν, | τὰ δ' ἀπ' αἰθερίου βλαστόντα γονῆς | εἰς οὐράνιον πάλιν
ἦλθε πόλον· | θνῄσκει δ' οὐδὲν τῶν γιγνομένων, | διακρινόμενον δ' ἄλλο
πρὸς ἄλλο⟨υ⟩[2] | μορφὴν ἑτέραν[3] ἀπέδειξεν.[4]

For the rest, the doctrine of *Corp.* VIII is mainly Platonic, but
partly Stoic. In his conception of the supracosmic and incorporeal
God, the writer is a Platonist; and in his account of the relation
between God and the Kosmos (§ 2), and his description of the
demiurgia (§ 3), he is dependent on the *Timaeus*. His conception
of ἄτακτος ὕλη is derived from Plato. But his division of ὕλη into
two separate portions, one of which is ' subject to God's will', and
the other is not, does not come directly from the *Timaeus*, but shows

---

[1] That passage of Euripides, or part of it, is quoted in Philo (?) *De incorrupt.
mundi* three times, cc. 2, 6, 27; and by Philo, *Leg. alleg.* 1. 3. 7, Cohn I, p. 65;
Aetius, Diels *Doxogr.* p. 430; Heraclitus *Alleg. Hom.* 22; Marcus Aurelius 7. 50;
Clem. Alex. *Strom.* 6. 24. It is translated into Latin by Lucretius, 2. 991 ff., and
by Vitruvius, 8 *praef.* § 1.

Euripides got the thought from Anaxagoras, fr. 17 Diels: τὸ δὲ γίνεσθαι καὶ
ἀπόλλυσθαι οὐκ ὀρθῶς νομίζουσιν οἱ Ἕλληνες· οὐδὲν γὰρ χρῆμα γίνεται οὐδὲ ἀπόλλυται,
ἀλλ' ἀπὸ ἐόντων χρημάτων συμμίσγεταί τε καὶ διακρίνεται. καὶ οὕτως ἂν ὀρθῶς
καλοῖεν τό τε γινέσθαι συμμίσγεσθαι καὶ τὸ ἀπόλλυσθαι διακρίνεσθαι. Compare also
Epicharmus *Gnom.*, fr. 9 Diels: συνεκρίθη καὶ διεκρίθη κἀπῆλθεν ὅθεν ἦλθεν πάλιν, |
γᾶ μὲν εἰς γᾶν, πνεῦμα δ' ἄνω (perhaps πνεῦμ' ἄνω). τί τῶνδε χαλεπόν; οὐδὲ ἕν.
But it was the verses of Euripides that fixed themselves in men's memory.

For a modern expression of the same thought, cf. Maeterlinck, *Our Eternity*,
Eng. tr. 1913, ch. 2: ' Total annihilation is impossible. We are the prisoners of
an infinity without outlet, wherein nothing perishes, wherein everything is dispersed,
but nothing lost. . . . We can no more conceive death than we can conceive
nothingness. . . . We give the name of death to anything that has a life a little
different from ours. . . . "There is no room for death!" . . . All that dies falls
into life.'

[2] ἄλλο πρὸς ἄλλου Clem. Alex.(?), Nauck, Diels; ἄλλο πρὸς ἄλλῳ Bernays.

[3] Variants, μορφὰς ἑτέρας and μορφὴν ἰδίαν.

[4] Variant, ἐπέδειξεν.

connexion with a later form of the Platonic doctrine of ὕλη. The comparison of the Kosmos to a cave may have been adopted from Numenius or some other Platonist of the same period. The description of the Kosmos as 'the second God' was doubtless suggested by the *Timaeus* (see *Tim.* 92 c). But the 'second God' of the Platonists is the supreme God of the Stoics ; and in his account of the Kosmos, and of man's relation to it, the writer has been influenced by Stoic authorities. The use of the word συμπάθεια (§ 5) is an indication of this. The words ἀποκατάστασις (§ 4), ποιόν and ποιότης (§ 3), probably came from Stoic sources. The writer of *Corp.* VIII apparently does not accept the Platonic doctrine that the individual man continues to exist as a separate person after the dissolution of the body. In this respect, he has rejected one of the most important tenets of Platonism, and his position more nearly resembles that of the Stoic Epictetus.

Date. The combination of Platonism and Stoicism which *Corp.* VIII presents cannot be earlier than the first century B.C. The date of this document must therefore lie somewhere between 100 B.C. and A. D. 300, if we take the latter date as the *terminus ad quem* of the *Hermetica* in general. Narrower limits cannot be fixed with absolute certainty ; but the probabilities are strongly in favour of the latter half of this period. The nearest parallels to § 3 *init.* (καὶ ὅσον ἦν τῆς ὕλης κ.τ.λ.) occur in the writings of Hermogenes and Methodius (A. D. 200–300) ; and the comparison of the Kosmos to a cave points towards the time of Numenius, Cronius, and Porphyry (A. D. 150–300), by whom the same comparison was employed. It is therefore most likely that *Corp.* VIII was written at some time between A. D. 150 and 300.

§ 1 a. περὶ ψυχῆς καὶ σώματος, ὦ παῖ, νῦν λεκτέον. This implies that something has preceded. If the *libellus* began with these words, its writer must have intended it to follow another 'discourse of Hermes to Tat'.

Hermes says that he is about to speak 'about the soul', and explain τρόπῳ ποίῳ ἀθάνατος ἡ ψυχή; but in the discourse which follows, there is not a word about ψυχή. The document might be described as περὶ ἀθανασίας; but no part of it can be described as περὶ ψυχῆς. However, there is undoubtedly a lacuna after καὶ διαλύσεως at the end of § 1 a; and it is possible that a passage of considerable length has disappeared there, and that these introductory words had more to do with the lost beginning of the discourse of Hermes than with the part of it which has been preserved.

ἐνεργείᾳ δὲ ποταπῇ ⟨συνίσταται καὶ διαλύεται (?) τὰ σώματα⟩. τὰ σώματα or τὸ σῶμα must have stood here, in correspondence to ἡ ψυχή in the preceding clause. The ἐνέργεια by which the σύστασις and διάλυσις of (earthly) bodies are carried on might be named either φύσις or εἱμαρμένη. The σύστασις and διάλυσις of bodies are spoken of in § 4; but the document, in the form in which we have it, contains no explanation of the nature of the ἐνέργεια by which these processes are effected,—unless indeed what is said in § 3 about God's imposition of ποιά on ἄτακτος ὕλη can be considered such an explanation.

§ 1 b. ⟨. . .⟩ περὶ οὐδὲν γὰρ αὐτῶν ὁ θάνατος. αὐτων must mean τῶν ἐν τῷ κόσμῳ. A passage in which 'the things in the Kosmos' were mentioned must therefore have been lost before these words.

ἀλλὰ ὄνομά ἐστιν ἡ θανάτου προσηγορία κενὸν ἔργου.—(ἀλλὰ νόημά ἐστιν ἀθανάτου προσηγορίας ἢ κενὸν ἔργον MSS.) For ὄνομα contrasted with ἔργον (as λόγος often is), cf. Eur. *Iph. Aul.* 128 : ὄνομ᾽, οὐκ ἔργον, παρέχων. *Ib.* 1115 : τοῖς ὀνόμασιν μὲν εὖ λέγεις, τὰ δ᾽ ἔργα σοῦ κ.τ.λ. For ὄνομα κενόν, cf. *Corp.* XI. i. 5 : ἀργία γὰρ ὄνομα κενόν ἐστι. We may suppose that ἀλλ᾽ ὄνομα was wrongly read as αλλο νομα, and this was wrongly corrected into ἀλλὰ νόημα.

There is no such thing as death. Cf. *Corp.* XII. ii. 18 : οὐδὲν δὲ φθαρτὸν ἢ ἀπολλύμενον· αἱ δὲ προσηγορίαι τοὺς ἀνθρώπους ταράττουσιν. *Corp.* XI. ii. 15 b : τὴν δὲ μεταβολὴν θάνατόν φασιν εἶναι κ.τ.λ.

Apollonius Tyaneus *Ep.* 58 (Kayser, *Philostrati opera* I, p. 359) [1] : θάνατος οὐδεὶς οὐδενὸς ἢ μόνον ἐμφάσει [2], καθάπερ οὐδὲ γένεσις οὐδενὸς

---

[1] This letter is a *consolatio* addressed to 'Valerius' on the death of his son. If the conclusions of Norden and Cichorius (Norden *Agnostos Theos* Anhang III, p. 337 sqq.), based on a combination of ingenious inferences, may be accepted, *Ep.* 58 is a genuine letter of Apollonius, written by him in A.D 81–83, and addressed to Valerius Festus, proconsul of Asia. The doctrine set forth in it is Stoic, not Platonic ; what the writer asserts is not that the individual man is immortal as an individual, but that at his death he is reabsorbed into the All, and the All is immortal. That same doctrine is taught in *Corp.* VIII, which may have been written one or two centuries later ; but the author of *Corp.* VIII has combined with it Platonic ingredients which are absent in the letter of Apollonius.

A similar thought occurs in Apollonius *Ep.* 55, a *consolatio* addressed by Ap. to his brother, whose wife had died : μηδέ, ἐπεὶ θάνατός τι λέγεται ('because men speak of a thing which they call death'), κρεῖττον αὐτοῦ τὸ ζῆν ὑπολάμβανε, χεῖρον ὂν τῷ παντὶ τοῖς νοῦν ἔχουσι. But in *Ep.* 55 (which may also be genuine, for aught that I know), there is no philosophic elaboration of this thought ; the bulk of the letter consists of advice to the widower (who was presumably not a philosopher) to marry again without delay.

[2] 'save only in appearance.'

ἢ μόνον ἐμφάσει. τὸ μὲν γὰρ ἐξ οὐσίας τραπὲν εἰς φύσιν¹ ἔδοξε γένεσις,
τὸ δὲ ἐκ φύσεως εἰς οὐσίαν κατὰ ταὐτὰ θάνατος, οὔτε γιγνομένου κατ᾽
ἀλήθειάν τινος οὔτε φθειρομένου ποτέ, μόνον δὲ ἐμφανοῦς ὄντος (for a
time) ἀοράτου δὲ ὕστερον, τοῦ μὲν διὰ παχύτητα τῆς ὕλης, τοῦ δὲ διὰ
λεπτότητα τῆς οὐσίας, οὔσης μὲν αἰεὶ τῆς αὐτῆς, κινήσει δὲ διαφερούσης καὶ
στάσει. τοῦτο γάρ που τὸ ἴδιον ἀνάγκη τῆς μεταβολῆς, οὐκ ἔξωθεν γινομένης
ποθέν, ἀλλὰ τοῦ μὲν ὅλου μεταβάλλοντος εἰς τὰ μέρη, τῶν μερῶν δὲ εἰς τὸ
ὅλον τρεπομένων ⟨. . .⟩² ἑνότητι τοῦ παντός. εἰ δὲ ἐρήσεταί τις τί τοῦτο
ἔστι τὸ ποτὲ μὲν ὁρατὸν ποτὲ δὲ ἀόρατον ἢ ⟨ἐν?⟩ τοῖς αὐτοῖς γινόμενον ἢ
ἄλλοις, φαίη τις ἂν ὡς ⌜ἔθος⌝³ ἑκάστου ἐστὶ τῶν ἐνθάδε γενῶν, ὃ πληρωθὲν
μὲν ⟨ὕλης?⟩ ἐφάνη διὰ τὴν τῆς παχύτητος ἀντιτυπίαν, ἀόρατον δέ ἐστιν, εἰ
κενωθείη, διὰ ⟨τὴν?⟩ λεπτότητα, τῆς ὕλης βίᾳ ⌜περιχυθείσης⌝⁴ ἐκρυείσης
τε τοῦ περιέχοντος αὐτὴν αἰωνίου μέτρου γεννητοῦ δ᾽ οὐδαμῶς⁵ οὐδὲ
φθαρτοῦ.⁶

¹ I. e. 'the change from the state of elemental matter (οὐσία in the Stoic sense)
to the state of an organism'. The meaning would be better expressed by writing
τὸ μὲν γὰρ ἐξ οὐσίας τραπῆν(αι) εἰς φύσιν ἔδοξε γένεσις ⟨εἶναι⟩.

² A few words have probably been lost here.

³ Perhaps μέτρον (or ⟨μέτρον⟩ ἑνὸς?).

⁴ Conybeare translates 'shed abroad', which seems to suit the context. The
word περιχυθείσης could hardly bear that meaning; but one might read περι⟨εκ⟩χυ-
θείσης.

⁵ The writer must have meant, and may have written, τοῦ περιέχοντος αὐτὴν
μέτρου, αἰωνίου ὄντος, γεννητοῦ δ᾽ οὐδαμῶς.

⁶ This obscure sentence may perhaps be translated thus : ' If some one asks what
is this thing that becomes visible at times, and invisible at other times, whether in
the same individuals or in different individuals, we may answer that each kind of
beings upon earth has a *measure*, which, when filled with gross matter, becomes
visible by reason of the solidity of its density, but if emptied of gross matter, is
invisible by reason of its rarity, the gross matter having been shed abroad by
violence and poured out from the *measure* which contained it. The *measure* is
eternal, and is neither generated nor subject to destruction.'

The 'thing which is now visible and now invisible' is, if I understand the passage
rightly, a sort of living gas (the πῦρ νοερόν or πνεῦμα of the Stoics), which
permeates the universe, and vivifies all individual organisms. It is thought of as
corporeal, but subtle, and is contrasted with ὕλη (*gross* matter). It is invisible in
itself; but when a portion of it, marked off by a definite boundary, is 'filled' with
ὕλη, the thing thus composed (i. e. the living organism) is visible and tangible.

But what is the meaning of μέτρον? The word seems to be here used to denote
the limiting surface of any one of these portions of πνεῦμα (if 'the thing which is
visible at times' may be called πνεῦμα). At the death of the organism, this limiting surface is, so to speak, shattered by a violent shock (βίᾳ), and the ὕλη with
which it was 'filled' escapes, and is dispersed. The portion of πνεῦμα which was
delimited by this μέτρον, and in which the life of the organism consisted, then
becomes invisible (and is presumably reabsorbed into the universal πνεῦμα).

I have failed to find any parallel to this use of the word μέτρον ; but it may
possibly have been suggested by the saying of Heraclitus, fr. 30 Diels, ἦν ἀεὶ καὶ ἔστι
καὶ ἔσται πῦρ ἀείζωον (= the πῦρ νοερόν of the Stoics), ἁπτόμενον μέτρα καὶ ἀποσβεν-
νύμενον μέτρα. Be that as it may, the notion which Apollonius here expresses by
μέτρον seems to be similar to that elsewhere expressed by the Pythagorean term
πέρας. Of the philosophic tenets of Apollonius little is known ; but a Stoicizing
Neopythagorean, such as we may suppose him to have been, might perhaps take

τί δὲ καὶ τὸ τῆς πλάνης ἐπὶ τοσοῦτον ἀνέλεγκτον; ¹ οἴονται γάρ τινες, ὃ
πεπόνθασιν, αὐτοὶ τοῦτο πεποιηκέναι, μὴ εἰδότες ὡς ὁ γεννηθεὶς διὰ γονέων
γεγέννηται, οὐχ ὑπὸ γονέων,² καθάπερ τὸ διὰ γῆς φυὲν οὐκ ἐκ γῆς φύεται,
πάθος τε οὐδὲν τῶν φαινομένων περὶ ἕκαστον, ἀλλὰ μᾶλλον περὶ ἓν ἑκάστου.³
τοῦτο δὲ (sc. τὸ ἕν) τί ἂν ἄλλο τις εἰπὼν ἢ τὴν πρώτην οὐσίαν ὀρθῶς ἂν
ὀνομάσειεν; ἢ δὴ μόνη ποιεῖ τε καὶ πάσχει, πᾶσι γινομένη πάντα διὰ
πάντων, θεὸς ἀίδιος,⁴ ὀνόμασι καὶ προσώποις ἀφαιρουμένη τὸ ἴδιον ἀδικου-
μένη τε.⁵

καὶ τοῦτο μὲν ἔλαττον. τὸ δὲ ⟨μεῖζον⟩· κλαίεταί τις, ὅταν θεὸς ἐξ
ἀνθρώπου γένηται τόπου μεταβάσει καὶ οὐχὶ φύσεως.⁶ ὡς δὲ ἔχει τὸ

the ἄπειρον of which Pythagoreans spoke to mean the universal πνεῦμα, and τὸ
πέρας to mean the μέτρον by which the πνεῦμα of an individual organism is marked
off from the universal πνεῦμα.

But the writer goes on to say that the μέτρον is αἰώνιον. What does he mean by
this? It seems to be an attempt to combine with the Stoic cosmology the Platonic or
Aristotelian conception of εἶδος. The μέτρον of a horse, so far as it is regarded merely
as belonging to this or that individual horse, is shattered at death; but regarded
as a type or general form (εἶδος), it is present in all horses; and the race of horses is
everlasting. (The *race* or *kind* is referred to in the words ἑκάστου τῶν ἐνθάδε γενῶν.)
The words ἢ ⟨ἐν?⟩ τοῖς αὐτοῖς γινόμενον ἢ ⟨ἐν?⟩ ἄλλοις are puzzling. The πνεῦμα
(and with it, the μέτρον by which the πνεῦμα is delimited) may be said to become
visible and invisible by turns ἐν ἄλλοις ⟨καὶ ἄλλοις⟩, i.e. in a succession of different
individuals; but how can it be said to do so ἐν τοῖς αὐτοῖς? Does τοῖς αὐτοῖς refer
to the heavenly bodies, which, though the life in them persists unchanged, are
alternately visible and invisible *to us* in the succession of day and night, and of the
seasons of the year?

¹ 'Why is it that this error (viz. the notion that men "die", or that there is
such a thing as "death") has so long remained unrefuted?'
² Valerius thinks '*I* have begotten a son' (and consequently mourns when he
loses his son). But that is a mistake; the begetting of his son, like all else that
takes place, is an act of God (God immanent in the universe, and identical with
φύσις),—or in other words, an operation of the all-permeating πῦρ νοερόν; and
Valerius (who is himself merely a temporarily marked off portion of God) is in
this, as in all else that he does (or rather, thinks that he does), a passive instrument
of God, who does all.
³ 'Nothing that takes place in the visible world is a thing that befalls an
individual; every incident in the life of an individual (ἑκάστου) is rather a thing
that befalls the One (περὶ ⟨τὸ?⟩ ἕν).' This must, I think, have been the meaning of
the clause; but περὶ ἓν ἑκάστου is obscure, and perhaps corrupt.
Valerius thinks 'the death of my son is a disaster that has befallen *me*'. But he
is wrong; it is an event that has to do, not with *him* as an individual, but with the
One who is all.—This is Stoic pantheism pushed to its extreme.
⁴ God (who is πῦρ νοερόν) is both the maker of the Kosmos and the πρώτη οὐσία
(i.e. the primary elemental substance) of which it is made. The other elements
(air, water, earth) have come into being by transmutation out of fire (and, according to the Stoics, will be wholly retransmuted into fire at the *ecpyrosis*, when God
will again be 'all in all'; but we have no evidence that Apollonius accepted the
Stoic doctrine of *ecpyrosis*).
⁵ 'This alone is agent and patient, . . . (and this,) in so far as it takes on the
names and persons of individuals, forfeits its peculiar character to its prejudice'
(Conybeare). Or perhaps, 'and when men impose on it the names and persons of
individuals (as Valerius does when he talks about "*me*" and "*my* son"), they
deprive it of its proper character, and do it wrong.'
⁶ To weep when this takes place is μεῖζον, i.e. 'a still greater error than that of

ἀληθές, οὐ πενθητέον σοι θάνατον, ἀλλὰ τιμητέον καὶ σεβαστέον.   . . .
υἱὸν δὲ ἔχεις καὶ νῦν τὸν τεθνηκότα, φήσει τις τῶν νοῦν ἐχόντων. τὸ γὰρ
ὂν οὐκ ἀπόλλυται, διὰ τοῦτο ὄν, ὅτι ἔσται διὰ παντός.¹ ἢ καὶ τὸ μὴ ὂν
γίνεται· πῶς δ᾽ ἂν γένοιτο [μὴ ἀπολλυμένου τοῦ ὄντος]; ²

Macrobius *Somn.* 2. 12. 12 : ' Quod autem ait (Cicero) "mundum
quadam parte mortalem", ad communem opinionem respicit, qua
mori aliqua intra mundum videntur, ut animal exanimatum, vel ignis
extinctus, vel siccatus humor ; haec enim omnino interisse credantur.
Sed constat secundum verae rationis adsertionem, quam et ipse
(Cicero) non nescit, nec Vergilius ignorat dicendo " nec morti esse
locum " (*Georg.* 4. 226), constat, inquam, nihil intra vivum mundum
perire, sed eorum quae interire videntur solam mutari speciem, et
illud in originem suam atque in ipsa elementa remeare, quod tale
quale fuit esse desierit.'

[ἢ κατὰ στέρησιν τοῦ πρώτου γράμματος λεγόμενος θάνατος ἀντὶ τοῦ
ἀθάνατος.] That is, when men say θάνατος, they mean, or ought to

which I have been speaking'. The man who has died ' has become θεός, by a
change of place, but not of nature '. This does not mean that he has become *a*
god,—i. e. a divine individual, one among a number, with a separate personality of
his own. He was (or at least, he seemed to be, and thought he was) an individual
person while he lived on earth, but he is such no longer ; he has been reabsorbed
into the All which is God. He has undergone 'a change of place, but not of
nature', in the same sense that this might be said of a bucket-full of water which
has been poured into the sea. His φύσις (his mode or kind of being) is unchanged ;
i. e. he still is what he was before. He was πνεῦμα upon earth ; (i. e. the man, *qua*
living, was πνεῦμα ; the ὕλη with which his μέτρον of πνεῦμα was 'filled ' to
constitute an organism was not he ;) and he is πνεῦμα still. But during his life on
earth he was a distinct portion of πνεῦμα, marked off and divided from the rest ;
now, that portion of πνεῦμα, which was he, is blended with the whole mass of
πνεῦμα in which the life of the universe resides.
    That is what the writer must have meant, if he adhered to the doctrine laid down
in the preceding part of the letter. But from this point onward, he speaks
ambiguously, and uses phrases which, to a reader who had not fully grasped the
meaning of his doctrine, might seem to imply a survival of the man as a distinct
and individual person ; e. g. ὅταν ἐξ ἀνθρώπου θεὸς γένηται, and υἱὸν ἔχεις καὶ νῦν
τὸν τεθνηκότα.
    ¹ 'That which is, *is* for this very reason, that it will be for ever.' This, I
suppose, means ' Only that which is everlasting can rightly be said to exist'. If it
could, at any time in the past, be truly said of your son that ' he is ', then it follows
that he can never cease to be. He must therefore be in existence now. (But he
does not now exist *as a separate person* ; he has been absorbed into God, or has
become one with God.)
    ² The thing to be proved is that τὸ ὂν οὐκ ἀπόλλυται ; and that being so, the
words μὴ ἀπολλυμένου τοῦ ὄντος appear to make the argument run in a circle. If
we cut out these words, the rest may be translated thus : ' Otherwise,' (i. e. if it
were true that τὸ ὂν perishes,) 'it would follow that τὸ μὴ ὂν comes into being ;
but how could τὸ μὴ ὂν come into being? ' (i. e. 'but that is impossible '). τὸ μὴ
ὂν γίνεται, 'the non-existent comes to be ', is merely another way of saying τὸ ὂν
ἀπόλλυται, 'the existent ceases to be ' ; but the writer seems to have thought that
the impossibility was more manifest when the statement was put in the form τὸ μὴ
ὂν γίνεται.

mean, ἀθάνατος, but have omitted the first letter. The writer should rather have said 'they mean ἀθανασία'; but he invents a substantive ἀθάνατος equivalent in sense to ἀθανασία, in order to give plausibility to his suggestion that θάνατος is a corruption of a word meaning 'deathlessness'.

The grammar of this clause is faulty. The grammatical defect might be removed by writing λέγεται in place of λεγόμενος; but it seems best to assume that ἢ ... ἀθάνατος has been inserted by a later hand.

ἀδύνατόν ἐστι τοῦ ἀθανάτου ζῴου μέρος τι ἀποθανεῖν. Cf. *Corp.* XII. ii. 15 b, 16. *Ascl. Lat.* III. 29 c : 'si enim animal mundus vivensque semper (ἀείζωος) et fuit et est et erit, nihil in mundo mortale est.'

[μάλιστα δὲ ⟨ἀθάνατος⟩ ὁ ἄνθρωπος, τὸ λογικὸν ζῷον.] According to the traditional text, μάλιστα δέ would mean μάλιστα δὲ μέρος ἐστὶ τοῦ κόσμου. But that is nonsense. The writer's meaning must have been that man is *immortal* in a higher sense than other creatures. (Cf. *Corp.* XII. ii. 19 : πάντων δὲ μᾶλλον ⟨ἀθάνατος⟩ ὁ ἄνθρωπος.) But the mention of man interrupts the sequence of thought here, and unduly anticipates § 5, τὸ δὲ τρίτον ὁ ἄνθρωπος κ.τ.λ. It is best therefore to bracket the words as an interpolation.

§ 2. δεύτερος δὲ ὁ κατ' εἰκόνα αὐτοῦ . . . ἀθάνατος γέγονε. This passage, as given in the MSS., is unintelligible ; but the writer's meaning was probably not far from that which is expressed by the Greek as I have rewritten it. God is ἀίδιος. (The word ἀίδιος here means 'without temporal beginning or end' ; it does not mean 'eternal' (αἰώνιος) in the Platonic sense, i. e. 'out of time'.) The Kosmos is not ἀίδιος, but is ἀείζωος or ἀθάνατος, these two words being used as synonyms. The Kosmos has had a beginning ; it has been made by God (ὑπ' αὐτοῦ γενόμενος). But having once been made, it is continually maintained in being, or unceasingly remade, by its Maker (ὑπ' αὐτοῦ συνεχόμενος καὶ τρεφόμενος,—ἀεὶ γίνεται). And it will be thus maintained in existence as a living being through all future time ; that is to say, God has made or makes it immortal. The contents of the paragraph are summed up in the concluding words, ὁ δὴ κόσμος ὑπὸ τοῦ πατρὸς ἀιδίου ὄντος ἀθάνατος γέγονε. This doctrine is evidently based on the *Timaeus.* See Herm. *ap.* Stob. *Exc.* XI. 2. (5), and *Corp.* XVIII. 14 a.

ὁ κατ' εἰκόνα αὐτοῦ . . . γενόμενος. See *Ascl. Lat.* I. 10 : 'dei, cuius sunt imagines duo mundus et homo.'

εἰ δὲ καὶ ἐγένετο, ὑφ' ἑαυτοῦ. God may be called αὐτογέννητος ;

but that is only another way of saying that he is ἀγέννητος. See *Ascl. Lat.* II. 14 b.

§ 3. ὅσον ἦν τῆς ὕλης ὑποκείμενον τῷ ἑαυτοῦ ⟨θελήματι⟩. These words imply that, of the total amount of ὕλη, a part only was 'subject to God's will', and the rest was not. This is a modification of the doctrine taught in the *Timaeus*, which is rather that *all* matter is *partly*, but *not wholly*, subject to God's will. Cf. Hermogenes *ap.* Hippol. *Ref. haer.* 8. 17 (quoted in prefatory note on *Ascl. Lat.* II): God ἐχώρισε (τὴν ὕλην) κατὰ μέρος, καὶ τὸ μὲν ἐκ τοῦ παντὸς λαβὼν ἡμέρωσε, τὸ δὲ εἴασεν ἀτάκτως φέρεσθαι. The 'Valentinian' in Methodius's dialogue Περὶ τοῦ αὐτεξουσίου c. 3 (quoted *ib.*) as emended: God ἀπὸ τῶν χειρίστων (τῆς ὕλης) τὰ κάλλιστα διακρίνας, οὕτως ἐδημιούργησεν ὅσα γοῦν ἥρμοζεν θεῷ δημιουργεῖν· τὰ δ' ὅσα αὐτῆς . . . τρυγώδη ἐτύγχανεν, ταῦτα ὡς εἶχεν κατέλιπεν.

The ἀταξία of which the speaker in Methodius' dialogue is thinking is wickedness, or moral evil. His view is that this ἀταξία exists in men alone, and that it has arisen out of that portion of ὕλη which God rejected as too bad to be brought to order by him, and which, we must suppose, has somehow entered into the composition of men,[1] though not into that of anything else in the universe. But the ἀταξία of which the writer of *Corp.* VIII is thinking is not (or at least, not solely or mainly) moral evil; it is rather αὔξησις and μείωσις (§ 3 *fin.*), i. e. the growth and decay, or composition and dissolution, of individual organisms,[2] as opposed to the permanent and un-changing existence of the heavenly bodies; and this kind of ἀταξία presents itself, not in men alone, but throughout the sublunar world.

οὖσαν καὶ αὐτὴν ἀθάνατον, καὶ ἔχουσαν ἀίδιον τὴν ὑλότητα. This is an *anacoluthon*. If the reading is right, the author has written οὖσαν &c. in agreement with ὕλην, which does not occur in the text, but might have stood above in place of ὅσον τῆς ὕλης. He ought rather to have written οὔσης τῆς ὕλης καὶ αὐτῆς ἀθανάτου, καὶ ἐχούσης κ.τ.λ. Matter is not merely ἀθάνατος, as is t e Kosmos, which has had a beginning; 'the materiality of matter' (i. e. matter as such, or unformed matter) is also ἀίδιος, as God is; that is to say, it has had no beginning, but has existed side by side with God from all eternity. Cf. *Ascl. Lat.* II.

---

[1] Compare the statement in *Pistis Sophia* (C. Schmidt, p. 160, l. 28 &c.) that men are 'the dregs of ὕλη'.

[2] Cf. Plut. *Is. et Os.*, quoted in prefatory note on *Ascl. Lat.* II.

πλέον δέ, τῶν ζώων (τῶν ἰδεῶν MSS.) τὰ ποιὰ ὁ πατὴρ ἐγκατασπείρας τῇ σφαίρᾳ ὥσπερ ἐν ἄντρῳ κατέκλεισε. God fashioned 'so much of ὕλη as was (wholly) subject to his will' into a hollow sphere; that is to say, out of this portion of ὕλη he made the heavens, that part of the universe in which there is perfect order. Moreover, he enclosed within this sphere the ὕλη which was *not* wholly subject to his will, and imposed a partial and imperfect order on this more refractory ὕλη; that is, he brought into being the mutable organisms of the sublunar world. And he did this by 'sowing' or 'planting' the qualities of the various kinds of ζῷα in the space within the sphere; that is, by imposing these qualities on the ὕλη with which that space was filled.

This writer uses the Stoic term ποιά, and not the Platonic term ἰδέαι or εἴδη, to denote the thing by the addition of which ὕλη is changed into ζῷα, that is, into organized and living σώματα. The word ἰδεῶν is unmeaning here, and must have been written by error.

The description of the sublunar world as a *cave* in which the refractory ὕλη is imprisoned, and in which the ζῷα composed of it (including man) are enclosed, must have been borrowed from writers by whom the point of the comparison was more fully explained. Cf. Porphyry *De antro nympharum* § 5 *sq.* (Nauck): ἄντρα μὲν δὴ . . . οἱ παλαιοὶ καὶ σπήλαια τῷ κόσμῳ καθιέρουν, . . . σύμβολον μὲν τῆς ὕλης ἐξ ἧς ⟨συνέστηκεν⟩ ὁ κόσμος τὴν γῆν παραδιδόντες, . . . τὸν δὲ ἐκ τῆς ὕλης γινόμενον κόσμον διὰ τῶν ἄντρων παριστάντες. . . . τὸ ἔνυδρον . . . τῶν ἄντρων . . . καὶ σκοτεινὸν . . . ἐδέξαντο εἰς σύμβολον τῶν προσόντων τῷ κόσμῳ διὰ τὴν ὕλην. . . . οὕτω καὶ Πέρσαι τὴν εἰς κάτω κάθοδον τῶν ψυχῶν καὶ πάλιν ἔξοδον μυσταγωγοῦντες τελοῦσι τὸν μύστην, ἐπονομάσαντες σπήλαιον ⟨τὸν⟩ τόπον· . . . εἰκόνα φέροντος [αὐτῷ] τοῦ σπηλαίου τοῦ κόσμου, ὃν ὁ Μίθρας ἐδημιούργησε, τῶν δὲ ἐντὸς κατὰ συμμέτρους ἀποστάσεις σύμβολα φερόντων τῶν κοσμικῶν στοιχείων ⌜καὶ κλιμάτων.⌝[1] *Ib.* § 8: οἱ Πυθαγόρειοι καὶ μετὰ τούτους Πλάτων (*Rep.* 7) ἄντρον καὶ σπήλαιον τὸν κόσμον ἀπεφήναντο. . . . ὅτι μὲν οὖν σύμβολον κόσμου τὰ ἄντρα καὶ τῶν ἐγκοσμίων δυνάμεων ἐτίθεντο οἱ θεολόγοι, διὰ τούτου δεδήλωται. Porphyry in the *De antr. nymph.* repeatedly refers to Cronius and Numenius, who had written on the same subject; e. g. § 21: 'Numenius and his friend Cronius

---

[1] Perhaps we ought to cut out καὶ κλιμάτων, which yields no satisfactory sense, and read τῶν δὲ ἐντὸς ⟨⟨κλιμάκων⟩⟩ κατὰ συμμέτρους ἀποστάσεις σύμβολα φερογϲῶν τῶν κοσμικῶν στοιχείων. The word στοιχείων may be taken to mean or include the planets. On the κλῖμαξ ἑπτάπυλος of the Mithraic cult, see note on *Corp.* I. 25.

say that the cave presents an image and symbol of the Kosmos.'
Thus it appears that the comparison of the Kosmos to a cave was
traditional among the Platonists of the second and third centuries
A. D., and that this symbolism may have been suggested to them
in part by the rites practised by the Mithraists in their subterranean
sanctuaries, as well as by reminiscences of the allegory of the cave
in Pl. *Rep.* 7. 515 *sq.*

πάσῃ ποιότητι κοσμῆσαι βουλόμενος τὸ μετ' αὐτοῦ ⟨ἄ⟩ποιον. If this
reading is right, τὸ μετ' αὐτοῦ ἄποιον must be taken to mean the
unformed matter 'which existed side by side with God'.

τῇ δὲ ἀθανασίᾳ περιέβαλε (περιβαλὼν MSS.) τὸ πᾶν σῶμα. God
conferred immortality on the universe which he had made. But the
immortality of the Kosmos resides more especially in the enclosing
sphere of heaven ; and the word περιέβαλε seems intended to
suggest the meaning 'God wrapped the Kosmos round with the
immortal heavens '.

τῆς τούτου συστάσεως θελήσασα ἀποστῆναι. The σύστασις is the
' putting together' or systematic arrangement of matter, by which
the Kosmos is constituted. It is nearly equivalent ·to τάξις ; and
so ἀταξία is contrasted with it. τούτου might perhaps be omitted
with advantage ; but if we retain it, we must take it to mean· τοῦ
παντὸς σώματος, i. e. τοῦ κόσμου.

If the matter of which the Kosmos is composed were not 'wrapped
in immortality' (i. e. enclosed by the immortal heavens), it might
break away, and all might go back to chaos. Cf. Numenius *ap.*
Euseb. *Pr. ev.* 11. 18. 24 (τὴν ὕλην . . . ξυνδησάμενος κ.τ.λ.),
quoted in prefatory note on *Corp.* II (p. 81).

ἔχει δὲ καὶ ἐνθάδε ἄτακτόν τι περὶ τὰ μικρὰ ζῷα εἰλούμενον.—(ἔχει
δὲ καὶ ἐνθάδε τὴν περὶ τὰ ἄλλα μικρὰ ποιὰ εἰλουμένην MSS.) Something like ἄτακτόν τι is needed to lead up to αὔτη ἡ ἀταξία in the
following sentence. τὰ μικρὰ ποιά is meaningless ; and there can be
little doubt that the author wrote τὰ μικρὰ ζῷα [1] (or σώματα). 'The
small ζῷα' are the individual organisms on earth (which are called
τὰ ἐπίγεια ζῷα below), as opposed to that great ζῷον the Kosmos,
and perhaps to the heavenly bodies also. ἄλλα is probably an
alternative reading for μικρά.

τὸ τῆς αὐξήσεως καὶ [τὸ τῆς] μειώσεως (*sc.* ἄτακτον) [ὃν θάνατον οἱ
ἄνθρωποι καλοῦσιν]. The μεταβολή to which all sublunar things are
subject takes the form of increase and decrease, or growth and decay.

_____
[1] Mr. G. R. S. Mead alters ποιά into ζῷα here.

Each living organism is continually taking into itself portions of the elements, and casting off other portions of them. But in the earlier stages of its existence it takes in more than it casts off, and so 'increases'; in the later stages it casts off more than it takes in, and so 'decreases'. Sooner or later, the advancing process of 'decrease' or 'decay' terminates in complete dissolution, 'which men call death'. But the relation between decrease and death is not explained in the text. It is not the decrease itself, or 'the disorderliness of the decrease', that men call death, but the dissolution in which the decrease terminates; and dissolution is not expressly mentioned. There is therefore reason to think that the words ὃν θάνατον οἱ ἄνθρωποι καλοῦσιν have been added by another hand.

The process of growth and decay to which sublunar organisms are subject is contrasted with the unvarying movement of the heavenly bodies, and is considered to be caused by the partial survival, in the lower part of the Kosmos, of the ἀταξία of unformed or chaotic matter.

§ 4. ἡ δὲ ἀποκατάστασις τῶν ἐπιγείων σωμάτων ⟨διαλυθείσης γίνεται τῆς⟩ συστάσεως· τῇ δὲ διαλύσει ταύτῃ (ἡ δὲ διάλυσις αὐτὴ MSS.) ἀποκαθίσταται εἰς τὰ ἀδιάλυτα σώματα. The 'indissoluble bodies' are the cosmic elements, which are immortal. When an organism is broken up, the earth, water, air, and fire of which it was composed are reabsorbed into the mass of cosmic earth, water, air, and fire (cf. *Corp.* XII. ii. 18); and this 'return to the former condition' is here described by the term ἀποκατάστασις, which, in its stricter sense, was applicable only to the heavenly bodies, and meant the return of any one of them (or of all of them simultaneously) to the same position which it (or they) had occupied before. In *Corp.* XI. i. 2, the ἀποκατάστασις of terrestrial bodies is called ἀνταποκατά-στασις.

καὶ οὕτω στέρησις γίνεται τῆς αἰσθήσεως, οὐκ ἀπώλεια ⟨⟨ζωῆς⟩⟩ [τῶν σωμάτων]. Cf. *Corp.* XII. ii. 18, as emended: οὐ γὰρ ἡ γένεσίς ἐστι ζωῆς ἀρχή, ἀλλ' αἰσθήσεως· οὐδὲ ἡ μεταβολὴ θάνατος, ἀλλὰ λήθη.

§ 5. τὸ δὲ τρίτον [[ζῷον]] ὁ ἄνθρωπος. If we retain ζῷον, these words imply that the Kosmos is τὸ δεύτερον ζῷον, and that God is τὸ πρῶτον ζῷον. But ζῷον usually means an animated body, i. e. a being composed of body and soul in combination; and in that sense, it is applicable to the Kosmos, but not to the supreme God, who is incorporeal. The Hermetists never, I think, call God a ζῷον. It seems best therefore to bracket ζῷον, which may have come from ζωῆς in the preceding sentence.

πρὸς τὸν δεύτερον θεὸν συμπάθειαν ἔχων. This use of the term συμπάθεια is of Stoic origin. Alex. Aphr. *De mixt.* 142 : ἠνῶσθαι μὲν ὑποτίθεται Χρύσιππος τὴν σύμπασαν οὐσίαν, πνεύματός τινος διὰ πάσης αὐτῆς διήκοντος, ὑφ᾽ οὗ συνάγεταί τε καὶ συμμένει καὶ συμπαθές ἐστιν αὐτῷ τὸ πᾶν. Cic. *Nat. deor.* 3. 28 : 'estque in (natura) iste quasi consensus, quam συμπάθειαν Graeci vocant.' (Compare *Nat. deor.* 2. 19. ' By such language the Stoics meant to express . . . the organic unity of the world as an animate body, and the correlation and mutual interdependence of all its parts,' J. B. Mayor *ad loc.*) Cic. *Div.* 2. 34 : ' ex coniunctione naturae, et quasi concentu atque consensu, quam συμπάθειαν Graeci appellant.' *Ib.* 2. 142 : ' continuatio coniunctioque naturae, quam, ut dixi, vocant συμπάθειαν.' Philo *De opif. mundi* 40. 117, Cohn I, p. 41 : ἐκ τῶν οὐρανίων τὰ ἐπίγεια ἤρτηται κατά τινα φυσικὴν συμπάθειαν. Epict. *Diss.* I. 14. 2 : συμπαθεῖν τὰ ἐπίγεια τοῖς οὐρανίοις οὐ δοκεῖ σοι; Sext. Emp. *Math.* 9. 78. Synesius *De providentia* 7, Migne Tom. 66 col. 1277 A : τὸν κόσμον ἐν ὅλον ἡγούμεθα, τοῖς μέρεσι συμπληρούμενον. σύρρουν τε οὖν καὶ σύμπνουν αὐτὸν οἰησόμεθα· τὸ γὰρ ἐν οὕτως ἂν σώζοι. καὶ οὐκ ἀσυμπαθῆ πρὸς ἄλληλα τὰ μέρη θησόμεθα· πῶς γὰρ ἂν ἐν ὦσιν, εἰ μή τι φύσει συνηρτημένα; καὶ ποιήσει δὴ καὶ πείσεται παρ᾽ ἀλλήλων τε καὶ εἰς ἄλληλα· καὶ τὰ μὲν μόνον ποιήσει, τὰ δὲ μόνον πείσεται. μετὰ τῆσδε τῆς ὑποθέσεως ἐπὶ τὸ σκέμμα βαδίζοντες, κατὰ λόγον ἂν αἰτιασόμεθα τῶν περὶ τὰ τῇδε τὸ μακάριον σῶμα τὸ κύκλῳ κινούμενον· μέρη γὰρ ἄμφω, καὶ ἔστιν αὐτοῖς τι πρὸς ἄλληλα. εἰ δὴ γένεσις ἐν τοῖς περὶ ἡμᾶς, αἰτία γενέσεως ἐν τοῖς ὑπὲρ ἡμᾶς, κἀκεῖθεν ἐνταῦθα καθήκει τὰ τῶν συμβαινόντων σπέρματα. Synesius *De insomniis* 2, Migne *ib.* col. 1285 A : ἔδει γάρ, οἶμαι, τοῦ παντὸς τούτου συμπαθοῦς τε ὄντος καὶ σύμπνου, τὰ μέρη προσήκειν ἀλλήλοις, ἅτε ἑνὸς ὅλου μέλη τυγχάνοντα. καὶ μή ποτε αἱ μάγων ἴυγγες αὗται· καὶ γὰρ θέλγεται παρ᾽ ἀλλήλων (τὰ τοῦ κόσμου μέρη), ὥσπερ σημαίνεται. καὶ σοφὸς ὁ εἰδὼς τὴν τῶν μερῶν τοῦ κόσμου συγγένειαν.

The Kosmos is one whole, all parts of which are συμπαθῆ, i. e. are interconnected and mutually affected ; man therefore, inasmuch as he is a part of the Kosmos, is συμπαθής with all other parts of it, and with the Kosmos as a whole. The Hermetist accepts this Stoic doctrine (cf. ὁ ἄνθρωπος ὑπὸ τοῦ κόσμου καὶ ἐν τῷ κόσμῳ below) ; but being, in the fundamentals of his theology, a Platonist, and not a Stoic, he goes on to say that man is something more than a part of the Kosmos, and that, in virtue of his νοῦς, he is capable of entering into relation with the supracosmic God.

ὡς ἀσωμάτου [καὶ νοῦ τοῦ ἀγαθοῦ]. God is ὁ ἀγαθὸς νοῦς. As ἀγαθός, he is distinguished from the human νοῦς, which might be called οὐ κακός, but could hardly be called ἀγαθός without undue presumption (cf. *Corp.* VI, and *Corp.* XII. ii *fin.*). Being νοῦς, God can be apprehended by the human νοῦς. But the words καὶ νοῦ τοῦ ἀγαθοῦ are awkwardly appended, and impair the symmetry of the sentence; and for this reason it seems probable that they have been added by another hand.

νόησον τί θεός, τί κόσμος, τί ζῷον ἀθάνατον, τί ζῷον διάλυτον. It is implied that reflection on these questions (that is, on the answers to them which Hermes has given in this discourse) will make it evident that man 'does not perish'. The ζῷα ἀθάνατα are the Kosmos itself, the heavenly bodies, and the cosmic elements (which are called τὰ ἀθάνατα σώματα in § 4); the ζῷα διάλυτα are the sublunar organisms. Man, as a terrestrial organism, must be reckoned among the διάλυτα ζῷα; and as such, he does not perish, but is resolved into the imperishable elements.[1] It seems to be in this sense alone that the writer holds man to be immortal; for he does not speak of any other sort of human immortality. He says nothing of a survival of the individual ψυχή;[2] and he appears to hold that in the case of man, as in that of other animals, the individual consciousness ceases at the dissolution of the body (στέρησις γίνεται τῆς αἰσθήσεως, § 4). If anything retains separate existence, it must be the νοῦς alone; but this writer gives no indication of a belief that the νοῦς of a particular man continues after death to exist as a separate person. We must conclude then that he rejected the Platonic doctrine of individual immortality.

ἀρχὴ δὲ καὶ περιοχὴ καὶ σύστασις πάντων ὁ θεός. In other words, γεννᾶται καὶ περιέχεται καὶ συνίσταται πάντα ὑπὸ τοῦ θεοῦ.

---

[1] Cf. Shelley, *Adonais* 42 : 'He is made one with Nature; there is heard his voice in all her music', &c.

[2] There is nothing in the extant text to correspond to the words of the introductory sentence, τρόπῳ μὲν ποίῳ ἀθάνατος ἡ ψυχή. If the writer had been asked what becomes of a man's ψυχή after the dissolution of the body, he might perhaps have answered that it is reabsorbed into the world-soul.

LIBELLVS IX

Contents

A. *Man's sense and thought.* §§ 1 b–5 a.

In men, sense and thought are inseparably united. In beasts, instinct takes the place of thought. § 1 b.

Thought is the function of mind. Thought and speech are inter-connected. § 1 c.

There cannot, in man, be thought without sense, nor sense without thought. (This holds good even in dreams.) § 2.

When a man's mind is impregnated by a daemon, it brings forth bad thoughts; when it is impregnated by God, it brings forth good thoughts. And to have good thoughts is to be religious, i. e. to know (and be devoted to) God. §§ 3, 4 a.

Those who know God are at variance with the many, and are persecuted by them. But the religious man will cling to his know-ledge of God in spite of persecution; and for him, all things are good. § 4 b.

All men possess thought; but the religious alone get good from it. All things are good to begin with, being made by God; but in the cosmic process, good turns to evil. The qualities of things are determined by the influence of the heavenly bodies; and by that influence some things are made bad, and others good. § 5.

B. *The sense and thought of the Kosmos.* §§ 6–8.

The sense and thought of the Kosmos are occupied in making and unmaking living organisms, and thereby accomplishing God's will. The Kosmos has received seed from God, and its function is to develop from this seed a perpetual succession of living beings. § 6.

The bodies of these beings are composed of the cosmic elements; their various qualities are imposed on them by the operation of the heavenly bodies; and their life is breathed into them from the life-breath of the Kosmos. §§ 7, 8.

C. *God's sense and thought.* § 9.

The sense and thought of all living beings are derived from the Kosmos; and the sense and thought of the Kosmos are derived from God. God's sense and thought are occupied in giving movement (i. e. life) to all things. All things owe their being to God. Nothing can ever cease to be; for all things are in God; or rather, God is all things.

D. *Teaching and belief.* § 10.

The teacher's words may serve to set the pupil on the right track; but only by his own thought can the pupil attain to assurance of the truth.

The opening words of *Corp.* IX imply that it was written as a sequel to the Λόγος τέλειος, i. e. the Greek original of the Latin *Asclepius.* (See notes on *Ascl. Lat. init.*) The writer of *Corp.* IX then had that document before him; and it is possible that he was the same person who joined together the Greek *Ascl.* I, *Ascl.* II, and *Ascl.* III, and gave the title Λόγος τέλειος to the composite treatise. At any rate, there seems to be good reason for ascribing to the writer of *Corp.* IX the insertion, in *Ascl.* I. 8, of the clause περὶ γὰρ τούτου, πότερον αὐτὸς (ὁ κόσμος) αἰσθάνεται ⟨ἢ μή, εἰσαῦθις ῥηθήσεται⟩, which points forward to *Corp.* IX. 6, καὶ γὰρ ὁ κόσμος . . . αἴσθησιν ἰδίαν καὶ νόησιν ἔχει κ.τ.λ.

The topic of 'sense and thought' is dealt with under three heads, viz. A. man's sense and thought: B. the sense and thought of the Kosmos: C. God's sense and thought. It is possible that this arrangement was suggested to the writer by *Ascl. Lat.* III. 32 b, where ὁ ἀνθρώπειος νοῦς, ὁ κοσμικὸς νοῦς, and ὁ θεῖος νοῦς are distinguished. But if so, he must have understood those three terms in a different sense from that intended by the author of *Ascl. Lat.* III. The 'cosmic' and 'divine' νοῦς of *Ascl. Lat.* III. 32 b, as well as the 'human' νοῦς there spoken of, are (if my explanation of that passage is right) primarily kinds or grades of νοῦς as it exists in men (ὁ ἄνθρωπος κοσμικῶς νοεῖ, ὁ ἀνθρ. θείως νοεῖ), and thus have little in common with the 'sense and thought of the Kosmos' and the 'sense and thought of God' discussed in *Corp.* IX, where the meaning is that ὁ κόσμος (and ὁ θεὸς) αἰσθάνεται καὶ νοεῖ. Moreover, the writer of *Corp.* IX differs from the writer of *Ascl. Lat.* III in speaking of 'thought' chiefly as connected with and issuing in action. The νόησις which he discusses is for the most part the function of the νοῦς πρακτικός, and not that of the νοῦς θεωρητικός; it is the operation of the will rather than of the intellect.

Sources. The writer's conception of the supracosmic God, and of the relation between God and the Kosmos, is Platonic. But in asserting the inseparability of νόησις and αἴσθησις, he is opposed to the teaching of the Platonists; and this part of his doctrine is probably derived from some Stoic authority. His conception of the cosmic πνοή is Stoic.

Date. The prophecy in *Ascl. Lat.* III was probably written about A. D. 270, under the stress of the troubles caused by the Palmyrene invasion of Egypt. *Corp.* IX then, being a sequel to *Ascl. Lat.*, was most likely written shortly after that date, i. e. about A. D. 280–300.

The only definite indication of date in the document itself is that which is given in § 4 b, where the writer says that οἱ ἐν γνώσει ὄντες (i. e. the adherents of his religion) are mocked at, hated, and despised, and that, if not actually put to death, they are at least in danger of being put to death by their enemies (τάχα που καὶ φονευό-μενοι). At what time, and under what circumstances, could this be said of an obscure group of Egyptian Platonists? It is true that descriptions of the philosopher despised and jeered at by the many occur repeatedly in Plato and elsewhere in Greek literature (e. g. Pl. *Gorgias* 521 D ff.; *Theaet.* 174 A ff.; *Phaedrus* 249 D); and the instance of Socrates would suffice to prove that a man might even be put to death on account of his devotion to philosophy. But the writer of *Corp.* IX would have had no reason to introduce the topic here, if it had not been suggested to him by present circumstances. There can be little doubt that he and his companions felt themselves to be exposed to such treatment as he describes; and the words ὁ θεοσεβὴς πάντα ὑποστήσει κ.τ.λ. show that they anticipated serious ill usage. The attitude which he ascribes to the enemies of 'the *gnosis*' closely resembles that which is ascribed to the enemies of religion in the Prophecy of Hermes, *Ascl. Lat.* III. 25 (compare μεμηνέναι δοκοῦσιν with *religiosus pro insano habebitur*, and γέλωτα ὀφλισκάνουσι with *anima et omnia circa eam . . . risui*); and it is to be presumed that in *Corp.* IX, as well as in *Ascl. Lat.* III, the enemies in question are the Christians. At the time at which we have found reason to think that *Corp.* IX was written (A. D. 280–300), the Palmyrene occupation of Egypt, which had given occasion for the prophecy in *Ascl. Lat.* III, was a thing of the past; but the aggressive energy of the Christians, which had forced the writer of that prophecy to recognize that Paganism was already doomed, must have been increasing year by year during the interval; and perhaps something of the temper which showed itself in the murder of Hypatia by a Christian mob in A. D. 415 was already visible among them.[1] The Hermetists, as well as other Egyptians who adhered to the old religion, must have known themselves to be despised and hated by their Christian neighbours ; and they must have seen that the Christians, if their present rate of progress was maintained, would soon get the upper hand. It was to be expected that, when this took place, the mass of the remaining Pagans would conform to the requirements of the new doctrine without serious resistance ; but the few who were in earnest about their religion, and were resolved to cling to it at all costs, may well have felt that, under Christian domination, their lives would be in danger.

Of Egyptian history during the last quarter of the third century, not much is known to us. The most striking event of the time is the rebellion which broke out in Egypt about A. D. 295, and was suppressed by Diocletian in 297.[2] What part the Christians of Egypt took in that struggle, we are not informed But it is not likely that they were passive and indifferent spectators ; and it may reasonably be conjectured that they sided against the imperial government,[3] and that their conduct on that occasion contributed to convince Diocletian that the existence of Christianity was a grave danger to the empire, and thus to bring about the systematic attempt to suppress it which began in A. D. 302. The reconquest of Egypt by Diocletian probably gave a temporary check to the growing power of the Christians in that country ; but it is not unlikely that in the confusion caused by the revolt, if not before it, their hatred of their Pagan countrymen may here and there have manifested itself in acts of open violence.

Title. The contents of the discourse are correctly described by the words περὶ νοήσεως καὶ αἰσθήσεως. The words which follow (ὅτι ἐν μόνῳ . . . οὐδαμοῦ) have been transferred to this place by error from the heading of *Corp.* VI.

§ 1 b. ὅτι ἡ μὲν (αἴσθησις) ὑλική ἐστιν, ἡ δὲ (νόησις) οὐσιώδης. The

---

[1] Compare Julian's accusation against the Christians, written in A.D. 362 (Jul. *c. Christianos*, Neumann, p. 199) : ζηλοῦτε δὲ 'Ιουδαίων τοὺς θυμοὺς καὶ τὴν πικρίαν, ἀνατρέποντες ἱερὰ καὶ βωμούς, καὶ ἀπεσφάξατε οὐχ ἡμῶν μόνον τοὺς τοῖς πατρῴοις ἐμμένοντας, ἀλλὰ καὶ τῶν ἐξ ἴσης ὑμῶν πεπλανημένων αἱρετικοὺς τοὺς μὴ τὸν αὐτὸν τρόπον ὑμῶν τὸν νεκρὸν θρηνοῦντας.

[2] Schiller, *Gesch. der röm. Kaiserzeit* II, pp. 138 ff. ; Mommsen, *Provs. of Rom. empire*, Eng. tr. II, p. 251. Mommsen says that the revolt lasted three or four years.

[3] Schiller (II, p. 140) says that prophecies extracted from the holy Scriptures were probably employed [by Christians ?] to stir up fanaticism in the interest of the rebellion.

words ὑλικός and οὐσιώδης are contrasted in *Ascl. Lat.* I. 7 b. In that passage, the human νοῦς is called *pars hominis* οὐσιώδης, which means that it consists of οὐσία in the Platonic sense, i. e. of incorporeal and eternal substance; and the body (including the ψυχὴ αἰσθητική?) is called ὑλικόν, which means that it is composed of material elements. The terms here used by the writer of *Corp.* IX were probably suggested to him by *Ascl. Lat.* I. 7 b; but he applies the words οὐσιώδης and ὑλικός somewhat differently. νόησις is not a *pars hominis*, but the function of a *pars hominis*; and when he says people think νόησις to be οὐσιώδης, he must mean that they hold, not that νόησις consists of οὐσία, but either that the 'part of man' which operates in νόησις consists of οὐσία, or that the object of νόησις is οὐσία. Similarly, when he says that they think αἴσθησις to be ὑλική, he must mean that they hold, not that αἴσθησις is composed of material elements, but either that the organs of sense consist of matter, or that the objects of sense-perception are material things.

ἐμοὶ δὲ δοκοῦσιν ἀμφότεραι ἡνῶσθαι. Cf. § 2 : οὔτε γὰρ χωρὶς αἰσθήσεως δυνατὸν νοῆσαι, οὔτε αἰσθέσθαι χωρὶς νοήσεως. In man, αἴσθησις and νόησις are inseparable; in every process of his conscious life, both are present together.

In saying this, the writer deliberately rejects the doctrine commonly taught by the Platonists, who held that in the higher activities of the human mind νόησις alone is present, and αἴσθησις is absent. The Platonic view of νόησις and νοητά is maintained in the Λόγος τέλεος (see especially *Ascl. Lat.* III. 17 b–19 c and 34 b–36); and the writer of *Corp.* IX must have intended to correct in this respect the teaching of that document.

But whence did he derive the doctrine of αἴσθησις and νόησις which he seeks to substitute for that taught by the Platonists? The pre-Socratics used the word νοῦς and its synonyms and derivatives to signify sense-perception as well as thought.[1] The first writer who made a clear and sharp distinction between αἴσθησις and νόησις was Plato;[2] and Plato's distinction was maintained by Aristotle, with

---

[1] Arist. *De an.* 3. 3, 427 a 21 : οἵ γε ἀρχαῖοι τὸ φρονεῖν καὶ τὸ αἰσθάνεσθαι ταὐτὸν εἶναί φασιν. . . . πάντες γὰρ οὗτοι τὸ νοεῖν σωματικὸν ὥσπερ τὸ αἰσθάνεσθαι ὑπολαμβάνουσιν. For them, the conception of τὸ οὐσιῶδες did not exist, and everything was ὑλικόν.

[2] Windelband, *Gesch. der alten Philosophie*, p. 117 : according to Plato, 'two worlds are to be distinguished (Pl. *Tim.* 27 D and 51 ff.). One of these two worlds consists of that which is and never becomes; the other consists of that which becomes and never is. The one is the object of αἴσθησις; the other is the object of νόησις.' That which 'becomes and never is' is corporeal; that which 'is and never becomes' is incorporeal.

some modifications. Aristotle held that νόησις can take place in man only when the νοῦς has been called into action by preceding αἴσθησις ;[1] and he would have admitted that, in this sense, ἄνθρωπος οὐ δύναται νοῆσαι χωρὶς αἰσθήσεως ; but he would not have said that ἀνθρ. οὐ δύναται αἰσθέσθαι χωρὶς νοήσεως. The view of the Peripatetic Strato, 290–270 B. C., was more like that expressed in *Corp.* IX. Strato denied the existence of the incorporeal νοητά recognized by Plato and, in a somewhat different sense, by Aristotle ; he held the objects of νόησις to be corporeal, and identical with those of αἴσθησις ; and accordingly, he regarded αἴσθησις and νόησις as inseparable.[2] Zeno, the founder of Stoicism, was a contemporary of Strato ; and the Stoics, as they agreed with Strato in holding that only the material is real, agreed with him also in rejecting the Platonic and Aristotelian separation of αἴσθησις and νόησις. Sext. Emp. *Math.* 7. 307 : ναί φασιν (οἱ δογματικοί, i. e. the Stoics), ἀλλὰ ταὐτόν ἐστι διάνοια καὶ αἴσθησις, οὐ κατὰ ταὐτὸ δέ, ἀλλὰ κατ᾿ ἄλλο μὲν διάνοια, κατ᾿ ἄλλο δὲ αἴσθησις· καὶ ὃν τρόπον τὸ αὐτὸ ποτήριον κοῖλόν τε καὶ περίκυρτον λέγεται, οὐ κατὰ ταὐτὸ δέ, ... οὕτως ἡ αὐτὴ δύναμις κατ᾿ ἄλλο μέν ἐστι νοῦς, κατ᾿ ἄλλο δὲ αἴσθησις. ' The Stoics' in Aetius, Diels *Doxogr.* p. 400 : τὸ γὰρ φάντασμα ἐπειδὰν λογικῇ προσπίπτει ψυχῇ, τότε ἐννόημα καλεῖται, εἰληφὸς τοὔνομα παρὰ τοῦ νοῦ. ' The Stoics' in Diog. Laert. 7. 51 : τῶν φαντασιῶν αἱ μέν εἰσι λογικαί, αἱ δὲ ἄλογοι· λογικαὶ μέν, αἱ τῶν λογικῶν ζῴων· ἄλογοι δέ, αἱ τῶν ἀλόγων. αἱ μὲν οὖν λογικαὶ νοήσεις εἰσίν· αἱ δ᾿ ἄλογοι οὐ τετύχασιν ὀνόματος. (This implies that all human φαντασίαι are νοήσεις ; and assuming that every act of αἴσθησις results in a corresponding φαντασία, it would follow that ' in man there is no αἴσθησις without νόησις ').[3]

---

[1] Ar. *De an.* 3. 8, 432 a 7 : οὔτε μὴ αἰσθανόμενος μηθὲν οὐθὲν ἂν μάθοι οὐδὲ ξυνείη· ὅταν τε θεωρῇ, ἀνάγκη ἅμα φάντασμά τι θεωρεῖν. ' Nihil est in intellectu quin fuerit in sensu.'

[2] Windelband, *Gesch. der alten Phil.* p. 179 : Strato ' identified God with the world, and on the other side, thought with sense. ... He regarded the soul as an indivisible ἡγεμονικόν, which has the senses for its organs, so that *the activity of the senses never takes place without thought*, and on the other hand *all thought is limited to a content given by sense-perception*.' No thought without sense ; Strato in Simplicius *Phys.* 225 a (Zeller *Arist.* II, p. 468) : ὅσα γὰρ μὴ πρότερον ἑώρακε (ἡ ψυχή), ταῦτα οὐ δύναται νοεῖν. No sense without thought ; Plut. *Sollert. animal.* 3. 6 : Στράτωνός γε τοῦ φυσικοῦ λόγος ἐστὶν ἀποδεικνύων ὡς οὐδ᾿ αἰσθάνεσθαι τοπαράπαν ἄνευ τοῦ νοεῖν ὑπάρχει· καὶ γὰρ γράμματα πολλάκις ἐπιπορευομένους τῇ ὄψει καὶ λόγοι προσπίπτοντες τῇ ἀκοῇ διαλανθάνουσιν ἡμᾶς καὶ διαφεύγουσι πρὸς ἑτέροις τὸν νοῦν ἔχοντας· εἶτ᾿ αὖθις ἐπανῆλθε καὶ μεταθεῖ καὶ διώκει τῶν προιεμένων ἕκαστον ἀναλεγόμενος. ἧ καὶ λέλεκται " νοῦς ὁρῇ καὶ νοῦς ἀκούει, τἄλλα κωφὰ καὶ τυφλά " (Epicharmus), ὡς τοῦ περὶ τὰ ὄμματα καὶ τὰ ὦτα πάθους, ἂν μὴ παρῇ τὸ φρονοῦν, αἴσθησιν οὐ ποιοῦντος.

[3] Cf. Philo *Leg. alleg.* 2. 18. 71, Cohn I, p. 104 : οὔτε γὰρ ὁ νοῦς δίχα αἰσθήσεως ἠδύνατο καταλαβεῖν ζῷον ἢ φυτὸν ἢ λίθον ἢ ξύλον ἢ συνόλως σῶμα, οὔτε ἡ αἴσθησις

A Hermetist of the third century A. D. is not likely to have been directly influenced by Strato ; and there can be little doubt that the writer of *Corp*. IX, in his doctrine of αἴσθησις and νόησις, has adopted a view suggested to him by some Stoic authority.

ἐν γὰρ τοῖς ἄλλοις (perhaps ἀλόγοις) ζῴοις ἡ αἴσθησις τῇ φύσει ἥνωται. The lower animals differ from man in this respect, that they are devoid of νοῦς, i. e. incapable of νόησις. But in place of νόησις, they have φύσις. Cf. *Corp*. XII. i. 1: ἐν δὲ τοῖς ἀλόγοις ζῴοις ⟨ἀντὶ νοῦ?⟩ ἡ φύσις ἐστίν. See also Herm. *Exc.* IV B.

The actions of men result from αἴσθησις supplemented by νόησις ; the actions of beasts result from αἴσθησις supplemented by φύσις. The word φύσις may here be translated 'instinct'. It means an impulse implanted in the animal by a force which operates throughout the universe, and which, in the view of the Hermetists, issues from the will of God. When a man acts, he is consciously aiming at a good (real or apparent) to be realized by his action ; and his conception of the good towards which he directs his action is called νόησις (ἀγαθοῦ). But a beast acts without conscious aim ; it has no conception of a good to be realized by its action ; and if its action is directed towards an end, the conception of that end or good must reside, not in the beast itself, but in the mind of God, who governs the forces by which the beast's action is determined. It is not the animal itself, but φύσις operating in the animal (or rather, God working through φύσις), that in this case aims at a good.

§ 1 C. νοήσεως δὲ ὁ νοῦς διαφέρει... χωρὶς λόγου. This is a digression. The writer here speaks of (1) the relation between νόησις and νοῦς, and (2) the relation between νόησις and λόγος. In § 2, he returns to the topic with which he began, viz. the relation between νόησις and αἴσθησις.

ἡ μὲν γὰρ θειότης ὑπὸ τοῦ θεοῦ γίνεται, ἡ δὲ νόησις ὑπὸ τοῦ νοῦ. What is the meaning of θειότης here ? ὁ νοῦς is the mind, i. e. the 'part of man' which thinks ; and νόησις is that which 'is done by the mind' (ὑπὸ τοῦ νοῦ γίνεται), or 'the action of the mind', i. e. the process of thinking. And since we are told that the relation between νόησις and νοῦς corresponds to that between θειότης and θεός, it follows that θειότης must mean 'what is done by God', or 'God's action'. The writer was probably thinking especially of God's

εἶχα τοῦ νοῦ περιποιῆσαι τὸ αἰσθάνεσθαι. ἐπειδὴ τοίνυν ἄμφω ταῦτα συνελθεῖν ἔδει πρὸς κατάληψιν τῶν ὑποκειμένων κ.τ.λ. The Stoics held that there is nothing which is not σῶμα ; and to one who took that view, Philo's statement would mean that (in man) there can neither be νόησις without αἴσθησις, nor αἴσθησις without νόησις.

action in or on the human soul; and in that respect, it might be said that as νόησις is that which takes place in him who is ἔννους, so θειότης is that which takes place in him who is ἔνθεος. If this is the writer's meaning, θειότης may be translated 'divine inspiration'; and the employment of the word in this sense may have been suggested by the common use of θεῖος to describe a man who is inspired. θειότης is similarly used in Clem. *Homil.* 2. 27 : Simon Magus τὰ μαγείᾳ γινόμενα θειότητι ποιεῖν ἔλεγεν. In that passage, θειότητι means 'by the operation of God', as μαγείᾳ means 'by the operation of demons'. Cf. περὶ θειότητος διαλεγόμενος in *Corp.* XIII. 1.

ἡ δὲ νόησις . . ., ἀδελφὴ οὖσα τοῦ λόγου. καὶ ὄργανα ⟨ταῦτα⟩ ἀλλήλων. λόγος here means 'speech'. See § 10, where λόγος is contrasted with νοῦς. Speech is an ὄργανον of thought; i. e. speech is the instrument by means of which thought is expressed. But what is meant by saying that thought is an ὄργανον of speech? Probably the meaning is that the speaker's words can influence the hearer only by acting through the hearer's thought; they are effective only so far as the hearer understands them. (That is the point which is insisted on in § 10.) But in order to obtain this meaning, we ought to read, in place of οὔτε γὰρ ὁ λόγος ἐκφωνεῖται χωρὶς νοήσεως, something like οὔτε γὰρ ὁ λόγος καταλαμβάνεται χ. ν. Perhaps ἐκφωνεῖται originally stood in the following clause (where the MSS. give οὔτε ἡ νόησις φαίνεται), and was thence transferred by error to this place, where it was substituted for the original verb.

§ 2. εἰς τὸν ἄνθρωπον συνεπεισρέουσιν ἀλλήλαις. See § 9, where we are told that the sense and thought of all ζῷα (including man) are derived from the sense and thought of the Kosmos, and that they pass into the individual ζῷον from the atmosphere in the process of breathing.

[δυνατὸν δὲ νόησιν] ⟨καίτοι λέγονται ἄνθρωποι ἐνίοτε (?)⟩ χωρὶς αἰσθή-σεως νοεῖσθαι, καθάπερ οἱ διὰ τῶν ὀνείρων φανταζόμενοι ὁράματα· ἐμοὶ δὲ δοκεῖ ⟨μᾶλλον εὔλογον εἶναι (?)⟩ τὸ γεγονέναι ἀμφοτέρας τὰς ἐνεργείας ἐν τῇ τῶν ὀνείρων ὄψει· ἐγρηγορῦσι γὰρ ⟨ἤνωται ἀεὶ ἡ νόησις τῇ (?)⟩ αἰσθήσει. I suppose the meaning of this mutilated passage to have been that some people say that νόησις takes place without αἴσθησις in dreams,[1] but that the writer denies this, and maintains that νόησις

---

[1] Compare the theory of sleep and dreams which is given in Lactant. *De opif. dei* 18. 4 : 'Requiescere nullo pacto possumus, nisi mens visionum imaginibus occupata teneatur. . . . Avocatur ergo (mens) simulacris, donec membra sopore irrigata vegetentur : corpus enim vigilante sensu, licet iaceat inmobile, tamen non est quietum, quia flagrat in eo sensus . . . Sed postquam mens ad contemplandas

and αἴσθησις are inseparable, not only in waking life, but in dreams also. I take [δυνατὸν δὲ νόησιν] to be a doublet of the preceding words δυνατὸν νόησαι. It is to be inferred from the phrase ἐμοὶ δὲ δοκεῖ that something like 'it is said by some' has preceded. The two ἐνέργειαι spoken of must be αἴσθησις and νόησις.

διῄρηται γὰ⟨ρ ἡ αἴσθησις⟩ (διῄρηταί γε MSS.) εἴς τε τὸ σῶμα καὶ εἰς τὴν ψυχήν. From the following words, καὶ ὅταν ἀμφότερα τὰ μέρη τῆς αἰσθήσεως κ.τ.λ., it may be inferred that the missing subject of διῄρηται was ἡ αἴσθησις. The 'two parts' of αἴσθησις are probably the two processes which Aristotle and the Stoics distinguished under the names αἴσθησις and φαντασία. According to Aristotle, the external object, acting through the bodily organ of sense, stamps an image of itself[1] on the ψυχὴ αἰσθητική; and the perception of this internal image (which persists after the external object has ceased to be present) is called φαντασία. He says that ἡ φαντασία ἐστὶν αἴσθησίς τις ἀσθενής (*Rhet.* 1. 11, 1370 a 28), and that τὰ φαντάσματα ὥσπερ αἰσθήματά ἐστι, πλὴν ἄνευ ὕλης (*De an.* 3. 8, 432 a 9). The Stoics adopted Aristotle's theory of αἴσθησις and φαντασία with little alteration. Cf. 'the Stoics' in Diog. Laert. 7. 46 : τὴν δὲ φαντασίαν εἶναι τύπωσιν ἐν ψυχῇ, τοῦ ὀνόματος [οἰκείως] μετενηνεγμένου ἀπὸ τῶν τύπων ⟨τῶν⟩ ἐν τῷ κηρῷ ὑπὸ τοῦ δακτυλίου γινομένων. A φαντασία may be ἀπὸ ὑπάρχοντος, i. e. it may be an impression stamped on the soul by a really existing external object ; in that case, it is called κατα-ληπτικὴ φαντασία (i. e. a φαντασία which gets hold of something real), and its evidence is true. On the other hand, it may be οὐκ ἀπὸ ὑπάρχοντος, i. e. it may have originated in the soul itself ; in that case, there is no external object to correspond to it, and the man who accepts it as evidence of reality is mistaken. (See Arnim, *Stoic. vet. fragm.* II, pp. 21 ff.) A dream is a series of φαντασίαι of the latter kind.

The Hermetist's doctrine of 'the two parts of αἴσθησις' is probably derived from the Stoic doctrine of αἴσθησις and φαντασία. The 'part of αἴσθησις' which he assigns to the body is the operation of the bodily sense-organs, and corresponds to the Stoic αἴσθησις ; the

---

imagines ab intentione traducta est, tunc demum corpus omne resolvitur in quietem. . . . Sibi avocamenta invenit (mens), ne saluberrimam quietem corporis interrumpat. . . . Dormiendi ergo causa tributa est a deo ratio somniandi.' This implies that in sleep *sensus* (αἴσθησις, i. e. the activity of the bodily sense-organs) is suspended, and the *mens* (νοῦς) alone is active, being occupied in the contemplation of *simulacra* or *imagines* (φαντάσματα).

[1] The simile of seal and wax, by which Aristotle (*De mem.* 1. 350 a) illustrates the process, had already been employed by Plato in the *Theaetetus*, 191 c *sqq.*

'part of αἴσθησις' which he assigns to the soul corresponds to the Stoic φαντασία.

ὅταν ἀμφότερα τὰ μέρη τῆς αἰσθήσεως πρὸς ἄλληλα συμφωνήσῃ. 'When the psychic αἴσθησις agrees with the bodily αἴσθησις (?).' This perhaps may mean ' when the φαντασία is an exact reproduction of an image impressed on the bodily sense-organs by an external object'; that is, in Stoic terms, 'when the φαντασία is ἀπὸ ὑπάρχοντος'. But the meaning of the paragraph as a whole is uncertain ; and that being so, there can be no certainty about the meaning of this or that clause of it.

§ 3. ὁ γὰρ νοῦς κύει πάντα τὰ νοήματα. In the words κύει and ἔσπειρε, the writer illustrates his meaning by a metaphor taken from human procreation. The man's νοῦς is the mother of his νοήματα ; but the father of every good νόημα is God, and the father of every bad νόημα is some daemon. That is to say, man's νοῦς does not produce νοήματα by its own unaided operation ; each of his designs or purposes is suggested to him from without, either by God or by a daemon.

As instances of κακὰ νοήματα, the writer mentions φόνοι, μοιχεῖαι, and the like; as instances of ἀγαθὰ νοήματα, he gives ἀρετή and σωφροσύνη. It is evident from this that the νοῦς here spoken of is νοῦς πρακτικός ; the νόησις is the process of deciding on a certain end to be aimed at by action, and is assumed to carry with it a corresponding act of will ; and the νόημα is the purpose thus formed, or the course of action thus decided on.

For the notion that good νοήματα are ' begotten' by God, cf. Philo De Cherubim 13. 43, Cohn I, p. 180 : ἀνὴρ μὲν γυναικὶ . . . τὰς ἐπὶ γενέσει παίδων ὁμιλίας . . . συνέρχεται ποιησόμενος· ἀρεταῖς δὲ πολλὰ καὶ τέλεια τικτούσαις θέμις οὐκ ἔστιν ἀνδρὸς ἐπιλαχεῖν θνητοῦ· μὴ δεξάμεναι δὲ παρά τινος ἑτέρου γονήν, ἐξ ἑαυτῶν μόνον οὐδέποτε κυήσουσι. τίς οὖν ὁ σπείρων ἐν αὐταῖς τὰ καλὰ πλὴν ὁ τῶν ὄντων πατήρ, ὁ ἀγένητος θεὸς καὶ τὰ σύμπαντα γεννῶν ; The ἀρεταί are here hypostatized, and are spoken of as if they were persons distinct and separate from the virtuous man ; but Philo's meaning appears to be that good thoughts and actions (the offspring of the ἀρεταί) are not originated by the man himself, but are implanted in him or bestowed on him by God. Philo expresses the same thought without metaphor in Leg. alleg. 3. 46. 136, Cohn I, p. 143 : δεῖ τὸν ὑπὲρ ἀρετῆς πόνον μὴ ἑαυτῇ προσάγειν τὴν ψυχήν, ἀλλ' ἀφελεῖν ἀφ' ἑαυτῆς καὶ θεῷ ἀνενεγκεῖν, ὁμολογοῦσαν ὅτι οὐχ ἡ ἰσχὺς αὐτῆς οὐδὲ ἡ δύναμις περιεποίησε τὸ καλόν, ἀλλὰ ὁ καὶ

τὸν ἔρωτα χαρισάμενος. Cf. Paul, *Phil.* 2. 13 : θεὸς γάρ ἐστιν ὁ ἐνεργῶν
ἐν ὑμῖν καὶ τὸ θέλειν καὶ τὸ ἐνεργεῖν.

[μηδενὸς μέρους τοῦ κόσμου κενοῦ ὄντος δαίμονος.] The following
ὅστις must be taken to refer, not to δαίμονος here, but to the preceding
τινος τῶν δαιμόνων. But that being so, the interposed words μηδενὸς
. . . δαίμονος awkwardly interrupt the sentence, and obscure the
construction. It seems best therefore to assume that they have been
inserted by a later hand.

ὁ κόσμος here means the sublunar world alone. It cannot include
the heavens ; for no Hermetist would have said that the heavens are
full of maleficent daemons. The writer of the clause presumably
held the view expressed in *Corp.* XVI and elsewhere, that all
physical processes in the sublunar world are carried on by the
agency of personal beings called daemons. He considered that
all bad thoughts and actions result from the influence on us of the
matter of which our bodies and their environment consist ; but he
attributed the influence of matter to the action of personal beings
residing in it.

⟨⟨ὑπεισελθών⟩⟩ τῷ ⟨μὴ⟩ ὑπὸ τοῦ θεοῦ πεφωτισμένῳ. If a man is
'illuminated' by God, he is secured against the action of the
daemons ; if not, they beget bad νοήματα in him. Cf. *Corp.* XVI.
16 : οὐδεὶς γὰρ οὐδὲν δύναται οὔτε δαιμόνων οὔτε θεῶν πρὸς μίαν ἀκτῖνα
τοῦ θεοῦ. Hermes in Lactant. *Div. inst.* 2. 15. 16 (*Ascl. Lat.* III.
29 b) : εὐσεβοῦς γὰρ ἀνθρώπου οὔτε δαίμων κακὸς οὔτε εἱμαρμένη
κρατεῖ.

In the word πεφωτισμένῳ, the writer employs a different and
inconsistent metaphor. To say that God 'pours light into' a man
is another way of saying that God begets good νοήματα in the
man's νοῦς.

ἔσπειρε τῆς ἰδίας ἐνεργείας τὸ σπέρμα. Each individual daemon
begets his own special kind of sin. Cf. Valentinus *ap.* Clem. Alex.
Strom. 2. 20. 114 : πολλὰ γὰρ ἐνοικοῦντα (τῇ καρδίᾳ) πνεύματα (= δαίμονες) οὐκ ἐᾷ καθαρεύειν· ἕκαστον δὲ αὐτῶν τὰ ἴδια ἐκτελεῖ ἔργα, πολλαχῶς
ἐνυβριζόντων ἐπιθυμίαις οὐ προσηκούσαις. Origen, *Hom. XV in Iesum
Nave* : 'per singulos homines sunt spiritus aliqui, diversa in iis
peccatorum genera molientes. Verbi causa, est aliquis fornicationis
spiritus, est irae spiritus alius, est avaritiae spiritus, alius vero
superbiae. Et si invenias esse aliquem hominem qui his omnibus
malis aut etiam pluribus agitatur, omnes hos vel etiam plures in se
habere inimicos putandus est spiritus.'

ἀσεβείας [ἀγχόνας, κατὰ κρημνῶν καταφοράς, καὶ ἄλλα πάντα ὅσα δαιμόνων ἔργα]. The enumeration of κακὰ νοήματα ought to end with ἀσεβείας, in which all wickednesses are summed up, as the enumeration of ἀγαθὰ νοήματα ends with εὐσεβεία. There is therefore reason to think that the words ἀγχόνας . . . δαιμόνων ἔργα have been subsequently added. The phrase κατὰ κρημνῶν καταφοράς recalls the words ὥρμησεν ἡ ἀγέλη κατὰ κρημνοῦ in the story of the Gadarene swine (*Mark* 5. 13, *Matth.* 8. 32, *Luke* 8. 33); and possibly the interpolator may have been a Christian, and may have been thinking of the δαιμονίων ἔργον which is described in that story.

§ 4 a. εὐσέβεια δέ ἐστι θεοῦ γνῶσις. Cf. Lactant. *Div. inst.* 2. 15. 8 : 'quid sit autem εὐσέβεια, ostendit (Hermes) alio loco his verbis : ἡ γὰρ εὐσέβεια γνῶσίς ἐστι τοῦ θεοῦ.' The words quoted by Lactantius are not quite identical with those of *Corp.* IX ; and they may perhaps have occurred in some other Hermetic document known to him.

ὃν ὁ ἐπιγνούς, πλήρης γενόμενος πάντων τῶν ἀγαθῶν, τὰς νοήσεις θείας ἴσχει. Cf. *Ascl. Lat.* 1 a : 'quem (sermonem) si intellegens ⟨deum⟩ videris, eris omnium bonorum tota mente plenissimus.' It appears from this that the writer of *Corp.* IX borrowed the phrase πλήρης γενόμενος πάντων τῶν ἀγαθῶν from the first paragraph of the Λόγος τέλειος.

§ 4 b. τὴν γὰρ κακίαν ἐνθάδε δεῖν οἰκεῖν εἶπον, ἐν (εἴπομεν MSS.) τῷ ἑαυτῆς χωρίῳ οὖσαν· χωρίον γὰρ αὐτῆς ἡ γῆ. The word εἶπον implies that this statement occurred in some earlier Hermetic document known to the writer. But the remoter source of it is Pl. *Theaet.* 176 A : οὔτ᾿ ἀπολέσθαι τὰ κακὰ δυνατόν . . ., ὑπεναντίον γάρ τι τῷ ἀγαθῷ ἀεὶ εἶναι ἀνάγκη, οὔτ᾿ ἐν θεοῖς αὐτὰ ἱδρύσθαι· τὴν δὲ θνητὴν φύσιν καὶ τόνδε τὸν τόπον περιπολεῖ ἐξ ἀνάγκης.

οὐχ ὁ κόσμος, ὡς ἔνιοί ποτε ἐροῦσι βλασφημοῦντες. The writer implies that some of his contemporaries assert that evil extends through the whole Kosmos ; but he holds that the heavens are free from evil, and that it exists on earth alone. Among the blasphemers who spoke evil of that 'second God', the Kosmos, were the Christians ; and perhaps it is of the Christians chiefly, if not solely, that the Hermetist is here thinking. Compare *Ascl. Lat.* III. 25 : when the Christians prevail, 'non admirandus videbitur mundus nec adorandus ' &c. But the writer of *Corp.* VI was guilty of similar blasphemy ; see VI. 4 a, ὁ γὰρ κόσμος πλήρωμά ἐστι τῆς κακίας.

The word κόσμος here includes the heavens ; whereas in § 3, in the clause μηδενὸς μέρους τοῦ κόσμου κενοῦ ὄντος δαίμονος, it means the sublunar world alone (the γῆ of § 4 b), and it is implied that the κόσμος (in that sense) *is* the abode of κακία. The verbal contradiction between the two statements confirms the suspicion that the clause in § 3 has been inserted by another hand.

ὁ μέντοι θεοσεβὴς πάντα ὑποστήσει ἀντισχόμενος (αἰσθόμενος MSS.) τῆς γνώσεως. He who has *gnosis* will endure pain and death, if need be, rather than abandon his religion.

πάντα ἀναφέρει εἰς τὴν γνῶσιν. Does this mean that he 'makes his sufferings contribute to the increase of his *gnosis*', i. e. that they bring him nearer to God ? Or, that he 'finds an explanation of them in his *gnosis*', in the light of which he sees that they are blessings in disguise ?

τὰ κακὰ μόνος ἀγαθοποιεῖ. He finds good in the sufferings inflicted on him. The Pagan writer here shows something of the spirit of those Christians who rejoiced in martyrdom. Cf. Paul, *Rom.* 8. 28 : τοῖς ἀγαπῶσι τὸν θεὸν πάντα συνεργεῖ εἰς ἀγαθόν. Plotinus 4. 3. 16 : εἰ δ᾽ ἀγαθὸς ὁ (ἄδικα πρὸς ἀνθρώπων) παθών, εἰς ἀγαθὸν ἡ τελευτὴ τούτων.

§ 5. οὐ πᾶς δὲ ἄνθρωπος . . . ἀπολαύει τῆς νοήσεως. All men νοοῦσιν, i. e. all men possess νοῦς and use it ; but some men do not use it rightly, and therefore get no good from their possession of it. This was implied in § 3, to which the words ὡς προεῖπον refer. In the *Hermetica*, νοῦς is sometimes used (as here) in a wider sense, to signify a faculty which all men possess, and by the possession of which they are distinguished from beasts ; and sometimes in a narrower sense, to signify a higher faculty, which is bestowed by God on a few among men, but is not possessed by the many. In the latter sense, it is the faculty by which men 'know God', and is thus correlative to γνῶσις, 'knowledge of God'.

[ἀλλ᾽ ὁ μὲν ὑλικός, ὁ δὲ οὐσιώδης.] The men who use their νόησις wrongly are ὑλικοί ; that is, they are dominated by material things, or in other words, by the daemons who reside in material things and operate by means of them. These men live in subjection to the πάθη bred by the material body, and their desires are directed to material objects. They are those who 'love the body', as some of the Hermetists say. On the other hand, those who use their νόησις rightly are οὐσιώδεις ; that is, they are freed from the domination of the body and its material surroundings ; it is the incorporeal and eternal part of them that has the upper hand, and their hearts are set on things incorporeal and eternal. Thus applied, the terms ὑλικός and οὐσιώδης correspond to χοϊκός and πνευματικός as used by some of the Christian Gnostics.

But the words ἀλλ' ὁ μὲν ὑλικὸς ὁ δὲ οὐσιώδης appear to be wrongly placed here. Their connexion with the preceding clause is obscure; and the sequence of thought becomes clearer if we cut them out, and read οὐ πᾶς δὲ . . . ἀπολαύει τῆς νοήσεως· [ ] ὁ μὲν γὰρ . . ., οἱ δὲ κ.τ.λ.

ὁ μὲν γὰρ μετὰ κακίας [ὑλικὸς] ⟨νοεῖ⟩, . . . οἱ δὲ μετὰ τοῦ ἀγαθοῦ [οὐσιωδῶς] (sc. νοοῦσιν). ὑλικός (or ὑλικῶς?) and οὐσιωδῶς may perhaps have been added by the same person who inserted ἀλλ' ὁ μὲν ὑλικὸς ὁ δὲ οὐσιώδης. The text is corrupt, and cannot be restored with certainty; but the writer's meaning must have been that some men's thinking produces bad results, and other men's thinking produces good results. The mention of 'evil' and 'good' in this sentence leads on to an attempt to account for the existence of evil.

ὑπὸ τοῦ θεοῦ σωζόμενοι. These men are saved by God from subjection to ὕλη and the daemons who operate in it.

πάντα ποιεῖ [μὲν] ἑαυτῷ ὅμοια. All things are made by God, and therefore all things, when first made, are 'like God', i. e. are good.

ταῦτα δ', ἀγαθὰ γενόμενα, ἐν τῇ χρήσει τῆς ἐνεργείας ⌜αφορα⌝. The sense required to suit the context is 'all things are good when first made, but some things afterwards become bad'. (Some things, not all, become bad; for the writer goes on to say that the κοσμικὴ φορά, while it makes some things bad, makes other things good). But it is doubtful how this sense is to be got out of the words. Perhaps ἐν τῇ χρήσει τῆς ἐνεργείας might be taken to mean 'when the operation of the (cosmic) forces is brought to bear on them'; but the phrase is obscure, and very likely corrupt. In place of αφορα, we might write ⟨ἐκβαίνει δι⟩άφορα, 'turn out various in quality' (i. e. some of them bad and others good). But it is also possible that αφορα has come by duplication from φορά, and that the original predicate is wholly lost.

For the thought, cf. Corp. XIV. 7 : 'evil has not been made by God, but breaks out, like a sort of rust, on the things which God has made.'

ἡ γὰρ κοσμικὴ φορά, τρέπουσα (τρίβουσα MSS.) τὰς γενέσεις, ποιὰς ποιεῖ. (Possibly ποι⟨κίλ⟩ας ποιεῖ· cf. ποικίλην in § 6, and τὴν ποικιλίαν τῶν γενέσεων in § 7.) 'The movement of the Kosmos' must here mean the movement of the heavenly bodies. The aspect of the stars changes from moment to moment; and the character (whether good or bad) of every living creature is determined by the aspect of the stars at the moment of its birth. (Cf. *Ascl. Lat.* III. 35.) This statement, if its logical implications were accepted, would involve absolute fatalism; it would throw all responsibility for evil on the heavenly bodies,[1] and therefore ultimately on God. If God has made the stars and determined their movements, and the stars, by their movements, determine that some men shall be bad, God is the author of moral evil. But the writer did not draw this inference.

§ 6. καὶ γὰρ ὁ κόσμος . . . αἴσθησιν ἰδίαν καὶ νόησιν ἔχει. The terms αἴσθησις and νόησις must be taken here in the same sense in which they were employed before with reference to man. αἴσθησις seems to be the perception that a certain state of things exists, and νόησις, a deliberate decision to take certain action in view of that state of things. Thus the statement that the Kosmos possesses αἴσθησις and νόησις means that the Kosmos is a conscious and rational agent.

οὐχ ὁμοίαν τῇ ἀνθρωπείᾳ, οὐδὲ ⟨οὔτ⟩ως ποικίλην. Man's νοήματα are ποικίλα; that is to say, they are sometimes good, but oftener bad; and when bad, they are bad in manifold ways (ἐσθλοὶ μὲν γὰρ ἁπλῶς, παντοδαπῶς δὲ κακοί). But the νοήματα of the Kosmos are invariably good, and therefore ἁπλᾶ. And it may be inferred that they are invariably begotten by God. (Yet if the νοήματα of the Kosmos are invariably good, how is it that the κοσμικὴ φορά gives rise to evil as well as good?)

ἡ γὰρ αἴσθησις καὶ νόησις τοῦ κόσμου μία ἐστί, τὸ (τῷ MSS.) πάντα ποιεῖν, καὶ εἰς ἑαυτὸν (ἑαυτὴν MSS.) ἀποποιεῖν. The correction τὸ for τῷ is confirmed by the parallel in § 9, τοῦτό ἐστιν ἡ α. καὶ ν. τοῦ θεοῦ, τὸ τὰ πάντα ἀεὶ κινεῖν. The Kosmos acts consciously and deliberately; and its action consists solely in making and unmaking things; i. e. all physical processes are directed to this end. By 'things' we must understand living organisms. When an organism is 'unmade', it is broken up into its component elements; and as these elements are parts of the Kosmos, the Kosmos is said to 'unmake things *into itself*'.

ὄργανον ⟨ὄντα⟩ τῆς τοῦ θεοῦ βουλήσεως. It seems necessary to insert ὄντα, in agreement with κόσμον, the understood subject of ποιεῖν and

---

[1] We were told in § 4 b that it is 'blasphemy' to say that there is evil in the heavens. But if a thing produces evil, how can it be denied that in that respect it is itself evil?

ἀποποιεῖν. The word ὄντως in the following clause yields no satis-factory sense; it is probable therefore that ὄντα was transferred to that place by error, and was subsequently altered into ὄντως. The word ὄργανον is wrongly repeated in [ὄργανο]ποιηθέν⟨τα⟩.

The Kosmos, in carrying on the physical processes by which living organisms are made and unmade, is executing the will of God, and therefore, though a conscious agent, may at the same time be called an 'instrument' by means of which God works. The same phrase occurs in *Ascl. Lat.* III. 25 ('mundus, . . . machina voluntatis dei'), whence the writer of *Corp.* IX presumably borrowed it.

ἀπὸ τοῦ θεοῦ λαβὼν τὰ σπέρματα. The Kosmos has received the 'seeds' of all things from God, retains these 'seeds' in itself, and produces from them a perpetual succession of living organisms. In using the word σπέρματα, the writer may have had in mind the σπερματικοὶ λόγοι of the Stoics. For its employment in this passage, cf. Basilides (or one of his followers) *ap.* Hippol. *Ref. haer.* 7. 21 :

ἦν ὅτε ἦν οὐδέν. . . . ἐπεὶ ⟨οὖν⟩ οὐδὲν ⟨ἦν⟩,—οὐχ ὕλη, οὐκ οὐσία, οὐκ ἀνούσιον, οὐχ ἁπλοῦν, οὔ[κ ἀ]σύνθετον, [οὐκ ἀνοητόν, οὐκ ἀναίσθητον,][1] οὐκ ἄνθρωπος, οὐκ ἄγγελος, οὐ θεός, οὐδὲ ὅλως τι τῶν ὀνομαζομένων ἢ δι᾽ αἰσθήσεως λαμβανομένων ἢ νοητῶν πραγμάτων,—. . . ⟨ὁ⟩ οὐκ ὢν θεὸς . . . ἀνοήτως, ἀναισθήτως,[2] ἀβούλως, ἀπροαιρέτως, ἀπαθῶς, ἀνεπιθυμήτως κόσμον ἠθέλησε ποιῆσαι. τὸ δὲ " ἠθέλησε " λέγω, φησί, σημασίας χάριν,[3] ἀθελήτως ⟨γὰρ ἠθέλησε⟩ καὶ ἀνοήτως καὶ ἀναισθήτως·[4] " κόσμον " δὲ οὐ τὸν κατὰ πλάτος καὶ διαίρεσιν γεγενημένον ὕστερον καὶ διεστῶτα,[5] ἀλλὰ γὰρ σπέρμα κόσμου. τὸ δὲ σπέρμα τοῦ κόσμου πάντα εἶχεν ἐν ἑαυτῷ, ὡς ὁ τοῦ σινάπεως κόκκος ἐν ἐλαχίστῳ συλλαβὼν ἔχει πάντα[6] ὁμοῦ, τὰς ῥίζας, τὸ πρέμνον, τοὺς κλάδους, τὰ φύλλα, τὰ ἀνεξαρίθμητα [τῶν κόκκων] (ἀπ)ὸ τοῦ φυτοῦ γεννώμενα[7] σπέρματα πάλιν ἄλλων καὶ ἄλλων πολλάκις φυτῶν ⌈κεχυμένα⌉.[8] οὕτως ⟨ὁ⟩ οὐκ ὢν θεὸς ἐποίησε κόσμον οὐκ ὄν⟨τα⟩[9] ἐξ οὐκ ὄντων, καταβαλ[λ]όμενος καὶ ὑποστήσας[10] σπέρμα τι ἕν,

---

[1] οὐκ . . . ἀναίσθητον *seclusi.* 'οὐ νοητόν, οὐκ αἰσθητόν susp. Iacobius'; but this would be a duplication of τῶν δι᾽ αἰσθήσεως κ.τ.λ. below.

[2] As to ἀνοήτως, ἀναισθήτως, see note on *Corp.* IX. 9 below.

[3] I.e. 'I use the word to indicate my meaning, but it is not to be understood literally'.

[4] καὶ ἀνοήτως καὶ ἀναισθήτως *secludendum*?

[5] Perhaps, τὸν [[ ]] κατὰ διαίρεσιν γεγενημένον ὕστερον καὶ ⟨⟨κατὰ πλάτος⟩⟩ διεστῶτα.

[6] πάντα Duncker and Schn. : πάσας MS.

[7] Perhaps γενησόμενα, or γεννησομένων.

[8] Perhaps ⟨ἅπαντα (?) συγ⟩κεχυμένα.

[9] ὄντα Duncker and Schn. : ὢν MS.

[10] Either καταβαλόμενος καὶ or καὶ ὑποστήσας ought, I think, to be struck out.

ἔχον πᾶσαν ἐν ἑαυτῷ τὴν τοῦ κόσμου πανσπερμίαν. ἵνα δὲ καταφανέστερον
ποιήσω τοῦτο ὅπερ ἐκεῖνοι λέγουσι· καθάπερ ὠὸν ὄρνιθος εὐποικίλ[λ]ου [1]
τινὸς καὶ πολυχρωμάτου, οἱονεὶ τοῦ ταῶνος ἢ ἄλλου τινὸς ἔτι μᾶλλον
πολυμόρφου [καὶ πολυχρωμάτου], ἐν ὄν, [οὕτως] [2] ἔχει ἐν ἑαυτῷ πολλὰς
οὐσιῶν πολυμόρφων καὶ πολυχρωμάτων καὶ πολυσυστάτων [3] ἰδέας, οὕτως
ἔχει [4] τὸ καταβληθέν, φησίν, ὑπὸ τοῦ οὐκ ὄντος θεοῦ οὐκ ὂν σπέρμα τοῦ
κόσμου ⌜πολύμορφον ὁμοῦ καὶ πολυούσιον⌝. [5]

ἵνα ... πάντα ποιῇ ἐνεργῶς. The Kosmos has received from God
the 'seeds' of things only, and not the things themselves; it
produces the things ἐνεργῶς by its own action. That is to say,
the things exist only δυνάμει (potentially) in the 'seeds', but are
made to exist ἐνεργείᾳ (actually) by the action of the Kosmos. With
the other reading, ἐναργῶς, the meaning would be that the Kosmos
brings the individual organisms into concrete and visible existence
by its own action.

⟨⟨φερόμενος δὲ πάντα ζωοποιεῖ.⟩⟩. This clause, where it stands in
the MSS., is an awkward and pointless repetition of οὐκ ἔστιν ὃ μὴ
ζωογονεῖ. I have therefore transposed it to this place, where something of the sort seems needed to lead on to καὶ διαλύων πάντα
ἀνανεοῖ. The word φερόμενος implies that it is the κοσμικὴ φορά,
i. e. the movement of the heavenly bodies, that produces life in each
individual organism at its birth.

ὥσπερ ἀγαθὸς [ζωῆς] γεωργὸς τῇ καταβολῇ ἀνανέωσιν αὐτοῖς [φερό-
μενος] παρέχων (παρέχει MSS.). καταβολή means 'a sowing of seed'.
As a farmer 'renews' his crop (i. e. brings a fresh crop into being in
place of that which has been reaped) by sowing seed, so the Kosmos
renews the life of all organisms by making them produce offspring.
Cf. *Corp.* III. 4 as emended: τὰ δὲ ἐλαττούμενα ἀνανεωθήσεται θεῶν
ἐγκυκλίων ἐναριθμίῳ δρομήματι. The word φερόμενος is out of place
here, since it has no application to the γεωργός. It has doubtless
come by duplication from φερόμενος δὲ πάντα ζωοποιεῖ.

For the simile of the γεωργός, cf. Numenius *ap.* Euseb. *Pr. ev.* 11.
18. 14, quoted in prefatory note on *Corp.* II.

Compare also *Pap. Mag. Berlin* Parthey I. 26, where the term
ἀγαθὲ γεωργέ is addressed to the Egyptian god Khnum (the Agathos

---

[1] εὐποικίλου Duncker and Schn.: ἐκ ποικίλλου MS.
[2] οὕτως *seclusi.* It has doubtless come from οὕτως ἔχει below.
[3] Two of these three adjectives might be struck out with advantage.
[4] ἔχει is here intransitive.
[5] ὁμοῦ is meaningless; and the σπέρμα, though it contains in itself πολλὰς οὐσιῶν
πολυμόρφων ἰδέας, is not itself πολύμορφον. *Legendum* πολυμόρφου ὄντος καὶ
πολυουσίου.

Daimon), who, as lord of the Nile, and fertilizer of Egypt, had come
to be regarded as the giver of all life on earth.

§ 7. τὰ δὲ σώματα ἀπὸ ὕλης. The writer distinguishes the material
body of the organism from the life (or soul) generated in it or infused
into it. His conception of ζωή resembles that of *anima* in *Ascl. Lat.*
I. 2 b, where the *anima* is distinguished from the *mundus* (ὕλη) of
which the body is composed.

ἐν διαφορᾷ. It would be possible to write ἐνδιάφορα, 'having
differences in or among them'. There seems to have been an
adjective ἐνδιάφορος with this meaning; cf. *Corp.* XII. i. 6, πῶς ἐνδιάφορός ἐστιν (ὁ νοῦς). See also *Corp.* V. 7.

[τὰ μὲν γάρ ἐστιν ἐκ γῆς, τὰ δὲ ἐξ ὕδατος, τὰ δὲ ἐξ ἀέρος, τὰ δὲ ἐκ
πυρός.] This appears to mean that the bodies of one kind of ζῷα
are made wholly and solely of earth, those of another kind wholly
and solely of water, and so on. But that is contradicted by the
following statement, πάντα δέ ἐστι σύνθετα, which implies that every
organized body is composed of different elements in combination.
It is most likely therefore that τὰ μὲν . . . ἐκ πυρός is a note inserted
by some reader.

The interpolator probably assumed that the bodies of men and
terrestrial animals are made of earth, and those of fishes, of water.
The only ζῷα that could be said to have bodies made of fire are the
celestial gods (sun, moon, and stars); and that being so, the ζῷα that
have bodies made of air are most likely the daemons.

πάντα δέ ἐστι σύνθετα, καὶ τὰ μὲν μᾶλλον, τὰ δὲ ἀπλούστερα· μᾶλλον
μὲν τὰ βαρύτερα, ἧττον δὲ τὰ κουφότερα. ἀπλούστερα is equivalent to
ἧττον σύνθετα, and (if the text is sound) is accordingly resumed by
ἧττον in the phrase which follows. But what kinds of ζῷα have
bodies that are ἧττον σύνθετα and consequently κουφότερα? If the
writer were speaking of men alone, one might suppose that he was
thinking of the doctrine of Posidonius concerning life after death.
Pos. seems to have said that men living on earth are composed of all
four elements, and when a man dies, he becomes first a 'hero',
composed of water, air, and fire, and dwelling in the lower atmosphere; then a 'daemon', composed of air and fire, and dwelling in
the upper atmosphere; and (in some few cases) finally a god, composed of fire alone, and dwelling in heaven. But that interpretation
of the sentence would not suit the context; for the author of *Corp.*
IX is speaking of the ζῷα produced by the Kosmos, and it is clear
that he includes among these ζῷα beasts as well as men, and that he

is thinking of them only as born on earth and living upon earth. There is reason therefore to suspect that not only the preceding sentence, but this passage also (πάντα δέ . . . κουφότερα) is an interpolation. Perhaps the best way out of the difficulty would be to cut out all that is here said about τὰ σώματα, and to assume that the original text ran thus: (ὁ κόσμος) ὁμοῦ τόπος ἐστὶ καὶ δημιουργὸς ζωῆς. [τὰ δὲ σώματα . . . ἧττον δὲ τὰ κουφότερα.] τὸ δὲ τάχος αὐτοῦ τῆς φορᾶς κ.τ.λ.

τὸ δὲ τάχος αὐτοῦ τῆς φορᾶς τὴν ποικιλίαν τῶν [ποιῶν] γενέσεων ἐργάζεται. This is explained by Ascl. Lat. III. 35. The qualities imposed on individuals at their birth are ποικίλα; that is to say, no two individuals are born alike; and this is accounted for by the fact that, owing to the rapid movement of the heavens, no two individuals are born under the same aspect of the stars. ποιῶν (qualities) may be an alternative reading for γενέσεων. It would be possible to write either τὴν ποικιλίαν τῶν γενέσεων (cf. τῇ ποικιλίᾳ τῆς γενέσεως below), or τ. π. τῶν ποιῶν, but hardly τ. π. τῶν ποιῶν γενέσεων.

πνοὴ γάρ, οὖσα πυκνοτάτη, προτείνει τὰ ποιὰ τοῖς σώμασιν. This πνοή is the Stoic πνεῦμα, i. e. the life-breath of the living Kosmos. (Cf. Ascl. Lat. I. 6 b, 'spiritus, quo plena sunt omnia, permixtus cunctis cuncta vivificat'; and Ascl. Lat. III. 17 a.) The writer identifies it with the atmosphere, and holds it to be the instrument by which the influences of the heavenly bodies are brought to bear on all organisms on earth. All ζῷα live by breathing, i. e. by taking into themselves a portion of the cosmic πνοή. (Cf. εἰσπνέουσα ἀπὸ τοῦ περιέχοντος below.)

The πνοή is πυκνοτάτη; that is to say, it operates without intermission, and so maintains a constant succession of changing qualities. It 'extends the qualities forward' (προτείνει τὰ ποιά); this seems to mean that it supplies a continuous series of them.

μετὰ ἑνὸς πληρώματος τῆς ζωῆς. The πνοή not only imposes on all bodies their sensible qualities (τὰ ποιά), but also conveys life into them. And since all bodies in the Kosmos (inorganic bodies as well as organisms) possess life in some degree, their lives, regarded collectively, constitute ἐν πλήρωμα τῆς ζωῆς; that is to say, the universe is, through the operation of the πνοή, wholly filled with one continuous mass of life. Cf. Corp. XII. ii. 15 b: ὁ δὲ σύμπας κόσμος οὗτος . . . πλήρωμά ἐστι τῆς ζωῆς.

§ 8. [πατὴρ μὲν . . . τοῦ κόσμου.] Placed in the midst of the discussion of the Kosmos, this passage is an interruption. It may perhaps have been a note appended to the words ἀπὸ τοῦ θεοῦ λαβὼν ἔχει in § 9, where the writer is passing on from the Kosmos to God. As to ὁ μὲν κόσμος υἱὸς τοῦ θεοῦ κ.τ.λ., cf. *Corp.* X. 14 b : καὶ γίνεται ὁ μὲν κόσμος τοῦ θεοῦ υἱός, ὁ δὲ ἄνθρωπος τοῦ κόσμου ⟨υἱός, καὶ τοῦ θεοῦ⟩ ὥσπερ ἔγγονος.

Numenius called the first God 'grandfather' of the Kosmos ; see Numen. *ap.* Procl. *In Tim.* 93 A, quoted in prefatory note on *Corp.* II.

ὁ αὐτὸς οὖν κόσμος ⌈ἀναγκαίως⌉ καὶ οἰκείως καλοῖτο. ἀναγκαίως, which is meaningless in this context, has probably come from ἀνάγκης above. The meaning must have been that the word κόσμος has two senses, viz. 'order' and 'universe', and that one of these is its 'proper' or primary sense, and the other is a transferred or secondary sense. Perhaps the original reading may have been ἀναλόγως, which, when contrasted with οἰκείως, would mean 'metaphorically'. Cf. Ar. *Rhet.* 3. 10. 7 : τῶν δὲ μεταφορῶν ... εὐδοκιμοῦσι μάλιστα αἱ κατ᾽ ἀναλογίαν.

For the omission of ἄν, cf. ὑποσταίη in *Corp.* XI. ii. 16 b. (In IX. 10, the MSS. give δόξειεν without ἄν, but the text is corrupt.) Whether ἄν was omitted from the first, or has been dropped out by a copyist, we have no means of knowing.

ὁ αὐτὸς ... καλοῖτο ends the paragraph feebly, and is an anticlimax after the more impressive sentence which precedes it ; I am therefore inclined to suspect that it is a note inserted by a later hand.

§ 9. πάντων οὖν τῶν ζῴων ἡ αἴσθησις καὶ νόησις ἔξωθεν ἐπεισέρχεται, εἰσπνέουσα ἀπὸ (ὑπὸ MSS.) τοῦ περιέχοντος. According to § 1 b, 'sense and thought' exist (on earth) in men alone, and in the lower animals their place is taken by 'sense and instinct'. But here, the phrase αἴσθησις καὶ νόησις is used in a wider sense, and means 'conscious life' in general, so that it becomes almost equivalent to ζωή. We have just been told that 'life' is conveyed into all bodies by the cosmic πνοή; and the same thing is expressed in other words by the statement that 'sense and thought' are breathed into them from the atmosphere. In adopting the Stoic doctrine of the cosmic πνεῦμα, the writer has not ceased to feel that πνεῦμα primarily means 'breath'; and his description of the process of vivification is based on the view that men and beasts draw into themselves, by the act of breathing, portions of the conscious life of the Kosmos, with which the atmosphere is filled. In this respect, he is still in touch with the theories of Heraclitus and Diogenes of Apollonia, out of which the Stoic doctrine of πνεῦμα was developed.

ὁ δὲ κόσμος, ἅπαξ λαβὼν ἅμα τῷ γενέσθαι. The writer assumes that the Kosmos has had a beginning. This was denied by the Aristotelians, and by some of the Platonists.

ὥσπερ ἐνίοις δόξει. Cf. § 4 b, ὡς ἔνιοί ποτε ἐροῦσι. The writer refers to his own time by putting a prediction into the mouth of the prehistoric Hermes. His meaning is that some of his contemporaries deny that God αἰσθάνεται καὶ νοεῖ. Who are the persons referred to? They can hardly be orthodox Christians; but some of the Christian Gnostics might be included among them. Cf. Basilides, quoted above, in note on § 6: the 'non-existent' God ἀνοήτως, ἀναισθήτως, ... κόσμον ἠθέλησε ποιῆσαι. But that is merely an extreme statement of a doctrine which was taught by some of the Pagan Platonists also; (see note on *Corp.* II. 5;) and the writer of *Corp* IX, when he spoke of certain men who blasphemously say that God is ἀναίσθητος καὶ ἀνόητος, may have been thinking either of Pagan Platonists or of Platonizing Christians.

ὑπὸ γὰρ δεισιδαιμονίας βλασφημοῦσι. It is their anxiety to exalt God to the utmost, and to separate him by the widest possible interval from the material world and the evil in it, that leads them into this error; and thus they may be said to 'blaspheme through excess of reverence'.

⟨⟨καὶ τοῦτο ἔστιν ἡ αἴσθησις καὶ νόησις τοῦ θεοῦ, τὸ τὰ πάντα ἀεὶ κινεῖν.⟩⟩ Cf. *Corp.* XI. ii. 17 c: τοῦτο γὰρ ὥσπερ (οὐσία?) ἐστὶ τοῦ θεοῦ, ⟨τὸ⟩ κινεῖν τὰ πάντα καὶ ζωοποιεῖν. God is the *primum movens*; it is his activity that takes effect in all subordinate activities. He infuses life and energy into the Kosmos, and thereby causes the Kosmos to infuse life and energy into all things contained in it. And his αἴσθησις and νόησις consist in doing this; that is to say, he does it consciously and deliberately, and is wholly occupied in doing it.

τὰ μὲν διὰ σωμάτων ἐνεργοῦντα, τὰ δὲ διὰ οὐσίας ψυχικῆς κινοῦντα. The writer probably adopted the view expressed in *Ascl. Lat.* I. 4, that plants, though they have ζωή, and even a kind of αἴσθησις, have no ψυχή. They are living and perhaps sentient bodies, but bodies without 'soul' or 'psychic substance'. Thus τὰ διὰ τῶν σωμάτων ἐνεργοῦντα may be taken to mean plants, as opposed to τὰ διὰ ψυχικῆς οὐσίας κινοῦντα, which means ἔμψυχα, i. e. beasts and men. ψυχή is 'self-moving' or 'self-moved' (Pl. *Phaedrus* 245 E, *Laws* 896 A); and the self-moving ψυχή of a man or animal originates movement in the body in which it resides, and thereby moves inanimate bodies also (*Corp.* II. 8 b, 9). ἔμψυχα are therefore κινοῦντα; but since this very power of self-movement is bestowed by God, the spontaneous movements of ἔμψυχα, as well as the mechanical movements of ἄψυχα, are caused by God.

τὰ δὲ διὰ πνεύματος ζωοποιοῦντα, τὰ δὲ τὰ κεκμηκότα ὑποδεχόμενα. This is obscure; but a comparison of *Ascl. Lat.* I. 2 b and 6 b (which the writer had before him in the Λόγος τέλειος) suggests that it is to be explained as follows. The two kinds of things here spoken of are the ἀνωφερῆ and κατωφερῆ of *Ascl. Lat.* I. 2 b, that is, the pair of light elements, fire and air, and the pair of heavy elements, earth and water. The ἀνωφερῆ are ζωοποιοῦντα (*vivifica, Ascl. Lat.* I); that is to say, portions of fire and air enter into the bodies of men and animals, (these bodies being composed mainly of τὰ κατωφερῆ, earth and water,) and convey life into them. And the fire and air do this διὰ πνεύματος, that is, by combining with one another to form a gaseous substance called πνεῦμα, which men and animals draw into their bodies by breathing. The κατωφερῆ 'receive into themselves dead organisms'; that is to say, when an animal 'expires', the invisible πνεῦμα by which it has hitherto been vivified passes away into the atmosphere, but the visible and tangible body is resolved into the gross elements of which it was composed, and is thus 'received back' into the mass of earth and water. If this is the meaning, the first and second of the four kinds of things distinguished are organic bodies (animals and vegetables), and the third and fourth are inorganic bodies (the lighter and heavier elements).

Perhaps it might also be possible to take the passage in another way; τὰ διὰ πνεύματος ζωοποιοῦντα might be taken to mean the heavenly bodies, which produce life in individual organisms by means of the cosmic πνεῦμα by which their influence is conveyed to earthly things; and τὰ τὰ κεκμηκότα ἀναδεχόμενα might be taken to mean the four elements, into which the organism (including the portion of πνεῦμα which has been infused into it, as well as the visible and tangible body) is decomposed at death.

[καὶ εἰκότως]. This phrase is evidently out of place; for it ought to be followed by an explanation introduced by γάρ, and there is no such explanation here. It may be a misplaced doublet of καὶ εἰκότως in § 8.

[[μᾶλλον δὲ λέγω ὅτι οὐκ αὐτὸς αὐτὰ ἔχει, ἀλλὰ ... αὐτὸς ἅπαντά ἐστιν.]] There can be little doubt that this was written as a correction of τὰ γὰρ ὄντα ὁ θεὸς ἔχει below. If we transpose it accordingly, the statement αὐτὸς ἅπαντά ἐστιν falls into its right place, as the climax with which the paragraph ends.

[οὐκ ἔξωθεν αὐτὰ προσλαμβάνων, ἔξω δὲ ἐπιδιδούς.] These words, in which God is spoken of as distinct from 'things', cannot have been meant to follow αὐτὸς ἅπαντά ἐστιν, in which he is identified with them. Perhaps οὐκ ... ἐπιδιδούς was intended to stand after τὰ γὰρ ὄντα ὁ θεὸς ἔχει below ; but if placed there, it would interrupt the sequence of thought ; and it seems most likely that it is a note inserted by a reader.

καὶ οὐκ ἔσται ποτὲ χρόνος ὅτε ἀπολειφθήσεταί τι τῶν ὄντων. See *Corp.* VIII, where it is maintained that οὐδὲν τῶν ἐν τῷ κόσμῳ ἀπόλλυται.

οὐκ ... ἀπολειφθήσεταί τι τῶν ὄντων· [ ] τὰ γὰρ ὄντα ὁ θεὸς ἔχει. Nothing that is can cease to be, because all things are contained [1] by God, or included in God. (Cf. ἐν τῷ θεῷ ἐστι above, and οὔτε αὐτοῦ οὐδὲν ἐκτός, which follows.) If things are 'in God', they partake of God's eternity, and cannot perish.

καὶ οὔτε αὐτοῦ οὐδὲν ἐκτὸς οὔτε αὐτὸς οὐδενός. The first of these two statements, 'there is nothing which is not in God', is a repetition of τὰ ὄντα ὁ θεὸς ἔχει in different words. But the second, 'there is nothing in which God is not', brings in a fresh thought which is hardly to the point ; and it may be suspected that the author wrote merely καὶ οὐδὲν αὐτοῦ ἐκτός, and that this was amplified by a transcriber.

§ 10. ὑπὸ τοῦ λόγου μέχρι τινὸς ὁδηγηθείς. The teacher's words may guide the pupil's thought in the right direction ; but they can do no more than that. Unless the pupil thinks for himself, he cannot grasp the truth which the teacher's words express ; (cf. *Ascl. Lat.* I. 3 b, and *Ascl. Lat.* III. 19 a ;) and it is only when his own thought has confirmed what another man tells him, that he arrives at an assured conviction. Cf. Plotinus 6. 9. 4 : διὸ οὐδὲ ῥητὸν οὐδὲ γραπτὸν (τὸ ἕν)· ἀλλὰ λέγομεν καὶ γράφομεν, πέμποντες εἰς αὐτό, καὶ ἀνεγείροντες ἐκ τῶν λόγων (by our teaching) ἐπὶ τὴν θέαν, ὥσπερ ὁδὸν δεικνύντες τῷ τι θεάσασθαι βουλομένῳ. μέχρι μὲν γὰρ τῆς ὁδοῦ καὶ τῆς πορείας ἡ δίδαξις, ἡ δὲ θέα αὐτοῦ ἔργον ἤδη τοῦ ἰδεῖν βεβουλημένου. I. e. a man may be led by his teacher to a standpoint from which it is possible to see 'the One' (or God) ; but he cannot see it unless he looks with his own eyes.

---

[1] It might be possible to translate ἔχει 'holds in his keeping'. But it suits the context better if we take it to mean 'contains within himself'.

The νόησις spoken of in this section is the operation of νοῦς θεωρητικός; whereas in the rest of the document the νόησις in question is mainly, if not solely, the operation of νοῦς πρακτικός.

ὁ δὲ νοῦς . . . φθάνει μέχρι (φθάνειν ἔχει MSS.) τῆς ἀληθείας. The repetition of the phrase φθάνει μέχρι τῆς ἀληθείας is clumsy; and perhaps it would be better to cut it out here, and write ὁ δὲ νοῦς . . . ὁδηγηθείς, [ ] καὶ περινοήσας κ.τ.λ.

τοιγαροῦν νοήσασι μὲν πιστὰ τὰ προειρημένα, μὴ νοήσασι δὲ ἄπιστα.— (τοῖς οὖν τὰ προειρημένα ὑπὸ τοῦ θεοῦ νοήσασι μὲν πιστά, μὴ νοήσασι δὲ ἄπιστα MSS.) In the traditional text, the position of μέν is impossible. ὑπὸ τοῦ θεοῦ may perhaps be a remnant of a note to the effect that it is only by God's help that a man can think rightly.

LIBELLVS X

Contents

A. §§ 1 b–4 a. *The relation between God and the Good.*

The action of God's will is one with the action of the Good. That action differs from the action of the cosmic forces, in that it has to do with things not subject to change. § 1 b.

God wills the existence of all things; and things exist only by his will. The Good appertains to God alone, and not to the Kosmos; for God alone is the author of life. The Kosmos may indeed be said to produce life, but only in a secondary sense; for the Kosmos is subject to God's will. §§ 2–4 a.

B. §§ 4 b–6. *The relation between man and the Good.*

Can man attain to the vision of the Good? Yes; but not until after death. While a man is still in the body, he can catch only faint and intermittent glimpses of the Good. But when released from the body, he may behold the Good in its full splendour; and if he does, he will thereby be changed from a man into a god.

C. §§ 6–19 a. *How do souls become bad, and how do they become good?*

All individual souls come into being by separation from the world-soul. The individual soul is incarnated on earth, first in an

animal body of the lowest grade, and then in animal bodies of
higher and higher grade, until it enters a human body. At that
stage, it may begin to be divine ; and if it does, that will be its last
earthly incarnation ; on its release from the human body, it will be
changed into a daemon, and subsequently into an astral god. But
if the soul, when it has entered a human body, continues to be bad,
it is reincarnated in the bodies of beasts. §§ 7–8 a.

The badness of a soul consists of lack of *gnosis* (i. e. knowledge
of God, or of the Good). A soul which has not *gnosis* is ruled by
the body, and is tossed about by the bodily passions. But the soul
which has got *gnosis* is good. *Gnosis* is not to be got by talk; nor
is it to be got by sense-perception. The senses operate by means of
the body; but *gnosis* has nothing to do with the body; its organ is
the mind, and mind is incorporeal. §§ 8 b–10 a.

Is the Kosmos good or bad? The Kosmos is immortal, and
therefore is not bad ; but it is material, and therefore is not good.
It is everlasting; but its existence is a perpetual becoming; and
becoming is movement. The Kosmos then is in ceaseless movement; and its movement is effected by something which is itself
incorporeal and motionless (i. e. by soul). The soul of the Kosmos
is incorporated in its body in the following way. The Kosmos
resembles a human head ; and its outermost sphere corresponds to
the cerebral membrane of the human head, that membrane which is
the seat of conscious life. Life or soul then pervades the whole
Kosmos, but is present in the highest degree in the outermost
sphere. The stars and planets, being closely connected with the
outermost sphere, have in them more soul than body, and are
consequently immortal; sublunar things, being remote from the
outermost sphere, have in them more body than soul, and are
consequently mortal. §§ 10 b, 11.

Man, *qua* mortal, is not merely 'not-good', but positively bad.
Like the Kosmos, he consists of a body with a soul in it; his soul
has for its vehicle the vital spirit; and the vital spirit, which is
intermingled with the blood, moves the body. When death takes
place, the soul quits the body; the vital spirit also then quits the
body, and the blood coagulates in the veins. §§ 12, 13.

The Kosmos is son of God; man is son of the Kosmos, and
grandson of God. God wills that man should know him ; and it is
by knowledge of God (*gnosis*) that a soul becomes good. §§ 14 b,
15 a.

The human soul is originally good, but necessarily becomes bad when incarnated. The soul of a young child is still good; for it is hardly yet separated from the world-soul. But as the body grows, it draws the soul down into its own gross substance, and makes it forget the Good; and thus the soul becomes bad. § 15 b.

When death takes place, not only does the soul separate from the vital spirit, but the mind also separates from the soul. The mind takes to itself a body of fire, and ranges through all space; and the soul, abandoned by the mind, suffers punishment according to its deserts. If a soul is pious, (i. e. if in this life it has attained to *gnosis*,) it becomes mind and nothing else; and in that case, it changes into a daemon when it quits the body. But the impious soul, after death, remains mere soul (as opposed to mind); it seeks another body into which it may enter, and thus suffers self-inflicted punishment. §§ 16–19 a.

D. §§ 22 b–25.   *The relations between men and beings of other grades.*

The Kosmos[1] is subject to God; man is subject to the Kosmos; and the lower animals are subject to man. God works on the Kosmos by the direct action of his will; the Kosmos works on man by its physical forces; and man works on what is subject to him by his arts and crafts. Thus all things are dependent on God, and are administered by mind, which is in both gods and men, and joins gods and men together. Not indeed all men; for some men have no mind in them; and such men are like the beasts. But the man whose soul is filled with mind (or in other words, the man who has got *gnosis*) is comparable, not to the beasts, but to the gods in heaven; indeed, we may even say that he is greater than a god in heaven. The Kosmos is an agent through whom God works; but not the Kosmos only; man also is God's agent. But it is God that governs all.

(A passage in which the reincarnation of human souls in bestial bodies is denied (§§ 19 b–22 a), and a short passage in which τὸ ἕν is spoken of (§ 14 a), have been added at a later date.)

The connexions of Libellus X with other Hermetica.   Among the

---

[1] 'The Kosmos' seems here to mean the astral gods regarded collectively. The Kosmos is a God composed of numerous individual gods, who are his 'members'. Compare the relation between the Demiurgus and his several δυνάμεις (identified with the several temple-gods), as described in *Abammonis resp.* 10. 6 (*Testim.*).

extant *Hermetica*, that with which *Corp*. X is most closely connected
is *Corp*. VI. Compare the following:—

Corp. VI.	*Corp*. X.

1 b. (τὸ ἀγαθὸν) οὐδενὶ ἄλλῳ
πρόσεστιν εἰ μὴ μόνῳ τῷ θεῷ.

2. τούτῳ ⟨δὲ πρόσεστι⟩ τὸ ἀγαθόν,
⟨τοιοῦτο ὂν⟩ ὃ μηδεν⟨ὶ⟩ πρόσεστι τῶν
ἄλλων.

1 a. τὸ ἀγαθὸν . . . ἐν οὐδενί
ἐστιν εἰ μὴ ἐν μόνῳ τῷ θεῷ.

3. (τὸ ἀγαθὸν) οὐ δυνατὸν ἐγγενέσθαι ἄλλῳ τινὶ ἢ μόνῳ ἐκείνῳ.

2 a. ἐν αὐτῷ τῷ ζώῳ τῷ πάντων
μείζονι (*sc*. τῷ κόσμῳ).

12. ὁ μὲν κόσμος πρῶτον ⟨⟨τῶν
ἄλλων ζῴων⟩⟩.

2 b. ὥσπερ δὲ μετουσία πάντων
ἐστὶν ἐν τῇ ὕλῃ ⟨δια⟩δεδομένη, οὕτω
καὶ τοῦ ἀγαθοῦ. τοῦτον τὸν τρόπον
ἀγαθὸς ὁ κόσμος, καθὰ καὶ αὐτὸς
πάντα ποιεῖ, ⟨ὡς⟩ ἐν τῷ μέρει τοῦ
ποιεῖν ἀγαθὸς εἶναι. ἐν δὲ τοῖς
ἄλλοις πᾶσιν οὐκ ἀγαθός· καὶ γὰρ
παθητός ἐστι.

2. ὁ μὲν γὰρ κόσμος [ ] τῶν
κατὰ μετουσίαν ⟨ἀγαθῶν⟩ καὶ αὐτὸς
πατήρ.

3. τὸ γὰρ ἀγαθόν ἐστι τὸ ποιητικόν.

10 b. οὐκέ[σ]τι δὲ ἀγαθὸς (ὁ
κόσμος)· ὑλικὸς γάρ, καὶ [εὐ]πα-
θητός.

5. ἐκεῖνο γὰρ τὸ κάλλος ἀσύγ-
κριτον, καὶ ἐκεῖνο τὸ ἀγαθὸν ἀμίμητον (*fortasse* ἀλάλητον).

5. τὸ κάλλος τοῦ ἀγαθοῦ, ἐκεῖνο[υ]
τὸ ἄφθαρτον, τὸ ⌜ἄληπτον⌝ (*lege*
ἀλάλητον).

These verbal similarities make it very probable that the writer of one
of the two documents had the other before him ; and *Corp*. X, being
the longer and more elaborate of the two, is presumably the later.
But a still stronger proof may be seen in the relation of the argument
of *Corp*. X as a whole to that of *Corp*. VI. The writer of *Corp*. VI
asserts with emphasis that man is wholly bad, and there is no good
in him ; and if he admits for a moment that there is a way which
leads to τὸ καλόν, viz. the way of 'piety combined with *gnosis*'
(VI. 5 *fin*.), he seems to forget this admission in the bitter
denunciation of man with which he concludes. Now *Corp*. X appears
to have been written with the express purpose of giving a different
answer to the question whether there is any good in man The
author of *Corp*. X accepts in part the statements of *Corp*. VI
concerning the relations of God, Kosmos, and Man respectively to
the Good ; but he counteracts the gloomy inferences which the
writer of *Corp*. VI drew from those statements, by directing attention
to the life beyond the grave (of which not a word was said in

Corp. VI), and pointing out that man is free to hope that after death he will enjoy the beatific vision, and attain to the 'crowning glory' of a life among the celestial gods. As regards the present life, he admits that the soul is necessarily made bad by its incarnation ; but he gives a different aspect to the matter, by insisting on the point (just hinted at in *Corp.* VI) that through *gnosis* the soul which has thus been made bad may become good again ; and he concludes with a glorification of 'the man who is a man indeed', which seems deliberately intended to contrast with the gloomy picture drawn in the concluding paragraph of *Corp.* VI. I think then that we may reasonably assume that the author of *Corp.* X had *Corp.* VI before him, and wrote with the object of supplying a corrective to the pessimism of that document.

Some verbal resemblances to *Corp.* II also are to be noted in *Corp.* X. Compare the following :—

Corp. II.	*Corp.* X.
4 a *sq.* σώματι δὲ ἐναντία φύσις τὸ ἀσώματον. . . . τὸ δὲ ἀσώματον ἢ θεῖόν ἐστιν (*sc.* νοῦς), ἢ ὁ θεός.	10 a. ὁ δὲ νοῦς τῷ σώματι ⟨ἐναντίος⟩.
8 a. πᾶσα οὖν κίνησις . . . ὑπὸ στάσεως κινεῖται.	11. ἡ δὲ νοητὴ στάσις κινεῖ τὴν ὑλικὴν κίνησιν.
16 (as emended): μία γὰρ ἡ φύσις τοῦ θεοῦ τῇ τοῦ ἀγαθοῦ. . . . ὁ γὰρ θεὸς ἀγαθός ἐστιν, ὡς ἅπαντα διδοὺς καὶ μηδὲν λαμβάνων.	1 b. ὁ μὲν οὖν θεὸς . . . καὶ τὸ ἀγαθὸν (*fortasse* τῷ ἀγαθῷ) τὴν αὐτὴν ἔχει φύσιν. 3. τῷ μηδὲν μὲν λαμβάνοντι, πάντα δὲ θέλοντι· εἶναι. οὐ γὰρ ἐρῶ . . . ποιοῦντι.

In the case of the statement about the φύσις of God (II. 16 = X. 1 b), if there was direct borrowing on either side, it must have been the writer of *Corp.* X who borrowed ; for he goes on to object to this use of the word φύσις. It seems probable therefore that the writer of *Corp.* X had before him *Corp.* II as well as *Corp.* VI. But if so, he merely took a few phrases from it ; he makes no attempt to deal with its argument as a whole, and he does not refer to the doctrine of the τόπος-νοῦς, which is peculiar to *Corp.* II. The phrase ὁ θεὸς καὶ πατήρ, used as a name of God in *Corp.* X, may possibly have been suggested by *Corp.* II. 17 a ; if so, that section must have been already appended to *Corp.* II at the time when *Corp.* X was written. The words καὶ τὸ ἀγαθόν, which occur repeatedly after ὁ θεὸς καὶ πατήρ in the traditional text of *Corp*. X, but were probably inserted by a later hand, may have been suggested to the interpolator by *Corp*. II. 16, ὁ οὖν θεὸς τὸ ἀγαθόν, καὶ τὸ ἀγαθὸν ὁ θεός.

The passage *Corp*. X. 22 b–25 has much in common with *Ascl. Lat.* I ; but there is no proof that the author of either of these two documents made use of the other ; and it is quite as likely that both were influenced by some common authority.

Sources. The doctrine of *Corp*. X is Platonic, with an ingredient of Stoicism. The influence of particular passages in Plato's dialogues may be recognized in § 19 a *fin.*, γήϊνον σῶμα ζητοῦσα εἰς ὃ εἰσέλθῃ (Pl. *Phaedo* 81 B ff.) ;—in the comparison of the Kosmos to a human head, § 11 (Pl. *Tim.* 44 D ff.) ;—and in the identification of the νοῦς with the ἀγαθὸς δαίμων, § 23 (Pl. *Tim.* 90 A). The doctrine of §§ 16–18, that the νοῦς, when it quits the earthy body, clothes itself in a body of fire, is characteristic of a certain sect of Platonists mentioned by Iamblichus, and may perhaps have been derived by them from Heraclides Ponticus. The statement in § 7 *fin.*, that an abode in the material heavens is the highest to which the soul can attain, may be attributed to the same sect of Platonists ; but it is also possible that it was suggested by Posidonius.

Stoic influence is to be seen in the doctrine taught n § 7, and implied in § 15 b, that all individual souls are ἀπὸ μιᾶς ψυχῆς τῆς τοῦ παντὸς ὥσπερ ἀπονενεμημέναι, which the writer tells us that he found in the Hermetic Γενικοὶ λόγοι ;—in the glorification of man in § 25, including the saying of Heraclitus (ἀθάνατοι θνητοί κ.τ.λ.) as there interpreted ;—and in the use of the terms ποιότητες and ποσότητες, ποιά and ποσά, in §§ 3 and 10 b (derived from Aristotle, but probably through Stoic intermediaries).

The physiological doctrine of § 11 concerning the function of the *meninx* was originated by Erasistratus. In his view of the function of the arteries (§ 13), the writer follows Herophilus. His conception of the ζωτικὸν πνεῦμα may have been derived from the same medical sources as the rest of his physiology.

The doctrine of the composition of opposites (§ 10 a) may be traced back to Heraclitus. The doctrine, mentioned in § 13, that 'the soul is the blood', was commonly ascribed to Empedocles. A quotation from Theognis occurs in § 24 a.

The contents of *Corp*. X are wholly derived from Greek sources. The document contains nothing Egyptian, except the names of the euhemerized gods Hermes, Tat, Asklepios, Uranos, and Kronos; and nothing Jewish, with the possible exception of the use of the word δόξα in § 7 *fin*. There is not the slightest trace of Christian influence.

Date. The blending of Stoic notions with Platonism in *Corp*. X makes it certain that this document cannot have been written before 100 B.C.; but beyond this, there is little to indicate any particular period, except so far as inferences can be drawn from the relations of *Corp*. X to other *Hermetica*. At the time when *Corp*. X was written, 'the Γενικοὶ λόγοι addressed to Tat' were already known as a collection of documents distinguished by that title from other Hermetic dialogues; *Corp*. X must therefore be later than the Γενικοὶ λόγοι, which were probably the earliest of the Greek *Hermetica*. But we know from *Corp*. X. 7 (ἀπὸ μιᾶς ψυχῆς κ.τ.λ.) that some of the Γενικοὶ λόγοι themselves contained an infusion of Stoic doctrine, and therefore cannot have been written before the first century B.C.; whence it follows that *Corp*. X can hardly have been written before the Christian era. It is most likely, however, that it is much later. Its author seems to have known *Corp*. VI, and probably *Corp*. II also. I have conjecturally assigned *Corp*. VI to the second or third century A.D., and *Corp*. II to the second century; *Corp*. X may therefore be provisionally placed in the second or third century A.D., and perhaps rather in the third century than the second.

The inserted passage 19 b–22 a was probably written at some date not far from A.D. 300; and the short passage about τὸ ἕν (§ 14 a) may be put with it.

Title. The title Κλείς may have been given to *Corp*. X by its author, or may have been applied to it at some later time. A key is the instrument by which a door is unlocked; and in this connexion, the door must be either that of a treasure-house, or that of a sanctuary. If the former, the title must be meant to imply that this document is a thing which gives access to the treasury in which *gnosis* is laid up. Cf. *Luke* 11. 52: ἤρατε τὴν κλεῖδα τῆς γνώσεως κ.τ.λ. But more probably, the meaning is that this document gives access to a sanctuary, in which holy secrets are revealed to those who are permitted to enter. Compare the use of κλειδοῦχος as applied to a priest or priestess. As an instance of the association of the word with mystery-cults, cf. Soph. *O. C.* 1051: ὧν καὶ χρυσέα κλῂς ἐπὶ γλώσσᾳ βέβακε προσπόλων Εὐμολπιδᾶν· 'on whose lips the ministrant Eumolpidae have laid the precious seal of silence' (Jebb). In that passage, however, κλείς means a thing used to *close* a door; as the title of *Corp.* X, it signifies a thing by means of which a door may be *opened*. The word occurs as the title of a 'Book of Moses' in which secrets of magic are revealed; Dieterich *Abraxas*, pp. 171–175 : ἐν τῇ Κλειδὶ τῇ Μωυσέους κ.τ.λ. Melito bishop of Sardis (who died before A. D. 195) wrote a book entitled ἡ Κλείς (Euseb. *Hist. eccl.* 4. 26. 2).

§ 1 a. Τὸν χθὲς λόγον . . . ἐπιτομή. The writer of § 1 a must have intended *Corp.* X to be read next after a discourse addressed to Asclepius, which he describes as 'the discourse delivered yesterday'. But did these introductory words form part of the original document, or were they inserted by the compiler of the *Corpus*? In the latter case, they must have been intended to refer to the document which immediately precedes *Corp.* X in the *Corpus*, i. e. to *Corp.* IX, which is addressed to Asclepius. There is no connexion between the contents of *Corp.* X and those of *Corp.* IX, and the juxtaposition of these two documents in the *Corpus* must be due to mere accident or caprice; but the compiler of the *Corpus* may have inserted these words with the object of linking them together ; and if so, the phrase τὸν χθὲς λόγον in *Corp.* X *init.* may have been suggested to him by *Corp.* IX *init.*, where the Τέλειος λόγος (i. e. *Ascl. Lat.*) is referred to as a discourse 'delivered yesterday'.

On the other hand, we have seen reason to think that *Corp.* X was written with the object of supplementing and correcting the teaching of *Corp.* VI, which is addressed to Asclepius ; and if the introductory words of *Corp.* X formed part of the original text, the preceding discourse to which they refer may perhaps be *Corp.* VI.

The writer of § 1 a assumes that both Asclepius and Tat are present, though in the rest of the dialogue Tat alone is addressed by Hermes. Compare *Ascl. Lat. init.*, where Tat and Ammon are present as well as Asclepius.

τῶν ⟨γ⟩ενικῶν λόγων. The statement that *Corp.* X is 'an abridgement of the Γενικοὶ λόγοι' is hardly to be taken in the strict and literal sense of the words ; but in § 7 the writer refers to the authority of the Γενικοὶ λόγοι ; and it may be presumed that he was more or less influenced by the same authority in other parts of his treatise also. Compare *Corp.* XIV. 1.

§ 1 b. ὁ μὲν οὖν θεὸς καὶ πατήρ, καὶ τὸ ἀγαθόν, ὦ Τάτ, τὴν αὐτὴν ἔχει φύσιν, μᾶλλον δὲ [καὶ] ἐνέργειαν. There can be little doubt that the writer is here thinking of *Corp.* II. 16, μία γὰρ ἡ φύσις τοῦ θεοῦ ⟨τῇ⟩ τοῦ ἀγαθοῦ ⟨τὸ ἀγαθόν MSS.⟩. But he rejects the word φύσις, as inapplicable to God, and substitutes ἐνέργεια. For the distinction between φύσις and ἐνέργεια, cf. § 22b : τοῦ μὲν θεοῦ καθάπερ ἀκτῖνες αἱ ἐνέργειαι, τοῦ δὲ κόσμου αἱ φύσεις.

God is here called ὁ θεὸς καὶ πατήρ. In *Corp.* II, πατήρ, as a name of God, occurs only in § 17a, which was probably added to the dialogue by a later hand. But in *Corp.* X, καὶ πατήρ must have occurred in the original text, in § 2 at least, if not in other places ; for it is presupposed there in the statement that the Kosmos is καὶ αὐτὸς πατήρ.

τὰ θεῖα [τε], ⟨⟨ὧν⟩⟩ καὶ ⟨τὰ⟩ ἀνθρώπεια [[ὧν]] αὐτὸς βούλεται εἶναι. The restoration of the sentence is doubtful ; but a satisfactory meaning can be obtained by the corrections which I have proposed. If a man is such as God wills or means him to be, he is exalted above τὰ μεταβλητὰ καὶ κινητά, and belongs to the world of eternal and changeless existence ; he is οὐσιώδης, and in that sense θεῖος In § 24 b we are told that ὁ ὄντως ἄνθρωπος (' he who is a man indeed ') ζῷόν ἐστι θεῖον.

ἀλλαχοῦ δὲ ⟨περὶ⟩ ἐνεργειῶν (ἐνέργειαν MSS.) [[ ]] ἐδιδάξαμεν. In Herm. *ap.* Stob. *Exc.* III, ἐνέργειαι are discussed at some length. In that document, the term is used to denote the cosmic forces put in action by the heavenly bodies. But in *Corp.* X, the word is applied only to the direct operation of God's will, as opposed to the operation of the cosmic forces. As τὸ ἀγαθόν is the τέλος towards which God's will is directed, the operation of God's will may be described either as ἡ ἐνέργεια τοῦ θεοῦ or ἡ ἐνέργεια τοῦ ἀγαθοῦ ; and so it may be said that ' God and the Good have the same ἐνέργεια '. God is the efficient cause of all ; τὸ ἀγαθόν is the final cause of all.

ἐνέργεια means ' a force in action ', and especially ' a divine force acting on earthly things '. (Cf. Herm. *ap.* Stob. *Exc.* XI. 2. (40) : αἱ ἐνέργειαι οὐκ εἰσὶν ἀνωφερεῖς, ἀλλὰ κατωφερεῖς.) Perhaps it was first applied in this sense to the influences of the star-gods, and thence transferred by Platonists to the action of the supracosmic God upon the Kosmos and the things contained in it. As to the use of the word in the New Testament, see note on ἐνεργεῖν and its cognates in Armitage Robinson, *St. Paul's Epistle to the Ephesians*, p. 241 f.

§ 2. ἡ οὐσία αὐτοῦ τὸ θέλειν πάντα εἶναι. Cf. *Corp.* XI ii. 13 b : νοήσεις τὸ τοῦ θεοῦ ἔργον ἐν ὄν, ἵνα πάντα γένηται τὰ γινόμενα κ.τ.λ.

Corp. IX. 9 : τοῦτο ἔστιν ἡ αἴσθησις καὶ νόησις τοῦ θεοῦ, τὸ τὰ πάντα ἀεὶ κινεῖν.

The οὐσία of God is spoken of in *Corp.* VI. 4 b : ἡ οὐσία τοῦ θεοῦ, εἴ γε οὐσίαν ἔχει, τὸ καλόν ἐστι. Cf. *Corp.* XII i. 1.

τί γάρ ἐστι⟨ν ὁ⟩ θεὸς καὶ πατὴρ [καὶ τὸ ἀγαθὸν] ἢ τὸ τῶν πάντων εἶναι οὐκέτι ὄντων ; Cf. *Ascl. Lat.* I. 2 a : 'dixi omnia unum esse et unum omnia, utpote quae in creatore fuerint omnia ante quam creasset omnia.' The παράδειγμα of the Kosmos, and of all things that come into being within it in course of time,—the 'builder's plan', as Philo calls it,—exists eternally in the mind of God. Before these things have come into being, God's will has already determined that they shall be ; and so they may be said to exist already in God, for whom there is no future, but all is one eternal present.

The writer of *Corp.* VI says that τὸ ἀγαθόν 'is in' God, or 'belongs to' God ; the writer of *Corp.* II says that τὸ ἀγαθόν *is* God. The writer of *Corp.* X, who probably had both *Corp.* VI and *Corp.* II before him, certainly adopted the first of these two forms of expression ; but owing to the uncertainties of the text, we can hardly make sure whether he employed the second also or not. If we read ὁ θεὸς καὶ πατήρ, ⟨ὁ ?⟩ καὶ τὸ ἀγαθόν, these words imply that God *is* the Good. But on the other hand, if we are right in reading ὁ μηδενὶ πρόσεστι τῶν ἄλλων below, the writer there employs the language of *Corp.* VI. 1 b, ⟨τὸ ἀγαθὸν⟩ οὐδενὶ ἄλλῳ πρόσεστιν εἰ μὴ μόνῳ τῷ θεῷ. Again, in *Corp.* X. 3, we are told that ⟨τὸ ἀγαθὸν⟩ οὐ δυνατὸν ἐγγενέσθαι ἄλλῳ τινὶ ἢ μόνῳ ⟨τῷ θεῷ⟩ ; and this agrees with *Corp.* VI *init.*, τὸ ἀγαθὸν ἐν οὐδενί ἐστιν εἰ μὴ ἐν μόνῳ τῷ θεῷ, but differs from *Corp.* II. Moreover, the writer of *Corp.* X speaks of the 'will' of God, and thereby implies the existence of τὸ ἀγαθόν as the object towards which God's will is directed, and as a thing distinct from him who wills (cf. *Corp.* VI. 4 b, ὁ θεὸς τοῦ καλοῦ καὶ τοῦ ἀγαθοῦ ἐρᾷ·) ; and this is hardly consistent with the statement that God *is* τὸ ἀγαθόν. There is therefore reason to think that the words καὶ τὸ ἀγαθόν, in which God and the Good are absolutely identified, have been inserted by a later hand, both here and elsewhere in *Corp.* X. The insertion of these words may have been suggested by a misunderstanding of the sentence ὁ θεὸς . . . καὶ τὸ ἀγαθὸν (originally τῷ ἀγαθῷ ?) τὴν αὐτὴν ἔχει φύσιν in § 1 b.

ὕπαρξις αὕτη τῶν ὄντων. αὕτη refers to ἡ τοῦ θεοῦ θέλησις. All things owe their existence to God's will ; it is only as willed by God that they exist.

ὃ μηδενὶ (ᾧ μηδὲν MSS.) πρόσεστι τῶν ἄλλων. The Good 'belongs
to' or 'is present to' God, and God alone; that is to say, the Good
which God wills is realized in his own eternal being, but is never
realized in the world of time, where, in place of the eternal οὐσία or
στάσις of God, there is only γένεσις or κίνησις, i. e. a process directed
towards the Good, but a process without end and without advance.

ὁ μὲν γὰρ κόσμος [   ] τῶν κατὰ μετουσίαν ⟨ἀγαθῶν⟩ καὶ αὐτὸς πατήρ.
Cf. *Corp.* VI. 2 b, ὥσπερ δὲ μετουσία κ.τ.λ.   *Ascl. Lat.* III. 27 a:
'sicuti enim deus ... dispensator ... est bonorum, id est sensus,
animae, et vitae, sic et mundus tributor est et praestitor omnium
quae mortalibus videntur bona.' The 'seeming goods' of *Ascl. Lat.*
III. (i. e. the material things or processes by means of which life ir.
the body is maintained) correspond to τὰ κατὰ μετουσίαν ἀγαθά of
Corp. X (of which the σπορὰ καὶ τροφή mentioned below are
instances); and the 'true goods' of *Ascl. Lat.* III (among which
vita is included) correspond to τὸ ἀγαθόν (coupled with τὸ ζῆν) in
this sentence of *Corp.* X.

[καὶ ὁ ἥλιος]. This must be one of the 'solar interpolations'.
Cf. [διὰ τοῦ ἡλίου], § 3; and see note on *Ascl. Lat.* III. 19 b, 'solis
οὐσιάρχης lumen est'.

οὐκέτι δὲ τοῦ ἀγαθοῦ τοῖς ζῴοις ἴσως αἴτιός ἐστιν· οὐδὲ ⟨γὰρ⟩ τοῦ ζῆν.
τὸ ἀγαθόν cannot here mean 'the Good' which was dealt with above
(i. e. the αὐτοαγαθόν, which 'belongs to none save God'); for 'the
good' here spoken of is, or includes, τὸ ζῆν, which exists in all living
creatures. The writer apparently regards life as a true good, and
distinguishes it, as such, from 'the things which are good merely by
participation' (τὰ κατὰ μετουσίαν ἀγαθά), but at the same time
distinguishes it also from the absolute Good, which does not enter
into the Kosmos.

εἰ δέ [   ], πάντως μέντοι ἀναγκαζόμενος. The Kosmos may in a
sense be said to produce life in the creatures contained in it; for
births are effected by the operation of the cosmic forces, and,
according to the view which prevails among the Hermetists, more
especially by the influence of the heavenly bodies. But life is a gift
of God, and the Kosmos is merely God's agent in its bestowal. It
is not clear, however, why the Kosmos is not held to be equally
subject to God's compelling will in the production of τὰ κατὰ
μετουσίαν ἀγαθά (e. g. the σπορὰ καὶ τροφή mentioned in § 3 *init.*).
Perhaps the author might have said that ψυχή is immortal, and, as
such, is not affected by the operation of the cosmic forces, but is

more directly connected with God himself; and that it is only the temporary incarnation of the immortal ψυχή (or of a separated portion of the cosmic ψυχή) in this or that particular body that can be ascribed to the relatively independent action of the Kosmos.

§ 3. ⟨παρὰ τοῦ θεοῦ⟩ τὴν [ὄρεξιν] ⟨χορηγίαν⟩ λαβὼν τοῦ ἀγαθοῦ. It might be said that the Kosmos, in its work of generating and maintaining living organisms, is impelled by 'a *desire* for the Good'; i. e. that the Kosmos, in the production of each individual creature, is seeking to produce something which shall 'partake of the Good', or in other words, something which shall be an εἰκών of the divine παράδειγμα. That statement would correspond to Aristotle's asser- tion that φύσις, in all its operations, 'aims at the good'; with the difference, however, that the Hermetist's Kosmos, unlike Aristotle's φύσις, is a conscious agent. But as there is nothing in the context to suggest a mention of this 'desire' of the Kosmos, it seems more likely that the author wrote, not ὄρεξιν, but some such word as χορηγίαν.

The word λαβών must have been accompanied by some phrase indicating the source from which the Kosmos gets its supply of 'good', or life-producing energy; and that source can only be God. I have therefore inserted παρὰ τοῦ θεοῦ.

τὸ γὰρ ἀγαθόν ἐστι τὸ ποιητικόν. The Good is 'the creative principle', in the sense that it is the τέλος or οὗ ἕνεκα of all ποίησις. But the Hermetist's thought seems to have been influenced by the fact that the word ἀγαθός, in addition to the sense 'desirable', may also bear the sense 'beneficent' or 'bountiful', and may in the latter sense be applied to the agent by whom things are made. In the following sentence (τῷ μηδὲν μὲν λαμβάνοντι κ.τ.λ.) it is clear that the writer regarded τὸ ἀγαθόν as connoting 'beneficence' or 'generosity'. Cf. Pl. *Tim.* 29 E: ἀγαθὸς ἦν (ὁ ποιητὴς καὶ πατὴρ τοῦδε τοῦ παντός), ἀγαθῷ δὲ οὐδεὶς περὶ οὐδενὸς οὐδέποτε ἐγγίγνεται φθόνος. . . . βουληθεὶς γὰρ ὁ θεὸς ἀγαθὰ μὲν πάντα, φλαῦρον δὲ μηδὲν εἶναι κ.τ.λ. Here Plato plays on the two senses of the word ἀγαθός. The Maker is 'bountiful' or 'beneficent'; the things which he makes are 'desirable', and are copies of τὸ ἀγαθόν, the supreme object of all desire. Those Platonists who completely identified God with τὸ ἀγαθόν, (among whom the writer of *Corp.* X is probably not to be reckoned,) meant in part that God is the supreme object of desire, but in part also that God is the source of infinite bounties. Cf. *Corp.* VI. 1 a as emended: πᾶν γὰρ τὸ ⟨ὁτιοῦν?⟩ χορηγοῦν ἀγαθὸν λέγεται. *Ib.* 2 b: ὡς ἐν τῷ μέρει τοῦ ποιεῖν ἀγαθὸς εἶναι.

τῷ μηδὲν μὲν λαμβάνοντι, πάντα δὲ θέλοντι εἶναι. Cf. *Corp.* II. 16 :
ὁ οὖν θεὸς πάντα δίδωσι καὶ οὐδὲν λαμβάνει.

οὐ γὰρ ἐρῶ . . . ποιοῦντι. The word ποιεῖν was applied to the action
of the Demiurgus in Pl. *Tim.*, and was habitually thus used by
Platonists ; but the writer of *Corp.* X gives reasons for rejecting it.
His first reason is that the action of a ποιητής is intermittent. When
the 'maker' has once finished making a thing, he has, as maker,
nothing more to do with it ; he begins to act again only when he
proceeds to make another thing. It is therefore better to say, not
that God is the 'maker' of all things, but that God 'wills the
existence of' all things ; for this phrase implies that God's will is
operative, not merely in bringing each thing into existence once for
all, but in maintaining each thing in existence as long as it continues
to exist. His second reason is that a 'maker' makes only 'quantities' and 'qualities' (but not 'substances') ; that is to say, he deals
with some already existing material, and merely adds to it or takes
from it, or in some way alters it, but does not bring it into being.
The writer holds that 'substances', as well as 'quantities' and
'qualities', owe their existence to God's will. This does not
necessarily imply that God has at some past time created the
universe out of nothing ; (see *Corp.* II. 13, where it is denied that
anything can come into existence out of nothing ;) for it is possible
to hold that the world has existed without beginning, but that it is
God's eternal will that has maintained it in its everlasting existence.
And this was probably the view held by the writer of *Corp.* X ; for
in § 10 b he speaks of the Kosmos as ἀεὶ ὤν.

ἐλλιπής ἐστι πολλῷ χρόνῳ, ⌈ἐν ᾧ⌉ ὅτε μὲν ποιεῖ, ὅτε δὲ οὐ ποιεῖ. This
may be a conflation of two alternative readings, viz. ἐ. ἐ. π. χ., ἐν ᾧ
οὐκέτι ποιεῖ, and ἐ. ἐ. π. χ., ὅς γε ὅτε μὲν ποιεῖ, ὅτε δὲ οὐ ποιεῖ.

ποτὲ μὲν γὰρ ποσὰ καὶ ποιὰ ⟨ποιεῖ⟩, ὅτε δὲ τὰ ἐναντία. The 'maker'
makes something large which was small before, or makes something
hard which was soft before, but does not, strictly speaking, 'make'
the thing itself, i. e. the ὑποκείμενον, or the οὐσία in the Stoic sense.
According to Aristotle (*Cat.* 5, 3 b 32, and 6, 5 b 11,) the term
ἐναντία is not applicable to quantities ; there is no contrary to 'three
feet long'. He admits that 'many' and 'few', or 'large' and
'small', may be called ἐναντία ; but he says that these terms belong
to the category of πρός τι, and not to that of ποσόν. The Stoics did
not recognize ποσόν as a distinct category.

§ 4 a. καὶ γὰρ ταῦτα (τοῦτο MSS.) θέλει εἶναι, καὶ ⟨⟨οὕτως ἄρα⟩⟩ ἔστι καὶ αὐτά (αὐτό MSS.). God wills things to be, and the things consequently exist. But they do not exist absolutely; for they are dependent on God. The only thing (besides God) that 'exists in the highest degree' (μάλιστα ἔστιν) is the Good, which is correlative to God, and is the final cause of the existence of all else (τὰ ἄλλα πάντα διὰ τοῦτο ἔστιν).

§ 4 b. ⟨. . .⟩ ἴδιον γὰρ τοῦ ἀγαθοῦ τὸ γνωρίζεσθαι ⟨θέλειν?⟩ [[ ]] ⟨⟨τῷ δυναμένῳ ἰδεῖν⟩⟩. Down to this point, the writer has been speaking of the relation between God and the Good. He now proceeds to speak of the relation between man and the Good; and in doing so, he begins by discussing the question whether, and under what conditions, it is possible for man to attain to the intuition of the Good, and to the union with God which is implied in that intuition (§§ 4 b–6). But the transition is abrupt, and it is probable that a connecting passage has been lost at the beginning of § 4 b.

The words τῷ δυναμένῳ ἰδεῖν are pointless where they stand in the MSS. Transposed to this place, they make good sense, and serve to lead on to the discussion of the θέα τοῦ ἀγαθοῦ.

Ἐπλήρωσας ἡμᾶς . . . τῆς . . . καλλίστης θέας. This passage (§§ 4 b–6) is discussed by Reitzenstein, Die hellen. Mysterienrel., pp. 115 ff.

In his joy at the new thought which has been awakened in him by his father's words, Tat imagines for a moment that he already 'sees the Good'. But Hermes undeceives him. In reality, he has caught but a faint glimpse of the beatific vision; and indeed, no more than a faint glimpse of it is possible for men, until they are released from the body by death.

ὀλίγου δεῖν ἐπεσκιάσθη (ἐσεβάσθη MSS.) μου ὁ τοῦ νοῦ ὀφθαλμὸς ὑπὸ τῆς τοιαύτης ⌈θέας⌉. If we retain ἐσεβάσθη, we must translate 'my mental eye was almost stricken with awe'. But why 'almost'? The writer must have meant to make Tat say 'my mental eye was dazzled, and almost blinded'; and this might be expressed by ἐπεσκιάσθη. (Cf. Philo, De opif. mundi 1. 6: τὰ . . . ὑπερβάλλοντα κάλλη, καὶ ταῖς μαρμαρυγαῖς τὰς τῶν ἐντυγχανόντων ψυχὰς ἐπισκιάζοντα.) Hermes proceeds to explain that the vision of the Good never produces the harmful effect which Tat thought it had 'almost' produced in his own case. It is true that the man who has once seen the Good 'can see nothing else thereafter' (§ 6 init.); but that does not mean that his mental eye is blinded; it is only the things of earth that he can no longer see. In Pl. Rep. VII init., it is said that those who come forth from the cave are at first dazzled by the light of day, i. e. by the splendour of the Good. Cf. Philo, *De opif. mundi* 23. 71, Cohn I, p. 24 : πρὸς τὴν ἄκραν ἁψῖδα παραπεμφθεὶς τῶν νοητῶν, ἐπ' αὐτὸν ἰέναι δοκεῖ τὸν μέγαν βασιλέα· γλιχομένου δ' ἰδεῖν, ἀθρόου φωτὸς ἄκρατοι καὶ ἀμιγεῖς αὐγαὶ χειμάρρου τρόπον ἐκχέονται, ὡς ταῖς μαρμαρυγαῖς τὸ τῆς διανοίας ὄμμα σκοτοδινιᾶν· It is not likely that the author ended two successive clauses with the same word θέας. The second θέας has probably been substituted by error for some other word, e. g. μαρμαρυγῆς.

πάσης ἀθανασίας ἀνάπλεως. ἀθανασία here, as often in the *Hermetica*, means the state of the ἀθάνατοι, i. e. of the gods. In so far as a man sees the Good, he is a god ; and a god is secured against all harm.

§ 5. οἱ δυνάμενοι πλέον τι ἀρύσασθαι τῆς θέας κατακοιμίζονται πολλάκις δὴ (δὲ MSS.) ὑπὸ τοῦ σώματος. Even those who are able to 'draw somewhat larger draughts' of the vision than others, are often made torpid by the body ; their mental eyes are at such times closed, as in sleep, and their glimpses of the Good are therefore necessarily intermittent. 'Our birth is but a sleep and a forgetting ;' and even those who have been awakened from the sleep or *lethe* of bodily life must many a time fall asleep again, as long as they are in the body. For the metaphor of sleep, cf. Philo, *De somn.* 1. 26. 165, Wendland III, p. 240 : ψυχαὶ δ' ὅσαι θείων ἐρώτων ἐγεύσασθε, καθάπερ ἐκ βαθέος ὕπνου διαναστᾶσαι, καὶ τὴν ἀχλὺν ἀποσκεδάσασαι, πρὸς τὴν περίβλεπτον θέαν ἐπείχθητε. The same metaphor is employed in the words addressed to the recently deceased Plotinus in an oracle quoted by Porphyry, *Vita Plotini* 22, l. 23 ff. : [1] 'Even in your earthly life, πολλάκι σεῖο νόοιο βολὰς ... | ὀρθοπόρους ἀνὰ κύκλα καὶ ἄμβροτον οἶμον ἄειραν | ἀθάνατοι, θαμινὴν φαέων ἀκτῖνα πορόντες | ὅσσοισιν δέρκεσθαι ἀπὸ σκοτίης λυγαίης· | οὐδέ σε παμπήδην βλεφάρων ἔχε νήδυμος ὕπνος, | ἀλλ' ἄρ' ἀπὸ βλεφάρων σκεδάσας κηλῖδα βαρεῖαν, | ἀχλύος ἐν δίνῃσι φορεύμενος, ἔδρακες ὄσσοις | πολλά τε καὶ χαρίεντα, τά κεν ῥέα οὔτις ἴδοιτο | ἀνθρώπων, ὅσσοι σοφίης μαιήτορες ἔπλευν. | νῦν δ', ὅτε δὴ σκῆνος μὲν ἐλύσαο, σῆμα δ' ἔλειψας | ψυχῆς δαιμονίης, you live a blessed life as a daemon.' Plotinus was one of those who are able πλέον τι ἀρύσασθαι τῆς θέας.

⟨ἀπολυθέντες δὲ τοῦ σώματος⟩ εἰς τὴν καλλίστην ὄψιν ⟨ἐνέτυχον⟩, ὥσπερ (ὅπερ or ὅσπερ MSS.) Οὐρανὸς καὶ Κρόνος, οἱ ἡμέτεροι πρόγονοι, ἐντετυ-

---

[1] Porphyry says that these verses were the response given by Apollo to the question put to him by Amelius, 'Where has the soul of Plotinus gone ?' Perhaps Amelius not only asked the question, but composed the answer also.

χήκασιν. It is clearly necessary to insert ἀπολυθέντες δὲ τοῦ σώματος, or something to that effect. It is only when death has freed a man from the encumbrance of the body, that the vision will burst upon his sight in its unclouded splendour. Uranos and Kronos once lived as men on earth; (cf. *Ascl. Lat.* III. 37, where the gods Thoth-Hermes and Imhotep-Asclepius are similarly spoken of;) but they have died, and become gods; and as gods they have attained to the vision of the Good. The human teacher Hermes and his son (and all devout Hermetists also) may hope that after death they will be as Uranos and Kronos now are.

Uranos and Kronos are here said to be ancestors of the teacher Hermes. According to *Ascl. Lat.* III. 37, the teacher Hermes was a grandson of the god Thoth-Hermes; and the writer of *Corp.* X may have held the same view. In the Greek theogonies, the list of gods was usually headed by Uranos and his son Kronos; Zeus was a son of Kronos, and the Greek Hermes was a son of Zeus. But the Hermetist probably intended Uranos and Kronos for Greek renderings of the names of two Egyptian gods. The earth-god Seb or Qeb was commonly identified with the Greek Kronos; and if Kronos here means Seb, Uranos ought to mean Shu (Σῶς or Σῶσις), the father of Seb. In the Heliopolitan theogony, Shu and his consort Tafnut were generated by the Propator Tum, and stood as the first συζυγία in the Ennead; and Seb and his consort Nut were the offspring of Shu and Tafnut. Seb and Nut were called Kronos and Rhea by the Greeks; (see Plut. *Is. et Os.* 12;)[1] it would there-fore be natural to identify their parents, Shu and Tafnut, with the Greek Uranos and Gaia. Shu was the god of the atmosphere,[2] and was called 'uplifter of heaven' and 'lord of heaven'; so that Uranos might very well be regarded as his Greek equivalent.

Thoth (Hermes) had no generally recognized place in the genealogy of the Egyptian gods. He was sometimes described as ungenerated, or self-generated (Brugsch, p. 445); he was sometimes said to be son of Ra (*ib.*), and sometimes son of Ptah (Wiedemann, *Rel. anc. Eg.*, p. 226). But we are also told (Brugsch, p. 188) that he was sometimes substituted for the maleficent Set in the list of the five children of Seb and Nut. Perhaps the writer of *Corp.* X may have adopted this variation of the Heliopolitan genealogy, and regarded

---

[1] Plutarch also says (*Is. et Os.* 44) ἐνίοις δὲ δοκεῖ Κρόνος ὁ Ἄνουβις εἶναι. But the Κρόνος of *Corp.* X cannot be Anubis.

[2] 'Sein Reich ist die Luftregion, der Wolkenhimmel' (Brugsch, *Rel. und Myth. der alten Aeg.* p. 431).

the god Thoth-Hermes as son of Seb (Kronos), and grandson of Shu (Uranos). See Lactantius, *Div. inst.* 1. 11. 16 (*Testim.*).

θεάσασθαι τὸ κάλλος τοῦ ἀγαθοῦ, ἐκεῖνο[υ] τὸ ἄφθαρτον, τὸ ἀλάλητον (ἄληπτον MSS.). Cf. *Corp.* VI. 5. The words ἐκεῖνο τὸ ἄφθαρτον (κάλλος) serve to contrast 'the beauty of the Good' with the perishable beauty of things on earth. The epithet ἄληπτον is hardly appropriate ; and there can be little doubt that the original reading was ἀλάλητον, which leads on to the words ὅταν μηδὲν περὶ αὐτοῦ ἐχῆς εἰπεῖν, and βαθεῖα σιωπή, in what follows.

ἡ γὰρ γνῶσις αὐτοῦ βαθεῖα (καὶ θεία MSS.) σιωπή ἐστι. Cf. § 9 : ὁ μὴ πολλὰ λαλῶν. *Corp.* I. 31 : ἀνεκλάλητε, ἄρρητε, σιωπῇ φωνούμενε. *Corp.* XIII. 2 as emended : σοφία ἡ μήτρα, ἐν σιγῇ ⟨κυοῦσα⟩. Compare also the name Σιγή applied by some of the Valentinians to the consort of the Propator. The Pythagorean injunction of σιγή was probably in the Hermetist's mind.

§ **6.** οὔτε γὰρ ἄλλο τι δύναται . . . θεάσασθαι ὁ τοῦτο θεασάμενος, . . . οὔτε τὸ σύνολον τὸ σῶμα κινῆσαι. If the Hermetist had written ὁ τοῦτο νοῶν, . . . ὁ τοῦτο θεώμενος, we might have understood him to be speaking of a temporary ecstasy or trance, from which the man will awake to resume the occupations of everyday life. But the aorist participles νοήσας, θεασάμενος, make this interpretation impossible. We are told that he who has once seen the Good in its full beauty can never thereafter see earthly things, or hear of earthly things, or move his body. But to say this of a man is equivalent to saying that he is either dead or dying. It is clear therefore that, in the writer's view, the θέα of which he speaks is incompatible with the continuance of earthly life. We may hope to see the beatific vision, but not until the moment of our release from the body. If a living man attains to it, his earthly life is then and there at an end ; the vision 'draws his soul up out of the body', and transforms him into pure οὐσία, or in other words, changes him from a man into a god. The writer seems to have regarded the cessation of earthly consciousness in a dying saint as the counterpart of his absorption in the dawning splendour of τὸ κάλλος τοῦ ἀγαθοῦ. Thus understood, the sentence is in agreement with the words ἀδύνατον . . . ψυχὴν ἀποθεωθῆναι ἐν σώματι ἀνθρώπου ⟨μένουσαν⟩ below. Cf. *Exc.* VI. 18 : ἀδύνατον τὸν ἐν σώματι τούτου (*sc.* τοῦ τὸν θεὸν θεάσασθαι) εὐτυχῆσαι.

πασῶν γὰρ τῶν σωματικῶν αἰσθήσεών τε καὶ κινήσεων ἐπιλαθόμενος (-λαβόμενος MSS.) ἀτρεμεῖ. The writer of the *Hermippus* (see notes on *Corp.* XVI) has borrowed from this passage. *Hermipp.* (Kroll and Viereck) 2. 20. 186 f. : ποίους ἂν ἔρωτας ἴσχοι ὁ τοιοῦτον κάλλος κατοπτεῦσαι δεδυνημένος, ἄφθαρτον, ἄκρατον ...; οἶμαι τὴν θείαν σιωπὴν ὑποστήσεται, λέγειν περὶ αὐτοῦ οὐχ οἷός τε ὤν, πασῶν τε τῶν σωματικῶν αἰσθήσεών τε καὶ κινήσεων ἐπιλαθόμενος ἀτρεμήσει.

τὴν ὅλην ψυχὴν ἀναλαμβάνει (ἀναλάμπει MSS.) καὶ ἀνέλκει διὰ τοῦ σώματος. 'The whole soul' is contrasted with the νοῦς, which is here regarded as a part of the soul. The relation between νοῦς and ψυχή is differently conceived in §§ 16 ff. The preposition διά must be taken in the sense of the Homeric διέκ; the beauty of the Good draws the soul forth from the body, as from a sheath. Cf. Corp. XIII. 3 : ἐμαυτὸν ⟨δι⟩εξελήλυθα εἰς ἀθάνατον σῶμα. Ib. 12 : τὸ σκῆνος τοῦτο ... ὃ διεξεληλύθαμεν. Both in Corp. XIII and in Corp. X. 6, the process described is an ἀποθέωσις; but the writer of Corp. XIII speaks of this ἀποθέωσις as taking place in a man who continues to live on earth,[1] whereas the writer of Corp. X holds that it can take place only at or after death.

εἰς οὐσίαν μεταβάλλει. 'Ins Göttliche und Uebersinnliche' Reitzenstein. Cf. Corp. XIII. 14, where the word οὐσιώδης is used in a similar connexion. The same thought is expressed in another way in Corp. X. 19 a, where it is said that after death the pious soul ὅλη νοῦς γίνεται.

ἀδύνατον ... ψυχὴν ἀποθεωθῆναι ἐν σώματι ἀνθρώπου ⟨μένουσαν· ἀλλὰ χρὴ μεταβληθῆναι αὐτήν, καὶ οὕτω δὴ⟩ θεασαμένην τοῦ ἀγαθοῦ ⟨τὸ⟩ κάλλος [τῷ] ἀποθεωθῆναι. [τῷ] may have arisen out of ⟨τό⟩ misplaced. My restoration of the text differs from that of Reitzenstein (Hellen. myst., p. 116); but he is right in saying that it is to be inferred from what follows that some form of the verb μεταβάλλειν occurred here. As to μεταβάλλειν and μεταβολή, cf. Pl. Legg. X. 904 c : μεταβάλλει μὲν τοίνυν πάνθ᾽ ὅσα μέτοχά ἐστι ψυχῆς, ἐν ἑαυτοῖς κεκτημένα τὴν τῆς μεταβολῆς αἰτίαν· μεταβάλλοντα δὲ φέρεται κατὰ τὴν τῆς εἱμαρμένης τάξιν καὶ νόμον. The word μεταβολή ('a change from one state to another') is sometimes used as a euphemism for death. Cf. Philostr. Vita Apollon. 8. 31 : τοῦ δὲ Ἀπολλωνίου ἐξ ἀνθρώπων μὲν ἤδη ὄντος, θαυμαζομένου δ᾽ ἐπὶ τῇ μεταβολῇ. Porphyry ap. Stob. 1. 49. 59, vol. i, p. 445 W. : ἑκατέραν γὰρ εἶναι τῆς ψυχῆς μεταβολήν, τὴν μὲν εἰς σῶμα γένεσιν, τὴν δὲ ἀπὸ σώματος θανατονπροσαγορευομένην.

§ 7. ἀπὸ μιᾶς ψυχῆς τῆς τοῦ παντὸς πᾶσαι αἱ ψυχαί εἰσιν αὗται ⟨⟨ὥσπερ ἀπονενεμημέναι⟩⟩. Cf. § 15 b, where the soul of a child is described as ἔτι σχεδὸν ἠρτημένη τῆς τοῦ κόσμου ψυχῆς. Ascl. Lat. I. 3 a:

[1] Cf. Ascl. Lat. 41 b: ἐν πλάσμασιν ἡμᾶς ὄντας ἀπεθέωσας.

'mundus unus, anima una.' See also *Corp.* IX. 9 *init.* The writer says that this doctrine was taught in the Γενικοὶ λόγοι. The conception of a world-soul occurs in the *Timaeus*, and must have been familiar to all Platonists ; but the doctrine that individual souls are derived from the world-soul, and have been 'parted off' from it, is not Plato's, and the Hermetists by whom the Γενικοὶ λόγοι were written must have got it from Stoic sources.

τούτων τοίνυν τῶν ψυχῶν πολλαὶ αἱ μεταβολαί. The individual souls, having been brought into existence by separation from the world-soul, pass through a series of transformations, in the course of which they may successively occupy all stations in the scale of life, from that of a reptile to that of a god. The writer seems to imply that their career begins by incarnation in animal bodies of the lowest order, viz. that of ἑρπετά. (Cf. § 8 a : τὴν ὁδὸν ὑποστρέφει τὴν ἐπὶ τὰ ἑρπετά.) If this is his view, he differs from Pl. *Tim.* 90 E ff., where we are told that, 'according to the probable account', the individual souls were first embodied as men (ἄνδρες), and that those of them who lived amiss in their first life on earth were afterwards reincarnated in the form of women, birds, quadrupeds, many-footed animals, reptiles, or fishes, according to the kind and degree of their decline from their original state.

τῶν μὲν ἐπὶ τὸ εὐτυχέστερον, τῶν δὲ ἐπὶ τὸ ἐναντίον. This is directly contradicted in § 22 a : εἰς μὲν οὖν τὸ κρεῖττον ψυχὴ μεταβαίνει, εἰς δὲ τὸ ἔλαττον ἀδύνατον.

αἱ δὲ ἀνθρώπειαι, ἀρχὴν ἀθανασίας [ι]σχοῦσαι. The soul which, in its successive transformations ἐπὶ τὸ εὐτυχέστερον, has risen to the condition of a man, may at that stage acquire something of ἀθανασία, i. e. of divinity. Such a soul is already a daemon or a god potentially (cf. § 19 a : ψυχὴ ἀνθρωπίνη, οὐ πᾶσα μέν, ἡ δὲ εὐσεβής, δαιμονία τίς ἐστι καὶ θεία) ; it may therefore, at its next transformation, actually become a daemon, and afterwards a god. The divine element (τὸ ἀθάνατον) in the human soul is νοῦς, by the possession of which man is distinguished from the lower animals.

In holding that the human soul must pass through an intermediate stage as a daemon before it becomes a god, the writer agrees with Posidonius ; but he does not recognize the stage of 'hero' which Posidonius interposed between 'man' and 'daemon'. In § 6 above, the daemon-stage is not mentioned, and *apotheosis* is spoken of as if it might follow immediately on death. In the oracle quoted by Porphyry, *Vita Plotini* 22 (see p. 239), Apollo says that Plotinus, now that he has departed from the body, is no longer a man, but a daemon (δαῖμον, ἄνερ τὸ πάροιθεν κ.τ.λ.), and the 'daemonic' life into which he has entered is described.

εἶθ' οὕτως εἰς τὸν τῶν θεῶν χορὸν χωροῦσι (χορεύουσι MSS.). They take their place among the star-gods. For the phrase ὁ τῶν θεῶν χορός, cf. Corp. XII. i. 12: ὁδηγηθήσεται . . . εἰς τὴν τῶν θεῶν καὶ μακάρων χορόν. Kaibel, Epigr. Gr. ex lapid. conl. 288 (Cyprus, 'recentioris aetatis'): ΗΤΙΣ . . (al. ΗΒΗΣΕΝ: legendum ἥρπασεν?) ἀ(θ)ανά(των με) χορός.

[χοροὶ δὲ δύο θεῶν, ὁ μὲν τῶν πλανωμένων, ὁ δὲ τῶν ἀπλανῶν]. This is an inserted note. The following αὕτη means τὸ εἰς τὸν τῶν θεῶν χορὸν χωρεῖν, and the interposed mention of two distinct χοροί (that of the planets and that of the fixed stars) is irrelevant.

Q gives ἀφανῶν in place of ἀπλανῶν. This seems to indicate an alternative reading, ὁ μὲν τῶν φανερῶν (= αἰσθητῶν), ὁ δὲ τῶν ἀφανῶν (= νοητῶν).

αὕτη ψυχῆς ἡ τελειοτάτη δόξα. A place among the star-gods is the highest to which the soul can attain. This again agrees with the system of Posidonius. In this paragraph, there is no suggestion of the Platonic notion that the soul may rise above the material heavens into the supracosmic and incorporeal world (as is said, for instance, in Corp. I).

The use of the word δόξα in this connexion may possibly be a sign of Jewish influence. Cf. Paul, 1 Cor. 15. 40: ἑτέρα μὲν ἡ τῶν ἐπουρανίων δόξα, ἑτέρα δὲ τῶν ἐπιγείων. . . . ἀστὴρ γὰρ ἀστέρος διαφέρει ἐν δόξῃ.

§ 8 a. οὔ[τε] γεύεται ἀθανασίας [οὔτε τοῦ ἀγαθοῦ μεταλαμβάνει]. A soul of this sort does not, in its human life on earth, acquire ἀρχὴν ἀθανασίας; for it has no νοῦς in it (§ 24 a), and is no better than that of a beast.

It is superfluous to tell us that a soul which remains bad does not 'partake of the Good'.

παλίσσυρτος (codd. Corp.), 'dragged back', or 'swept back as by an adverse current', seems better than παλίσσυτος (codd. Stob.).

⟨⟨καὶ ἡ κακοδαίμων . . . δουλεύει σώμασιν ἀλλοκότοις καὶ μοχθηροῖς.⟩⟩ These words are out of place in the MSS., where they form part of the description of κακία ψυχῆς. 'Servitude to uncouth and noxious bodies', i. e. incarnation in the bodies of beasts, is not κακία, but is the penalty of κακία; the mention of it ought therefore to precede the words αὕτη καταδίκη ψυχῆς κακῆς. Cf. Ascl. Lat. I. 12 a: 'secus enim inpieque qui vixerint, . . . constituitur in corpora alia, indigna animo sancto, [et] foeda migratio.'

ἀγνοήσασα ἑαυτήν. The soul forgets, or fails to recognize, its kinship with the divine; hence the νοῦς in it (if νοῦς has entered into it at all) becomes dormant or departs, and only the lower and merely animal part of the man is active. A soul thus degraded is fit only to animate the body of a beast, and is accordingly incorporated in a bestial body at its next incarnation. The Platonic *locus classicus* on τὸ γνῶναι ἑαυτόν is *Alcib.* I, in which compare especially 133 c: τῷ θείῳ ἄρα τοῦτ' ἔοικεν αὐτῆς ('this part of the soul', viz. the νοῦς)· καί τις εἰς τοῦτο βλέπων, καὶ πᾶν τὸ θεῖον γνούς, οὕτω καὶ ἑαυτὸν ἂν γνοίη μάλιστα. Cf. ὁ ἀναγνωρίσας ἑαυτόν in *Corp.* I. 18–21.

§ 8 b. μηδὲν γνοῦσα τῶν ὄντων, μηδὲ τὴν τούτων φύσιν, μηδὲ τὸ ἀγαθόν. By τὰ ὄντα are here meant τὰ ὄντως ὄντα, i. e. τὰ νοητά or τὰ θεῖα. The soul which does not recognize the existence of things incorporeal and eternal is wholly subject to the influences of the body. μηδὲ τὴν τούτων φύσιν seems a pointless repetition of μηδὲν . . . τῶν ὄντων (unless indeed we take τούτων to mean τῶν γιγνομένων, as opposed to τῶν ὄντων); and the sentence would be improved by cutting out μηδὲ τὴν . . . τὸ ἀγαθόν.

ἐντινάσσε⟨τα⟩ι τοῖς σωματικοῖς πάθεσι. . . . αὕτη κακία ψυχῆς. Cf. Plotinus 1. 2. 3: ἐπειδὴ κακὴ μέν ἐστιν ἡ ψυχὴ συμπεφυρμένη τῷ σώματι καὶ ὁμοπαθὴς γινομένη αὐτῷ καὶ πάντα συνδοξάζουσα, εἴη ἂν ἀγαθὴ καὶ ἀρετὴν ἔχουσα, εἰ μήτε συνδοξάζοι, ἀλλὰ μόνη ἐνεργοῖ· ὅπερ ἐστὶ νοεῖν τε καὶ φρονεῖν· μήτε ὁμοπαθὴς εἴη· ὅπερ ἐστὶ σωφρονεῖν· μήτε φοβοῖτο ἀφισταμένη τοῦ σώματος· ὅπερ ἐστὶν ἀνδρίζεσθαι· ἡγοῖτο δὲ λόγος καὶ νοῦς, τὰ δὲ μὴ ἀντιτείνοι· δικαιοσύνη δ' ἂν εἴη τοῦτο. τὴν δὴ τοιαύτην διάθεσιν τῆς ψυχῆς, καθ' ἣν νοεῖ τε καὶ ἀπαθὴς οὕτως ἐστίν, εἴ τις ὁμοίωσιν λέγοι πρὸς θεόν, οὐκ ἂν ἁμαρτάνοι. (This last sentence corresponds to καὶ ἤδη θεῖος in *Corp.* X. 9 *init.*)

ὥσπερ φορτίον βαστάζουσα τὸ σῶμα. In *Corp.* II. 9 we are told that in all men and animals alike the soul φέρει (i. e. κινεῖ) τὸ σῶμα. But here, the meaning is different. The vicious soul is weighed down by the body, as by an oppressive burden; the virtuous soul is not thus weighed down. Cf. ὥσπερ φόρτον τινὰ βαστάζει in § 13.

The conception of the body as a thing by which the soul *is weighed down* does not agree well with the conception of it as a thing by which the soul *is governed* (οὐκ ἄρχουσα ἀλλ' ἀρχομένη); and for this reason it might perhaps be better to bracket ὥσπερ φορτίον . . . καί.

246   CORPVS HERMETICVM

§ 9. Ὁ μὴ πολλὰ λαλῶν, μηδὲ πολλὰ ἀκούων. The writer's meaning must have been that the wordy disputations of the schools are not a help to the attainment of *gnosis*, but rather a hindrance. This meaning might have been more clearly expressed by writing οὐχ ὁ πολλὰ λέγων, οὐδὲ ὁ πολλὰ ἀκούων. Cf. Porphyry, *Ad Marcellam* 20 : θεοῦ γὰρ γνῶσις ποιεῖ βραχὺν λόγον (*lege* βραχυλόγον). Stobaeus, vol. v Hense, *praef.*, p. vii : βραχυλόγον μάλιστα ἡ θεοῦ γνῶσις ποιεῖ. ·Sexti *Sent.* 430 Elter : ἄνθρωπον θεοῦ γνῶσις βραχυλόγον ποιεῖ.

σκιαμαχεῖ. ' He fights without any real opponent matched against him ; ' he is like a boxer going through the motions for practice, who strikes at an imaginary adversary, and beats the empty air.[1] That is to say, the philosophizing of such men is not directed to any serious purpose ; it is a vain repetition of empty formulas. Cf. Pl. *Apol.* 18 D : ἀνάγκη ἀτεχνῶς ὥσπερ σκιαμαχεῖν . . . καὶ ἐλέγχειν μηδενὸς ποκρινομένου. Philo, *De plantatione* 42. 175, II, p. 169 Wendland : οὐδεὶς καθ' αὑτὸν ἀγωνιζόμενος ἀναγράφεται νικῶν, ⌐εἰ δὲ ἀγωνίζεται⌐ (εἰ δὲ ἀγωνίζοιτο Wendland : rather, εἰ δὲ ⟨οὕτως⟩ ἀγωνίζοιτο), σκιαμαχεῖν μᾶλλον ἂν εἰκότως δόξαι. Plutarch, *De sanitate praecepta* 130 E, couples together σφαιρίζειν (ball-playing) and σκιαμαχεῖν (sparring) as two modes of bodily exercise. Pausanias 6. 10. 3, of the statue of a famous boxer : σκιαμαχοῦντος δὲ ὁ ἀνδριὰς παρέχεται σχῆμα· i. e. the man is represented in a fighting attitude, but with no opponent facing him. Numenius *ap.* Euseb. *Pr. ev.* 14. 6. 13 : Zeno would not dispute directly with his living opponent Arcesilaus, πρὸς δὲ τὸν οὐκέτι ἐν ζῶσιν ὄντα Πλάτωνα ἐσκιαμάχει, . . . ὡς οὔτ' ἂν τοῦ Πλάτωνος ἀμυνομένου κ.τ.λ. Lucian, *Piscator* 35 (of philosophers who do not practise what they preach) : οὐκ οἶδ' ὅποι ποτὲ οἴχεται πάντα ταῦτα ἀποπτάμενα, πτερόεντα ὡς ἀληθῶς ἔπη, μάτην πρὸς αὐτῶν ἐν ταῖς διατριβαῖς σκιαμαχούμενα.

[[τούτου δὲ . . . χωρὶς αὐτοῦ]]. This passage has no meaning as it stands in the MSS. I have found possible places for τούτου . . . οὖσιν and διὰ τὸ . . . χωρὶς αὐτοῦ ; but I propose these transpositions with diffidence. The words αἱ αἰσθήσεις εἰσί may be a remnant of a sentence containing some mention of αἴσθησις which led on to the statement that *gnosis* is something very different from it (γνῶσις δὲ

---

[1] The same comparison is employed by Paul, 1 *Cor.* 9. 26 : οὕτως πυκτεύω ὡς οὐκ ἀέρα δέρων (= σκιαμαχῶν)· ἀλλὰ ὑπωπιάζω μου τὸ σῶμα. The body is no σκιά ; it is a real and solid opponent. And τὸ σῶμα is the enemy with whom the Hermetists also were engaged in combat.

In Liddell and Scott, σκιαμαχεῖν is said to mean ' to fight in the shade ' ; but that is a mistake.

αἰσθήσεως πολὺ διαφέρει). Having said that ἀρετὴ ψυχῆς is γνῶσις, the writer proceeds to explain what γνῶσις is, by contrasting it with αἴσθησις.

§ 10 a. [ἔστιν ἐπιστήμης . . . γὰρ ἐπιστήμη]. The mention of ἐπιστήμη is irrelevant; and these words have probably passed into the text from a marginal note.

ὀργάνῳ χρωμένη αὐτῷ τῷ νοΐ. The νοῦς is the 'organ' of gnosis, in the same sense that the eye is the organ of sight.

ὁ δὲ νοῦς τῷ σώματι ⟨ἐναντίος⟩. According to the reading of the MSS., the meaning would be that the νοῦς uses the body as its organ. But that cannot be right ; for the body is not the organ of the mind in the same sense that the mind (or mental eye) is the organ of gnosis. By inserting ἐναντίος, we get a statement which suits well with what precedes, and leads on naturally to what follows. Man consists of two opposites in combination ; and this is an instance of a law which applies to all things alike.

τά τε νοητὰ καὶ τὰ ὑλικά. The human soul 'admits into itself both things incorporeal and things material'; or in other words, it performs the two contrasted operations of νόησις and αἴσθησις. This, or something like it, must have been the writer's meaning ; and this meaning can be obtained by writing εἰς σῶμα ⟨εἰσδῦσα ψυχή⟩.

ἐξ ἀντιθέσεως γὰρ καὶ ἐναντιότητος δεῖ τὰ πάντα συνεστάναι. This must be more or less remotely derived from Heraclitus. Ar. *Eth. Nic.* 9. 2, 1155 b 4: Ἡράκλειτος τὸ ἀντίξοον συμφέρον, καὶ ἐκ τῶν διαφερόντων καλλίστην ἁρμονίαν, καὶ πάντα κατ' ἔριν γίνεσθαι. Pseudo-Ar. *De mundo* 5, 396 b 7: ἴσως δὲ τῶν ἐναντίων ἡ φύσις γλίχεται, καὶ ἐκ τούτων ἀποτελεῖ τὸ σύμφωνον, οὐκ ἐκ τῶν ὁμοίων. . . . ταὐτὸ δὲ τοῦτο ἦν καὶ τὸ παρὰ τῷ σκοτεινῷ λεγόμενον Ἡρακλείτῳ· συνάψιες ὅλα καὶ οὐχ ὅλα, συμφερόμενον διαφερόμενον, συνᾷδον διᾷδον, καὶ ἐκ πάντων ἓν καὶ ἐξ ἑνὸς πάντα. Heracl. fr. 51 Diels: οὐ ξυνιᾶσιν ὅκως (τὸ ἓν or τὸ πᾶν) διαφερόμενον ἑωυτῷ ὁμολογέει· παλίντροπος ἁρμονίη ὅκωσπερ τόξου καὶ λύρης. The Hermetist says in this section that man is composed of νοητά and ὑλικά, just as he says in § 11 that τὸ πᾶν (the universe) ἔκ τε ὑλικοῦ καὶ νοητοῦ συνέστηκεν; and he regards τὰ νοητά (i. e. ἀσώματα) as ἐναντία to τὰ ὑλικά (i. e. σωματικά). Cf. *Corp.* II. 4 a : σώματι δὲ ἐναντία φύσις τὸ ἀσώματον. . . . ἀσώματος οὖν ὁ τόπος. (The τόπος there spoken of is identified with νοῦς.)

§ 10 b. Τί[ς] οὖν ὁ ὑλικὸς θεὸς ὁδί, ⟨ὁ κόσμος⟩; In §§ 7–10 a, the writer has been considering the question whether, and under what conditions, man (or the human soul) is good. His answer to that question has been given in the words κακία ψυχῆς ἀγνωσία (§ 8 b) ; ἀρετὴ ψυχῆς γνῶσις (§ 9) ; ὁ γνοὺς ἀγαθός (*ib.*). Man is good if he has *gnosis*, and bad if he has not *gnosis*. And this answer was probably more fully explained in the lost passage at the end of § 10 a. E.g. it may have been there said that the human soul is good in so far as it detaches itself from the material body, and identifies itself with νοῦς (the 'organ' of *gnosis*), which is 'contrary to the body'. In § 10 b, the writer passes on from man to the Kosmos, and considers the question whether the Kosmos is good.

Οὐ κακὸς ὁ κόσμος, οὐκέτι δὲ ἀγαθός.—(ὁ καλὸς κόσμος, οὐκ ἔστι δὲ ἀγαθός MSS.) Cf. § 12 : ὁ μὲν γὰρ κόσμος οὐκ ἀγαθός, ὡς κινητός, οὐ κακὸς δέ, ὡς ἀθάνατος. See *Corp.* VI. 2 b.

[καὶ αὐτοδεὴς] καὶ αὐτὸς [ποτὲ μὲν γενόμενος] ἀεὶ [δὲ] ὤν, ὧν δὲ ἐν γενέσει. The meaning might be made more unmistakable by transposing καὶ αὐτός, and writing ἀεὶ ⟨μὲν ?⟩ ὢν καὶ αὐτός, ὢν δὲ ἐν γενέσει. The Kosmos καὶ αὐτός (i. e. as well as God) is ever-existent ; but it is not ever-existent in the same sense that God is ; for its everlasting existence takes the form of perpetual γένεσις.

The word αὐτοδεής does not occur elsewhere ; and it is difficult to assign any meaning to it. καὶ αὐτο- has probably come by duplication from the following καὶ αὐτός. The words ποτὲ μὲν γενόμενος and δέ were most likely inserted by some one who held the view that the Kosmos has had a beginning. The author himself, on the other hand, seems to have held that the Kosmos has always been in existence.

γινόμενος ἀεὶ ⟨τῇ⟩ γενέσει (γένεσις or -σιν MSS.) τῶν ποιῶν καὶ τῶν ποσῶν. Cf. ποιότητας καὶ ποσότητας ποιεῖ (ὁ ποιῶν) in § 3 as emended. The οὐσία (substance) of the κόσμος is everlasting ; but (in the sublunar world at least) every part of this substance is continually having fresh qualities imposed on it, and every individual thing that is made of it is continually increasing or decreasing.

§ 11. ἡ δὲ νοητὴ στάσις κινεῖ τὴν ὑλικὴν κίνησιν τὸν τρόπον τοῦτον. Cf. *Corp.* II. 8 a : πᾶσα οὖν κίνησις . . . ὑπὸ στάσεως κινεῖται. All changes of quality and quantity that take place in the Kosmos are modes of material movement (ὑλικὴ κίνησις) ; and τὸ κινοῦν must be something which is itself immaterial and motionless (νοητὴ στάσις). The writer assumes that τὸ κινοῦν is ψυχή (see *Corp.* II), and proceeds to explain how the cosmic ψυχή (i. e. the immaterial thing by which all material things are moved) is incorporated in the structure of the Kosmos.

ὁ κόσμος σφαῖρά ἐστι, τουτέστι κεφαλή. The notion that the spherical Kosmos is like a human head was doubtless suggested by Pl. *Tim.* 44 D ff., where the making of the human body by the 'created gods' is described: τὰς μὲν δὴ θείας περιόδους (i. e. the movements of νοῦς) . . ., τὸ τοῦ παντὸς σχῆμα ἀπομιμησάμενοι περιφερὲς ὄν, εἰς σφαιροειδὲς σῶμα ἐνέδησαν, τοῦτο ὃ νῦν κεφαλὴν ἐπονομάζομεν, ὃ θειότατον τ' ἐστὶ καὶ τῶν ἐν ἡμῖν πάντων δεσποτοῦν κ.τ.λ. In the *Timaeus* the human head is said to resemble the spherical Kosmos; in *Corp.* X the spherical Kosmos is said to resemble a human head. Cf. Synesius, *Calvitii encomium* 8, Migne tom. 66, col. 1181 B: τί δ' ἂν σφαίρας γένοιτο . . . θεσπεσιώτερον; . . . ὁ τρίτος θεός, ἡ τοῦ κόσμου ψυχή· ἦν ὁ πατὴρ μὲν αὐτῆς, τοῦ δὲ σωματικοῦ κόσμου δημιουργός, ἐπεισήγαγε τῷ κόσμῳ, τέλεον αὐτὸν . . . ἀπεργασάμενος, ἀποδοὺς διὰ τοῦτο καὶ σχῆμα σχημάτων τὸ περιεκτότατον (i.e. a spherical shape). . . . ἥ τε οὖν ὅλη ψυχὴ σφαῖραν ὄντα τὸν ὅλον κόσμον ψυχοῖ, αἵ τε ἀπὸ τῆς ὅλης ῥυεῖσαι καὶ μέρη γενόμεναι θέλουσιν ἑκάστη τοῦθ' ὅπερ ἡ πᾶσα ψυχή, διοικεῖν σώματα καὶ κόσμων εἶναι ψυχαί, ὃ καὶ τοῦ μερισμοῦ γέγονεν αὐταῖς αἴτιον. οὕτως ἐδέησε τῇ φύσει σφαιρῶν μερικῶν. ἄνω μὲν οὖν ἀστέρες, κάτω δὲ κεφαλαὶ διεπλάσθησαν, ἵν' εἶεν οἶκοι ψυχῶν, ἐν κόσμῳ κόσμοι μικροί· ἔδει γάρ, οἶμαι, εἶναι τὸν κόσμον ζῷον ἐκ ζῴων συγκείμενον.

[κεφαλῆς δὲ οὐδὲν ὑπεράνω ὑλικόν, ὥσπερ οὐδὲ ποδῶν οὐδὲν νοητὸν ὑποκάτω, πᾶν δὲ ὑλικόν]. I can make no sense of this. The words must be taken to refer to man, and not to the Kosmos; for the Kosmos is a head without trunk or limbs, and has no feet. But what can be meant by saying that in a man 'there is nothing material above the head, and nothing immaterial below the feet'? The words κεφαλῆς οὐδὲν ὑπεράνω ὑλικόν might possibly be taken to mean that the head is the highest part of man's material frame, and therefore the part best suited to be the abode of ψυχή; but the mention of the feet and what lies below them seems utterly irrelevant.

[⌈νοῦς δὲ κεφαλὴ αὕτη⌉ σφαιρικῶς κινουμένῃ, τοῦτο ἔστι κεφαλικῶς]. This also is meaningless. It is absurd to say that a head is νοῦς; for a head is a material thing, and νοῦς is immaterial. Perhaps νοῦς . . . αὕτη is a corruption of ⟨ἔν⟩νους δὲ ⟨ἡ⟩ κεφαλὴ αὕτη, 'this head (viz. the Kosmos) has νοῦς in it'. That statement would be intelligible in itself, and would agree with the doctrine of the *Timaeus*, according to which man's νοῦς is situated in his head; but it would not be to the point here; for in this paragraph the writer is speaking about the embodiment of ψυχή, and not that of νοῦς. The words κεφαλὴ . . . σφαιρικῶς κινουμένη, τοῦτο ἔστι κεφαλικῶς, suggest the grotesque notion of a man's head spinning round like a top. If a thing moves σφαιρικῶς (i. e. like a sphere revolving on its axis), then it does *not* move κεφαλικῶς (i. e. as a human head moves). The Kosmos (or, to speak more exactly, the celestial part of the Kosmos) 'moves spherically'; and it might be said in a metaphorical sense that νοῦς 'moves spherically'; but it is nonsense to say that the human head 'moves spherically'. The Kosmos resembles the human head in its spherical shape, but differs from the human head in its movement; and a writer who is seeking to show that these two things resemble one another ought to avoid mentioning their movement.

ὅσα οὖν προσήνωται τῷ ὑμένι τῆς κεφαλῆς ταύτης . . . ἀθάνατα πέφυκεν. The ὑμήν is the *meninx* or *pia mater*, i. e. the membrane in which the brain is enclosed.[1] Ar. *Hist. animal.* 1. 16, 494 b 29: ὑμένες δὲ (τὸν ἐγκέφαλον) δύο περιέχουσιν, ὁ μὲν περὶ τὸ ὀστοῦν (the *dura mater*) ἰσχυρότερος, ὁ δὲ περὶ αὐτὸν τὸν ἐγκέφαλον (the *pia mater*) ἥττων ἐκείνου. *Ib.* 495 a 8: ἔστι δ' ὑμὴν δερματικὸς ἡ μῆνιγξ ὁ περιέχων τὸν ἐγκέφαλον. The writer of *Corp.* X holds this membrane to be the seat or organ of conscious life and thought in the human body. Here, as in § 13, he shows some acquaintance with the physiological theories of his time.

The Platonists in general, adhering to the teaching of the *Timaeus*, held the seat of νοῦς or τὸ λογιστικόν to be the brain.[2] Chrysippus and most of the Stoics placed the ἡγεμονικόν in the heart. The Aristotelian Strato, about 280 B.C., said that the seat of the ἡγεμονικόν is τὸ μεσόφρυον (the space between the eyebrows), or rather, the part of the brain which lies behind that region.[3] The view adopted by the writer of *Corp.* X is that of the physician Erasistratus[4] (about 300–250 B.C.). Aetius, Diels, *Doxogr.*, p. 391:

[1] Suidas (Bernhardy) : Μῆνιγξ· ὑμὴν τὸν ἐγκέφαλον σκέπων. . . . ὅτι αἱ αἰσθήσεις ἀπὸ τοῦ ἐγκεφάλου ἀρχόμεναι διὰ τῶν νεύρων ἄχρι τῶν αἰσθητηρίων προΐασι. . . . ἔστιν οὖν ἀπειλημμένος τις ἀὴρ ἐν τῷ κοιλώματι τῆς ἀκοῆς, συμφυὴς ὢν τῇ μήνιγγι καὶ τῷ ὑμένι. οὗτος οὖν ὁ ἀήρ, δεχόμενος ἐκ τοῦ ἔξωθεν ἀέρος τοὺς ψόφους, . . . δι' ἑαυτοῦ εἰς τὴν μήνιγγα διαπορθμεύει τοὺς ψόφους.

[2] Alcmaeon of Croton, about 500 B.C., 'was the first to recognize the brain as the central organ of intellectual activity' (Gomperz, *Greek Thinkers*, Eng. tr. 1901, vol. i, p. 148).

[3] Aetius (Diels *Doxogr.* p. 391) says that Strato placed the *hegemonikon* ἐν τῷ μεσοφρύῳ (*in superciliorum meditullio*, Tertull. *De an.* 15). Pollux, *Onomast.* 2. 226, says that he placed it κατὰ τὸ μεσόφρυον. The latter phrase, no doubt, gives Strato's meaning more exactly.

[4] The doctrines of Erasistratus continued to be maintained by a succession of followers for several centuries. A medical school of *Erasistrateioi* at Smyrna stood

Ἐρασίστρατος (τὸ τῆς ψυχῆς ἡγεμονικὸν λέγει εἶναι) περὶ τὴν μήνιγγα τοῦ ἐγκεφάλου, ⌜ἣν ἐπικρανίδα λέγει⌝.[1] The almost equally celebrated physician Herophilus (about 300 B. C.) placed the ἡγεμονικόν in the ventricles of the brain (ἐν τῇ τοῦ ἐγκεφάλου κοιλίᾳ, ἥτις ἐστὶ καὶ βάσις, Aetius ib.); and there can be no doubt that Erasistratus was the first to place it in the *meninx*.[2]

The Hermetist compares the Kosmos to a human head. The ' cerebral membrane' of the Kosmos is the outermost sphere;[3] and ' the things which are united to' this cosmic *meninx* are the fixed stars and the planets. They, like the Kosmos itself and all living things within it, are composed of soul (νοητόν) and body (ὑλικόν); but being in or near the outermost sphere, in which the soul or life of the Kosmos is concentrated, they have in them ' more soul than body'; whence it results that they are ἀθάνατα (and consequently ' not bad'). On the other hand, all living organisms in the sublunar region have in them 'more body than soul'; whence it results that they are θνητά (and consequently ' bad').

Compare Plotinus 4. 3. 17 on the descent and embodiment of souls : ὅτι δὲ ἐκ τοῦ νοητοῦ εἰς τὴν οὐρανοῦ ἴασιν αἱ ψυχαὶ τὸ πρῶτον χώραν, λογίσαιτο ἄν τις ἐκ τῶν τοιούτων. εἰ γὰρ οὐρανὸς ἐν τῷ αἰσθητῷ τόπῳ ἀμείνων, εἴη ἂν προσεχὴς τῶν νοητῶν τοῖς ἐσχάτοις. ἐκεῖθεν τοίνυν (sc. ἐκ τῶν νοητῶν) ψυχοῦται ταῦτα (sc. τὰ οὐράνια) πρῶτα [καὶ μεταλαμβάνει], ὡς ἐπιτηδειότερα μεταλαμβάνειν· τὸ δὲ γεηρὸν ὕστατόν τε καὶ ψυχῆς ἧττον πεφυκὸς μεταλαμβάνειν,[4] καὶ τῆς ἀσωμάτου φύσεως πόρρω.

in high repute in the first century B. C. (Strabo 12. 20, 580); and ' the school of Erasistratus was still flourishing at Rome in the second century A. D.' (Puschmann, *Gesch. der Medizin*, p. 309).

[1] There must be some error here; perhaps there is a lacuna before ἣν ἐπικρανίδα λέγει. According to Liddell and Scott, ἐπικρανίς means ' the membrane of the *cerebellum*', not that of the brain. (But does it not rather mean the *cerebellum* itself?) Puschmann, *op. cit.*, p. 300, says 'Das Seelencentrum, ἡγεμονικόν, verlegte (Erasistratos) in die Meninx *und in das kleine, für sich umhautete Hirn*, ἐπικρανίς'; but the text of Aetius does not yield that meaning.

[2] ' According to Rufus Ephesius,' Erasistratus ' divided the nerves into those of sensation and those of motion; the former he considered to be hollow, and to arise from the membranes of the brain' (W. A. Greenhill, in Smith's *Dict. Biogr.* II. 43 b). He held that these hollow nerves serve to convey *pneuma*. ' He recognized the purpose of the larger number of cerebral convolutions in man, as compared with the stag and the hare' (Puschmann, p. 300). His theory of the function of the *meninx* was founded on his own anatomical investigations.

[3] Cf. the teaching of the Naassenes, as reported by Hippolytus, *Ref. haer.* 5. 9 : Ἐδὲμ (Eden) δὲ εἶναι λέγουσι τὸν ἐγκέφαλον, οἱονεὶ δεδεμένον καὶ κατεσφιγμένον ἐν τοῖς περικειμένοις χιτῶσιν ὥσπερ οὐρανοῖς· παράδεισον δ' εἶναι νομίζουσι τὸν μέχρι μόνης τῆς κεφαλῆς ἄνθρωπον (i. e. the human head).

[4] Perhaps : τὸ δὲ γεηρὸν ὕστατον (sc. ψυχοῦται), ὡς ψυχῆς ἧττον πεφυκὸς μεταλαμβάνειν κ.τ.λ.

ἐμψύχου δὲ τοῦ σώματος πεποιημένου, τὸ πᾶν δὴ ζῷον. I have reconstructed this sentence by mere guesswork, out of the two misplaced scraps ἐν ψυχῇ δὲ σώματος πεποιημένου and πᾶν δὲ ζῷον. But something to this effect seems wanted to lead on to what follows. If we assume that the words are rightly restored, the writer, having explained the relation between ψυχή and σῶμα in the case of the Kosmos, ends the paragraph by saying that the Kosmos is an ἔμψυχον σῶμα ('a body with soul in it'), that is, a ζῷον; and he then goes on to say that it is the first of all ζῷα, and that man is the second.

§ 12. ὁ δὲ ἄνθρωπος δεύτερον ζῷον. Having disposed of the Kosmos, the Hermetist returns to the discussion of man. The treatment of man in §§ 12, 13 is parallel in arrangement to the treatment of the Kosmos in §§ 10 b, 11. The writer first gives his decision on the question whether man is good or bad, and then explains how the human soul is incorporated in the human body.

οὐκέτι δὲ [[μόνον]] οὐκ ἀγαθὸς ⟨⟨μόνον⟩⟩. Man is not, as the Kosmos is, merely not-good; he is positively bad. The reading of the MSS. would rather mean 'man is not, as the Kosmos is, almost good'; and that cannot be the sense intended.

The statement that man is κακός is verbally inconsistent with § 24 b, ὁ γὰρ ἄνθρωπος ζῷόν ἐστι θεῖον κ.τ.λ. (compare also ὁ γνοὺς ἀγαθός in § 9 init.). These apparently conflicting statements are probably derived from different sources; the language used in § 12 may have been suggested by Corp. VI, and that in § 24 b, by some document similar in tone to Ascl. Lat. I. 6 a, 'magnum miraculum est homo' &c. But there is no real contradiction. In § 12 we are told that man ὡς θνητός (i. e. in respect of his body, and the θνητὸν εἶδος ψυχῆς which is inseparably connected with the body,) is κακός. In § 24 b we are told that ὁ ὄντως ἄνθρωπος (i. e. man as identified with νοῦς, or with the higher and immortal part of the soul,) stands on a par with the astral gods, or perhaps above them. And ὁ γνούς (§ 9), 'the man who has got gnosis', is ὁ ὄντως ἄνθρωπος.

§ 13. ψυχὴ δὲ ἀνθρώπου ὀχεῖται τὸν τρόπον τοῦτον κ.τ.λ. The connexion of § 13 with § 12 may be explained thus. Man is bad in so far as he is a θνητὸν ζῷον; and he is a θνητὸν ζῷον in so far as his soul is enclosed in a material body. Hence arises the question how soul and body are connected during earthly life.

The writer here says that the πνεῦμα is the 'vehicle' (ὄχημα) of the ψυχή, and the ψυχή is the 'vehicle' of the νοῦς. In § 16, he describes the same relation by a different metaphor, speaking of the πνεῦμα as the 'garment' or 'envelope' (ἔνδυμα, περιβολή) of the ψυχή. Both these metaphors are employed together in Iambl. Περὶ ψυχῆς, Stob. 1. 49. 43, vol. i, p. 385 W. : οἱ μὲν γὰρ εὐθὺς αὐτὴν τὴν ψυχὴν αὐτῷ τῷ σώματι τῷ ὀργανικῷ συνοικίζουσιν, ὥσπερ οἱ πλεῖστοι τῶν Πλατωνικῶν· οἱ δὲ μεταξὺ τῆς τε ἀσωμάτου ψυχῆς καὶ τοῦ[1] ⌜ἀγγελιώδους⌝ (lege γεώδους) ⟨σώματος τίθενται[2]⟩ αἰθέρια ⟨τινὰ?⟩ καὶ οὐράνια καὶ πνευματικὰ περιβλήματα, ⟨ἅ[3] φασι⟩ περιαμπέχοντα τὴν νοερὰν ζωὴν προβεβλῆσθαι μὲν αὐτῆς φρουρᾶς ἕνεκεν, ὑπηρετεῖν δὲ αὐτῇ καθάπερ ὀχήματα, [συμμέτρως δ' αὖ] καὶ πρὸς τὸ στερεὸν σῶμα συμβιβάζειν ⟨⟨αὐτὴν⟩⟩ μέσοις τισὶ [κοινοῖς] συνδέσμοις [[αὐτὴν]] συνάπτοντα. The word ὄχημα is used in a similar connexion in Pl. Tim. 69 c : the created gods, when they fashioned man, παραλαβόντες ἀρχὴν ψυχῆς ἀθάνατον, τὸ μετὰ τοῦτο θνητὸν σῶμα αὐτῇ περιετόρνευσαν, ὄχημά τε πᾶν τὸ σῶμα ἔδοσαν. In that passage, the σῶμα in which the immortal soul is enclosed is the human head (περιετόρνευσαν implies a circular shape), and the ὄχημα is the trunk and limbs, which were added as means of locomotion (Tim. 44 E) ; but Plato's phrase may have suggested to later writers the metaphor by which they described either the whole body, or the corporeal pneuma, as ὄχημα ψυχῆς.

This section is copied in the Hermippus, 1. 13. 96–99 : λόγος μὲν ὄχημα νοῦ, τοῦ δὲ λόγου ψυχή, τὸ δὲ πνεῦμα τῆς ψυχῆς· τοῦτο δὲ διῆκον διὰ φλεβῶν καὶ ἀρτηριῶν καὶ αἵματος κινεῖ τὸ ζῷον καὶ πρὸς τὰς οἰκείας ἐνεργείας καθίστησιν. ... ὥσπερ τοίνυν ἐκεῖνα ἐν τῇ συστάσει δι' ἀλλήλων χωρεῖ καὶ τὸ ζῷον ἐμπνεῖ, οὕτω κἂν τῇ διαλύσει αὖθις πρὸς ἄλληλα ἐπαναχωρεῖ καὶ συστέλλεται·[4] αἷμα μὲν εἰς τὸ πνεῦμα, πνεῦμα δὲ εἰς ψυχήν, ψυχὴ δ' αὖ εἰς λόγον, καὶ ὁ λόγος εἰς νοῦν, καὶ οὗτος αὖ εἰς τὸ συγγενές. The writer of the Hermippus had before him the same corrupt text which presents itself in our MSS. of the Corpus.

ὁ νοῦς [ἐν τῷ λόγῳ, ὁ λόγος] ἐν τῇ ψυχῇ. λόγος is spoken of as a human faculty inferior to νοῦς in Corp. IV. 3 : τὸν μὲν λόγον ... πᾶσι τοῖς ἀνθρώποις ἐμέρισε, τὸν δὲ νοῦν οὐκέτι. See also Corp. XII. i. 12 sq. But in Corp. X, λόγος is nowhere interposed between νοῦς and ψυχή, except in this one sentence; and in § 16, νοῦς is spoken of as contained in ψυχή without any intermediate 'envelope'. It is clear therefore that the mention of λόγος here must be an interpolation.

---

[1] τοῦ P : τῆς F.
[2] 'Fort ante αἰθέρια intercidit τίθενται' Wachsmuth.
[3] 'Fort. post προβλήματα intercidit ἃ' Wachsmuth.
[4] Cf. Corp. X. 16 : συστέλλεται τὸ πνεῦμα εἰς τὸ αἷμα, ἡ δὲ ψυχὴ εἰς τὸ πνεῦμα.

Plotinus, 2. 9. 1, says that it is an error to interpose λόγος ('discursive reason'?), as a separate entity, between νοῦς and ψυχή.[1] The words ἐν τῷ λόγῳ, ὁ λόγος must have been inserted in *Corp.* X by some one whose doctrine of λόγος resembled that which Plotinus rejects.

For the series νοῦς, ψυχή, πνεῦμα, cf. *Corp.* XI. i. 4 b : ὁ μὲν θεὸς ἐν τῷ νῷ, ὁ δὲ νοῦς ἐν τῇ ψυχῇ, ἡ δὲ ψυχὴ ἐν τῇ ὕλῃ. (πνεῦμα is ὕλη qualified in a certain way.) *Corp.* XII. i. 14 a (= V. 11 *fin.*): τῆς μὲν ὕλης τὸ λεπτομερέστατον ἀήρ, ἀέρος δὲ ψυχή, ψυχῆς δὲ νοῦς, νοῦ δὲ θεός. (ἀήρ there takes the place of πνεῦμα.) The writer of *Corp.* X holds νοῦς and ψυχή to be ἀσώματα ; yet at the same time he pictures each of them to himself as a material thing enclosed in another material thing of denser substance.

But why should νοῦς be spoken of at all in § 13 ? At this stage, the writer's business is to explain the relation between ψυχή and σῶμα in man, as he has just explained the relation between ψυχή and σῶμα in the Kosmos ; and this mention of νοῦς unduly anticipates the contents of § 16 f., where he passes on to a discussion of the relation between νοῦς and ψυχή. Moreover, the words are awkwardly put together ; a man composing freely would hardly write ψυχὴ . . . ὀχεῖται τὸν τρόπον τοῦτον, ὁ νοῦς ἐν τῇ ψυχῇ. I am therefore inclined to suspect that τὸν τρόπον τοῦτον, ὁ νοῦς . . . ἡ δὲ ψυχή is a later addition, and that the original text ran thus : ψυχὴ δὲ ἀνθρώπου ὀχεῖται [ ] ἐν τῷ πνεύματι, τὸ δὲ πνεῦμα, διῆκον κ.τ.λ., κινεῖ τὸ σῶμα. (Perhaps the puzzling words νοῦς δὲ κεφαλὴ αὐτη κ.τ.λ. in § 11 may have been inserted by the same interpolator.)

ἡ δὲ ψυχὴ ἐν τῷ πνεύματι. τὸ ⟨δὲ⟩ πνεῦμα, διῆκον κ.τ.λ. Turn. gives ἡ δὲ ψυχὴ ἐν τῷ πνεύματι· τὸ πνεῦμα ἐν τῷ σώματι. τὸ πνεῦμα διήκει κ.τ.λ. But the words τὸ πνεῦμα ἐν τῷ σώματι are not wanted ; for the relation between the πνεῦμα and the σῶμα is sufficiently described by the following sentence, τὸ πνεῦμα, διῆκον . . . ⟨μετὰ τοῦ⟩ αἵματος, κινεῖ τὸ σῶμα καὶ . . . βαστάζει. Moreover there would be a

---

[1] Plot. 2. 9. 1 (Volkmann) : ἔστι γὰρ ὡς ἔστι νοῦς ἀεὶ ὡσαύτως ἐνεργείᾳ κείμενος ἑστώσῃ· κίνησις δὲ πρὸς αὐτὸν καὶ περὶ αὐτὸν ψυχῆς ἤδη ἔργον. καὶ λόγος ἀπ' αὐτοῦ (sc. τοῦ νοῦ) εἰς ψυχήν, ψυχὴν νοερὰν ποιῶν, οὐκ ἄλλην τινὰ μεταξὺ νοῦ καὶ ψυχῆς φύσιν. (Perhaps οὐκ ἄλλη τις μεταξὺ ν. καὶ ψ. φύσις· 'λόγος is not a thing distinct from νοῦς and ψυχή, and intermediate between them.') . . . τὸν δὲ λόγον ὅταν τις ἀπὸ τοῦ νοῦ ποιῇ (i. e. when a man says that the absolute or universal λόγος is derived from the absolute or universal νοῦς), εἶτα [ἀπὸ τούτου] γίνεσθαι ἐν ψυχῇ (λόγον) ἄλλον ἀπ' αὐτοῦ τοῦ λόγου, ἵνα μεταξὺ ψυχῆς καὶ νοῦ ᾖ οὗτος (sc. ὁ λόγος), ἀποστερήσει τὴν ψυχὴν τοῦ νοεῖν, εἰ μὴ παρὰ τοῦ νοῦ κομιεῖται, ἀλλὰ παρὰ ἄλλου τοῦ μεταξύ, τὸν λόγον· καὶ εἴδωλον λόγου, ἀλλ' οὐ λόγον ἕξει, καὶ ὅλως οὐκ εἰδήσει νοῦν οὐδ' ὅλως νοήσει.

verbal contradiction in saying that τὸ πνεῦμα ὀχεῖται ἐν τῷ σώματι
(= βαστάζεται ὑπὸ τοῦ σώματος), and at the same time, that τὸ πνεῦμα
(*nom.*) βαστάζει τὸ σῶμα (*acc.*)

The *pneuma* spoken of in *Corp.* X is the 'vital spirit' (ζωτικὸν πνεῦμα)
of the individual organism. It is a gaseous substance, which serves
as the corporeal 'vehicle' or 'integument' of the incorporeal soul.
Pneuma in this sense occupied a prominent place in the theories
of the medical writers, from Erasistratus onward (i. e. from about
300 B. C.), if not earlier (Puschmann, *Gesch. Med.*, p. 299 ff.). The
cosmic *pneuma* of the Stoics, which is the 'vital spirit' of the
universe (the Kosmos being conceived by them as a ζῷον organized
on the same plan as an individual man or animal), is not mentioned
in *Corp.* X.

τὸ ⟨δὲ⟩ πνεῦμα, διῆκον διὰ ⟨τῶν⟩ [φλεβῶν καὶ] ἀρτηριῶν [καὶ] ⟨μετὰ τοῦ⟩
αἵματος. If we retain the words φλεβῶν καί, we must understand the
writer to say that the veins and arteries alike convey both blood and
pneuma. It is not quite impossible that he held that view ;[1] but it
seems more probable that φλεβῶν καί was inserted by a later hand,
perhaps in consequence of the corruption of κατὰ τὰς φλέβας into καὶ
τὰς φλέβας below. As to the function of the arteries, opinions
differed among the medical writers. Praxagoras of Cos (about
340–320 B. C.) said that the veins contain blood alone, and the
arteries contain air alone ; and his view was adopted by the Stoics
(Puschmann, p. 276). Herophilus held that the arteries convey
both blood and *pneuma* (Galen iv. 731 ; Puschmann, p. 288) ;
Erasistratus held that the veins convey the blood by which the
tissues are nourished, and the arteries serve as canals for the ζωτικὸν
πνεῦμα alone (Puschmann, p. 300).[2] If my restoration of the sentence
is right, the writer of *Corp.* X agrees with Herophilus and differs
from Erasistratus on this question.

κινεῖ τὸ σῶμα (ζῷον MSS.) καὶ ὥσπερ φόρτον (τρόπον MSS.) τινὰ
βαστάζει. The Platonic doctrine was that ψυχή is τὸ κινοῦν (see

---

[1] For the opinion that the φλέβες contain air as well as blood, cf. Aetius (Diels
Doxogr. p. 436): Διογένης (Apolloniates)· εἰ (ἐὰν ?) ἐπὶ πᾶν τὸ αἷμα διαχεόμενον
πληρώσει (-ση ?) μὲν τὰς φλέβας, τὸν δὲ ἐν αὐταῖς περιεχόμενον ἀέρα ὤσει (-ση ?) εἰς
τὰ στέρνα καὶ τὴν ὑποκειμένην γαστέρα, ὕπνον γίγνεσθαι. . . · ἐὰν δὲ ἅπαν τὸ ἀερῶδες
ἐκ τῶν φλεβῶν ἐκλίπη, θάνατον συντυγχάνειν.

[2] Cf. Simon Magus, as reported by Hippolytus, *Ref. haer.* 6. 14 : ἑκατέρωθεν γὰρ
τοῦ ὀμφαλοῦ δύο εἰσὶν ἀρτηρίαι παρατεταμέναι, ὀχετοὶ πνεύματος, καὶ δύο φλέβες,
ὀχετοὶ αἵματος. . . . αἱ δὲ ἀρτηρίαι, ἃς ἔφημεν ὀχετοὺς εἶναι πνεύματος, . . . πρὸς τὴν
μεγάλην συνάπτουσιν ἀρτηρίαν, τὴν κατὰ ῥάχιν καλουμένην ἀορτήν· καὶ οὕτως διὰ τῶν
παραθύρων ἐπὶ τὴν καρδίαν ὁδεύσαν τὸ πνεῦμα κίνησιν ἐργάζεται τῶν ἐμβρύων.

Corp. II. 8 b, 9); but the writer of *Corp.* X holds that the ψυχή acts on the gross matter of the body, not immediately, but through the interposed *pneuma*. The function of the *pneuma*, as he conceives it, corresponds to that of the nervous system in modern physiology.

As to ὥσπερ φόρτον τινὰ βαστάζει, see ὥσπερ φορτίον βαστάζουσα τὸ σῶμα in § 8 b.

διὸ καί τινες τὴν ψυχὴν αἷμα ἐνόμισαν εἶναι. This is what Empedocles said, or rather, what he was commonly understood to have meant. Emped. *fr.* 105, Diels *Vorsokr.* p. 202: (ἡ καρδία) αἵματος ἐν πελάγεσσι τεθραμμένη ἀντιθορόντος, | τῇ τε νόημα μάλιστα κικλήσκεται ἀνθρώποισιν· | αἷμα γὰρ ἀνθρώποις περικάρδιόν ἐστι νόημα. Pl. *Phaedo* 96 B: πότερον τὸ αἷμά ἐστιν ᾧ φρονοῦμεν (Emped.), ἢ ὁ ἀήρ (Anaximenes and Diog. Apoll.), ἢ τὸ πῦρ (Heraclitus), ἢ τούτων μὲν οὐδέν, ὁ δὲ ἐγκέφαλος κ.τ.λ. (Alcmaeon). Theophrast. *De sensu*, Diels *ib.* p. 168, l. 43: διὸ καὶ τῷ αἵματι μάλιστα φρονεῖν (λέγει ὁ Ἐμπεδ.)· ἐν τούτῳ γὰρ μάλιστα κεκρᾶσθαι [ἐστι] τὰ στοιχεῖα τῶν μερῶν. Cic. *Tusc.* I. 9. 19: ' Empedocles animum esse censet cordi suffusum sanguinem.' Galen *Dogm. Hipp. et Plat.* 2, V. 283 K.: Empedocles αἷμά φησιν εἶναι τὴν ψυχήν. In the extant fragments of Empedocles himself, the word ψυχή nowhere occurs; and the apparent inconsistency between his Περὶ φύσεως and his Καθαρμοί may be best explained by assuming him to have held that man has two 'souls', viz. (1) the νοητικόν (including the αἰσθητικόν), which resides in (or is identical with) the blood about the heart, and comes into being and perishes simultaneously with the bodily organism, with which it is inseparably connected, and (2) the δαίμων, which existed before the body in which it is imprisoned, and will survive it. If this is the case, the view of Empedocles was an anticipation of the Platonic theory of the soul; cf. the θνητὸν εἶδος ψυχῆς in Pl. *Tim.*, and the 'two souls' of the Hermetists as reported in *Abammonis resp.* 8. 6 (*Testim.*).

The opinion that the soul is the blood was maintained by Critias, shortly before 400 B.C. (Aristot. *De an.* I. 2, 405 b 5); and it seems to have been asserted, but probably in a modified sense, by the Stoic Diogenes Babylonius, about 160 B.C. Galen, *Dogm. Hipp. et Plat.* 2. 8, 110, quotes Diog. Bab. as saying that τὸ κινοῦν τὸν ἄνθρωπον τὰς κατὰ προαίρεσιν κινήσεις ψυχική τίς ἐστιν ἀναθυμίασις, πᾶσα δὲ ἀναθυμίασις ἐκ τῆς τροφῆς ἀνάγεται· but he adds that Diogenes, αὐτὸς ἐπιλανθανόμενος τῶν οἰκείων δογμάτων, αἷμά φησιν εἶναι τὴν ψυχήν, ὡς Ἐμπεδοκλῆς καὶ Κριτίας ὑπέλαβον. εἰ δέ γε ἕποιτο Κλεάνθει καὶ Χρυσίππῳ καὶ Ζήνωνι, τρέφεσθαι μὲν ἐξ αἵματος φήσασι τὴν ψυχήν, οὐσίαν δ' αὐτῆς εἶναι τὸ πνεῦμα, πῶς ἔτι ταὐτὸν ἔσται τὸ τρέφον καὶ τὸ κινοῦν, εἴπερ τρέφει μὲν τὸ αἷμα, κινεῖ δὲ τὸ πνεῦμα; In the Διασυρμὸς τῶν ἔξω φιλοσόφων of the Christian Hermias (Diels *Doxogr.* p. 651), the doctrine that the soul is the blood is mentioned as one of those taught by Pagan philosophers.

The Hebrews held·that 'the life is the blood', and gave this as a reason for the law which forbade them to eat flesh in which the blood is retained. *Gen.* 9. 4: κρέας ἐν αἵματι ψυχῆς οὐ φάγεσθε. Cf. Philo *De special. leg.* 4. 10. 119–123, Cohn V, p. 236 f.: κελεύει μέντοι μήτε θνησιμαῖον μήτε θηριάλωτον προσίεσθαι. . . . ἔνιοι δὲ . . . ἄθυτα παρασκευάζουσιν, ἄγχοντες καὶ ἀποπνίγοντες, καὶ τὴν οὐσίαν τῆς ψυχῆς, ἣν ἐλεύθερον καὶ ἄφετον ἐχρῆν ἐᾶν, ⟨ἐν⟩τυμβεύοντες τῷ σώματι, τὸ αἷμα· σαρκῶν γὰρ αὐτὸ μόνον ἀπολαύειν αὐταρκες ἦν, μηδενὸς ἐφαπτομένους τῶν συγγένειαν πρὸς ψυχὴν ἐχόντων. ὅθεν ἐν ἑτέροις τίθησι νόμον περὶ αἵματος, μήθ' αἷμα μήτε στέαρ προσφέρεσθαι· τὸ μὲν αἷμα δι' ἣν εἶπον αἰτίαν, ὅτι οὐσία ψυχῆς ἐστίν, οὐχὶ τῆς νοερᾶς καὶ λογικῆς, ἀλλὰ τῆς αἰσθητικῆς, καθ' ἣν ἡμῖν τε καὶ τοῖς ἀλόγοις κοινὸν τὸ ζῆν συμβέβηκεν· ἐκείνης γὰρ οὐσία πνεῦμα θεῖον (*Gen.* 2. 7). Philo must have met with the doctrine that the blood is οὐσία ψυχῆς in Pagan writings, as well as in the Books of Moses. In the time of the Roman empire, Jewish¦ influence may perhaps have helped to revive this primitive belief among the Pagan Greeks.

σφαλλόμενοι τῆς φύσεως (τὴν φύσιν MSS.). It would be possible to say σφαλλόμενοι τὴν γνώμην, but not σφαλλόμενοι τὴν φύσιν. If we read τῆς φύσεως, the phrase may be taken as equivalent to σφαλλόμενοι τοῦ περὶ τῆς φύσεως ἀληθοῦς.

πρῶτον δεῖ [[ ]] ⟨ἐξελθεῖν⟩ τὴν ψυχήν, καὶ τότε, ⟨⟨τοῦ πνεύματος ἀναχωρήσαντος εἰς⟩⟩ ⟨τὸ περιέχον⟩, τὸ αἷμα παγῆναι κατὰ (καὶ MSS.) τὰς φλέβας, καὶ τὰς ἀρτηρίας κενωθείσας [τὸ ζῷον] καταλ[ε]ιπεῖν. The argument appears to be that the soul cannot be identical with the blood, because at death the soul departs, while the blood remains in the corpse. But the details are obscure. We are told that at death the arteries (or, according to the MSS., the veins and arteries) 'are emptied'. It was said above that during life the [veins and] arteries contain both blood and *pneuma*. What then becomes of the blood and *pneuma* at death? The blood 'is coagulated'. It certainly remains in the body (except in the case of death by bleeding); and as the writer says that the arteries are left empty after death, his view must be that at the time of death that part of the blood which was previously contained in the arteries passes from them into the veins,[1] so that all the blood in the body is collected in the veins, and is there coagulated. This meaning may be obtained by writing τὸ αἷμα παγῆναι κατὰ τὰς φλέβας, καὶ τὰς ἀρτηρίας κ.τ.λ. in place of τὸ αἷμα παγῆναι, καὶ τὰς φλέβας καὶ τὰς ἀρτηρίας κ.τ.λ.

But what becomes of the *pneuma* when it quits the arteries? According to the text of the MSS., it passes εἰς τὴν ψυχήν; but that is absurd. The ψυχή might be said to be in the πνεῦμα, which is its ἔνδυμα; but the πνεῦμα cannot be said to be in the ψυχή, either during life or after death. We must therefore conclude that the Hermetist either omitted to say where the *pneuma* goes, or wrote something like εἰς ⟨τὸ περιέχον⟩. With the alterations which I have proposed, the passage yields a satisfactory sense. The ψυχή quits the body; and the vital *pneuma*, which is the vehicle or envelope of the ψυχή, quits the body with it. Thereupon the blood, no longer conveyed along the arteries by the *pneuma*, coagulates in the veins; and the arteries are left empty of blood as well as of *pneuma*. This physical change, which follows and results from the departure of the ψυχή, is 'the death of the body'.

A theory similar in part, but not identical with that of the Hermetist, is mentioned in Iambl. Περὶ ψυχῆς, Stob. 1. 49. 43, vol. i, p. 383 W.: ἀρά γε (γίγνεται ὁ θάνατος) πνιγμῷ τῶν ἀρτηριῶν, ἀποκλειομένων τοῦ δέχεσθαι τὸ ἐκτὸς πνεῦμα; Cf. *Exc.* XXIII (*Kore Kosmu*) 67.

§ 14 a. ἐκ μιᾶς δὲ ἀρχῆς . . . οὐ κινεῖται. This passage has no connexion with the context, and interrupts the train of thought. It may have been written at the top or bottom of a page by some reader, and inserted into the text by a copyist's error.

The writer of these words introduces the Neoplatonic conception of τὸ ἕν, of which there is no mention in the rest of the document. 'The One' of which he speaks is something which is prior to the ἀρχή. But what is this ἀρχή? The writer can hardly have omitted to give it a name; and he most likely named it νοῦς. It is possible that he wrote ἐκ μιᾶς ἀρχῆς ⟨τοῦ νοῦ⟩, and that the superfluous words καὶ μόνου have arisen out of τοῦ νοῦ misplaced. On τὸ ἕν, as distinguished from νοῦς, and placed above it, see Plotinus *passim*.

ἡ μὲν ἀρχὴ κινεῖται. If the ἀρχή is νοῦς, this statement can hardly

---

[1] Cf. Aetius (Diels *Doxogr.* p. 435): Πῶς ὕπνος γίνεται καὶ θάνατος. Ἀλκμαίων ἀναχωρήσει τοῦ αἵματος εἰς τὰς αἱμόρρους φλέβας ὕπνον γίνεσθαί φησι, τὴν δὲ ἐξέγερσιν διάχυσιν (*sc.* τοῦ αἵματος: perhaps διαχύσει)· τὴν δὲ παντελῆ ἀναχώρησιν (*sc.* εἰς τὰς φλέβας) θάνατον. But where did Alcmaeon suppose the blood to be during waking life, when it has not 'withdrawn into the veins'?

LIBELLVS X: §§ 13–15 a 259

be reconciled with § 11 *init.*, ἡ δὲ νοητὴ στάσις κινεῖ τὴν ὑλικὴν κίνησιν. But it agrees with Plotinus 6. 7. 13: νοῦς τε κινούμενος κινεῖται μὲν ὡσαύτως καὶ κατὰ ταῦτα καὶ ὅμοια ἀεί.... ἐπὶ πάντα οὖν κινεῖσθαι δεῖ ⟨νοῦν⟩, μᾶλλον δὲ κεκινῆσθαι.... εἰ δ᾽ ἔστηκεν (ὁ νοῦς), οὐ νοεῖ·... εἰ δὲ τοῦτο, οὐδ᾽ ἔστιν.

τὸ δὲ ἕν ... ἔστηκεν. This is not quite in agreement with Plotinus, who says (6. 9. 3) that τὸ ἕν is οὐ κινούμενον οὐδ᾽ αὖ ἑστώς, but is πρὸ κινήσεως, πρὸ στάσεως.

§ 14 b. τρία τοίνυν ταῦτα, ὁ θεός [ ], καὶ ὁ κόσμος, καὶ ὁ ἄνθρωπος. Cf. *Ascl. Lat.* I. 10: 'deus primus est, secundus est mundus, homo est tertius.' Herm. *ap.* Stob. *Exc.* XI. 2. (6): πρῶτον ὁ θεός, δεύτερον ὁ κόσμος, τρίτον ὁ ἄνθρωπος.

τὸν μὲν κόσμον ὁ θεὸς ἔχει, τὸν δὲ ἄνθρωπον ὁ κόσμος. ἔχει probably means 'contains' (ἐμπεριέχει). In other words, the Kosmos is 'in God', or God is the τόπος of the Kosmos. Cf. *Corp.* IX. 9: τὰ γὰρ ὄντα ὁ θεὸς ἔχει.

γίνεται ὁ μὲν κόσμος τοῦ θεοῦ υἱός, ὁ δὲ ἄνθρωπος τοῦ κόσμου ⟨υἱός, καὶ τοῦ θεοῦ⟩ ὥσπερ ἔγγονος (ἔκγονος MSS.). Cf. *Corp.* IX. 8: πατὴρ μὲν οὖν ὁ θεὸς τοῦ κόσμου, ὁ δὲ κόσμος τῶν ἐν τῷ κόσμῳ. The word ἔγγονος ('grandson') is preferable to ἔκγονος ('offspring' or 'descendant').

§ 15 a. οὐκ ἄρα (οὐ γὰρ MSS.) ἀγνοεῖ τὸν ἄνθρωπον ὁ θεός. God does not ignore his grandson man; he recognizes the relationship. Cf. Paul, 1. *Cor.* 13. 12: τότε δὲ ἐπιγνώσομαι καθὼς καὶ ἐπεγνώσθην.

καὶ θέλει γνωρίζεσθαι. Cf. *Corp.* I. 31: ἅγιος ὁ θεός, ὃς γνωσθῆναι βούλεται. At this point the writer of *Corp.* X recurs to the thought, already suggested in §§ 4 b–6, that man on earth, though sunk in matter, is yet not wholly estranged from God (or from 'the Good', which is correlative to God), and that through *gnosis* he may rid himself of the evil which adheres to him in consequence of his incarnation, and may thus become good (τούτῳ μόνῳ ἀγαθὴ γίνεται ψυχή).

αὕτη εἰς τὸν Ὄλυμπον ἀνάβασις. In the Greek poets, from the Odyssey downward, Olympus means heaven; and the word was employed by some of the Pythagoreans in the sense of the highest or outermost sphere of heaven. Aetius, Diels *Doxogr.* p. 337: τὸ μὲν οὖν ἀνωτάτω μέρος τοῦ περιέχοντος ... Ὄλυμπον καλεῖ (ὁ Φιλόλαος)· τὰ δὲ ὑπὸ τὴν τοῦ Ὀλύμπου φοράν, ἐν ᾧ τοὺς πέντε πλανήτας μεθ᾽ ἡλίου καὶ σελήνης τετάχθαι, κόσμον· τὸ δ᾽ ὑπὸ τούτοις ὑποσέληνόν τε καὶ περίγειον μέρος τοῦ περιέχοντος ... οὐρανόν. Cf. Kaibel *Epigr.*

S 2

Gr. 649. 7 (Rome, third century A. D.) : ζώεις γὰρ ἀμέμπτως | αὐγαῖς ἐν καθαραῖσιν Ὀλύμπου. *Ib.* 159. 2 : ψυχὴ δ᾽ ἐν Ὀλύμπῳ. *Ib.* 261. 11 (Corcyra, second century A. D. ?) : ἀθάνατος ψυχὴ τὰ μὲν οἰκία τῶν ἐν Ὀλύμπῳ | ναίω. The phrase εἰς τὸν Ὄλυμπον ἀναβαίνειν is equivalent to εἰς τὸν τῶν θεῶν χορὸν χωρεῖν in § 7.

This statement, if it stood alone, might be taken to imply that it is possible for a man to 'ascend to Olympus', i. e. to become a god, while he is still in the body. But that is expressly denied in §§ 5 and 6 ; and it appears from § 7 that the τελειοτάτη δόξα is beyond man's reach as long as he lives on earth, and that the soul must be released from its earthly prison, and must afterwards pass through an intermediate stage as a daemon, before it becomes a god. We must therefore take the writer's meaning in § 15 a to be that those who, while still in the body, have attained to such *gnosis* as is possible for them on earth, will, after death, eventually ascend to heaven, and become astral gods.

§ 15 b. ⟨. . .⟩ καὶ οὐδέποτε (οὐκέτι ?) ἀγαθὴ ⟨μένει⟩, κακὴ δὲ [[ ]] κατ᾽ ἀνάγκην γίνεται. A connecting passage must have been lost before these words. The sense required might be expressed by writing ⟨φύσει μὲν γὰρ ἀγαθὴ ἡ ψυχή· ἐνσωματωθεῖσα δὲ μολύνεται,⟩ καὶ οὐκέτι ἀγαθὴ ⟨μένει⟩. In this life, the human soul is bad, and can become good only by acquiring *gnosis*; for though it was good in its antenatal state, it has necessarily been made bad by its incarnation. Cf. Philo, *Quis rer. div. heres* 55. 272, Wendland III, p. 62 : ἀνάγκη γὰρ θνητὸν ὄντα τῷ τῶν παθῶν ἔθνει πιεσθῆναι καὶ τὰς οἰκείους τῷ γενομένῳ κῆρας ἀναδέξασθαι, βούλημα δὲ θεοῦ[1] τὰ σύμφυτα κακὰ τοῦ γένους ἡμῶν ἐπικουφίζειν· ὥστε καὶ ἡμεῖς ἐν ἀρχῇ τὰ οἰκεῖα πεισόμεθα, ὠμῶν γενόμενοι δεσποτῶν δοῦλοι, καὶ ὁ θεὸς τὸ οἰκεῖον ἐργάσεται ἑαυτῷ, ἄφεσιν καὶ ἐλευθερίαν ταῖς ἱκέτεσιν αὐτοῦ ψυχαῖς προκηρύξας.

Ψυχὴν παιδὸς θέασαι, . . . πῶς καλὴ[ν] . . ., ἔτι σχεδὸν ἠρτημένη τῆς τοῦ κόσμου ψυχῆς. πῶς καλή, 'how beautiful it is!' This use of πῶς is post-classical. It occurs several times in the New Testament; *Matth.* 21. 20 : ἐθαύμασαν λέγοντες Πῶς παραχρῆμα ἐξηράνθη ἡ συκῆ. *Mark* 10. 23 : πῶς δυσκόλως . . . εἰσελεύσονται. *Luke* 12. 50 : πῶς συνέχομαι ἕως ὅτου τελεσθῇ. *John* 11. 36 : ἴδε πῶς ἐφίλει αὐτόν.

The thought expressed in this passage closely resembles that of

---

[1] Similarly, the writer of *Corp.* X says that it is 'the will of God' that men should get *gnosis*, and thereby be ' made good '.

Wordsworth's *Ode on intimations of immortality*.[1] It contrasts with the Christian doctrine of 'original sin'; but there is no reason to suppose that the writer knew of that doctrine and was consciously opposing it.

It is here assumed that the soul of the child comes directly ἀπὸ τῆς τοῦ παντὸς ψυχῆς (§ 7 *init.*). This assumption is hardly consistent with the doctrine of successive incarnations which is taught in § 7, and from which it would seem to follow that the child's soul must have been (or at any rate may have been) previously incorporated in a series of bestial bodies, and that traces of the connexion of the individual soul with the world-soul from which it was originally parted off ought to be more clearly visible in a ἑρπετόν than in a human child. On this subject, the writer of *Corp.* X seems to have set down side by side statements derived from different sources, without asking himself how they were to be reconciled.

Iamblichus (Περὶ ψυχῆς, Stob. 1. 49. 40, vol. i, p. 380 W) distinguishes the case of a soul which comes to its embodiment fresh from enjoyment of the beatific vision in the world above, from that of one which has been corrupted in a preceding incarnation : δεῖ δέ που καὶ τοὺς βίους τῶν ψυχῶν κατανοεῖν πρὶν ἐλθεῖν εἰς σῶμα, ὡς ἄρα καὶ οὗτοι πολλὴν ἔχουσιν ἐν ἑαυτοῖς διάστασιν· ἀπὸ δὲ διαφόρων τρόπων ζωῆς διάφορον ποιοῦνται ἑαυτῶν καὶ τὴν πρώτην σύνοδον.[2] οἵ τε γὰρ νεοτελεῖς[3] καὶ πολυθεάμονες τῶν ὄντων, οἵ τε συνοπαδοὶ καὶ συγγενεῖς τῶν θεῶν,[4] οἵ τε παντελεῖς καὶ ὁλόκληρα[5] τὰ εἴδη τῆς ψυχῆς περιέχοντες, πάντες ἀπαθεῖς καὶ ἀκήρατοι ἐμφύονται πρώτως εἰς τὰ σώματα· οἱ δὲ ἀπὸ τῶν ἐπιθυμιῶν ἄδην ἀναπεπλησμένοι, καὶ ἄλλων παθῶν μεστοί, μετὰ παθῶν συνέρχονται πρώτως τοῖς σώμασι. The soul described by the Hermetist as ἔτι σχεδὸν ἠρτημένη τῆς τοῦ κόσμου ψυχῆς corresponds, in some respects at least, to the νεοτελεῖς κ.τ.λ.

---

[1] Perhaps one might compare *Mark* 10. 14 (*Matth.* 19. 14, *Luke* 18. 16) : τὰ παιδία . . ., τῶν γὰρ τοιούτων ἐστὶν ἡ βασιλεία τοῦ θεοῦ. . . . ὃς ἂν μὴ δέξηται τὴν βασιλείαν τοῦ θεοῦ ὡς παιδίον, οὐ μὴ εἰσέλθῃ εἰς αὐτήν.

Abelson, *The immanence of God in Rabbinical literature*, p. 281 : 'The Rabbins emphasize untiringly the spotless purity of the new-born babe. "The good inclination", say they, "is thirteen years older than the evil inclination" (because the latter only begins to assert itself at the age of thirteen).'

[2] The σύνοδος is the junction of the soul with the body.

[3] 'Recently initiated'; i.e. fresh from the antenatal ἐποπτεία of the νοητὸν κάλλος. This is a reference to Pl. *Phaedr.* 250 E f.: ὁ μὲν οὖν μὴ νεοτελής, ἢ διεφθαρμένος, οὐκ ὀξέως ἐνθένδε ἐκεῖσε φέρεται πρὸς αὐτὸ τὸ κάλλος. . . . ὁ δὲ ἀρτιτελής, ὁ τῶν τότε πολυθεάμων κ.τ.λ.

[4] Pl. *Phaedr.* 248 C : ἥτις ἂν ψυχὴ θεῷ ξυνοπαδὸς γενομένη κατίδη τι τῶν ἀληθῶν.

[5] Pl. *Phaedr.* 250 C : ὁλόκληροι μὲν αὐτοὶ ὄντες καὶ ἀπαθεῖς κακῶν . . ., ὁλόκληρα δὲ . . . φάσματα μυούμενοί τε καὶ ἐποπτεύοντες.

of Iamblichus, who ἀκήρατοι ἐμφύονται πρώτως εἰς τὰ σώματα; but
those who have been polluted in previous incarnations, and who μετὰ
παθῶν συνέρχονται πρώτως τοῖς σώμασι,[1] are ignored in *Corp.* X. 15 b.

αὐτὴν (ἑαυτὴν MSS.) διάλυσιν αὐτῆς μηδέπω ἐπιδεχομένην. The
διάλυσις of the individual soul must mean its separation from the
world-soul. The soul of the young child does not accept, or admit
to itself, its separation; i. e. it feels itself to be still a part of the
world-soul from which it has only just been separated. The opposite
of this is expressed by διαλύσασα ἑαυτήν below.

ὅταν δὲ ὀγκωθῇ τὸ σῶμα, . . . ⟨⟨ἐγγεννᾷ λήθην⟩⟩. If the arrangement
of the words in the MSS. is retained, the subject of ἐγγεννᾷ λήθην is
ἡ ψυχή; and in order to make sense of that, it would be necessary to
write ⟨ἑαυτῇ⟩ ἐγγεννᾷ λήθην. But the meaning required is rather τὸ
σῶμα τῇ ψυχῇ ἐγγεννᾷ λήθην; and I have transposed the words so as
to obtain that meaning.

The λήθη of which Orphici and Platonists spoke is here said to
result inevitably from the διάλυσις of the individual soul, i. e. its
severance from the world-soul. An incarnated soul must necessarily
be an individual soul, and must, as such, be in some degree separated
from the world-soul; but the writer regards this separation as a
gradual process, which is not completed until after the first years of
childhood.

§ 16. ἀναδραμοῦσα γὰρ ἡ ψυχὴ εἰς τὰ ἑαυτῆς (εἰς ἑαυτὴν MSS.) ⟨τοῦ
πνεύματος χωρίζεται, καὶ ὁ νοῦς τῆς ψυχῆς⟩. The Platonists held that
the home or natural place of the soul (τὰ ἑαυτῆς) is above; and the
Stoics said that all souls, when they quit the body, rise into the
atmosphere.

A few lines below, we are told that Hermes has said that ὁ νοῦς
τῆς ψυχῆς χωρίζεται καὶ ἡ ψυχὴ τοῦ πνεύματος. A statement to that
effect must therefore have occurred somewhere; and it is precisely
what is needed here to complete the sentence.

The separation of the ψυχή from the πνεῦμα in which it is enveloped
is pictured in Plutarch's 'Vision of Thespesius', *De sera numinis
vindicta* 22, 564 A. Thespesius sees fiery bubbles rising through the
air; the bubbles break, and little figures in human shape come forth
from them. These human figures are newly disembodied souls; and
the bubble must be intended to represent the πνεῦμα in which the
soul is enclosed.

---

[1] I. e. who have πάθη already adhering to them when their life on earth (in the
present incarnation) begins.

ὁ δὲ νοῦς . . . σώματος πυρίνου ⟨ἐπι⟩λαβόμενος περιπολεῖ πάντα τόπον.
The νοῦς, when it quits the earthy body, does not remain bodiless,
but assumes another sort of body, which consists of fire. This
corresponds to what is described in § 7 by the words αἱ δὲ ἀνθρώπειαι
(ψυχαὶ) . . . εἰς δαίμονας μεταβάλλουσιν. The νοῦς incorporated in a
fiery body, and ranging through all space, must be a daemon. But
in § 7, it is the ψυχή, and not the νοῦς, that is said to be thus transformed ; that is, the word ψυχή is there used in a wider sense, and
the νοῦς is included under it. Cf. § 19 a : (ἡ εὐσεβὴς ψυχὴ) ὅλη νοῦς
γίνεται κ.τ.λ.

For the notion of a 'fiery body', cf. Plotinus 4. 3. 4 : καίτοι τινές
φασι τόδε μὲν (τὸ σῶμα) καταλείψειν (τὴν ἡμετέραν ψυχήν), οὐ πάντη δὲ
ἔξω σώματος ἔσεσθαι. Ib. 4. 3. 9 : διττὸς ὁ τρόπος τῆς εἰς τὸ σῶμα
ψυχῆς εἰσόδου· ἡ μὲν γὰρ γίνεται ψυχῇ ἐν σώματι οὔσῃ, τῇ τε μετενσω-
ματουμένῃ καὶ τῇ ἐκ σώματος ἀερίνου ἢ πυρίνου εἰς γήινον γινομένῃ, ἣν
δὴ μετενσωμάτωσιν οὐ λέγουσιν εἶναι, ὅτι ἄδηλον τὸ ἀφ' οὗ ἡ εἴσκρισις·
ἡ δὲ ἐκ τοῦ ἀσωμάτου εἰς ὁτιοῦν σῶμα, ἢ δὴ καὶ πρώτη ἂν εἴη ψυχῇ
κοινωνία σώματος. Plot. 4. 3. 15 : ἴασι δὲ (αἱ ψυχαὶ) ἐκκύψασαι τοῦ
νοητοῦ εἰς οὐρανὸν μὲν πρῶτον, καὶ σῶμα ἐκεῖ προσλαβοῦσαι, δι' αὐτοῦ
ἤδη χωροῦσι καὶ ἐπὶ τὰ γεωδέστερα σώματα. Iambl. Περὶ ψυχῆς, Stob.
1. 49. 39, vol. i, p. 378 W : (ἄλλη αἵρεσις τῶν Πλατωνικῶν), τιθεμένη
τὴν ψυχὴν ἀεὶ εἶναι ἐν σώματι, ὥσπερ ἡ Ἐρατοσθένους καὶ Πτολεμαίου
τοῦ Πλατωνικοῦ καὶ ἄλλων, ἀπὸ σωμάτων αὐτὴν λεπτοτέρων εἰς τὰ
ὀστρεώδη¹ πάλιν εἰσοικίζει σώματα· διατρίβειν μὲν γὰρ αὐτὴν ⌜εἰς μοῖράν
τινα⌝ (lege ἀεὶ ἐν μοίρᾳ τινὶ) τοῦ αἰσθητοῦ, καθήκειν γε μὴν εἰς τὸ στερεὸν
σῶμα ἄλλοτε ἀπ' ἄλλων τοῦ παντὸς τόπων. καὶ τούτους (sc. τοὺς τόπους)
Ἡρακλείδην μὲν τὸν Ποντικὸν ἀφορίζειν περὶ τὸν γαλαξίαν, ἄλλους δὲ
καθ' ὅλας τοῦ οὐρανοῦ τὰς σφαίρας, ἀφ' ὧν δὴ δεῦρο κατιέναι τὰς ψυχάς·
τοὺς δὲ περὶ σελήνην ἢ ἐν τῷ ὑπὸ σελήνην ἀέρι λέγειν αὐτὰς κατοικεῖν, καὶ
ἀπ' αὐτῶν κάτω χωρεῖν εἰς τὴν περίγειον γένεσιν· τοὺς δὲ ἀπὸ σωμάτων
ἀεὶ στερεῶν πίπτειν εἰς ἕτερα ⟨στερεὰ ?⟩ σώματα διισχυρίζεσθαι.

It appears from this passage that Iamblichus knew of certain
Platonists who held that the soul, when not incorporated in an
earthy body, is at all times incorporated in a material body of finer
substance.² They may perhaps have derived this doctrine from

---

¹ I. e. γήινα or στερεά. This use of the word ὀστρεώδης must have been suggested
by Pl. *Phaedr.* 250 C : καθαροὶ ὄντες καὶ ἀσήμαντοι τούτου, ὃ νῦν σῶμα περιφέροντες
ὀνομάζομεν, ὀστρέου τρόπον δεδεσμευμένοι.
² This opinion was adopted by Origen, *De princip.* 2. 2 : 'Quaerendum primo
videtur, si possibile est penitus incorporeas remanere rationabiles naturas, cum ad
summum sanctitatis ac beatitudinis venerint,—quod mihi quidem difficillimum et

Heraclides Ponticus. We are told that Heraclides φωτοειδῆ τὴν ψυχὴν ὡρίσατο (Aetius, Diels *Doxogr.*, p. 388), or said that the soul is *lumen* (Tertull. *De an.* 9; Macrob. *Somn.* 1. 14); and that he considered the soul to be an οὐράνιον σῶμα (Philoponus *De an.*). If these statements are correct, it follows that Heraclides must have rejected the Platonic doctrine that the soul is incorporeal. But if he had done so, how could he have come to be reckoned a Platonist? It seems more probable that he considered the soul itself to be incorporeal, but held that, when released from its earthy body, it is incorporated in a body of another sort; that the τελειοτάτη δόξα of a soul is to be incorporated in a body consisting of light, or luminous fire; and that the ζῷον formed by the combination of the incorporeal soul with this luminous body is of like nature with a star, and shines as a point of light in the Milky Way. If Heraclides held some such view as this, Posidonius's theory of disembodied souls may be regarded as a modified version of that of Heraclides, adapted to the principles of the Stoic physics. The Platonist Heraclides may be presumed to have said that the soul, before and after its embodiment in gross matter upon earth, has for its ἔνδυμα either an aerial body (i. e. the body of a daemon), or an aetherial body (i. e. the body of an astral god), and is situated in the atmosphere in the one case, and in the highest heaven in the other case;[1] the Stoic Posidonius said that the soul, before and after its embodiment on earth, *is* either a mass of air and fire mingled with watery vapour and situated in the lower atmosphere (i. e. a 'hero'), or a mass of air and fire situated in the upper atmosphere (i. e. a 'daemon'), or a mass of pure fire situated in the fiery heaven (i. e. an astral god). The Platonists whom Iamblichus describes as holding that the soul 'is always in a body' may have been influenced by Posidonius; but being Platonists and not Stoics, and therefore holding that the soul

---

paene impossibile videtur,—an necesse est eas semper coniunctas esse corporibus. . . . Si vero impossibile est hoc ullo modo affirmari, id est, quod vivere praeter corpus possit ulla alia natura praeter Patrem et Filium et Spiritum sanctum, necessitas consequentiae ac rationis coarctat intelligi, principaliter quidem creatas esse rationabiles naturas, materialem vero substantiam opinione quidem et intellectu solum separari ab iis, . . . sed nunquam sine ipsa eas vel vixisse vel vivere : solius namque Trinitatis incorporea vita exsistere recte putabitur. Ut ergo superius diximus, materialis ista substantia . . . cum ad inferiores quosque trahitur, in crassiorem corporis statum solidioremque formatur . . .; cum vero perfectioribus ministrat et beatioribus, in fulgore caelestium corporum micat, et spiritualis corporis indumentis vel angelos Dei, vel filios resurrectionis exornat.'

[1] Cf. the classification of ζῷα in the Platonic *Epinomis*, the writer of which must have been contemporary with Heraclides.

is incorporeal, they necessarily rejected Posidonius's way of putting it, and reverted to that of Heraclides. The writer of *Corp.* X appears to have belonged to this sect of Platonists, or at least to have been influenced by them.

The Hermetist's conception of the σῶμα πύρινον of the liberated νοῦς is to some extent similar to Paul's conception of the σῶμα πνευματικόν or ἐπουράνιον in 1 *Cor.* 15. 35–50.

καταλιπὼν τὴν ψυχὴν κρίσει καὶ τῇ κατ' ἀξίαν δίκῃ. Here we have a notion of which the writer has hitherto given no hint. At death, the man splits into two distinct persons,[1] called respectively the νοῦς and the ψυχή. The νοῦς assumes a fiery body, becomes a daemon, and is employed in God's service as a ministering spirit (§ 19 a); but the ψυχή, after the νοῦς has quitted it, continues to exist with a separate personality of its own,[2] and is subjected to punishment, which presumably takes the form of reincarnation in an animal body (§§ 7, 8 a). The man of whom this is said must be the ordinary man, neither very good nor very wicked; for in the case of the εὐσεβής, the ψυχή is wholly absorbed into the νοῦς (ὅλη νοῦς γίνεται), and ceases to exist as a separate entity; and on the other hand, the wicked man has no νοῦς in him (§ 24 a), so that after death nothing is left of him except a ψυχή subject to punishment.

A somewhat similar view of the relation between the νοῦς and the ψυχή is expressed in Plutarch's 'Tale of the stranger from the western continent' (*Fac. in orbe lunae* 28, 943 ff.). We are there told that man is composed, not of two parts only (σῶμα and ψυχή), but of three distinct parts, viz. σῶμα, ψυχή, and νοῦς. When death takes place on earth, the σῶμα is cast off; and after a term of purgation in the atmosphere, the disembodied man, consisting of νοῦς and ψυχή still linked together, passes to the moon, and resides there. In the moon takes place a 'second death', by which the

---

[1] For a modern presentment of the same notion, see Edward Carpenter, *The drama of love and death*, p. 264: 'We have once or twice in the foregoing chapters alluded to the possibility of the self dividing into two personalities, or even more. We have supposed, for instance, that at death the psychic organism may possibly split up—some more terrestrial portion remaining operant and active on the earth-plane, and some other portion removing to a subtler and more ethereal region.'

[2] Cf. Iambl. *De an.*, Stob. 1. 49. 43, vol. i, p. 384 W. According to one of the views there mentioned, χωρισθεῖσα ἀπὸ τῆς διανοίας ἡ ὅλη ἄλογος ζωὴ μένει καὶ αὐτὴ διασωζομένη ἐν τῷ κόσμῳ, ὥσπερ οἱ παλαιότατοι τῶν ἱερέων ἀποφαίνονται. The διάνοια of Iambl. corresponds to the νοῦς of *Corp.* X. 16, and the ἄλογος ζωή of Iambl., to the ψυχή of *Corp.* X. 16. But who are the 'most ancient priests' who taught this doctrine? That term might be used by Iamblichus to denote either Orpheus, or Egyptian priests; and among the latter he might possibly include Hermes Trismegistus.

νοῦς is separated from the ψυχή. The νοῦς then ascends to the sun, whence it originally came; the ψυχή is left on the moon, and retains for a time a dreamlike life of its own, but sooner or later fades away, and is resolved into the substance of the moon.

Πῶς τοῦτο λέγεις, ὦ πάτερ, ⟨ὅτι⟩ ὁ νοῦς τῆς ψυχῆς χωρίζεται [καὶ ἡ ψυχὴ τοῦ πνεύματος]; The relation between the ψυχή and the πνεῦμα has been sufficiently described already, and Tat has no reason to ask for any further explanation about that. But he may well be surprised and puzzled by what Hermes has just said about the separation of the νοῦς from the ψυχή. It is therefore most likely that his question originally ended at χωρίζεται, and that the words καὶ ἡ ψυχὴ τοῦ πνεύματος were subsequently added. The person who added these words must have read something like ἡ ψυχὴ τοῦ πνεύματος χωρίζεται in the second sentence of § 16.

[σοῦ εἰπόντος ἔνδυμα εἶναι τοῦ μὲν νοῦ τὴν ψυχήν, τῆς δὲ ψυχῆς τὸ πνεῦμα.] This seems to be a clumsy attempt to account for Tat's question; and it was probably inserted after the point of that question had been obscured by the addition of καὶ ... πνεύματος. The words πῶς τοῦτο λέγεις ... σοῦ εἰπόντος κ.τ.λ. imply that Tat finds it difficult to reconcile the two statements of Hermes (viz. 'the νοῦς is separated from the ψυχή' &c. and 'the ψυχή is a garment of the νοῦς' &c.) with one another. That is, the interpolation makes it appear that Tat thought it impossible for a thing to be separated from its ἔνδυμα. But no one could think that; every one knows that it is possible to take one's coat off.

The phrase καθαρὸς γενόμενος τῶν ἐνδυμάτων occurred a few lines above; but Hermes has not expressly said that the ψυχή is an ἔνδυμα of the νοῦς, or that the πνεῦμα is an ἔνδυμα of the ψυχή.

§ 17. Συννοεῖν δεῖ ... τὸν ἀκούοντα τῷ λέγοντι [καὶ συμπνεῖν]. Cf. Corp. IX fin.—συμπνεῖν (or συμπνέειν) is probably a variant for συννοεῖν. The meaning seems to be this: 'If you have understood what I have told you about the relation between ψυχή and πνεῦμα, you ought to be able to anticipate the conclusion at which I have been aiming, namely, that the relation between νοῦς and ψυχή is analogous to that between ψυχή and πνεῦμα, and consequently, that νοῦς is united with ψυχή only so long as both are contained in an earthy body.'

ἡ σύνθεσις [τῶν ἐνδυμάτων] τούτων ἐν σώματι γηΐνῳ γίνεται. The σύνθεσις of which Hermes is speaking is that of νοῦς and ψυχή; and νοῦς is not an ἔνδυμα. It is therefore necessary to bracket τῶν ἐνδυμάτων.

ἀνέχεσθαι συγχρωτιζόμενον αὐτῇ παθητὸν σῶμα. συγχρωτίζεσθαι is derived from χρώς, and means 'to be in contact with another person, skin against skin'; hence, 'to be in defiling contact'. Cf. *Corp.* XII. i. 10 as emended: καὶ ὁ νοῦς ἄρα παθητός ἐστι, συγχρωτιζόμενος τοῖς πάθεσι. Diog. Laert. 7. 1. 2: Zeno was told by an oracle that he would live the best life εἰ συγχρωτίζοιτο τοῖς νεκροῖς. He took this to mean that he must study the writings of dead authors.[1] The use of συγχρωτ. here might be made to agree more exactly with its use elsewhere by writing ἀνέχεσθαι συγχρωτιζομένην παθητῷ σώματι, 'to endure being defiled by contact with'.

§ 18. νοῦς δέ, ὀξύτατος ὢν πάντων τῶν [θείων] νοη[μα]τῶν. νοῦς cannot be called a νόημα; but it may be called a νοητόν. ψυχή also is a νοητόν; but νοῦς is ὀξύτερος ψυχῆς. The word νοητόν is here equivalent to ἀσώματον, and the writer is hardly conscious of its etymological connexion with νοῦς. θείων may be an alternative reading for νοητῶν.

δημιουργὸς γὰρ ὢν [πάντων] ὁ νοῦς. Compare the corresponding Stoic doctrine in Arius Didymus, Diels *Doxogr.*, p. 469: οὔτε γὰρ τῆς οὐσίας (material substance) ἀρχὴν κἀνάπαυσιν οἷόν τε γίνεσθαι, οὔτε τοῦ διοικοῦντος αὐτήν. οὐσίαν τε γὰρ τοῖς γινομένοις ὑφεστάναι δεῖ, πεφυκυῖαν ἀναδέχεσθαι τὰς μεταβολὰς πάσας, καὶ τὸ ⌜δημιουργῆσαν⌝ (-σον Usener) ἐξ αὐτῆς· οἷα [γὰρ] ἐφ᾽ ἡμῶν τίς ἐστι φύσις δημιουργοῦσα, τοιούτου τινὸς κατ᾽ ἀνάγκην ὄντος καὶ ἐν τῷ κόσμῳ ἀγενήτου. The Stoics held that τὸ ἐν τῷ κόσμῳ δημιουργοῦν is πῦρ νοερόν; the Platonist writer of *Corp.* X holds that it is νοῦς using πῦρ as its instrument.

ὀργάνῳ τῷ πυρὶ πρὸς τὴν δημιουργίαν χρῆται. See *Ascl. Lat.* II. 16 a (III. 17 a): 'spiritu ... qui quasi organum vel machina summi dei voluntati subiectus est.' The fire which the divine νοῦς uses as its instrument in its demiurgic activity (i. e. in the administration of the universe, not its 'creation', for this writer appears to hold that the Kosmos is without beginning, § 10 b,) is primarily the light and heat emitted by the heavenly bodies. But perhaps the writer thought that the νόες incorporated in fiery bodies, and 'ranging through all

---

[1] The word occurs in the anonymous fragment appended to *Ep. ad Diognetum* (12. 8 Funk): τρυγήσεις ἀεὶ τὰ παρὰ θεῷ ποθούμενα, ὧν ὄφις οὐχ ἅπτεται, οὐδὲ πλάνη συγχρωτίζεται, οὐδὲ Εὔα φθείρεται, ἀλλὰ παρθένος πιστεύεται. I can make no sense either of πλάνη συγχρωτίζεται or of παρθένος πιστεύεται. Perhaps the author wrote something like this: ὧν ὄφις οὐχ ἅπτεται, οὐδὲ πλάνη ⟨⟨πιστεύεται⟩⟩ (cf. ὑπὸ τοῦ ὄφεως πλανᾶται a few lines above), οὐδὲ Εὔα ⟨⟨συγχρωτίζεται⟩⟩ (' is defiled '), ἀλλὰ παρθένος ⟨διασώζεται⟩. Eve believed the deceptive words of the serpent; she ate, and was defiled. φθείρεται may have been inserted as an explanation of συγχρωτίζεται.

space', (i. e. the 'daemons',) are employed in subordination to the divine νοῦς by which the whole is governed, and that the cosmic processes are carried on, in part at least, through their agency.

ὁ δὲ τοῦ ἀνθρώπου (νοῦς) τῶν ἐπιγείων μόνον (δημιουργός). The writer probably had in mind the primary meaning of δημιουργός, 'a skilled workman'. The sort of δημιουργία to which the human νοῦς is limited is the tendance of things upon earth (the θεραπεία τῶν ἐπιγείων spoken of in *Ascl. Lat.* I) by means of the arts and crafts. In the human arts and crafts, as well as in the divine administration of the universe, fire is an indispensable ὄργανον. The δημιουργία of the human νοῦς cannot mean the operation of the vital force by which our bodies are fashioned; for that process is not carried on by the human νοῦς, i. e. by man as a conscious and rational agent, but by the same power which operates in all natural processes throughout the universe.

§ 19 a. τὸν τῆς εὐσέβειας ἀγῶνα ἀγωνισαμένη. This clause refers to man's life in the body; the words μετὰ τὸ ἀπαλλαγῆναι τοῦ σώματος, which precede it in the MSS., ought therefore to be placed after it.

καὶ μηδένα ἀνθρώπων ἀδικῆσαι. Cf. § 21, πάντας ἀνθρώπους . . . εὖ ποιοῦσα. This is one of the few mentions of social obligation, or of man's 'duty towards his neighbour', which occur in the *Hermetica.* See *Ascl. Lat.* I. 8: 'commodationes alternae.'

ἡ δὲ ἀσεβὴς ψυχὴ μένει ἐπὶ τῆς ἰδίας οὐσίας. The impious soul is ψυχή in the more restricted sense of the word, i. e. ψυχή as distinct from and opposed to νοῦς. The ordinary human soul (ψυχή in the wider sense), during its life on earth, is a combination of νοῦς with παθητόν τι; and this παθητόν is called ἡ ψυχή in the narrower sense. The pious soul (ψυχή in the wider sense), when it quits the body, throws off whatever it has hitherto retained of τὸ παθητόν, so that only ὁ νοῦς remains; in other words, the ψυχή in the narrower sense, as a thing distinct from νοῦς, ceases to exist. But the impious soul (ψυχή in the wider sense), when disembodied, is abandoned by the νοῖς, (if indeed there was any νοῦς in it during its life in the body), and thenceforth consists of τὸ παθητόν (= ψυχή in the narrower sense) alone. Consequently, it seeks to enter another earthy body, in which it may find satisfaction for its gross desires. The wicked soul is punished, both by the misery of unsatisfied desire in its disembodied state, and by reincarnation; but the punishment is self-inflicted. This description of the destiny of the ἀσεβὴς ψυχή is based on Pl. *Phaedo* 81 B ff. With ὑφ' ἑαυτῆς κολαζομένη, compare *Phaedo* 82 E : τοῦ εἰργμοῦ τὴν δεινότητα κατιδοῦσα, ὅτι δι' ἐπιθυμίας ἐστίν, ὡς ἂν μάλιστα αὐτὸς ὁ δεδεμένος ξυλλήπτωρ εἴη τῷ (τοῦ Schanz) δεδέσθαι.

§§ 19 b–22 a. ἀνθρώπινον δέ ... εἰς δὲ τὸ ἔλαττον ἀδύνατον. In § 19 b it is denied that a human soul can enter the body of a beast. This denial is in direct contradiction to §§ 7, 8 a : it is therefore certain that § 19 b cannot have been written by the author of § 7 f. The same argument applies to § 20 *fin.* and § 22 a *fin.*, where the denial is repeated. The only doubt is whether we ought to assign to a different writer those sentences only in which the doctrine taught in § 7 is denied, or the whole passage in which these sentences are contained. But on further examination it appears that the whole passage 19 b–22 a is written from a different point of view from the rest of *Corp.* X. The writer of § 20 no doubt intended that section for an explanation of the phrase ὑφ' ἑαυτῆς κολαζομένη in § 19 a ; but he has misunderstood the words on which he comments. The punishment spoken of in § 19 a is that which the *disembodied* soul inflicts upon itself ; but the self-punishment described in § 20 takes place *while the soul is still in the body.* Also, the maleficent νοῦς which suddenly makes its appearance in § 21 is ignored in the rest of the *libellus*, and what is there said about νοῦς cannot be reconciled with what is said about νοῦς in other parts of *Corp.* X. We must therefore conclude that the whole passage 19 b–22 a has been inserted by a later hand.

§ 19 b. οὐδὲ θέμις ἐστὶν εἰς ἀλόγου ζῴου σῶμα ψυχὴν ἀνθρωπίνην καταπεσεῖν. The doctrine that human souls migrate into the bodies of beasts was adopted by Plato from the Pythagoreans.[1] Aristotle

---

[1] The Orphici agreed with the Pythagoreans in holding that the human soul is incarnated in a series of bodies in succession ; but it may be doubted whether the Orphici, in earlier times at least, spoke of its reincarnation in bodies other than human. The only evidence for this that I have met with is an Orphic fragment quoted by Proclus *In rem. publ.* p. 339 Kroll (Abel *Orphica* fr. 223): ἔπειθ' ὅτι καὶ εἰς τὰ ἄλλα ζῷα μετάβασίς ἐστι τῶν ψυχῶν τῶν ἀνθρώπων, καὶ τοῦτο διαρρήδην Ὀρφεὺς ἀναδιδάσκει, ὁπηνίκα ἂν διορίζηται· Οὕνεκ' ἀμειβομένη ψυχὴ κατὰ κύκλα χρόνοιο | ἀνθρώπων ζώοισι μετέρχεται ἄλλοθεν ἄλλοις· | ἄλλοτε μέν θ' ἵπποις,... ἄλλοτε δὲ πρόβατον, τότε δ' ὄρνεον κ.τ.λ. But the date of these verses is unknown ; they may have been written in a period when the original distinction between the Orphic doctrine of reincarnation and that of the Pythagoreans had been obliterated. In a second passage quoted from ' Orpheus ' by Proclus *ib.* (Abel 222 = 225), reincarnation in human bodies alone is spoken of ; and in a third (Abel 224), the lot of the disembodied souls of beasts is expressly distinguished from that of the disembodied souls of men ; for the Orphic poet there says that the soul of a beast, when it quits the body, hovers in the air εἰσόκεν αὐτὴν | ἄλλο ἀφαρπάζῃ μίγδην ἀνέμοιο πνοῇσιν· but human souls, when they quit the body, are led down by Hermes γαίης εἰς κευθμῶνα πελώριον. The fact that the destination of all disembodied human souls

pointed out a serious difficulty in the Pythagorean and Platonic doctrine of *metensomatosis*; *De an.* 1. 3, 407 b : οἱ δὲ μόνον ἐπιχειροῦσι λέγειν ποῖόν τι ἡ ψυχή, περὶ δὲ τοῦ δεξομένου σώματος οὐθὲν ἔτι προσδιορίζουσιν, ὥσπερ ἐνδεχόμενον κατὰ τοὺς Πυθαγορικοὺς μύθους τὴν τυχοῦσαν ψυχὴν εἰς τὸ τυχὸν ἐνδύεσθαι σῶμα κ.τ.λ. *Ib.* 2. 2, 413 b. The Platonists agreed with Aristotle that man is distinguished from the beasts by the possession of νοῦς; and according to the *Timaeus*, the νοῦς is the only part of the soul which is immortal.[1] If then the body of a beast is not receptive of νοῦς, how can it be animated by a human soul?

But in spite of this objection, the Platonists in general, down to the latter part of the third century A. D., adhered to the Pythagorean doctrine of transmigration into bestial bodies, which they found set forth in Plato's dialogues;[2] and this view was still maintained by Plotinus, who asserted that the human soul may descend so low as to take to itself not only the body of a beast, but even (as Empedocles had said) that of a vegetable. Plot. 3. 4. 2 : the human soul is at once λογική, αἰσθητική, and φυσική. ἐξελθοῦσα δὲ τοῦ σώματος, ὅ τι περ ἐπλεόνασε, τοῦτο γίνεται. . . . ὅσοι μὲν οὖν τὸν ἄνθρωπον ἐτήρησαν, πάλιν ἄνθρωποι· ὅσοι δὲ αἰσθήσει μόνον ἔζησαν, ζῷα· ἀλλ' εἰ μὲν αἰσθήσει μετὰ θυμοῦ, τὰ ἄγρια, ὅσοι δὲ μετ' ἐπιθυμίας . . ., τὰ ἀκόλαστα τῶν ζῴων καὶ γαστρίμαργα. εἰ δὲ μηδὲ αἰσθήσει μετὰ τούτων, ἀλλὰ νωθείᾳ αἰσθήσεως μετ' αὐτῶν, καὶ φυτά· μόνον γὰρ τοῦτο (ἐν αὐτοῖς) ἢ μάλιστα ἐνήργει, τὸ φυτικόν,

is in these verses placed beneath the earth indicates an early date ; and it is possible that this may be the very passage to which Aristotle refers in *De an.* 1. 5, 410 b 27 : τοῦτο δὲ πέπονθε καὶ ὁ ἐν τοῖς Ὀρφικοῖς ἔπεσι καλουμένοις λόγος· φησὶ γὰρ τὴν ψυχὴν ἐκ τοῦ ὅλου εἰσιέναι ἀναπνεόντων, φερομένην ὑπὸ τῶν ἀνέμων. οὐχ οἷόν τε δὴ τοῖς φυτοῖς τοῦτο συμβαίνειν, οὐδὲ τῶν ζῴων ἐνίοις, εἴπερ μὴ πάντα ἀναπνέουσιν. There is no reason to assume that the Orphic abstinence from flesh-eating (ἄψυχος βορά, Eur. *Hippol.* 952) was founded on a belief that the bodies of beasts are animated by human souls. The Pythagoreans, who did hold that belief, alleged it as one reason among others for their traditional practice of abstinence from flesh-food ; but the prohibition itself, in the case of Orphici and Pythagoreans alike, is analogous to the taboos or ' laws of holiness ' by which in many primitive religions the worshippers are required to abstain from certain kinds of food. The Hebrews and other Semites abstained from pork, but did not suppose that the souls of their deceased fathers inhabited the bodies of pigs.

[1] In this respect the teaching of the *Timaeus* approximates to that of Aristotle. Cf. Ar. *De an.* 2. 2 : περὶ δὲ τοῦ νοῦ καὶ τῆς θεωρητικῆς δυνάμεως οὐδέν πω φανερόν, ἀλλ' ἔοικε ψυχῆς γένος ἕτερον εἶναι· καὶ τοῦτο μόνον ἐνδέχεται χωρίζεσθαι, καθάπερ τὸ ἀίδιον τοῦ φθαρτοῦ. τὰ δὲ λοιπὰ μόρια τῆς ψυχῆς φανερόν . . . ὅτι οὐκ ἔστι χωριστά.

[2] The writer of the *Timaei Locri de anima mundi* (before A. D. 200) must be excepted. In the last paragraph of the *Tim. Locr.* (Mullach *Fr. Ph. Gr.* II, p. 46) it is clearly implied (though not expressly said) that the doctrine of penal reincarnation in the bodies of beasts is untrue, but may be useful as a ' medicinal lie '.

καὶ ἦν αὐτοῖς ⟨ἡ ?⟩ μελέτη δενδρωθῆναι. Plot. 4. 3. 12 *fin.*: κάτεισι δὲ οὐκ ἀεὶ τὸ ἴσον (ἡ ψυχή) . . .· κάτεισι δὲ εἰς ἕτοιμον ἑκάστη καθ' ὁμοίωσιν τῆς διαθέσεως. ἐκεῖ γάρ, ᾧ ἂν ὁμοιωθεῖσα ᾖ, φέρεται, ἡ μὲν εἰς ἄνθρωπον, ἡ δὲ εἰς ζῷον ἄλλη ἄλλο. *Ib.* 6. 7. 6 f. But the successors of Plotinus were more strongly impressed by the objections to this view. As to Porphyry, the evidence is conflicting. In a passage preserved in Stob. 1. 49. 60, vol. i, p. 445 W., Porphyry, like his teacher Plotinus, accepts the statements of Plato on this matter in their literal sense. Pythagoras and Plato, he says, teach that the soul μεταβολὴν ἴσχει καὶ μετακόσμησιν εἰς ἕτερα σωμάτων εἴδη. . . . Hence πολλῆς μὲν εὐτυχίας αἱ ψυχαὶ δέονται, πολλῆς δὲ σωφρο- σύνης, ὅπως μὴ . . . κακοδαίμονα καὶ θηριώδη βίον ἀμείψωσιν. ἡ γὰρ . . . τῶν ἐν Ἅιδου τρίοδος ἐνταῦθά που τέτακται, περὶ τὰ τῆς ψυχῆς σχιζόμενα μέρη, τὸ λογιστικὸν καὶ θυμοειδὲς καὶ ἐπιθυμητικόν, ὧν ἕκαστον ἀρχὴν ἐξ ἑαυτοῦ καὶ ῥοπὴν ἐπὶ τὸν οἰκεῖον βίον ἐνδίδωσι. καὶ οὐκέτι ταῦτα μῦθος οὐδὲ ποίησις, ἀλλὰ ἀλήθεια καὶ φυσικὸς λόγος.[1] ὧν μὲν γὰρ ἐν τῇ μεταβολῇ καὶ γενέσει τὸ ἐπιθυμητικὸν ἐξανθοῦν ἐπικρατεῖ καὶ δυναστεύει, τούτοις εἰς νωθῆ [καὶ][2] σώματα . . . φησὶ (Plato) γενέσθαι τὴν μεταβολήν· ὅταν δὲ . . . ἐξηγριωμένον ἔχουσα παντάπασιν ἡ ψυχὴ τὸ θυμοειδὲς εἰς δευτέραν γένεσιν ἀφίκηται, . . . ἔρριψεν ἑαυτὴν εἰς λύκου φύσιν ἢ λέοντος.[3] Nemesius[4] does not expressly say that Porphyry adhered to the doctrine of transmigration

---

[1] It may be inferred from these words that some Platonists known to Porphyry thought that what Plato had written about transmigration into the bodies of beasts was merely 'myth' or 'poetry'.

[2] εἰς νωθῆ καὶ F : ἰσονωθῆ καὶ P : εἰς ὀνώδη καὶ ⟨ὑώδη⟩ conj. Canter.

[3] In *De abst.* 1. 19, Porphyry represents an advocate of flesh-eating as arguing ' if the soul of the beast I kill for food is immortal, I am doing it a kindness by expelling it from its present lodging; it will make its way back into a human body all the sooner'. But Porphyry does not there give his own opinion.

[4] Nemesius *De nat. hom.* 2 : κοινῇ μὲν οὖν πάντες Ἕλληνες οἱ τὴν ψυχὴν ἀθάνατον ἀποφηνάμενοι τὴν μετενσωμάτωσιν δογματίζουσι· διαφέρονται δὲ περὶ τὰ εἴδη τῶν ψυχῶν· οἱ μὲν γὰρ ἐν εἶδος τὸ λογικὸν εἶναι λέγουσι, τοῦτο δὲ καὶ εἰς φυτὰ καὶ εἰς τὰ τῶν ἀλόγων σώματα μεταβαίνειν· . . . ἄλλοι δὲ οὐχ ἓν εἶδος ψυχῶν, ἀλλὰ δύο, λογικόν τε καὶ ἄλογον· τινὲς δὲ πολλά, τοσαῦτα ὅσα τῶν ζῴων τὰ εἴδη. μάλιστα δὲ οἱ ἀπὸ Πλάτωνος περὶ τὸ δόγμα τοῦτο διηνέχθησαν· εἰπόντος γὰρ Πλάτωνος τὰς μὲν θυμικὰς καὶ ὀργίλους καὶ ἁρπακτικὰς ψυχὰς λύκων καὶ λεόντων σώματα μεταμφιέννυσθαι, τὰς δὲ περὶ τὴν ἀκολασίαν ἠσχολημένας ὄνων καὶ τῶν τοιούτων ἀναλαμβάνειν σώματα, οἱ μὲν κυρίως ἤκουσαν τοὺς λύκους καὶ τοὺς λέοντας καὶ τοὺς ὄνους, οἱ δὲ τροπικῶς αὐτὸν εἰρηκέναι διέγνωσαν, τὰ ἤθη διὰ τῶν ζῴων παρεμφαίνοντα. Κρόνιος μὲν γὰρ ἐν τῷ Περὶ παλιγγενεσίας—οὕτω δὲ καλεῖ τὴν μετενσωμάτωσιν—λογικὰς πάσας εἶναι βούλεται· ὁμοίως δὲ καὶ Θεόδωρος ὁ Πλατωνικὸς (a disciple of Porphyry) ἐν τῷ Ὅτι ἡ ψυχὴ πάντα τὰ εἴδη ἐστί· καὶ Πορφύριος ὁμοίως. Ἰάμβλιχος δέ, τὴν ἐναντίαν τούτοις δραμών, κατ' εἴδη ζῴων ψυχῆς εἴδος εἶναι λέγει, ἤγουν εἴδη διάφορα· γέγραπται γοῦν αὐτῷ μονόβιβλον ἐπίγραφον ὅτι οὐκ ἀπ' ἀνθρώπων εἰς ζῷα ἄλογα, οὐδὲ ἀπὸ ζῴων ἀλόγων εἰς ἀνθρώπους αἱ μετενσωματώσεις γίνονται, ἀλλὰ καὶ ἀπὸ ζῴων εἰς ζῷα, καὶ ἀπὸ ἀνθρώπων εἰς ἀνθρώπους.

into the bodies of beasts; but he names him among those who held that all souls, including those of beasts, are (at least potentially) λογικαί;[1] and from this it may be inferred that Porphyry saw no force in the objection which prevented others from admitting that a human soul may animate the body of a brute.   But Augustine gives evidence on the other side; *Civ. dei* 10. 30 : 'Platonem animas hominum post mortem revolvi usque ad corpora bestiarum scripsisse certissimum est.   Hanc sententiam Porphyrii doctor tenuit [et] Plotinus; Porphyrio tamen iure displicuit.'   *Ib.* 12. 26 : 'Porphyrius . . . cum suo Platone aliisque Platonicis sentit eos, qui immoderate inhonesteque vixerint, propter luendas poenas ad corpora redire mortalia, Plato quidem etiam ad bestiarum, Porphyrius tantum modo ad hominum.'   *Ib.* 13. 19 : 'Porphyrium . . . ab animis humanis removisse corpora bestiarum.'   And Aeneas of Gaza (quoted below) speaks of Porphyry as Augustine does. It seems therefore that Porphyry must have expressed different opinions on the question in different writings.   Iamblichus then is (with the exception of the writer of *Tim. Locr.*) the earliest Platonist of whom it can be said with certainty that he rejected the Pythagorean form of the doctrine of transmigration, and maintained ὅτι οὐκ ἀπ' ἀνθρώπων εἰς ἄλογα ζῷα αἱ ἐνσωματώσεις γίνονται (Nemesius above).   Aeneas of Gaza 'in Theophrasto p. 16 ed. Barth' (Mullach *F. P. G.* II, p. xi): ἐπιγενόμενοι δὲ Πορφύριος καὶ Ἰάμβλιχος, καὶ τοὺς πρὸ αὐτῶν σοφίᾳ περιφρονοῦντες, καὶ ἐρυθριῶντες τὸν Πλάτωνος ὄνον καὶ λύκον καὶ ἰκτῖνον, καὶ κατανοήσαντες ὡς ἄλλη μὲν λογικῆς ψυχῆς ἡ οὐσία, ἄλλη δὲ ἀλόγου, καὶ ὅτι οὐ μετανίστανται, ἀλλ' ὡσαύτως ἔχουσιν αἱ οὐσίαι οἷαι τὸ πρῶτον προῆλθον· οὐ γὰρ τῇ ψυχῇ τὸ λογικὸν συμβέβηκός, ὡς μεταχωρεῖν, ἀλλ' οὐσίας διαφορὰ βεβαίως ἱδρυμένη· καὶ ὅλως ἀδύνατον τὸν λόγον εἰς ἀλογίαν μετατίθεσθαι, εἰ μὴ καὶ τὸ ἄλογον φήσουσιν ὑφαρπάζειν τοῦ λόγου τὴν φύσιν· ταῦτα ὀψέ ποτε διαλογισάμενοι, ⌜ὑπερπηδήσαντες τὰ ἄλογα τῶν ζῴων, μεταβαλόντες οὐκ εἰς ὄνον φασίν (ὄνου φύσιν Wyttenbach), ἀλλ' ὀνώδη ἄνθρωπον.[1][2]   Thus according to Aeneas, the view which we

---

[1] As to the view that all souls are λογικαί, cf. Aetius, Diels *Doxogr.* p. 432 : Πυθαγόρας, Πλάτων, λογικὰς μὲν εἶναι καὶ τῶν ἀλόγων ζῴων καλουμένων τὰς ψυχάς, οὐ μὴν λογικῶς ἐνεργούσας, παρὰ τὴν δυσκρασίαν τῶν σωμάτων καὶ τὸ μὴ ἔχειν τὸ φραστικόν, ὥσπερ ἐπὶ τῶν πιθήκων καὶ τῶν κυνῶν· νοοῦσι μὲν γὰρ οὗτοι, οὐ φράζουσι δέ.   Porphyry *De abst.* 3. 1 asserts the truth of the 'Pythagorean' doctrine that every ψυχή (including the souls of beasts), ᾗ μέτεισιν αἰσθήσεως καὶ μνήμης, is λογική ; and he says it follows from this that we have duties towards the beasts.

[2] The sense required is ὑπερ(ε)πήδησαν[τες] τὰ ἄλογα τῶν ζῴων, μεταβάλ(λειν τὴν ψυχὴν λέγ)οντες οὐκ εἰς ὄνου φύσιν, ἀλλ' (εἰς) ὀνώδη ἄνθρωπον.

find expressed in *Corp.* X. 19 b–22 a was first put forward by Platonists not long before A. D. 300. It was adopted by many Platonists of later times, e. g. by Hierocles,[1] Olympiodorus,[2] and Chalcidius.[3] Sallustius tried to find a *via media;* he says (*De diis et mundo* 20) αἱ δὲ μετεμψυχώσεις εἰ μὲν εἰς λογικὰ γίνοιντο, αὐτὸ τοῦτο ψυχαὶ γίνονται τῶν σωμάτων· εἰ δὲ εἰς ἄλογα, ἔξωθεν ἔπονται, ὥσπερ καὶ ἡμῖν οἱ εἰληχότες ἡμᾶς δαίμονες. οὐ γὰρ ἄν ποτε λογικὴ ἀλόγου ψυχὴ γένοιτο. Proclus agreed in part with the view of the earlier Platonists down to Plotinus, that human souls are sometimes reincarnated in beast-bodies, but stated that view in a modified form; Procl. *in Tim.* 329 D: ὁ δὲ ἀληθὴς λόγος εἰσκρίνεσθαι μὲν εἰς θηρία φησὶ τὴν ἀνθρωπίνην ψυχήν, ἔχοντα δὲ τὴν οἰκείαν ζωήν,[4] καὶ ἐπὶ ταύτῃ τὴν εἰσκριθεῖσαν (human) ψυχὴν οἷον ἐποχουμένην, καὶ τῇ πρὸς αὐτὴν (*sc.* τὴν τοῦ θηρίου ζωὴν) συμπαθείᾳ δεδεμένην. See also Procl. *in Phaedrum*, and *in Remp.* II. 309, 28–312, 5; 315, 18; 324, 11; 325, 11 *sqq.*; 333, 2–341, 8.

The opinion which Aeneas of Gaza thought to have originated with Porphyry and Iamblichus can hardly have been so complete a novelty in their time as he represents it. An obvious objection to the Pythagorean doctrine of transmigration had long before been pointed out by Aristotle; and a Platonist of any period might be driven to admit that the difficulty was insuperable. Lucretius (3. 748 ff.), after speaking of *metensomatosis* in the Pythagorean sense, proceeds to say ' Sin animas hominum dicent in corpora semper | ire humana, tamen quaeram' &c. He must therefore have known of some one who held that human souls are reincarnated, but only

---

[1] Hierocl. *In aureum carmen* 23, Mullach *F. P. G.* I. 469 b: ὁ θηρίου μεταμφιάσασθαι σῶμα ἐλπίζων καὶ ζῷον ἄλογον γενέσθαι διὰ κακίαν, ἢ καὶ φυτὸν δι' ἀργίαν αἰσθήσεως, ... πρὸς τὰ κάτω (τὴν τοῦ ἀνθρώπου οὐσίαν) συνωθεῖ, πεπλανημένος καὶ μὴ νοῶν τὸ ἀμετάβλητον τοῦ κατ' οὐσίαν ὑπάρχοντος εἴδους τῇ ἀνθρωπίνῃ ψυχῇ. ἀεὶ γὰρ μένουσα ἄνθρωπος, τῇ τῆς ἀρετῆς καὶ κακίας ἀνὰ μέρος κτήσει θηρίον λέγεται ἢ θεὸς γίνεσθαι· φύσει δὲ οὐδέτερον, ἀλλὰ σχέσει τῆς πρὸς ἑκάτερον ὁμοιώσεως.

[2] Mullach II, p. xi.

[3] Chalcid. *In Tim.* 194 f., Mullach II, p. 223 a: ' Porro (anima) si deterior facta sit deteriusque vivet, propter nimiam corporis amplexationem vitae destinabitur infeliciori, quoadusque ad ferae naturae perveniat immanitatem. Empedocles tamen, Pythagoram secutus, ait eas non naturam modo agrestem et feram sortiri, sed etiam formas varias (i. e. that human souls are actually reincarnated in bestial bodies).... Sed Plato non putat rationabilem animam vultum atque os ratione carentis animalis induere, sed ad vitiorum reliquias accedente corpore, incorporatione[m] auctis animae vitiis efferari ex instituto vitae prioris, et iracundum quidem hominem eundemque fortem provehi usque ad feritatem leonis, ferum vero et eundem rapacem ad proximam luporum similitudinem pervenire, ceterorum item. Sed ... anima quondam hominis nequaquam transit ad bestias iuxta Platonem.'

[4] I. e. the beasts into which human souls have entered retain the sort of life that is proper to them as beasts.

T

in human bodies. But there is no reason to think that those who held this view in or before the time of Lucretius were Platonists. The Platonizing Stoic Posidonius certainly held that the human soul exists before its incarnation, and probably held also that the same soul is or may be repeatedly incarnated; but as far as I know, there is no trace of evidence that he thought a human soul might be reincarnated in a body other than human. It is probable therefore that the teacher of whom Lucretius was thinking was Posidonius.

The opinion that a human soul 'is not permitted to sink into the body of a beast' may have been held by a Platonist here and there [1] before the time of Porphyry; but it was not until about the end of the third century A. D. that it was definitely adopted by the leaders of Platonic thought, and became, so to speak, the orthodox doctrine [of the Platonic school. It is therefore probable that the passage X. 19 b–22 a, in which this doctrine is maintained, was written either after A. D. 300, or at any rate, not long before that date.

§ 20. ποῖον πῦρ τοσαύτην φλόγα ἔχει ὅσην ἡ ἀσέβεια; . . . "καίομαι, φλέγομαι". Cf. Origen De princip. 2. 10. 4: 'hoc videtur indicari, quod unusquisque peccatorum flammam sibi ipse proprii ignis accendat, et non in aliquem ignem qui antea iam fuerit accensus ab alio . . . demergatur. Cuius ignis materia atque esca nostra sunt

---

[1] Origen, De princip. lib. I fin. (Lommatzsch), discussed the question whether it is possible for a human soul to be reincarnated in the body of a beast, but apparently did not make it clear to which side his own opinion inclined. His words are quoted thus (Justinianus Imp. ad calcem epist. ad Mennam Patriarch. Constant.): ἡ ψυχὴ ἀπορρέουσα τοῦ καλοῦ, καὶ τῇ κακίᾳ προσκλιναμένη, καὶ ἐπὶ πλεῖον ἐν ταύτῃ γινομένη, εἰ μὴ ὑποστρέφοι, ὑπὸ τῆς ἀνοίας ἀποκτηνοῦται, καὶ ὑπὸ τῆς πονηρίας ἀποθηριοῦται. This is followed by three or four lines which are hopelessly corrupt, but contain the words αἱρεῖται . . . τὸν ἔνυδρον, ἵν' οὕτως εἴπω, βίον (which seem to imply that, according to the view there stated,—though not necessarily according to the view of Origen himself,—a human soul may come to inhabit the body of a fish), and ἐνδύεται σῶμα[τα] . . . τοιοῦδε ζῴου ἀλόγου. Hieronymus Ep. ad Avitum p. 764: 'Ad extremum (primi libri) sermone latissimo disputavit (Origenes) angelum, sive animam, aut certe daemonem, quos unius asserit esse naturae sed diversarum voluntatum, pro magnitudine negligentiae et stultitiae iumentum posse fieri; et pro dolore poenarum et ignis ardore magis eligere ut brutum animal sit, et in aquis habitet et fluctibus; ac corpus assumere huius vel illius pecoris; ut nobis non solum quadrupedum, sed et piscium corpora sint timenda. Et ad extremum, ne teneretur Pythagorici dogmatis reus, qui asserit μετεμψύχωσιν, post tam nefandam disputationem, qua lectoris animum vulneravit, "haec" inquit "iuxta nostram sententiam non sint dogmata, sed quaesita tantum atque proiecta, ne penitus intractata viderentur".' Rufinus, in his Latin version of Origen's De principiis, has struck out this 'nefanda disputatio', and substituted for it the following inoffensive statement: 'Illa nos nequaquam recipienda censemus, quae et a quibusdam superfluo vel requiri vel adstrui solent, id est, quod animae in tantum sui decessum veniant, ut, naturae rationabilis ac dignitatis oblitae, etiam in ordinem irrationabilium animantium, vel bestiarum vel pecudum, devolvantur.'

peccata. . . . Anima cum multitudinem malorum operum et abun-
dantiam in se congregaverit peccatorum, competenti tempore omnis
illa malorum congregatio effervescit ad supplicium, atque inflammatur
ad poenas; cum mens ipsa . . . omnia in memoriam recipiens . . .
historiam quandam scelerum suorum ante oculos suos videbit exposi-
tam; tunc et ipsa conscientia propriis stimulis agitatur atque com-
pungitur. . . . Ex quo intelligitur quod circa ipsam animae substantiam tormenta quaedam ex ipsis peccatorum noxiis affectibus'
generantur.' Origen is there speaking of penal suffering *after death*;
but he adds, with reference to the present life, 'Et ne satis tibi
huius rei intellectus difficilis appareat, considerari possibile est ex
his passionum vitiis quae animabus accidere solent, id est, cum vel
flammis amoris exuritur anima, vel zeli, vel livoris ignibus maceratur,
aut cum ira agitatur, vel cum insaniae vel tristitiae immensitate
consumitur, quomodo horum malorum nimietates aiiquanti intolera-
biliter ferentes, mortem subire quam huiusmodi cruciatus perpeti
tolerabilius habuere.'

The early Buddhists also were accustomed to speak of the (tor-
turing) 'fire' of passion. Mrs. Rhys Davids, *Buddhism*, pp. 175–177,
quotes from Buddhist documents 'My sense with passion burns, my
mind's aflame', and 'There is no fire like unto passion's greed';
and the word *nirvana* is said to have primarily meant the 'quenching'
of this fire.

ἢ οὐχ ὁρᾷς ὅσα κακὰ πάσχει κ.τ.λ.; This is an appeal to observation; the punishment here spoken of must therefore be that which
the wicked soul inflicts upon itself *in the present life*.

[οὔτε βλέπω οὔτε ἀκούω]. Cf. οὔτε βλέπει ἡ ψυχὴ οὔτε ἀκούει in § 24 a.
But the cry of the tortured soul cannot have been meant to end with
these comparatively feeble words. They would perhaps be less
objectionable if placed after οὐκ οἶδα; but the passage would gain
in force if the words τί εἴπω, τί ποιήσω οὐκ οἶδα (which correspond
to οὔτε τι εἰπεῖν οὔτ' ἔρξαι δύναται in § 24 a) were also cut out.

ὡς οἱ πολλοὶ δοκοῦσι. It appears from this that, in the society
known to the writer, even 'the many' were Platonists, so far at
least as to accept the doctrine of *metensomatosis*. But it is possible
that οἱ has been wrongly inserted.

§ 21. ὁ γὰρ νοῦς, [[ὅταν δαίμων γένηται, πυρίνου τυχεῖν σώματος
τέτακται πρὸς τὰς τοῦ θεοῦ ὑπηρεσίας,]] [καὶ] εἰσδὺς . . . αἰκίζεται
αὐτὴν κ.τ.λ. The words ὅταν . . . ὑπηρεσίας are manifestly out of
place here. We were told in § 18 that a νοῦς must put off its fiery

integument in order to enter a human body. The contradiction of that statement in § 21 might be accounted for on the ground that the two passages were written by different persons; but there is another difficulty, which cannot be thus got over. The νοῦς spoken of in § 21 is a bad νοῦς (cf. δεῖ εὔχεσθαι καλοῦ τοῦ νοῦ τυχεῖν in § 22 a); it is one which drives a man to sin; therefore it could not be described as employed in 'the service of God' (τὰς τοῦ θεοῦ ὑπηρεσίας). There can be little doubt that the words which I have bracketed belong to the description of the disembodied εὐσεβὴς ψυχή in § 19 a.

As to the bad νοῦς here spoken of, cf. *Corp.* IX. 3. In that passage, it is said that κακὰ νοήματα are begotten in the human νοῦς by maleficent daemons; in *Corp.* X. 21, the κακὰ νοήματα are attributed to a bad νοῦς which has entered into the soul from without, and is itself regarded as a maleficent daemon.

αἰκίζεται αὐτὴν . . . τρέπεται ⟨γὰρ⟩ ἐπὶ κ.τ.λ. I am by no means confident that my restoration of this corrupt passage is right; but the general meaning seems fairly clear. We must be guided by the analogy of the following sentence concerning the εὐσεβὴς ψυχή. We are told that a νοῦς of one kind enters the pious soul and guides it to all that is good; the writer must therefore have said that a νοῦς of another kind enters the impious soul and impels it to all that is evil. The μάστιγες τῶν ἁμαρτημάτων must be taken to mean the miseries which sin brings with it in the present life, and which have been described in § 20 (ὅσα κακὰ πάσχει ψυχὴ ἡ ἀσεβής κ.τ.λ.). In the view of this writer, sin is its own punishment, and there is no need for any doctrine of penal reincarnation.

τρέπεται ⟨γὰρ⟩ ἐπὶ ⟨⟨βλασφημίας, καὶ⟩⟩ φόνους καὶ ὕβρεις καὶ [[ ]] βίας ποικίλας δι' ὧν ἄνθρωποι ἀδικοῦνται. It is necessary to place βλασφημίας before φόνους κ.τ.λ.; cf. ⟨τὸν θεὸν⟩ εὐφημοῦσα . . . ⟨καὶ⟩ πάντας ἀνθρώπους . . . εὖ ποιοῦσα below. Perhaps some phrase corresponding to δι' ὧν ἄνθρωποι ἀδικοῦνται has fallen out after βλασφημίας; one might write, for instance, ἐπὶ βλασφημίας ⟨δι' ὧν ὁ θεὸς ἀσεβεῖται⟩, καὶ φόνους κ.τ.λ.

⟨τὸν θεὸν⟩ ὑμνοῦσα εὐφημοῦσά τε, ⟨καὶ⟩ πάντας ἀνθρώπους . . . εὖ ποιοῦσα. Cf. Marc. Aurel. 5. 33: τί ἀρκεῖ; τί δ' ἄλλο ἢ θεοὺς μὲν σεβεῖν καὶ εὐφημεῖν, ἀνθρώπους δὲ εὖ ποιεῖν κ.τ.λ.

22 a. δεῖ εὔχεσθαι καλοῦ τοῦ νοῦ τυχεῖν. The νοῦς dealt with in this passage is regarded as a personal being, distinguishable from the soul into which it enters; it is a δαίμων, as in § 23. But according

to the writer of §§ 19 b–22 a, this guiding *genius* may be either good or bad. If it is good, it is a guardian angel by whom the man is led ; if it is bad, it is a devil by whom he is possessed.

§ **22 b**. κοινωνία δέ ἐστι ψυχῶν κ.τ.λ. From this point to the end of the document, the Hermetist speaks of man's station in the universe, and his relations to beings of other grades ; and the thoughts expressed have much in common with those of *Ascl. Lat.* I, *De homine*. On the κοινωνία between human souls and beings of other grades, cf. *Ascl. Lat.* I. 5 f.

αἱ τῶν θεῶν (ψυχαί). The word ψυχή is here used in its wider sense ; i. e. it includes νοῦς. If a pious human soul becomes unmixed νοῦς (§ 19 a), it follows *a fortiori* that the soul of a god must be νοῦς and nothing else.

ἄνθρωποι δὲ τῶν ἀλόγων (ἐπιμελοῦνται). Compare the doctrine of *Ascl. Lat.* I, that one of man's two functions is ἡ τῶν ἐπιγείων θεραπεία, and that in discharging this function he co-operates with the Creator in the administration of the universe.[1] The words would apply in their most obvious sense to a man who is occupied in keeping cattle. The relation between gods and men is analogous to that between men and domestic animals ; ' we are the sheep of His pasture ' (*Ps.* 100. 3).

τοῦ δὲ κόσμου (καθάπερ ἀκτῖνες) αἱ φύσεις. The influences ' radiated ' by the Kosmos (or more especially by the heavenly bodies) are αἱ φύσεις, that is to say, the forces by which individual organisms are brought into being and maintained in being. These forces operate διὰ τῶν στοιχείων ; i.e. it is through the action of the heavenly bodies on the elements contained in the sublunar region that the organisms are built up. In this process, the demiurgic activity of God (αἱ ἐνέργειαι) is the first cause ; but God acts upon man (who is here regarded as an earthly organism) not directly, but through the medium of the Kosmos, and by means of its φυσικαὶ ἀκτῖνες. The same view might be expressed in more personal terms by saying that the astral gods (who are ' members ' of that ' second God ', the Kosmos,) are the intermediaries through whom the action of God's will is brought to bear on men. As we were told above, the Kosmos is the ' son ' of God, and man is his ' grandson '.

---

[1] Cf. J. Abelson, *The immanence of God in Rabbinical literature*, p. 114 : ' A favourite Rabbinic expression is that of man, under certain circumstances, being " a co-worker with God in the work of creation ". . . . When man adds his quota of usefulness, he *ipso facto* becomes a co-worker with God. The sum of Divine blessedness is (thereby) increased.'

τοῦ δὲ ἀνθρώπου, αἱ τέχναι καὶ ἐπιστῆμαι. Here we have the familiar antithesis between φύσις and τεχνή, between 'works of nature' and 'works of art'. It is by means of the arts and crafts that man fulfils his function of 'tending earthly things', and thereby supplements the operation of the cosmic forces. Cf. *Ascl. Lat.* I. 8 : 'quae pars terrena mundi artium (τεχνῶν) disciplinarumque (ἐπιστημῶν) cognitione atque usu servatur, sine quibus mundum deus noluit esse perfectum.' In the interpolated passage *Ascl. Lat.* I. 5, the works of nature are described as 'things made by gods and daemons', in contrast to 'things made by men'; that is, the φύσεις or φυσικαὶ ἀκτῖνες spoken of in *Corp.* X. 22 b are there personified as gods and daemons.

[οἱ δὲ ἄνθρωποι διὰ τῶν τεχνῶν καὶ ἐπιστημῶν.] If we retain these words, we get the statement that οἱ ἄνθρωποι do something ἐπὶ τὸν ἄνθρωπον by means of the arts and crafts. But there is no sense in that; and it seems clear that the clause must have been inserted by some one who failed to understand the passage.

§ 23. ἐκ τῆς ἑνὸς ⟨τοῦ θεοῦ⟩ φύσεως. Here the writer inadvertently uses the word φύσις with reference to God, though in § 1 b he objected to such use of it.

καὶ διοικουμένων (διήκουσα or διοίκουσα MSS.) δι' ἑνὸς τοῦ νοῦ. The several ἀκτῖνες spoken of above are all of them operations or manifestations of νοῦς. In the ἐνέργειαι of God, the divine νοῦς is at work; in the cosmic φύσεις, the νοῦς of the Kosmos; in the arts and crafts, the human νοῦς. And in all its different manifestations, νοῦς is one. This implies that the νοῦς of the Kosmos and the νόες of individual men are ἀπόρροιαι of the divine νοῦς, and are consubstantial with it. Cf. *Corp.* XII. i *init.*

οὗτός ἐστιν ὁ ἀγαθὸς δαίμων. The word δαίμων here means ὁ ἴδιος ἑκάστου δαίμων. A man's δαίμων is the power by which happiness or unhappiness is assigned to him,—that power being conceived as a person who attends on the man and watches over him.

This use of the word δαίμων must be distinguished from that in which it means one of a class of beings intermediate between gods and men (as in Pl. *Sympos.* 202 E), and located in the atmosphere. What is the relation between the two uses? It is difficult to understand how a word meaning 'a man's good or ill fortune' could have come to mean 'one of a class of superhuman beings who hover in the air',[1] or *vice versa*; and it may be suspected

[1] We are told, however, that the French word *fée*, 'a fairy', is derived from the

that the two main senses of the word are of different and independent origin.[1] But the meaning of ὁ ἴδιος ἑκάστου δαίμων was doubtless modified by the influence of the other use of the word. The δαίμων in the one sense was assumed to be a δαίμων in the other sense also; that is, the power by which a man's fortune is determined was regarded as a personal being who belongs to the class of ἀέρια ζῷα, and has been told off to watch over that particular man; and so the ἴδιός τινος δαίμων came to be pictured in imagination as a sort of 'familiar spirit' or 'guardian angel'.[2]

The ἴδιος ἑκάστου δαίμων is spoken of by Plato in *Rep.* 10. 620 D: (τὴν Λάχεσιν) ἑκάστῳ, ὃν εἵλετο δαίμονα, τοῦτον φύλακα ξυμπέμπειν τοῦ βίου καὶ ἀποπληρωτὴν τῶν αἱρεθέντων. (In that passage, 'to choose one's δαίμων' means to choose the life which one is to live in one's next embodiment.)[3] Cf. Pseudo-Pl. *Axiochus* 371 C: ὅσοις μὲν οὖν ἐν τῷ ζῆν δαίμων ἀγαθὸς ἐπέπνευσεν, εἰς τὸν τῶν εὐσεβῶν χῶρον οἰκίζονται. Hor. *Ep.* 2. 2. 183 ff.: why two brothers differ in disposition, 'scit genius, natale comes qui temperat astrum, | naturae deus

Latin *fata* (= *Parca*), which meant 'the being who presides over our *fatum*' (Brachet); and it is possible that a corresponding change of meaning may have taken place in the case of the word δαίμων.

[1] δαίμων in the sense of 'a man's fortune' (ὁ ἴδιος ἑκάστου δαίμων) may perhaps be connected with δαίειν, δαΐζειν, 'to divide' or 'distribute'; cf. μοῖρα. The word may have originally meant 'a distributor'; and a man's δαίμων may thence have come to mean the power which assigns to him his share of good things or of bad things. On the other hand, it might be conjectured that δαίμων in the sense of a ζῷον ἀέριον is possibly connected with δαίς, δαίνυσθαι, δαιτυμών (cf. θεοδαίσια); i. e. that it may have originally meant 'a feaster', and may thence have come to be applied to the invisible guest (or host) at the sacrificial meal or funeral banquet,— the superhuman being with whom the worshippers enter into communion by partaking of the holy food. On this hypothesis, we may see a trace of the primary meaning of the word in the belief, still prevalent in Christian times, that the 'daemons' feed on the blood or reek of sacrifices.

In the Homeric poems, as well as in later literature, two uses of the word can be distinguished. δαίμων in Homer sometimes means a man's fate or fortune, as in the compound ὀλβιοδαίμων, Γ. 182. In other Homeric passages it means a superhuman being; but when thus used, it is a mere synonym of θεός, and does not, as in later times, signify a being of lower order than 'the gods'. It does not, however, necessarily follow from this that the distinction between δαίμων (in the sense of a ἀέριον ζῷον) and θεός first originated in post-Homeric times. The Homeric poems are separated from the popular religion of the Greeks by a wider gulf than much of the later literature; and the distinction between θεός and δαίμων, though the Homeric poets ignored it, may have existed before their time, and may have been maintained throughout in other regions or in other social strata. A trace of a more primitive conception survives in the Homeric word δαιμόνιε, which may be rendered 'What (spirit) has possessed you?' There is no analogous use of the word θεῖος.

[2] See Ammian. Marcell. 21. 14 (*Testim.*); Apuleius *De deo Socr.* 16. 155 f.

[3] In the myth of the *Phaedo*, 107 D, we are told that the δαίμων who has presided over a man's life continues to discharge his function after the man's death: τελευτήσαντα ἕκαστον ὁ ἑκάστου δαίμων, ὅσπερ ζῶντα εἰλήχει, οὗτος ἄγειν ἐπιχειρεῖ εἰς δή τινα τόπον κ.τ.λ. But this is merely an invention of the myth-maker, and not an ancient and traditional belief.

humanae, mortalis in unum | quodque caput, vultu mutabilis, albus an ater'. (Horace's description of the *genius* is based, in part at least, on the Greek conception of the ἴδιος ἑκάστου δαίμων.) If a man lives a happy life, his δαίμων is ἀγαθός; if he lives an unhappy life, his δαίμων is κακός. Hence the adjectives εὐδαίμων and κακοδαίμων. Sometimes a man's ἀγαθὸς δαίμων (the author of his happiness) and his κακὸς δαίμων (the author of his unhappiness) were spoken of as two distinct persons. Plut. *De tranq. an.* 15, 474 B : οὐ γάρ, ὡς Μένανδρός φησιν, " ἅπαντι δαίμων ἀνδρὶ συμπαρα-στατεῖ | εὐθὺς γενομένῳ μυσταγωγὸς τοῦ βίου | ἀγαθός·" ἀλλὰ μᾶλλον, ὡς Ἐμπεδοκλῆς,[1] διτταί τινες ἕκαστον ἡμῶν παραλαμβάνουσι καὶ κατάρ-χονται μοῖραι καὶ δαίμονες.[2]

The δαίμων of an individual man might be thought of either as determining his external circumstances, or as influencing his character and directing his actions. Where the former notion prevails, the word means a man's 'fortune' or 'luck'.[3] Thus the σπονδὴ τοῦ ἀγαθοῦ δαίμονος at a meal (Ar. *Eq.* 106) perhaps meant little more than 'here's luck'. And in a similar sense people sometimes spoke of ὁ ἀγαθὸς δαίμων τῆς οἰκίας, i. e. 'the luck of the house' personified.[4] On the other hand, moralists expressed their conviction that the sources of happiness and unhappiness are within us by saying that a man's character is his δαίμων. Heraclitus, fr. 119 Diels : ἦθος ἀνθρώπῳ δαίμων. Cf. the verse attributed to Epicharmus,

---

[1] It does not appear that the *word* δαίμων was thus used by Empedocles; in the verses which Plutarch here quotes from him, that word does not occur, and there is only a list of good and evil influences personified under various other names, e. g. Δῆρις and Ἀρμονίη, Καλλιστώ and Αἴσχρη.

[2] Compare the Jewish and Christian conception of a man's 'good angel' and 'bad angel'. Hermas, *Mand.* 6. 2 : δύο εἰσὶν ἄγγελοι μετὰ τοῦ ἀνθρώπου, εἷς τῆς δικαιοσύνης καὶ εἷς τῆς πονηρίας κ.τ.λ.

[3] The building in which men who intended to descend into the cave of Trophonius were housed during the preparatory rites was called δαίμονος ἀγαθοῦ καὶ τύχης ἀγαθῆς ἱερόν (Paus. 9. 39. 4), probably with reference to the good fortune which it was hoped that the oracle would announce to them. In a system of astrology described by Bouché-Leclercq *L'astrol. grecque* p. 280, the phrase ἀγαθὸς δαίμων was employed as a technical term. In the diagram which B.-L. gives to illustrate that system, one of the twelve divisions of the zodiacal circle is inscribed ' ἀγαθὸς δαίμων, *bonus genius* '; while another, diametrically opposite to it, is inscribed ' ἀγαθὴ τύχη, *bona fortuna* '. Here ἀγαθὸς δαίμων differs little in meaning from ' good fortune '. A planet situated in the division marked ἀγαθὸς δαίμων was described as ἀγαθοδαιμονῶν (*ib.* p. 513).

[4] Diog. Laert. 6. 74 : Xeniades, having bought Diogenes the Cynic as a slave, said ἀγαθὸς δαίμων εἰς τὴν οἰκίαν μου εἰσελήλυθε, meaning that all went well with his household when Diogenes had the management of it. Timoleon dedicated his house in Syracuse ἀγαθῷ δαίμονι (Plut. *De se ipso laud.* 11. 542 E); this is under-stood by Plutarch as meaning that Timoleon did not take credit to himself for his achievements, but attributed his success τὸ μὲν εἰς τὴν τύχην, τὸ δ' εἰς τὸν θεόν.

fr. 17 Diels : ὁ τρόπος ἀνθρώποισι δαίμων ἀγαθός, οἷς δὲ καὶ κακός. And Platonists, holding that man's welfare consists in the supremacy of νοῦς over the irrational impulses, expressed this by saying that a man's νοῦς is his δαίμων, or his ἀγαθὸς δαίμων. But at the same time, this form of expression may also have been suggested in part by the Orphic and Pythagorean belief that the human soul (or τὸ ἐν ἡμῖν θεῖον, the higher of the two parts of the soul,) is a δαίμων in the other sense, i. e. an immortal being, temporarily incarnated in a human body. The identification of ὁ ἑκάστου νοῦς with ὁ ἑκάστου δαίμων occurs in Pl. *Tim.* 90 A : τὸ δὲ περὶ τοῦ κυριωτάτου παρ' ἡμῖν ψυχῆς εἴδους (i. e. τοῦ νοῦ) διανοεῖσθαι δεῖ τῇδε, ὡς ἄρα αὐτὸ δαίμονα θεὸς ἑκάστῳ δέδωκε, τοῦτο ὃ δή φαμεν οἰκεῖν μὲν ἡμῶν ἐπ' ἄκρῳ τῷ σώματι κ.τ.λ. *Ib.* 90 c : ἅτε δὲ ἀεὶ θεραπεύοντα τὸ θεῖον, ἔχοντά τε αὐτὸν εὖ κεκοσμημένον τὸν δαίμονα ξύνοικον ἐν αὐτῷ, διαφερόντως εὐδαίμονα εἶναι. Cf. Plutarch's ' Vision of Timarchus ', *De gen. Socr.* 591 D f. : ψυχὴ πᾶσα νοῦ μέτεσχεν . . . · ἀλλ' αἱ μὲν ὅλαι κατέδυσαν εἰς σῶμα, . . . αἱ δὲ πῆ μὲν ἀνεκράθησαν, πῆ δ' ἔλιπον ἔξω τὸ καθαρώτατον. . . . τὸ μὲν οὖν ὑποβρύχιον ἐν τῷ σώματι φερόμενον ψυχὴ λέγεται· τὸ δὲ φθορᾶς λειφθὲν οἱ πολλοὶ νοῦν καλοῦντες ἐντὸς εἶναι νομίζουσιν αὐτῶν . . . · οἱ δ' ὀρθῶς ὑπονοοῦντες, ὡς ἐκτὸς ὄντα, δαίμονα προσαγορεύουσιν. In the symbolism of the Vision of Timarchus, the νοῦς or δαίμων is described as floating in a higher world, but connected by a cord with the ψυχή embodied on earth below. Dio Chrysost. 4, vol. i, p. 77 Dindorf : Diogenes says to Alexander, οὐ πρότερον ἔσει βασιλεύς, πρὶν ἂν ἱλάσῃ τὸν σαυτοῦ δαίμονα, καὶ θεραπεύσας ὡς δεῖ ἀποδείξῃς . . . βασιλικόν. . . . οὐκ εἰσὶν ἔξωθεν τῶν ἀνθρώπων οἱ κακοὶ καὶ ἀγαθοὶ δαίμονες, οἱ τὰς συμφορὰς καὶ τὰς εὐτυχίας φέροντες αὐτοῖς, ὁ δὲ ἴδιος ἑκάστου νοῦς, οὗτός ἐστι δαίμων τοῦ ἔχοντος ἀνδρός, ἀγαθὸς μὲν ὁ τοῦ φρονίμου καὶ ἀγαθοῦ δαίμων, πονηρὸς δὲ ὁ τοῦ πονηροῦ. Marc. Aurel. 5. 27 : συζῇ δὲ θεοῖς ὁ συνεχῶς δεικνὺς αὐτοῖς τὴν ἑαυτοῦ ψυχήν. . . . ποιοῦσαν . . . ὅσα βούλεται ὁ δαίμων ὃν ἑκάστῳ προστάτην καὶ ἡγεμόνα ὁ Ζεὺς ἔδωκεν, ἀπόσπασμα ἑαυτοῦ· οὗτος δέ ἐστιν ὁ ἑκάστου νοῦς καὶ λόγος.

The statement that ὁ (ἑκάστου) νοῦς is in this sense ὁ (ἑκάστου) ἀγαθὸς δαίμων must have been familiar to all Platonists. But among the Hermetists, the term ὁ ἀγαθὸς δαίμων carried with it also a second and quite different set of associations. It was employed by the Greeks of Egypt in Ptolemaic and Roman times as a name of an Egyptian god, probably the god Khnum or Kmeph. The Egyptian god called Ἀγαθὸς Δαίμων is spoken of in *Corp.* XII. i and elsewhere as the teacher from whom Hermes learnt his wisdom. But in other *Hermetica* the teacher of Hermes is called Νοῦς. (See *Corp.* XI ; and compare *Corp.* I. 2, ἐγώ εἰμι ὁ Ποιμάνδρης, ὁ τῆς αὐθεντίας νοῦς.) The words ὁ νοῦς ἐστιν ὁ ἀγαθὸς δαίμων might therefore be taken as conveying, in addition to their more obvious meaning, a suggestion that the Egyptian god called Agathos Daimon is a personification of the divine νοῦς.

Πῶς τοῦτο πάλιν λέγεις ; 'This' (τοῦτο) is the statement that some souls are devoid of νοῦς, which is implied in the preceding words of Hermes, ἡ τούτου κενή. As to the view that some men have νοῦς and others not, see *Corp.* I. 21 *fin.*, *Corp.* IX. 5 *init.*, and *Ascl. Lat.* I. 7 a.

[τὸν ἀγαθόν . . . τῆς δίκης.] I take these words to have been added to the text after §§ 19 b–22 a had been inserted. The writer of the original document spoke of νοῦς as a thing bestowed on the elect alone. According to his view, there is no other kind of νοῦς to be contrasted with the ἀγαθὸς νοῦς ; the wicked are not men who have a κακὸς νοῦς, but men who have no νοῦς at all. But the writer of 19 b–22 a (see especially § 21) spoke of νοῦς as a thing which enters into all men, and which may be either good or bad. Hence, when 19 b–22 a had been inserted, it appeared desirable to point out that, in what follows, the ἀγαθὸς νοῦς alone is in question. The words τοῦ ὑπηρετικοῦ περὶ οὗ ἔμπροσθεν εἰρήκαμεν κ.τ.λ. refer to § 21 in the corrupted form in which it appears in our MSS., viz. ὁ γὰρ νοῦς, ὅταν δαίμων γένηται, πυρίνου τυχεῖν σώματος τέτακται πρὸς τὰς τοῦ θεοῦ ὑπηρεσίας, καὶ εἰσδὺς εἰς τὴν ἀσεβῆ ψυχὴν αἰκίζεται αὐτὴν κ.τ.λ. That passage then must have been already corrupted when the words τὸν ἀγαθόν . . . ὑπὸ τῆς δίκης were inserted in § 23 by a still later hand.

§ 24 a. πολλάκις γὰρ ἐξίσταται ὁ νοῦς . . . . ἀλλ᾽ οὐδὲ νωθρᾶς ψυχῆς ἀνέχεται κ.τ.λ. In the first of these two sentences, the writer speaks of temporary withdrawals of νοῦς ; in the second, he speaks of its permanent abandonment of the 'torpid soul'.

οὔτε τι εἰπεῖν οὔτ᾽ ἔρξαι δύναται. This phrase is quoted from Theognis 177, but is used with an altered application. In Theognis, the subject is ἀνὴρ πενίῃ δεδμημένος. The Hermetist, if he remembered the context of his quotation, may have intended to imply that it is the man who is in want of νοῦς that is truly πένης.

The clause ψυχὴ γὰρ . . . ἔρξαι δύναται is out of place in the MSS. It most likely followed ἀλόγῳ ζώῳ ἔοικε, and was meant to confirm that statement. (An ἄλογον ζῷον is a creature which 'cannot speak'.) But it is not indispensable there; and it may perhaps have been added later.

ὑπ' αὐτοῦ ἀγχομένην κάτω. Cf. *Corp*. VII. 3 : ἄγχων σε κάτω πρὸς αὐτόν. *Ascl. Lat*. I. 12 a : 'animam obtorto, ut aiunt, detinet collo.'

§ 24 b. ὁ γὰρ ἄνθρωπος ζῷόν ἐστι θεῖον κ.τ.λ. Cf. *Ascl. Lat*. I. 6 a : 'magnum miraculum est homo' &c. Cic. *De legg*. 1. 22 (from Panaetius?) : 'animal hoc providum, sagax, multiplex, acutum, memor, plenum rationis et consilii, quem vocamus hominem, praeclara quadam condicione generatum esse a supremo deo. Solum est enim ex tot animantium generibus atque naturis particeps rationis et cogitationis, cum cetera sint omnia expertia. Quid est autem, non dicam in homine, sed in omni caelo atque terra, ratione divinius?' Macarius Aegyptius (an Egyptian monk of the fourth century), *Hom*. 15. 22, Migne 34. 589 D : μεγάλου γὰρ ἀξιώματός ἐστιν ὁ ἄνθρωπος. ἴδε πόσος ἐστιν ὁ οὐρανὸς καὶ ἡ γῆ, ὁ ἥλιος καὶ ἡ σελήνη, καὶ οὐκ εὐδόκησεν ἐν αὐτοῖς ὁ Κύριος, εἰ μὴ ἐν τῷ ἀνθρώπῳ μόνῳ, ἐπαναπαύεσθαι. τιμιώτερος οὖν ἐστιν ὁ ἄνθρωπος ὑπὲρ πάντα τὰ δημιουργήματα, τάχα δὲ τολμήσω λέγειν ὅτι μὴ μόνον τῶν ὁρατῶν δημιουργημάτων, ἀλλὰ καὶ τῶν ἀοράτων, ἤγουν τῶν λειτουργικῶν πνευμάτων. οὐ γὰρ περὶ Μιχαὴλ καὶ Γαβριὴλ τῶν ἀρχαγγέλων εἶπεν ὅτι "ποιήσωμεν κατ' εἰκόνα καὶ ὁμοίωσιν ἡμετέραν", ἀλλὰ περὶ τῆς νοερᾶς οὐσίας τοῦ ἀνθρώπου, τῆς ἀθανάτου λέγω ψυχῆς.

Compare the *Hermippus*, 1. 6. 40 : τούτων δ' (*sc*. of beasts and plants) ἡγεμὼν ὁ ἄνθρωπος πέπλασται, ὕλην μὲν τῆς συστάσεως τὴν αὐτὴν αὐτοῖς ἐσχηκώς, ἔχων δέ τι νοερᾶς οὐσίας ἐν αὐτῷ πλέον, καθ' ἣν γῆν τε περιπολεῖ καὶ οὐρανοῦ ἐμβατεύει καὶ θαλάττης ὑγρὰ τέμνει κέλευθα, καὶ τούτων τὰ μεγέθη μετρεῖ, ἔτι τε ⟨τὰς⟩ τῶν ἀστέρων κατὰ μῆκος καὶ πλάτος πορείας ἐπίσταται.

καὶ ὑπὲρ ἐκείνους ἐστὶν ὁ ὄντως ἄνθρωπος. Cf. *Ascl. Lat*. III. 22 b *fin*.: 'hominem . . . esse meliorem et diis' &c.

§ 25. οὐδεὶς μὲν γὰρ τῶν οὐρανίων θεῶν ἐπὶ γῆν (γῆς MSS.) κατελεύσεται. Is this directed against the Christian belief that God the Son 'came down to earth'? I think not. The 'heavenly gods' of whom the writer speaks are the sun, moon, and stars; and he takes it to be an undisputed truth that they will never quit the stations which God has assigned to them. Yet there were Pagans who said that gods had come down from heaven to earth; Horace, for instance, spoke thus of Augustus ('serus in caelum redeas', *Od*. 1. 2. 45).

τὸν μὲν ⟨⟨ἐπίγειον⟩⟩ ἄνθρωπον [[ ]] εἶναι θνητὸν θεόν, τὸν δὲ οὐράνιον θεὸν ἀθάνατον ἄνθρωπον. Cf. *Corp.* XII. i. 1: ὁ Ἀγαθὸς Δαίμων τοὺς μὲν θεοὺς εἶπεν ⟨ἀνθρώπους⟩ ἀθανάτους, τοὺς δὲ ἀνθρώπους θεοὺς θνητούς. The ultimate source of this is Heraclitus, fr. 62 Diels: ἀθάνατοι θνητοί, θνητοὶ ἀθάνατοι, ζῶντες τὸν ἐκείνων θάνατον, τὸν δὲ ἐκείνων βίον τεθνεῶτες. Whatever Heraclitus may have meant by these obscure words,[1] he certainly did not mean what the Hermetist takes them to mean, viz. that a man stands as high as a star-god in the scale of being. But the Stoics, who adopted and popularized the sayings of Heraclitus, often put into them meanings of which their author had never thought. Thus the words ἀθάνατοι θνητοί, θνητοὶ ἀθάνατοι, detached from their context, were taken to mean that gods are men and men are gods, or that mortal men are on a level with the immortal gods; and the saying was paraphrased and expanded in this sense.[2]

The interest of the earlier Stoics was almost entirely limited to man's present life; and to them, the saying would mean that man (or at least the ideally wise and good man) is the equal of the gods, save that his life is shorter. Cic. *Nat. deor.* 2. 61. 153 (Stoic): 'virtutes, e quibus vita beata exsistit[3] par et similis deorum, nulla alia re nisi immortalitate, quae nihil ad bene vivendum pertinet, cedens caelestibus.' Chrysippus, in Plut. *Comm. not.* 33. 1076: ἀρετῇ οὐχ ὑπερέχειν τὸν Δία τοῦ Δίωνος· . . . ἀρετῇ δὲ μὴ ὑπολειπόμενον ἄνθρωπον οὐδὲν ἀποδεῖν εὐδαιμονίας, ἀλλ' ἐπίσης εἶναι μακάριον τῷ Διὶ τῷ σωτῆρι τὸν ἀτυχῇ. Plut. *Sto. rep.* 13. 1038: τοῖς ἀγαθοῖς πᾶσι

[1] Perhaps he was speaking of the living elements (fire, water, earth), regarded as θεοί, and therefore masculine. If so, he may have meant that each of these elements is 'mortal', in the sense that portions of it are ceaselessly changing into another element; but that at the same time each of them is 'immortal', either in the sense that the thing into which it changes is still a living thing, or else, in the sense that the whole mass of water, for instance, is maintained in perpetual existence by the ceaseless change of other elements into water, which goes on simultaneously with the change of water into other elements. Cf. Heraclitus fr. 50 Diels: ⟨ἕν⟩ φησιν εἶναι τὸ πᾶν, διαιρετὸν ἀδιαίρετον, γενητὸν ἀγένητον, θνητὸν ἀθάνατον. The universe is mortal in each several part, but immortal as a whole.

[2] Maximus Tyrius, 4. 4 h, p. 45 Hobein: Heraclitus said θεοὶ θνητοί, ⌐θεοὶ⌐ (*al.* ἄνθρωποι) ἀθάνατοι.—Clem. Alex. *Paed.* 3. 1. 2: Heraclitus said ἄνθρωποι θεοί, θεοὶ ἄνθρωποι.—Heraclitus *Alleg. Hom.* 24 p. 51 Mehler: Heraclitus said θεοὶ θνητοί ⌐τ΄⌐ ἄνθρωποι ἀθάνατοι, κ.τ.λ.—Lucian, Βίων πρᾶσις 14: (*Buyer*) Τί δαὶ οἱ ἄνθρωποι; (*Heraclitus*) Θεοὶ θνητοί. (*Buyer*) Τί δαὶ οἱ θεοί; (*Heracl.*) Ἄνθρωποι ἀθάνατοι.— Hippol. *Ref. haer.* 9. 10: Heraclitus said ἀθάνατοι θνητοί, θνητοὶ ἀθάνατοι, κ.τ.λ.— Dio Cass. *fr.* 30. 3, p. 40 Dind.: εἰ γὰρ δεῖ δή τι καὶ θρασυνόμενον εἰπεῖν, οὔτ' ἄνθρωπος οὐδὲν ἄλλο ἐστὶν ἢ θεὸς σῶμα θνητὸν ἔχων, οὔτε θεὸς ἄλλο τι ἢ ἄνθρωπος ἀσώματος καὶ διὰ τοῦτο καὶ ἀθάνατος.

[3] Is there not a lacuna after *exsistit*? The subject to which *par et similis deorum* is predicate ought to be *homo*.

. . . κατ' οὐδὲν προεχομένοις ὑπὸ τοῦ Διός. Stob. 2. 7. 11 g, vol. ii,
p. 98 W.: τὴν (τῶν ἀγαθῶν ἀνθρώπων) εὐδαιμονίαν μὴ διαφέρειν τῆς
θείας εὐδαιμονίας, μηδὲ τὴν ἀμεριαίαν ὁ Χρύσιππός φησι διαφέρειν τῆς
τοῦ Διὸς εὐδαιμονίας, ⟨καὶ⟩ κατὰ μηδὲν αἱρετωτέραν εἶναι μήτε καλλίω
μήτε σεμνοτέραν τὴν τοῦ Διὸς εὐδαιμονίαν τῆς τῶν σοφῶν ἀνδρῶν. Seneca
De prov. 1. 5: 'bonus ipse tempore tantum a deo differt.' Sen. Ep.
73. 13: 'Iuppiter quo antecedit virum bonum? Diutius bonus est.'
Sen. Ep. 53. 11: 'est aliquid quo sapiens antecedat deum: ille
naturae beneficio, non suo sapiens est.' Sen. De prov. 6. 6: 'hoc
est quo deum antecedatis; ille extra patientiam malorum est, vos
supra patientiam.'

The Platonists, unlike the Stoics, regarded man's life on earth
as a mere episode in the everlasting existence of the soul; and
consequently, when a Platonist adopted the saying of Heraclitus,
he would have reason to indicate that he was speaking of man upon
earth, and not merely expressing the thought, familiar to his school,
that a *disembodied* soul may become a god. Hence the insertion of
the word ἐπίγειος in *Corp.* X. 25.

Plato called the philosopher 'divine', but did not go so far as
to say that a man upon earth can be a god, or the equal of a god.
Pl. *Rep.* 6. 500 D: the philosopher θεῖος εἰς τὸ δυνατὸν ἀνθρώπῳ
γίγνεται. Pl. *Soph.* 216 B (Theodorus *loq.*): καί μοι δοκεῖ θεὸς μὲν
ἀνήρ (sc. the Eleatic stranger) οὐδαμῶς εἶναι,[1] θεῖος μήν· πάντας γὰρ
ἐγὼ τοὺς φιλοσόφους τοιούτους προσαγορεύω. (Socr.) Καὶ καλῶς γε.[2]
The instances of a glorification of man such as we find in *Corp.* X.
24 b, 25 are mostly Stoic; and there can be little doubt that the
contents of this paragraph, including the saying of Heraclitus, were
transmitted to the Hermetist from some Stoic source.

ὑπὸ δὲ τοῦ ἑνὸς ⟨θεοῦ⟩ τὰ πάντα. In the text of the MSS., God
is here called either ὁ εἷς or τὸ ἕν ('the One') instead of ὁ θεός.
But the writer is not likely to have introduced without explanation,

---

[1] Perhaps Plato was here thinking of Empedocles, who spoke of himself as θεὸς
ἄμβροτος, οὐκέτι θνητός, *fr.* 112 Diels.

[2] Cf. Plotinus 4. 7. 10: ὅτι δὲ τῇ θειοτέρᾳ φύσει συγγενὴς ἡ ψυχὴ καὶ τῇ ἀιδίῳ, . . .
ἐκ τῶνδε ἔστι δεικνύναι. . . . λάβωμεν δὲ ψυχὴν μὴ τὴν ἐν σώματι ἐπιθυμίας ἀλόγους
καὶ θυμοὺς προσλαβοῦσαν, . . . ἀλλὰ τὴν ταῦτα ἀποτριψαμένην. . . . καθηραμένη δὲ
αὐτῇ ἐνυπάρχει τὰ ἄριστα, φρόνησις καὶ ἡ ἄλλη ἀρετή, οἰκεῖα ὄντα. εἰ οὖν τοιοῦτον ἡ
ψυχὴ ὅταν ἐφ' ἑαυτὴν ἀνέλθῃ, πῶς οὐ τῆς φύσεως (ἐστὶν) ἐκείνης, οἷον φαμὲν τὴν τοῦ
θείου καὶ ἀιδίου παντὸς εἶναι; φρόνησις γὰρ καὶ ἀρετὴ ἀληθής, θεῖα ὄντα, οὐκ ἂν
ἐγγένοιντο φαύλῳ τινὶ καὶ θνητῷ πράγματι, ἀλλ' ἀνάγκη θεῖον τὸ τοιοῦτον εἶναι, ἅτε
θείων μετὸν αὐτῷ διὰ συγγένειαν καὶ τὸ ὁμοούσιον. διὸ καὶ ὅστις τοιοῦτος ἡμῶν,
ὀλίγον ἂν παραλλάττοι τῶν ἄνω τῇ ψυχῇ αὐτῇ, μόνον τοῦτο, ὅσον ἐστὶν ἐν σώματι,
ἐλαττούμενος. This amounts to saying that a good man on earth is almost, but not
quite, a god.

in the last line of his treatise, a name of God which he has not
hitherto employed. He has been speaking of the triad ὁ θεός, ὁ
κόσμος, ὁ ἄνθρωπος (see § 14 b) ; and he doubtless here wrote either
τοῦ ἑνὸς θεοῦ, or ἑνὸς τοῦ θεοῦ, in contrast to τῶν δύο, κόσμου καὶ
ἀνθρώπου. All things are governed *by* God ; but God governs them
through his two subordinate agents, viz. the Kosmos (which works
by means of its φυσικαὶ ἀκτῖνες), and man (who works by means
of his arts and crafts). It is possible that ἑνὸς τοῦ θεοῦ was intentionally altered into τοῦ ἑνός by the person who inserted § 14 a, in
which τὸ ἕν is spoken of.

LIBELLVS XI. i

It is evident that the beginning of *Corp.* XI has been in some
way tampered with. Firstly, a discourse cannot start with a sentence
introduced by οὖν. Secondly, the words ὡς δέ μοι ἐπῆλθεν κ.τ.λ.
(§ 1 b), which must be assigned to the pupil, are not rightly connected with § 1 a, in which the teacher is speaking. δέ is impossible
in this context; and if the teacher bids the pupil remember his
instruction (§ 1 a), that injunction ought to follow, and not to
precede, the speech in which the pupil asks the teacher to instruct
him (§ 1 b). The words ἄκουε ὦ τέκνον κ.τ.λ. (§ 1 b *fin.*), follow
rightly on the pupil's request;[1] but κατάσχες . . . λεγομένων (§ 1 a)
is clearly out of place.

The text of the MSS. may be accounted for by the following
hypothesis.[2] Some collection of *Hermetica* contained two distinct
discourses of Nous to Hermes, which I call XI. i and XI. ii. The
marks of division between the two (including the title of the second)
accidentally disappeared, and the two discourses came to be read
as one. The introductory sentences of XI. ii now stood in the
middle of the composite document. A redactor, noticing that they
were unsuitable for that position, cut out these sentences, and
inserted at the beginning of the whole document (where it now
stands in the MSS., as § 1 b,) so much of the original introduction
of XI. ii as it seemed to him possible or desirable to retain. But
he wrongly took the concluding sentence of XI. i (κατάσχες οὖν . . .

---

[1] ὁ χρόνος, inserted by error before ἄκουε in § 1 b *fin.*, has come from ὁ κόσμος,
ὁ χρόνος in § 2 *init.*

[2] Merely a hypothesis; but I can think of no other hypothesis that would account
for the facts before us.

τῶν λεγομένων, § 1 a) to be connected with the introductory sentences of XI. ii, and transposed it along with them.

At the beginning of XI. ii, something which preceded and led on to ὡς δέ μοι κ.τ.λ. (§ 1 b) has disappeared; and at the end of XI. i, it is possible that τὰ γινόμενα ὑπ' αὐτῷ in § 6 a was followed by some sentences which are now lost. But each of the two documents appears to be nearly, if not quite, complete. They differ markedly in style, and exemplify two strongly contrasted methods of teaching. In XI. i, the thought is petrified in rigid formulas; in XI. ii, the thought is fresh and living. In XI. i, the teacher recites a sort of creed (§ 2), which would be utterly meaningless to a beginner; the explanations which he adds (§§ 3–6 a) are intelligible in themselves, but do not throw much light on the obscurity of § 2; and he expects his pupil to learn the words by rote (μέμνησο τῶν λεγομένων). In XI. ii, on the other hand, the teacher takes nothing for granted, and presupposes no previous knowledge in the pupil. He does his utmost to make his meaning clear, and to carry the learner with him at every step. He appeals repeatedly to the pupil's personal experience (§ 12 a, σοῦ τοσαῦτα ποιοῦντος: § 14 a, ἴδε τί σοι ἐγγίνεται: § 19 *init.*, τοῦτο νόησον ἀπὸ σεαυτοῦ); and he ends by telling him to think things out for himself.

It must not be inferred from the straightforward simplicity of XI. ii, and the dogmatic elaboration of XI. i, that the former is necessarily of earlier date than the latter. The writer of XI. ii, though he thinks fit to conceal his learning rather than to obtrude it, is at home among the conceptions of Platonism and Stoicism; and the apparent *naïveté* of his tone may be due to a reaction against that sort of ματαιολογία of which the author of *Corp.* XIV speaks with contempt, and of which XI. i. 2 is a specimen.

The two documents, while differing greatly in style and tone, present close resemblances in doctrine. In both alike, God is regarded as the author of *life*, and his creative function is described as that of putting life into matter; in both alike, it is asserted with emphasis that God 'is always at his work' of generating life in the universe; and in both, the two modes of life, ἀθανασία in heaven and μεταβολή on earth, are similarly contrasted. It is therefore probable that the author of the later of the two documents had the earlier before him; and it is most likely that XI. i was the earlier. If so, we may suppose that the writer of XI. ii was dissatisfied with the cut-and-dried formulas of XI. i. 2, and wrote a second 'discourse

of Nous to Hermes' with the object of putting fresh meaning into
so much of the doctrine of the earlier document as he held to be
of value. He rejected the hypostatized αἰών of XI. i; but he
accepted the conception of God as the author of all life, and made
his exposition of it serve to lead up to that exhortation to 'expand
yourself' (§§ 20 b, 21 a) which is the most significant part of his
own treatise.

Contents of Libellus XI. i

§ 2. The relations between God, the Aeon (or Eternity), the
Kosmos, Time, and Birth (or Coming-into-being), are set forth in
tabular form.

§§ 3, 4 a. The universe is the work of God; and the power by
which God works is the Aeon. The universe is ever being made
by the Aeon, and therefore will never cease to be. The Aeon
makes things by putting life into matter. But life is put into matter
in one way in heaven, and in another way on earth. In heaven, the
same beings are made to live for ever; on earth, a succession of
mortal creatures is produced.

§ 4 b. The universe is filled with soul. The body of the Kosmos
is animated by a soul; the heavenly bodies are animated by souls
which persist in them without change; each earthly organism is
animated by a soul which stays in it only for a time.

§§ 5, 6 a. That which holds the universe together (and maintains
life throughout it) is the Aeon; and the Aeon is God at work.
God then is the sole author of life. His work is to make things
live; and he is present in all things, and is always and everywhere
at work.

Corp. XI. i deals only with God and the universe. Man is not
expressly spoken of, but is implicitly included among the perishable
organisms of earth; and there is no mention of human immortality.
Possibly the writer may have held that man has before him the
prospect of rising from the condition of an earthly and mortal
ζῷον to that of a heavenly and immortal ζῷον; but in this document
he gives no hint of any such belief.

Sources. The doctrine of XI. i is founded on Platonism, but
includes some things not derived from Plato. The conception of
the supracosmic God is Platonic. The use of the word αἰών to
express the notion of 'eternity' as distinguished from 'time' comes
from the *Timaeus.* The description of the Kosmos as a great ζῷον

in which all ζῷα, both mortal and immortal, are included,—the statement that the Kosmos is both pervaded and encompassed by 'soul',—and the assertion that 'the Kosmos makes time',—may also be traced back to the *Timaeus*. The use of the phrase κοσμεῖ τὴν ὕλην to describe the demiurgic process is Platonic; and the Platonic term τὸ ἀγαθόν occurs in § 2.

But in saying that God is the author of 'life', and that God, or God's ἐνέργεια, is present in all things in the form of 'life' (or 'soul'), the writer hardly speaks as a Platonist. Something not unlike this may perhaps be implied in the mythical description of the making of the cosmic ψυχή and the individual ψυχαί which is given in the *Timaeus*; but the language used on this subject by the writer of XI. i has little resemblance to that of Plato. The Platonists said that the Demiurgus κοσμεῖ τὴν ὕλην by imposing 'forms' on matter, not by putting 'life' into matter; and the substitution of 'life' for 'form' must be due to some influence independent of Platonism.

The writer's conception of 'God at work' as entering into all things, and manifesting himself in the form of life throughout the universe, is not very different from the Stoic notion of πνεῦμα διῆκον δι' ὅλου τοῦ κόσμου [1] (if we leave out of account the fact that the Stoics regarded this πνεῦμα as a material substance); but the terms employed by the Hermetist to express that conception are not those used by the Stoics.

Parallels to the language of *Corp.* XI. i concerning 'life' are to be found in documents of the old religion of Egypt. The word *ānkh* or *ōnkh*, the Egyptian equivalent of ζωή, was much used in the Egyptian cults. Take, for instance, the following phrases, which occur in a hymn of King Ikhnaton to the Sun-god, about 1370 B.C. (Breasted, *Hist. of Egypt*, p. 371, and *Religion and Thought in Ancient Egypt*, p. 324): 'O living Aton, Beginning of life (ἀρχὴ ζωῆς)! . . . Thou art he who giveth life to the son in the body of his mother, . . . who giveth breath to animate every one that he maketh. . . . By thee man liveth.' In the carvings of

---

[1] Cf. Orig. *c. Cels.* 6. 7 : τῶν Στωικῶν φασκόντων ὅτι ὁ θεὸς πνεῦμά ἐστι διὰ πάντων διεληλυθὸς καὶ πάντ' ἐν ἑαυτῷ περιέχον.

Some resemblance to XI. i. 4 b–6 a may be seen in the words of Paul's speech at Athens, *Acts* 17. 24 ff.: ὁ θεὸς ὁ ποιήσας τὸν κόσμον καὶ πάντα τὰ ἐν αὐτῷ, . . . αὐτὸς διδοὺς πᾶσι ζωὴν καὶ πνοὴν καὶ τὰ πάντα. . . . ἐν αὐτῷ γὰρ ζῶμεν καὶ κινούμεθα καὶ ἐσμέν. The writer of *Acts* represents Paul as here using language which would be familiar to a Pagan audience ; and the doctrine expressed in these words is that of Stoicism, slightly modified by a tinge of Jewish thought.

Ikhnaton's reign, the sun-disk is seen sending forth rays which terminate in hands holding the emblem of life, and in this way 'God at work' is visibly depicted as 'putting life into' the bodies of the king and queen. It is true that Ikhnaton was a heretic, in the sense that he sought to overthrow the ecclesiastical supremacy of the Theban priesthood, and to suppress the established cults of Amon and other local gods; but the thoughts which he expressed in his hymns to the Sun were in accordance with the spirit of Egyptian religion, and similar phrases were used by worshippers of the traditional deities. Brugsch, *Rel. und Myth.*, p. 287, quotes an inscription of the time of Augustus: 'Hor-Samta, the lord of Tentyra, the god *Anch* (i. e. Life), lord of life, who causes the living (men) to live, in whose hand is life, and by whose look we live.' Brugsch, *ib.*, says that the most frequently recurring epithet of the god Tum of Heroopolis (Pithom) is *Anch* or *Anchi* ('life' or 'the living one'). Thus it is possible that, when the Hermetist describes the function of the creative Power as that of putting *life* into matter, his Platonism was modified by Egyptian influence. But the conception of God as the author or giver of life occurs in the Old Testament also, and is too widespread to be traced back to any one source.[1]

Another sign of Egyptian influence may perhaps be seen in the writer's peculiar treatment of the Platonic αἰών. He has hypostatized 'the Aeon', and interposed it between God and the Kosmos. Its function in his system is analogous to that of Philo's λόγος, and the 'Second God' of Numenius; and though Philo's doctrine of the λόγος can be adequately accounted for as the result of a blending of Greek and Jewish thought, it is possible that certain Egyptian speculations also contributed to it. Moreover, the Hermetist's personification of αἰών was probably suggested in part by the employment of the term in Roman Egypt as a title or epithet of a god. (See note on *Ascl. Lat.* III. 26 b–32 a.) The use of the word

---

[1] In the use of the word ζωή in Paul's Epistles and the Fourth Gospel, phrases resembling some of those used in the old cults of Egypt have been turned to a new purpose. (See *Rom.* 8. 10; 2 *Cor.* 4. 11 and 5. 4; *Col.* 3. 3; *Eph.* 4. 18; *Acts* 3. 15; *Ev. Joh.* 1. 4; 5. 26; 6. 33; 8. 12; 11. 25; 14. 6; *Ep. Joh.* 1. 1. 1 ff. and 5. 11.) The Egyptians spoke of their Sun-god as the author of earthly life; Christians spoke of God or Christ as the author of spiritual and eternal life. The *ankh* of the Egyptian priests is the life which enters into men by carnal birth; the ζωή of the Fourth Gospel is the life which enters into men by 'the second birth'. The writer of *Corp.* XI. i speaks of two different forms of life, which he distinguishes by the words ἀθανασία and μεταβολή; if he had gone on to say, as other Hermetists do, that ἀθανασία is attainable by men, this ἀθανασία might have been compared with the ζωή (αἰώνιος) of Paul and *Ev. Joh.*

αἰῶνες by some of the Christian Gnostics to signify hypostatized δυνάμεις of God is to be connected with this Graeco-Egyptian habit of calling a god αἰών, rather than with the Platonic use of αἰών in the sense of 'eternity'.

Marks of Stoic influence are to be seen in the words ποιότης ⟨καὶ ποσότης⟩ and ἀποκατάστασις ; and the terms ἀνάγκη, πρόνοια, and φύσις, mentioned in § 5 as possible substitutes for ὁ αἰών or ἡ τοῦ θεοῦ ἐνέργεια, are characteristic of Stoicism.

The use of the phrase δύναμις τοῦ θεοῦ to describe the hypostatized αἰών may perhaps have been derived from a Jewish source. The document contains no trace of Christian influence.

Date. The occurrence of Stoic terms in a document mainly Platonic excludes the possibility of any date earlier than the first century B. C. This argument applies to nearly all the other *Hermetica* also ; but the fact that Hermes here appears as a pupil, and not as a teacher, seems to indicate that *Corp.* XI. i belongs to a comparatively late stage of the Hermetic literature. It may be presumed that the earlier Hermetists regarded Hermes as the founder of their religion, and that it was not until a considerable number of dialogues in which he took the part of teacher had been written, that the question whence he himself had derived his *gnosis* was asked and answered. It seems probable that the first answer given to this question was that Hermes had been instructed by the Agathos Daimon (i. e. the god Khnum), and that the substitution of Νοῦς for ᾽Αγαθὸς Δαίμων as the name of his teacher did not take place till a yet later stage in the development of the Hermetic tradition. We may conclude then that *Corp.* XI. i was probably written in the second or third century A. D., and that the balance of probability is in favour of the third century rather than the second.

Title. The title of *Corp.* XI, as given in the MSS., is Νοῦ (*al.* Νοῦς) πρὸς ῾Ερμῆν. There is no reason to doubt that this was the heading of XI. i from the first ; and XI. ii may very well have borne the same heading. In XI. ii, the teacher is not expressly named ; but Hermes uses the word δέσποτα (§ 1 b), which would not be employed in addressing a mere man ; and the phrase δι᾽ ἐμοῦ (§ 6 b) seems to imply that the teacher's name is Νοῦς.

Cyril,[1] quoting part of XI. ii. 22, says that the discourse from

---

[1] *C. Julianum* 2. 52, Migne 76. 580: ἃ γέγραφέ ποτε καὶ ὁ τρισμέγιστος ῾Ερμῆς πρὸς τὸν ἑαυτοῦ νοῦν· ὀνομάζεται γὰρ ὡδὶ τὸ βιβλίον.

which he took the words was addressed by Hermes 'to his own mind'. In supposing Hermes to be the teacher and Nous the pupil, Cyril has blundered; but his statement shows that in his copy of *Corp.* XI the word νοῦς occurred in the title.

In some of the *Hermetica*, the Egyptian god Agathos Daimon was represented as the teacher from whom Hermes learnt the *gnosis*; and some of the Hermetists held the Agathos Daimon to be the divine νοῦς (see *Abammonis Resp.* 8. 3). In *Corp.* I, the divine νοῦς manifests itself in the form of a person named Poimandres, and in that form gives instruction to an unnamed prophet. In XI. i, and probably in XI. ii also, the personal name (Agathos Daimon or Poimandres) is dropped, and the divine instructor is called simply Νοῦς. The writers of XI. i and XI. ii can hardly have intended their readers to suppose that the divine νοῦς had in fact manifested itself in personal form to the founder of their religion; it is more likely that, in putting their teaching into this form, they merely meant to suggest that the human prophet Hermes derived his wisdom from the divine νοῦς which had entered into him.

§ **2**. ὁ θεὸς ⟨τὸν⟩ αἰῶνα ποιεῖ. In XI. i, αἰών means 'eternity' in the Platonic sense; but the writer has hypostatized eternity. He interposes it, as a divine person, between God and the Kosmos, and assigns to it a function partly analogous to that of the αὐτόζῳον (i. e. the νοητὸς κόσμος, the παράδειγμα of the αἰσθητὸς κόσμος) in the *Timaeus*, but more closely corresponding to that of the extracosmic νοῦς (also called ὁ τόπος) in *Corp.* II, and to that of the divine λόγος of Philo, and the 'Second God' of Numenius. I have found no precisely similar use of the word αἰών elsewhere; but a partial analogy may be seen in Philo, *Quod deus sit immutabilis* 6. 31, Wendland II, p. 63 (quoted in note on *Ascl. Lat.* III. 26 b ff.). Philo there says that the νοητὸς κόσμος is God's elder son; that the αἰσθητὸς κόσμος is God's younger son; that χρόνος is son of the αἰσθητὸς κόσμος, and therefore grandson of God; and that αἰών, which is the ἀρχέτυπον and παράδειγμα of χρόνος, is the mode of life (ὁ βίος) of God. In that passage, Philo does not indeed personify αἰών; but he personifies χρόνος in the same way that the writer of *Corp.* XI. ii personifies both χρόνος and its archetype αἰών. The practice of using αἰών as a name or title of an individual god[1] must

---

[1] The god Κρόνος or Χρόνος (Zerwan) of the Mithraic religion was also called Αἰών; and in Roman Egypt the god Khnum was sometimes called αἰών. Possibly those who applied the term to Khnum may have borrowed it from the Mithraists.

have been known to the writer of XI. i, and no doubt made it easier for him to speak of αἰών ('eternity' or 'eternal life') as a personal being, distinct from the supreme God.

ὁ κόσμος δὲ τὸν χρόνον (ποιεῖ). In the *Timaeus*, time is spoken of as constituted by the movement of the heavenly bodies, and therefore as coming into being together with the material Kosmos. *Tim.* 37 E : ἡμέρας γὰρ καὶ νύκτας καὶ μῆνας καὶ ἐνιαυτούς, οὐκ ὄντας πρὶν οὐρανὸν γενέσθαι, τότε ἅμα ἐκείνῳ ξυνισταμένῳ . . . μηχανᾶται· ταῦτα δὲ πάντα μέρη χρόνου. *Ib.* 38 B : χρόνος δ' οὖν μετ' οὐρανοῦ γέγονεν. ('If there is to be succession, there must be things to succeed each other', Archer-Hind *ad loc.*) See also Aristotle, *Phys.* 8. 1, 251 b 9 ff. The Greeks commonly conceived time in a less abstract way than we do ; they could hardly think of it except in connexion with something which is going through a process ; and the process with which they usually connected it was the movement of the heavenly bodies. Hence the writer of XI. i says that the Kosmos (by its movement) 'makes' time; and Philo expresses the same thought by saying that the Kosmos is the 'father' of time (πατὴρ δὲ χρόνου κόσμος).

ὁ χρόνος δὲ τὴν γένεσιν (ποιεῖ). In literature of all periods, time is often spoken of as producing things or causing events by its action, when the meaning is merely that the things come into being or the events take place in the course of time. The writer here adopts this way of speaking, in order to maintain the symmetry of his scheme; but his meaning is more exactly expressed by the subsequent phrase, ἡ γένεσις γίνεται ἐν τῷ χρόνῳ.

τοῦ δὲ θεοῦ [ὥσπερ] οὐσία ἐστὶ τὸ ἀγαθόν. Cf. *Corp.* VI. 4 b as emended : ἡ οὐσία τοῦ θεοῦ, εἴ γε οὐσίαν ἔχει, τὸ καλόν ἐστι καὶ τὸ ἀγαθόν. See also *Corp.* XII. i *init.* The word ὥσπερ has been inserted in recognition of the doctrine that God is ὑπερούσιος or ἐπέκεινα τῆς οὐσίας. (See notes on *Corp.* II. 4 b and 13.) If ὥσπερ applied to this clause alone, there would be no objection to it. But if we retain it here, we must understand ὥσπερ οὐσία in the following clauses also ; and there would be no point in saying that 'sameness is, *as it were*, the essence of the Aeon', and so on. It seems clear therefore that ὥσπερ must have been inserted by a later hand.

τῆς δὲ γενέσεως (οὐσία) ἡ ζωή [καὶ ὁ θάνατος]. This is vaguely expressed. The meaning implied seems to be that 'in birth life begins', or 'through birth ζῶντα come into being'; but the writer of this document attaches more importance to the neat grouping of words than to exactness of statement.

The words καὶ ὁ θάνατος must be cut out. In the first place, they violate the law of verbal symmetry which the writer has imposed upon himself; and in the second place, they are inconsistent with the context. It would be possible in some connexions to use γένεσις as a term covering all processes in time, and therefore including φθορά; but the writer of XI. i, wherever he uses the words γένεσις and γίνεσθαι, is thinking of the process by which things are made, or come into being, and not of that by which they are destroyed, or cease to be. Cf. οὐδὲ ἀπολεῖταί τι τῶν ἐν τῷ κόσμῳ a few lines below.

ἐνέργειαι δὲ τοῦ θεοῦ νοῦς καὶ ψυχή. For the word ἐνέργεια, see *Corp.* X. 1 b. Its proper meaning is 'a force in action'; but here, the things described as ἐνέργειαι seem to be rather the results produced by the action of God, the Aeon, &c., than the forces which God, the Aeon, &c., put in action.

νοῦς and ψυχή are the results produced by God's action. They are a higher and a lower grade of ζωή; and ζωή comes from God. Cf. *Ascl. Lat.* III. 27 a: 'deus . . . dispensator . . . est bonorum, id est sensus (νοῦ), animae (ψυχῆς), et vitae (ζωῆς).'

τοῦ δὲ αἰῶνος (ἐνέργειαι) ἀθανασία καὶ διαμονή (διαμονὴ καὶ ἀθανασία MSS.). Cf. § 4 a: ὁ αἰὼν . . . ἀθανασίαν καὶ διαμονὴν ἐνθεὶς τῇ ὕλῃ. The word διαμονή is here contrasted with ἀθανασία, and must therefore be taken to mean 'duration for a finite time'. ἀθανασία refers to things celestial, and διαμονή to things terrestrial. In heaven, it results from the action of αἰών that the star-gods live for ever. On earth, it results from the action of αἰών that this or that man (as an earthly organism) lives on for seventy years. Perhaps the writer may have had in mind the fact that in common usage αἰών bears the two distinct senses 'endless time' and 'a man's lifetime'.

The Hermetist doubtless wrote the words in the order ἀθανασία καὶ διαμονή, as in § 4 a. Heaven ought to come before earth, as it does in the corresponding phrase of the next clause, ἀποκατάστασις καὶ ἀνταποκατάστασις.

τοῦ δὲ κόσμου (ἐνέργειαι) ἀποκατάστασις καὶ ἀνταποκατάστασις. As to ἀποκατάστασις, see *Corp.* VIII. 4, *Ascl. Lat.* I. 13, and *Ascl. Lat.* III. 26 a. I have not met with the word ἀνταποκατάστασις elsewhere; but there can be no doubt that the writer meant by it the *quasi-apocatastasis* of terrestrial organisms (*Corp*. VIII. 4). The movement of the heavenly bodies is cyclic ; each of them, after a fixed interval of time, will again be in the same position which it occupies at this moment ; and after a longer interval (the ' Great Year '), all of them will simultaneously be in the same positions as before, relatively to one another and to the universe as a whole. This periodical return to the old position, or recurrence of an identical state of things, is what is meant by ἀποκατάστασις ; and it is characteristic of heaven as opposed to earth. The course of life on earth is not cyclic ;[1] an old man does not ' return to his former position ' and become young again. But the father lives again in his son ; and though the individuals die, and return no more, the life of the race is perpetually renewed. It is this ' renewal of things by substitution ' that is here called ἀνταποκατάστασις.

τοῦ δὲ χρόνου (ἐνέργειαι) αὔξησις καὶ μείωσις. Cf. *Corp*. XIII. 5 : τὸ γὰρ θνητὸν εἶδος (i. e. τὸ σῶμα) καθ᾽ ἡμέραν ἀλλάσσεται· χρόνῳ γὰρ τρέπεται εἰς αὔξησιν καὶ μείωσιν.

τῆς δὲ γενέσεως (ἐνέργειαι) ποιότης ⟨καὶ ποσότης⟩. Since each of the four other things has two ἐνέργειαι, γένεσις also must have had two ἐνέργειαι assigned to it ; and if the writer wanted a word to pair with ποιότης, the first to present itself would be ποσότης. Cf. *Corp*. X. 3 as emended : (ὁ ποιῶν) ποιότητας καὶ ποσότητας ποιεῖ. But assuming that he wrote καὶ ποσότης, how is the production of ποσότητες, which is the work of γένεσις, to be distinguished from αὔξησις καὶ μείωσις, the work of χρόνος ? Perhaps it might be said that γένεσις determines the weight of a baby at birth, and χρόνος is responsible for the child's gains and losses of weight during life. But the writer probably did not ask himself this question ; it was enough for him that the words by which he described the ἐνέργειαι of γένεσις had no obvious resemblance to those by which he described the ἐνέργειαι of χρόνος.

ὁ οὖν αἰὼν ἐν τῷ θεῷ κ.τ.λ. The five entities are here imagined in the form of five concentric spheres,—or rather, perhaps, four concentric spheres contained within a boundless space, which is God. Even χρόνος and γένεσις may be thus pictured, if we take χρόνος to stand for the heavenly bodies which constitute time by

---

[1] The Stoic doctrine that after each *ecpyrosis* the course of things on earth also will repeat itself (e. g. that the same lecturer—or a precisely similar lecturer—will again address the same or precisely similar pupils in the same words) is ignored by the writer of XI. i.

their movement,[1] and γένεσις for sublunar things. But at the same time, we are not debarred from taking the words ἡ γένεσις ἐν τῷ χρόνῳ in the more obvious sense 'the births of things take place in the course of time' (cf. ἡ δὲ γένεσις γίνεται ἐν τῷ χρόνῳ below). The statement ὁ κόσμος ἐν τῷ αἰῶνι is repeated below in the words τοῦ κόσμου ὑπὸ τοῦ αἰῶνος ἐμπεριεχομένου.

ὁ μὲν αἰὼν ἔστηκε περὶ τὸν θεόν. *Ascl. Lat.* III. 26 b–32 a would serve as a commentary on these words. περί does not mean 'around' in a local sense; for if thus taken, it would conflict with ὁ αἰὼν ἐν τῷ θεῷ. It is rather comparable to πρός in *Ev. Joh.* I. I, ὁ λόγος ἦν πρὸς τὸν θεόν.

ὁ δὲ κόσμος κινεῖται ἐν τῷ αἰῶνι. In this clause, 'the Aeon' corresponds exactly to the extracosmic νοῦς spoken of in *Corp.* II, and there called ὁ τόπος (ἐν ᾧ κινεῖται ὁ κόσμος).

§ 3. δύναμις δὲ τοῦ θεοῦ ὁ αἰών. As to this use of the word δύναμις, see note on *Corp.* I. 26 a. The αἰών of *Corp.* XI. i is δύναμις τοῦ θεοῦ in nearly the same sense in which Philo (*De fuga et invent.* 18. 94 ff., Wendland III, p. 130) says that the θεῖος λόγος is the supreme δύναμις of God.

ὁ κόσμος, γενόμενος οὔποτε, καὶ ἀεὶ γινόμενος. We might rather have expected γενόμενος μὲν οὔποτε, γινόμενος δὲ ἀεί. The Kosmos has had no beginning. Cf. *Corp.* X. 10 b as emended: (ὁ κόσμος) ἀεὶ ὤν, ὢν δὲ ἐν γενέσει, καὶ γινόμενος ἀεί.

οὐδὲ ἀπολεῖταί τι τῶν ἐν τῷ κόσμῳ. Cf. *Corp.* VIII, Ὅτι οὐδὲν τῶν ὄντων ἀπόλλυται.

[ἡ δὲ τοῦ θεοῦ [[σοφία]] ⟨οὐσία⟩ τί[ς] ἐστι; τὸ ἀγαθὸν καὶ τὸ καλόν]. This is a misplaced doublet of τοῦ δὲ θεοῦ οὐσία ἐστὶ τὸ ἀγαθόν in § 2.

§ 4 a. ἀθανασίαν καὶ διαμονὴν ἐνθεὶς τῇ ὕλῃ. The demiurgic power puts life into matter throughout the Kosmos, but does so in two different ways; it produces immortal ζῷα in the heavens, and ζῷα of finite duration on earth.

The Platonists were accustomed to describe the function of the Demiurgus as that of imposing *forms* on matter. But to impose forms on matter is to make living organisms; and this writer conceives the demiurgic work of God (executed through his minister the Aeon) as that of putting *life* into lifeless matter.

[ἡ γὰρ ἐκείνης γένεσις] . . . μεταβλητῶν καὶ φθαρτῶν (μεταβλητοὶ καὶ φθαρτοί MSS.). No sense can be made of this except by

---

[1] Pseudo-Galen *Hist. Phil.* 37, Diels *Doxogr.* p. 619 : τὸν χρόνον εἶναι Πυθαγόρας ὑπείληφε τὴν σφαῖραν τοῦ περιέχοντος.

sweeping alteration of the text. It seems clear, firstly, that the sentence containing the words ἐν μὲν οὐρανῷ . . . ἐν δὲ γῇ must have been intended to explain the distinction implied in ἀθανασίαν καὶ διαμονήν, and consequently must have immediately followed ἀθανασίαν καὶ διαμονὴν ἐνθεὶς τῇ ὕλῃ; secondly, that the words ἤρτηται ἐκ τοῦ αἰῶνος καθάπερ καὶ ὁ αἰὼν ἐκ τοῦ θεοῦ, which in the MSS. separate that explanation from the phrase explained by it, ought to stand immediately before καὶ τοῦ μὲν αἰῶνος κ.τ.λ.; and thirdly, that the subject of ἤρτηται must have been ὁ κόσμος.

I take [ἡ γὰρ ἐκείνης γένεσις] to be a doublet of the following ἡ γὰρ γένεσις. (ἐκείνης may perhaps have come from the preceding clause, where it would be possible to write ἐνθεὶς ἐκείνη in place of ἐνθεὶς τῇ ὕλῃ.)

The MSS. give ἡ γὰρ γένεσις καὶ ὁ χρόνος ἐν οὐρανῷ καὶ ἐν γῇ εἰσιν, ὄντες διφυεῖς, ἐν μὲν οὐρανῷ ἀμετάβλητοι καὶ ἄφθαρτοι, ἐν δὲ γῇ μεταβλητοὶ καὶ φθαρτοί. This cannot be right; there is no sense in saying that χρόνος is ἄφθαρτος in heaven and φθαρτός on earth. Moreover, it is difficult to think of any possible subject to which the masculine adjectives ἀμετάβλητοι &c. could be made to apply. (οἱ θεοί might be called ἀμετάβλητοι καὶ ἄφθαρτοι; but the only beings that could be called μετάβλητοι καὶ φθαρτοί are οἱ ἄνθρωποι, and there is no occasion here for speaking of men apart from other ἐπίγεια ζῷα.) It can hardly be doubted therefore that the termination -τοι is a misreading. I have expressed what I suppose to have been the author's meaning, by writing ἡ γὰρ γένεσις [ ] διφυής, ἐν μὲν οὐρανῷ ἀμεταβλήτων κ.τ.λ. This is equivalent to γίνεται ἐν μὲν οὐρανῷ ἀμετάβλητα κ.τ.λ. The οὐράνια ζῷα, like the Kosmos as a whole, οὔποτε ἐγένετο, but ἀεὶ γίνεται.

καὶ τοῦ μὲν αἰῶνος ⌜ἡ ψυχὴ⌝ ὁ θεός, τοῦ δὲ κόσμου ὁ αἰών. [τῆς δὲ γῆς ὁ οὐρανός.] ἡ ψυχή is certainly wrong. God, working through the Aeon, puts ψυχή into things; but neither God nor the Aeon is ψυχή. A satisfactory sense might be got by substituting ἀρχή or πηγή for ἡ ψυχή.

If we retained τῆς δὲ γῆς ὁ οὐρανός, it would be necessary to make the series continuous by inserting another clause before it, and writing

καὶ τοῦ μὲν αἰῶνος (ἀρχὴ ?) ὁ θεός,
τοῦ δὲ κόσμου ὁ αἰών,
⟨τοῦ δὲ οὐρανοῦ ὁ κόσμος,⟩
τῆς δὲ γῆς ὁ οὐρανός.

But it could hardly be said that earth is dependent on heaven, and heaven on the Kosmos, in the same sense that the Kosmos is dependent on the Aeon, and the Aeon on God; and it seems more likely that τῆς δὲ γῆς ὁ οὐρανός is an interpolation, suggested by the preceding words ἐν μὲν οὐρανῷ . . . ἐν δὲ γῇ.

§ 4 b. [καὶ ὁ μὲν θεὸς ἐν τῷ νῷ, ὁ δὲ νοῦς ἐν τῇ ψυχῇ, ἡ δὲ ψυχὴ ἐν τῇ ὕλῃ.] [πάντα δὲ ταῦτα διὰ τοῦ αἰῶνος.] This is evidently out of place. When it is removed, the sentence τὸ δὲ πᾶν τοῦτο σῶμα κ.τ.λ. follows naturally on what has been said about the Kosmos in § 4 a. The words καὶ ὁ μὲν θεὸς . . . ἐν τῇ ὕλῃ are a superfluous repetition of τὸ δὲ πᾶν τοῦτο σῶμα ψυχῆς πληρές ἐστιν . . . καὶ ὁ νοῦς τοῦ θεοῦ. The clause πάντα δὲ ταῦτα διὰ τοῦ αἰῶνος cannot have been meant to follow ὁ μὲν θεὸς . . . ἐν τῇ ὕλῃ; for in this position, πάντα ταῦτα can only mean θεός, νοῦς, ψυχή, and ὕλη; and it would be impossible to say that God is 'by means of' something other than himself. If πάντα δὲ ταῦτα διὰ τοῦ αἰῶνος occurred at all in the original text, it may possibly have stood at the end of § 6 a. Placed there, it would form a fitting conclusion to the discourse, and would serve to lay stress on the novel conception of αἰών which the writer has been expounding.

⟨ἡ δὲ⟩ ψυχὴ πλήρης τοῦ νοῦ, καὶ ⟨ὁ νοῦς⟩ τοῦ θεοῦ. νοῦς is here regarded as something which resides within ψυχή. (Cf. Corp. X. 16 f., where it is said that νοῦς, when embodied, has ψυχή for its integument.) But the writer adds that God in like manner resides within νοῦς. Hence it may be inferred that God is present throughout the universe; and that is expressly asserted below (ὁ γὰρ ποιῶν ἐν πᾶσίν ἐστιν, § 6 a). It is not quite clear how this is to be reconciled with the preceding sections, in which God is set apart from the Kosmos, and separated from it by the interposed αἰών. Perhaps the writer drew his doctrine of αἰών (§§ 2–4 a) from one source, and his doctrine of ψυχή and νοῦς (§ 4 b) from another, and did not completely succeed in harmonizing them.

⟨ψυχὴ δὲ⟩ ἐντὸς μὲν αὐτὸ (sc. τὸ πᾶν τοῦτο σῶμα) πληροῖ, ἐκτὸς δὲ περιλαμβάνει. A feminine subject is required by the following participles ζωοποιοῦσα &c.; and there can be little doubt that the missing subject is ψυχή. Cf. Pl. Tim. 34 B : ψυχὴν δὲ εἰς τὸ μέσον αὐτοῦ (sc. τοῦ σώματος, the body of the Kosmos) θεὶς διὰ παντός τε ἔτεινε καὶ ἔτι ἔξωθεν τὸ σῶμα αὐτῇ περιεκάλυψε ταύτῃ. The writer divides 'soul' into two parts. One part of it is the world-soul, i. e. the soul which animates the Kosmos as a whole (ζωοποιεῖ τοῦτο τὸ μέγα καὶ τέλειον ζῷον); and this part is located 'without' (ἐκτός), i. e. in the outermost sphere. The other part is distributed among the individual organisms within the Kosmos (ζωοποιεῖ πάντα τὰ ζῷα), and is the sum of their several souls. Cf. *Corp.* X. 11 on the embodiment of the cosmic ψυχή.

τοῦτο τὸ μέγα καὶ τέλειον ζῷον. Cf. Pl. *Tim.* 69 c: πᾶν τόδε, ζῷον ἐν ζῷα ἔχον τὰ πάντα ἐν αὐτῷ θνητὰ ἀθάνατά τε.

̤ ἄνω μὲν ἐν τῷ οὐρανῷ διαμένουσα ⟨ἐν⟩ τῇ ταυτότητι, κάτω δὲ ἐπὶ τῆς γῆς ⟨ἅμα⟩ τῇ γενέσει (τὴν γένεσιν MSS.) μεταβάλλουσα. The ζῷα within the Kosmos are of two different kinds. In the οὐράνια ζῷα (i. e. the heavenly bodies), which are immortal, soul or life 'remains in its sameness'. In the ἐπίγεια ζῷα, which are mortal, soul or life shifts from one body to another by successive births.

§ 5. συνέχει δὲ τοῦτο ⟨τὸ πᾶ⟩ν ὁ αἰών. Cf. Philo *De fuga et invent.* 20. 112, Wendland III, p. 133 : ὅ τε γὰρ τοῦ ὄντος (i. e. τοῦ θεοῦ) λόγος, δεσμὸς ὢν τῶν ἁπάντων, . . . καὶ συνέχει τὰ (τοῦ κόσμου) μέρη πάντα καὶ σφίγγει, κωλύων αὐτὰ διαλύεσθαι καὶ διαρτᾶσθαι, κ.τ.λ. It is through the action of the αἰών (as through that of the λόγος in Philo) that 'all things are one'.

ὁ αἰών, . . . τοῦτο ἔστι [πᾶ]ν ὁ θεὸς ἐνεργῶν. In the earlier sections, the Aeon was spoken of as an entity distinct from God. But here, we are told that the Aeon is a certain aspect of God's being; it is God at work upon the world. God and the Aeon are two Persons, yet the two are one.

εἴτε [δι'] ἀνάγκην, εἴτε πρόνοιαν, εἴτε φύσιν, [καὶ] εἴ⟨τε⟩ τι ἄλλο οἴεται ἢ οἰηθήσεταί τις. ἀνάγκη, πρόνοια, and φύσις are mentioned as terms which some people may prefer to employ in place of αἰών to express the conception of 'God at work'. These three terms were thus used by the Stoics. Philodemus (Diels *Doxogr.*, p. 545): Chrysippus Δία φη(σὶν εἶναι τὸ)ν ἄπαντ(α διοικοῦ)ντα λόγον . . .· καὶ (πρόνο)ιαν ὀν(ομάζεσ)θαι τὸν Δία, καὶ τὴν κοινὴν πάντων φύσιν, καὶ εἱμαρμ(έ)νην, καὶ ἀνά(γ)κην.

But the words εἴτε ἀνάγκην . . . οἰηθήσεταί τις are awkwardly interposed; and it is possible that they were inserted later, and that the original text was συνέχει δὲ τοῦτο τὸ πᾶν ὁ αἰών, [ ] τοῦτο ἔστιν, ὁ θεὸς ἐνεργῶν.

ἡ δὲ ἐνέργεια ⟨τοῦ⟩ θεοῦ δυνάμει (δύναμις MSS.) [οὖσα] ἀνυπέρ-βλητος. It might be possible to call God's ἐνέργεια a δύναμις, just as ὁ αἰών was called δύναμις τοῦ θεοῦ in § 3 *init.*; but δυνάμει suits the context better.

οὐδὲν γὰρ ὅμοιον τῷ [ἀνομοίῳ καὶ] μόνῳ καὶ ἑνί. The meaningless ἀνομοίῳ may perhaps have been substituted for some word (e. g. ἀνωτάτω) which was written as an alternative for μόνῳ καὶ ἑνί.

⟨τίς ἄλλος αἴτιος⟩ [εἴτε] ζωῆς, καὶ ἀθανασίας καὶ μεταβολῆς ποιητής (ποιότητος MSS.); Cf. *Corp.* XII. ii. 22 : ὑπὸ τίνος οὖν ζωοποιεῖται τὰ πάντα ζῷα ; ὑπὸ τίνος ἀθανατίζεται τὰ ἀθάνατα ; ὑπὸ τίνος μεταβάλλεται τὰ μεταβλητά; God is the maker of ἀθανασία in heaven, and the maker of μεταβολή, i. e. of the perpetual renewal of life by fresh births, on earth. To the question 'Who else is the maker of ἀθανασία and μεταβολή?' a reader of §§ 2–4 a might be inclined to answer, 'the Aeon'. Cf. § 2 : τοῦ αἰῶνος (ἐνέργειαι) ἀθανασία καὶ διαμονή. § 4 a : ὁ αἰὼν . . . ἀθανασίαν καὶ διαμονὴν ἐνθεὶς τῇ ὕλῃ. But the distinction between ὁ θεός and ὁ αἰών, which was insisted on before, is minimized in § 5. The writer at one time regards the Aeon as an intermediary agent δι' οὗ ὁ θεὸς ἐνεργεῖ, and at another time, as ὁ θεὸς ἐνεργῶν.

τί δὲ αὐτοῦ ἄλλο ⟨ἔργον ἢ⟩ τὸ ποιεῖν ; (τί δὲ αὐτὸς ἄλλο τι ποιήσειεν MSS.). The reading which I propose is very doubtful; but the author must have written something to this effect; and it may be inferred from the following ἀργός and ἀργία that the word ἔργον occurred in this sentence.

οὐ γὰρ ἀργὸς ὁ θεός. Cf. Philo *Leg. alleg.* 1. 3. 5, Cohn I, p. 62 (commenting on *Gen.* 2. 2, 'God finished his work which he had made, and he rested on the seventh day') : παύεται γὰρ οὐδέποτε ποιῶν ὁ θεός, ἀλλ' ὥσπερ ἴδιον τὸ καίειν πυρὸς καὶ χιόνος τὸ ψύχειν, οὕτως καὶ θεοῦ τὸ ποιεῖν· καὶ πολύ γε μᾶλλον, ὅσῳ καὶ τοῖς ἄλλοις ἅπασιν ἀρχὴ τοῦ δρᾶν ἐστιν.[1] Origen *De princip.* 3. 5. 2 : 'Solent nobis obiicere, dicentes : Si coepit mundus ex tempore, quid ante faciebat Deus quam mundus inciperet? Otiosam enim et immobilem dicere naturam Dei, impium est simul et absurdum, vel putare quod bonitas aliquando bene non fecerit, et omnipotentia aliquando non egerit potentatum.' (Origen's answer is, that this world has had a beginning and will have an end, but that God made other worlds before it, and will make others after it.)

ἅπαντα γὰρ πλήρη τοῦ θεοῦ. All things are filled with ψυχή. But ψυχή is filled with νοῦς, and νοῦς is filled with God (§ 4 b); therefore, it may be said that all things are filled with God. In other words,

---

[1] Compare *Ev. Joh.* 5. 17 : ὁ πατήρ μου ἕως ἄρτι ἐργάζεται, κἀγὼ ἐργάζομαι (said in answer to a charge of sabbath-breaking).

there is life everywhere, and all life is a manifestation of God's presence and working.

These words imply that God, as the source or root of life, is *in* things; whereas in the rest of the paragraph God is spoken of rather as an external agent, who 'makes' living things, or 'puts life into' things. These two conceptions are combined together in the phrase ὁ γὰρ ποιῶν ἐν πᾶσίν ἐστιν, § 6 a.

οὐδὲ ἐν τῷ κόσμῳ ἐστὶν ἀργία οὐδαμοῦ. Cf. Pseudo-Galen *Hist. philos.* 24 (Diels *Doxogr.*, p. 613): τοῖς δὲ σώμασι συνδεῖσθαι (τὰς ψυχὰς) νομίζουσιν οἱ μὲν ⌐αὐτοφυεῖς ἠκούσας ἐγκρατεῖς οὔσας ὥστε ταύτας πασχούσας,⌐¹ τῷ ἐπιθυμεῖν ἡδονῶν τῶν διὰ τῶν σωμάτων αὐταῖς προσγινομένων·² οἱ δέ, κατὰ θεὸν ἐγγίνεσθαι τοῖς σώμασι, ⌐βουλόμενοι⌐³ μηδὲν τῶν στοιχείων ἀργὸν μηδὲ ⌐ζῴου⌐⁴ ἄμοιρον εἶναι διὰ τέλους. The second of these two doctrines resembles that of *Corp.* XI. i. God's work is to put soul or life into matter. Soul is τὸ κινοῦν; and matter without soul in it would be ἀργόν. But God is always and everywhere at work; there is therefore no matter without soul in it, i. e. no matter which is not alive and active.

[οὐδὲ ἔν τινι ἄλλῳ]. This is meaningless. There is nothing else beside God, the Kosmos, and the things in the Kosmos (except the hypostatized αἰών of §§ 2–4 a, which cannot here be meant).

ἀργία γὰρ ὄνομα κενόν ἐστι. ἀργία is a word to which nothing in actual existence corresponds. For this phrase, compare *Corp.* VIII. 1 b as emended: ὄνομά ἐστιν ἡ θανάτου προσηγορία κενὸν ἔργου.

§ 6 a. πάντα δὲ δεῖ γίνεσθαι καὶ ἀεὶ καὶ καθ' ἕκαστον τόπον (καθ' ἑκάστου τόπου ῥοπήν MSS.). The writer must have meant 'always and everywhere'. ῥοπήν might be combined with χρόνον, but hardly with τόπον. Perhaps the reading of the MSS. has resulted from a conflation of καθ' ἕκαστον τόπον and καθ' ἑκάστην (χρόνου) ῥοπήν.

LIBELLVS XI. ii

Contents

The Kosmos is an organized whole, each part of which discharges its special function. The Sun is the (proximate) source of life; for the fire which the Sun emits is transmuted into light, ⟨and this light

---

¹ Perhaps: οἱ μὲν ἐκούσας, αὐτοφυεῖ ἀκρατείᾳ τοῦτο πασχούσας.
² This opinion is based on Pl. *Phaedo.*
³ Al. βουλομένων: *legendum* βουλόμενον, in agreement with θεόν.
⁴ *Legendum* ζωῆς.

conveys life into all organic bodies.) The Moon fashions matter into a succession of organic bodies here below. The Earth supplies material nutriment to these bodies. And all things in the Kosmos, both the immortals in heaven (i. e. the heavenly bodies) and the mortal creatures on earth, are filled with 'soul' or life. §§ 6 b–8 a.

Since all things in the Kosmos are *living* bodies, there must be some one who puts 'soul' or life into them ; that is to say, there must be a Maker. § 8 b.

And since all things are wrought together into one ordered whole, there cannot be more than one Maker. The theory that the immortals in heaven owe their life to one Maker, and the mortal creatures on earth to another, must be rejected. §§ 9, 10.

The one Maker of all is God. God is one ; and the one life which runs through all things is the work of the one God. §§ 11, ⟨⟨14 b⟩⟩.

Why should not the one God be the author of two different modes of life,—immortal life in heaven, and mortal life on earth,—seeing that you yourself are active in different ways ? § 12 a.

God's work then is to make living things. God could not exist without doing good ; and to do good is to make things live. Human procreation is a type of God's life-generating energy. And God is ever at his work ; if he were to cease from it for a moment, all things would perish. §§ 12 b–14 a.

⟨But he never ceases, and therefore life never ceases.⟩ What men call 'death' should rather be called 'change'. When a living creature 'dies', the life that was in it departs out of our sight, but does not perish. And inasmuch as life is ever shifting and changing in the bodies of which the Kosmos is composed, the Kosmos itself is ever changing, and may be said to 'assume all forms'. §§ 15 b, 16 a.

Does God likewise change, and 'assume all forms'? No. God has one form, and one alone ; but it is an *incorporeal* form. §§ 16 b, 17 a.

God contains all things. All things 'are in God', but not in the same sense in which bodies are contained in a larger body ; for God is incorporeal. The incorporeal (i. e. mind) is capable of containing everything. Is it not so in the case of your own mind? You can place yourself in thought at any point in the universe, and even beyond its outermost limits ; that is, your mind is capable of containing anything ; potentially, it contains everything. And God (being mind, not body,) contains things in the same sense that your mind contains things. But God contains all things in his thought, not merely potentially, or severally and successively, but actually, and all at once. All things are thoughts which God thinks. §§ 17 b–20 a.

If you would know God, you must be as God is. You must get quit of everything corporeal, and expand yourself to the magnitude of all existence ; you must rise above all limitations of time, and become eternal. You must include all things in yourself, or identify yourself with all things. Do this, and you will know God. But if you shut yourself up in the body, and cower within the narrow cell of your separate being, a poor feeble wretch, self-centred and self-seeking, then you have nothing in common with God, and cannot know him. §§ 20 b, 21 a.

Not to know God is the height of evil ; to know God is the good, and to seek to know him is to be on the way to the good. Seek him, and he will come to meet you at all times and places. God is not invisible ; for he is in all things, and you may see him everywhere at work. §§ 21 b, 22 a.

The most significant passage in this document, and that which contains the essence of the writer's religion, is §§ 20 b, 21 a. The Hermetist there states, in the special form in which he has realized it in his own experience, the principle that ' he who would find himself must lose himself'.[1] But how does he conceive the larger whole in which a man may 'lose' his falsely narrowed self, and 'find' his true self? For this writer, the one alternative to 'shutting oneself up' in one's separate personality is to 'expand oneself to the measureless magnitude' of the universe, and the God who fills the universe with life. Most people are more ready to agree with

---

[1] Cf. Inge, *Personal idealism and mysticism*, p. 102 : ' How does a man " lose his soul " so as to gain it ! . . . To be willing to lose our ψυχή must mean to forget ourselves entirely, to cease to revolve round our own selfish interests, to pass out freely into the great life of the world, constructing our universe on a . . . cosmocentric basis, not a self-centred one. To do this is to lose and then to find ourselves.' Caird, quoted by James, *Varieties of religious experience*, p. 451 : ' As a thinking being, it is possible for me to suppress and quell in my consciousness every movement of self-assertion, every notion and opinion that is merely mine, every desire that belongs to me as this particular self, and to become the pure medium of a thought that is universal,—in one word, to live no more my own life, but let my consciousness be possessed and suffused by the Infinite and Eternal life of spirit. And yet it is just in this renunciation of self that I truly gain myself, or realize the highest possibilities of my own nature. For whilst in one sense we give up self to live the universal and absolute life of reason, yet that to which we thus surrender ourselves is in reality our truer self.'

those who find the alternative to selfish isolation in identifying oneself in feeling and interest with one's *fellow men*, or with some of them. The *human* whole in which a man 'loses himself, and losing, finds himself', may assume many different forms. For some Greeks, it took the form of the city-state, as in the ideal Sparta and Athens of the fifth century B. C., and in Plato's Republic ; by Stoics, it was recognized in the human race at large. The larger whole with which the individual identifies himself,—the 'body' of which he feels himself to be a 'member',—may, in the case of one man, be restricted to his own household ; for another, it may be some larger human group, or several different groups in turn ; and for one here and there, it may include every human being with whom the chances of life bring him into connexion. But the recognition of a human whole, larger or smaller, into which the separate self may expand, does not conflict with the recognition of a cosmic or supracosmic All ; often the two are combined, and men's sense of union with the one is intensified by their sense of union with the other. Citizens of Sparta and Athens expressed and heightened their civic patriotism by their worship of the gods who watched over the city ; in Plato's Republic, it is because the 'guardian' is a votary of the Good on which all existence hangs, that in his social life he has no private use for the word 'mine' ; and the Cosmopolis of the Stoics is a world-wide brotherhood of men united by the common fatherhood of the God who pervades the universe. Among the many different religions included under the vague term 'Christianity', all possible modes and forms of 'self-expansion' might be exemplified. In the language of Paul and the Fourth Gospel, 'Christ' means at once the Head or common Life of the body of believers, and the Power 'by whom all things were made' ; and he who, using the name of Christ in this sense, says 'I live, and yet no longer I, but Christ lives in me', [1] identifies himself at once with his human brothers and with the life of the whole universe. The writer of XI. ii, when he bids a man break out of his narrow cell

---

[1] *Gal.* 2. 20 : ζῶ δὲ οὐκέτι ἐγώ, ζῇ δὲ ἐν ἐμοὶ Χριστός. The 'old man' of whom Paul speaks,—the man who has died in the Christian,—corresponds to the man whom the Hermetist describes as 'shutting up his soul in his body'; the 'new man' who is born in the Christian corresponds to the man whom the Hermetist describes as having risen above the limitations of time and space. In *Corp.* XIII, the change from the one state to the other is described by the simile of a 'second birth', just as it is in the Fourth Gospel. The old narrow self ceases to exist, and a new and larger self comes into being in its place. The change may be called either 'self-surrender' or 'self-realization'; it is at once the surrender of a smaller self, and the realization of a larger self.

in space and time, and 'become eternal', is at one with what may
be called the 'cosmic' side of the religion of Paul and the Fourth
Gospel, as distinguished from its 'human' side; but he has nothing
to say about the brotherhood of men, or the 'love of one's neighbour'.
For him, as for most of the Hermetists, human society hardly exists,
and the only human relation recognized is that between teacher and
pupil. The individual man stands solitary, face to face with the
universe at large; and if he would escape from his isolation, it is
in the life which fills the universe, and the God whom he sees
behind that universal life, that he must 'lose himself to find
himself'.

Sources. The theoretic doctrine of XI. ii closely resembles that
of XI. i, apart from the conception of αἰών which is peculiar to XI. i;
and the mode of regarding God and the universe which is common
to both documents seems to have resulted from a fusion of Platonic
and Stoic theories, modified by some other influence. In § 1 b,
there is a verbal reminiscence of a sentence of Pl. *Tim.* The application of the term κόσμοι to the planets may be taken as a sign that
the teachers by whom the Platonic tradition was transmitted to the
writer had adopted some distinctively Pythagorean notions. In the
discussion of the μορφή of God (§ 16 b), and the assertion that God
is ἀσώματος, the author maintains the Platonic position against that
of the Stoics. The conception of 'one soul' or 'one life' pervading
the universe is more akin to Stoicism than to Platonism; but in the
form in which it is here presented, it appears to have been derived
in part from some other source, which may possibly have been
Egyptian. The physical theory of fire and light (with the words
ἡ φιλία τῶν ἐναντίων) in § 7, and the phrases τὰς ἀντιθέσεις τῶν
ποιοτήτων and πράγματα, ποιότητας, ποσότητας in § 20 b, are marks
of Stoic influence. The theory of two Makers, which is discussed
and rejected in § 9, must be one which was held by some of the
writer's contemporaries; theories more or less resembling it are
to be found in the writings of some of the Christian Gnostics, but
it is not clear against whom the Hermetist is here contending.
   In the passage on 'self-expansion' (§§ 20 b, 21 a), the author is
presumably describing a state of mind which was known to him by
his own experience, and which perhaps reached its greatest intensity
in occasional ecstasies, but also took the form of an abiding or
frequently recurring consciousness in everyday life (§ 21 b, 'every-

where God will come to meet you' &c.). In this, the most original part of his teaching, his attitude differs from that of the earlier Platonists and Stoics, and more nearly approximates to that of Plotinus. If a discourse of Ammonius Saccas, the Egyptian teacher of Plotinus, had been preserved in writing, we might perhaps have found in it a close resemblance to this document. The sort of religion in which the limits of the man's individual personality melt away, and he becomes one with the object of his worship, ('I am Thou, and Thou art I',) is restricted to no one race or country; but it seems to have been specially prevalent in Egypt, from the earliest ages down to Roman times; and the writer of XI. ii, when he speaks in this tone, shows that, beneath his Hellenic culture, he is still a true Egyptian.

I find no trace of Jewish or Christian influence in this document.

Date. What I have said about the date of XI. i applies to XI. ii also. If we are right in assuming that its author had XI. i before him, XI. ii must be placed a little later; and its affinity to the teaching of Plotinus points to the same direction. I would therefore assign it conjecturally to the third century after Christ.

§ 1 b. ὡς δέ μοι ἐπῆλθεν εἰπεῖν οὐκ ὀκνήσω. Hermes feels that it needs some courage to speak frankly to his divine visitant. It is to be presumed that Nous has asked him on what subject he wishes to be instructed; and he answers that he wishes to be told the truth περὶ τοῦ παντὸς καὶ τοῦ θεοῦ. Cf. *Corp.* I *init.*, where Poimandres (i.e. the divine νοῦς) asks Τί βούλει ... μαθεῖν καὶ γνῶναι; and the prophet answers Μαθεῖν θέλω τὰ ὄντα ... καὶ γνῶναι τὸν θεόν.

πολλὰ πολλῶν καὶ ταῦτα διάφορα περὶ τοῦ παντὸς καὶ τοῦ θεοῦ εἰπόντων. This is an echo of Pl. *Tim.* 29 C: πολλὰ πολλῶν εἰπόντων περὶ θεῶν καὶ τῆς τοῦ παντὸς γενέσεως.

§ 6 b. δι' ἐμοῦ: i.e. διὰ τοῦ νοῦ. Cf. § 13 b: ἄν μοι σεαυτὸν ἐπίδῳς. It is not enough to look at the world with our bodily eyes; we must also reflect on what we see.

[τό τε κάλλος αὐτοῦ ἀκριβῶς κατανόησον.] This clause breaks the grammatical construction. σῶμα ought to be in apposition to κόσμον; but in the text of the MSS., it can only be taken as standing in apposition to κάλλος; and so taken, it does not make sense. It would be possible to avoid this difficulty by transposing the clause τό τε ... κατανόησον, and placing it after ἀκμαῖον καὶ νέον; but even in that position it would still be superfluous, and would rather weaken the force of the passage. It seems most likely, therefore, that it has been added by a later hand.

§ 7. τοὺς ὑποκειμένους ἑπτὰ κόσμους. These 'seven worlds' are the planets. In the astronomical system ascribed to the Pythagorean Philolaus (Aetius, Diels *Doxogr.* p. 337), the word κόσμος did not signify the universe as a whole (τὸ πᾶν), but was used to denote the region occupied by the seven planets, in contradistinction both to the outermost sphere (called Ὄλυμπος) above that region, and to the sublunar atmosphere (called οὐρανός) below it. Heraclides Ponticus and some of the Pythagoreans (perhaps by a modification of the usage of Philolaus) called each of the planets a κόσμος. Aetius, Diels *ib.* p. 43: Ἡρακλείδης καὶ οἱ Πυθαγόρειοι, ἕκαστον τῶν ἀστέρων κόσμον ὑπάρχειν, γῆν περιέχοντα[1] καὶ ἀέρα, ἐν τῷ ἀπείρῳ αἰθέρι. ταῦτα δὲ τὰ δόγματα ἐν τοῖς Ὀρφικοῖς φέρεσθαι· κοσμοποιοῦσι γὰρ ἕκαστον τῶν ἀστέρων. Some Pythagoreans said that the moon is a world like ours, and is inhabited; Plutarch (*Fac. lunae*) speaks of this theory, and makes the moon an abode of disembodied human souls. Anaxagoras also is reported to have said that the moon is inhabited (Diog. Laert. 1. 8). Cf. the Orphic fragment 81 Abel (Proclus, *In Tim.* 3. 154 A): μήσατο δ' ἄλλην γαῖαν ἀπείριτον, ἥν τε σελήνην | ἀθά-νατοι κλήζουσιν, ... ἢ πόλλ' οὔρε' ἔχει, πόλλ' ἄστεα, πολλὰ μέλαθρα. Perhaps there were Pythagoreans who held that not only the moon, but all the planets are inhabited worlds, and consequently called them κόσμοι. At any rate, this use of the word κόσμος seems to be a mark of either Pythagorean or Orphic influence.

κεκοσμημένους τάξει αἰωνίῳ, καὶ δρόμῳ διαφόρῳ τὸν αἰῶνα ἀναπληροῦντας. The planets 'fill endless time with their movements'; i.e. their movements endure through endless time. The writer of XI. ii uses αἰών differently from the writer of XI. i; he does not hypostatize 'the Aeon'; and he does not here use the word in the Platonic sense of 'eternity' as distinguished from endless time. In § 20 b, however, αἰών⟨ιος⟩ γενοῦ means 'free yourself from the limitations of existence in time'.

πῦρ δὲ οὐδαμοῦ ⟨. . .⟩. It would be impossible for a Hermetist to say that there is no region of fire in any part of the Kosmos; and the contrary is expressly asserted in § 19 (τὸ τοῦ ἡλίου πῦρ). The meaning must therefore have been that there is no (cosmic or

---

[1] Perhaps [περι]έχοντα. Each of the planets is an earth surrounded by an atmosphere of its own; but all of them are situated 'in the boundless aether'.

unmixed) fire *in the sublunar world*, or *in the terrestrial atmosphere*;
and some phrase expressing that limitation must have fallen
out of the text.

τῇ γὰρ φιλίᾳ τῶν ἐναντίων καὶ τῇ συγκράσει τῶν ἀνομοίων (ἡ γὰρ φιλία
καὶ ἡ σύγκρασις τῶν ἐναντίων καὶ τῶν ἀνομοίων MSS.) ⟨τὸ πῦρ⟩ φῶς
γέγονε, καταλαμπόμενον ὑπὸ τῆς τοῦ [θεοῦ] ⟨ἡλίου⟩ ἐνεργείας. A mention
of God would be premature here. The pupil does not yet know
that there is one supreme God; that truth is demonstrated to him
later on, in §§ 9–11. On the other hand, since the teacher, after
speaking of the seven planets together, describes the special function
of the moon, he must also have described the special function of
the sun. It may therefore be considered certain that the Hermetist
here wrote ἡλίου, and not θεοῦ. After the mark of division between
XI. i and XI. ii had disappeared, a person who had just been
reading about the ἐνέργεια τοῦ θεοῦ in §§ 4 b–6 a might easily be led
to substitute that phrase for ἐνέργεια τοῦ ἡλίου in § 7.

The meaning must have been that the fiery heat emitted by the
sun, which would be destructive to all earthly things if it reached
them unaltered, is transmuted into mild and beneficent light in the
course of its passage downward through the atmosphere. The fire
there meets with 'unlike' and 'opposite' elements, viz. air and
watery vapour, and enters into combination with them; and the
substance produced by the combination of fire with air and water
takes the form of light. This theory is based on the Stoic physics.
On the Stoic doctrine as to the illumination of the atmosphere, see
Arnim, *Stoic. vet. fragm.* II, p. 142 f. The phrase ἡ φιλία τῶν ἐναντίων is doubtless a Stoic reminiscence of certain well-known sayings
of Heraclitus. For the notion that the celestial fire would burn up
all earthly things if they were not protected from it, cf. *Corp.* X. 18,
γῇ γὰρ πῦρ οὐ βαστάζει κ.τ.λ.

⟨τοῦ⟩ παντὸς ἀγαθοῦ γεννήτορος, καὶ πάσης τάξεως ἄρχοντος, καὶ
ἡγεμόνος τῶν ἑπτὰ κόσμων. The Sun is the generator of every good
thing; he is the ruler by whom order is maintained throughout
the universe; and he is the governor to whom the other planets
are subject. Of course the writer held that the Sun himself is
subject to the supreme God; his view must have been similar to
that expressed by Plutarch, *Quaest. Plat.* 8 *fin.*: (ὁ ἥλιος) τῶν μεγί-
στων καὶ κυριωτάτων τῷ ἡγεμόνι καὶ πρώτῳ θεῷ γίνεται συνεργός. In
Corp. XI. ii, as in *Corp.* XVI, and in Herm. *ap.* Stob. *Exc.* XXI. 2,
the Sun holds the position of 'second God', which in some of the

other *Hermetica* is assigned to the Kosmos; but in this paragraph, the time for speaking of the 'first God' has not yet come.

What are we to understand by παντὸς ἀγαθοῦ? Since we are told below that the function of the Moon is τὸ τὴν κάτω ὕλην μεταβάλλειν (i. e. to build up terrestrial matter into a succession of organic bodies), it may be presumed that the corresponding function of the Sun is to put ψυχή into the bodies fashioned by the moon, and thereby produce ζῷα.[1] 'Life' is closely associated with 'light'; and the writer's view was probably that the Sun (operating as the highest agent or minister of the supreme God) conveys ζωή or ψυχή into material bodies by means of the πῦρ which he emits, and which, by the time it reaches the earth, has been transmuted into φῶς. Now all that is good in the Kosmos may be comprehended under the term 'life' (cf. *Ascl. Lat.* III. 27 a); it is therefore possible to take the statement that the Sun is παντὸς ἀγαθοῦ γεννήτωρ as meaning that the Sun is the generator of life, or the dispenser of ψυχή. But if this is what the writer meant, we should have expected him to express it more clearly and directly; and it may be suspected that παντὸς ἀγαθοῦ has been substituted for some other term (e. g. πάσης ζωῆς), perhaps by the same person who substituted θεοῦ for ἡλίου.

σελήνην ⟨ἴ⟩δε, ἐκείνων πρόδρομον πάντων. πρόδρομος usually means one who goes in advance of others travelling in the same direction. The moon might be called πρόδρομος in this sense, because her *eastward* movement (i. e. her movement relatively to the fixed stars) is swifter than that of any of the other planets.

ὄργανον τῆς φύσεως. φύσις means either the process of birth and growth, or the power which operates in that process. Taking the word in the former sense, we may translate 'The Moon is the instrument by which birth and growth are wrought' (by a higher deity, viz. either the Sun, or the Supreme God,—though the latter has not yet been mentioned). But if we take φύσις to mean the force which operates, we must understand that force to be here personified, and translate 'The Moon is the instrument by means of which Nature works'.

τὴν κάτω ὕλην μεταβάλλουσαν. The Moon works up terrestrial matter into organic bodies, and replaces them by others as they successively suffer dissolution. Cf. Firmicus Maternus *Math.* 4. 1 :

---

[1] A different, but partly analogous, view of the respective functions of Sun, Moon, and Earth, occurs in Plut. *Fac. lunae* 28. 3: τὸ μὲν σῶμα ἡ γῆ, τὴν δὲ ψυχὴν ἡ σελήνη, τὸν δὲ νοῦν ὁ ἥλιος πάρεσχεν εἰς τὴν γένεσιν (of man).

'omnis enim substantia humani corporis ad istius pertinet numinis (*sc.* lunae) potestatem. Nam . . . compositi corporis formam pro qualitate cursus sui luna sustentat. . . . Quare scire debemus quod corpus hominis luna susceperit, et quod lunae sit potestatibus deputatum; nam et crescentis lunae augmenta in corporibus nostris et deficientis [luminis] damna sentimus. . . . Sic omnis ₛsubstantia terrenae corporis istius numinis providentia gubernatur. In posterioribus enim caeli regionibus collocata, et terrae imperium ex vicinitate sortita, omnia corpora, quae inspiratione divinae mentis animantur, cursus sui multiplici varietate sustentans, et per signa omnia festina celeritate [1] discurrens, et omnibus stellis adsiduis se coniunctionibus socians, ex contrariis mixturis et ex disparibus elementis integra compositi operis substantia mutuata, omnia animantium corpora et concepta procreat et generata dissolvit.' In *Ascl. Lat.* I. 3 c, a similar function is assigned to Sun and Moon together: '(omnium corporum) augmenta detrimentaque sol et luna sortiti sunt.'

ὑποστάθμην τοῦ καλοῦ κόσμου. Cf. 'the Stoics' in Diog. Laert. 7. 137 : ἀνωτάτω μὲν οὖν εἶναι τὸ πῦρ, ὃν δὴ αἰθέρα καλεῖσθαι, ἐν ᾧ πρώτην τὴν τῶν ἀπλανῶν σφαῖραν γεννᾶσθαι, εἶτα τὴν τῶν πλανωμένων· μεθ' ἣν τὸν ἀέρα· εἶτα τὸ ὕδωρ· ὑποστάθμην δὲ πάντων τὴν γῆν, μέσην ἁπάντων οὖσαν. Plutarch, *Fac. lunae* 25. 28, 940 F, says that the earth, seen from the moon, would appear to be οἷον ὑποστάθμη καὶ ἰλὺς τοῦ παντός, 'a muddy sediment at the bottom of the universe'. But perhaps the Hermetist took the word, as applied to the earth, to mean 'foundation' rather than 'sediment'; cf. Diod. 3. 44. 3, παλαιῶν οἰκιῶν λιθίνας ὑποστάθμας, 'stone foundations'.

τροφὸν καὶ τιθήνην τῶν ἐπιγείων. The Earth is nurse, not mother The Sun gives life to terrestrial organisms; the Moon fashions their material structure; the Earth supplies them with material nutriment. Pl. *Tim.* 40 B : γῆν δέ, τροφὸν μὲν ἡμετέραν κ.τ.λ. But in *Tim.* 88 D, the phrase is differently applied ; it is the ὑποδοχή (i. e. ὕλη) that is there called τροφὸς καὶ τιθήνη τοῦ παντός.

μέσην δὲ ἀμφοτέρων [ ] τὴν σελήνην περιπορευομένην. The lunar sphere is the boundary between the abode of τὰ ἀθάνατα ζῷα above and that of τὰ θνητὰ ζῷα below.

§ 8 a. πάντα δὲ πλήρη ψυχῆς, καὶ πάντα κινούμενα. ψυχή is τὸ κινοῦν ; see *Corp.* II.

[καὶ μήτε τὰ δεξιὰ . . . μήτε τὰ κάτω ἄνω.] This is irrelevant, and

---

[1] Cf. ἐκείνων πρόδρομον πάντων in *Corp.* XI. ii. 7.

interrupts the argument, which should run thus : ' all things, whether mortal or immortal, are alive (πάντα δὲ πλήρη ψυχῆς ... περὶ τὴν γῆν) ; and there must be some one who generates life in them (καὶ ὅτι πάντα ταῦτα γεννητά κ.τ.λ.) '. Also, these interposed phrases are obscure and awkwardly constructed. The negative μήτε (not οὔτε) shows that they are meant to be dependent on θέασαι ; and κινούμενα must be supplied ; but the sense intended is clumsily expressed. It might be possible to defend μήτε τὰ ἄνω κάτω μήτε τὰ κάτω ἄνω, taking it to mean ' the immortal ζῷα in heaven do not descend to earth, and the mortal ζῷα on earth do not ascend to heaven ' ; though, if the writer had wished to say this, it would have been better, instead of putting it here, to write ⟨ὥστε⟩ μήτε τὰ ἄνω κάτω ⟨χωρεῖν⟩ μήτε τὰ κάτω ἄνω after μέσην ... τὴν σελήνην περιπορευομένην above. But what can be meant by ' those on the right do not move to the left, nor those on the left to the right ' ? This cannot be said of the θνητὰ ζῷα, which move irregularly in all directions; it must be meant to apply only to the ἀθάνατα, i. e. the heavenly bodies ; but there is nothing in the text to limit it to them. And even if we assume that the heavenly bodies alone are here spoken of, the statement is still inaccurate. 'Right' and 'left' may be taken to mean 'North' and 'South';[1] but the sun, for instance, moves northward and southward in the course of the year, as well as westward in his daily round. I conclude. then that καὶ μήτε ... κάτω ἄνω is an interpolation.

§ 8 b. πάντα ταῦτα γεννητά. Having described the universe, the teacher goes on to show that there must be a maker of it, and that there cannot be more than one maker. γεννητά is here equivalent to ποιητά, and therefore implies a ποιητής. The verbs γεννᾶν and ποιεῖν are often interchanged ; in Pl. Tim., the Demiurgus is called πατήρ (' generator ') as well as ποιητής (' maker ') of the universe ; and τεκνοποιεῖν or τεκνοποιεῖσθαι means τέκνα γεννᾶν. The sense would be the same if we wrote γενητά ; for γίγνεσθαι is often used as the passive of ποιεῖν. Pl. Phileb. 27 A : τό γε ποιούμενον καὶ τὸ γιγνόμενον οὐδὲν πλὴν ὀνόματι ... διαφέρον εὑρήσομεν. The Hermetists probably made no distinction of meaning between γεννητός and γενητός.

When the writer of XI. ii calls God the ποιητής of the universe,

---

[1] Aetius, Diels Doxogr. p. 339 : Πυθαγόρας Πλάτων Ἀριστοτέλης δεξιὰ τοῦ κόσμου τὰ ἀνατολικὰ μέρη (East), ἀφ' ὧν ἡ ἀρχὴ τῆς κινήσεως, ἀριστερὰ δὲ τὰ δυτικά (West). ... Ἐμπεδοκλῆς δεξιὰ μὲν τὰ κατὰ τὸν θερινὸν τροπικόν (North), ἀριστερὰ δὲ τὰ κατὰ τὸν χειμερινόν (South).

he is not thinking of a divine act of creation in the past, such as is
described in the first chapter of *Genesis*, or in the mythical narrative
of the *Timaeus*. His God is not one who made the world in six
days and 'rested on the seventh day'; he holds (as does also the
writer of XI. i. 4 b–6 a) that God 'is ever at his work' (§ 14 a),
and that if he were to desist from it for a moment, all things would
perish. And this ceaseless work of God consists, not in creating
things out of nothing, but in 'bringing ὕλη and ψυχή together', that
is to say, in putting life into lifeless matter, and maintaining that
life from moment to moment. His work is τὸ κινεῖν τὰ πάντα καὶ
ζωοποιεῖν (§ 17 c). ὕλη not animated by ψυχή does not exist in
actuality; and the only 'things' which this writer recognizes are
ζῶντα. To say that God is the ποιητής of all things is therefore
merely another way of saying that God is the author of all life.

§ 9. μιᾶς δὲ κατὰ πάντων τάξεως τεταμένης (ταχύτητος τεταγμένης
MSS.), ἀδύνατον δύο ἢ πλείους ποιητὰς εἶναι. Cf. Psellus *De daemonum
operatione*, Migne *P. G.* 122, 828 B (*Testim.*).

εἰ ἕτερος ἦν ὁ ποιητὴς τῶν μεταβλητῶν [ζῴων] καὶ θνητῶν. Against
whom is this argument directed? The writer evidently knew of
some persons who taught that τὰ ἀμετάβλητα καὶ ἀθάνατα have been
made by one Demiurgus, and τὰ μεταβλητὰ καὶ θνητά have been
made (or are ceaselessly being made) by another. That theory
may have been first suggested by Pl. *Tim.* 41 c, where the Demiurgus
says to the gods whom he has made, δι' ἐμοῦ δὲ ταῦτα (*sc.* τὰ θνητὰ
γένη) γενόμενα καὶ βίου μετασχόντα θεοῖς ἰσάζοιτ' ἄν· ἵνα οὖν θνητὰ ...
ᾖ ..., τρέπεσθε κατὰ φύσιν ὑμεῖς ἐπὶ τὴν τῶν ζῴων δημιουργίαν,
μιμούμενοι τὴν ἐμὴν δύναμιν περὶ τὴν ὑμετέραν γένεσιν.[1] 'I myself',
he adds, 'will generate and hand over to you the immortal part
of them;' τὸ δὲ λοιπὸν ὑμεῖς, ἀθανάτῳ θνητὸν προσυφαίνοντες, ἀπεργά-
ζεσθε ζῷα καὶ γεννᾶτε, τροφήν τε διδόντες αὐξάνετε, καὶ φθίνοντα πάλιν
δέχεσθε.[2] (Cf. Herm. *ap.* Stob. *Exc.* V. 2, where the maker of men,

---

[1] 'Imitating my power that was put forth in the generation of you' (Archer-
Hind). This meaning would be more clearly expressed if τήν were added before
περί.

[2] Cf. Philo *Opif. mundi* 24. 73, Cohn I, p. 24 (commenting on the plural verb in
ποιήσωμεν ἄνθρωπον, *Gen.* I. 26): τῶν ὄντων τὰ μὲν οὔτ' ἀρετῆς οὔτε κακίας μετέχει,
ὥσπερ φυτὰ καὶ ζῷα ἄλογα ... · τὰ δ' αὖ μόνης κεκοινώνηκεν ἀρετῆς, ἀμέτοχα πάσης
ὄντα κακίας, ὥσπερ οἱ ἀστέρες· ... τὰ δὲ τῆς μικτῆς ἐστι φύσεως, ὥσπερ ἄνθρωπος, ὃς
ἐπιδέχεται τἀναντία, ... ἀρετὴν καὶ κακίαν. τῷ δὴ πάντων πατρὶ θεῷ τὰ μὲν σπουδαῖα
(the heavenly bodies) δι' αὐτοῦ μόνου ποιεῖν οἰκειότατον ἦν, ... τὰ δὲ ἀδιάφορα (the
plants and beasts) οὐκ ἀλλότριον ... · τὰ δὲ μικτὰ τῇ μὲν οἰκεῖον τῇ δ' ἀνοίκειον. ...
διὰ τοῦτ' ἐπὶ μόνης τῆς ἀνθρώπου γενέσεώς φησιν ὅτι εἶπεν ὁ θεὸς " ποιήσωμεν ", ὅπερ
ἐμφαίνει συμπαράληψιν ἑτέρων ὡς ἂν συνεργῶν, ἵνα ταῖς μὲν ἀνεπιλήπτοις βουλαῖς τε

and presumably of θνητά in general, is a single subordinate Demiurgus. See also *Exc.* XXI *fin.*) But the 'gods' (i. e. the cosmic forces) to whom the making of mortal ζῷα is assigned in the *Timaeus* have themselves been made by the supreme God, and work under his orders, so that, on the principle that 'qui facit per alium facit per se', there is after all but one Maker; whereas what is said in *Corp.* XI. ii seems to imply that those against whom the writer is contending taught that τὰ θνητά are made by some one who works independently of the maker of τὰ ἀθάνατα.[1]

Doctrines more or less resembling this were taught by some of the Christian Gnostics. Compare, for instance, Basilides *ap.* Hippol. *Ref. haer.* 7. 24: the 'great Archon' (not the supreme God) made τὰ αἰθέρια (i. e. the heavens and the heavenly bodies); and thereafter, πάλιν ἀπὸ τῆς πανσπερμίας ἄλλος ἄρχων ἀνέβη, . . . πολὺ ὑποδεέστερος τοῦ πρώτου ἄρχοντος· . . . καὶ πάντων τῶν ὑποκειμένων (*sc.* of all sublunar things) οὗτός (*sc.* the ἄλλος ἄρχων) ἐστι διοικητὴς καὶ δημιουργός. The Hermetist is not likely to have been directly concerned with the teachings of Christian Gnostics; but he may have been thinking of some Pagan theory by which Basilides and other Christian Gnostics were influenced. The view discussed and rejected in *Corp.* XI. ii has something in common with the Zoroastrian and Manichaean doctrine of two hostile Powers, the authors respectively of good and evil; for change and death might be regarded as forms of evil, though the writer of XI. ii does not so regard them.

ἐπεθύμησεν ἂν καὶ ἀθανάτους ποιῆσαι, ὥσπερ καὶ ὁ τῶν ἀθανάτων (ποιητὴς) θνητούς. If the reading is right, we must understand ἀθανάτους (θεούς) and θνητοὺς (ἀνθρώπους); though we should rather have expected ἀθάνατα and θνητά. The masculines ἀμετάβλητοι καὶ ἄφθαρτοι, μεταβλητοὶ καὶ φθαρτοί, occur (in the MSS.) in a similar context in XI. i 4 a.

μιᾶς οὔσης τῆς ὕλης καὶ μιᾶς τῆς ψυχῆς, παρὰ τίνι [ἂν] αὐτῶν ἡ χορηγία [τῆς ποιήσεως]; The χορηγία must mean the supply of the

---

καὶ πράξεσιν ἀνθρώπου κατορθοῦντος ἐπιγράφηται θεὸς ὁ πάντων ἡγεμών, τοῖς δ' ἐναντίαις ἕτεροι τῶν ὑπηκόων· ἔδει γὰρ ἀναίτιον εἶναι κακοῦ τὸν πατέρα τοῖς ἐκγόνοις. Philo must have had Pl. *Tim.* 41 in mind when he wrote this passage.

Arnobius (2. 36) says ʻ Christ has told us that our souls were generated, not by the supreme God, but by another *genitor*, many grades below him, yet of his court, and of lofty birth'. Did Arnobius get this from some Gnostic Gospel ?

[1] This would mean that φύσις (in the sense of the force which works birth and growth in the sublunar world) is not subject to the direction or control of the God who governs the heavens. On the question whether φύσις is subject to God, see *Corp.* III.

materials (viz. ὕλη and ψυχή) needed for ποίησις. (We might either cut out τῆς ποιήσεως, or take it to be a corruption of something like εἰς τὴν ποίησιν.) In the view of the writer, ποίησις is the making of ζῶντα; and ζῶντα are made by joining together ὕλη and ψυχή. This work can only be done if there is in existence a stock of ὕλη and a stock of ψυχή for the ποιητής to draw on. Assuming that there are two ποιηταί, which of the two has the stock of ὕλη and ψυχή at his disposal?

With μιᾶς οὔσης τῆς ὕλης καὶ μιᾶς τῆς ψυχῆς, compare *Ascl. Lat.* I. 3 a : *mundus* (ὕλη) *unus, anima* (ψυχή) *una*. The writer's notion of μία ψυχή may have been suggested by the Stoic conception of living fire or πνεῦμα pervading the universe. See *Corp.* X. 7 : ἀπὸ μιᾶς ψυχῆς τῆς τοῦ παντὸς κ.τ.λ.

The view that ψυχή as well as ὕλη existed before the making of the Kosmos occurs in Plut. *Quaest. Plat.* 4. 1003 : ἡ μὲν γὰρ ἄνους ψυχὴ καὶ τὸ ἄμορφον σῶμα συνυπῆρχον ἀλλήλοις ἀεί, καὶ οὐδέτερον αὐτῶν γένεσιν ἔσχεν οὐδ' ἀρχήν· ἐπεὶ δὲ ἡ ψυχὴ νοῦ μετέλαβε καὶ ἁρμονίας, καὶ γενομένη διὰ συμφωνίας ἔμφρων, μεταβολῆς αἰτία γέγονε τῇ ὕλῃ, . . . οὕτω τὸ σῶμα τοῦ κόσμου γένεσιν ἔσχεν ὑπὸ τῆς ψυχῆς. And the same doctrine is more fully expounded in Plut. *De an. procr. in Timaeo* 5–7, 1013 F ff. Plutarch there says that, before the *demiurgia*, there existed, not mere empty space, but ὕλη ἀτάκτως κινουμένη,[1] that is to say, ὕλη animated by ἄτακτος ψυχή. The Demiurgus did not create either σῶμα or ψυχή out of nothing; both already existed, but existed in a chaotic condition. But the Demiurgus brought the ἄτακτος ψυχή to order by putting νοῦς into it; the ἔννους ψυχή which was thus brought into existence changed the disorderly movement of ὕλη into an orderly movement; and so the Kosmos came into being. The disorder of Chaos was not however completely abolished; in the world as we know it, ἄτακτος ψυχή is still at work side by side with ἔννους ψυχή; and the evil in the world is wrought by the ἄτακτος ψυχή. (In Plut. *Is. et Os.*, this ἄτακτος ψυχή is mythically symbolized by Typhon.) In this theory of Plutarch we may see a partial analogy to the Hermetist's notion of a pre-existing stock of ψυχή. But there is an important difference; the writer of XI. ii speaks of ὕλη and ψυχή as existing apart from one another until

---

[1] In the *Timaeus*, two different and inconsistent accounts of what existed before the *demiurgia* stand side by side. In *Tim.* 52 A, the ὑποδοχή is identified with χώρα, i. e. empty space; but in other passages, we are told that the Demiurgus found already in existence something ἀτάκτως κινούμενον. Plutarch adopts and amplifies the second of these two notions.

the 'Maker' joins them together, whereas Plutarch's view is that the chaotic ψυχή was already embodied in the chaotic ὕλη. In this respect then, the pre-existing ψυχή of XI. ii corresponds to the νοῦς which Plutarch's Demiurgus introduced into the pre-existing chaos, rather than to Plutarch's ἄτακτος ψυχή.

§ 10. τὰ δὲ μὴ ζῶντα ὕλη [πάλιν] καθ' ἑαυτήν ἐστι. There are no 'things without life' in actual existence. (Cf. § 14 b, πάντα ζῷά ἐστι.) The Maker never desists from his work of maintaining, or renewing from moment to moment, the union of ψυχή with ὕλη; and ὕλη by itself never presents itself in our experience. It is possible, however, to form an abstract conception of τὰ μὴ ζῶντα, and to talk about them, as one might talk about τὸ μὴ ὄν; and at this stage of his argument, the teacher falls into the common practice of speaking of the activity of the Maker as if it were occasional and intermittent, or had taken place once for all.

καὶ ψυχὴ ὁμοίως καθ' ἑαυτήν, τῷ ποιητῇ παρακειμένη, τῆς ζωῆς οὐσία (αἰτία MSS.). The meaning must be that ψυχή is the substance of which life is made, and that, before the Maker does his work of making ζῶντα, this substance exists apart from ὕλη. The word αἰτία could hardly be used to signify 'the substance of which a thing is made'; and the Hermetist probably wrote οὐσία, which was commonly used in that sense by the Stoics. The construction of this sentence is not clear; what verb is to be supplied with καὶ ψυχὴ κ.τ.λ.? Perhaps there is some slight error in the text.

Where and how does ψυχή exist 'by itself'? It does not follow, because 'ὕλη by itself' is a mere abstraction, that the same must be said of 'ψυχή by itself' also; and perhaps the writer held that there is a universal unembodied ψυχή, which exists in close connexion with God (τῷ θεῷ παρακειμένη), and of which the several ψυχαί of individual organisms are separated portions. (Cf. Corp. X. 7.) A Platonist of the usual type might have said that 'ψυχή by itself' exists ἐν τῷ νοητῷ; and the writer of XI. ii might accordingly have said that it exists ἐν τῷ ἀσωμάτῳ (that is, in God's mind), since τὸ ἀσώματον is his equivalent for Plato's νοητόν; but it is assumed that the pupil is not yet acquainted with the conception of τὸ ἀσώματον. (See § 17 a.)

πῶς οὖν . . . ⟨⟨τῆς . . . τῶν ἀθανάτων.⟩⟩ My rewriting of this corrupt passage probably gives the author's meaning, or something not far from it, though his exact words can hardly be recovered.

§ 11. καὶ γὰρ μία ψυχή, καὶ μία ζωή, καὶ μία ὕλη. The order of the three substantives is hardly satisfactory. It would seem better either to omit καὶ μία ζωή, or to write μία ψυχὴ καὶ μία ὕλη, καὶ μία ζωή· 'soul is one and matter is one, and life (resulting from the union of soul with matter throughout the universe) is one.'

τὸν μὲν κόσμον ὡμολόγησας ἕνα εἶναι. Neither the teacher nor the pupil has expressly said this before; but it may perhaps be held to be implied in the description of the ordered universe in § 7, to which the pupil gave tacit assent.

καὶ τὸν ἥλιον ἕνα, καὶ τὴν σελήνην μίαν. It might be objected that, if the Sun is one and the Moon is one, Sun and Moon are two; and that the recognition of Sun and Moon as distinct deities, if it has any bearing on the question at all, tells in favour of pluralism rather than monism. But if the text is sound, the writer's meaning must have been that each of these deities discharges a certain function for the whole universe, and not for a part of it alone, and therefore *a fortiori* the higher function of putting life into matter throughout the universe must be assigned to a single Being. Yet a difficulty remains; for it would seem from § 7 that the operation of the Moon is limited to the sublunar region; and if so, how can the instance of the Moon be used to prove that all ζῷα, celestial and terrestrial alike, are made by one God? There is certainly some confusion of thought; but that is hardly a sufficient reason for concluding that the words καὶ τὸν ἥλιον . . . μίαν are an interpolation.

καὶ [θειότητα] ⟨τὴν γῆν⟩ μίαν. θειότητα is meaningless; and as γῆ was spoken of in connexion with ἥλιος and σελήνη in § 7, it is to be presumed that τὴν γῆν is the right reading.

εἰ πολλοί (ἐν πολλῷ MSS.), γελοιότατον. There are many θεοί; but there is only one Being to whom the name ὁ θεός applies. γελοιότατον has been duplicated by error; it is rightly placed here, and wrongly above.

§ 14 b. ⟨⟨εἷς ἄρα . . . γίνεται πάντα.⟩⟩ This passage has no connexion with the topic discussed in the latter part of § 14 a, viz. the ceaselessness of God's life-giving work. On the other hand, it fits in well at the place where I have put it. At the beginning of § 11, the writer sets out to prove that all things are made by one God; and that is precisely the conclusion arrived at in § 14 b. But the conclusion is reached by two stages; it is shown, firstly, that God is one (εἷς ἄρα καὶ ὁ θεός), and secondly (καὶ πάλιν), that all things are made by this one God (ὑπὸ τοῦ θεοῦ ἄρα γίνεται πάντα).

In εἰς ἄρα καὶ ὁ θεός, the καί may be taken as referring back to κόσμον, ἥλιον, σελήνην, and γῆν.

καὶ τὰ ἐν οὐρανῷ καὶ τὰ ἐν τῇ γῇ. Both here and in § 12 a *init.* (καὶ ἀθανασίαν καὶ μεταβολὴν ποιεῖν), the writer is still contending against the theory that τὰ ἀθάνατα are made by one Demiurgus, and τὰ θνητά by another.

§ 12 a. [ζωὴν καὶ ψυχὴν] καὶ ἀθανασίαν καὶ μεταβολὴν ποιεῖν. ἀθανασίαν and μεταβολήν stand for ἀθάνατα and μεταβλητά (i. e. θνητά). The writer's doctrine is not that God makes ψυχή, but that God puts pre-existing ψυχή into pre-existing ὕλη, and thereby makes ζῶντα. The words καὶ ψυχήν must therefore be struck out. We might either strike out ζωήν also, or write ζωῆς ⟨αἰτίῳ ὄντι⟩. Compare XI. i. 5 as emended: τίς ἄλλος αἴτιος ζωῆς, καὶ ἀθανασίας καὶ μεταβολῆς ποιητής;

σοῦ τοσαῦτα ποιοῦντος. God 'makes' different things, viz. immortal and mortal ζῷα; the same man 'does' different things, e. g. he both speaks and hears. But ποιεῖν may signify either 'to make' or 'to do'; and by the use of the same verb with reference to both God and man, the analogy between God's actions and man's actions is made to appear closer than it really is. The effect of the Greek can be more nearly reproduced in French than in English; 'Quoi d'étonnant que Dieu *fasse* . . . l'immortalité ⟨et⟩ le changement, quand toi-même tu *fais* tant d'actions différentes?' (Ménard.)

καὶ γὰρ βλέπεις . . . καὶ πνεῖς. The human functions mentioned in this list are oddly selected and arranged. Why should 'speaking' be put among the bodily senses? And why should 'thinking' be inserted between 'walking' and 'breathing'? There can be little doubt that the list was originally shorter; but it is difficult to guess which of the verbs were included in its earliest form. Perhaps νοεῖς may have come by duplication from πνεῖς, and the corresponding words καὶ ἄλλος ὁ νοῶν may have been subsequently added below. Possibly the author wrote only καὶ γὰρ λαλεῖς καὶ ἀκούεις, καὶ περιπατεῖς καὶ ⟨ἀνα⟩πνεῖς. Since the pupil is taking part in a dialogue, he may be said to be actually 'speaking and hearing'; and loco-motion and respiration might be mentioned as functions which belong to him in common with all terrestrial animals.

§ 12 b. ἂν τούτων καταργηθῇς, οὐκέτι ζῷον εἶ. A man does not cease to be a ζῷον if he is deprived of sight or hearing; we must therefore understand τούτων to mean 'all these functions together'. It might be held that some kind of αἴσθησις, some kind of spontaneous κίνησις (such as τὸ περιπατεῖν), and ἀναπνοή, are indispensable for the existence of a ζῷον.

ἂν ἐκείνων καταργηθῇ, ὁ θεός ... οὐκέτι ἐστὶ θεός. ἐκείνων means τοῦ τὰ ἀθάνατα καὶ τὰ θνητὰ ποιεῖν. Cf. XI. i. 5 : οὐ γὰρ ἀργὸς ὁ θεός κ.τ.λ. *Corp.* XVI. 19 : οὐκ ἄν ποτε παύσαιτο (ποιῶν ὁ θεός), ἐπεὶ καὶ αὐτὸς ἄπαυστος.

§ 13 b. τοῦτο δέ ἐστι τὸ ἀγαθόν. [τοῦτο ἔστιν ὁ θεός.] The words τοῦτο ἔστιν ὁ θεός were probably added by some one who wished to insist on the identification of the Good with God. Cf. καὶ τὸ ἀγαθόν, repeatedly inserted after ὁ θεὸς καὶ πατήρ in *Corp.* X.

§ 17 c. ⟨⟨ὥσπερ γὰρ ... καὶ ζωοποιεῖν.⟩⟩ This passage, misplaced in the MSS., deals with the subject discussed in §§ 13 and 14 ; and the term τὸ ἀγαθόν connects it especially with § 13 b *fin.* It seems clear therefore that it must have originally stood here. There is some obscurity in the transition from the first sentence of 17 b (ὥσπερ γὰρ ... τὸ ἀγαθόν) to the second (τοῦτο γὰρ ... ζωοποιεῖν) ; and the meaning becomes clearer if we insert between them the words ἔστι δὲ τοῦτο, ὦ φίλτατε, ζωή, which make confusion where they stand in the MSS. God's work is to produce that which is good ; and that means, to make things live.

ὁ ἄνθρωπος χωρὶς [ζωῆς] ⟨πνοῆς⟩ οὐ δύναται ζῆν. ζωῆς is certainly wrong ; and πνοῆς is probably the right correction. We were told above that breathing is one of the things without doing which a man cannot be a ζῷον.

τοῦτο γὰρ ὥσπερ [ζωὴ καὶ ὥσπερ κίνησις] ⟨οὐσία⟩ ἐστὶ τοῦ θεοῦ, ⟨τὸ⟩ κινεῖν τὰ πάντα καὶ ζωοποιεῖν. Cf. XI. i. 2 : τοῦ δὲ θεοῦ [ὥσπερ] οὐσία ἐστὶ τὸ ἀγαθόν.

§ 14 a. ἴδε τί σοι ἐγγίνεται θέλοντι γεννῆσαι. God is 'the Father' of the universe and all things in it ; and human procreation is a type or image of God's creative energy. The human father generates life in a single child ; God generates life in all things. Cf. *Ascl. Lat.* III. 20 b., and *Corp.* II. 17 a.

οὐδὲ γὰρ ἄλλο ἔχει συνεργόν. Cf. *Corp.* VI. 1 b : οὔτε σύζυγόν ἐστιν αὐτῷ, [ ] οὗ ἐρασθήσεται.

αὐτὸς ὢν ὁ ποιεῖ. If the text is sound, the writer here says that God not only makes ζωή (or ζῶντα), but is himself the ζωή (or the ζῶντα) which he makes. Cf. *Corp.* XVI. 19 : πάντα οὖν ποιῶν ἑαυτὸν ποιεῖ. It is of course possible to say that 'God is life' ; but it seems strange to combine in one clause the two verbally inconsistent propositions 'God *makes* life' and 'God *is* life'. (There is the same sort of difficulty in § 14 b, in the words αὕτη (*sc.* ἡ ζωὴ) ἐστι θεός, followed by ὑπὸ τοῦ θεοῦ ἄρα γίνεται πάντα.) Possibly the author may have written αὐτὸς ὢν ἐν ᾧ ποιεῖ; cf. XI. i. 6 a, ὁ γὰρ ποιῶν ἐν πᾶσίν ἐστι.

εἰ γὰρ χωρισθείη αὐτοῦ, πάντα μὲν συμπεσεῖσθαι, πάντα δὲ τεθνήξεσθαι ἀνάγκη. Cf. Augustine, quoted by Inge, *Personal idealism and mysticism*, p. 79 : 'If God were to cease speaking the Word even for a moment, heaven and earth would vanish.'

εἰ δὲ πάντα ζῷα (*legendum* ζῶ⟨ντ⟩α?), [μία δὲ καὶ ἡ ζωή,] ⟨. . .⟩. The sentence here breaks off, and three unconnected fragments follow. The words μία δὲ καὶ ἡ ζωή are probably a misplaced doublet of μία δὲ κατὰ πάντων ζωή in § 14 b.

§ 14 c. [ζωὴ δέ ἐστιν ἔνωσις [νοῦ] ⟨σώματος⟩ καὶ ψυχῆς. θάνατος δὴ οὐκ ἀπώλεια τῶν συναχθέντων, διάλυσις δὲ τῆς ἐνώσεώς ἐστι.] In place of νοῦ, we must read either σώματος or ὕλης. If we read σώματος, the definition of θάνατος agrees with Pl. *Phaedo* 67 D : τοῦτό γε θάνατος ὀνομάζεται, λύσις καὶ χωρισμὸς ψυχῆς ἀπὸ σώματος.

But this definition of the terms ζωή and θάνατος is inconsistent with what precedes and follows. ζωή is spoken of elsewhere in this Libellus as if it were a substantive thing ; but ἔνωσις σώματος καὶ ψυχῆς is merely a συμβεβηκός of things. We have been told in § 14 b that μία κατὰ πάντων ζωὴ ὑπὸ τοῦ θεοῦ γίνεται ; but what could be meant by saying that there is μία κατὰ πάντων ἔνωσις σώματος καὶ ψυχῆς? And in § 15 b, we are told that at the dissolution of the body ἡ ζωὴ εἰς τὸ ἀφανὲς χωρεῖ (i. e. disappears from our view, but continues to exist) ; but how could this be said of the ἔνωσις σώματος καὶ ψυχῆς? Moreover, in § 14 c θάνατος is spoken of as something that really occurs ; but the words τὴν μεταβολὴν θάνατόν φασιν εἶναι in § 15 b imply that there is in reality no such thing as θάνατος. And to this it may be added that the meaning of διάλυσις in § 14 c differs from that of διαλύεσθαι in § 15 b. The διάλυσις spoken of in § 14 c is the separation of soul and body from one another ; the διάλυσις spoken of in § 15 b is the 'dissolution' or 'decomposition' of the body, i. e. the separation and dispersion of the material elements of which the body is composed. Hence it may be inferred that § 14 c was not written by the author of the Libellus, but is a note appended by some one else.

§ 15 a. [τοίνυν εἰκὼν τοῦ θεοῦ ὁ αἰών, . . . τοῦ δὲ ἡλίου ὁ ἄνθρωπος.] This passage has nothing to do with the subject discussed in XI. ii. It was evidently written in imitation of the sentences in XI. i. 2 ;

320 CORPVS HERMETICVM

but it would not be in place there, as it substitutes a different series,
viz. θεός, αἰών, κόσμος, ἥλιος, ἄνθρωπος, for the series dealt with in all
the formulae of XI. i. 2, viz. θεός, αἰών, κόσμος, χρόνος, γένεσις.

εἰκὼν τοῦ θεοῦ ὁ αἰών. Cf. Philo *De fuga et invent.* 19. 101, Wendland III, p. 132 : αὐτὸς (ὁ θεῖος λόγος) εἰκὼν ὑπάρχων θεοῦ.

τοῦ δὲ αἰῶνος (εἰκὼν) ὁ κόσμος. Cf. Pl. *Tim.* 92 C : ὅδε ὁ κόσμος,
. . . εἰκὼν τοῦ ποιητοῦ (*al.* νοητοῦ) θεὸς αἰσθητός. *Ascl. Lat.* I. 10 :
'(deus) cuius sunt imagines duae mundus et homo.' *Corp.* VIII. 2 :
πρῶτος . . . ὁ δημιουργὸς τῶν ὅλων θεός· δεύτερος δὲ ὁ κατ᾽ εἰκόνα αὐτοῦ
ὑπ᾽ αὐτοῦ γενόμενος (i. e. the Kosmos).[1] The writer of § 15 a had
some such statement as that in mind, and modified it by interposing
the αἰών of XI. i between God and the Kosmos. Perhaps he
identified 'the Aeon' with the νοητὸς κόσμος, of which the αἰσθητὸς
κόσμος is an image or copy.

τοῦ δὲ κόσμου (εἰκὼν) ὁ ἥλιος, τοῦ δὲ ἡλίου ὁ ἄνθρωπος. The Sun,
being the greatest of individual ζῷα, might be called an εἰκών of the
Kosmos, which is the all-inclusive ζῷον ; and worshippers of the
Sun-god, whether Mithraists or adherents of the old solar cults of
Egypt and Syria, would readily accept the statement that man is
made in the image of Helios, who was depicted in human form in
their temples. It was a commonplace to say that man is a microcosm, i. e. εἰκὼν τοῦ κόσμου ; and the writer of § 15 a interposed the
Sun between the Kosmos and man, just as he interposed 'the Aeon'
between God and the Kosmos.

§ 15 b. ⟨. . .⟩ τὴν δὲ μεταβολὴν θάνατόν φασιν εἶναι. Some connecting words have been lost ; but the lacuna is probably not large.
The words πάντα δὲ τεθνήξεσθαι ἀνάγκη in § 14 a suggested the
thought of death ; and the writer here proceeds to explain that
there is really no such thing as death (cf. *Corp.* VIII *init.*), and
that what men call death ought rather to be called μεταβολή. The
lost beginning of § 15 b may perhaps have been to this effect :
⟨ἀποθνήσκει μὲν γὰρ οὐδέν, μεταβάλλεται δὲ τὰ ἐπίγεια πάντα·⟩ τὴν δὲ
μεταβολὴν κ.τ.λ.

τὴν δὲ ζωὴν εἰς τὸ ἀφανὲς χωρεῖν. ζωή is imperishable ; but at
the dissolution of an individual organism, the ζωή which was in it

[1] Compare Plut. *Quaest. Plat.* 8. 4. 6, 1007 D (Duebner) : εἰκόνες δέ εἰσιν ἄμφω
(*sc.* ὅ τε κόσμος καὶ ὁ χρόνος) τοῦ θεοῦ, τῆς μὲν οὐσίας ὁ κόσμος, τῆς δ᾽ ἀιδιότητος ὁ
χρόνος ἐν κινήσει, ⌐καθάπερ ἐν γενέσει θεὸς ὁ κόσμος⌐. The passage might be emended
thus : εἰκόνες δέ εἰσιν ἄμφω τοῦ θεοῦ, τῆς μὲν οὐσίας ὁ κόσμος ⟨⟨ἐν γενέσει⟩⟩, τῆς δ᾽
ἀιδιότητος ὁ χρόνος ἐν κινήσει. The words καθάπερ [[ἐν γενέσει]] (αἰσθητὸς ?) θεὸς ὁ
κόσμος (cf. Pl. *Tim.* 92 C quoted above) are probably an appended note.

(or the ψυχή in which its ζωή resided) 'passes away out of our sight'. Where does it go ? The writer does not here tell us ; but we must suppose his view to have been either that the portion of life which has quitted the individual goes back into the undivided stock of life or soul which is 'laid up in God's keeping' (ψυχὴ ... καθ' ἑαυτήν, τῷ ποιητῇ παρακειμένη, § 10), or else, that it passes immediately into other organisms which are just coming into existence. When we are observing the cessation of life in this or that particular ζῷον, we do not notice the beginnings of fresh life which are simultaneously taking place elsewhere ; and so that portion of the universal life may be said to 'pass away out of our sight'. If the author were speaking as a Platonist, he ought rather to have said that the disembodied ψυχή, with its inherent ζωή, retains its individual personality, and continues to exist as a distinct and separate being ; but his conception of ψυχή and ζωή resembles that of the Stoics rather than that of Plato.

ταῦτά ἐστι τὰ τοῦ κόσμου πάθη, ⌈δινήσεις τε καὶ κρύψεις· καὶ ἡ μὲν δίνησις στροφή, ἡ δὲ κρύψις ἀνανέωσις.⌉ The meaning which the context seems to require is that 'the things which befall the Kosmos' are not deaths, but renewals of life, which vanishes in one place only to reappear in another ; and the ἀνανέωσις spoken of must be this perpetual renewal of life. But I can make nothing of the words given by the MSS.[1]

§ 16 a. παντόμορφος δέ ἐστιν (sc. ὁ κόσμος). In Ascl. Lat. III. 19 b, παντόμορφος is a name or epithet of the Zodiac, regarded as the deity who assigns to all individuals born on earth their several forms. But in Corp. XI. ii, the word is used without any suggestion of astral influences ; and the meaning is that the Kosmos, in its various parts, assumes (successively) all possible forms, or passes through all possible changes. Cf. Ascl. Lat. III. 36 : ' et mundus speciem mutat' &c. Plut. Is. et Os. 53 : ἡ γὰρ Ἶσίς ἐστι μὲν τὸ τῆς φύσεως θῆλυ καὶ δεκτικὸν ἁπάσης γενέσεως . . .· ὑπὸ δὲ τῶν πολλῶν μυριώνυμος κέκληται, διὰ τὸ πάσας ὑπὸ τοῦ λόγου τρεπομένη μορφὰς δέχεσθαι καὶ ἰδέας.

οὐ τὰς μορφὰς ἐγκειμένας ἔχων ἐν ἑαυτῷ, [[δὲ]] αὐτὸς ⟨⟨δὲ⟩⟩ μεταβάλλων. The writer seems to be guarding against a possible misinterpretation of the word παντόμορφος. It might be supposed that the Kosmos

---

[1] A sense consistent with what precedes could be got by writing ταῦτά ἐστι τὰ τοῦ κόσμου πάθη, διαλύσεις τε καὶ κρύψεις (i. e. διαλύσεις σωμάτων and κρύψεις ζωῆς). καὶ τῇ μὲν διαλύσει ⟨ἕπεται συ⟩στροφή (= σύστασις), τῇ δὲ κρύψει ⟨φ⟩ανέρωσις.

is itself changeless, but contains within it things which change their forms. He rejects this view, and asserts that the Kosmos itself changes, i. e. assumes different forms in succession. But if this is his meaning, it is obscurely expressed; he ought rather to have written something like οὐ τὰ μεταμορφούμενα ἐγκείμενα ἔχων ἐν ἑαυτῷ.

§ 16 b. ἐπεὶ οὖν ὁ κόσμος παντόμορφος γέγονεν, ὁ ποιήσας τί ἂν εἴη; Does God himself 'assume all forms'? It was frequently said that he does; as for instance in an invocation addressed to the Creator (Magic Papyrus, Dieterich *Abraxas*, p. 176, Reitzenstein *Poim.* p. 22): ἐπικαλοῦμαί σε . . . τὸν τὰ πάντα κτίσαντα, σὲ τὸν αὐτογέννητον θεόν· . . . οὖ οὐδεὶς θεῶν δύναται ἰδεῖν τὴν ἀληθινὴν μορφήν· ὁ μεταμορφούμενος εἰς πάντα[ς] ἐν ταῖς ὁράσεσιν ἀόρατος αἰὼν αἰῶνος.[1] ἐπικαλοῦμαί σε, κύριε, ἵνα μοι φανῇ ἡ ἀληθινή σου μορφή. This implies that God has one 'true' form, but usually appears in other and 'untrue' forms; i. e. that he is usually seen, not as he is in his own being, but only as manifested in the things that he has made.

Plato, *Rep.* 2. 380 ff., criticizes the popular mythology, according to which the gods either 'change their own εἶδος into many μορφαί', or deceive men by appearing to them ἄλλοτε ἐν ἄλλαις ἰδέαις; and he there asserts that ὁ θεὸς ἁπλοῦς τέ ἐστι καὶ πάντων ἥκιστα τῆς ἑαυτοῦ ἰδέας ἐκβαίνει, and that ἥκιστα ἂν πολλὰς μορφὰς ἴσχοι ὁ θεός. The writer of *Corp.* XI. ii was very likely thinking of that passage. According to the Platonic doctrine, the Kosmos is σωματικός and μεταβλητός, but the supreme God is ἀσώματος and ἀμετάβλητος; it must therefore be an error to say that the supreme God assumes different forms in succession; and if any μορφή or ἰδέα is attributed to him, it must be a μορφή or ἰδέα ἀσώματος (i. e. νοητή, as opposed to αἰσθητή). The Stoics, on the other hand, ignored the supracosmic God of Platonism; their supreme God corresponded to the Kosmos (αἰσθητὸς θεός) of the Platonists, and might be said to 'assume all forms'. Orig. *c. Cels.* 1. 21 : ὁ θεὸς τοῖς Στωικοῖς ἐστι σῶμα, οὐκ αἰδουμένοις λέγειν αὐτὸν τρεπτὸν καὶ δι᾽ ὅλων ἀλλοιωτὸν καὶ μεταβλητόν. Plut. *Fac. lunae* 12. 926 D: ὁ δὲ Ζεὺς ⌜ἡμῖν⌝ (*lege* ὑμῖν, *sc.* τοῖς Στωικοῖς) οὗτος οὐ τῇ μὲν αὑτοῦ φύσει χρώμενος[2] ἕν ἐστι μέγα πῦρ καὶ συνεχές, νυνὶ δ᾽ ὑφεῖται καὶ κέκαμπται καὶ διεσχημάτισται, πᾶν χρῆμα γεγονὼς καὶ γιγνόμενος ἐν ταῖς μεταβολαῖς; The author of XI. ii then, in his discussion of the question whether one or many

---

[1] Perhaps αἰὼν αἰώνων.　　　　[2] I. e. at the *ecpyrosis*.

μορφαί are to be attributed to God, is maintaining the Platonic doctrine against that of the Stoics.

ἄμορφος μὲν γὰρ μὴ γένοιτο. ἄμορφος often means 'misshapen' or 'ugly', and in that sense at least cannot be applicable to God. Besides, to deny that God has any μορφή would almost amount to denying his existence. The writer does not belong to that school of Platonists who refused to ascribe any qualities or attributes to God, and defined him only by negatives. He differs from Plotinus, who says (6. 9. 4) that 'the One' is ἄμορφον καὶ μορφῆς νοητῆς, and ἀνείδεον, πρὸ εἴδους ὂν παντός.

μίαν οὖν ἔχει ἰδέαν. The words ἰδέα and μορφή are here synonymous, as they are in Pl. Rep. 2. 380, referred to above. But the writer probably preferred to use ἰδέα in speaking of God, because μορφή was more commonly used in the sense of forma visibilis, and ἀσώματος μορφή would therefore sound more paradoxical than ἀσώματος ἰδέα.

[εἴ τις ἔστιν αὐτοῦ ἰδέα (ἰδία MSS.)]. This is inconsistent with ἄμορφος μὴ γένοιτο. It must have been added by some one who hesitated to ascribe 'form' to God. Cf. Corp. XII. i. 1 : εἴ γέ τις ἔστιν οὐσία θεοῦ.

οὐχ ὑποσταίη. For the omission of ἄν, cf. Corp. IX. 8 fin.

[καὶ πάσας διὰ τῶν σωμάτων δείκνυσι.] If we retain these words, we must take them to mean that God, though he does not himself appear in visible forms, imposes such forms on bodies, and thereby enables us to see the forms. But this is not satisfactory. The phrase πάσας μορφὰς δεικνύναι ought rather to mean 'to present all forms', i. e. 'to appear in all forms'; the subject ought therefore to be ὁ κόσμος rather than ὁ θεός. Perhaps the clause originally formed part of the missing passage before παντόμορφος δέ ἐστιν in § 16 a, where the writer was speaking of the forms assumed by the Kosmos.

§ 17 a. μὴ θαυμάσῃς εἰ ἔστι τις ἀσώματος ἰδέα. The teacher assumes that the conception of τὸ ἀσώματον is new to his pupil. If so, Platonists could not have been included among the 'many men' whom the pupil had already heard speaking 'about the All and God' (§ 1 b).

ἔστι γάρ· ὥσπερ [ἡ τοῦ λόγου] καὶ ἐν ταῖς γραφαῖς κ.τ.λ. The phrase ἡ (ἰδέα) τοῦ λόγου might perhaps mean the rhetorical or literary style of a speech. Cf. Isocr. 5. 143, ἀλλὰ γὰρ εἱλόμην ἀποσχέσθαι τῆς τοιαύτης ἰδέας, 'to abstain from such a style, sc. τοῦ λόγου' (A. E.

Taylor). Compare also σχῆμα λέξεως, 'a figure of speech'. Literary style is a form, but not a 'corporeal' form; it is not a thing that we can perceive with our bodily senses. But if the writer had intended to mention literary style as an instance of an ἀσώματος ἰδέα, he would surely have expressed his meaning more fully and clearly. It seems best therefore to bracket ἡ τοῦ λόγου.

ἐν ταῖς γραφαῖς ἀκρώρειαι ὁρῶνται μὲν [γὰρ] πάνυ ἐξέχουσαι. Suppose that you are looking at a picture of an undulating tract of country. The ἰδέα in this case is the shape of the undulations. But there are no undulations in the σῶμα at which you are looking; the object before you is a flat surface daubed with colours. The ἰδέα then is not in the σῶμα; it is an ἀσώματος ἰδέα. It exists; but (supposing the landscape depicted to be imaginary) it exists only in someone's mind, and not in any σῶμα.

The instance however does not seem very happily chosen. It is not true that there are no undulations of any sort in the picture; for the vertical undulations of the mountain-ridge are represented in the picture on the wall by vertically undulating lines. The writer's meaning would therefore have been more clearly expressed if, instead of speaking of the varying *height* of the parts of the thing depicted, he had spoken of their varying *distance* from the eye, and said that the ἰδέα of a scene including *near* and *distant* objects is presented to us, though the σῶμα at which we are looking is a flat board.

According to the Platonists, the best preparation for dealing with νοητά or ἀσώματα is the study of geometry. The writer of XI. ii is precluded from using the conceptions of geometry for this purpose, because he has determined to assume no previous training in the pupil. But the instance of the picture is a geometrical instance in disguise; the ἰδέα ἀσώματος in this case, viz. the shape of the mountain, is a geometrical figure in three dimensions, represented by a diagram in two dimensions.

§§ 17 b-20 a. ἐννοήσας δὲ ... ἑαυτόν, ⟨τὸ⟩ ὅλον. In this passage the order and connexion of the sentences is very doubtful; but I suppose the meaning to have been as follows: 'Grasp boldly the conception of an ἀσώματος ἰδέα, and realize that God is ἀσώματος; then you will see the true meaning of the statement that God contains all things. Things are in God, not as bodies are in another body, but as thoughts are in the mind of the thinker.'

§ 17 b. ἀληθέστερον [δὲ] ⟨⟨νοήσεις τὸν περιέχοντα τὰ πάντα⟩⟩. The

words νόησον τὸν περιέχοντα τὰ πάντα are unintelligible where they
stand in § 18 ; and something of the sort is wanted here. The whole
paragraph is an explanation of the statement 'God contains all
things', or 'all things are in God'.

§ 18. ἔνια δὲ τῶν λεγομένων ἰδίαν ἔννοιαν ἔχειν ὀφείλει. Some terms
or phrases must (under special circumstances) be taken in a special
sense. Thus the phrase τὸ περιέχειν ('to contain things'), when
used with reference to God, must be taken in a sense compatible
with the truth that God is ἀσώματος, and not in the sense in which
it is used when we are speaking of bodies.

ὁ μὲν γὰρ τόπος [καὶ] σῶμά ἐστι. It seems strange to say that
τόπος is a body. The statement is in verbal contradiction to *Corp.*
II. 4 a (ἀσώματος οὖν ὁ τόπος) ; but in that passage, ὁ τόπος means
extracosmic space, or rather, the divine νοῦς with which extracosmic
space is filled.   Here, if σῶμα is the right reading, ὁ τόπος must
mean the larger body in which a smaller body is contained..   But
perhaps the author wrote σωμά⟨των περιεκτικός⟩ ἐστι, or something to
that effect.

καὶ ⟨πᾶν⟩ σῶμα ⟨κινητόν· τὸ δὲ ἀσώματον⟩ ἀκίνητον. The preceding
μέν requires an answering δέ ; it is therefore certain that some words
have fallen out here.

τὰ ⟨ἐν αὐτῷ⟩ κείμενα κίνησιν οὐκ ἔχει. 'Things situated in the
incorporeal' (i. e. thoughts in the mind) are not κινητά, if we take
κίνησις in the literal and physical sense ; they do not move from
place to place.

§ 19. καὶ τοῦτο (οὕτω MSS.) νόησον ἀπὸ σεαυτοῦ. 'This' (τοῦτο)
is the fact that τὸ ἀσώματον (i. e. mind or thought) is capable of
containing all things (πάντων περιοριστικόν). Any man can see that
this is true of his own mind or thought ; therefore *a fortiori* it must
be true of the mind or thought of God. The difference between
man and God is this, that a man can (in thought) place himself
anywhere, whereas God is *everywhere at once*. But we are afterwards
told that it is possible for a man to free himself from his limitations,
and 'make himself equal to God' in this respect.

Your mind 'contains all things', at least potentially. You can
think of anything in the universe, and even of things beyond the
limits of the universe ; and anything of which you think is 'contained in' your mind. The point of this passage is somewhat
obscured by the use of the phrase 'bid your soul go to' this place
or that, which might seem to imply that the mind does not 'contain'

things, but merely travels through space from one thing to another. But the writer guards against this misunderstanding by adding οὐχ ὡς μεταβᾶσα ἀπὸ τόπου εἰς τόπον, ἀλλ' ὡς ἐκεῖ οὖσα. Before you thought of that particular place, your mind was already there; it is (potentially) everywhere, and therefore must be capable of including all things. The ταχυτής spoken of does not mean swiftness of movement through space; but the writer employs this word to express the instantaneousness with which the mind finds itself present anywhere at will.

Compare Lactantius *De opif. dei* 16. 9 f. : ' An potest aliquis non admirari quod sensus ille vivus atque caelestis, qui mens vel animus nuncupatur, . . . tantae celeritatis (est), ut uno temporis puncto caelum omne conlustret, si velit, maria pervolet, terras et urbes peragret, omnia denique quae libuerit, quamvis longe lateque sub-mota sint, in conspectu sibi ipse constituat? Et miratur aliquis si divina mens dei per universas mundi partes intenta discurrit et omnia regit, omnia moderatur, ubique praesens, ubique diffusa, cum tanta sit vis ac potestas mentis humanae intra mortale corpus in-clusae, ut ne saeptis quidem gravis huius ac pigri corporis, cum quo inligata est, coerceri ullo modo possit quominus sibi liberam vagandi facultatem quietis impatiens largiatur ? '

κέλευσόν σου τῇ ψυχῇ εἰς ἣν δὴ (δὲ MSS.) καὶ ⟨βούλει γῆν⟩ πορευ-θῆναι. By ψυχή is here meant the νοερὰ ψυχή or νοῦς. The word ἐκεῖσε, which is substituted for εἰς ἣν δὴ καί in Turn., must have come from the following ἐκεῖ. We need γῆν to contrast with ὠκεανόν.

The reflection that a man can send his thought, or transfer himself in thought, to any place at will, occurs in Homer; and the 'swift-ness' of thought was already proverbial in Homeric times. *Il.* 15. 80 : ὡς δ' ὅτ' ἂν ἀΐξῃ νόος ἀνέρος, ὅς τ' ἐπὶ πολλὴν | γαῖαν ἐληλουθὼς φρεσὶ πευκαλίμῃσι νοήσῃ | "ἔνθ' εἴην ἢ ἔνθα", . . . | ὡς κραιπνῶς μεμαυῖα διέπτατο ποτνία Ἥρη. *Od.* 7. 36 : τῶν νέες ὠκεῖαι ὡσεὶ πτερὸν ἠὲ νόημα. *Hymn. Apoll.* 186 (*Pyth.* 8): ἔνθεν δὲ πρὸς Ὄλυμπον ἀπὸ χθονός, ὥς τε νόημα, | εἶσι Διὸς πρὸς δῶμα. Compare the saying ascribed to Thales in Diog. Laert. 1. 35 : τάχιστον νοῦς· διὰ παντὸς γὰρ τρέχει. *Ascl. Lat.* I. 6 a : ' omnia illi licent (i. e. omnia acumine mentis adire homini licet); . . . omnia idem est, et ubique idem est.' Also *Corp.* X. 25.

οὐ τὸ τοῦ ἡλίου πῦρ, [οὐχ ὁ αἰθήρ,] οὐχ ἡ ⟨τῶν ἀστέρων⟩ δίνη. The solar sphere is a region of burning heat; cf. πῦρ δὲ οὐδαμοῦ κ.τ.λ. in § 7. If we retain οὐχ ὁ αἰθήρ, we must understand the αἰθήρ to be an element distinct from πῦρ, and situated above the region of fire ; and it must in that case be presumed that the writer borrowed the notion of αἰθήρ as a distinct element from the Aristotelians. But the view that αἰθήρ in that sense is limited to the region above the solar sphere does not, as far as I know, occur elsewhere ; and it seems most likely that the words οὐχ ὁ αἰθήρ have been inserted by a later hand. The δίνη cannot be the movement of the outermost sphere, or that of the fixed stars ; for we are told that τὸ ἔσχατον σῶμα is not reached until the δίνη has been passed. It must therefore be the movement of the planet-spheres ; and τῶν ἀστέρων is needed to give it that meaning.

[οὐχὶ τὰ τῶν ἄλλων ἀστέρων σώματα.] This cannot be right. σώματα does not correspond satisfactorily with πῦρ and δίνη ; and the chance of colliding with ' the body ' of one of the six ' other planets ' in the course of the imaginary ascent is too small to be worth mentioning. But it is necessary for the ascending mind to pass through the δίνη of the planets, i. e. the revolving spheres to which they are affixed.

αὐτὸ (τὸ) ὅλον διαρρήξασθαι· ' to break your way out of the material universe ' ; i. e. to break through the outermost sphere, and pass out into extracosmic space. Cf. Lucr. 1. 73 (of Epicurus) : ' ergo vivida vis animi pervicit, et extra | processit longe flammantia moenia mundi, | atque omne immensum peragravit mente animoque.' In *Corp.* I. 13 b, we are told that the Archanthropos ἠβουλήθη ἀναρρῆξαι τὴν περιφέρειαν τῶν κύκλων κ.τ.λ. ; i. e. he broke a passage for himself downward through the sky.

τὰ ἐκτός, εἴ γέ τι ἐκτὸς τοῦ κόσμου. Cf. *Corp.* IV. 5 : τὰ ἐν οὐρανῷ, καὶ εἴ τι ἐστιν ὑπὲρ οὐρανόν. *Ascl. Lat.* III. 33 a : ' quod dicitur extra mundum, si tamen est aliquid.' In *Ascl. Lat.* III, we are told that the extracosmic space is ' plenum intellegibilium rerum ' (πλῆρες νοητῶν).

§ 20 a. τοῦτον οὖν τὸν τρόπον νόησον τὸν θεόν, ὥσπερ νοήματα, πάντα ἐν ἑαυτῷ ἔχειν. The emphasis is on τοῦτον τὸν τρόπον, ὥσπερ νοήματα. When it is said that ' all things are in God ', the meaning of the statement is that all things are thought by God, or are God's thoughts.[1]

Most of the later Platonists regarded τὰ νοητὰ εἴδη as τοῦ θεοῦ νοήματα (see e. g. Albinus, *Epitome*, 9 : ἡ ἰδέα, ὡς μὲν πρὸς τὸν θεόν,

---

[1] Cf. W. James, *Pragmatism*, p. 145 : ' The great monistic *Denkmittel* for a hundred years past has been the notion of *the one Knower*. The many exist only as objects for his thought—exist in his dream, as it were.'

νόησις αὐτοῦ κ.τ.λ.); but the Platonists in general, whether they spoke of τὰ νοητά as existing independently of God or as existing in God's thought, sharply distinguished τὰ νοητά from τὰ αἰσθητά, and did not say that the latter are τοῦ θεοῦ νοήματα. The position of the writer of XI. ii appears to be somewhat different. He seems here to imply that the concrete and spatially extended world in all its detail exists in and is constituted by God's thought. A Platonist of the usual type might have said that God 'contains in himself', as his thought, a νοητὸς κόσμος which exists apart from the αἰσθητὸς κόσμος, and is the παράδειγμα of the latter; but this writer recognizes only one Kosmos, and not two; he says simply that God 'contains in himself, as his thought, *the universe*'. It is not quite clear, however, how this is to be reconciled with the statement in § 18, τὰ (ἐν τῷ ἀσωμάτῳ—i. e. ἐν τῷ νῷ) κείμενα κίνησιν οὐκ ἔχει. In that passage, the 'things situated in the incorporeal' seem to be νοητά in the ordinary Platonic sense, and to be distinguished as such from the contents of the αἰσθητὸς κόσμος, which are κινητά. Perhaps the writer's meaning might be expressed by saying that the Kosmos exists in God's mind, but exists there ἄνευ ὕλης, and consequently without spatial extension or movement. The Kosmos and all things in it are composed of ὕλη and ψυχή; but ὕλη, apart from ψυχή, has a merely potential existence. It is in virtue of their ψυχή (i. e. as ζῶντα) that things actually exist; and it is the ψυχή, i. e. the *life* of things, that God 'contains in himself as his thought'.

We were told before, in §§ 8 b–14 a, that God 'makes' all things (i. e. puts life into them); we are here told that God 'thinks' all things. The writer does not bring these two propositions into connexion; but they might be combined by saying that it is God's νόησις that makes things live, or that God generates life in things by thinking them. In *Corp.* X. 2, a different term is used; we are there told that it is God's 'will' (θέλησις, not νόησις,) that constitutes the existence of all things.

τὸν κόσμον, ἑαυτόν, ⟨τὸ⟩ ὅλον. The term τὸ ὅλον, which was used above to signify the material universe, has here a wider meaning, and includes both God and the Kosmos. God not only 'thinks himself', as Aristotle said, but 'thinks the Kosmos' also.

§§ 20 b, 21 a. ἐὰν οὖν μὴ σεαυτὸν ἐξισάσῃς τῷ θεῷ, . . . φιλοσώματος ὢν καὶ κακός. This paragraph contains the lesson which it is the writer's object to impress upon his readers, and to which all that has preceded is preparatory. The good of man is τὸ τὸν θεὸν νοῆσαι (§ 20 b), or τὸ τὸν θεὸν γνῶναι (§ 21 b), that is, to 'know' God, and in knowing him, to become one with him. How is a man to attain to that supreme good? The writer of XI. ii here gives his answer to that question. Spread yourself over all space and all time; expand your notion of 'yourself' till it includes the whole universe; identify yourself in thought and feeling with all living beings in all times and places, and regard the life of each and all as your own life; then you will 'know' God, for you will be as God is. The state of consciousness described is that of the man who is 'born again' in *Corp*. XIII. 11 b : ἐν οὐρανῷ εἰμί, ἐν γῇ, ἐν ὕδατι, ἐν ἀέρι· ἐν ζῴοις εἰμί, ἐν φυτοῖς· ἐν γαστρί, πρὸ γαστρός, μετὰ γαστέρα· πανταχοῦ ⟨πάρειμι⟩. And he who can speak thus θεὸς πέφυκεν, *ib*. 14. In *Corp*. XIII, these phrases are perhaps traditional, and it may be doubted whether the writer of that document fully realized their meaning. But the author of XI. ii seems to be speaking of a state of mind known to him by personal experience. He knows that it is possible to 'leap clear of all body' and 'expand oneself to the measureless magnitude' of Him who is everywhere,—to 'rise above all time' and 'become eternal',—because he himself, in some sense and in some degree, has done so.

Many people in other times and countries have had a like experience. Numerous parallels are to be found in W. James, *Varieties of religious experience*,[1] and in W. R. Inge, *Christian mysticism*, Lectures 7 and 8, 'on Nature-mysticism'. To the instances there given may be added R. Jefferies, *The story of my heart*, p. 8 ff. : 'Having drunk deeply of the heaven above, and felt the most glorious beauty of the day, . . . I now became lost, and absorbed into the being or existence of the universe. I felt down deep into the earth under, and high above into the sky, and farther still into the sun and stars, still farther beyond the stars into the hollow of space, and losing thus my separateness of being, came to seem like a part of the whole. . . . I came to feel the long-drawn life of the earth back into the dimmest past. . . . From all the ages my soul desired to take that soul-life which had flowed through them. . . . I prayed . . . that I might take from all their energy, grandeur, and beauty, and gather it into me. . . . (I prayed) that

---

[1] See R. W. Trine, quoted by James, p. 101 : Leuba, *ib*. p. 247; Tennyson, *ib*. p. 384; Anon., *ib*. p. 394; Amiel, *ib*. p. 395; Malwida von Meysenberg, *ib*. p. 395; R. M. Bucke, *ib*. p. 398; Vivekananda, *ib*. p. 400.

I might have the deepest of soul-life, the deepest of all, deeper far than all this greatness of the visible universe and even of the invisible. . . . The same prayer comes to me at this very hour. It is now less solely associated with (outward things). . . . It is always with me. I am it.' *Ib.* p. 38 : 'I cannot understand time. It is eternity now. I am in the midst of it. . . . Nothing has to come ; it is now. . . . To the soul there is no past and no future ; all is and will be ever, in now. . . . There may be time for the clock, there is none for me. . . . My soul has never been, and never can be, dipped in time.' E. Carpenter, *The art of creation*, p. 230 : 'The true and ultimate Self therefore in each of us is universal and common to all beings, and yet it is also individual and specialized in a certain direction. When the more universal nature of the Self descends and becomes revealed, the consciousness of the individual necessarily takes certain forms corresponding.—One of these is Love and Sympathy. The self, hitherto deeming itself a separate atom, suddenly becomes aware of its inner unity with these other human beings, animals, plants even. It is as if a veil had been drawn aside. A deep understanding, knowledge, flows in. Love takes the place of ignorance and blindness ; and to wound another is to wound oneself. It is the great deliverance from the prison-life of the separate self,[1] and comes to the latter sometimes with the force and swiftness of a revelation.—Another form is Faith, Courage, Confidence. If I have my home in these other bodies as well as my own, if my life is indeed so wide-reaching, so universal, if I *feel* that it is so, what is there to fear, how can I fear?[2] All things are given into my hands.[3] My life checked here may flow on there ; innumerable are my weapons, my resources ; and rooted down, deep, below all accidents, is my real being.—Or again a strange sense of Extension[4] comes on me, and of presence in distant space and time. Mine is an endless Life, unconquerable, limitless in subtlety and expanse ; and strange intimations that it is so come to me even in my tiny earth-cell,—intimations of power inexhaustible, of knowledge mysterious and unbounded, and of far presence through all forms and ranges of being.—These are some of . . . the new modes of consciousness that come. . . . Let them be *felt* first.

---

[1] Cf. *Corp.* XI. ii. 21 a : ἐὰν δὲ κατακλείσῃς σου τὴν ψυχὴν ἐν τῷ σώματι.
[2] XI. ii. 21 a : ἐὰν εἴπῃς "φοβοῦμαι γῆν καὶ θάλασσαν" κ.τ.λ.
[3] XI. ii. 20 b : μηδὲν ἀδύνατον σεαυτῷ ὑπόστησαι.
[4] XI. ii. 20 b : συναύξησον σεαυτὸν τῷ ἀμετρήτῳ μεγέθει κ.τ.λ.

Do not *think* too much about them. When you have merged your being, if it be but for a moment, in its source, then inevitably on emerging (if union has really been effected) will one or other of these feelings that I have mentioned be found occupying your mind."[1]

When the teacher bids his pupil πάντα ὁμοῦ νοεῖν, he is not bidding him merely to 'think of' things, or to form concepts of them; the νόησις of which he speaks is rather what Bergson calls 'intuition', as opposed to 'analysis'.[2] To 'think' things, in the sense in which the term is here used, is to identify oneself with them, or include them in one's own being.

The notion of 'expanding oneself to the magnitude of the All' is expressed by Plotinus in language partly similar to that of the Hermetist. Plot. 6. 5. 7 : ἀνάγεται γὰρ καὶ τὸ ἡμέτερον καὶ ἡμεῖς εἰς τὸ ὄν, . . . καὶ νοοῦμεν ἐκεῖνα, οὐκ εἴδωλα αὐτῶν οὐδὲ τύπους ἔχοντες,[3] εἰ δὲ μὴ τοῦτο, ὄντες ἐκεῖνα.[4] εἰ οὖν ἀληθινῆς ἐπιστήμης μετέχομεν, ἐκεῖνα ἐσμέν. . . . ὄντων δὲ καὶ τῶν ἄλλων, οὐ μόνον ἡμῶν, ἐκεῖνα,[5] πάντες ἐσμὲν ἐκεῖνα· πάντα[6] ἄρα ἐσμὲν ἕν. ἔξω μὲν οὖν ὁρῶντες ἢ ὅθεν ἐξήμμεθα, ἀγνοοῦμεν ἓν ὄντες, οἷον πρόσωπα πολλὰ εἰς τὸ ἔξω, κορυφὴν ἔχοντα εἰς τὸ εἴσω μίαν. εἰ δέ τις ἐπιστραφῆναι[7] δύναιτο, . . . θεόν τε καὶ αὐτὸν καὶ τὸ πᾶν ὄψεται. ὄψεται δέ, τὰ μὲν πρῶτα, οὐχ ὡς ⟨αὐτὸς ὤν⟩ τὸ πᾶν· εἶτ᾽, οὐκ ἔχων ὅπη αὐτὸν στήσας ὁριεῖται μέχρι τίνος αὐτός ἐστιν,[8] ἀφεὶς περιγράφειν ἀπὸ τοῦ ὄντος ἄπαντος αὐτόν, εἰς ἄπαν τὸ πᾶν ἥξει, προελθὼν οὐδαμοῦ, ἀλλ᾽ αὐτοῦ μείνας οὗ ἵδρυται τὸ πᾶν. *Ib.* 6. 5. 12 : ⟨τῷ⟩ παντὶ προσῆλθες, καὶ οὐκ ἔμεινας ἐν μέρει αὐτοῦ, οὐδ᾽ εἶπας

[1] A state of mind which has some resemblance to the 'self-expansion' of *Corp.* XI. ii is described in a lighter tone by A. Daudet, *Lettres de mon moulin* : 'J'y restais presque tout le jour dans cette espèce de stupeur et d'accablement délicieux que donne la contemplation de la mer. Vous connaissez, n'est-ce pas, cette jolie griserie de l'âme? On ne pense pas, on ne rêve pas non plus. Tout votre être vous échappe, s'envole, s'éparpille. On est la mouette qui plonge, la poussière d'écume qui flotte au soleil entre deux vagues, la fumée blanche de ce paquebot qui s'éloigne, ce petit corailleur à voile rouge, cette perle d'eau, ce flocon de brume, tout excepté soi-même.'

[2] Bergson, *Introduction to metaphysics*, Eng. tr. 1913, p. 6 : to have *intuition* of a thing means ' possessing a reality absolutely instead of knowing it relatively,—placing oneself within it instead of looking at it from outside points of view'. (When Wordsworth's Peter Bell looked at the ' primrose by the river's brim ', his mind presumably worked only by 'analysis', and not by 'intuition'.)

[3] I. e. not merely having within us 'images' or 'impressions' of things which are outside of us.

[4] Aristotle said (*De an.* 3. 4) that ἐπὶ τῶν ἄνευ ὕλης τὸ αὐτό ἐστι τὸ νοοῦν καὶ τὸ νοούμενον.

[5] ' Since not only I, but all others also are identical with those objects.'

[6] Perhaps πάντες ?

[7] This ἐπιστροφή corresponds to τὸ συναυξῆσαι ἑαυτὸν τῷ ἀμετρήτῳ μεγέθει in *Corp.* XI. ii. 20 b, and to the παλιγγενεσία of *Corp.* XIII.

[8] He cannot find any fixed limit by which his personality is bounded.

οὐδὲ σὺ "τοσοῦτός εἰμι ". ¹ ἀφεὶς δὲ ⟨τὸ⟩ τοσοῦτον, γέγονας πᾶς. καίτοι καὶ πρότερον ἦσθα πᾶς· ἀλλ', ὅτι καὶ ἄλλο τι προσῆν σοι μετὰ τὸ πᾶν, ἐλάττων ἐγίνου τῇ ⟨⟨ἐκ τοῦ μὴ ὄντος⟩⟩ προσθήκῃ· ² οὐ γὰρ ἐκ τοῦ ὄντος ἦν ἡ προσθήκη,—οὐδὲν γὰρ ἐκείνῳ προσθήσεις,—ἀλλὰ τοῦ μὴ ὄντος. γενόμενος δέ τις,³ [καὶ] [[ἐκ τοῦ μὴ ὄντος]] (a man) ἐστιν οὐ πᾶς· ἀλλ' (ἔσται πᾶς) ὅταν τὸ μὴ ὂν ἀφῇ.⁴ αὔξεις τοίνυν σεαυτὸν ἀφεὶς τὰ ἄλλα· καὶ πάρεστί σοι τὸ πᾶν (τὰ ἄλλα) ἀφέντι, μετὰ δὲ ἄλλων ὄντι οὐ φαίνεται (παρεῖναι τὸ πᾶν). The All was really present to you all the time, but you were unconscious of its presence. You had not 'departed from' it, for that is impossible; ἀλλὰ παρὼν (τῷ παντί), ἐπὶ τὰ ἐναντία ἐστράφης.

Cf. Proclus *In Remp.* 121. 32 : διὸ καὶ τὰ λόγια (i. e. the *Oracula Chaldaica*) παρακελεύεται πλατύνειν ἡμῖν διὰ τῆς ἀπολύτου ζωῆς (i. e. by detachment from the body) ἑαυτούς, ἀλλὰ μὴ ἀποστενοῦν, " πνιγμὸν ἔρωτος ἀληθοῦς " ἐφελκομένους ἀντὶ τῆς εἰς τὰ ὅλα ἀνατάσεως.

§ 20 b. τὸ γὰρ ὅμοιον τῷ ὁμοίῳ νοητόν. (I have altered τῶν ὁμοίων into τῷ ὁμοίῳ.) Cf. Sext. Emp. *Math.* 7. 116 : παλαιὰ . . . δόξα περὶ τοῦ τὰ ὅμοια τῶν ὁμοίων εἶναι γνωριστικά. Philolaus, as reported *ib.* 7. 92 : ὑπὸ τοῦ ὁμοίου τὸ ὅμοιον καταλαμβάνεσθαι πέφυκεν. Ar. *Metaph.* B. 4, 1000 b 5 : ἡ δὲ γνῶσις τοῦ ὁμοίου τῷ ὁμοίῳ.

πάντα χρόνον ὑπεράρας αἰών⟨ιος⟩ γενοῦ. Eternity is here contrasted with time, as in Pl. *Tim.* The meaning must be 'become eternal'. But to express this meaning, an adjective is needed. The substantive αἰών would hardly serve the purpose; neither the use of αἰών as a name or epithet of a god,⁵ nor its use in XI. i to signify the hypostatized δύναμις or ἐνέργεια of God, would justify its employment in the sense here required. But a transcriber who was not aware that XI. i and XI. ii were two different documents might easily be led to substitute αἰών for αἰώνιος, in consequence of the prominence of αἰών in XI. i. I have therefore written αἰώνιος.

σεαυτὸν ἥγησαι ἀθάνατον, καὶ πάντα δυνάμενον νοῆσαι, πᾶσαν μὲν τέχνην, πᾶσαν δὲ ἐπιστήμην. ' Art is long, and life is short ', said

---

¹ I. e. you have not set a limit to the extent of your *self.*

² The μὴ ὄν is ὕλη. A material body has been added to you, and you have become smaller by the addition. As the Hermetist expresses it, your soul has been 'shut up in the body '.

³ I. e. having become a separate individual person (by the narrowing or separating influence of the body).

⁴ I. e. ὅταν τὴν ὕλην or τὸ ὑλικὸν σῶμα ἀφῇ.

⁵ As αἰών (understood as meaning ἀεὶ ὤν) seems to have been sometimes used as a synonym for θεός (see note on *Ascl. Lat.* III. 26 b–32 a), it would perhaps be possible to take αἰὼν γενοῦ as equivalent to θεὸς γενοῦ. But no instance of that use of αἰών occurs elsewhere in the *Hermetica.*

Hippocrates. You must reject this limitation of man's power to get knowledge. What matter if the *ego* whose life is bound up with this perishable body has but a few years to learn in? That narrowly restricted *ego* is not your true self. Realize that you are one with all that lives, and that all life is *your* life ; then you will be actually, what you already are potentially, ἀθάνατος and αἰώνιος.[1]

παντὸς ζῴου ἤθη (ἦθος MSS.) ⟨. . .⟩. A verb in the imperative ('find your home in') must have been lost. The word ἤθη in the sense of the 'haunts' of animals is frequent in all periods ; but I have found no instance of ἦθος, singular, in this sense. It must be remembered that ζῷον includes every kind of corporeal and animated being, from a star-god to an insect.

[πυρός, ὕδατος,] ⟨θερμοῦ καὶ ψυχροῦ,⟩ ξηροῦ καὶ ὑγροῦ. Fire and water are not ποιότητες ; and the words πυρός, ὕδατος are probably a gloss, which has been substituted for θερμοῦ καὶ ψυχροῦ. The meaning is 'identify yourself simultaneously with all parts of the universe'.

τὰ μετὰ τὸν θάνατον. The text may be sound, though the grammar is confused. With this phrase we must supply νόησον alone, and not νοῆσον εἶναι, which the preceding words require.

'The things after death' are left undescribed ; this writer has nothing to say about the destiny of the individual soul when disembodied. To one who has learnt to 'contemplate all time and all existence', and to identify himself with all that he contemplates, the question what will become of *him*, as an individual person, after the dissolution of the body, would be negligible, if not unmeaning.

---

[1] The thought agrees in part with that of Browning in *A Grammarian's Funeral* : 'Let me know all! . . . Others mistrust, and say—" But time escapes! Live now or never!"' He said, "What's time? Leave Now for dogs and apes! Man has Forever."' And he who says this 'throws himself on God, and unperplexed Seeking shall find him'. But the Hermetist is not here thinking, as Browning presumably was, of a continuance of the man's individual and separate personality beyond the grave ; and perhaps his attitude may better be compared with that of Shelley in *Adonais* : 'Dust to the dust! but the pure spirit shall flow Back to the burning fountain whence it came, A portion of the Eternal, which must glow Through time and change, unquenchably the same. . . . He lives, he wakes —'tis Death is dead, not he. . . . He is made one with Nature : there is heard His voice in all her music, from the moan Of thunder, to the song of night's sweet bird ; He is a presence to be felt and known In darkness and in light, from herb and stone, Spreading itself where'er that Power may move Which has withdrawn his being to its own : Which wields the world with never-wearied love, Sustains it from beneath, and kindles it above.' Shelley is speaking of one who has ceased to live in the body ; but the Hermetist holds that even in this life a man may, if he will, become one with 'the Power which wields the world', and so 'become eternal'.

πράγματα, ποιότητας, ποσότητας. Here πράγματα means οὐσίας or ὑποκείμενα, the 'substances' in which qualities and magnitudes inhere. The use of these terms in a document in which the technical language of philosophy is deliberately avoided shows that by this time a scheme of categories based on those of Aristotle and the Stoics had passed into popular usage.

§ 21 a. ἐὰν δὲ κατακλείσῃς σου τὴν ψυχὴν ἐν τῷ σώματι. Cf. Philo *Quis rer. div. heres* 14. 68, Wendland III, p. 16 : τίς οὖν γενήσεται κληρονόμος; οὐχ ὁ μένων ἐν τῇ τοῦ σώματος εἱρκτῇ [λογισμὸς] καθ' ἑκούσιον γνώμην, ἀλλ' ὁ λυθεὶς τῶν δεσμῶν καὶ ἐλευθερωθεὶς καὶ ἔξω τειχῶν προεληλυθώς, καὶ καταλελοιπώς, εἰ οἷόν τε τοῦτο εἰπεῖν, αὐτὸς ἑαυτόν.

If you 'shut your soul up in your body', you have nothing in common with God, and cannot 'know' God, or have that intuition of him which would make you one with him. There is no Greek word equivalent to 'person' or 'personality'; but σῶμα, in such a connexion as this, serves to express the notion of the separate and isolated *ego*. To 'shut one's soul up in one's body' means to shut oneself up in one's separate personality,[1] and to be concerned solely about one's petty personal interests. The body (or τὸ αἰσθητικόν, which has its root in the body,) is that which isolates the individual man ; it is through embodiment that the human soul is individualized, and severed from 'the soul of the All' (*Corp.* X. 7). The body exists only at one particular place and time ; and as long as a man limits himself to his body, he is tethered to that one place and that one time. Such a man is interested in things only as they affect him through his body, i. e. only so far as they are or may be productive of pleasure or pain to him through his bodily senses. He is φιλοσώματος ; that is to say, he is φίλαυτος in the bad sense of that ambiguous term ; he is 'self-seeking'. For him, the universe is centred in his separate and narrowly limited *ego*; and his life is consequently filled with selfish anxieties. He is afraid of everything around him (φοβεῖται γῆν καὶ θάλασσαν), because he thinks

---

[1] John Smith, the 'Cambridge Platonist', speaks with similar contempt of 'a soul confined within the private and narrow cell of its own particular being'. (Inge, *Christian Mysticism*, p. 292.)

Something like this was already taught by Heraclitus, who seems to have held that it is the earthy element in man that separates him from the universal soul, and so causes delusion and moral evil (O. Gilbert, *Griechische Religionsphilosophie*, pp. 77–79). Compare Apollonius Tyaneus, *Ep.* 58, quoted in note on *Corp.* VIII. 1 b.

of things only as affecting his own private interests; he is always asking with a shudder 'what is going to happen to *me*?'

On the subject of separate personality, and the meaning of 'self-expansion', see Inge, *Personal idealism and mysticism*, ch. 4, 'The problem of personality'.

§ 21 b. ἡ γὰρ τελεία κακία τὸ ἀγνοεῖν τὸν θεόν (τὸ θεῖον MSS.). Cf. *Corp.* X. 8 b, 9 : κακία δὲ ψυχῆς ἀγνωσία. . . . ἀρετὴ ψυχῆς γνῶσις.

ὁδός ἐστιν εὐθὺ τοῦ ἀγαθοῦ φέρουσα.—(ὁ. ἐ. εὐθεῖα, ἰδία τ. ἀ. φ. MSS.) Probably ῥᾳδία was inserted here by error from the following clause, and ευθυραιδια was changed into ευθειαιδια. To know God is the good; therefore, if a man is capable of knowing God, and wills and hopes to do so, he is on the way which leads to the good. The pupil has not yet attained to *gnosis*, but he is starting on the way to it.

πανταχοῦ συναντήσει ⟨⟨σοι⟩⟩ ⟨ὁ θεός⟩. In everything which meets your eyes, God will manifest himself to you; for wherever there is life, there God is at work. Cf. Philo *De fuga et invent.* 25. 141, Wendland III, p. 140 : ἡ δὲ τοῦ . . . θεοῦ ζήτησις εὐφραίνει μὲν εὐθὺς ἰόντας ἐπὶ τὴν σκέψιν, ἀτελὴς δ' οὐ γίνεται, προϋπαντῶντος (τοῦ θεοῦ) . . . καὶ ἐπιδεικνυμένου ἑαυτὸν τοῖς γλιχομένοις ἰδεῖν, οὐχ οἷός ἐστιν, ἀμήχανον γάρ . . ., ἀλλ' ὡς ἐνεχώρει γενητὴν φύσιν τῇ ἀπερινοήτῳ δυνάμει προσβαλεῖν.[1] 'Ophite *Eva-evangelium*' (Reitzenstein *Poim.* p. 242) : I heard a voice like thunder, which spoke to me and said ἐγὼ σὺ καὶ σὺ ἐγώ, καὶ ὅπου ἐὰν ᾖς, ἐγὼ ἐκεῖ εἰμι, καὶ ἐν ἅπασίν εἰμι ἐσπαρμένος, καὶ ὅθεν ἐὰν θέλῃς συλλέγεις με, ἐμὲ δὲ συλλέγων ἑαυτὸν συλλέγεις.

οὐδὲν γάρ ἐστιν ὁ οὐκ ἔστιν [εἰκόνι] ⟨ἐκεῖνος⟩. It would also be possible to write ἐν ᾧ οὐκ ἔστιν ἐκεῖνος, or ὁ οὐκ ἔστιν ἐν ἐκείνῳ (cf. § 20 a, τὸν θεὸν . . . πάντα ἐν ἑαυτῷ ἔχειν). Perhaps εἰκόνι may have come from εἰκὼν ⟨ἐκείνου⟩; the words εἰκών εἶτα φῄς might easily be altered into εἰκόνι ταφῆς, the reading of codd. Corp.

§ 22 a. εἶτα φῄς "ἀόρατος ὁ θεός"; Platonists commonly said that God is ἀόρατος; in saying that God is ὅρατος, the writer is asserting a paradox. Cf. *Corp.* V *tit.*: Ὅτι ⟨πῇ μὲν?⟩ ἀφανὴς ⟨ὁ⟩ θεός, ⟨πῇ δὲ?⟩ φανερώτατός ἐστι. *Corp.* XIV. 3 as emended : ἐπεὶ δὲ τὰ γεννητὰ ὁρώμενά ἐστι, κἀκεῖνος δὴ ὁρατός· διὰ τοῦτο γὰρ ποιεῖ, ἵνα ὅρατος ᾖ.

---

[1] Cf. Martineau, quoted by James, *Varieties of religious experience*, p. 475 : 'If we cannot find God in your house or in mine, upon the roadside or the margin of the sea, in the bursting seed or opening flower; . . . in the procession of life ever entering afresh, and solemnly passing by and dropping off; I do not think we should discern him any more on the grass of Eden, or beneath the moonlight of Gethsemane.' The 'procession of life' is the μεταβολή of *Corp.* XI. ii.

⟨ὁ⟩ νοῦς ὁρᾶται ἐν τῷ νοεῖν, ὁ θεὸς ἐν τῷ ποιεῖν. ὁ νοῦς here means
'one's own mind'. Neither ὁ νοῦς nor ὁ θεός is 'visible' in the
literal sense of the word; but both are 'visible' in the sense that
we can apprehend them through their working. My mind, as
a substance, is hidden from me; but I am conscious of my thoughts,
which are the workings of my mind, and in that way I can 'see'
my mind. Similarly, God, as a substance, is hidden from me;
but I see his workings around me, and feel them within me, and
thereby I can 'see' God. In the view of this writer, God is the
universal νοῦς, ('the one Knower', as W. James expresses it,) and
πάντα τὰ ὄντα are his νοήματα (§ 20 a).

§ 22 b. ταῦτά σοι ἐπὶ τοσοῦτον πεφανέρωται. The teacher refers back
to the words of the pupil in § 1 b: σοὶ γὰρ ἂν καὶ μόνῳ πιστεύσαιμι
τὴν περὶ τούτου φανέρωσιν.

τὰ δὲ ἄλλα πάντα ὁμοίως κατὰ σεαυτὸν νόει. Having once been
started on the right track, the pupil will be able to think things
out for himself. Cf. Corp. IX. 10: ὁ δὲ νοῦς (the pupil's mind),
. . . ὑπὸ τοῦ λόγου (the teacher's words) μέχρι τινὸς ὁδηγηθείς, φθάνει
μέχρι τῆς ἀληθείας. Corp. XIII. 15: ὁ Ποιμάνδρης . . . πλέον μοι
. . . οὐ παρέδωκεν, εἰδὼς ὅτι ἀπ' ἐμαυτοῦ δυνήσομαι πάντα νοεῖν.

LIBELLVS XII. i

It is evident that Corp. XII consists of two distinct documents,
which I call XII. i and XII. ii. We may suppose that XII. ii stood
next after XII. i in a collection of 'discourses of Hermes to Tat',
and that the two documents came to be read as one, in consequence of the disappearance of the title of the second. The
contents of XII. i, which ends at § 14 a, are summed up in § 6:
'We are now concerned with mind; and the questions we have
to consider are these:—what mind can do, and how it admits of
differences; . . . for not in all men does it quench angry passion
and desire.' This document then might be described as περὶ νοῦ
ἀνθρωπίνου, 'concerning mind in man'. The beginning of XII. ii
is lost; but what remains of it (§§ 14 b–23 b) might be described as
περὶ ζωῆς. It has nothing to do with νοῦς, and is in no way connected with the teaching of XII. 1.

Contents

Mind is of the very substance of God. It is diffused by God, as light is diffused by the sun. It enters into men, and makes some of them divine; but the souls of beasts are devoid of it. In men, mind works good, by counteracting their natural impulses; but in beasts, it 'co-operates with'(?) the natural impulses. The human soul, when embodied, is depraved by the evil influence of pleasure; mind heals this disease of the soul by means of medicinal pain. But those men in whose souls mind does not bear rule are like the beasts; they indulge their appetites without restraint, and thereby incur the worst of evils, and suffer the punishment ordained for them by God. §§ 1–4.

But are not men compelled by Fate to do evil deeds? And if so, how can they justly be punished for these deeds? The answer to this question is that it is only 'irrational' men (i. e. those men whose souls are not governed by mind) that are compelled by Fate to do wicked deeds; ⟨and such men deserve the punishment which follows, because it is their own fault that they have rejected the guidance of mind, and by doing so, have put themselves under the dominion of Fate.⟩ The rational man and the irrational alike are subject to Fate in respect of what befalls their bodies; ⟨e. g. both alike must suffer death;⟩ but the rational man is not subject to Fate in respect of his actions; Fate cannot compel him to commit a crime. Mind is superior to Fate, and has power to place above the reach of Fate the human soul in which it resides. §§ 5–9.

Is mind liable to 'passive affections' ($\pi\acute{a}\theta\eta$)? All things which enter into body are passively affected; mind therefore, when it is embodied (i. e. when it resides in a man's soul during his earthly life), is passively affected; but it ceases to be passively affected when it is freed from the body. §§ 10, 11.

Men are distinguished from beasts by the possession of mind and speech. If a man rightly uses these two gifts of God, he is almost an equal of the gods in this life, and after death he will dwell among the gods. The beasts do not possess speech; and among men, though languages differ, speech is one and the same in all nations. Speech is an image of mind; and mind is an image of God. §§ 12, 13a.

Soul is in body, mind is in soul, and God is in mind. As air is finer than gross matter, so soul is finer than air, mind than soul, and God than mind. God acts on all things; mind acts on soul, soul acts on air, and air acts on gross matter. §§ 13 b, 14 a.

Sources. The doctrine of XII. i is mainly Platonic; but it shows signs of Stoic influence. The writer's conception of νοῦς, and of the function of νοῦς in the human soul, is Platonic. His account of the effect of embodiment on a previously unembodied human soul (§ 2, ψυχὴ . . . ἐν σώματι γενομένη . . . κακίζεται) is derived from Plato (cf. Pl. *Tim.* 42 A); and his description of vice as disease of the soul (§ 3) may have been suggested by Pl. *Tim.* 86 B. He follows Plato in coupling θυμός and ἐπιθυμία (§ 4 and § 6). His notion of νοῦς παθητός (§§ 10, 11) may perhaps have been suggested by the Aristotelian doctrine of ὁ παθητικὸς νοῦς. The influence of Stoicism is to be seen in the discussion of εἱμαρμένη (§§ 5–9); in the sentence τῆς μὲν ὕλης τὸ λεπτομερέστατον . . . θεός (§ 14 a); and perhaps in the meaning given to the word οὐσία (§ 1). The term ὁ προφορικὸς λόγος (§ 12) is of Stoic origin; but the clause in which it occurs is probably an interpolation. The ἀήρ of § 14 a corresponds to the πνεῦμα of the Stoics; but I do not know from what source the Hermetist derived this use of ἀήρ.

The writer quotes three sayings from Hermetic dialogues in which the part of teacher was assigned to the Agathos Daimon; and one of these sayings (§ 1, τοὺς μὲν θεοὺς ἀνθρώπους εἶπεν ἀθανάτους κ.τ.λ.) is derived from Heraclitus, presumably through Stoic intermediaries. He also refers to an earlier discourse of Hermes to Tat concerning εἱμαρμένη.

It is possible that the writer's use of νόμος in place of δίκη (§§ 4 *fin.* and 9) came from a Jewish source. I can find nothing else of Jewish origin in XII. i: and there is no trace of Christian influence.

Date. The combination of Stoic conceptions with Platonism excludes the possibility of any date earlier than the first century B. C. The discourse referred to in § 5 was probably one of the διεξοδικοὶ λόγοι; and if so, some of the documents known by that name must have been in existence before XII. i was written.

The fact that the writer quotes from dialogues in which the Agathos Daimon gave instruction to Hermes may be taken to indicate that this document is one of the later *Hermetica*; and we may conclude that it was written in the second or third century A. D., and more probably in the third century than in the second.

Title. περὶ νοῦ ⌜κοινοῦ⌝. The epithet κοινοῦ, which yields no satisfactory sense, may be accounted for as a corruption of ἀν̄ίνου, i. e. ἀνθρωπίνου.

§ 1. Ὁ νοῦς ... ἐξ αὐτῆς τῆς τοῦ θεοῦ οὐσίας ἐστίν. What is meant by οὐσία here? In Plato, οὐσία is commonly contrasted with γένεσις, and applied to τὰ νοητά as opposed to τὰ αἰσθητά. Aristotle distinguishes three uses of the word οὐσία, *Metaph.* Z. 3, 1029 a 2 : τρόπον μέν τινα ἡ ὕλη λέγεται (οὐσία), ἄλλον δὲ τρόπον ἡ μορφή (*i. q.* τὸ εἶδος), τρίτον δὲ τὸ ἐκ τούτων (i. e. τὸ σύνθετον ἐξ εἴδους καὶ ὕλης, the concrete individual thing). The Stoics, who did not accept either the Platonic doctrine of νοητά or the Aristotelian doctrine of εἴδη, used the word οὐσία in the first of Aristotle's three senses. To them, the οὐσία of a thing meant the material substance of which the thing consists. The word ἐξ shows that the writer of XII. i, in his use of οὐσία, has been influenced by the Stoic usage. The meaning of his opening sentence is that νοῦς, wherever it presents itself, (e. g. the νοῦς which operates in an individual human soul,) 'comes out of', or is a portion of, the very substance of which God consists. But he is conscious that this statement might seem to imply that God consists of some *material* substance, such as fire (cf. *Corp.* IV. 1 b) ; and in order to guard against this mis-understanding, he adds εἴ γέ τις ἐστιν οὐσία θεοῦ κ.τ.λ. The 'sub-stance of which God consists' is not material; what it is, 'God only knows'. It is the ἀσώματον spoken of in *Corp.* IV ; but what that is, no man can say precisely.

εἴ γέ τις ἐστιν οὐσία θεοῦ. Cf. *Corp.* VI. 4 b as emended : ἡ οὐσία τοῦ θεοῦ, εἴ γε οὐσίαν ἔχει, τὸ καλόν ἐστι καὶ τὸ ἀγαθόν.

οὐκ ἔστιν ἀποτετμημένος τῆς οὐσιότητος τοῦ θεοῦ. When οὐσία, through Aristotelian and Stoic influence, had acquired the meaning of 'a concrete (material or quasi-material) substance', it became necessary to coin the word οὐσιότης to express the abstract notion of 'substantial existence'. The writer hesitates to attribute οὐσία to God, and therefore here prefers to use the abstract term.

ὥσπερ ἡπλωμένος, καθάπερ τὸ τοῦ ἡλίου φῶς. ἡπλωμένος, 'unfolded', is here used in the sense 'spread abroad', 'diffused'. (Perhaps we ought to read ἐξηπλωμένος.) God radiates νοῦς, as the sun radiates light. Cf. *Corp.* II. 12 b. Plotinus 5. 1. 6 (speaking of the generation of νοῦς from the One) : δεῖ οὖν, ἀκινήτου ὄντος (τοῦ ἑνός), εἴ τι δεύτερον μετ' αὐτό, οὐ προσνεύσαντος οὐδὲ βουληθέντος οὐδὲ ὅλως κινηθέντος ὑποστῆναι αὐτό. πῶς οὖν ; ... (δεῖ νοῆσαι) περίλαμψιν ἐξ αὐτοῦ μέν, ἐξ αὐτοῦ δὲ μένοντος, οἷον ἡλίου τὸ περὶ αὐτὸν λαμπρὸν φῶς περιθέον, ἐξ αὐτοῦ ἀεὶ γεννώμενον μένοντος. *Ib.* § 7 : δεῖ πως εἶναι ἐκείνου τὸ γεννώ-μενον, καὶ ἀποσώζειν πολλὰ αὐτοῦ, [καὶ εἶναι ὁμοιότητα πρὸς αὐτόν,] ὥσπερ καὶ τὸ φῶς τοῦ ἡλίου. Plotinus 5. 3. 12 : κατὰ λόγον θησόμεθα τὴν μὲν ἀπ᾽ αὐτοῦ (sc. τοῦ ἑνὸς) οἷον ῥυεῖσαν ἐνέργειαν ὡς ἀπὸ ἡλίου (φῶς). φῶς τι οὖν θησόμεθα καὶ πᾶσαν τὴν νοητὴν φύσιν, αὐτὸν δὲ ἐπ᾽ ἄκρῳ τῷ νοητῷ ἑστηκότα βασιλεύειν ἐπ᾽ αὐτοῦ, οὐκ ἐξώσαντα ἀπ᾽ αὐτοῦ τὸ ἐκφανέν. . . . οὐδὲ γὰρ ἀποτέτμηται τὸ ἀπ᾽ αὐτοῦ, οὐδ᾽ αὖ ταὐτὸν αὐτῷ. Abammonis resp. 8. 2 (Testim.) : the second God (the Demi-urgus-νοῦς) ἀπὸ τοῦ ἑνὸς ἑαυτὸν ἐξέλαμψε.

οὗτος δὲ ὁ νοῦς ἐν μὲν ἀνθρώποις ⌜θεός⌝ ἐστι. The words ἐν μὲν ἀνθρώποις point forward to ἐν δὲ τοῖς ἀλόγοις ζῴοις below. The statement that ʻin men indeed νοῦς is a god' would imply that under other conditions, e. g. when it acts on beasts, νοῦς is not a god. But this cannot be right. Mind operates differently in the case of men and beasts, but must be equally divine in all its different operations; as we have just been told, it is of one substance with God, and is emitted by God. The author's meaning might perhaps be expressed by writing ἐν μὲν ἀνθρώποις θειότητος ἐνεργητικός ἐστι. ʻIn men, mind produces divinity by its working'; i. e. mind makes men divine, but it does not make beasts divine· This would serve to lead on to the following statement, ʻtherefore some men are divine'.

διὸ καί τινες ἀνθρώπων θε⟨ῖ⟩οί εἰσι. A Hermetist might say that ʻsome men are gods'; but if he said this, he could not go on to say that ʻthe humanity of these men is *near to* deity', i. e. that they are nearly gods, but not quite. It is therefore necessary to alter θεοί into θεῖοι.

ὁ Ἀγαθὸς Δαίμων . . . εἶπεν. Three utterances of the Agathos Daimon are quoted by Hermes in XII. 1. (See § 8 and § 13 b.) ʻThe Agathos Daimon' is a name given by Greeks to the Egyptian god Khnum; and the writer assumes that this god was the first teacher of the *gnosis*, and had given oral instruction to Hermes. We know that there were written dialogues in which the Agathos Daimon took the part of teacher; and the writer of XII. i probably found in one or more of those dialogues the three sayings which he attributes to the Agathos Daimon.

τοὺς μὲν θεοὺς ⟨ἀνθρώπους⟩ εἶπεν ἀθανάτους, τοὺς δὲ ἀνθρώπους θεοὺς θνητούς. This is a Stoic adaptation of a saying of Heraclitus. See *Corp.* X. 25.

ἐν δὲ τοῖς ἀλόγοις ζῴοις ⟨. . .⟩ ἡ φύσις ἐστίν. The predicate is lost. Perhaps the Hermetist wrote something like ⟨ἀντὶ νοῦ⟩ ἡ φύσις ἐστίν· ʻin the irrational animals instinct takes the place of mind'.

Cf. *Corp.* IX. 1 b as emended : ἐν γὰρ τοῖς ἄλλοις ζῴοις ἡ αἴσθησις τῇ φύσει ἥνωται, ἐν δὲ ἀνθρώποις τῇ νοήσει.

§ 2. ὅπου γὰρ [ψυχή, ἐκεῖ καὶ νοῦς ἐστιν, ὥσπερ ὅπου καὶ] ζωή, ἐκεῖ καὶ ψυχή ἐστιν. The traditional text cannot be right; for the statement 'wherever there is soul there is mind' is contradicted by the following words, 'in the irrational animals the soul is devoid of mind'. If we cut out ψυχή, ἐκεῖ . . . ὅπου καί, what remains becomes intelligible. There is ψυχή wherever there is ζωή (i. e. in all ζῷα, whether rational or irrational); but in the irrational ζῷα, the ψυχή is devoid of νοῦς. It would be possible to make sense in another way, by writing ὅπου γὰρ ψυχὴ ⟨ἀνθρωπίνη⟩, ἐκεῖ καὶ νοῦς ἐστιν, and cutting out ὥσπερ ὅπου καὶ ζωή, ἐκεῖ καὶ ψυχή ἐστιν. The meaning would then be 'wherever there is a human soul, there is mind; but the souls of irrational animals are devoid of mind'.

ἡ ψυχὴ [ζωή] ἐστι κενὴ τοῦ νοῦ. ζωή seems to have been inserted as an alternative for ψυχή.

ἐργάζεται γὰρ αὐταῖς (αὐτὰς εἰς MSS.) τὸ ἀγαθόν. Beasts cannot attain to the good ; but men can attain to it, through the operation of νοῦς in them.

τοῖς μὲν ἀλόγοις τῇ ⟨ἰ⟩δί⟨ᾳ⟩ ἐκάστου φύσει συνεργεῖ. Cf. § 4 : συνεργὸς γὰρ αὐταῖς γενόμενος κ.τ.λ. § 10 : ἔλεγες γὰρ τὸν νοῦν ἐν τοῖς ἀλόγοις ζῴοις φύσεως δίκην ἐνεργεῖν, συνεργοῦντα αὐτῶν ταῖς ὁρμαῖς. What does the Hermetist mean by saying that νοῦς 'co-operates with' the instincts or impulses of beasts? We were told above that 'in beasts the soul is devoid of νοῦς'; and in § 12, it is said that God has given νοῦς (and λόγος) to man παρὰ πάντα τὰ ἄλλα ζῷα, which implies that νοῦς has not been given to beasts. We might therefore have expected the writer to say that νοῦς does not operate at all in beasts. But he tells us that it does operate in them, though not in the same way that it operates in men, or at least in 'rational' men. (Cf. § 6 : ἐνδιάφορός ἐστιν (ὁ νοῦς), ἐν μὲν ἀνθρώποις τοιόσδε, ἐν δὲ τοῖς ἀλόγοις ζῴοις ἠλλαγμένος.) We might perhaps reconcile these apparently inconsistent statements by assuming the writer's view to be that νοῦς acts on men from within, and on beasts from without.[1] The human soul has νοῦς within it ; and the νοῦς within, if it 'takes command' of the soul, works against the natural impulses. A beast's soul has no νοῦς within it ; but a beast, being a part of the universe,

---

[1] It would be possible so to alter § 1 as to make it express this view ; e. g. one might write there οὗτος δὲ ὁ νοῦς ἐν μὲν ἀνθρώποις [θεὸς] ⟨ἔνδον ἔνοικός⟩ ἐστι· . . . ἐν δὲ τοῖς ἀλόγοις ζῴοις ⟨ἀντὶ νοῦ ἔνοικος⟩ ἡ φύσις ἐστίν.

is governed by the divine νοῦς to which the whole universe is subject, and by which the laws of nature are determined; and thus its instinctive actions result from the working of νοῦς, in the same sense that the falling of a stone results from the working of νοῦς. But if this was the Hermetist's meaning, he ought to have said that the instincts are implanted in the beast by νοῦς (i. e. by the mind which governs the universe); and he does not say that. He speaks of instinct as something which exists apart from the action of νοῦς, and says, not that νοῦς produces the instincts, but that νοῦς ' co-operates with' them; and this I am unable to explain.

ψυχὴ γὰρ πᾶσα, ἐν σώματι γενομένη, εὐθέως ὑπό τε τῆς λύπης καὶ τῆς ἡδονῆς κακίζεται. Cf. Corp. X. 15 b : ψυχὴν παιδὸς θέασαι κ.τ.λ. Pl. Tim. 42 A : ὁπότε δὴ σώμασιν ἐμφυτευθεῖεν (αἱ ψυχαί) . . ., πρῶτον μὲν αἴσθησιν ἀναγκαῖον εἴη μίαν πᾶσιν ἐκ βιαίων παθημάτων ξύμφυτον γίγνεσθαι, δεύτερον δὲ ἡδονῇ καὶ λύπῃ μεμιγμένον ἔρωτα κ.τ.λ.

§ 3. ἀντιπράσσων αὐτῶν τοῖς προλήμμασιν. It is to be inferred from the context that the προλήμματα of the soul are its animal instincts or natural impulses. But does the word mean ' things which the soul has taken hold of ', or ' things which have taken hold of the soul' ? As the writer goes on to speak of σῶμα προειλημμένον ὑπὸ νόσου, it appears that he meant προλήμματα to be understood in the latter sense.

ὥσπερ ⟨γὰρ⟩ ἰατρὸς ἀγαθὸς λυπεῖ τὸ σῶμα . . . καίων ἢ τέμνων. This simile may have been suggested by Pl. Gorg. 477 E–481 B. Compare especially Gorg. 480 C: one ought to force oneself and one's friends μὴ ἀποδειλιᾶν, ἀλλὰ παρέχειν μύσαντα καὶ ἀνδρείως ὥσπερ τέμνειν καὶ κάειν ἰατρῷ, τὸ ἀγαθὸν καὶ καλὸν διώκοντα, μὴ ὑπολογιζόμενον τὸ ἀλγεινόν, . . . ὅπως ἂν . . . ἀπαλλάττωνται τοῦ μεγίστου κακοῦ, ἀδικίας.

ὁ νοῦς ⟨τὴν⟩ ψυχὴν λυπεῖ, ἐξυφαιρῶν αὐτῆς τὴν ἡδονήν. We were told above that both λύπη and ἡδονή deprave or vitiate the soul; i. e. a man becomes vicious through seeking to escape from pain and to get pleasure. But here, λύπη is spoken of differently; it is ἡδονή alone that vitiates the soul, and νοῦς counteracts the evil influence of ἡδονή by employing λύπη medicinally. The thwarting of the natural impulses is painful; but by enduring this pain, the man is cured of the moral disease which ' pleasure' (i. e. indulgence of the natural impulse to seek pleasure and avoid pain) has produced in him. Cf. Synesius De insomniis 5, Migne 66. 1293 D : ἀναγωγὸν ἡ μετάνοια. . . . καὶ διὰ τοῦτο τῇδέ τε κἀκεῖ χρείαν τὴν μεγίστην τε καὶ ἀρίστην τῇ τάξει τῶν ὄντων αἱ ⌜κράσεις⌝ (lege κολάσεις) παρέχονται, τὸ λυπηρὸν ἀντεισάγουσαι, καὶ τῆς ἐμπλήκτου χαρᾶς τὴν ψυχὴν ἐκκαθαίρουσαι· αἵ τε

παρ' ἀξίαν καλούμεναι συμφοραὶ μέγα μέρος συμβάλλονται πρὸς τὸ
λῦσαι τὴν σχέσιν ἣν ἔχομεν πρὸς τὰ τῇδε. . . . ὡς οὐκ ἔστιν ὅπως ποτ'
ἂν ἀποστραφείη τὴν ὕλην ψυχὴ μηδενὶ κακῷ περὶ τὰ τῇδε προσκόπτουσα.
τὴν ἡδονήν, ἀφ' ἧς πᾶσα νόσος ψυχῆς γίνεται. Cf. Pl. *Tim.* 86 B:
νόσον μὲν δὴ ψυχῆς ἄνοιαν ξυγχωρητέον. . . . ἡδονὰς δὲ καὶ λύπας ὑπερ-
βαλλούσας τῶν νόσων μεγίστας θετέον τῇ ψυχῇ.

νόσος δὲ μεγάλη ψυχῆς ἀθεότης. In the ἄθεος, ἡδονή or ἐπιθυμία
rules unchecked; he is governed wholly by his προλήμματα. The
νοῦς, by which alone this disease of the soul can be cured, is the
organ of *gnosis*; it rids the man of ἀθεότης, and makes him εὐσεβής.

§ 4. ὅσαι δὲ ψυχαὶ ἀνθρώπιναι οὐκ ἔτυχον κυβερνήτου τοῦ νοῦ. It is
not quite clear whether the writer holds that νοῦς is present in all
human souls, or that it is present in some only, and not in others.
At any rate, it is in some men only that νοῦς acts as κυβερνήτης,
i. e. takes command. (Cf. § 3 *init.*: ὅσαις ἂν οὖν ψυχαῖς ὁ νοῦς ἐπι-
στατήσῃ. § 7: οἱ δὲ ἐλλόγιμοι, ὧν ἔφαμεν τὸν νοῦν ἡγεμονεύειν.) In
other men, νοῦς fails to discharge its proper function of checking and
thwarting the natural impulses; and if the writer considers it to be
present at all in such men, his view must be that it aids and abets
the ὁρμαί instead of counteracting them. The words συνεργὸς γὰρ
αὐταῖς γενόμενος, if they were used with regard to men alone, might
be thought to decide the question in favour of the latter alternative;
but the writer says that ὁ νοῦς συνεργεῖ ταῖς ὁρμαῖς in the case of
beasts also (§ 10), and he denies that νοῦς is present in the souls
of beasts (§ 2).

συνεργὸς γὰρ αὐταῖς γενόμενος (ὁ νοῦς), καὶ ἀνέσας τὰς ἐπιθυμίας,
⟨. . .⟩ εἰς ἃς φέρονται (αἱ ψυχαί). The verb of which ὁ νοῦς was the
subject has been lost. According to the text of the MSS., εἰς ἃς
means εἰς τὰς ἐπιθυμίας. But it would be more correct to say that
the souls εἰς τὰς ἡδονὰς φέρονται τῇ ῥύμῃ τῆς ὀρέξεως (i. e. τῇ ἐπιθυμίᾳ).
Perhaps the missing phrase contained the word ἡδονάς; in that case,
εἰς ἃς would mean εἰς τὰς ἡδονάς.

ταύταις δὲ ὥσπερ τιμωρὸν καὶ ἔλεγχον ὁ θεὸς ἐπέστησε τὸν νόμον.
Does ταύταις mean ταύταις ταῖς ψυχαῖς, or ταύταις ταῖς κακίαις?
Probably the former. The νόμος is the penal law of God. It is
elsewhere called δίκη; cf. Herm. *ap.* Stob. *Exc.* VII. 2: ἡ δὲ δίκη
τέτακται τιμωρὸς τῶν ἐπὶ γῆς ἁμαρτανόντων. In the words τιμωρὸν καὶ
ἔλεγχον, punishment is placed before conviction, as in Virgil's
description of the procedure of Rhadamanthus, *Aen.* 6. 567: 'casti-
gatque auditque dolos subigitque fateri.'

§ 5. ὁ περὶ τῆς εἱμαρμένης λόγος, ὃ⟨ν⟩ ἔμπροσθέν μοι ⟨δι⟩εξελήλυθας
(ὁ . . . ἐξεληλυθώς MSS.). The writer refers to a discourse of Hermes
to Tat concerning εἱμαρμένη; and we may perhaps infer from the
word διεξελήλυθας that it was one of the διεξοδικοὶ λόγοι. Cf. *Corp.*
V. 1 a: καὶ τόνδε σοι τὸν λόγον, ὦ Τάτ, διεξελεύσομαι. See the extract
from *Hermes to Tat* on πρόνοια, ἀνάγκη, and εἱμαρμένη, Stob.
Exc. VIII.

διὰ τί κολάζεται ὁ ἀναγκασάσης (ὁ ἐξ ἀνάγκης MSS.) τῆς εἱμαρμένης
δράσας τὸ ἔργον; The Stoics asserted, in their physics, that all
things without exception are determined by εἱμαρμένη; and from
this it would seem to follow that men are not responsible for their
actions.   Chrysippus refused to accept that inference; but his
endeavours to reconcile his doctrine of Fate with his belief in τὸ ἐφ'
ἡμῖν were not very successful.   His arguments on this topic are
criticized by Alexander Aphrod. *De fato* (Arnim, *Stoic. vet. fragm.*
II, pp. 295–297).   Cf. Aulus Gellius 7. 2: 'the opponents of
Chrysippus say, "Si Chrysippus fato putat omnia moveri et regi, . . .
peccata quoque hominum et delicta non suscensenda neque indu-
cenda sunt ipsis voluntatibusque eorum, sed necessitati cuidam et
instantiae quae oritur ex fato; . . . et propterea nocentium poenas
legibus inique constitutas, si homines ad maleficia non sponte
veniunt, sed fato trahuntur." Contra ea Chrysippus tenuiter multa
et argute disserit. . . . Negat (Chrysippus) oportere ferri audirique
homines aut nequam aut ignavos et nocentes et audaces, qui, cum
in culpa et in maleficio revicti sunt, perfugiunt ad fati necessitatem
tamquam in aliquod fani asylum, et quae pessime fecerunt, ea non
suae temeritati, sed fato esse attribuenda dicunt.'

The Hermetists, being Platonists, had a way of escape from this
ἀπορία which was not open to a Stoic.   They accepted the Stoic
doctrine of Heimarmene *so far as things corporeal are concerned*
(χωρὶς ἐκείνης οὐδὲν τῶν σωματικῶν . . . γενέσθαι συμβαίνει); and
holding that the animal impulses, in beasts and men alike, result
from the influence of the body on the soul, they admitted that these
impulses are determined by Fate, and that the lives and actions
of those men in whom the 'bodily passions' work unchecked are
wholly subject to that external power.   Men of this class then they
considered to be mere puppets, moved from without, like the beasts,
by physical forces which are set in action by the movements of the
heavenly bodies.   But unlike the Stoics, they held that the corporeal
world is not all; beside or above it is 'the incorporeal', and the

incorporeal is not subject to Heimarmene. νοῦς is incorporeal; and the man in whose soul νοῦς rules lives in another world, on which physical forces have no bearing. (See Herm. *ap.* Stob. *Exc.* XVIII. 3.) Such a man has 'escaped from Heimarmene'. He is content to 'let Heimarmene do what she will with her own clay, that is, with his body' (Hermes in Zosimus i. 7, *Testim.*); his heart is set on other and higher things, and nothing corporeal has power to influence him. (See *Abammonis resp.* 10. 5 (*Testim.*) on 'release from the bonds of εἱμαρμένη'.) According to the writer of *Corp.* IV, the gift of νοῦς is offered to all men; if a man wilfully rejects that gift, it is by his own fault that he remains a slave to Fate, and he deserves the punishment which follows.

εἵμαρται δὲ καὶ ⟨τὸν⟩ τὸ κακὸν ποιήσαντα [τὸ] ⟨κακὸν⟩ παθεῖν. Cf. Diog. Laert. 7. 23: Zeno the Stoic δοῦλον ἐπὶ κλοπῇ, φασίν, ἐμαστίγου· τοῦ δ' εἰπόντος " εἵμαρτό μοι κλέψαι", " καὶ δαρῆναι ", ἔφη. But the writer of XII. i says not only that both the crime and the punishment which follows it are ordained by Heimarmene, but also (if I understand the passage rightly) that the crime is ordained for the purpose of bringing about the punishment (διὰ τοῦτο ⟨εἵμαρται αὐτὸν⟩ δρᾶ⟨ν⟩(?), ἵνα πάθῃ); that is to say, Heimarmene determines that a man shall suffer, and compels him to commit the crime in order that he may incur the suffering. This in itself is no answer to Tat's question, 'Why are men punished for that which they are compelled to do?' On the contrary, it would appear at first sight to emphasize the injustice of God's government, and to represent Fate, the agent through whom God works, as a wantonly malignant power. But it must be interpreted in the light of what follows. The ἄλογος ἄνθρωπος, by the very fact that he has rejected God's offered gift of νοῦς, (or rejected the guidance of the νοῦς which God has implanted in him,) already deserves punishment. Through his own fault, he is subject to Heimarmene; and to Heimarmene is assigned the task of punishing him. Heimarmene discharges this task by compelling him to commit crimes, and thereby causing him to incur penal suffering.

§ 6. νῦν δὲ περὶ νοῦ ἐστιν ἡμῖν ὁ λόγος. The subject of *Corp.* XII. i is νοῦς, and not εἱμαρμένη; but the doctrine of νοῦς has an important bearing on the problem of εἱμαρμένη, as Hermes proceeds to show.

πῶς ἐνδιάφορός ἐστιν. ἐνδιάφορος must be taken to mean 'having διαφοραί within it'; cf. ἔννους and ἔνθεος. See *Corp.* V. 7 and IX. 7, where the MSS. give ἐν διαφορᾷ, but perhaps we ought to read ἐνδιάφορα.

ἐν δὲ τοῖς ἀλόγοις ζῴοις ἠλλαγμένος. In the case of the beasts, νοῦς operates differently. The writer probably means, not that there is νοῦς *in* beasts, but that the νοῦς by which the universe is governed acts on beasts from without, through the forces of nature, and the πάθη which those forces produce in the soul. In the case of beasts then, νοῦς operates in the form of εἱμαρμένη (the power by which corporeal things are governed); in the case of 'rational' men, in whose souls it works from within, νοῦς is opposed to εἱμαρμένη, and counteracts it.

ἐν μὲν τοῖς ἀλόγοις ζῴοις οὐκ ἔστιν εὐεργετικός, ⟨ἐν δὲ τοῖς ἀνθρώποις ἀγαθὸν ἐργάζεται,⟩ ἀλλ᾽ ἀνομοίως (ἀνόμοιος MSS.). The words ἐν μὲν τοῖς ἀλόγοις ζῴοις κ.τ.λ. must have been followed by a corresponding statement introduced by ἐν δὲ τοῖς ἀνθρώποις; and as it is clear that in the phrase τό τε θυμικὸν καὶ τὸ ἐπιθυμητικὸν σβεννύων the writer is speaking of the action of νοῦς in men, and not in beasts, the words ἐν δὲ τοῖς ἀνθρώποις must have stood where I have placed them. The conjecture ἀγαθὸν ἐργάζεται is suggested by § 2: ὁ γὰρ νοῦς ψυχῶν ἐστιν εὐεργέτης ἀνθρώπων· ἐργάζεται γὰρ αὐταῖς τὸ ἀγαθόν.

τοὺς μὲν ἐλλογίμους [ἄνδρας] δεῖ νοεῖν. If the reading of the MSS. is sound, ἄνδρας must here mean 'true men', or 'fully developed men' (τέλειοι, *Corp.* IV. 4), as opposed to mere ἄνθρωποι. But the combination of the two distinct predicates ἐλλογίμους and ἄνδρας is awkward; and it seems best to cut out ἄνδρας. The word ἐλλόγιμος here means ἔλλογος, 'having reason in oneself'. The ἐλλόγιμος is the man οὗ ὁ νοῦς ἡγεμονεύει. I have not found any instance elsewhere of the use of ἐλλόγιμος in this sense.

πάντες δὲ οἱ ἄνθρωποι εἱμαρμένῃ ὑπόκεινται. 'All men are subject to destiny,' *sc.* in respect of their bodies. As it is expressed below, πάντες πάσχουσι τὰ εἱμαρμένα. All men must suffer bodily pain and death. But the ἐλλόγιμος does not care what befalls his body, and does not allow himself to be influenced by πάθη which have their origin in the body; he is therefore, as far as his true self is concerned, free from the dominion of εἱμαρμένη.

⟨ἐπεὶ⟩ καὶ γενέσει καὶ μεταβολῇ· ἀρχὴ γὰρ καὶ τέλος ταῦτα εἱμαρμένης. μεταβολή here, as often, is a euphemism for θάνατος. Since εἱμαρμένη deals only with things corporeal, it can have power over a man only during his embodiment; its hold on him begins at his birth, and ends at his death. The unembodied soul before birth, and the disembodied soul after death, are beyond the reach of εἱμαρμένη.

§ 7. ὁ μοιχὸς οὐ κακός; . . . Ἀλλ' ὁ ἐλλόγιμος . . . οὐ μοιχεύσας πείσεται, ἀλλ' ὡς ⟨ὁ⟩ μοιχεύσας. The irrational man is subject to εἱμαρμένη in two distinct ways; Fate first compels him to commit crimes, and then inflicts pain or death on him by way of punishment for the crimes he has committed. (Perhaps the case of which the writer is thinking is that in which these penalties are inflicted by the sentence of a human judge.) Hence Tat, having been told that the rational man, as well as the irrational, πάσχει τὰ εἱμαρμένα, infers that the rational man also is compelled by Fate to commit crimes; and if he commits crimes, how can it be said that he is not κακός? Hermes' answer amounts to this, that the rational man is subject to Heimarmene in one of the two ways spoken of, but not in the other. Fate inflicts pain and death on the rational man as well as on the irrational, but does not and cannot compel the rational man to do wicked deeds. The rational man then πείσεται ὡς ⟨ὁ⟩ μοιχεύσας, i. e. will undergo pain and death even as the wicked man does, but οὐ μοιχεύσει, and therefore οὐ μοιχεύσας πείσεται. (E. g. Fate may cause a rational man to be unjustly condemned by a human judge, and to suffer the same penalty as the guilty; but Fate cannot make him guilty.) ' It is impossible for any man to escape from death; but the man who has mind can escape from wickedness.'

It might be objected that, if this is so, Fate acts unjustly in inflicting on the rational and innocent man the same sufferings which she inflicts on the irrational and guilty. But to this objection the Hermetist could have given an answer. The irrational man undergoes death κακὸς ὤν; and the κακός is φιλοσώματος. (Cf. φιλοσώματος ὢν καὶ κακός, *Corp.* XI. ii. 21 a.) He has identified himself with his body, and his interests with corporeal things; the destruction of his body is therefore felt by him as an evil; and this evil comes upon him as a punishment for the crimes he has committed. To the rational man, on the other hand, death is no evil; he 'hates his body' (*Corp.* IV. 6 b), and quits it willingly. He has deserved no punishment; and he suffers no punishment in dying.[1] Fate can deal only with his body; and nothing that may be done to his body concerns him. We may suppose that the

---

[1] 'You can kill me, but you cannot do me any harm,' says Socrates, Pl. *Apol.* 30 C, D.

writer would have answered to this effect if the objection had been raised. But the objection is an obvious one, and it seems somewhat surprising that he did not think it worth while to give his answer to it. Perhaps the matter had been more fully dealt with in the earlier treatise on εἱμαρμένη to which he refers, and he was unwilling to interrupt his exposition of the doctrine of νοῦς in *Corp.* XII. i by further discussion of the problem of Fate. It is possible that there is a lacuna of some length before μεταβολῆς ἀδύνατόν ἐστι διεκφυγεῖν, and that the passage would be less obscure if we had the lost words before us.

§ **8.** τοῦ Ἀγαθοῦ Δαίμονος . . . ἤκουσα λέγοντος ἃ εἰ καὶ [εἰ] ἐγγράφως ⟨ἐξ⟩εδεδώκει κ.τ.λ. The MSS. give ἤκουσα λέγοντος ἀεί· καὶ εἰ κ.τ.λ. But ἀεί yields no satisfactory sense ; (if any temporal adverb were used, it should rather be ποτέ, as below, ἤκουσα γοῦν αὐτοῦ ποτε λέγοντος ;) and the object wanted for the verb ⟨ἐξ⟩εδεδώκει may be supplied by writing ἃ εἰ in place of ἀεί.

The tradition which the writer presupposes is that the god Agathos Daimon was the first teacher of the *gnosis*, and taught it orally to the man Hermes, but that Hermes was the first to set it down in writing. Hermes here expresses regret that the Agathos Daimon had not himself set down in writing, and so made more widely known, the saying which he proceeds to quote from him.

ὡς πρωτόγονος θεός. The Agathos Daimon (Khnum) was the 'first-born' god. In *Kore Kosmu*, Herm. *ap.* Stob. *Exc.* XXIII. 32, Kamephis (i. e. Khnum) is called ὁ προπάτωρ and ὁ πάντων προγενέστερος. According to the ancient theogony of Heliopolis, the epithet πρωτόγονος should rather have been applied to Tum, who was said to have issued from the waters of the primal Ocean (Nu), and generated the other gods (Wiedemann, *Rel. of Anc. Eg.*, Eng. tr. p. 31). But Khnum seems to have held at Philae a position similar to that of Tum at Heliopolis ; and in Hellenistic times, the primacy of Khnum was recognized in Lower Egypt also. The term πρωτόγονος was applied by the Orphici to their god Phanes ; the parts of the Orphic Theogonia in which Phanes was spoken of were probably composed in the Ptolemaic period, and may have been influenced by Egyptian doctrines concerning Tum or Khnum. Lactant. *Div. inst.* I. 5 : 'Orpheus . . . deum verum et magnum πρωτόγονον, primogenitum, appellat, quod ante ipsum nihil sit genitum, sed ab ipso sint cuncta generata. Eundem etiam Φάνητα nominat.' Philo applies the adjectives πρωτόγονος and πρωτότοκος to the divine λόγος.

τὰ πάντα κατιδών. The Agathos Daimon, being the 'first-born' of the gods, (i. e. 'second God', and older than all except the 'first God', who would be called, not πρωτόγονος, but ἀγέννητος,) was the only person who 'had seen all things' (i. e. had witnessed the creation of the universe from its first beginning?); therefore, he alone knew the whole truth and could reveal it.

⌜ἕν ἐστι τὰ πάντα . . . ποιεῖν ὅπερ βούλεται⌝. This saying of the Agathos Daimon has lost all meaning through the corruption of the text; and its sense can only be guessed from what Hermes afterwards says about it (§ 9). He sums up its contents in the words πάντων ἐπικρατεῖ ὁ νοῦς, . . . καὶ οὐδὲν αὐτῷ ἀδύνατον κ.τ.λ.; and something like this may be recognized in the concluding words of the quotation (νοῦν, ἄρχοντα πάντων, . . . ποιεῖν ὅπερ βούλεται). But Hermes also says that Tat will find in the saying of the Agathos Daimon an answer to his question about Destiny, i. e. to the question 'Why is a man punished for his crimes, when Destiny has compelled him to commit them?' (§ 5). The passage quoted contains no trace of the word εἱμαρμένη; but it must have included something which might be taken to mean what Hermes expresses in the words οὐδὲν (τῷ νῷ) ἀδύνατον, οὔτε εἱμαρμένης ὑπεράνω θεῖναι ψυχὴν ἀνθρωπίνην κ.τ.λ. We may presume then that the Agathos Daimon spoke of the relation between νοῦς and ψυχή in man, and asserted the sovereign power of νοῦς in the soul of which it takes command. But there is little hope of restoring the text. It is impossible to discover any connexion with the subject under discussion in the words ἕν ἐστι τὰ πάντα; and perhaps we ought to read ἔνεστι (or ἔξεστι) τῷ ⟨νῷ⟩ πάντα, 'all things are possible for mind'. The author cannot have written νοητὰ σώματα, which would be equivalent to ἀσώματα σώματα. He may possibly have written ⟨τὰ⟩ νοητὰ ⟨καὶ ἀ⟩σώματα; but if so, the rest of that sentence has been lost. The words ζῶμεν δὲ δυνάμει καὶ ἐνεργείᾳ καὶ αἰῶνι are utterly devoid of meaning. It may be conjectured that οὖν δυνατόν is a corruption of οὐδὲν ἀδύνατον, which occurs in Hermes' paraphrase below. The statement that νοῦς is the ψυχή of the supreme God (νοῦν . . . ψυχὴν ὄντα τοῦ θεοῦ) is unparalleled; and it seems probable that the only ψυχή spoken of in this passage was the human soul. But if these words are corrupt, a similar, and perhaps consequent, corruption must be assumed in the corresponding words in § 9 (ὁ νοῦς, ἡ τοῦ θεοῦ ψυχή).

Perhaps the last part of the passage may have been something like this : ὥσ⟨τε⟩ οὐ⟨δὲ⟩ν ⟨ἀ⟩δύνατον νοῦν, ἄρχοντα πάντων, καὶ [[ψυχὴν]] ⟨ἐνέργειαν?⟩ ὄντα τοῦ θεοῦ, ⟨⟨ψυχὴν⟩⟩ ποιεῖν ὅπερ βούλεται. ' It is not impossible for mind . . . to make what it wills of the soul (in which it resides)'.

§ 9. τοὺς ἐριστικοὺς λόγους. The argument implied in Tat's question (§ 5, διὰ τί κολάζεται κ.τ.λ.) is merely ' contentious '. It may serve to disconcert an opponent ; but it gives no help to those who are seeking the truth.

ὁ νοῦς [ἡ τοῦ θεοῦ ψυχή]. It is difficult to believe that the phrase ἡ τοῦ θεοῦ ψυχή was written by the author. It may have been inserted by some one to whom it was suggested by the words ὅπερ ἐστὶν αὐτοῦ καὶ ψυχή and νοῦν . . . ψυχὴν ὄντα τοῦ θεοῦ in the corrupt passage which precedes ; or it may be a corruption of ἡ τοῦ θεοῦ ⟨τῇ⟩ ψυχῇ ⟨ἐνοῦσα ἐνέργεια⟩, ' the force of God at work in the (human) soul', or something to that effect. (A possible meaning could be got by writing ὁ νοῦς ⟨τ⟩ῇ τοῦ θε⟨ί⟩ου ⟨ἀνθρώπου ἐνὼν⟩ ψυχῇ.)

καὶ εἱμαρμένης, καὶ νόμου. In the case of the soul in which νοῦς rules, both the power of Destiny which impels to crime, and the penal law by which crime is punished, are reduced to impotence.

οὔτε ἀμελήσασαν . . . ὑπὸ τὴν εἱμαρμένην ⟨θ⟩εῖναι. If a soul ' is heedless ' of νοῦς, i. e. declines to be ruled by it, (or, in the language of *Corp*. IV, rejects God's offered gift of mind,) the divine νοῦς punishes this heedlessness by making the soul subject to εἱμαρμένη.

[τὰ τοῦ Ἀγαθοῦ Δαίμονος ἄριστα.] If these words are retained, they must be assigned to Tat. But as his assent is sufficiently expressed by what follows (Καὶ θείως κ.τ.λ.), it is more likely that τὰ . . . ἄριστα was inserted by some admiring reader. A verb such as λέλεκται must be understood after θείως, ὦ πάτερ.

§ 10. ἔλεγες γὰρ τὸν νοῦν ἐν τοῖς ἀλόγοις ζῴοις φύσεως δίκην ἐνεργεῖν, συνεργοῦντα αὐτῶν ταῖς ὁρμαῖς. This refers to § 2 : τοῖς μὲν ἀλόγοις τῇ ἰδίᾳ ἑκάστου φύσει συνεργεῖ. In the case of beasts, the operation of νοῦς takes the form of instinct. In both passages alike, it is not clear why the (external) νοῦς is said to ' co-operate with ' the animal's impulses, and not simply to produce them.

αἱ δὲ ὁρμαὶ . . . πάθη εἰσίν. The word πάθη originally meant *quae quis patitur*, ' things which are done to one', or ' things which befall one '. It was applied to the feelings of pleasure and pain (regarded as states produced by the action of external objects on

the senses), and was thence extended to signify emotional disturb-
ances (*animi perturbationes*) in general, including the impulses
(ὁρμαί) which result from feelings of pleasure and pain. νοῦς, being
unaffected by τὰ αἰσθητά, was usually considered to be ἀπαθής; hence
Tat finds a difficulty in a doctrine which brings νοῦς into close
connexion with the.πάθη..

καὶ ὁ νοῦς ἄρα παθ⟨ητ⟩ός ἐστι, συγχρω[μα]τίζων τοῖς πάθεσιν. It is
hardly possible to call νοῦς a πάθος; but νοῦς might be said to be
παθητός, i. e. to be affected by πάθη. The verb συγχρωτίζεσθαι
means 'to be in defiling contact with'. Cf. *Corp.* X. 17 : οὔτε τὴν
τοσαύτην ἀρετὴν (*sc.* τὸν νοῦν) ἀνέχεσθαι συγχρωτιζόμενον αὐτῇ παθητὸν
σῶμα. The active form of this verb does not, as far as I know,
occur elsewhere ; and the sense of mutual contact which is required
would be better expressed by the middle form συγχρωτιζόμενος.

§ 11. πάντα, ὦ τέκνον, τὰ ἐν σώματι . . . ὀνόματι χρήσασθαι οὐ λυπεῖ.
This passage is the teacher's answer to Tat's objection that, if νοῦς
co-operates with the impulses of beasts, and those impulses are
πάθη, then νοῦς must be παθητός. Tat calls the answer lucid (σαφέ-
στατα τὸν λόγον ἀποδέδωκας); but as given in the MSS., it is obscure
in the extreme. Tat's difficulty appears to be directly referred to
only in the clause ἀπαλλαγεὶς δὲ τοῦ σώματος (ὁ νοῦς) ἀπηλλάγη καὶ
τοῦ πάθους. This must have been preceded by another clause, now
lost, to the effect that, as long as νοῦς is in the body, or operates
in the body, it is παθητός. But the writer prepares the way for
this statement about νοῦς by first laying down some general propositions concerning the question what things are παθητά. His doctrine
appears to be that bodies are παθητὰ κυρίως (i. e. παθητά in the strict
or primary sense of the term), but that in a wider sense 'all things
which are in a body', including things which are themselves incorporeal, are παθητά;[1] whence it follows that νοῦς is παθητός as
long as it is in a body. But what are 'the things which are in
a body'? Presumably the ψυχή and the νοῦς of a man living on
earth are included under this term; whether the writer meant to
include under it any other things as well, I do not know. At any
rate, the particular 'thing in a body' with which he is chiefly
concerned is embodied νοῦς, i. e. the νοῦς which resides in the soul
of an individual man during his earthly life ; and his point is that

---

[1] Cf. Porphyry, *Sententiae ad intellegibilia ducentes*, 18 : ἄλλο τὸ πάσχειν τῶν
σωμάτων, ἄλλο τὸ τῶν ἀσωμάτων, κ.τ.λ. But the ἀσώματον of which Porphyry
speaks in that passage is ψυχή, and not νοῦς.

νοῦς in this condition is παθητός. His conception of παθητὸς νοῦς may perhaps have some connexion with Aristotle's conception of ὁ παθητικὸς νοῦς (*De an.* 3. 5, 430 a), which might be understood to mean νοῦς as affected by embodiment.

[[καὶ τὰ ἀσώματα δὲ]] [κινεῖται ὑπὸ τοῦ νοῦ]. According to the MSS., we are here told that 'incorporeals also are moved'. But this contradicts the preceding statement, 'everything that is moved is body'. It is therefore certain that there is something wrong in the traditional text. I have assumed that καὶ τὰ ἀσώματα δέ has been shifted, and ought to precede πᾶν γὰρ τὸ κινοῦν ἀσώματον ; that some words which followed καὶ τὰ ἀσώματα δέ in its original position have been lost ; and that some one tried to fill the gap by inserting κινεῖται ὑπὸ τοῦ νοῦ. If I am right in thinking that νοῦς is one of the ἀσώματα spoken of, and indeed the very one with which the Hermetist is chiefly concerned, the statement that these ἀσώματα 'are moved by νοῦς' must have been written by some one who misunderstood the meaning of the paragraph. In the lost words, the author must have said that ἀσώματα also, under certain conditions, (*sc.* when embodied,) are παθητά. He supports this statement by the words πᾶν γὰρ . . . τὸ δὲ ἀρχόμενον, in which he brings in the conception of κίνησις ; and thereupon follows the conclusion at which he has been aiming : '⟨νοῦς then, as long as it is embodied, is παθητός ;⟩ but when it is freed from the body, it is freed from the πάθος also'.

[κίνησις δὲ πάθος.] In order to make these words relevant, κίνησις must be taken to mean τὸ κινεῖν, and not τὸ κινεῖσθαι. It is obvious that τὸ κινεῖσθαι is πάθος ; but the point on which the writer is here insisting is that τὸ κινεῖν also is (or involves) πάθος, and that consequently ἀσώματα (νοῦς and ψυχή), when they are 'in bodies' and are occupied in moving those bodies, are affected by πάθη. But the phrase κίνησις δὲ πάθος is too ambiguous and obscure to help the argument ; and perhaps it is a fragment of a note inserted by a reader.

⌜μᾶλλον δέ ποτε, ὦ τέκνον, οὐδὲν ἀπαθές, . . . διὰ τοῦτο παθητά ἐστι.⌝ I can make no sense of this passage. It would be possible to put a meaning into it (or into some of the clauses at least) by rewriting the text as follows : μᾶλλον δέ [ποτε], ὦ τέκνον, ⟨. . .⟩. οὐδὲν ⟨γὰρ τῶν ἐν σώματι⟩ ἀπαθές, πάντα δὲ (*sc.* τὰ ἐν σώματι) παθητά. διαφέρει δὲ παθητὸν παθητοῦ· τὸ μὲν γὰρ ἐνεργεῖ ⟨τε καὶ πάσχει⟩, τὸ δὲ πάσχει ⟨μόνον⟩. τὰ δὲ ⟨ἀ⟩σώματα (e. g. νοῦς) καὶ καθ' αὐτὰ ἐνεργεῖ (i. e. are

capable of acting by themselves, as well as of acting on the body) ;
⟨καθ' αὐτὰ δ' ἐνεργοῦντα ἀπαθῆ ἐστι⟩. [[ ]] τὰ δὲ [α]σώματα ἀεὶ
ἐνεργεῖται, καὶ διὰ τοῦτο ⟨ἀεὶ⟩ παθητά ἐστι. ⟨⟨ἡ γὰρ ἀκίνητά ἐστιν
(sc. τὰ σώματα) ἢ κινεῖται· ὁπότερον δὲ ἂν ᾖ, παθητά ἐστι.⟩⟩ But this
is mere guesswork.

⌜ἥ τε γὰρ ἐνέργεια καὶ τὸ πάθος ταὐτόν ἐστι⌝. This can hardly be
right. What the author probably meant to say might be expressed
by writing τὸ γὰρ ἐνεργοῦν καὶ τὸ πάσχον ταὐτόν ἐστι. The embodied
νοῦς both ἐνεργεῖ and πάσχει.

εὐφημοτέρῳ δὲ τῷ ὀνόματι χρήσασθαι οὐ λυπεῖ. This seems to mean
that there are two terms which are equally applicable to embodied
νοῦς, but there is no harm in using the 'better-sounding' of the two,
and avoiding the use of the other. (This meaning would be more
clearly expressed by writing τῷ δὲ εὐφημοτέρῳ ὀνόματι.) The two
terms are probably ἐνεργητικός and παθητός ; and the former is ' the
better-sounding ' of the two, because παθητός is commonly regarded
as implying depreciation.

The writer's view appears to be that embodied νοῦς works actively
(ἐνεργεῖ) in checking (or, in the case of the irrational man, 'co-oper-
ating with ') the ὁρμαί of the human soul, but that, in doing this,
it is itself affected or modified by that on which it works, and
therefore not only ἐνεργεῖ, but also πάσχει. When it is freed from
the body, it no longer πάσχει, but ἐνεργεῖ only. Tat, in putting
forward his objection (§ 10), spoke only of beasts, and not of men ;
but Hermes, in his answer, seems to be speaking of men, and not
of beasts ; for it is only in the case of men that νοῦς can be said to
be ἐν σώματι.

§ 12. δύο ταῦτα τῷ ἀνθρώπῳ ὁ θεὸς παρὰ πάντα τὰ θνητὰ ζῷα
ἐχαρίσατο, τόν τε νοῦν καὶ τὸν λόγον. Cf. Corp. IV. 3 as emended :
ὁ δὲ ἄνθρωπος τῶν ἄλλων ζῴων πλεονεκτεῖ τὸν λόγον καὶ τὸν νοῦν.
Ascl. Lat. 41 b : χαρισάμενος ἡμῖν νοῦν, λόγον, γνῶσιν· νοῦν μέν, ἵνα
σὲ νοήσωμεν, λόγον δέ, ἵνα σὲ ἐπικαλέσωμεν.

ἰσότιμα τῇ ἀθανασίᾳ. ἰσότιμα means ' equal in value '. νοῦς and λόγος
are, so to speak, promissory notes, in exchange for which ἀθανασία
(i. e. the life or condition of a god) can be obtained on demand.

[τὸν δὲ προφορικὸν λόγον [1] λέγει (ἔχει MSS.).] It would be possible
to write λέγω, and take this to be an explanation added by the
author himself ; ' the λόγος of which I am speaking is the προφορικὸς

---

[1] In vol. i, p. 230 l. 8, λόγον has been omitted by mistake.

λόγος, and not the ἐνδιάθετος λόγος'. But it seems more likely that the note 'he means the προφορικὸς λόγος' was inserted by some reader. In either case, the explanation given is correct; the λόγος of which Hermes is speaking in this passage is 'speech', and not 'thought'. The terms ὁ προφορικὸς λόγος (thought expressed by utterance, i. e. speech), and ὁ ἐνδιάθετος λόγος (thought which exists only ἐν τῇ διαθέσει, i. e. unuttered thought), were first used by the Stoics.

ὁδηγηθήσεται ὑπὸ ἀμφοτέρων εἰς τὸν¹ τῶν θεῶν . . . χορόν. It seems strange to say that speech, as well as νοῦς, will act as a guide to lead the disembodied soul to the abode of the gods. But the writer probably meant that speech (whether in the form of oral teaching and discussion,—cf. ὑπὸ τοῦ λόγου μέχρι τινος ὁδηγηθείς in Corp. IX. fin.,—or in the form of verbal adoration,—cf. λόγον δέ, ἵνα σὲ ἐπικαλέσωμεν in Ascl. Lat. 41 b —) is an indispensable aid or supplement to thought, and that the right use of both together in this life is needed to qualify a man for attainment to the divine life after death.

§ 13 a. εἰς δὲ ὁ ἄνθρωπος· οὕτω καὶ ὁ λόγος εἷς ἐστι. λόγος means speech considered with respect to its meaning, and not with respect to its sound. All men are of one species ; and so, though men of different nations express their thought by different sounds, the thought expressed by these different sounds is the same. This is proved by the fact that a term or proposition can be translated from one language into another. E. g. the words ἄνθρωπος and *homo* differ in sound, but are identical *qua* λόγος, i. e. in respect of their meaning. Cf. Tertullian *On the witness of the soul*, 6 : ' Throughout the world man is one, though his names are various ; the soul is one, though its language is various ; the spirit is one, though its voice is various. Every nation has its own proper speech ; but the matter of all speech is the same in all.' Both Tertullian and the Hermetist probably got the thought from some Stoic writer.

ἐν Αἰγύπτῳ καὶ Περσίδι καὶ Ἑλλάδι. As instances of different languages, Hermes mentions those of Egypt, *Persia*, and Greece. To a man residing in Egypt under the Roman empire, Egyptian, Greek, and *Latin* would have been the first languages to present themselves ; but as it would have been a glaring anachronism to make Hermes speak of Latin, the writer makes him mention the language spoken in Persia instead. The Persian kingdom of the Sassanidae was founded in A. D. 226; for some centuries before

---

¹ In vol. i, p. 230 l. 12, τὴν has been printed by mistake for τὸν.

that date, the kingdom beyond the Euphrates was more properly
called Parthian, and not Persian. But the earlier name Persia
never died out in literature; (Horace, for instance, *Od*. 1. 2. 22,
speaks of *Persae*, meaning the Parthians;) and the Hermetist would
probably be aware that the Parthian dominion was of recent date,
and could not have been known to the prehistoric Hermes.
Corp. XII. i may have been written after A. D. 226; but the use of
the word Περσίδι cannot be held to prove it.

⟨⟨ὁ οὖν λόγος ἐστὶν εἰκὼν ⟨τοῦ νοῦ⟩, καὶ ⟨ὁ⟩ νοῦς τοῦ θεοῦ.⟩⟩ In the
text of the MSS., the discussion of λόγος breaks off abruptly, and
the γάρ of the following sentence (ὁ γὰρ . . . Ἀγαθὸς Δαίμων κ.τ.λ.)
has no meaning. It is evident therefore that something has been
lost here. As the subject of the whole dialogue is νοῦς, it may
be presumed that the Hermetist concluded the paragraph on λόγος
by explaining the relation of λόγος to νοῦς, and then went on, in a
fresh paragraph, to explain the relation of νοῦς to God on the one
hand, and to ψυχή and σῶμα on the other hand. A better connexion
can be obtained by transposing to this place the words ὁ οὖν λόγος
. . . τοῦ θεοῦ; but it is probable that, when these words have been
inserted, there still remains an unfilled gap.

If my reconstruction of the passage is right, Hermes, after dis-
posing of λόγος, proceeds to say (1) that νοῦς is an 'image' of God,
and (2) that God is 'in' νοῦς. The relation between God and νοῦς
is described in two different ways; but both descriptions alike imply
that νοῦς is connected with and subordinate to God.

§ 13 b. ὁ γὰρ . . . Ἀγαθὸς Δαίμων ψυχὴν μὲν ἐν σώματι ἔφη εἶναι,
νοῦν δὲ ἐν ψυχῇ, [λόγον] ⟨θεὸν⟩ δὲ ἐν τῷ νῷ. Cf. *Corp.* XI. i. 4 b (Νοῦς
loquitur): ὁ μὲν θεὸς ἐν τῷ νῷ, ὁ δὲ νοῦς ἐν τῇ ψυχῇ, ἡ δὲ ψυχὴ ἐν τῇ
ὕλῃ. It is possible that this is the passage to which the writer of
XII. i is referring. If so, he must have assumed the Νοῦς who
speaks in XI. i to be identical with the Agathos Daimon.

Compare also *Corp.* X. 13: ὁ νοῦς [ ] (ὀχεῖται) ἐν τῇ ψυχῇ, ἡ δὲ
ψυχὴ ἐν τῷ πνεύματι· τὸ ⟨δὲ⟩ πνεῦμα . . . κινεῖ τὸ ⟨σῶμα⟩.

[τὸν οὖν θεὸν τούτων πατέρα.] If these words are retained, τούτων
must be taken to mean νοῦ καὶ ψυχῆς καὶ σώματος. But the writer
can hardly have said at the same time that God is 'in' νοῦς and
that God is 'the father of' νοῦς.

§ 14 a. [καὶ τὸ σῶμα δὲ (ἐστιν εἰκὼν) τῆς ἰδέας, ἡ δὲ ἰδέα τῆς
ψυχῆς.] I can see no sense in this. What is meant by ἡ ἰδέα?

ἔστιν οὖν τῆς μὲν ὕλης τὸ λεπτομερέστατον ἀήρ, . . . νοῦ δὲ θεός. This statement occurs again (with λεπτομερέστερον in place of -έστατον) at the end of *Corp.* V, where it is manifestly out of place. In XII. i, it leads on to the mention of θεός, νοῦς, ψυχή, ἀήρ, and ὕλη in the following sentence. The word λεπτομερής is properly applicable only to that which is corporeal; and this sentence, taken literally, would imply that θεός, νοῦς, and ψυχή are material substances. It must therefore have been derived from some source in which Stoic influence was predominant. The Hermetist himself, however, did not hold that God, mind, and soul are corporeal; he must have meant rather that the relation between the incorporeals θεός and νοῦς, and that between the incorporeals νοῦς and ψυχή, are analogous to the relation between the incorporeal ψυχή and the corporeal ἀήρ, and that this relation again is analogous to that between fine matter (ἀήρ) and gross matter (ὕλη). The ἀήρ which he interposes between ψυχή and ὕλη corresponds to the πνεῦμα ('vital spirit', the corporeal vehicle or integument of the incorporeal soul,) which is interposed between ψυχή and σῶμα in *Corp.* X and elsewhere.

ὁ μὲν θεὸς περὶ πάντα καὶ διὰ πάντων. Cf. XII. ii. 20 b, where these words are repeated; and *ib.* 23 a, πᾶν γάρ ἐστι (*sc.* ὁ θεός), τὸ δὲ πᾶν διὰ πάντων καὶ περὶ πάντα. God is περὶ πάντα; i. e. God 'is concerned with' or 'has to do with' all things; there is nothing which is not included under his control. And God is διὰ πάντων; i. e. God penetrates and pervades all things (διήκει πάντα, as the Stoics said); he is present everywhere, and is everywhere at work. Cf. *Ep. ad Eph.* 4. 6: εἷς θεὸς καὶ πατὴρ πάντων, ὁ ἐπὶ πάντων καὶ διὰ πάντων καὶ ἐν πᾶσιν.

ὁ δὲ νοῦς περὶ τὴν ψυχήν, ἡ δὲ ψυχὴ περὶ τὸν ἀέρα, ὁ δὲ ἀὴρ περὶ τὴν ὕλην. νοῦς 'has to do with' ψυχή; that is to say, νοῦς (which issues from God, and is of one substance with God, § 1) acts on ψυχή, and so indirectly acts on ὕλη or σῶμα also, through the medium of ἀήρ, which here takes the place of πνεῦμα. This statement may be applied both to the Kosmos as a whole and to individual organisms. The universal νοῦς acts on the world-soul, and the operation of the world-soul is transmitted to gross matter by the universal air; the νοῦς of an individual man acts on his soul, and the operation of his soul is transmitted to his bodily organs by the air (or *pneuma*) contained within his body. Thus God, by means of νοῦς, administers all things. This description of the position of νοῦς in the scale of existence, and of its function in the administration of the universe and the individual organism, forms a fitting conclusion to the discussion of νοῦς in *Corp*. XII. i ; and the *libellus* may very well have ended at this point.

LIBELLVS XII. ii

Contents

(*The beginning is lost.*) . . . And God uses ⟨Destiny ?⟩, Necessity, Providence, and Nature as his instruments in the administration of the Kosmos.   § 14 b.[1]

The Kosmos is full of life.   There is nothing in it that is not alive ; and no part of it ever dies.   It is a mistake to say that men or animals die.   They undergo dissolution ; but dissolution is not death, but renewal of life.   All things in the Kosmos are in motion ; and wherever there is motion, there is life.   Life shifts from one organism to another ; and for each several organism, there is a beginning and end of consciousness ; but there is no beginning or end of life.   Every living organism is composed of gross matter, vital spirit,[2] and soul ; and each of these three component parts is immortal.   §§ 15 b–18.

But man is immortal in a higher sense than the beasts ; for (1) God imparts to him knowledge of the future, through divination ; and (2) whereas each kind of beasts is confined to one of the three lower elements, man not only makes use of all three, but also looks up to heaven.[3]   §§ 19, 20 a.

(*Something has been lost here.*)

The life with which the Kosmos is filled is the work of God ; and you can see God in his work.   The forces by which life is put into matter are Destiny, Necessity, Providence, and Nature ; but these forces are parts of God.   God then is everywhere at work.   Matter, apart from God, would have no real existence ; it is God that gives it reality, by putting life into it.   Material things, with all their qualities, are manifestations of God's activity.   God is the All, and there is nothing beside him.   §§ 20 b–23 a.

[1] A disconnected fragment concerning unity and plurality (§§ 14 c, 15 a) has been inserted after § 14 b.
[2] Consisting of fine matter.
[3] Heaven is the region of fire, the fourth and highest element.

Worship God then. And the one way to worship God is to keep oneself free from evil. § 23 b.

Sources. The doctrine of XII. ii is partly Platonic; but marks of Stoic influence are to be seen in the use of the terms πρόνοια (and εἱμαρμένη?), §§ 14 b and 21 ; πνεῦμα, § 18 ; and οὐσία (coupled with ὕλη and σῶμα), § 22. The importance attached to divination (§ 19) is characteristic of Stoicism ; and the paragraph in which divination is spoken of may have been suggested by Posidonius.

But in his employment of the conception of *life*, and his description of God's work as that of putting *life* into matter, (not that of imposing *forms* on matter,) the writer is not closely following either Platonic or Stoic authorities. The language of *Corp.* XII. ii concerning life resembles that of *Corp.* XI. i and XI. ii ; and the resemblance indicates either direct borrowing on one side or the other, or derivation from a common source. The doctrine that ' nothing dies ' is that which is taught in *Corp.* VIII also ; but in XII. ii it is asserted in an exaggerated and paradoxical form.

There is no sign of Jewish or Christian influence in this document.

Date. For the same reason which has been repeatedly given in dealing with other *Hermetica*, *Corp.* XII. ii cannot have been written before the first century B. C. Between this *terminus a quo*, and the *terminus ad quem* given by Lactantius's quotation (*circa* A. D. 310), I can find no definite indication of date ; but on the ground of its resemblances to other Hermetic documents, and especially to *Corp.* XI. i, XI. ii, and VIII, this *libellus* may be conjecturally assigned to the second or third century A. D.

§ 14 b. ἀνάγκη δὲ καὶ [ἡ] πρόνοια καὶ [ἡ] φύσις ὄργανά ἐστι ⟨τῆς διοικήσεως⟩ τοῦ κόσμου. Necessity, Providence, and Nature are instruments used by God in his administration of the universe. If we retain ἀνάγκη, we must either strike out the article before πρόνοια and φύσις, or write ἡ δὲ ἀνάγκη in place of ἀνάγκη δέ. Compare § 21 as emended : μέρη ἐστὶ τοῦ θεοῦ εἱμαρμένη καὶ ἀνάγκη καὶ πρόνοια καὶ φύσις. Possibly the same four powers were mentioned in § 14 b also ; the original reading may have been εἱμαρμένη δὲ καὶ ἀνάγκη καὶ πρόνοια καὶ φύσις. But it is also possible that ἀνάγκη δέ is out of place, and that πρόνοια and φύσις alone were mentioned in § 14 b. The group ἀνάγκη, πρόνοια, φύσις occurs in *Corp.* XI. i. 5. πρόνοια, ἀνάγκη, and εἱμαρμένη are grouped together in Herm. *ap.* Stob. *Exc.* VIII and *Exc.* XIV ; [φύσις?], πρόνοια, ἀνάγκη, and εἱμαρμένη, in Herm. *ap.*

Stob. *Exc.* XII. In *Ascl. Lat.* III. 39 f., εἱμαρμένη, ἀνάγκη, and τάξις are spoken of as inseparably connected, and the three together are subordinated to the νόμος καὶ λόγος τοῦ θεοῦ (which is equivalent to πρόνοια). Cf. Herm. *ap.* Stob. *Exc.* XI. 2. (46): πρόνοια θεία τάξις· ἀνάγκη προνοίᾳ ὑπήρετις.

§§ 14 c, 15 a. [καὶ τῶν μὲν νοητῶν . . . καὶ ἡ ὕλη μία.] This passage deals with the topic of unity and plurality. It has no connexion with the rest of the dialogue ; and it is probably a misplaced fragment of some other document. The writer of XII. ii presumably began by giving an account of God's government of the Kosmos, the concluding words of which are preserved in § 14 b, and then went on at once to speak of the life with which the Kosmos is filled(§ 15 b ff.).

§ 14 c. τῶν μὲν νοητῶν ἕκαστόν ἐστιν ⟨ἕν⟩ [οὐσία], οὐσία δὲ κ.τ.λ. The phrase τῶν νοητῶν (i. e. ἀσωμάτων) ἕκαστον is contrasted with the following phrase τῶν σωμάτων ἕκαστον ; and the author must have written ἐστιν ἕν, in contrast to πολλά ἐστιν. When ἕν had fallen out, the missing predicate was supplied by writing οὐσία twice. In the absence of the preceding context, it is uncertain what sort of νοητά the writer was thinking of. He may have meant by τὰ νοητά the Platonic ' ideas ' (τὰ νοητὰ εἴδη); cf. Pl. *Phileb.* 15 A: ὅταν δέ τις ἕνα ἄνθρωπον ἐπιχειρῇ τίθεσθαι, καὶ βοῦν ἕνα, καὶ τὸ καλὸν ἕν, καὶ τἀγαθὸν ἕν, περὶ τούτων τῶν ἑνάδων καὶ τῶν τοιούτων ἡ πολλὴ . . . ἀμφισβήτησις γίγνεται. But it is possible that he meant rather such incorporeal entities as ὁ θεός and ὁ νοῦς.

οὐσία δὲ αὐτῶν ἡ ταυτότης. It is the 'essence' of the νοητά, (i. e. it is that which constitutes their existence,) that each of them is ταυτόν. This means that a νοητόν is always the same *with itself*, that is to say, that it never changes. If the writer adopted the Platonic conception of eternity, he must have held that the νοητά are eternal (i. e. out of time), and therefore necessarily exempt from change ; if not, he must have meant that the νοητά persist unchanged through endless time. In the following sentence (ἔχεται γὰρ κ.τ.λ.), ταυτότης is contrasted with μεταβολή ; cf. *Corp.* XI. i. 2 : τοῦ δὲ αἰῶνος (οὐσία ἐστὶν) ἡ ταυτότης, . . . τοῦ δὲ χρόνου, ἡ μεταβολή. But ταυτότης also implies unity, as opposed to plurality.

The word ταυτότης is not used by Plato ; it occurs first in Aristotle. But its employment by the Hermetists was, no doubt, suggested by Plato's use of ταὐτόν as a philosophic term. See Pl. *Tim.* 35 A, where ταὐτόν (' the principle of unity and identity ', Archer-Hind *ad loc.*) is contrasted with θάτερον (' the principle of multiplicity and difference'); and *Soph.* 254 E ff.

⟨⟨καὶ ἡ ὕλη μία⟩⟩. These words appear to be irrelevant where they occur in the MSS.; and something of the kind is needed here, to account for the following γάρ. The sequence of thought might be more clearly indicated by writing καὶ ἡ ⟨μὲν⟩ ὕλη μία· (ἔχεται γὰρ τῆς ταυτότητος τὰ ἀσύνθετα σώματα κ.τ.λ.·) ἐν δὲ τοῖς συνθέτοις πᾶσι σώμασιν ἀριθμὸς ἐκάστου ἐστί (i. e. in all composite bodies there is plurality). See Herm. *ap.* Stob. *Exc.* II A. 13 on τὰ ἀίδια σώματα. For the statement 'matter is one', compare *Corp.* XI. ii. 9 : μιᾶς οὔσης τῆς ὕλης. *Ib.* 11 : μία ψυχή, καὶ μία ζωή, καὶ μία ὕλη.

ἔχεται γὰρ τῆς ταυτότητος τὰ ἀσύνθετα σώματα.—(ἔχοντα γὰρ τὴν ταυτότητα τὰ σύνθετα σώματα MSS.) It may be considered certain that the author wrote ἀσύνθετα. The 'incomposite bodies' are the four cosmic elements, fire, air, water, and earth; and they are contrasted with the 'composite bodies' spoken of below (ἐν δὲ τοῖς συνθέτοις κ.τ.λ.). The material elements do not exist for ever in absolute 'sameness'; that is, they are not absolutely exempt from change, as the νοητά are; for they are transmuted into one another (τὴν μεταβολὴν εἰς ἄλληλα ποιοῦνται). Yet they 'hold on to sameness' (ἔχεται τῆς ταυτότητος); that is, they maintain their identity in another way; for though each of them is perpetually changing into the others, these transmutations compensate one another, so that the total amount of each of the four elements persists unaltered, and in this sense each of them 'maintains its sameness unimpaired for ever' (ἀεὶ τῆς ταυτότητος τὴν ἀφθαρσίαν σώζει). Hence it follows that 'matter (i.e. the sum of the four elements regarded collectively)[1] is one'.

If this explanation is right, μία must here be equivalent to ταὐτόν; and the words ἡ ὕλη μία must be taken to mean, not that all the matter in the universe forms a single whole, nor that it is all of one nature, but that (considered as a whole) it persists unchanged through all time. Cf. ὧν γὰρ ὁμοῦ σύμπας ὁ κόσμος ἀμετάβλητός ἐστι, § 18.

§ 15 a. ἐν δὲ τοῖς [ἄλλοις] συνθέτοις πᾶσι σώμασιν ἀριθμὸς ἐκάστου ἔστι. What is meant by saying that a composite body 'has number', or that there is number in it? What are the things that are numbered? As we are told that 'there cannot be composition without number', it seems that the things numbered must be the parts or elements of which the body is composed. If so, the meaning is that every composite body consists of a certain number of distinct parts or elements, and is therefore 'many' (cf. τῶν . . . σωμάτων ἕκαστον πολλά ἐστιν above).

---

[1] ὕλη does not here mean ἄμορφος or ἄποιος ὕλη.

Perhaps, however, the words might be understood in a different way; they might be taken to mean that the *proportional quantities* of the different elements of which the body is composed are 'numbered', or measured by number, i. e. that the elements are combined in fixed proportions. Cf. Ar. *De an.* 1. 5, 409 b 32 (Emped. *fr.* 96 Diels): ὁμοίως δὲ καὶ ἄλλο ὁτιοῦν τῶν συνθέτων· οὐ γὰρ ὁπωσοῦν ἔχοντα τὰ στοιχεῖα τούτων ἕκαστον, ἀλλὰ λόγῳ τινὶ ⌐καὶ συνθέσει⌐ (συντεθέντα ?), καθάπερ φησὶ καὶ Ἐμπεδοκλῆς τὸ ὀστοῦν· Ἡ δὲ χθὼν ... | τὼ δύο τῶν ὀκτὼ μερέων λάχε νήστιδος αἴγλης, | τέσσαρα δ' Ἡφαίστοιο· τὰ δ' ὀστέα λευκὰ γένοντο. These verses are thus explained by Simplicius (Diels *ad loc.*): μίγνυσι δὲ πρὸς τὴν τῶν ὀστῶν γένεσιν τέσσαρα μὲν πυρὸς μέρη, δύο δὲ γῆς, καὶ ἓν μὲν ἀέρος, ἓν δὲ ὕδατος. But, taken in this sense, the statement that 'each composite body has number' would be less directly connected with the question whether each thing is 'one' or 'many', which seems to be the main subject of the paragraph.

αἱ δὲ ἑνάδες τὸν ἀριθμὸν γεννῶσι καὶ αὔξουσι. Number is 'generated' and 'increased' by units; i.e. the number two is produced by adding one to one, and each larger number in succession is produced by adding one to the preceding number. Cf. *Corp.* IV. 10: ἡ γὰρ μονὰς ... πάντα ἀριθμὸν γεννᾷ. This is a general proposition concerning number as such, and has no apparent connexion with the preceding statements that each νοητόν is one, and each composite body is many, or 'has number'; for the writer cannot have held that a composite body is formed by adding νοητά together.

§ 15 b. οὐδέν ἐστιν . . . ὃ οὐχὶ ζῇ. νεκρὸν γὰρ οὐδὲ ἓν κ.τ.λ. Cf. *Corp.* VIII *tit.*: Ὅτι οὐδὲν τῶν ὄντων ἀπόλλυται. *Corp.* XI. ii. 15 b: τὴν δὲ μεταβολὴν θάνατόν φασιν εἶναι κ.τ.λ.

⟨⟨ἀπὸ⟩⟩ τῆς πρώτης [[ἀπο]]καταστάσεως. This phrase implies that the universe has had a beginning.

§ 16. ἵνα νέα γένηται. These words might mean either 'in order that the same ζῷα may be renewed', or 'in order that new ζῷα may come into being in the place of those which suffer dissolution'. The ambiguity is convenient for the writer's argument. The statement is true in the latter sense only; but in order to support the paradoxical thesis that no animal dies, it must be taken in the former sense.

τίς τῆς ζωῆς ἐστιν ἡ ἐνέργεια; οὐχὶ κίνησις; The syllogism implied is this: 'All things which are in motion are alive; all things in the Kosmos are in motion; therefore all things in the Kosmos are alive'. But instead of saying 'All things which are in motion are alive', Hermes says 'The ἐνέργεια of life (i. e. the result produced by the working of life) is motion'; and this amounts to no more than 'all things which are alive are in motion'. The argument therefore is not formally valid. In order to make it valid, we must assume that there is no motion other than that which results from life.

§ 17. καὶ πολυκίνητος μόνη ἥδε καὶ στάσιμος. All material things except the earth are κινητά and not στάσιμα. The earth differs from all the rest in being στάσιμος; but though στάσιμος in one respect, it is at the same time κινητή in other respects. It is στάσιμος, in that it is fixed at the centre of the universe, and does not either move indefinitely, like the water and the air, or revolve, like the celestial spheres. But it is κινητή, in that it puts forth plants and animals at its surface, and that portions of its substance enter into the bodies of the plants and animals.

γελοιότατον δὲ ἐπύθου, εἰ τὸ τέταρτον μέρος ἀργόν ἐστ[α]ι. The earth is one of the four μέρη of the Kosmos, the other three being water, air, and fire. The future ἔσται cannot stand in combination with ἐπύθου. We must either write γελοιότατον δὲ ἐπύθου, εἰ . . . ἀργόν ἐστι ('it is absurd to ask, as you did, whether the earth is idle'); or omit ἐπύθου, and write γελοιότατον δὲ εἰ . . . ἀργὸν ἔσται ('it is absurd if the earth is to be idle', i. e. 'it is absurd to try to make out that the earth is idle'). For the word ἀργόν in this connexion, cf. Corp. XI. i. 5 : ἀλλ' οὐδὲ ἐν τῷ κόσμῳ ἐστὶν ἀργία οὐδαμοῦ.

§ 18. πᾶν τοίνυν ἴσθι . . . τὸ ὂν ἐν ⟨τῷ ?⟩ κόσμῳ κινούμενον [ἢ κατὰ μείωσιν ἢ αὔξησιν]. The words ἢ κατὰ . . . αὔξησιν must be cut out. If they are retained, the statement is (according to the writer's cosmology) untrue; for the heavenly bodies do not 'increase or decrease'. It is true of earthly organisms; but the earth is only 'a fourth part of the Kosmos'.

τὸ δὲ ζῶ[ο]ν πᾶν οὐκ ἀνάγκη τὸ αὐτὸ ⟨ἀεὶ⟩ εἶναι. There is life in all matter at all times; but life does not through all time maintain itself in the same organisms. A living organism sooner or later ceases to exist as such; but when it suffers dissolution, its material substance either is absorbed into the mass of the unorganized elements, which are themselves alive, or enters into the composition of other living organisms. As the writer of Corp. XI. ii. 15 b puts it, life does not perish at the dissolution of an organism, but only departs out of our sight, to reappear elsewhere.

οὐ γὰρ ἡ γένεσίς ἐστι ζωῆς ἀρχή, ἀλλ' αἰσθήσεως.—(οὐ γὰρ ἡ γένεσίς ἐστι ζωή, ἀλλ' ἡ αἴσθησις MSS.) In order to make sense of this, it seems necessary to take αἴσθησις to mean 'individual consciousness', and λήθη 'the cessation of individual consciousness'. The *life* which for a time resides in a particular animal has no beginning or end; it has come from elsewhere, and will depart only to reappear elsewhere; but an animal's *consciousness* begins when that animal is born, and ceases when that animal suffers dissolution. (Cf. *Corp.* VIII. 4: οὕτω στέρησις γίνεται τῆς αἰσθήσεως, οὐκ ἀπώλεια ⟨ζωῆς⟩.) Life (ζωή) may exist without consciousness (αἴσθησις); for instance, it was commonly said that plants have ζωή, but not αἴσθησις. The writer may have held that the unorganized elements have life without consciousness; or he may have held that each of them has a consciousness of its own, but that this consciousness is distinct and separate from that of individual organisms, and that the former persists continuously, but the latter begins at the birth of the organism, and ends at its dissolution. In *Corp.* IX. 6, we are told that the Kosmos has an αἴσθησις καὶ νόησις (i. e. a consciousness) of its own; and it would be possible to say the same of the several elements, which were called 'parts' of the Kosmos, and were sometimes regarded as gods.

ἀθάνατα πάντα ⟨⟨ἐξ ὧν πᾶν ζῷον συνέστηκε⟨ν⟩⟩⟩, ἡ ὕλη [ζωή], τὸ πνεῦμα [ὁ νοῦς], ⟨ἡ⟩ ψυχή. ζωή is evidently out of place here. νοῦς, if mentioned at all, ought to stand after ψυχή (as it does in R), and not before it; but as beasts have no νοῦς, it ought not to be spoken of here. If we cut out ζωή and ὁ νοῦς, there remain (1) ὕλη (gross matter, i. e. earth and water), (2) πνεῦμα ('vital spirit', consisting of fine matter, i. e. air and fire), and (3) ψυχή (incorporeal); and these three are correctly described as 'the things of which every (earthly) ζῷον is composed'. At the dissolution of the individual organism, its ὕλη goes back into the mass of cosmic ὕλη; its πνεῦμα goes back into the cosmic πνεῦμα, or the mass of cosmic air and fire; and it seems to be implied that its ψυχή is likewise reabsorbed into the cosmic ψυχή, i. e. the mass of undivided ψυχή whence it was parted off to enter into the individual animal. For the notion of an undivided mass of ψυχή, cf. *Corp.* XI. ii. 9, μιᾶς οὔσης τῆς ὕλης καὶ μιᾶς τῆς ψυχῆς. *Ib.* 10, ψυχὴ ·." . . καθ' ἑαυτήν, τῷ ποιητῇ παρακειμένη. *Corp.* X. 7: ἀπὸ μιᾶς ψυχῆς τῆς τοῦ παντὸς πᾶσαι αἱ ψυχαί εἰσιν . . . ὥσπερ ἀπονενεμημέναι.

πᾶν ἄρα ζῷον ἀθάνατον δι⟨ὰ τὴν ἀθανασίαν⟩ αὐτῶν. The cosmic ὕλη, the cosmic πνεῦμα, and the cosmic ψυχή are immortal; and the portions of them which enter into the individual organism share the immortality of the mass from which they are temporarily parted off. Thus the parts of which the organism is composed are immortal; and the writer considers this enough to justify his paradoxical assertion that the organism itself is immortal.

§ 19. πάντων δὲ μᾶλλον ⟨ἀθάνατος⟩ ὁ ἄνθρωπος. Beasts can be called ἀθάνατα only by a strained and unnatural use of the term; but men are ἀθάνατοι in a different and higher sense. But in what sense? What does the writer mean by ἀθάνατος when he applies the word to men? The two reasons given for holding men to be ἀθάνατοι are these: (1) men receive from God revelations by which future events are made known to them; and (2) men are superior to beasts in that they are not restricted to one element, and look up to heaven. Neither of these facts can be considered to prove that men survive the dissolution of the body; but both may be held to show that man is a being of higher order than the beasts. It seems therefore that ἀθάνατος here means 'of like nature with the gods', and is equivalent to θεῖος. It is possible however that a passage containing some further explanation of the ἀθανασία of men has been lost at the end of § 20 a.

ὁ καὶ τοῦ θεοῦ δεκτικὸς καὶ τῷ θεῷ συνουσιαστικός. Man is 'receptive of God'; that is, he is capable of becoming ἔνθεος. And man is 'capable of holding intercourse with God'; that is, God speaks to men by dreams and signs.

For the notion that man is exalted above the beasts, and brought near to God, by the gift of μαντεία, cf. Synesius *De insomniis* I, Migne Tom. 66 col. 1284 A: μαντεία δὲ ἀγαθῶν ἂν εἴη τὸ μέγιστον. τῷ μὲν γὰρ εἰδέναι, καὶ ὅλως τῷ γνωστικῷ τῆς δυνάμεως, θεός τε ἀνθρώπου καὶ ἄνθρωπος διαφέρει θηρίου. ἀλλὰ θεῷ μὲν εἰς τὸ γινώσκειν ἡ φύσις ἀρκεῖ· ἀπὸ δὲ μαντείας ἀνθρώπῳ πολλαπλάσιον παραγίνεται τοῦ τῇ κοινῇ φύσει προσήκοντος. ὁ γὰρ πολὺς τὸ παρὸν μόνον οἶδε, περὶ δὲ τοῦ μήπω γενομένου στοχάζεται· ὁ δὲ Κάλχας εἰς ἄρα . . . μόνος ἠπίστατο "τά τ' ἐόντα τά τ' ἐσσόμενα πρό τ' ἐόντα".[1] . . . σημαίνει μὲν διὰ πάντων πάντα, ἅτε ἀδελφῶν ὄντων τῶν ἐν ἑνὶ ζῴῳ τῷ κόσμῳ· καὶ ἔστι ταῦτα γράμματα παντοδαπὰ καθάπερ ἐν βιβλίῳ τοῖς οὖσι, . . . ἀναγινώσκει δὲ ὁ σοφός, . . . καὶ ἄλλος ἄλλα, καὶ ὁ

---

[1] Hom. *Il.* I. 70. The Hermetist's words, ἐπαγγέλλεται ὁ ἄνθρωπος ἐπίστασθαι τὰ προγεγενημένα καὶ ἐνεστῶτα καὶ μέλλοντα, show that he had in mind the same Homeric verse.

μὲν μᾶλλον, ὁ δὲ ἧττον. . . . οὕτως ὁρῶσι σοφοὶ τὸ μέλλον, οἱ μὲν
ἄστρα εἰδότες,[1] . . . οἱ δὲ ἐν σπλάγχνοις αὐτὰ ἀναγνόντες, οἱ δὲ ἐν
ὀρνίθων κλαγγαῖς καὶ καθέδραις καὶ πτήσεσι. τοῖς δὲ καὶ τὰ καλούμενα
σύμβολα τῶν ἐσομένων ἐστὶν ἀρίδηλα γράμματα, φωναί τε καὶ συγκύρ-
σεις ἐπ' ἄλλῳ γενόμεναι, σημαντικῶν ὄντων ἄπασι πάντων. The
resemblance between the Hermetist's summary treatment of μαντεία,
and Synesius's fuller discussion of it, makes it probable that they
drew from a common source; and it is not unlikely that both of
them were directly or indirectly influenced by Posidonius. Cic.
Div. 1. 6: 'Chrysippus . . . totam de divinatione duobus libris
explicavit sententiam, uno praeterea de oraculis, uno de somniis:
quem subsequens unum librum Babylonius Diogenes edidit, eius
auditor; duo Antipater; quinque noster Posidonius.' *Ib.* 1. 1:
'magnifica quidem res (μαντική), et salutaris, . . . quaque proxime
ad deorum vim natura mortalis possit accedere.'

διὰ ὀρνέων, διὰ σπλάγχνων, διὰ πνεύματος, διὰ δρυός. Cf. *Ascl. Lat.*
III. 24 a: 'statuas futurorum praescias, eaque sorte, vate, somniis,
multisque aliis rebus praedicentes.' Observation of the flight and
cries of birds, and inspection of the livers of animals slaughtered in
sacrifice, were two of the commonest forms of Greek μαντική.
The mention of divination διὰ δρυός is perhaps a literary allusion to
the oracle of Dodona. But there may have been tree-oracles in
Egypt also.[2] It is not likely that there were many *oaks* in Egypt;
but the Hermetist may have used δρῦς as a synonym for δένδρον.

The word πνεῦμα was sometimes used to mean the divine 'breath'
by which a human being is inspired;[3] and if διὰ δρυός is an allusion
to the oracle of Dodona, διὰ πνεύματος might possibly be meant to
allude to the inspiration of the Pythia at Delphi.[4] But as the word

---

[1] The writer of *Corp.* XII. ii does not mention astrology among the ways of
getting knowledge of the future; and as it was one of those most commonly
employed in his time, the omission is probably deliberate.

[2] In Philostratus *Vita Apollon.* 6. 10, the chief of the *Gymni*, on the upper Nile,
makes an elm-tree talk. "τὸ δεῖνα" ἔφη "δένδρον", πτελέα δὲ ἦν, . . . "προσεῖπε
τὸν σοφὸν Ἀπολλώνιον." καὶ προσεῖπε μὲν αὐτόν, ὡς ἐκελεύσθη, ἡ φωνὴ δὲ ἦν
ἔναρθρός τε καὶ θῆλυς. The story is no doubt a free invention; but the man who
invented it may perhaps have heard of talking trees in Egypt.

[3] E. g. Democritus fr. 18 Diels (Clem. Alex. *Strom.* 6. 18. 167): ποιητὴς δὲ
ἄσσα μὲν ἂν γράφῃ μετ' ἐνθουσιασμοῦ καὶ ἱεροῦ πνεύματος, καλὰ κάρτα ἐστίν. Ps.-
Plato *Axiochus* 370 c: man could not have acquired the knowledge he possesses
εἰ μή τι θεῖον ὄντως ἐνῆν πνεῦμα τῇ ψυχῇ, δι' οὗ τὴν τῶν τηλικῶνδε περίνοιαν καὶ
γνῶσιν ἔσχεν.

[4] The πνεῦμα by which the Pythia was inspired was sometimes supposed to issue
from the chasm above which she was seated. Cic. *Div.* 1. 38: 'potest autem vis
illa terrae, quae mentem Pythiae divino afflatu concitabat, evanuisse vetustate, ut

πνεῦμα has been used in a different sense a few lines before, and is barely intelligible here without some explanation, it may be suspected that it has been inserted by a Christian, who wished to make the sentence applicable to the prophets of his own religion.

ἐπίστασθαι τὰ προγεγενημένα καὶ ἐνεστῶτα καὶ μέλλοντα. The emphasis is on μέλλοντα. To know the future is a privilege of the gods ; and man, in so far as he knows the future, is godlike (ἀθάνατος).

§ 20 a. ἕκαστον τῶν ζῴων ἐνὶ μέρει ἐπιφοιτᾷ τοῦ κόσμου. This is a singularly futile argument. It might have been said with some show of reason that man is the only animal that has to do with all four elements ; but the Hermetist shows a strange disregard of obvious facts in saying that every other animal is restricted to one element. There are amphibious animals, which haunt both earth and water ; birds haunt both air and earth, and some birds swim and dive in water also. Moreover, man uses air only as the beasts use it ; both men and beasts breathe air. A more plausible statement of the same argument occurs in Philo *De opif. mundi* 51. 147, Cohn I, p. 51 : Man πᾶσι τοῖς λεχθεῖσι (*sc.* γῇ, ὕδατι, ἀέρι, πυρὶ) ὡς οἰκειοτάτοις καὶ συγγενεστάτοις χωρίοις ἐνδιαιτᾶται, τόπους ἀμείβων, καὶ ἄλλοτε ἄλλοις ἐπιφοιτῶν, ὡς κυριώτατα φάναι τὸν ἄνθρωπον πάντα εἶναι, χερσαῖον, ἔνυδρον, πτηνόν, οὐράνιον· ᾗ μὲν γὰρ οἰκεῖ καὶ βέβηκεν ἐπὶ γῆς, χερσαῖον ζῷόν ἐστιν, ᾗ δὲ δύεται καὶ νήχεται καὶ πλεῖ πολλάκις, ἔνυδρον, . . . ᾗ δὲ μετέωρον ἀπὸ γῆς ἀνώφοιτον ἐξῆρται τὸ σῶμα (i. e. stands erect) λέγοιτ᾿ ἂν ἐνδίκως ἀεροπόρον εἶναι, πρὸς δὲ καὶ οὐράνιον, διὰ τῆς ἡγεμονικωτάτης τῶν αἰσθήσεων ὄψεως ἡλίῳ καὶ σελήνῃ καὶ ἑκάστῳ τῶν ἄλλων ἀστέρων πλανήτων καὶ ἀπλανῶν συνεγγίζων. The common source is probably Stoic.

ὁ δὲ ἄνθρωπος τούτοις πᾶσι χρῆται, γῇ, ὕδατι, ἀέρι [πυρί]· ὁρᾷ δὲ καὶ οὐρανόν. ' All these ' (τούτοις πᾶσι) must mean the three elements which have just been mentioned, viz. earth, water, and air ; πυρί must therefore be cut out. The fourth cosmic region, that of fire, is here called, not πῦρ, but οὐρανός. Cf. § 21 : τοῦ κόσμου μέρη εἰσὶν οὐρανὸς καὶ γῆ καὶ ὕδωρ καὶ ἀήρ.

ὁρᾷ δὲ καὶ οὐρανόν, ἅπτεται δὲ καὶ τούτου αἰσθήσει.. Men do not indeed ' make use of ' the celestial fire, as they make use of the other three elements ; but they look up at it, and are in that way brought into connexion with it. It could hardly be denied that beasts and birds, as well as men, are able to ' see the sky ' in the

quosdam exaruisse amnes aut in alium cursum contortos et deflexos videmus.' Here the prophetic πνεῦμα is regarded as a gaseous substance.

literal sense of the words ; but the Hermetist considers that men are,
by their bodily form, better fitted than beasts to look upward ; and
he holds that, in consequence of the direction of our eyes towards
the sky, our thoughts are turned towards things heavenly and divine,
or at any rate, that the upturning of man's eyes is symbolic of the
elevation of his thought.   As to the significance of ' looking up to
heaven', cf. *Ascl. Lat.* I. 6 a : 'suspicit caelum.'   *Ib.* 9 : ' caeli sus-
piciendi venerabilem curam.'   *Ascl. Lat.* III. 25 : 'nemo suspiciet
caelum.'   Pl. *Tim.* 47 A : ὄψις δὲ . . . αἰτία τῆς μεγίστης ὠφελείας
γέγονεν ἡμῖν, ὅτι τῶν νῦν λόγων περὶ τοῦ παντὸς λεγομένων οὐδεὶς ἂν
ποτε ἐρρήθη μήτε ἄστρα μήτε ἥλιον μήτε οὐρανὸν ἰδόντων· νῦν δ᾿ . . . .
ἐπορισάμεθα φιλοσοφίας γένος.   Cic. *Nat. deor.* 2. 140, probably from
Posidonius : '(di homines) humo excitatos celsos et erectos consti-
tuerunt, ut deorum cognitionem caelum intuentes capere possent.
Sunt enim . . . homines . . . quasi spectatores superarum rerum atque
caelestium, quarum spectaculum ad nullum aliud genus animantium
pertinet.'   Cic. *Legg.* 1. 26 : 'nam cum ceteras animantes abiecisset
ad pastum, solum hominem erexit (natura), ad caelique quasi cogna-
tionis domiciliique pristini conspectum excitavit.'   Ov. *Metam.* i.
84 : 'pronaque cum spectent animalia cetera terram, | os homini
sublime dedit, caelumque videre | iussit, et erectos ad sidera tollere
vultus.'   In the *cosmogonia* of 'Sanchuniathon' (quoted in introductory note on *Corp.* III) men are called οὐρανοῦ κατόπται.   Sen.
Ep. 94. 56 : '(natura) vultus nostros erexit in caelum, et quicquid
magnificum mirumque fecerat videri a suspicientibus voluit.'   Lactantius *Opif. dei* 8. 2 : ' cum igitur statuisset deus ex omnibus ani-
malibus solum hominem facere caelestem, caetera universa terrena,
hunc ad caeli contemplationem rigidum erexit bipedemque con-
stituit, scilicet ut eodem spectaret unde illi origo est, illa vero
depressit ad terram.'   Lactant. *Div. inst.* 2. 1. 14–19, and 7. 5. 6.
This commonplace is criticized by Galen, *Us. part.* 3. 3 (J. B. Mayor
ad Cic. *N. D.* 2. 140) : 'Those who believe man to have been made
erect in order that he might look up to heaven . . . can never have
seen thê fish called *uranoscopus*, not to mention various birds, which
are much better adapted for looking up than man. The true upward
looking, as Plato said (*Rep.* 7. 529), is to fix the mental eye on that
which really exists.'   The notion is more plausible from the point of
view of a Stoic, who identifies the visible sky with the supreme deity,
than from that of a Platonist ; and it may have been Posidonius that
first expressed it in the form in which it was adopted by later writers.

§ 20 b. [ὁ δὲ θεὸς καὶ περὶ πάντα καὶ διὰ πάντων.] These words occur in XII. i. 14 a, and have probably been repeated here by error. Compare διὰ πάντων καὶ περὶ πάντα in § 23 a.

καὶ οὐδὲν δύσκολόν ἐστι νοῆσαι τὸν θεόν, . . . εἰ δὲ θέλεις, [[αὐτὸν]] καὶ θεωρῆσαι ⟨⟨αὐτόν⟩⟩. The writer distinguishes θεωρῆσαι, 'to see', from νοῆσαι, 'to apprehend in thought'. Cf. Corp. XI. ii. 21 b sq.: πανταχοῦ ὀφθήσεται (σοι ὁ θεὸς). . . . εἶτα φῇς " ἀόρατος ὁ θεός"; εὐφήμησον. . . . ὁ θεὸς (ὁρᾶται) ἐν τῷ ποιεῖν.

Having shown in §§ 15 b–18 that the Kosmos is full of life, Hermes proceeds to say in this paragraph (§§ 20 b–23 a) that all the life in the Kosmos is a manifestation of God's working, and that God can therefore be seen in all things. But the transition is abrupt; and the new topic is in no way suggested by the preceding demonstration that man is ἀθάνατος (§§ 19, 20a). It is therefore probable that a connecting passage has been lost. The unintelligible words ⌜ἐνέργεια γάρ ἐστι δύναμις⌝ are presumably a fragment of the lost passage.

§ 21. ἴδε τὴν ἀνάγκην τῶν φαινομένων. If the text is sound, the meaning must be ' see how, in the visible world, one event necessarily follows another'. The sequence of cause and effect is unvarying and inevitable. Cf. Ascl. Lat. III. 39 : 'necessitas vero cogit ad effectum quae ex illius (sc. εἱμαρμένης) primordiis pendent. . . . necessitas, qua ad effectum vi coguntur omnia.'

καὶ τὴν πρόνοιαν τῶν γεγονότων τε καὶ γινομένων. ' Observe the indications of God's providence (i.e. the proofs of design) in past and present events' (or, ' in things that have come into being in the past, and things that come into being in the present'). This topic was much dwelt on by the Stoics ; see e.g. Cic. Nat. deor. 2. §§ 73–167.

⟨ἴδε⟩ τὸν τηλικοῦτον θεὸν κινούμενον μετὰ πάντων ⟨τῶν ἐνόντων⟩ [ἀγαθῶν καὶ καλῶν] [θεῶν τε καὶ δαιμόνων καὶ ἀνθρώπων]. ' This great god' is the Kosmos. The Kosmos and all things in it are ever in motion ; and that which is in motion must be alive. These words then amount to a repetition of the statement that the Kosmos is πλήρωμα τῆς ζωῆς.

Something like τῶν ἐνόντων is needed to complete the sense. When this had been lost, two different attempts were made to fill the gap ; hence we have the two alternatives ἀγαθῶν καὶ καλῶν and θεῶν τε καὶ δαιμόνων καὶ ἀνθρώπων.

Ἀλλ᾽ αὗται, ὦ πάτερ, ἐνέργειαι ὅλως εἰσίν. What is meant by αὗται? The things last spoken of were the Kosmos and its contents ; but these cannot be called ἐνέργειαι. The word αὗται must therefore be taken to mean ἡ ἀνάγκη and ἡ πρόνοια. Tat says that Necessity and Providence are ' energies ', i. e. forces at work ; and he assumes that ' energies' are things distinct from God, and consequently, that if the life in the Kosmos is produced by ' energies', it cannot be the work of God. Hermes corrects his error by explaining that the ἐνέργειαι of which he is speaking (viz. Necessity, Providence, and the like) ὑπὸ τοῦ θεοῦ ἐνεργοῦνται ; that is, they are ἐνέργειαι τοῦ θεοῦ, modes of God's activity ; they are therefore ' parts of God ', and not, as Tat imagined, entities distinct from God. Cf. *Ascl. Lat.* III. 39 as emended : ἡ δὲ εἱμαρμένη ἐστὶν ἢ αὐτὸς ὁ θεός, ἢ ἡ μετ' ἐκεῖνον τεταγμένη ἐνέργεια. *Corp.* III *fin.* : ἐν γὰρ τῷ θεῷ καὶ ἡ φύσις καθέστηκεν.

ἢ ἀγνοεῖς ὅτι . . . μέρη (μέλη MSS.) ἐστὶ ⟨τοῦ⟩ θεοῦ [ζωὴ καὶ ἀθανασία καὶ] εἱμαρμένη (αἷμα MSS.) καὶ ἀνάγκη καὶ πρόνοια καὶ φύσις [   ] ; There can be little doubt that the author gave a list of four ' parts ' of God to match the four ' parts ' of the Kosmos. Among the ' parts ' of God, ἀνάγκη and πρόνοια, the two ἐνέργειαι which have just been mentioned, must have been included ; with these, φύσις is fittingly coupled ; and the first of the four, which has been corrupted into αἷμα, was almost certainly εἱμαρμένη. For the association of εἱμαρμένη with ἀνάγκη, πρόνοια, and φύσις, see note on § 14 b above.

[καὶ ψυχὴ καὶ νοῦς] [καὶ τούτων πάντων ἡ διαμονὴ] [τὸ λεγόμενον ἀγαθόν]. The author cannot have coupled ψυχή and νοῦς with ἀνάγκη &c. These phrases, as well as [ζωὴ καὶ ἀθανασία καὶ] above, may be misplaced fragments of the lost passage which preceded § 20 b. Perhaps it was there said that God is the author or source of νοῦς and ψυχή, and of life in its two different forms of ἀθανασία and διαμονή. Cf. *Corp.* XI. i. 2 : ἐνέργειαι δὲ τοῦ θεοῦ νοῦς καὶ ψυχή. *Ib.* 4 a as emended : ὁ αἰὼν κοσμεῖ τὴν ὕλην, ἀθανασίαν καὶ διαμονὴν ἐνθεὶς τῇ ὕλῃ. XI. ii. 17 c as emended : οὐδὲ ὁ θεὸς δύναται ⟨εἶναι⟩ μὴ ποιῶν τὸ ἀγαθόν· ἔστι δὲ τοῦτο . . . ζωή.

οὐκ [ἔτι] ἔστι τι . . . ὅπου οὐκ ἔστιν ὁ θεός. Cf. *Corp.* XI. i. 6 a as emended : ὁ γὰρ ποιῶν ἐν πᾶσίν ἐστιν, . . . πανταχοῦ ὢν ἐνεργής.

§ 22. Ἡ γὰρ ὕλη . . . χωρὶς θεοῦ ⟨τί⟩ ἐστιν, ἵνα τόπον (ποιὸν MSS.) αὐτῇ ἀπομερίσῃς ; Matter, if it were not ' energized ' by God (i. e. if God did not put life into it), would have no actual existence. Lifeless ὕλη is a mere abstraction ; the writer holds it to be μὴ ὄν, as the Platonists said that ἄμορφος or ἄποιος ὕλη is μὴ ὄν. You cannot ' assign a place to it ', i. e. you cannot say that it is to be found in this or that part of the universe. All existent matter is alive ; and its life must have been put into it by the vivifying activity (ἐνέργεια) of God.

τί δὲ [ουσ] ἂν ἢ σωρὸν αὐτὴν οἴει εἶναι, μὴ ἐνεργουμένην ; If the text is right, σωρός must here mean ' an inert and lifeless mass '. But I have found no instance elsewhere of the use of the word in this sense ; and some qualification of σωρόν may have been lost. Perhaps the author may have written ⟨νεκρῶν⟩ σωρόν ; cf. Diod. 12. 62. 5 : πολλοὺς τῶν πολεμίων νεκροὺς σωρεύσας. Or possibly the true reading may be σορόν ; matter, if it were not energized by God, would be a σορός, i. e. a thing that contains nothing but dead bones or ashes.

ὑπὸ τίνος οὖν ζωοποιεῖται τὰ πάντα ζῷα ; ὑπὸ τίνος ἀθανατίζεται τὰ ἀθάνατα ; ὑπὸ τίνος μεταβάλλεται τὰ μεταβλητά ; The two different forms which life takes, viz. immortal life (ἀθανασία) and mortal life (μεταβολή), are here distinguished, as in Corp. XI. i and ii. Compare especially XI. i. 5 as emended : τίς ἄλλος αἴτιος ζωῆς, καὶ ἀθανασίας καὶ μεταβολῆς ποιητής ; It is to be noted that the writer has already forgotten his reckless assertion that all ζῷα are ἀθάνατα (§ 18 fin.).

εἴτε δὲ ὕλην, εἴτε σῶμα, εἴτε οὐσίαν φῇς. ὕλη is here, not ἄποιος or ἄμορφος ὕλη, but matter as it presents itself to our senses, i. e. matter formed and vivified. In this sense, ὕλη is an alternative for σῶμα ; and that being so, οὐσία also must be taken as an alternative for σῶμα. The three terms ' matter ', ' body ', and ' substance ' are equally applicable to τὸ αἰσθητον, and you may use which of them you will in speaking of it. The word οὐσία then is here used as it was used by the Stoics, and not as it was used by Plato.

ἴσθι καὶ ταύτας οὔσας (αὐτὰς MSS.) ἐνεργείας τοῦ θεοῦ. ἐνέργεια here means, not ' a force at work ', but ' the result produced by a force at work '. Cf. Corp. XI. i. 2 : ἐνέργειαι δὲ τοῦ θεοῦ νοῦς καὶ ψυχή κ.τ.λ.

⟨ὁ γὰρ θεὸς⟩ . . . ἐνεργεῖ . . . τῶν σωμάτων ⟨τὴν⟩ σωματότητα. It is God's ἐνέργεια that makes body what it is. If God did not put life into it, it would be lifeless ; and to be lifeless is to be non-existent.

§ 23 a.   οὔτε μέγεθος οὔτε τόπος οὔτε ποιότης οὔτε σχῆμα οὔτε χρόνος παρὰ (περὶ MSS.) τὸν θεόν ἐστι. If this sentence stood alone, we might retain περί, and take the words to mean that magnitude, position in space, &c. cannot be attributed to God,—in short, that

God is ἀσώματος. (Cf. Herm. *Exc.* II A. 15.) But that statement would be irrelevant here. The connecting word ὅθεν shows that οὔτε μέγεθος κ.τ.λ. is an expansion of the preceding *dictum*, 'God is the All, and there is nothing that is not included in the All'; the meaning must therefore be that no attribute of material things exists 'beside' (παρά) God, i. e. in independence of him.

χρόνος is oddly placed; if the word were used at all here, it would most naturally be put next to τόπος. As σχῆμα and χρῶμα are often coupled together, (e. g. ἀχρώματός τε καὶ ἀσχημάτιστος in Pl. *Phaedr.* 247 c, copied in Herm. *ap.* Stob. *Exc.* II A. 15,) it seems probable that the author wrote οὔτε σχῆμα οὔτε χρῶμα.

τὸ δὲ πᾶν διὰ πάντων καὶ περὶ πάντα. The phrase resembles that in XII. i. 14 a, ὁ μὲν θεὸς περὶ πάντα καὶ διὰ πάντων; but it does not necessarily follow that the writer of either document borrowed from the other.

§ 23 b. τοῦτον [τὸν λόγον], ὦ τέκνον, προσκύνει. This sentence had already been corrupted in the copy used by Lactantius, who read τοῦτον τὸν λόγον . . . προσκύνει, 'worship this λόγος', and took 'this λόγος' to mean the Second Person of the Christian Trinity. But *Corp.* XII. ii contains no trace elsewhere of a personified λόγος; and that being so, the Hermetist cannot possibly have spoken of 'this λόγος' as a God to be worshipped. The simplest remedy is to strike out τὸν λόγον (which may perhaps have been inserted by a Christian through whose hands the text had passed before it reached Lactantius), and to take τοῦτον to mean τὸν θεόν. But it is also possible that the author wrote ⟨κατὰ⟩ τοῦτον τὸν λόγον (in accordance with this my teaching), ὦ τέκνον, ⟨τὸν θεὸν⟩ προσκύνει, or something to that effect.

μὴ εἶναι κακόν. The Hermetist has chosen to write 'not to be bad' rather than 'to be good', presumably because he considers that God alone can properly be called good (see *Corp.* VI), and that 'not to be bad' is the utmost to which man, while yet in the body, can attain. The 'not being bad' of which he is thinking is probably not abstinence from wrong-doing towards one's fellow men (the *iustitia* which Lactantius, in his comment on the passage, takes this phrase to imply); he would doubtless have said, like other Hermetists, that the chief and all-inclusive virtue is not δικαιοσύνη (justice towards men), but εὐσέβεια (piety towards God); and for him, μὴ εἶναι κακόν would perhaps mean first and chiefly μὴ εἶναι φιλοσώματον.

LIBELLVS XIII

Contents

A. *The teacher describes the Rebirth.*   §§ 1–8 a.

The doctrine of the Rebirth is to be taught only to those who are
ready to be estranged from the material world.   § 1.

The man whom the Rebirth brings into being is a son of God ;
he belongs to the world of Mind ; he is composed of divine Powers.
He who has been born again has become an incorporeal being ;
he is no longer a thing visible to bodily eyes.   §§ 2–4.

The human body is subject to change, and is unreal, as are all
material and sensible things.   That only is real which is changeless
and incorporeal.   §§ 5, 6.

He who would be born again must suppress the working of his
bodily senses, and rid himself of the evil passions which spring from
matter.   That is not impossible ; but it can be accomplished only
by God's mercy.   §§ 7 a–8 a.

B. *The pupil experiences the Rebirth.*   §§ 8 b–14.

The Powers of God enter into the man, and there is built up in
him an incorporeal organism, of which those Powers are the
members.   Knowledge (of God), Reality, the Good, Life and Light
are now present in him ; no evil passion can henceforth trouble him ;
he is changed into a god.   §§ 8 b–10.

He sees things no longer by bodily sense ; he sees with the eye
of Mind.   And thus seeing, he finds himself to be one with
all that exists ; he feels himself to be omnipresent and eternal.
§§ 11 a–11 b.

The new self which has thus come into being is imperishable.   He
who has once become a god, and son of God, can never cease to be
that which he has become.   § 14.

C. *Teacher and pupil give thanks to God for the Rebirth.*
§§ 15–22 a.

The Powers, who sing praise to God in their supracosmic abode,
are present in the human teacher also (inasmuch as he has been

born again), and sing within him, Thus inspired, he now sings a hymn of thanksgiving, in which he praises God (1) as maker of the material universe, and (2) as operating, through his Powers, in the mind of the man who has been born again. §§ 15–20.

The pupil, further illuminated through the influence of his teacher's hymn, gives thanks to God in a short hymn of his own devising. § 21.

Having been born again, and having thereby come to know himself and God, the pupil will bring forth good fruit. § 22 a.

The doctrine of the Rebirth must be kept secret. § 22 b. (13 b.)

Relations of Libellus XIII to other Hermetica. The Γενικοὶ λόγοι of Hermes to Tat are known to the writer as a collection of documents bearing that title (§ 1). *Corp.* XIII, since it explains a matter which was spoken of obscurely in one of the Γενικοὶ λόγοι, is presumably one of the documents entitled Διεξοδικοὶ λόγοι.

The writer knows *Corp.* I as a document ascribed to Hermes. He expressly refers to it in § 15, and repeatedly shows acquaintance with it in other passages. In § 11 b, he appears to have copied from *Corp.* XI. ii. 20 b; and in § 15 there is perhaps a reference to the concluding words of XI. ii. In § 6, he has probably borrowed from §§ 9 and 15 of the Hermetic Περὶ ἀληθείας (Herm. *ap.* Stob. *Exc.* II A).

The term παλιγγενεσία occurred in one of the Γενικοὶ λόγοι; but in the extant *Hermetica*, the metaphor or figure of 'rebirth' is employed in *Corp.* XIII alone, and the thing signified by it is elsewhere expressed in other ways. E. g. in *Corp.* I, this transformation is described by the phrases εἰς τὸ ἀγαθὸν χωρεῖν (§§ 18, 19, 21); εἰς ζωὴν καὶ φῶς χωρεῖν (§§ 21, 32); ἡ τοῦ νοῦ παρουσία (§ 22); γνῶσιν ἐσχηκέναι (§ 26 a *fin.*); σωθῆναι (§§ 26 b, 29); τῆς ψυχῆς νῆψις,— ἀληθινὴ ὅρασις (§ 30); θεόπνους γενόμενος ⟨ἐπὶ τὸ πεδίον ?⟩ τῆς ἀληθείας ἦλθον (*ib.*); τῆς ἀθανασίας μεταλαβεῖν (§ 28). *Corp.* XI. ii: ἑαυτὸν ἐξισάσαι τῷ θεῷ (§ 20 b); συναυξῆσαι ἑαυτὸν τῷ ἀμετρήτῳ μεγέθει, κ.τ.λ. (*ib.*); νοῆσαι τὸν θεόν (*ib.*). *Corp.* X: ἡ τοῦ ἀγαθοῦ θέα (§ 4 b); ἡ ἐπεισροὴ τῆς νοητῆς λαμπηδόνος (*ib.*); ἀναπετάσαι ἡμῶν τοὺς τοῦ νοῦ ὀφθαλμούς, καὶ θεάσασθαι τὸ κάλλος τοῦ ἀγαθοῦ (§ 5); ἡ γνῶσις τοῦ ἀγαθοῦ (*ib.*); εἰς οὐσίαν μεταβληθῆναι,—ἀποθεωθῆναι (§ 6); γενέσθαι ἀθανασίας,—τοῦ ἀγαθοῦ μεταλαμβάνειν (§ 8 a); γνῶσις (§ 9); ἡ γνῶσις τοῦ θεοῦ (§ 15 a); τὸ τῆς γνώσεως φῶς (§ 21). In *Corp.* IV, the process which corresponds to the 'rebirth' of *Corp.* XIII is called 'dipping oneself in the basin of νοῦς'; i. e. in that document it is figuratively described as a baptism.

Sources. The doctrine of *Corp.* XIII is based on Platonism. The Platonic antitheses of αἴσθησις and νόησις, αἰσθητά and νοητά, τὸ ἀληθές (= τὸ ὄντως ὄν) and τὸ ψευδές (= τὸ φαινόμενον), the corporeal and the incorporeal, are present in the writer's thought throughout the dialogue; and in § 2 *fin.* there is a reference to the Platonic doctrine of ἀνάμνησις. But in describing the change which takes place in a man when he ' comes forth from the cave ', the Platonists in general were not accustomed to employ the metaphor of 're-birth'; and the source of the conception expressed in *Corp.* XIII by the term παλιγγενεσία must be looked for in some other quarter. The group of Hermetists to which the author of *Corp.* XIII belonged probably got this conception either from the Christians, who held that men are reborn by the sacrament of baptism, or from some Pagan mystery-cult in which men were held to be reborn by a sacramental operation. But the author of *Corp.* XIII rejects all *theurgia*, as did the Hermetists in general ; and accordingly, while adopting the notion of rebirth, he differs both from the Christians and from the adherents of those Pagan mystery-cults in which a rebirth was spoken of, in that he does not regard παλιγγενεσία as effected by any sacramental action.

Date. Corp. XIII is certainly later than *Corp.* I, which I con-jecture to have been written between A. D. 100 and 200 ; and it is probably later than *Corp.* XI. ii, which I have assigned to the third century. (See note on XIII. 11 b.) It also appears to be later than Herm. *ap.* Stob. *Exc.* II A. (See note on XIII. 6.) Moreover, *Corp.* XIII differs from almost all the other *Hermetica* in presenting indications that its writer was a member of a religious fraternity which already possessed established traditions and fixed forms of worship (see note on § 21), and which therefore had presumably been in existence for some considerable time. This *libellus* then is probably one of the latest of the extant *Hermetica* ; and we may conclude that it was written in the third century after Christ, and most likely towards the end of that century.

Title. The insertion of ἐν ὄρει must have been suggested by the words ἐπὶ τῆς τοῦ ὄρους μεταβάσεως in § 1. But those words have to do with the earlier dialogue of which Tat is there speaking, and not with the dialogue reported in *Corp*. XIII. There is no reason to suppose that in *Corp*. XIII itself Hermes and Tat are situated 'on a mountain'.

The words καὶ σιγῆς ἐπαγγελίας refer to § 22 b, where Hermes says to Tat σιγὴν ἐπάγγειλαι. But *Corp*. XIII cannot be called 'a discourse *about* a promise of silence'; and if the phrase occurred at all in the title, it must have been connected differently.

§ 1. περὶ θειότητος (*al*. θεότητος) διαλεγόμενος. If περὶ θειότητος meant merely 'about divinity', or 'about things divine', all the *Hermetica* alike might be said to be περὶ θειότητος. But the term is here used to indicate the special subject of one particular dialogue, and must therefore bear some more definite sense. Perhaps the meaning is 'concerning the state of *a man* who has become θεῖος or ἔνθεος'. Cf. *Corp*. IX. 1 c, where we are told that θειότης is something done by God (to a man?), and that it is related to God as νόησις to νοῦς.

μηδένα δύνασθαι σωθῆναι πρὸ τῆς παλιγγενεσίας. Cf. *Ev. Joh*. 3. 3: ἐὰν μή τις γεννηθῇ ἄνωθεν, οὐ δύναται ἰδεῖν τὴν βασιλείαν τοῦ θεοῦ.

ἐμοῦ τε σοῦ ἱκέτου γενομένου ⌜ἐπὶ τῆς τοῦ ὄρους μεταβάσεως⌝ μετὰ τὸ σὲ ἐμοὶ διαλεχθῆναι [πυθομένου] τὸν τῆς παλιγγενεσίας λόγον μαθεῖν. In the dialogue περὶ θειότητος, which was one of the Γενικοὶ λόγοι, Hermes had told Tat that 'no man can be saved until he has been born again'. At the end of that dialogue, or in another which followed it, (μετὰ τὸ σὲ ἐμοὶ διαλεχθῆναι,) Tat had begged Hermes to explain what he meant by 'being born again', and Hermes had refused, on the ground that Tat was not yet ready to be 'estranged from the world'. The words ἐπὶ τῆς τοῦ ὄρους μεταβάσεως appear to refer to the place where the scene of the dialogue referred to was laid; but as that dialogue is not extant, it is impossible to discover their meaning. One might conjecture ἐπὶ τῆς ⟨ἀπὸ?⟩ τοῦ ὄρους καταβάσεως, 'when we were coming down from the mountain'. That would imply that Hermes had taken Tat up to the desert plateau above the Nile-valley, to talk with him there in private, and that it was when their talk was ended, and they were on their way back, that Tat made his request.

The infinitive μαθεῖν depends on ἱκέτου γενομένου; 'I besought you to let me learn'.

ὅταν μέλλῃς ⟨τοῦ⟩ κόσμου ἀπαλλοτριοῦσθαι [[ ]] ⟨παραδώσω⟩ (*sc*. τὸν τῆς παλιγγενεσίας λόγον). The doctrine of the Rebirth must not be taught to the disciple until he is ready to experience the Rebirth in his own person; and the condition of experiencing it is 'alienation from the (material) world'. The meaning of this alienation is explained in Tat's reply, ἀπηλλότριωσα τὸ ἐν ἐμοὶ φρόνημα ἀπὸ τῆς τοῦ κόσμου ἀπάτης. If a man is to be changed into an incorporeal being, he must rid himself of all that binds him to the body, and must therefore put away from him all interest in things corporeal. Cf. *Ep. Joh.* I. 2. 15: μὴ ἀγαπᾶτε τὸν κόσμον μηδὲ τὰ ἐν τῷ κόσμῳ, κ.τ.λ. A similar thought is expressed in different terms elsewhere in the *Hermetica*; e.g. *Corp.* I. 19: ὁ δὲ ἀγαπήσας . . . τὸ σῶμα, οὗτος μένει ἐν τῷ σκότει κ.τ.λ. *Corp.* IV. 5: καταφρονήσαντες πάντων τῶν σωματικῶν. *Ib.* 6 b: ἐὰν μὴ πρῶτον τὸ σῶμα μισήσῃς κ.τ.λ. *Corp.* XI. ii. 21 a: οὐδὲν γὰρ δύνασαι τῶν καλῶν καὶ ἀγαθῶν νοῆσαι, φιλοσώματος ὤν.

παλιγγενεσίαν παραδοῦναι προθέμενος. 'You promised to transmit the Rebirth to me when I should be fit to receive it; I am now fit to receive it, and I ask you to fulfil your promise.' It may be doubted whether παλιγγενεσίαν παραδοῦναι means 'to transmit to me the doctrine of the Rebirth', or 'to cause me to be born again'. In this dialogue, the Rebirth takes place in Tat immediately after the doctrine has been expounded to him; and the two things are not very clearly distinguished. On the use of παραδοῦναι and παράδοσις in connexion with religion, see Norden, *Agnostos Theos*, pp. 288–293.

[ἐκ φωνῆς ἢ κρυβήν]. (Perhaps κρυβῇ or κρύβδην.) The writer of these words must have intended to say 'either openly or in secret'. But the antithesis is not correctly expressed; Hermes must speak to Tat ἐκ φωνῆς (*viva voce*), even if he teaches him in private. Besides, Tat has no motive for mentioning the alternatives here.

ἀγνοῶ . . . ἐξ οἵας μήτρας ἄνθρωπος ἀναγεννηθείη ἄν (ἐγεννήθη MSS.). The aorist indicative can hardly be right; the sense required is ' I do not know how a man *could be* born again', and this might be expressed by the optative. Tat's perplexity resembles that of Nicodemus in *Ev. Joh.* 3. 4: πῶς δύναται ἄνθρωπος γεννηθῆναι γέρων ὤν; μὴ δύναται εἰς τὴν κοιλίαν τῆς μητρὸς αὐτοῦ δεύτερον εἰσελθεῖν καὶ γεννηθῆναι;

§ 2. σοφία ἡ μήτρα, ἐν σιγῇ ⟨κύουσα⟩.—(σοφία νοερὰ ἐν σιγῇ MSS.) It can hardly be doubted that νοερά is a corruption of μήτρα. Tat has asked two parallel questions, ἐξ οἵας μήτρας and (ἐκ) σπορᾶς ποίας; and since Hermes repeats the word σπορά in his reply (ἡ σπορὰ τὸ ἀληθινὸν ἀγαθόν), he must have repeated the word μήτρα also.

The restoration of κύουσα is less certain ; but something of the sort is needed to provide a construction for ἐν σιγῇ.

The statement that σοφία is the μήτρα is equivalent to saying that God's Wisdom is the mother who gives birth to the new man ;[1] and Hermes goes on to say that God's Will (θέλημα) is the father who begets him. (A few lines below, we are told more simply that the new man is θεοῦ παῖς, a son of God himself.) The σπορά (= σπέρμα), i. e. the vital germ from which the new man springs, is 'the true Good', which is regarded as a thing emitted by God's Will.

The new man is conceived, or his birth is prepared, 'in silence'.[2] The New Birth cannot be brought about by verbal teaching or discussion. (Cf. § 2 *fin.* : τοῦτο τὸ γένος οὐ διδάσκεται. *Corp.* X. 5 : ἡ γὰρ γνῶσις αὐτοῦ βαθεῖα σιωπή ἐστιν.) It agrees with this statement that Hermes is represented as having refused to talk to Tat about the παλιγγενεσία until the new man that was to be born in him had already been conceived, and the embryo was ripe for birth.

⟨⟨Λέγε μοι καὶ τοῦτο· τίς ἐστι τελεσιουργὸς . . . θελήματι θεοῦ⟩⟩ ⟨ὑπουργῶν⟩. This passage is certainly out of place in § 4, where it interrupts the train of thought ; and the question 'who is the ministrant ?' would most naturally be asked in close connexion with the question 'who is the father ?'

The MSS. give τίς ἐστι γενεσιουργὸς τῆς παλιγγενεσίας ; 'Who is the worker of the birth of the Rebirth ?' The repetition of γενεσι- is awkward ; and it is most likely that the author wrote τελεσιουργός, intending by this word to suggest an analogy[3] between the Rebirth and the process of initiation in a mystery-cult. (Cf. τέλος, τελετή, 'initiation'; τελεῖν, 'to initiate'; τέλειος, 'one whose initiation has been completed'.[4]) The word τελεσιουργός was frequently employed

---

[1] In the Valentinian system, Sophia (Achamoth) is the mother of the πνευματικόν in man (Irenaeus 1. 6). 'The mother of the New Man, says Boehme, is the Virgin Sophia, the Divine Wisdom, or Mirror of the Being of God' (E. Underhill, *Mysticism*, 1912, p. 147).

[2] Cf. Eckhart, *Pred.* ii (E. Underhill, *Mysticism*, p. 381) : 'It may be asked whether this Birth is best accomplished in man when he does his work, and forms and thinks himself into God, or when he keeps himself in silence, stillness, and peace, so that God may speak and work in him. . . . The best and noblest way in which thou mayst come into this work and life is by keeping silence, and letting God work and speak.'

[3] Analogy, but not identity. In the mystery-cults, the thing aimed at was accomplished by means of certain ritual actions of sacramental efficacy ; but no sacramental action is mentioned or implied in *Corp.* XIII.

[4] According to Miss J. E. Harrison, 'The meaning of the word τελετή', *Class. Rev.* March 1914, the mystery-rites were originally adolescence-rites, and τέλειος, in this connexion, primarily meant 'admitted to the *status* of an adult'. It may

with reference to religious initiation. In *Abammonis Resp.* 2. 11, the performance of a sacramental action is described as ἡ τῶν ἔργων τῶν ἀρρήτων καὶ ὑπὲρ πᾶσαν νόησιν θεοπρεπῶς ἐνεργουμένων τελεσιουργία. The word is much used by Dionysius Areopag., in combination with other terms borrowed from the language of the Pagan mysteries, and doubtless transmitted to him by Pagan Neoplatonists ; e. g. *Cael. hierarch.* 3. 3 : τοὺς δὲ τελεσιουργοὺς (χρή), ὡς ἐπιστημονικοὺς τῆς τελεστικῆς μεταδόσεως, τελεῖν τοὺς τελουμένους τῇ πανιέρῳ μυήσει τῆς τῶν ἐποπτευθέντων ἱερῶν ἐπιστήμης. Dionysius calls the bishops τελεσιουργοί, as being the agents by whom the most holy sacraments are administered, and through whom the supreme consecration is conferred ; he says the deacons καθαίρουσι, the priests φωτίζουσι, and the bishops τελεσιουργοῦσι. The τελεσιουργός then is the man through whose ministration the process of initiation is completed, and the *mystes* is made τέλειος. The New Birth of *Corp.* XIII is analogous to the achievement of that union of the worshipper with his god which it was the object of mystery-rites to bring about ; and the man who does that which gives occasion for another man to be ' born again ' may accordingly be called ' the τελεσιουργός of the Rebirth '.

In the particular case of Tat, the τελεσιουργός is Hermes. But answering the question in general terms, Hermes says that the τελεσιουργός is 'some one man who is a son of God'. Hermes himself is such a man ; he has been born again, and has thereby become a son of God.

Ἄλλος [ἔσται] ὁ γεννώμενος. As Hermes is here speaking generally, and not referring to an expected παλιγγενεσία of Tat, the use of the future tense cannot be justified ; and we must either strike out ἔσται, or alter it into ἐστίν.

The man who has been born again is 'another man'. The νοερὸς ἄνθρωπος differs so completely from the σωματικὸς ἄνθρωπος, that the change which takes place in a man when he passes from the one state to the other can be described by saying that he ceases to exist, and another man comes into being in his place. Something like this is necessarily implied when the term παλιγγενεσία is used. But the statement must not be insisted on in its literal sense. Tat becomes ' another man' in the course of the dialogue ; yet the

have been so in a remote past ; but if so, it had ceased to be so in the times known to us. The Greeks of history, when they spoke of a τελετή, were not thinking of adolescence.

Tat who 'sees with the eyes of the mind' after his transformation is after all the same person as the Tat who previously saw only with his bodily eyes.

τὸ πᾶν, ἐν παντί. The New Man 'is the All', and 'is in all'. This is more fully expressed in § 11 b, where Tat says ἐν οὐρανῷ εἰμι, ἐν γῇ, κ.τ.λ. The writer intentionally made the phrases by which Hermes here describes the new man obscure enough to invite Tat's reply, 'you are speaking in riddles'. But he had no reason to make the obscurity extend to the grammatical construction; and perhaps some word or words by which τὸ πᾶν ἐν παντί was connected with the context may have fallen out.

⟨⟨ἄμοιρος γάρ ⟨ἐστι⟩ τῆς ⌜ἐν ἐμοὶ⌝ οὐσίας, καὶ τῆς νοητῆς⟩⟩ ⟨μοῖραν ἔχει⟩. These words have been wrongly assigned to Tat; they must have formed part of Hermes' answer.

ἐν ἐμοί is meaningless. We need some word which may stand in contrast to νοητῆς (e. g. αἰσθητῆς, σωματικῆς, or ὑλικῆς); and as the speaker, Hermes, is one who has been born again, the οὐσία 'which is in him' (or of which he consists) is νοητή, and not σωματική. It is conceivable that ἐν ἐμοί might be a corruption of ἐναίμου, used as an equivalent for σαρκίνης; cf. Hdt. 3. 29: θεοὶ . . . ἔναιμοί τε καὶ σαρκώδεες (with reference to the bull-god Apis).

ἐκ πασῶν δυνάμεων συνεστώς. The word δυνάμεις is used in *Corp.* XIII, as in *Corp.* I, to signify the hypostatized 'Powers of God'. But in *Corp.* I, the 'Powers' are spoken of as residing in the supracosmic region, and collectively constituting the Noetos Kosmos. The writer of *Corp.* XIII adopts this conception; but he adds that the man who has been born again consists of these same Powers of God. Thus the man of whom he speaks τῆς νοητῆς οὐσίας μοῖραν ἔχει. He is consubstantial with the Noetos Kosmos, and is a Noetos Kosmos in himself.

ἐκ πασῶν δυνάμεων συνέστηκε means, not 'he consists of all the Powers' (which would be ἐκ πασῶν τῶν δυνάμεων), but 'the things of which he consists are all of them Powers', i. e. 'he consists of Powers and nothing else'. Cf. Pl. *Rep.* 579 B: κύκλῳ φρουρούμενος ὑπὸ πάντων πολεμίων ('those who keep watch around him are all of them enemies').

ὑπὸ τοῦ θεοῦ, ⟨⟨ὅταν θέλῃ,⟩⟩ ἀναμιμνήσκεται. This is a reference to the Platonic doctrine of ἀνάμνησις. In its antenatal state, the soul was united with God and the Noetos Kosmos, and possessed all knowledge of things divine. Through its embodiment, it has been overcome by λήθη (cf. *Corp.* X. 15 b); but, God willing, it may be enabled to recall to memory its former knowledge. Mere human teaching is powerless to impart this knowledge, and can, at most, only give occasion for the ' reminiscence '.

§ 3. ⟨ἆρ'⟩ ἀλλότριος [υἱὸς] πέφυκα τοῦ πατρικοῦ γένους; With these corrections, which improve the sense, we get an iambic *senarius*. The line is presumably quoted from some play, but perhaps not quite exactly. πατρικοῦ may possibly have been substituted for πατρός.

οὐδὲ τῷ πλαστῷ τούτῳ ⌜στοιχείῳ⌝, δι' οὗ ⟨σὺ ὁρᾷς⟩, ἔστιν ἰδεῖν. The thing ' by means of which you see ' is the bodily eye. But the eye cannot be called a στοιχεῖον; and we must suppose either that στοιχείῳ has been wrongly substituted for some other word (e. g. ὀργάνῳ), or that it is a remnant of some longer phrase (e. g. τῷ πλαστῷ τούτῳ ἐκ στοιχείων ὀργάνῳ).

οὐκ ἔχω λέγειν πλὴν τοῦτο· ὁρῶ[ν] τι⟨ν'⟩ ἐν ἐμοὶ κ.τ.λ. Hermes knows what the Rebirth is, because he has himself experienced it; but he cannot find words to describe it adequately. It is impossible to make one who has not experienced it understand what it is by means of a mere verbal statement.

ἄπλαστον ἰδέαν (θέαν MSS.). Cf. *Corp.* XI. ii. 16 b on the ἀσώματος ἰδέα of God.

ἐμαυτὸν ⟨δι⟩εξελήλυθα εἰς ἀθάνατον σῶμα. ἐμαυτόν here means ' myself as identified with my material body '. Hermes has passed forth out of this self, and has ' entered into ' (or become) a new self, which he describes, by a paradoxical ˙metaphor, as an immortal (i. e. divine) ' body '. This ' body ', his new self, is incorporeal, and is composed of divine δυνάμεις.

καὶ διαλέλυταί (διὸ ἠμέληταί MSS.) μοι τὸ πρῶτον [σύνθετον] εἶδος. The reading διὸ ἠμέληται may be accounted for by assuming that διΑΛέλυται was read as δι Μέλυται, and that this was altered into διὸ ἠμέληται in an attempt to make sense.

It seems best to cut out σύνθετον. The material ' form ' (εἶδος), i. e. the body, is indeed composite, but there is no reason to call attention to that fact; for the new man, with whom it is contrasted, is also composite (ἐκ δυνάμεων συνεστώς). The word διαλέλυται (if that is the right reading) must be taken to mean ' has been put away (from me) ', and not ' has been broken up '. It is not true that Hermes' material body has been broken up; it still exists, but it is no longer identical with *him*, or a part of him; it is a thing

alien to him,—a mere external object, like anything else in the
sensible world,—and in that sense 'it has been put away from
him'. A reader may however have supposed διαλέλυται to mean
'it has been broken up into its component parts', and may thus
have been led to insert σύνθετον.

[ὁρᾷς με ὦ τέκνον, ὀφθαλμοῖς.] This is perhaps a misplaced doublet
of ὀφθαλμοῖς τούτοις θεωροῦμαι νῦν, ὦ τέκνον below.

οὐκ ὀφθαλμοῖς τ⟨οι⟩ούτοις θεωροῦμαι. τοιούτοις means σωματικοῖς.
The new man, being incorporeal, can be seen only with 'the eyes
of the mind'. Cf. Porphyr. *Ad Marcellam* 8 : ἐγὼ οὐχ ὁ ἁπτὸς
οὗτος καὶ τῇ αἰσθήσει ὑποπτωτός, ὁ δὲ ἐπὶ πλεῖστον ἀφεστηκὼς τοῦ σώματος, ὁ ἀχρώματος καὶ ἀσχημάτιστος, καὶ χερσὶ μὲν οὐδαμῶς ἐπαφητός,
διανοίᾳ δὲ μόνῃ κρατητός. But Porphyry's meaning is that the *ego*
is the incorporeal soul, and not the body ; and that might be said
of every man alike. In *Corp.* XIII, on the other hand, it is implied
that only he who has been born again is incorporeal, and that all
other men *are* identical with their bodies.

§ 4. ἐμαυτὸν γὰρ νῦν οὐχ ὁρῶ ; Taking this as a question, we may
explain the meaning thus : 'You tell me that I do not see *you* ;
you might as well tell me that I do not see *myself*. Both statements
alike contradict the evidence of my senses'. (If this is what is
meant, it might have been more clearly expressed by writing οὐδὲ
γὰρ ἐμαυτὸν νῦν ὁρῶ ;) Hermes replies, 'Would that you too, like
me, had passed forth out of yourself', i. e. had been born again,
and so had put the body away from you. 'In that case', it is implied,
'it would have been true to say that you do not see yourself', i. e.
that the body which you see is not yourself. 'But as you have not
yet been born again, it cannot be denied that you see yourself when
you look at your body.'

⟨ἵνα εἶδες, μὴ⟩ ὡς οἱ ἐν ὕπνῳ ὀνειροπολούμενοι, ⟨ἀλλὰ⟩ χωρὶς ὕπνου.
'It is true that you see your body (and therefore "yourself", since
you are still identified with your body) ; but when you see your
body, or anything else, with your bodily eyes, the thing you see
is no more real than the things seen in dreams; for all sense-
perception is illusion. If you would see truly, you must wake from
your present sleep (i. e. from the state of one whose soul is sunk
in the body), and look with waking eyes (i. e. with the eyes of the
mind).'

The same meaning might be got in another way, by writing
⟨ἵνα εἶδες ⟨⟨χωρὶς ὕπνου⟩⟩· νῦν δὲ ὁρᾷς⟩ ὡς οἱ ἐν ὕπνῳ ὀνειροπολούμενοι.

§ 5. τὸ γὰρ μέγεθος βλέπω τὸ σὸν τὸ αὐτό, ὦ πάτερ, σὺν τῷ χαρακτῆρι. This is clumsily expressed, and perhaps corrupt ; but the meaning must be ' (I certainly do see you ;) for when I look at you, I see a man of the same stature as before, and the bodily features by which I am accustomed to recognize you are unaltered '.

Καὶ ἐν τούτῳ ψεύδῃ. You are mistaken in saying that what you see when you look at me now is 'the same' as what you have seen before ; for the human body is continually changing. My body is an illusory appearance (ψεῦδος); for all that changes is illusory ; it is only that which exists in eternal changelessness that is real (ἀληθές, = ὄντως ὄν). Cf. Herm. ap. Stob. Exc. XI. 2. (16): οὐδὲν ἐν σώματι ἀληθές· μόνον τὸ ἀσώματον ἀψευδές. Exc. II A. passim ; e. g. § 10, πᾶν γὰρ τὸ ἀλλοιούμενον ψεῦδός ἐστι κ.τ.λ.

§ 6. Τί οὖν ἀληθές ἐστιν . . .; Τὸ μὴ θολούμενον κ.τ.λ. Cf. Herm. ap. Stob. Exc. II A. 9 : ἡ γὰρ ἀλήθειά [ ] ἐστι . . . τὸ μὴ ὑπὸ ὕλης θολούμενον μήτε ὑπὸ σώματος περιβαλλόμενον, γυμνόν, φανόν, ἄτρεπτον, [ ] ἀναλλοίωτον [ἀγαθόν]. Ib. § 15 as emended : Τί οὖν ἂν εἴποι τις ἀληθὲς τὴν πρώτην ἀλήθειαν, ὦ πάτερ ; Ἕνα καὶ μόνον, ὦ Τάτ, τὸν μὴ ἐξ ὕλης, τὸν μὴ ἐν σώματι, τὸν ἀχρώματον, τὸν ἀσχημάτιστον, τὸν ἄτρεπτον, τὸν μὴ ἀλλοιούμενον, τὸν ἀεὶ ὄντα. It seems clear that the writer of Corp. XIII has copied from Exc. II A. He has borrowed τὸ μὴ θολούμενον, γυμνόν, φανόν, ἀγαθόν, from Exc. II A. 9 ; ἀχρώματον, ἀσχημάτιστον, from ib. 15 ; and ἄτρεπτον, ἀναλλοίωτον, from both passages ; and he has added τὸ μὴ περιοριζόμενον and τὸ αὐτῷ καταληπτόν. Compare the Hermippus (Kroll and Viereck) 2. 20. 186 : ποίους ἂν ἐρωτᾷς ἴσχοι ὁ τοιοῦτον κάλλος κατοπτεῦσαι δεδυνημένος, ἄφθαρτον, ἄκρατον, μὴ ὑφ' ὕλης θολούμενον, ἄτρεπτόν τε καὶ ἀναλλοίωτον.

τὸ μὴ περιοριζόμενον (διοριζόμενον MSS.). Cf. Corp. XI. ii. 18 as emended : τοῦ ἀσωμάτου οὐδέν ἐστι περιοριστικόν, αὐτὸ δὲ πάντων περιοριστικόν. In Corp. I. 7, the Noetos Kosmos is called κόσμος ἀπεριόριστος.

τὸ γυμνόν is obscure here ; but in Exc. II A. 9, its meaning is explained by the preceding phrase, μήτε ὑπὸ σώματος περιβαλλόμενον. The writer would have said that the human soul, when unembodied, is ἀληθής, but ceases to be ἀληθής when it is incarnated, and in this life, becomes ἀληθής only when it has put the body away from it by the Rebirth.

τὸ αὐτῷ καταληπτόν. The incorporeal can be apprehended only by νοῦς, which is itself incorporeal ; for 'like is known only by like '.

It would be possible to write τὸ αὐτοκατάληπτον, taking it in the same sense.

[[τὸ ἀσώματον]]. This can hardly have been written here by the author ; the series ought to end with ἀγαθόν, as in *Exc.* II A. 9 MSS. But some one rightly summed up the meaning of the whole sentence by putting τὸ ἀσώματον at the end of it.

ἐνεφράχθησαν αἱ αἰσθήσεις. Cf. *Corp.* VII. 3 : τὰ . . . αἰσθητήρια ἀναίσθητα ποιῶν, τῇ πολλῇ ὕλῃ αὐτὰ ἀποφράξας. As the writer of *Corp.* XIII had certainly read *Corp.* I, it is probable that he had also read *Corp.* VII, which is closely connected with *Corp.* I.

Tat cannot apprehend 'the thought which has been put before him ', i. e. understand what Hermes has said ; he cannot grasp the notion of the incorporeal. And for that very reason, he makes no distinction between αἴσθησις and νόησις ; he thinks he ought to be able to apprehend the thing spoken of *with his senses,* i. e. to see or hear it,—in imagination at least, if not by actual sense-perception. Hermes therefore has to explain to him that it is impossible αἰσθητῶς νοεῖν τὸ ἀσώματον.

τὸ μὲν ἀνωφερὲς [ὡς πῦρ] κ.τ.λ. The explanation that τὸ ἀνωφερές here means fire, τὸ κατωφερές means earth, &c., is correct ; but the author would hardly have thought it necessary to explain the terms ; and ὡς is used improperly. I have therefore bracketed ὡς πῦρ &c.

καὶ σύμπνοον [ὡς ἀήρ]. Does this mean the air ' which is breathed by all of us together ', i. e. the common life-breath of us all ?

τὸ ⌜ἀσφίγγωτον⌝ (ἀσύνθετον ?), τὸ μὴ διαλυόμενον. Bodies are σύνθετα and διάλυτα, i. e. are composed of the four elements, and resolved into the elements of which they were composed.

τὸ μόνον δυνάμει [καὶ ἐνεργείᾳ] νοούμενον. δύναμις may be taken to mean here, as before, 'a Power of God ', i. e. one of the ' Powers ' which are the component parts both of the divine νοῦς, and of the mind of the individual man into whom a portion of the divine νοῦς has entered. The incorporeal can be apprehended only by νοῦς, or by a δύναμις which is, so to speak, one of the members of νοῦς. But the writer was at the same time conscious of the more ordinary meaning of δύναμις, ' power ' or ' faculty ' ; and this suggested to him the phrase which follows, τοῦ δυναμένου νοεῖν.

The word ἐνέργεια is used by some of the Hermetists in the sense of ' a power of God at work ', or ' an operation of God's power ' ; and in this sense it would be possible to say that the incorporeal ἐνεργείᾳ νοεῖται. But the combination δυνάμει καὶ ἐνεργείᾳ is puzzling ; and it seems best to assume that καὶ ἐνεργείᾳ was inserted by some one who did not understand the author's peculiar use of δύναμις.

[τὴν ἐν θεῷ γένεσιν]. These words, which are equivalent to τὴν παλιγγενεσίαν, seem to have been inserted in order to provide an object for νοεῖν. But the object required is not τὴν παλιγγενεσίαν, but τὸ μὴ σκληρὸν κ.τ.λ., i. e. the incorporeal ; and as τὸ ἀσώματον seems to have been wrongly inserted above, the simplest remedy is to transpose it to this place.

§ 7 a. ἐπίσπασαι εἰς ἑαυτόν. Here again, the object is 'the in-corporeal', that is, in this connexion, τὸν θεῖον νοῦν, or τὰς δυνάμεις. Two lines below, this same thing, which is to be 'drawn into him', or 'born within him', is called ἡ θεότης.

§ 7 b. ⟨. . . δεῖ⟩ καθᾶραι σεαυτὸν ἀπὸ τῶν ἀλόγων τῆς ὕλης τιμωριῶν. The editors print κάθαραι, imperative middle, and connect it closely with the preceding imperatives (ἐπίσπασαι, θέλησον, κατάργησον). But the use of the middle voice with σεαυτόν is hardly possible ; and the description of the purification required is sufficiently distinct from what precedes it to make a fresh paragraph desirable.

The purging away of evil passions would most naturally be regarded as *preliminary* to the reception of that which is divine ; and assuming that the author took this view, we might write ⟨πρῶτον δὲ δεῖ⟩ καθᾶραι. In the following sentences, however, we are told that the evil passions do not depart until after the δυνάμεις have arrived. But there is reason to suspect that those sentences have been inserted by a later hand.

The vices or evil passions are here called τιμωρίαι. The word τιμωρίαι properly means 'punishments'. In *Corp*. I. 23, evil passions are spoken of as punishments inflicted on the impious by the τιμωρὸς δαίμων ; and in *Corp*. XII. i. 5-7, they are similarly spoken of as punishments inflicted by Heimarmene. But the writer of *Corp*. XIII does not speak of them as punishments of previous sin ; and in this passage, τιμωρίαι must be taken to mean, not 'punishments', but 'tortures' resembling those which are inflicted on criminals.

Τιμωροὺς γὰρ ἐν ἐμαυτῷ ἔχω, ὦ πάτερ ; The writer personifies the evil passions, and therefore calls them τιμωροί, 'torturers', as well as τιμωρίαι, 'tortures'. He does not himself call them 'daemons' ; but his use of the word τιμωροί may have been suggested to him by writings in which the evil in men was attributed to the operation of

τιμωροὶ δαίμονες.   Cf. Lydus *De mens.* 4. 32 (*Ascl. Lat.* III. 33 b):
τοὺς μὲν τιμωροὺς τῶν δαιμόνων κ.τ.λ.

δευτέρα λύπη . . . δωδεκάτη κακία. It seems probable that this list
of τιμωρίαι, and the later passages in which it is presupposed (viz.
§§ 8 c–9, 11 c–12, and a few lines in § 18), were not written by the
original author, but were inserted by some person or persons into
whose hands the document afterwards passed. When these excre-
scences have been removed, *Corp.* XIII is less unworthy to take its
place among the other *Hermetica*. It is true that we have no right
to assume that the author's canons of good sense and taste agreed
with ours, and to conclude that passages are spurious merely because
we think them silly; but it will be found that several difficulties and
inconsistencies in detail are cleared away when these parts of the
text have been excised.

The list of τιμωρίαι is based on no logical classification; the writer
was chiefly interested in making up the number to twelve, and was
content to include in his list any word signifying a bad emotion,
quality, or disposition. δόλος, ἐπιθυμία, ἀπάτη, and προπέτεια may
have been suggested to him by the list of planetary πάθη in *Corp.* I.
25. The twelfth and last is κακία, 'vice',[1] which does not stand on
a par with the particular vices (πλεονεξία &c.), but includes them all;
and inasmuch as 'vice is ignorance.', the same might be said of the
first, ἄγνοια, and perhaps of the seventh, ἀπάτη, also. The number
twelve was fixed on because that is the number of the Signs of the
Zodiac. See § 12, where it is implied that each of the twelve
τιμωρίαι results from the influence of one of the twelve zodiacal Signs.
The astral theory presupposed differs from that in *Corp.* I, according
to which each of the evil passions results from the influence of
one of the seven planets. In both alike, the astral influences are
held to be maleficent; but *Corp.* I takes into account the planets
only, and ignores the zodiac, whereas *Corp.* XIII takes into account
the zodiac only, and ignores the planets.

αἱ διὰ τῆς αἰσθήσεως ⟨κακὰ?⟩ πάσχειν ἀναγκάζουσι τὸν ἐν τῷ δεσμω-
τηρίῳ τοῦ σώματος δεδεμένον ἄνθρωπον.—(διὰ τοῦτο δεσμωτηρίου τοῦ
σώματος αἰσθητικῶς πάσχειν ἀναγκάζουσι τὸν ἐνδιάθετον ἄνθρωπον MSS.)
There can be little doubt that this conjectural restoration expresses
the author's meaning, though the exact words are uncertain. When

---

[1] Ménard translates κακία 'la méchanceté', and Mead 'malice'. Cf. *Ep. Col.*
3. 8 : ὀργήν, θυμόν, κακίαν (R. V. 'malice'), βλασφημίαν, αἰσχρολογίαν. But could
κακία be understood in the restricted sense of 'malice' where there is nothing in the
context to suggest this limitation of its meaning?

a man is 'bound in the prison of the body', the τιμωροί (who are compared to the agents by whom sentence is executed on imprisoned criminals) have him in their power, and can inflict their torments on him.

If we retain τὸν ἐνδιάθετον ἄνθρωπον, we must translate 'the inner man'. But there is no authority for this use of ἐνδιάθετος; it could not be justified by the Stoic phrase ὁ ἐνδιάθετος λόγος. Besides, 'the inner man' would rather mean the incorporeal man who is brought into being by the Rebirth; whereas the man here spoken of is the natural or earthly man, who is sunk in or identified with the body. It seems certain therefore that ἐνδιάθετον is corrupt.

ἀφίστανται δὲ αὗται [οὐκ] ἀθρόως. Cf. § 12, as emended : τὴν ἀπό-στασιν ποιοῦνται, καθὼς ⟨εἶπον, ἀθρόως⟩. On the hypothesis that the list of τιμωρίαι was added by a later hand, we may suppose that οὐκ was inserted here in order to avoid an apparent inconsistency with the interpolated sentences, in which the expulsion of each of the first six τιμωρίαι is separately and successively described.

οὕτω συνίσταται ὁ ⟨⟨λόγος⟩⟩. Cf. § 8 b, εἰς συνάρθρωσιν τοῦ λόγου, and § 19, ὁ σὸς λόγος δι' ἐμοῦ ὑμνεῖ σέ. The λόγος is the incorporeal organism which is composed of divine δυνάμεις, and is brought into being by the παλιγγενεσία. It is identical with the ἀθάνατον σῶμα spoken of in § 3, the σῶμα τὸ ἐκ δυνάμεων συνεστός in § 14, and the νοερὰ οὐσία (?) in § 10. It corresponds more or less to what Plato called τὸ λογιστικόν, and Aristotle (*Eth. Nic.* 1. 13) τὸ λόγον ἔχον; and it might equally well have been called ὁ νοῦς. It is quite distinct from the λόγος of *Corp.* I. 5 a, &c., which is a personification of the 'word' or *fiat* by which God made the world; and if we are to look for a Jewish parallel, it corresponds more nearly to the 'word of the Lord' by which he spoke to or through the prophets.

⟨οὗτος ὁ⟩ τῆς παλιγγενεσίας τρόπος. Hermes has now answered Tat's question (§ 3, διάφρασόν μοι τῆς παλιγγενεσίας τὸν τρόπον), as far as it is possible to answer it by mere words. But Tat is already on the verge of experiencing the Rebirth in his own person; and in what follows, it is described as actually taking place in him. It would hardly be correct to say that the words of the teacher *cause* the transformation of the pupil. Hermes is indeed in this instance the τελεσιουργός; but that means no more than that by his teaching and influence, culminating in the words which he has spoken in this dialogue, Tat has been brought into a fit state to be born again. The efficient cause of the Rebirth, as we are repeatedly told, is God's will' or 'God's mercy'. Hermes, however, has judged his time well, and has consented to talk to Tat about the Rebirth only when Tat is ready to experience it.

§ 8 a. ⌜καὶ διὰ τοῦτο οὐ καταπαύσει⌝ τὸ ἔλεος εἰς ἡμᾶς ἀπὸ τοῦ θεοῦ. οὐ καταπαύσει cannot be right; the meaning must be, not that God's mercy will *continue* to operate, but that it will *now begin* to operate in Tat's case, i. e. that it will bring the Rebirth to pass in him. Besides, εἰς and ἀπό require a verb of motion. The sense wanted might be obtained by writing οὕτω κατελεύσεται τὸ ἔλεος κ.τ.λ. Hermes might rather have been expected to say something like εὐφήμησον, εἴ πως κατελεύσεται κ.τ.λ.; 'wait in silence, and let us see whether it will come'. But if he is confident of its near approach, he may very well say positively 'it will come'. Cf. § 7 a : ἐπίσπασαι εἰς ἑαυτὸν (τὸ ἀσώματον), καὶ ἐλεύσεται.

Hermes himself has been reborn already, and it is on Tat alone, and not on him, that 'God's mercy' is now about to operate ; but he says εἰς ἡμᾶς instead of εἰς σέ, because he is deeply interested in the rebirth of his son.

After these words, we must assume an interval of solemn and prayerful silence, which is ended by the exclamation χαῖρε λοιπόν, ὦ τέκνον, κ.τ.λ. At that point, Hermes, in virtue of his God-given insight, perceives that his expectation is fulfilled, and that Tat's παλιγγενεσία has actually begun. In this dialogue, as in the *Hermetica* in general, there is no trace of any sacramental action. The Rebirth is wrought by God alone ; and the ministrations of the human τελεσιουργός, by which the way is prepared for it, consist of nothing but teaching.

§ 8 c. ἦλθεν ἡμῖν [γνῶσις] χαρά[ς]. There is some awkwardness in speaking of the arrival of χαρά, when Hermes has said χαῖρε ὦ τέκνον just before. This tends to confirm the suspicion that the list of τιμωρίαι, and the corresponding list of δυνάμεις, are interpolations.

ἡ λύπη φεύξεται εἰς τοὺς χωροῦντας αὐτήν. 'Grief' is imagined as an evil demon, which, when expelled from one man, seeks another into whom it may enter.

§ 9. ὁ βαθμὸς οὗτος . . . δικαιοσύνης ἐστὶν ἔδρασμα. 'Justice' is pictured as enthroned on her judgement-seat, like a Roman magistrate seated on his tribunal to administer the law. The 'Justice' here spoken of is the justice of God, by which men are judged, rather than the human virtue of justice, which enters into the reborn man

C C 2

and becomes part of him. But according to the doctrine of this document, the δυνάμεις which enter into the man are consubstantial with the δυνάμεις of God, and it is therefore easy for the writer to pass from the one to the other.

《《χωρὶς γὰρ κρίσεως (κτίσεως MSS.)》》 ἐδικαιώθημεν, ὦ τέκνον, ἀδικίας ἀπούσης. 'There is no need for our case to be tried and judged; we are *justified* without trial; for there is no injustice in us.' The writer takes advantage of the ambiguity of the word ἐδικαιώθημεν, which may mean either 'we have been *pronounced* just (by the judge)', or 'we have been *made* just'. In the former sense, it agrees with the preceding picture of the law-court; but it is in the latter sense only that it has any direct bearing on the Rebirth. The reborn man 'has been made just'; i. e. the vice of injustice has gone out of him, and the virtue of justice has entered into him.

Paul also would have said that the new man is 'justified'. Cf. *Ep. Rom.* 3. 21–24: χωρὶς νόμου δικαιοσύνη θεοῦ πεφανέρωται. . . . δικαιούμενοι δωρεὰν τῇ αὐτοῦ χάριτι. *Ib.* 6. 6 ff.: ὁ παλαιὸς ἡμῶν ἄνθρωπος συνεσταυρώθη, ἵνα καταργηθῇ τὸ σῶμα τῆς ἁμαρτίας . . . ὁ γὰρ ἀποθανὼν δεδικαίωται ἀπὸ τῆς ἁμαρτίας. Had the writer of this Hermetic passage read *Ep. Rom.*? At any rate, it is possible that he had talked with Christians who used phrases taken from that epistle.

τὴν κατὰ τῆς πλεονεξίας, ⟨τὴν⟩ κοινωνίαν. πλεονεξία is 'a grasping disposition'; it is the disposition of the man who claims more than his fair share, and seeks to take from others more than he has a right to. Its opposite, κοινωνία, must therefore be the disposition of one who is ready to share with his neighbours, and seeks nothing for himself alone.

ἰδὲ πῶς τὸ ἀγαθὸν πεπλήρωται κ.τ.λ. The incoherence of this and the following paragraphs down to the end of § 12 can hardly be accounted for except on the hypothesis of interpolation; and it seems probable that two different interpolators have been at work in succession. In the traditional text, Hermes gives a list of twelve τιμωρίαι, and a list of seven δυνάμεις, the last of which is ἀλήθεια. He pairs off the first six τιμωρίαι with the first six δυνάμεις; and having done so, he has no course open to him but to say that the other six τιμωρίαι are expelled on the arrival of the seventh and last δύναμις, viz. ἀλήθεια, and that 'the Good' is thereby 'completed'. He does say this; indeed, he says it twice over, first in the words ἰδὲ πῶς τὸ ἀγαθὸν πεπλήρωται παραγενομένης τῆς ἀληθείας, and then in the words τῇ δὲ ἀληθείᾳ καὶ τὸ ἀγαθὸν ἐπεγένετο κ.τ.λ. But in § 10 *init.*, we are told, to our surprise, that the δυνάμεις are not seven, but ten in number; and in §§ 11 c–12, the fact that there are ten of them is discussed at some length. It seems therefore that the passage must have been altered. In an earlier form of it, the δυνάμεις were seven in number; but a redactor thought fit to increase their number to ten (presumably because he held ten to be 'the perfect number'), and did so by counting in the three terms τὸ ἀγαθόν, ζωή, and φῶς, which happened to occur in § 9 *fin.*, but were not there used as names of distinct and individual δυνάμεις.

But there is reason to suspect that even the list of seven δυνάμεις was not present in the earliest form of the text; and if this suspicion is justified, we must distinguish three different stages. (1) The original author spoke of the τιμωρίαι and the δυνάμεις collectively, but did not enumerate them. He described the Rebirth as the coming of ἀλήθεια (the unique significance of which he had previously pointed out in § 6); and he may have spoken also of γνῶσις, not as an entity sharply distinguished from ἀλήθεια, but rather as its correlate, or the subjective aspect of it. (2) A first interpolator inserted in the text a list of twelve τιμωρίαι, and a list of seven δυνάμεις, making ἀλήθεια the seventh and last of the latter. (3) A second interpolator increased the number of the δυνάμεις from seven to ten, and inserted §§ 11 c–12, in which the numbers twelve and ten are discussed.

The passages which I ascribe to the first interpolator are printed in small type, but not bracketed; those which I ascribe to the second interpolator are printed in small type and also bracketed.

φθόνος γὰρ ἀφ' ἡμῶν ἀπέστη ⟨καὶ αἱ λοιπαὶ τιμωρίαι⟩. φθόνος is the eighth of the twelve τιμωρίαι in the preceding list; and the departure of the remaining four must also have been mentioned.

τὸ ἀγαθὸν . . . ἅμα ζωῇ καὶ φωτί. The writer has taken over the phrase ζωὴ καὶ φῶς from *Corp.* I, where it stands for God, or the substance of which God consists. The New Man consists of that same substance. τοῦ σκότους is also a reminiscence of *Corp.* I.

ἐξέπτησαν [νικηθεῖσαι] ῥοίζῳ. ῥοίζῳ must be taken with ἐξέπτησαν, and is wrongly separated from it by the participle. We might either strike out νικηθεῖσαι, or shift it, writing ἐξέπτησαν ῥοίζῳ νικηθεῖσαι; but the former seems preferable.

§ 10. [τῆς δεκάδος παραγινομένης.] ⟨οὕτω δή,⟩ ὦ τέκνον, συνετέθη ⟨ἡ⟩ νοερὰ [γένεσις] ⟨οὐσία⟩ [καὶ τὴν δωδεκάτην ἐξελαύνει]. If we cut out the words which refer to 'the ten' and 'the twelve', what remains may be taken in close connexion with § 9 *fin.* It is impossible to say that a 'birth' was 'put together'; γένεσις must therefore have been wrongly substituted for some other word, such as οὐσία.

The phrase καὶ τὴν δωδεκάτην ἐξελαύνει appears to be misplaced. The text as altered by the interpolator may perhaps have run as Reitzenstein has rewritten it; τῆς δεκάδος παραγινομένης (or rather π ιραγεν.), ὦ τέκνον, ἡ ⟨⟨τὴν δωδεκάδα ἐξελαύνει⟩⟩, συνετέθη κ.τ.λ.

καὶ ἐθεώ[ρη]θημεν τῇ ⟨ταύτης⟩ γενέσει (συνθέσει?). ταύτης means τῆς νοερᾶς οὐσίας. For ἐθεώθημεν, cf. θεοῦ θεὸς παῖς in § 2 ; ἡ γένεσις τῆς θεότητος in § 7 a ; θεὸς πέφυκας in § 14. The new man is a god. The verb θεοῦσθαι is frequently used with a similar application by Dionysius Areop.

ἑαυτὸν γνωρίζει ἐκ [τούτων] ⟨δυνάμεων⟩ συνιστάμενον (-νος MSS.), καὶ ⟨γνωρίσας⟩ εὐφραίνεται. The speech of Hermes ends, as it began, with a word expressing joy. Cf. *Corp.* I. 30 : πληρωθεὶς ὧν ἤθελον ἐξηυφράνθην. The phrase ἑαυτὸν γνωρίζει was suggested by *Corp.* I. 18–22 (ὁ ἀναγνωρίσας ἑαυτὸν εἰς τὸ ἀγαθὸν χωρεῖ κ.τ.λ.). As to ἐκ δυνάμεων συνιστάμενον, cf. § 2, ἐκ πασῶν δυνάμεων συνεστώς, and § 14, τὸ σῶμα τοῦτο τὸ ἐκ δυνάμεων συνεστός.

§ 11 a. ⟨Οὐσί⟩α καινὴ γενόμενος—('Ακλινὴς γενόμενος MSS.). If the New Man were called ἀκλινής, that might mean either that he is not (or cannot be) brought down to a lower level,[1] or that he is not (or cannot be) turned from his course. But neither of these thoughts is suggested by the preceding context ; and the expression of either by a single word would be abrupt and obscure. It seems probable therefore that ἀκλινής is a corruption of οὐσία καινή, or something similar. Cf. καινὴ κτίσις in Paul, *Gal.* 6. 15 and 2 *Cor.* 5. 17.

ἀλλὰ τῇ [διὰ δυνάμεων] νοητικῇ ἐνεργείᾳ. διὰ δυνάμεων was probably written as an alternative for τῇ νοητικῇ ἐνεργείᾳ. Either phrase might stand, but hardly both together.

§ 13 a. ⟨⟨Αὕτη ἐστὶν ἡ παλιγγενεσία, . . . τὸ μηκέτι φαντάζεσθαι [εἰς] τὸ σῶμα τὸ τριχῇ διάστατον.⟩⟩ This is appropriate here, as a comment on Tat's statement about bodily and mental sight, in which the same verb φαντάζεσθαι was used. It is true that the sentence would

---

[1] This meaning might be illustrated by Synesius, *Hymn* 3, 296 : ψυχά τ' ἀκλινὴς καὶ κλινομένα | ἐς μελαναυγεῖς χθονίους ὄγκους (μέλπε σε)· 'both when it is not brought down (into an earthly body), and when it is brought down.'

also serve as a comment on Πάτερ, τὸ πᾶν ὁρῶ . . . ἐν τῷ νοΐ, which it follows in the MSS. ; but Πάτερ, τὸ πᾶν κ.τ.λ. is wanted to introduce ἐν οὐρανῷ εἰμι κ.τ.λ., which, without some such introduction, is intolerably abrupt. I have therefore interchanged the two sentences of § 13 a.

εἰς must be cut out. φαντάζεσθαι means 'to present something to oneself by φαντασία', i. e. 'to perceive'. It can be used in this sense either without expressed object, as in the preceding sentence, or with an object in the accusative, as here (φαντάζεσθαι τὸ σῶμα) ; but φαντάζεσθαι εἰς τὸ σῶμα is impossible.

τὸ μηκέτι φαντάζεσθαι κ.τ.λ. corresponds to the negative part of Tat's preceding statement (φαντάζομαι οὐχ ὁράσει ὀφθαλμῶν) ; and something more is needed, to correspond to the positive part of it (ἀλλὰ τῇ νοητικῇ ἐνεργείᾳ). I have therefore added ἀλλὰ τὸ ἀσώματον.

⟨⟨Πάτερ, τὸ πᾶν ὁρῶ [καὶ] ἐμαυτὸν ⟨ὄντα⟩, ἐν τῷ νοΐ⟩⟩ ⟨ὁρῶν⟩. The connexion of this with what precedes might be shown more clearly by writing Πάτερ, ἐν τῷ νοΐ ὁρῶν, τὸ πᾶν ὁρῶ ἐμαυτὸν ὄντα. 'Now that I look with my mind (and no longer with my bodily eyes), I see that I am the All.' Cf. § 2, where the new man is said to be τὸ πᾶν, ἐν παντί.

The statement 'I am the All' is expanded in the following clauses, ἐν οὐρανῷ εἰμι κ.τ.λ. By virtue of his παλιγγενεσία, Tat has done what the pupil is exhorted to do in *Corp.* XI. ii. 20 b ; he is freed from the limits of space and time ; he has 'grown to a like expanse with that greatness which is beyond all measure' ; he has 'risen above all time, and become eternal'. The phrases by which his self-expansion is described closely resemble those employed in *Corp.* XI. ii, and were doubtless borrowed thence.

Corp. XI. ii. 20 b.	*Corp.* XIII. 11 b.
ὁμοῦ πανταχῇ ⟨νόησον⟩ εἶναι, ἐν γῇ, ἐν θαλάττῃ, ἐν οὐρανῷ.	ἐν οὐρανῷ εἰμι, ἐν γῇ, ἐν ὕδατι, ἐν ἀέρι.—πανταχοῦ ⟨πάρειμι⟩.
παντὸς ζῴου ἤθη ⟨. . .⟩.	ἐν ζῴοις εἰμί, ἐν φυτοῖς.
μηδέπω γεγεννῆσθαι, ἐν τῇ γαστρὶ εἶναι, νέος, γέρων, τεθνηκέναι.	ἐν γαστρί, πρὸ γαστρός, μετὰ γαστέρα.

§ 11 b. **πανταχοῦ ⟨πάρειμι⟩.** If πανταχοῦ is not provided with a verb of its own, it must be closely connected with the preceding words, ἐν γαστρί, πρὸ γαστρός, μετὰ γαστέρα. But in that case, a word meaning 'at all times', and not 'in all places', would be required.

⟨⟨Ἔγνωκας, ὦ τέκνον, τῆς παλιγγενεσίας τὸν τρόπον.⟩⟩ In § 10, this is pointless ; and the repetition of ὦ τέκνον there, in two successive sentences spoken by Hermes, is an indication that one of the two at least is out of place. But the words are appropriate when placed at the end of § 11 b, as a comment on Tat's description of his new experience. ' Now at last you *know* what the Rebirth is.' Hermes had previously tried to tell Tat what the Rebirth meant, and ended his account of it by saying οὗτος ὁ τῆς παλιγγενεσίας τρόπος (§ 7 b *fin.*). But it was impossible to make Tat understand by merely talking to him about it. He *now* knows what it is, because he has now himself experienced it.

§§ 11 c–12. ['Αλλ' ἔτι τοῦτο . . . ἡ δεκὰς τὴν ἑνάδα.] Tat has just passed through the most stupendous of all conceivable experiences. He has been changed from a man into a god ; he feels himself to be omnipresent and eternal. And this new-made god can find no more fitting occupation than to talk about the fact that the Powers of which he is composed differ in number from the vices which they have expelled ! Our respect for the original author of *Corp.* XIII is much increased when we find that there are sufficient reasons for thinking that he is not responsible for this absurdity.

§ 12. τὸ σκῆνος τοῦτο . . . ἐκ τοῦ ζῳοφόρου κύκλου συνέστη, κ.τ.λ. This section has been much corrupted ; but it seems clear that the writer's meaning must have been that which is expressed by my conjectural reconstruction of the text. It is the influence of the zodiac that brings to pass the birth of the individual man, and determines his bodily form ; and the zodiac is consequently here regarded as the source or cause of his bad qualities or vicious dispositions.

⟨γεννῶντος⟩ φύσεως μιᾶς παντομόρφου⟨ς⟩ ἰδέας εἰς πλάνην τοῦ ἀνθρώπου. The φύσις μία is the character of the natural or corporeal man as a whole ; the παντόμορφοι ἰδέαι of it are the several τιμωρίαι (i. e. vices or bad passions), which are so many different aspects or manifestations of that one character. The word παντόμορφος is specially associated with the zodiac ; see *Ascl. Lat.* III. 19 b and 35.

⟨⟨καὶ τούτου συνεστῶτος ἐκ ζῳδίων (ἐξ ἀριθμῶν MSS.) δώδεκα ὄντων τὸν ἀριθμόν,⟩⟩ διαζυγ⟨ί⟩αι ἐν αὐταῖς εἰσιν, ὦ τέκνον, ⟨δώδεκα⟩. αὐταῖς means ταῖς τῆς μιᾶς φύσεως ἰδέαις, i. e. the evil passions. The twelve divisions (διαζυγίαι) into which they fall are the τιμωρίαι enumerated in § 7 b ; and we are meant to understand that each of the τιμωρίαι is caused by one of the zodiacal Signs. Hence, the Signs being twelve in number, the τιμωρίαι also are necessarily twelve in number.

ἀχώριστος ⟨γάρ⟩ ἐστιν ἡ προπέτεια τῆς ὁρμῆς (ὀργῆς MSS.). ὁρμή is irrational impulse in general ; and ἡ προπέτεια τῆς ὁρμῆς is merely another name for the μία φύσις spoken of above.

εἰκότως οὖν [[κατὰ τὸν ὄρθον λόγον]] τὴν ἀπόστασιν ποιοῦνται, καθὼς ⟨εἶπον, ἀθρόως⟩. As the several τιμωρίαι are merely subdivisions or different modifications of one and the same ὁρμή, there is nothing to be surprised at in the fact that they all depart together on the arrival of the Powers. καθὼς εἶπον is a reference to § 7 b (ἀφίστανται δὲ αὗται ἀθρόως). The words κατὰ τὸν ὄρθον λόγον are superfluous after εἰκότως ; I have therefore transferred them to the following sentence, where something of the sort is wanted. But the original reading there was probably κατὰ λόγον, which may be taken as equivalent to εὐλόγως.

καὶ ⟨⟨κατὰ [   ] λόγον⟩⟩ ἀπὸ δέκα δυνάμεων ἐλαύνονται (ἐλαυνόμεναι MSS.). Having discussed the fact that the number of the τιμωρίαι is twelve, the writer now proceeds to discuss the fact that the number of the δυνάμεις is ten. This matter is so far distinct from the other, that it ought to be dealt with in a fresh sentence ; I have therefore written ἐλαύνονται.

ἀπό has the meaning of ὑπό after a passive verb, as often in the traditional text of the *Hermetica*. Whether in these cases the author wrote ἀπό or ὑπό, we have no means of knowing.

ἡ γὰρ δεκὰς . . . ἐστὶ ψυχογόνος. This notion is of Pythagorean origin. Philolaus, Diels *Vorsokr.* p. 243 : μεγάλα γὰρ καὶ παντελὴς καὶ παντοεργὸς καὶ θείω καὶ οὐρανίω βίω καὶ ἀνθρωπίνω ἀρχὰ καὶ ἁγεμὼν (ἁ δεκάς). Speusippus, the successor of Plato, 'raised a hymn of praise to the number Ten' (Gomperz, *Gk. thinkers* IV, p. 4).

The number ten is 'generative of soul'. It may be doubted whether the writer attached any definite meaning to this obscure statement; but he accepted it on traditional authority, and inferred that, if the number ten is generative of 'soul' or life in the natural man, it must also be generative of the higher life which is brought into being at the birth of the new man, and that the δυνάμεις which operate in the Rebirth must consequently be ten in number.

ζωὴ δὲ καὶ φῶς ἡνωμέναι εἰσὶν ἑνάς (εἰσὶν ἔνθα MSS.). The phrase ζωὴ καὶ φῶς is used in *Corp.* I to denote God ; and Pythagorizing Platonists frequently said that God is the ἑνάς or μονάς.

ὁ ⟨δὲ⟩ τῆς ἐνάδος ἀριθμὸς πέφυκε τοῦ [πνεύματος] ⟨τῆς δεκάδος (ἀριθμοῦ) ἀρχή⟩. A mention of πνεῦμα, in any of the various senses of that word, would be irrelevant here; what is wanted is some statement about the relation between the ἐνάς and the δεκάς.

ἡ ἐνὰς οὖν κατὰ λόγον τὴν δεκάδα ⟨ἐμπερι⟩έχει. Cf. *Corp.* IV. 10 : ἡ γὰρ μονὰς . . . πάντα ἀριθμὸν ἐμπεριέχει, καὶ πάντα ἀριθμὸν γεννᾷ. Dionys. Areop. *De div. nomin.* 5. 6 : ἐν μονάδι πᾶς ἀριθμὸς ἐνοειδῶς προϋφέστηκε, καὶ ἔχει πάντα ἀριθμὸν ἡ μονὰς ἐν ἑαυτῇ μοναχῶς. The δεκάς is connected with the μονάς by the Gnostic Monoimus, Hippol. *Ref. haer.* 8. 13 : ἔστιν οὖν . . . ἡ μονὰς . . . καὶ δεκάς, κ.τ.λ.

The ἐνάς in question here is ζωὴ καὶ φῶς; and the implied conclusion is that in this 'unit' all the ten δυνάμεις are comprehended, and that the arrival of ζωὴ καὶ φῶς consequently involves the arrival of all the ten δυνάμεις together. The following phrase [καὶ ἡ δεκὰς τὴν ἐνάδα] is a meaningless addition to a futile argument.

§ 13 b. [[διὰ τὸν λόγον τοῦτον . . . ὁ θεὸς αὐτὸς θέλει.]] This note must have been intended by its writer to stand at the end of the document to which it refers. Assuming it to be in its right place, we should be forced to infer that *Corp.* XIII originally ended here, and that §§ 14–22 b are an appendage subsequently added. But there is nothing in those sections to suggest a different author; they are written with reference to the παλιγγενεσία described in §§ 1–12, and deal with it from the same point of view. It therefore seems most likely that § 13 b has been accidentally shifted, and ought to stand after § 22 b.

§ 14. τὸ σῶμα τοῦτο . . . λύσιν ἕξει (ἴσχει MSS.) ποτέ; Having been born again, Tat wishes to know whether the incorporeal 'body' (or self) into which he has been transformed is perishable or imperishable, i. e. whether the effect of the Rebirth which he has experienced will be permanent or transient. At the present moment, he feels himself to be a god; but can he be sure that he will not at some future time cease to be what he is now?

The question whether it is possible for one who has attained to *gnosis*, or union with God, to fall away from it, is touched on in several of the *Hermetica*. In Herm. *ap.* Stob. *Exc.* II B. 3, the possibility of such a fall is denied (as it is in the answer given to Tat's question here): οὐδέποτε . . . ὀλισθῆναι δύναται ἐπὶ τὸ ἐναντίον. On the other hand, the possibility appears to be asserted in

Corp. XII. i. 9 as emended : οὐδὲν ⟨τῷ νοΐ⟩ ἀδύνατον, οὔτε εἱμαρμένης ὑπεράνω θεῖναι ψυχὴν ἀνθρωπίνην, οὔτε ἀμελήσασαν, ἅπερ συμβαίνει, ὑπὸ τὴν εἱμαρμένην θεῖναι. In *Corp.* I. 32, and in *Ascl. Lat.* 41 b, the worshipper prays that he may not fall away. Compare a sacramental prayer in the Mithraic *Apathanatismos*, Dieterich's 'Mithrasliturgie' (see Appendix on Rebirth) : μένε σὺν ἐμοὶ ἐν τῇ ψυχῇ μου, . . . ἵνα μὴ πάλιν γενόμενος ἀπογένωμαι.

μὴ ἀδύνατα φθέγγου, ἐπεὶ [ἁμαρτήσεις καὶ] ἀσεβή⟨σεις. μὴ ἐσβέσ⟩θη [σεται] σου ὁ ὀφθαλμὸς τοῦ νοῦ ; It is hardly worth while to tell a person that if he says impossible things he ' will make a mistake '; and ἁμαρτήσεις was most likely inserted to provide a verb after ἐπεί, when ἀσεβήσεις had been partly obliterated. Cf. *Corp.* II. 15 as emended : μὴ οὖν εἴπῃς ἄλλο τι ἀγαθὸν ἢ μόνον τὸν θεόν, ἐπεὶ ἀσεβήσεις.

τὸ αἰσθητὸν τῆς φύσεως σῶμα πόρρωθέν ἐστι [τῆς] τοῦ οὐσιώδους ⟨*sc.* σώματος⟩ [γενέσεως]. 'You must not suppose, because the material body is dissoluble, that the incorporeal " body " into which you have been changed is also dissoluble ; for the one differs widely from the other.'

§ 15. Ἐβουλόμην . . . τὴν διὰ τοῦ ὕμνου εὐλογίαν ⟨μαθεῖν⟩. Tat wishes to give thanks to God for his παλιγγενεσία ; and since he is now composed of δυνάμεις, he feels that the best form which his act of worship could take would be to sing the hymn which is sung by the δυνάμεις in their supracosmic abode. He therefore says that he wishes he could be taught that hymn (*sc.* in order that he might join in it, or use it in his own worship).

In making Tat speak of what ' Poimandres foretold ', the writer is referring to *Corp.* I. 26 a, where an unnamed person is told by Poimandres that, when he has departed from the body and ascended to the eighth sphere of heaven, he will ' hear the δυνάμεις, who are above that sphere, singing praise to God with a voice (or in a language) that is theirs alone '. But the writer of *Corp.* XIII assumes that Hermes was the man to whom Poimandres spoke on that occasion. This shows that, at the time when *Corp.* XIII was written, it had come to be assumed that the anonymous prophet who narrates his vision and preaching in *Corp.* I was Hermes.

ἧν, ⟨⟨καθὼς⟩⟩ ἔφης, ἐπὶ τὴν ὀγδοάδα γενομένου σου (μου MSS.) ἀκούσ⟨εσθ⟩αι ⟨σε⟩ τῶν δυνάμεων [[ ]] [ ] ὁ Ποιμάνδρης ἐθέσπισε. καθὼς ἔφης means 'as you wrote in *Corp.* I ', which is taken to have been written by Hermes. With the alterations which I have proposed, the passage is a correct report of what Poimandres is there said to have predicted. It is true that, in the particular sentence referred to, the verb is in the third person (ἀκούει, sc. ὁ ἄνθρωπος); but the speech of Poimandres in which it occurs deals especially with the destiny of the person addressed; the verbs in the opening sentences of it are in the second person (εἶχες &c.); and if my transposition of the words πῶς εἰς ζωὴν χωρήσω is accepted, the whole speech is an answer to the question 'by what process shall *I* pass into life?' If we retained ἀκοῦσαι here, we should be obliged to suppose that the writer of *Corp.* XIII assumed that Hermes had, at some time subsequent to the vision described in *Corp.* I, gone through the experience which Poimandres there foretells; but this can be avoided by altering ἀκοῦσαι into ἀκούσεσθαι, which suits better with ἐθέσπισε ('prophesied').

καλῶς σπεύδεις· κεκάθαρσαι γάρ, λυσάμενος τὸ σκῆνος.—(καλῶς σπεύδεις λῦσαι τὸ σκῆνος, κεκαθαρμένος γάρ MSS.) 'Your eagerness to be taught that hymn has my approval; for now that you have cast off the body (through your New Birth), you are purified (from evil passions, and are therefore worthy to hear it).' The terminations of λυσάμενος and κεκάθαρσαι seem to have been interchanged. For λυσάμενος τὸ σκῆνος, cf. the oracle in Porphyr. *Vita Plotini* 22 : νῦν δ', ὅτε δὴ τὸ σκῆνος ἐλύσαο κ.τ.λ. The active λῦσαι could hardly be used in this sense.

ὁ Ποιμάνδρης . . . πλέον μοι τῶν ἐγγεγραμμένων οὐ παρέδωκεν. τῶν ἐγγεγραμμένων means 'what stands written in *Corp.* I'. It may be inferred from these words that the writer of *Corp.* XIII knew of no document other than *Corp.* I in which teachings of Poimandres were recorded.

εἰδὼς ὅτι ἀπ' ἐμαυτοῦ δυνήσομαι πάντα νοεῖν, καὶ ἀκούειν ὧν βούλομαι, καὶ ὁρᾶν τὰ πάντα. He knew that through his revelation my mental eyes were opened, and the power of apprehending the divine realities by direct intuition was conferred upon me. (Cf. *Corp.* I. 30: ἐγένετο . . . ἀληθινὴ ὅρασις. . . . θεόπνους γενόμενος ⟨ἐπὶ τὸ πεδίον?⟩ τῆς ἀληθείας ἦλθον.) There was therefore no need for him to tell me all particulars. It would have been superfluous to recite to me the hymn sung by the Powers; he knew that I could find out for myself how God ought to be adored.

καὶ ἐπέτρεψέ μοι ἐκεῖνος ⌜ποιεῖν τὰ καλά⌝. The context requires, in place of ποιεῖν τὰ καλά, something like νοεῖν τὰ ἄλλα (or τὰ λοιπά), 'to think out for myself what he did not tell me'. The clause looks like a reference to some particular sentence in *Corp.* I ; but *Corp.* I, in the form in which we have it, contains no such injunction. (The phrases most nearly resembling it are νοεῖ τὸ φῶς καὶ γνώριζε τοῦτο, I. 7, and οὐκ ἔφην σοι νοεῖν; I. 20.) On the other hand, *Corp.* XI. ii, in which Νοῦς is the teacher, ends with the very injunction which is here implied: τὰ δὲ ἄλλα πάντα ὁμοίως κατὰ σεαυτὸν νόει, καὶ οὐ διαψευσθήσῃ. Is that the passage to which the writer of *Corp.* XIII is here referring? And if so, did he, by a slip of memory, imagine that he had read it in *Corp.* I? Or did he identify the Νοῦς who speaks in XI. ii with the Poimandres of *Corp.* I?

διὸ αἱ ἐν πᾶσι δυνάμεις καὶ ἐν ἐμοὶ ᾄδουσι.—(διὸ καὶ ἐν πᾶσιν αἱ δυνάμεις καὶ ἐν ἐμοὶ ᾄδουσι MSS.) The divine δυνάμεις which pervade the universe are identified with those which were spoken of in *Corp.* I as residing in extracosmic space, and singing to God there. But those same δυνάμεις are also present in the 'reborn' man; indeed, he is wholly composed of them (ἐκ πασῶν δυνάμεων συνεστώς) ; and they sing within him, as well as 'above the Ogdoad'. It is their voice then which speaks in the hymn which Hermes now proceeds to sing.

Θέλω, πάτερ, ἀκοῦσαι ⟨⟨ταῦτα⟩⟩, καὶ βούλομαι [[ ]] νοῆσαι. 'I wish to hear the words of the hymn which the Powers sing within you, and to grasp its meaning', or perhaps rather 'to make it the expression of my own thought'. For the distinction between ἀκοῦσαι and νοῆσαι, cf. *Corp.* I. 1 : Τί βούλει ἀκοῦσαι καὶ θεάσασθαι, καὶ νοήσας μαθεῖν καὶ γνῶναι;

§ 16. τῆς ἁρμοζούσης ⟨⟨τῇ παλιγγενεσίᾳ⟩⟩ νῦν ἄκουε εὐλογίας τὸν ὕμνον. The hymn of Hermes is the thanksgiving of one who has been born again. By joining in it as Hermes sings it, Tat will fittingly give thanks to God for his own παλιγγενεσία.

The word νῦν comes in awkwardly, and might perhaps be struck out with advantage. If we retain it, we must take it in connexion with the following words, ὃν οὐκ ἔκρινα οὕτως εὐκόλως ἐκφάναι ⟨⟨σοι⟩⟩. 'I will let you hear it now, though I had not meant to make it known to you so readily.'

[ὅθεν τοῦτο οὐ διδάσκεται . . . πρὸς ἀπηλιώτην.] As addressed by Hermes to Tat, this passage is quite out of keeping with the context. Why should Hermes, when 'the Powers' are about to 'sing within him', interrupt himself or them in order to state the conditions under which this hymn is to be transmitted to people who are not now present, and lay down regulations for its use at other times? The passage is a liturgical rubric, and must have been inserted after the hymn had come to be used in worship by a religious brotherhood.

τοῦτο οὐ διδάσκεται, ⟨⟨εἰ μὴ ἐπὶ τέλει τοῦ παντός.⟩⟩ The hymn must not be taught to catechumens; only those whose course of religious instruction is completed, and who have become τέλειοι (or in other words, have been born again), are to be permitted to hear it. As the hymn is a thanksgiving for παλιγγενεσία, those who have not themselves been born again can have no concern with it, and it would be a profanation to make it known to them.

By the insertion of this rubric, the words ἡσύχασον, ὦ τέκνον were too widely separated from the hymn which they had been intended to introduce; and they were consequently written again immediately before the hymn.

§ 17. ['Υμνωδία κρυπτή.] This title must have been inserted by a later hand. λόγος δ', which is added in some of the MSS., probably means 'the fourth hymn'. In the extant *Hermetica*, hymns of more or less similar character occur in *Corp.* I. 31, *Corp.* V. 10 b, and *Ascl. Lat.* 41 b. When the Hermetic documents had come to be used for liturgical purposes, special attention must have been given to the hymns contained in them; and it is possible that these hymns and others like them were extracted and put together in a hymn-book, and that this one was the fourth in that collection.

As given in the MSS., a large part of the hymn is unintelligible. I have tried to put meaning into it by freely altering the text; but much remains doubtful and obscure. It falls into two distinct parts. In the first part, God is spoken of as the creator of the material universe; in the second part, God is spoken of as present in the 'reborn' man. In other words, the first part deals with γένεσις, and the second, with παλιγγενεσία. The second part consists mainly of an amplification of the thought expressed by Hermes above, αἱ ἐν πᾶσι δυνάμεις καὶ ἐν ἐμοὶ ᾄδουσι. When the reborn man praises God, it is the Powers of God that speak in him.

⟨⟨'Ανοιγήτω μοι πᾶς μοχλὸς (μυχὸς ?)⟩⟩⟩ ⟨τοῦ⟩ ⟨⟨κόσμου⟩⟩·
πᾶσα φύσις [[κόσμου]] προσδεχέσθω τοῦ ὕμνου τὴν ἀκοήν.

This mode of beginning a hymn seems to be of Jewish origin; it may be traced back to the Song of Moses, *Deut.* 32. 1 : πρόσεχε

οὐρανέ, καὶ λαλήσω· καὶ ἀκουέτω ἡ γῆ ῥήματα ἐκ στόματός μου.
(The formula recurs, with a different application, in *Isaiah* i. 2 :
ἄκουε, οὐρανέ, καὶ ἐνωτίζου, γῆ, ὅτι Κύριος ἐλάλησεν.) In Philo
In Flaccum 14. 123, Cohn VI, p. 142, the thanksgiving of the
Alexandrian Jews at the downfall of their oppressor begins thus :
γῆν καὶ θάλασσαν, ἀέρα τε καὶ οὐρανόν, τὰ μέρη τοῦ παντὸς καὶ σύμπαντα
τὸν κόσμον, ὦ μέγιστε βασιλεῦ θνητῶν καὶ ἀθανάτων, παρακαλέσοντες
εἰς εὐχαριστίαν τὴν σὴν ἥκομεν. Compare also a prayer embedded
in the longer Paris *Papyrus magicus*, Wessely l. 1168 *sqq*. (Dieterich,
Abraxas, p. 25), which may be conjecturally reconstructed as
follows :

σὲ τὸν ἕνα καὶ μάκαρα ⟨α⟩ἰὼν⟨α⟩ αἰώνων [1] πατέρα τε κόσμου κοσμικαῖς
κλῄζω λιταῖς [2]. δεῦρό μοι ὁ ⌈ἐνφυσήσας⌉ [3] τὸν σύμπαντα κόσμον,
ὁ τὸ πῦρ κρεμάσας ⌈ἐκ τοῦ ὕδατος⌉, [4] καὶ τὴν γῆν χωρίσας ἀπὸ τοῦ
ὕδατος. [5]

⟨⟨ἀνοίγηθι [6] οὐρανέ, δέξαι μου τὰ φθέγματα·⟩⟩ πρόσεχε ⌈μορφῇ⌉ [7] καὶ
πνεῦμα καὶ γῆ καὶ θάλασσα [ῥῆμα τοῦ σοφοῦ] [θείας ἀνάγκης], καὶ
πρόσδεξαί μου τοὺς λόγους [8] [ὡς βέλη πυρός]· [9] ὅτι ἐγώ εἰμι [ἄνθρωπος]
θεοῦ τοῦ ἐν οὐρανῷ [ω] πλάσμα κάλλιστον, [10] γενόμενον ἐκ ⟨πυρὸς
καὶ?⟩ πνεύματος καὶ δρόσου καὶ γῆς.   [[ἀνοίγητι οὐρανέ, δέξαι μου τὰ
φθέγματα.]]

ἄκουε, [ἥλιε,] πάτερ κόσμου· ἐπικαλοῦμαί σε τῷ ὀνόματί σου κ.τ.λ.

ἀνοιγήτω is to be taken in connexion with προσδεχέσθω τὴν ἀκοήν
(' let every region be flung open to receive the sound of my voice '),
and ought to precede it. κόσμου is superfluous after πᾶσα φύσις;

[1] μάκαρα τῶν αἰώνων Pap.
[2] κοσμικαις κληζωνταις Wessely : corr. Dieterich. Cf. *Corp.* XIII. 20: ταῦτα
βοᾷ . . . διὰ τῶν κτισμάτων σου, ἀπὸ τοῦ αἰῶνος κ.τ.λ.
[3] ' Thou who didst *inflate* the whole Kosmos.' This cannot be right. Perhaps
ὁ φυτεύσας τὸν σ. κ.
[4] It could not be said that the fire of heaven is 'suspended from the water'.
Perhaps ὑπὲρ τοῦ πνεύματος (' above the air '). This would give an exact repetition
of accentual rhythm :

ὁ τὸ πῦρ κρεμάσας | ὑπὲρ τοῦ πνεύματος,
καὶ τὴν γῆν χωρίσας | ἀπὸ τοῦ ὕδατος.

[5] Cf. *Corp.* XIII. 17: τὸν κτίσαντα τὰ πάντα, τὸν πήξαντα τὴν γῆν καὶ οὐρανὸν
κρεμάσαντα. The verb κρεμάσαι occurs in a similar connexion both in the *cosmogonia*
of *Corp.* I and in that of *Corp.* III.
[6] ἀνοίγητι Pap. Perhaps a second and distinct prayer or hymn begins here.
[7] Perhaps μου τῇ φωνῇ.
[8] Cf. *Corp.* XIII. 17 : ἀνοιγήτω μοι . . . προσδεξάσθω μου τὸν λόγον.
[9] It looks as if the sentence ⟨τὰ⟩ ῥήμα⟨τα⟩ τοῦ σοφοῦ ὡς βέλη πυρός, ' the words of
the wise are as shafts of fire ', had been cut in two, and the two parts inserted at
different points. But any such statement would be irrelevant here.
[10] Cf. a Jewish spell πρὸς δαιμονιζομένους, in *Pap. mag.* Par. i. 3009 (Dieterich,
Abraxas, p. 138): ἐκκρινέτω (ὁ ἄγγελος τὸν δαίμονα) τοῦ πλάσματος τούτου, ὃ
ἔπλασεν ὁ θεὸς ἐν τῷ ἁγίῳ ἑαυτοῦ παραδείσῳ.

and something of the sort is needed to complete the first line. It seems that, after the phrase ἀνοιγήτω μοι πᾶς μοχλός had been shifted, some one added ὄμβρου (a poetical substitute for ὕδατος), thinking that, after ἀνοίγηθι γῆ, a corresponding mention of *water* would be appropriate.

ἀνοίγηθι γῆ, [[ ]] τὰ δένδρα μὴ σείεσθε· ὑμνεῖν μέλλω κ.τ.λ. The verb 'open' is obscure in this connexion, unless closely followed by some phrase meaning 'receive my song'; and the earth could hardly 'open', except by splitting asunder, or forming a chasm. This difficulty might be avoided by writing σίγησον ἡ γῆ in place of ἀνοίγηθι γῆ; and τὰ δένδρα μὴ σείεσθε ('hush the sound of your rustling leaves') would then follow more naturally. σιγη- might easily be corrupted into (ἀν)οιγη-, under the influence of the preceding ἀνοιγήτω.

ὑμνεῖν μέλλω τὸν [τῆς κτίσεως κύριον]. This looks like a misplaced doublet of μέλλω γὰρ ὑμνεῖν τὸν κτίσαντα τὰ πάντα a few lines below; and if so, its insertion here may have caused the loss of some words which originally preceded καὶ τὸ πᾶν καὶ τὸ ἕν.

ὁ κύκλος ὁ ἀθάνατος [τοῦ θεοῦ] προσδεξάσθω μου τὸν λόγον. ὁ κύκλος ὁ ἀθ., 'the immortal sphere' (i. e. the sphere of heaven), might very well stand here without a following genitive. But if a genitive followed, it is most likely to have been τοῦ αἰθέρος.

⟨τὸν⟩ ⌜ἐπιτάξαντα⌝ . . . τὸ γλυκὺ ὕδωρ εἰς τὴν οἰκουμένην [καὶ ἀοίκητον]. ἐπιτάξαντα has come from the parallel phrase below, and has taken the place of the original word, which may have been ὀχετεύσαντα.

It is impossible to retain καὶ ἀοίκητον. In Egypt especially, 'inhabited land' and 'watered land' are synonymous terms, and the desert (ἡ ἀοίκητος γῆ) is waterless. And the absurdity is increased by the following words, which, taken with ἀοίκητον, would imply that men are maintained in uninhabited land.

Even when καὶ ἀοίκητον has been struck out, what remains is still too long to correspond to the parallel clause (καὶ ἐπιτάξαντα πῦρ φανῆναι); and it is probable that either some words have been inserted in the one clause, or some words have fallen out of the other.

ἐκ τοῦ ὠκεανοῦ. In Egypt, life is maintained, not by rain, but by the water of the Nile; and ὁ ὠκεανός must mean an imaginary Ocean-stream out of which the Nile is supposed to flow.

εἰς διατροφὴν [ ] πάντων ⌜ἀνθρώπων⌝. ἀνθρώπων can hardly be right, because (1) it too closely resembles ἀνθρώποις in the parallel phrase, and (2) water maintains life in beasts and plants as well as in men. ζώων or ζωὴν ἐχόντων would be more appropriate.

εἰς πᾶσαν πρᾶξιν θεοῖς τε καὶ ἀνθρώποις. Fire is used by the gods (i. e. by the Sun and the other astral gods) in their administration of the universe; and it is used by men in their arts and crafts. Cf. *Corp.* X. 18: δημιουργὸς γὰρ ὢν ὁ νοῦς ὀργάνῳ τῷ πυρὶ πρὸς τὴν δημιουργίαν χρῆται, κ.τ.λ.

δῶμεν πάντες ὁμοῦ αὐτῷ τὴν εὐλογίαν. πάντες ὁμοῦ may be taken to mean 'all we on whom his bounty falls' (θεοί τε καὶ ἄνθρωποι); or, 'all we his creatures'. For the latter, cf. 'O all ye works of the Lord, bless ye the Lord '.

§ 18. οὗτός ἐστιν ὁ τοῦ νο⟨ός⟩ μου ὀφθαλμός. Hitherto, Hermes has been praising God as the creator of the material universe. In the second part of the hymn, which begins with this line, he praises God as operating, through his δυνάμεις, in the mind of the man who has been born again. The first part is merely preparatory to the second, in which the hymn becomes a thanksgiving for the Rebirth.

He who has created the universe is also 'the eye of my mind'; i. e. it is through the presence of God or his δυνάμεις within me that I am enabled to see τὰ νοητά. Cf. τὸ νοητὸν φῶς below.

συνάσατε τῷ θελήματί μου. As we have been told that the reborn man consists wholly of divine δυνάμεις, there is some inconsistency in speaking of his 'will' as a thing distinct from 'the δυνάμεις which are in him '. But in dealing with such a topic as this, precise consistency of language is hardly to be expected. At this moment, the writer thinks of the δυνάμεις as portions of the divine Mind, which have entered into the man, but have not wholly absorbed him into themselves, and do not constitute his whole being; there still remains a human will, which is distinguishable from them, though wholly in accord with them.

γνῶσις ἁγία . . . ⟨χαίρετε⟩ σὺν ἐμοί. Compare § 8 b : χαῖρε λοιπόν, . . . ἦλθεν ἡμῖν γνῶσις θεοῦ. The original author may very well have spoken of the γνῶσις by which the reborn man is illumined, and of the joy which results from this illumination; though it was probably an interpolator that made γνῶσις and χαρά the first and second in a list of named and numbered δυνάμεις.

[καὶ σύ μοι, ἐγκράτεια, . . . τὴν ἀληθείαν.] The writer of these lines was referring to the list of δυνάμεις in § 8 b f., and must have

2806·2   D d

mentioned καρτερία among the rest, though it does not appear here in the traditional text.

τὸ ἀγαθόν . . . ὔμνει· ζωὴ καὶ φῶς, ἀφ' ὑμῶν (ἡμῶν MSS.) εἰς ὑμᾶς χωρεῖ ἡ εὐλογία.   Cf. § 9 : τῇ δὲ ἀληθείᾳ τὸ ἀγαθὸν ἐπεγένετο ἄμα ζωῇ καὶ φωτί. The praise is uttered by the 'Life and Light' which is in me ; it is addressed to 'Life and Light', i. e. to God.

ἐνέργεια τῶν δυνάμεων (μου). 'When my δυνάμεις operate, it is God that operates in them.' According to the Aristotelian usage of δύναμις and ἐνέργεια, the words might mean 'that which exists potentially in me is actualized in God'; but there is no reason to think that the writer attached this meaning to the phrase.

It is difficult to find any sense in δύναμις τῶν ἐνεργειῶν μου ; and it seems probable that the original ending of the clause was lost, and that some one filled the gap with words taken from the preceding line.

§ 19. ταῦτα βοῶσαι (βοῶσιν MSS.) . . . σῇ βουλῇ. It may be conjectured that τὸ πᾶν ὑμνοῦσαι originally stood in correspondence to ταῦτα βοῶσαι, and σὴ βουλή to τὸ σὸν θέλημα.

⟨⟨ὁ σὸς λόγος . . .⟩⟩ . . . ⟨⟨. . . ἐπὶ σὲ τὸ πᾶν.⟩⟩ I have assumed that the words δέξαι ἀπὸ πάντων λογικὴν θυσίαν | τὸ πᾶν are in their right place ; and I have restored some coherence to the passage by transposing, and connecting with these words, two other clauses in which λόγος is spoken of. The last phrase of § 18 (δέξαι ⌜τὸ πᾶν λόγῳ⌝ λογικὴν θυσίαν) appears to be a misplaced doublet of δέξαι ἀπὸ πάντων λογικὴν θυσίαν in § 19 ; and this makes it probable that the preceding clause in § 18 (ὁ σὸς λόγος δι' ἐμοῦ ὑμνεῖ σε) is also misplaced. According to my arrangement of the passage, Hermes first speaks about the δυνάμεις, and then proceeds to speak about the λόγος. By the λόγος of the man is meant the sum of the δυνάμεις which are in him, or the incorporeal organism composed of them ; cf. § 7 b fin. as emended, οὕτω συνίσταται ὁ λόγος, and § 8 b, εἰς συνάρθρωσιν τοῦ λόγου. And the λόγος ('Word') of God may be similarly regarded as made up of the δυνάμεις of God ; whence it would follow that the λόγος of the man is consubstantial with the λόγος of God. But the writer seems to have had in mind at the same time the primary meaning of λόγος, viz. 'speech'.

ὁ σὸς λόγος δι' ἐμοῦ ὑμνεῖ σέ. Cf. a eucharistic prayer of Sarapion, bishop of Thmuis in Egypt, c. A.D. 350 (Wobbermin, Texte und Unters. N. F. II. 3 b, p. 5) : λαλησάτω ἐν ἡμῖν ὁ κύριος Ἰησοῦς καὶ

ἅγιον πνεῦμα, καὶ ὑμνησάτω σὲ δι' ἡμῶν. In the language of a
Christian, Ἰησοῦς and ἅγιον πνεῦμα take the place of the λόγος
and δυνάμεις of Corp. XIII. (In 1 Cor. 1. 24, Christ is called θεοῦ
δύναμις.)

⟨⟨λόγον γὰρ τὸν ἐμὸν (σὸν MSS.) ποιμαίνει⟨s σὺ⟩ ὁ νοῦς.⟩⟩ The
word ποιμαίνεις may have been suggested by Ποιμάνδρης, the name
by which the divine νοῦς is called in Corp. I. If so, the writer
of Corp. XIII must have taken Ποιμάνδρης to mean 'Shepherd
of men'. For the identification of God with νοῦς, cf. σὺ ὁ νοῦς
in § 21.

⟨⟨δι' ἐμοῦ⟩⟩ δέξαι ἀπὸ πάντων (or perhaps ἀπὸ ⟨τοῦ⟩ παντὸς ?) λογικὴν
θυσίαν. The man who has been born again contains all things
within himself (cf. § 13 a as emended: τὸ πᾶν ὁρῶ ἐμαυτὸν ὄντα
κ.τ.λ.); therefore, when he adores God, the universe adores God
through him. As to λογικὴν θυσίαν, cf. δέξαι λογικὰς θυσίας in
Corp. I. 31.

τὸ πᾶν ⟨γὰρ⟩ ⟨⟨ἀπὸ σοῦ, ⟨καὶ⟩ ἐπὶ σὲ τὸ πᾶν.⟩⟩ τὸ πᾶν appears
to refer to ἀπὸ πάντων in the preceding line; and if we put
after it the misplaced fragment ἀπὸ σοῦ ἐπὶ σὲ τὸ πᾶν, we get an
intelligible statement. 'The universe has come from God; and it
is fitting that what has come from God should seek and adore
him, as it now does through me.' In the MSS., the subject of
ἀπὸ σοῦ (ἐστι) is ἡ βουλή; but it would be superfluous to say a
thing so self-evident as that 'God's purpose issues from God'.

The formula here employed by the Hermetist can be traced
back to the early Ionian physicists. From them it was adopted
by the Stoics, and through Stoic influence, became widely current
among religious writers of the Hellenistic age. Heraclitus, fr. 10
fin. Diels: ἐκ πάντων ἓν καὶ ἐξ ἑνὸς πάντα. Xenophanes, fr. 27
Diels: ἐκ γαίης γὰρ πάντα, καὶ εἰς γῆν πάντα τελευτᾷ. Arist. Met.
A. 3, 983 b 6: τῶν δὴ πρώτων φιλοσοφησάντων οἱ πλεῖστοι τὰς ἐν
ὕλης εἴδει μόνας ᾠήθησαν ἀρχὰς εἶναι πάντων· ἐξ οὗ γὰρ ἔστιν ἅπαντα
τὰ ὄντα, καὶ ἐξ οὗ γίγνεται πρῶτον, καὶ εἰς ὃ φθείρεται τελευταῖον,
. . . ταύτην ἀρχήν φασιν εἶναι τῶν ὄντων. (In the view of the Stoics,
this physical ἀρχή,—which, in their system, is fire,—is at the same
time the supreme God.) Paul, Rom. 11. 36: ἐξ αὐτοῦ καὶ δι' αὐτοῦ
καὶ εἰς αὐτὸν τὰ πάντα. 1 Cor. 8. 6: ἐξ οὗ τὰ πάντα, καὶ ἡμεῖς εἰς
αὐτόν. M. Aurel. 4. 23 (addressed to φύσις): ἐκ σοῦ πάντα, ἐν σοὶ
πάντα, εἰς σὲ πάντα. Oppianus (c. A. D. 180), Hal. 1. 409: Ζεῦ
πάτερ, ἐς δὲ σὲ πάντα, καὶ ἐκ σέθεν ἐρρίζωται. In a hymn to the

Moon, *Pap. mag. Par.* i. 2838 (Abel *Orphica*, p. 249, Dieterich *Abraxas*, p. 81): ἀρχὴ καὶ τέλος εἶ . . .· ἐκ σέο γὰρ πάντ' ἐστι, καὶ εἰς σὲ τὰ πάντα τελευτᾳ.[1] See Norden, *Agnostos Theos*, p. 240 ff.

⟨τὸν νοῦν⟩ τὸ⟨ν⟩ ἐν ἡμῖν [[   ]] φώτιζε φῶς·
⟨τὴν ψυχὴν . . .⟩ ⟨⟨σῷζε ζωή⟩⟩.

In *Corp.* I. 17, the human νοῦς is derived from the divine φῶς, and the human ψυχή from the divine ζωή.

[⌈πνεῦμα θεέ . . . σὺ εἶ ὁ θεός[1].] As the series νοῦς, ψυχή, πνεῦμα repeatedly occurs in other *Hermetica*, some one may have been led by the mention of νοῦς and ψυχή in the preceding couplet to add a clause about πνεῦμα. But this clause is not likely to have been written by the original author; for πνεῦμα, in the sense in which it is usually associated with νοῦς and ψυχή (i. e. in the sense of 'vital spirit'), is a corporeal thing, and the reborn man has put away from him all things corporeal. Nor is πνεῦμα in the Christian sense (i. e. that which is highest and divinest in man) likely to have been spoken of by the author; for he uses other terms (νοῦς, δυνάμεις, λόγος) to express that conception.

§ **20.** ὁ σὸς ἄνθρωπος. Cf. *Corp.* I. 32 : ὁ σὸς ἄνθρωπος συναγιάζειν σοι βούλεται. In both passages alike, we should rather have expected ὁ σὸς υἱός or ὁ σὸς παῖς.

ταῦτα βοᾷ [διὰ πυρός, δι' ἀέρος, διὰ γῆς, διὰ ὕδατος,] [διὰ πνεύματος,] διὰ τῶν κτισμάτων σοῦ. The meaning is undoubtedly ' by means of my bodily organs, which are composed of the material elements '. This might be expressed by naming the four elements; but as the clause is too long to be matched by that which follows, it is most likely that the author wrote merely ταῦτα βοᾷ διὰ τῶν κτισμάτων σοῦ, and that some one afterwards inserted διὰ πυρός . . . διὰ ὕδατος to make the meaning clearer. The explanation is correct, but is not necessary. διὰ πνεύματος was probably added by the same interpolator who inserted the clause about πνεῦμα above. *Pneuma* in the sense of ' vital spirit' consists of fire and air, which have already been mentioned; and the *pneuma* of the Christians ought not to be coupled with the material elements.

ἀπὸ τοῦ (σοῦ MSS.) αἰῶνος τὴν εὐλογίαν εὑρών (εὗρον MSS.).   ὁ αἰών

---

[1] A last echo of this ancient phrase occurs in Anatole France, *La Révolte des anges*, 1914, p. 103 : ' Votre science humaine . . . enseigne que tout sort de l'éther et que tout y rentre.' The modern opinion described in that sentence is a return to the position of the Ionian physicists,—with this difference, however, that the modern man of science does not usually, as they did, regard his material ἀρχή as a living being.

here means the world of τὰ νοητά or τὰ οὐσιώδη, of things incorporeal
and eternal, in contrast to the material world to which the body
belongs. The worshipper gives voice to his adoration by means of
his bodily organs; but the thoughts and feelings which he thus
expresses come to him from another and a higher world. But
perhaps Reitzenstein may be right in reading ἀπὸ ⟨τοῦ⟩ σοῦ αἰῶνος,
'from thine eternity'.

ὁ ζητῶ ⟨⟨εἶδον⟩⟩. 'I have found what I have been seeking'; I have
attained to that to which I aspired.

βουλῇ τῇ σῇ ἀναπέπαυμαι [[ ]]·
θελήματι τῷ σῷ ⟨ἀνεγεννήθην⟩.

God's βουλή and God's θέλημα are spoken of side by side, as in
§ 19. ἀναπέπαυμαι, 'I have found rest for my soul'. Cf. *Sap. Sirach*
6. 28: ἐπ' ἐσχάτων γὰρ εὑρήσεις τὴν ἀνάπαυσιν αὐτῆς (*sc.* τῆς σοφίας),
καὶ στραφήσεταί σοι εἰς εὐφροσύνην. *Ib.* 51. 27: ὀλίγον ἐκοπίασα, καὶ
εὗρον ἐμαυτῷ πολλὴν ἀνάπαυσιν. *Ev. Matth.* 11. 28 f.: κἀγὼ ἀναπαύσω
ὑμᾶς. . . . καὶ εὑρήσετε ἀνάπαυσιν ταῖς ψυχαῖς ὑμῶν.

Since the hymn as a whole is a thanksgiving for παλιγγενεσία, it
may be considered certain that the Rebirth was mentioned in the
concluding words; and from § 2, where God's θέλημα was said to be
the begetter of the new man, it may be inferred that the missing
verb after θελήματι τῷ σῷ is ἀνεγεννήθην, or some equivalent.

The three short clauses with which the hymn ends are comparable
to the cries by which the initiated in some of the Pagan mysteries
declared themselves to have received the sacramental grace; e. g.
ἔφυγον κακόν, εὗρον ἄμεινον, Dem. *De cor.* 323 (313) (see Dieterich,
Mithrasliturgie, p. 213 ff.).

§ 21. τέθεικα⟨ς⟩ καὶ ἐν κόσμῳ τῷ ἐμῷ . . . δύναμιν (δύναμαι MSS.) ἐκ
τοῦ σοῦ ὕμνου. Tat's sentence is interrupted by the words which his
father interposes, but is resumed and completed after the interruption. ὁ κόσμος ὁ ἐμός means 'the universe which is in me' (τὸ πᾶν
τὸ ἐν ἐμοί), i. e. 'myself, as containing the universe, or identified with
it'. But Hermes reminds Tat that, inasmuch as he has put the body
from him, 'the universe which is in him' must be an incorporeal
universe, made up of divine δυνάμεις; he ought therefore to have
said ἐν τῷ νοητῷ κόσμῳ τῷ ἐμῷ.

Tat has already been illumined by the divine Light, from the first
moment of his παλιγγενεσία; but the effect of the hymn sung by
Hermes has been to produce in him a further or fuller illumination
(ἐπι-πεφώτισταί μου ὁ νοῦς); and the result is that he now feels

capable, not merely of joining in his father's thanksgiving, but of giving thanks to God in words of his own choosing.

There is no need to infer from this passage that the writer adhered to the old Egyptian belief in the magical or sacramental efficacy of verbal formulae. He does not ascribe Tat's παλιγγενεσία to the working of the hymn ; for the hymn is a thanksgiving for a παλιγγενεσία which has already taken place. And without attributing any magic potency to the sound of the words, it might well be thought that the religious emotion of the pupil would be heightened when he heard his revered father and teacher pouring out his heart in adoration. The writer assumes that spiritual 'power' and 'illumination' may be conveyed from one man to another by such means ; but in making this assumption, he is not adopting an Egyptian superstition ; he is recognizing a fact of universal experience.

ὦ τέκνον, μὴ ἀσκόπως (sc. πέμψῃς ἐξ ἰδίας φρενὸς εὐλογίαν, with the emphasis on ἐξ ἰδίας φρενός). Even for one who has been born again, it is no light matter to address the supreme God without the guidance of a recognized authority ; think well before you venture on it. A beginner might easily go wrong, and unwittingly incur the guilt of impiety. The writer's attitude appears to be that of a member of a religious community which possesses a traditional liturgy, made up of prayers and hymns composed by inspired teachers. Fixed forms of worship have already been established ; and a new hymn to the supreme God is not to be admitted without due consideration.

ἐν τῷ νῷ, ὦ πάτερ, ἃ θεωρῶ λέγω. The more natural order of the words would be ἃ ἐν τῷ νῷ θεωρῶ λέγω ; but if the MSS. are right, ἐν τῷ νῷ has been placed first for emphasis. ' Do not fear that I shall go wrong ; for the words I am about to utter are the expression of what I see in Mind' (or, as a Christian might have said, 'in the Spirit '). The insight into things divine which has come to him through the Rebirth will secure him against error.

γενάρχα τῆς γενεσιουργίας. It may be suspected that the author wrote τελεσιουργίας ; cf. τελεσιουργός (MSS. γενεσιουργός) in § 2. The meaning might have been more simply expressed by writing τῆς παλιγγενεσίας.

σοῦ γὰρ βουλομένου πάντα ⟨μοι⟩ τελεῖται. σοῦ βουλομένου refers back to ἃς θέλεις. ' It is by thy will that I am born again ; it is therefore fitting that I should do thy will by giving thanks to thee.' Cf. θελήματι τῷ σῷ ⟨ἀνεγεννήθην⟩ in § 20, and ἐπὶ τέλει τοῦ παντός in

§ 16. We should rather have expected πάντα μοι τετέλεσται, ' I have been made τέλειος ', i. e. I have been born again. If the present tense τελεῖται is the right reading, the παλιγγενεσία must here be regarded as a process still continuing.

ἀλλὰ καὶ προσθές, ὦ τέκνον, "διὰ τοῦ ⟨σοῦ ?⟩ λόγου". Hermes amends his son's wording, as before in § 21. The meaning appears to be that Tat ought to have said δέξαι εὐλογίας ἀπ᾽ ἐμοῦ διὰ τοῦ λόγου.[1] The word λόγος cannot here mean merely ' speech '; for there would be no need to insist that Tat's ' speech of praise ' (εὐλογία) was uttered ' by means of speech '. It must mean either ' the divine Logos ' or ' the human reason '; and in the view of this writer, there is no essential distinction between the one and the other. The divine λόγος is the sum of the divine δυνάμεις; my λόγος is the sum of ' the δυνάμεις which are in me '; and the δυνάμεις which are in me are identical or consubstantial with the divine δυνάμεις. ' Accept ǀpraise from me through the λόγος' means, 'accept praise offered by thy λόγος, which has entered into me '. Cf. § 19 : ὁ σὸς λόγος δι᾽ ἐμοῦ ὑμνεῖ σε.

Εὐχαριστῶ σοι, πάτερ [⟨ὅτι⟩ ταῦτά μοι αἰνεῖς (αἰνεῖν MSS.) εὐξαμένῳ]. ' I thank you, father, for your approval of my hymn.' But this makes Tat ignore what his father has last said (ἀλλὰ καὶ πρόσθες κ.τ.λ.). It seems most likely then that ὅτι ταῦτα ... εὐξαμένῳ is an explanation added by a later hand, and that the author wrote simply Εὐχαριστῶ σοι, πάτερ. ' I thank you (for your correction).' Cf. εὐχαριστῶ δὲ ἅμα in Corp. I. 20.

§ 22 a. Χαίρω, τέκνον, ⟨ὡς ?⟩ καρποφορήσοντός (-σαντός MSS.) ⟨σου ...⟩. Tat has not as yet had time to bring forth any ' fruit ' since his New Birth, except his little hymn ; and that can hardly be meant. It seems clear therefore that Hermes must here be speaking of what Tat may be expected to do during the remainder of his life on earth. Now that he has been born again, and has thereby escaped from the illusions of sense, and entered into the world of ἀλήθεια (i. e. of eternal reality), he will bring forth the good fruits which belong to that world ; that is, (as the following words explain,) he will live a life of virtuous action. Cf. Ep. Joh. i. 3. 9 : πᾶς ὁ γεγεννημένος ἐκ τοῦ θεοῦ ἁμαρτίαν οὐ ποιεῖ, κ.τ.λ. The use of καρποφορεῖν to express this notion is probably of Jewish origin; cf. Matth.

---

[1] Or, that he ought to have said πάντα μοι τελεῖται διὰ τοῦ λόγου ? But since he *has* in that clause said σοῦ βουλομένου, there seems to be less reason for any further addition there.

3. 8, where John the Baptist says ποιήσατε οὖν καρπὸν ἄξιον τῆς μετανοίας. Paul, *Gal.* 5. 22 : ὁ δὲ καρπὸς τοῦ πνεύματός ἐστιν ἀγάπη κ.τ.λ. *Eph.* 5. 9 : ὡς τέκνα φωτὸς περιπατεῖτε· ὁ γὰρ καρπὸς τοῦ φωτὸς ἐν πάσῃ ἀγαθωσύνῃ κ.τ.λ. *Matth.* 7. 16 : ἀπὸ τῶν καρπῶν αὐτῶν ἐπιγνώσεσθε αὐτοὺς κ.τ.λ. The thought, as well as the expression, is rather Jewish than Platonic ; the Platonists were inclined to regard virtuous action as a preparation for the *gnosis* of the θεωρητικὸς βίος, or a precedent condition of it, rather than as a result produced by it.

[τὰ ἀγαθὰ] τὰ ἀθάνατα ⟨⟨τῆς ἀρετῆς⟩⟩ γεννήματα. τὰ ἀγαθά is probably a variant for τὰ ἀθάνατα. A genitive is required with τὰ γεννήματα ; and τῆς ἀρετῆς, which is an obstruction where it stands in the MSS., is exactly what is wanted here. τὰ τῆς ἀρετῆς γεννήματα are virtuous actions ; and they are ἀθάνατα (divine), inasmuch as they issue from and belong to the divine world of ἀλήθεια.

⟨⟨νοερῶς ἔγνως σεαυτὸν καὶ τὸν πατέρα τὸν ἡμέτερον.⟩⟩ The Rebirth which Tat has just experienced is what other Hermetists call ' attaining to *gnosis* '. When a man ' knows himself ', he knows himself to be a son of God. Cf. ἀναγνωρισάτω . . . ἑαυτὸν ὄντα ἀθάνατον in *Corp.* I. 18. A similar thought occurs in a *Logion* of Jesus, Oxyrhynchus 654 (Lietzmann's *Kleine Texte*, Klostermann *Apocrypha* II, p. 17) : ἡ βασ(ιλεία τῶν οὐρανῶν) ἐντὸς ὑμῶν (ἐ)στι· (καὶ ὅστις ἂν ἑαυτὸν) γνῷ, ταύτην εὑρή(σει. ἐὰν γὰρ ἀληθῶς [1]) ἑαυτοὺς γνώσεσθε [2], (καὶ εἰδήσετε ὅτι υἱοὶ) ἐστὲ ὑμεῖς τοῦ πατρός.

§ 22 b. μηδενὶ [[ ]] ἐκφανεῖν (ἐκφαίνων MSS.) τῆς παλιγγενεσίας τὴν παράδοσιν. The injunctions of secrecy in this document contrast strongly with the attitude of the writer of *Corp.* I, who goes forth to preach his gospel to all mankind.

ἵνα μὴ ὡς διάβολοι ⟨τοῦ παντὸς⟩ λογισθῶμεν. These words give a reason for the secrecy enjoined. But what *is* the reason given ? διάβολοι (' maligners ') is unintelligible unless defined by a following genitive ; I therefore assume the original reading to have been διάβολοι τοῦ παντός, as in the writer's note added below. This may be taken to mean ' maligners of the Kosmos '. It is implied in § 1 that he who would be born again must be ready to ' be estranged from the Kosmos ' ; and the teacher speaks in the same tone throughout the dialogue. (The reborn man ἄμοιρός ἐστι τῆς (αἰσθητῆς?) οὐσίας, § 2 ; the material world is an illusion, §§ 5, 6 ; we must ' stop the working of our bodily senses ', § 7 a ; the body is a prison and a torture-chamber, § 7 b.) The ' illuminated ' man will know how to

---

[1] Swete's restoration.   [2] γνώσεσθαι Pap.

reconcile such language with a belief that the material world, with all that it contains, has been created by God, and manifests his goodness (§ 17); he will understand that it is not in the universe itself that the evil resides, but in the men who use God's κτίσματα amiss, and allow themselves to be dominated by material things. But others might mistakenly suppose that Hermes is expressing a hatred of the Kosmos such as that with which the writer of *Ascl. Lat.* III (c. 25) reproaches the Christians, or that with which Plotinus charges the Gnostics (*Enn.* 2. 9 : superscription, Πρὸς τοὺς κακὸν τὸν δημιουργὸν τοῦ κόσμου καὶ τὸν κόσμον κακὸν εἶναι λέγοντας). Compare Herm. *ap.* Stob. *Exc.* XI. 5, where the writer gives it as one of his reasons for enjoining secrecy, that the unworthy, if they hear his doctrine, καταφρονήσουσι τοῦ παντὸς ὡς γενητοῦ.

⟨. . .⟩ ἱκανῶς γὰρ ἕκαστος ἡμῶν ⟨ἑαυτοῦ⟩ ἐπεμελήθη, ἐγώ τε [ὁ] λέγων σύ τε [ὁ] ἀκούων. These are evidently the concluding words of Hermes. The meaning is '⟨I will say no more ;⟩ for we have done enough to satisfy our respective wants'. ἑαυτοῦ ἐπιμέλεσθαι in the literal sense would mean 'to take food'. Cf. *Ascl. Lat.* 40 d : 'satis enim nos de divinis rebus tractantes velut animi pabulis saturavimus.'

§ 13 b. ⟨⟨⟨ἰ⟩δίᾳ τὸν λόγον τοῦτον . . . διάβολοι τοῦ παντός⟩⟩. This is not said by Hermes. It is a note appended either by the author of the dialogue, or by a transcriber of it ; and the writer of the note speaks in his own person. ὑπεμνηματισάμην means ' I have recorded in writing'. διά is, no doubt, a corruption of ἰδίᾳ ; but ἰδίᾳ would be better placed if it stood immediately before εἰς οὓς κ.τ.λ. It is necessary to cut out εἰς ὄν, which was presumably written as a variant for εἰς οὓς.

Were the two hymns in *Corp.* XIII (§§ 17–20 and § 21) intended to be literally 'sung', and not merely 'said'? If their author meant them to be sung, and composed words and tune together, traces of the rhythm of the music ought to be discoverable in the words, and we might expect to find in them some sort of metre. But there is nothing here that resembles the metres of classical Greek poetry ; and if any regularity of rhythm is to be found in the Hermetic hymns, we must look rather for something similar to the accentual rhythm of the hymns sung in the Byzantine churches.[1] That form of com-

---

[1] An account of the Byzantine hymns is given by Krumbacher *Gesch. der byzant. Litt.*, 1897, pp. 655–705. See also Bardenhewer *Patrologie*, 1910, pp, 485 ff. The rhythm of the Byz. hymns is discussed by W. Meyer, *Ges. Abhandl. zur mittel-*

position is known to have been already fully developed in the fifth century;[1] and there is nothing unreasonable in supposing that accentual rhythm of the same kind may have been used in less elaborately constructed Pagan hymns in Egypt before the end of the third century A. D.,[2] i. e. at the time at which it is probable that *Corp*. XIII was written.

The rhythm of the Byzantine hymns may be illustrated by two specimens taken from hymns of Romanos (Krumbacher, pp. 694, 667).

(1) ἡ παρθένος σήμερον | τὸν ὑπερούσιον τίκτει,
καὶ ἡ γῆ τὸ σπήλαιον | τῷ[3] ἀπροσίτῳ προσάγει.

– – ‿́ – ‿́ – ‿ | – – – ‿́ – – ‿

ἄγγελοι | μετὰ ποιμένων | δοξολογοῦσιν,
μάγοι δὲ | μετὰ ἀστέρος | ὁδοιποροῦσιν.

‿́ – – | – – – ‿́ – | – – – – ‿́ –

(2) ψυχή μου, ψυχή μου, | ἀνάστα, τί καθεύδεις;
τὸ τέλος ἐγγίζει, | καὶ μέλλεις θορυβεῖσθαι.

– ‿́ – – ‿́ – – ‿́ – {‿́⁄–} – ‿́ –

As another instance, we may take the ἀκάθιστος ὕμνος,[4] a hymn to the Virgin Mary, which is generally attributed to Sergius, patriarch of Constantinople, A. D. 610–641, and is still used in the Eastern Church. The Greek text of it has recently been republished by Birkbeck and Woodward, London, 1917. It consists of twenty-four stanzas, preceded by a prelude. I here give as a specimen a group

lateinischer Rhythmic, 1905, vol. ii, pp. 62–94. Krumbacher, p. 649: ' An Stelle der Quantität tritt hier als Hauptprinzip die Silbenzählung und der Schlussaccent. Unter sich ungleiche Verse sind zu Perioden und diese zu Strophen vereinigt.'

[1] The greatest of the composers of Byzantine hymns was Romanos, 'the Pindar of accentual poetry', as to whose date opinions vary between A. D. 491–518 and 713–716. But the names of several men who composed hymns of the same character in the fifth century are given by Bardenhewer, p. 486.

[2] Two of the poems of Greg. Nazianz., c. A. D. 360 (viz. 1. 1. 32, *Hymnus vespertinus*, and 1. 2. 3, *Exhortatio ad virgines*) are ' accentual ', at least in the sense that the distinction between long and short syllables is disregarded. A critical edition of those two poems is given by W. Meyer, *Mittellatein. Rhythmic* II, pp. 141 ff.; and their rhythm is discussed *ib.* pp. 48–51. They consist of verses most of which, though not all, conform to the type – – – – – – | – – – – – ‿́ –; e. g. σὺ φωστῆρσιν οὐρανὸν | κατηύγασας ποικίλοις. That is, the typical verse is composed of two *cola*, each of which contains seven syllables; and in the second *colon*, there is an accent on the last syllable but one. (There seems to be no regularity in the positions of the other accents.) Whether the divergences from this type which occur in some of the verses were admitted by the author, or are (some of them at least) due to corruption of the text, it is difficult to say.

[3] τῷ apparently counts as an unstressed syllable.

[4] It is called ἀκάθιστος, because during its recital the congregation ' does not sit ', but stands.

of six couplets, which forms part of the 19th stanza. It is one of
twelve rhythmically corresponding passages, which occur in alternate
stanzas of the hymn (the 1st, 3rd, 5th, &c.); so that the metrical
scheme of this group of couplets is twelve times repeated, syllable
for syllable and accent for accent.

> { χαῖρε, ἡ στήλη | τῆς παρθενίας·
> { χαῖρε, ἡ πύλη | τῆς σωτηρίας.
>
> { χαῖρε, ἀρχηγὲ | νοητῆς ἀναπλάσεως·
> { χαῖρε, χορηγὲ | θεϊκῆς ἀγαθότητος.
>
> { χαῖρε, σὺ γὰρ ἀνεγέννησας [1] | τοὺς συλληφθέντας αἰσχρῶς·
> { χαῖρε, σὺ γὰρ ἐνουθέτησας | τοὺς συληθέντας τὸν νοῦν.[2]
>
> { χαῖρε, ἡ τὸν φθορέα | τῶν φρενῶν καταργοῦσα·
> { χαῖρε, ἡ τὸν σπορέα | τῆς ἁγνείας τεκοῦσα.
>
> { χαῖρε, παστὰς | ἀσπόρου νυμφεύσεως·
> { χαῖρε, πιστοὺς | Κυρίῳ ἁρμόζουσα.
>
> { χαῖρε, καλὴ | κουροτρόφε παρθένων·
> { χαῖρε, ψυχῶν | νυμφοστόλε ἁγίων.

Now in the two hymns of *Corp.* XIII there is a strongly marked
parallelismus membrorum; and the agreement between the parallel
members, both in the number of syllables and in the positions of the
accents, is close enough to make it appear possible that, if we had
the text before us in its original form, we should find the accentual
rhythm of the first of each pair of corresponding phrases repeated in
the second with as much precision as in the Byzantine hymns. I here
give a tentative reconstruction of the text, based on the assumption
that it was metrical in the sense explained; and it will be seen that
the alterations required for this purpose are not very large.

The rules which I have provisionally assumed and applied [3] are these:

(1) Corresponding phrases contain the same number of syllables.

(2) No distinction is made between long and short syllables.

---

[1] An allusion to the doctrine of rebirth.

[2] The rhythm of the second and third couplets, for instance, might be roughly
reproduced in English thus:

  ‘ Háil thou, who hast wroúght | a resháping of mínd in us ;
  haíl thou, who dost gíve | what is goód and of Gód in us.

Haíl, for thou hast given bírth anew | to men conceivèd in sháme ;
haíl, for thou hast taught to thínk anew | men who were réft of sane thought.’

[3] These appear to be the rules observed in the Byzantine hymns. But I know
too little about those hymns to be certain that my statement of the rules is wholly
right ; and assuming it to be right with respect to the Byzantine hymns, one cannot
be sure that precisely the same rules would be observed by a Pagan hymn-writer in
Egypt two or three centuries earlier.

(3) A stress falls on every syllable which is written with an acute or circumflex accent,[1] with the exception that circumflexed cases of the article (τοῦ, τῆς, &c.) may be treated as unstressed syllables.

(4) Corresponding *cola* invariably agree in the position of the *last* stress (which is here indicated by a double accent).

(5) In the positions of the other stresses, corresponding *cola* agree for the most part, but some divergence is permitted.

It will be noticed that instances of rhyme, and of assonance approximating to rhyme, present themselves here and there, just as in the Byzantine hymns.

Tat's hymn.

Σοὶ ἐγώ, | ὦ γενάρχα τῆς γενεσιουργίας,
Τὰτ θεῷ | πέμπω ⟨– – –⟩[2] λογικὰς θυσίας.
– – ″ | ᴸ – ᴸ – ᴸ – – – – ″ –

θεέ, σὺ ὁ πατήρ·
κύριε, σὺ ὁ νοῦς.
{ – ᴸ / ᴸ – } – – – ″

δέξαι εὐλογίας | ἀπ᾽ ἐμοῦ ἃς σὺ θέλεις·
σοῦ γὰρ βουλομένου | τὰ πάντα μοι τελεῖται.
ᴸ – – – ″ – | – { – ᴸ / ᴸ – } – – ″ –

Hymn of Hermes.

(The first couplet is difficult to dispose of. Its rhythm somewhat resembles that of the two following couplets ; and the resemblance might be increased by rewriting it thus :

Ἀνοιγήτω μοι | ἅπας μυχὸς τοῦ κόσμου·
ἡ φύσις προσδεχέσθω μου | τὴν ἀκοὴν τοῦ ὕμνου.

But to make the correspondence perfect, there ought to be a stress on μοι, and one more syllable in the last *colon*.)

---

[1] What is to be said about syllables written with a grave accent? They are certainly stressed in some cases ; e. g. in the sixth of the group of couplets quoted above from the *acathist* hymn, the last syllable of καλὴ must be stressed, since the word corresponds to ψυχῶν ; and in the case of ἀρχηγὲ and χορηγὲ in the second couplet, and πασταὶ and πιστοὺς in the fifth couplet, it is to be inferred from corresponding couplets in other stanzas that the last syllable is stressed. But there are also syllables written with a grave accent which are unstressed, and I cannot formulate any general rule on this point.

[2] ⟨ἐκ ψυχῆς⟩?

σίγησον ἡ γῆ, | μὴ σείεσθε τὰ δένδρα·
ὑμνήσω ⟨– – – – –⟩ | τὸν τὸ πᾶν καὶ τὸ ἐν ὄντα.
σιγᾶτ᾽ οὐρανοί, | οἱ ἄνεμοι κοιμᾶσθε·
ὁ κύκλος ὁ ἀθάνατος | προσδεξάσθω μου τὸν λόγον.

$$\left\{ \begin{array}{c} \acute{} \ \bar{} \\ \bar{} \ \acute{} \end{array} \right\} \ \_ \ \_ \ '' \ | \ \_ \ \acute{} \ \_ \ \_ \ \_ \ '' \ \_$$

$$\_ \ \acute{} \ \_ \ \_ \ \_ \ '' \ \_ \ \_ \ | \ \_ \ \_ \ \acute{} \ \_ \ \_ \ \_ \ '' \ \_$$

μέλλω γὰρ ὑμνεῖν | τὸν τὰ πάντα κτίσαντα,
τὸν πήξαντα γῆν | κοὐρανὸν κρεμάσαντα·

$$\left\{ \begin{array}{c} \acute{} \ \bar{} \\ \bar{} \ \acute{} \end{array} \right\} \ \_ \ \_ \ '' \ | \ \_ \ \_ \ \_ \ \acute{} \ \_ \ \acute{} \ \_ \ \_$$

τὸν ὀχετεύσαντα | τὸ γλυκὺ ὕδωρ
    εἰς τροφὴν πάντων | ⟨– – – – – –⟩[1]
καὶ ἐπιτάξαντα | τὸ πῦρ φανῆναι
    εἰς πᾶσαν πρᾶξιν | θεοῖς τε καὶ ἀνθρώποις.[2]

$$\_ \ \_ \ \_ \ \acute{} \ \_ \ \_ \ | \ \_ \left\{ \begin{array}{c} \bar{} \\ \acute{} \end{array} \right\} \ \_ \ '' \ \_$$

$$\_ \left\{ \begin{array}{c} \bar{} \\ \acute{} \end{array} \right\} \ \_ \ '' \ \_ \ \_ \ \acute{} \ \_ \ \_ \ \_ \ '' \ \_$$

δῶμεν πάντες ὁμοῦ | αὐτῷ τὴν εὐλογίαν,
    τῷ ἐπ᾽ οὐρανῶν μετεώρῳ·
⟨. . . .   .⟩
    τῷ συμπάσης φύσεως κτίστῃ.

$$\acute{} \ \_ \ \acute{} \ \_ \ \_ \ '' \ | \ \_ \ \acute{} \ \_ \ \_ \ \_ \ '' \ \_$$

$$\acute{} \ \left\{ \begin{array}{c} \bar{} \\ \acute{} \end{array} \right\} \ \_ \ \acute{} \ \_ \ \_ \ '' \ \_$$

οὗτός ἐστιν ὁ τοῦ νοός μου ὀφθαλμός·
δέξαιτο τῶν δυνάμεών μου τὴν φωνήν.

$$\acute{} \ \left\{ \begin{array}{c} \acute{} \\ \bar{} \end{array} \right\} \ \_ \ \_ \ \_ \ \acute{} \ \_ \ \acute{} \ \_ \ \_ \ \_ \ ''$$

    αἱ δυνάμεις αἱ ἐν ἐμοί,
    ὑμνεῖτε τὸ ἐν καὶ τὸ πᾶν.

$$\_ \ \left\{ \begin{array}{c} \bar{} \ \acute{} \\ \acute{} \ \bar{} \end{array} \right\} \ \_ \ \_ \ \_ \ \_ \ ''$$

    συνᾴσατε τῷ θελήματί μου
    ἅπασαι αἱ ἐν ἐμοὶ δυνάμεις.

$$\left\{ \begin{array}{c} \bar{} \ \acute{} \\ \acute{} \ \bar{} \end{array} \right\} \ \_ \ \_ \ \_ \ \_ \ \acute{} \ \_ \ '' \ \_$$

---

[1] ⟨τῶν ζωὴν ἐχόντων⟩?
[2] θεοῖς one syllable? Or θε-οῖς τε κἀνθρώποις? Or θε-οῖς καὶ ἀνθρώποις?

γνῶσις ἁγία, | φωτισθεὶς ἀπὸ σοῦ,
    διὰ σοῦ τὸ νοητὸν φῶς ὑμνῶ.
⟨ – – – – – ⟩ | χαίρω ἐν χαρᾷ νοῦ·
    αἱ δυνάμεις χαίρετε σὺν ἐμοί.

‿ – ″ – – – | · { – / – } – – – – ‿ ″

– – – ‿ – { – / – } – – ‿ – ″

τὸ ἀγαθόν, | ἀγαθὸν ⟨ – – – – – – – – ⟩ ὑμνει·
ζωὴ καὶ φῶς, | ἀφ' ὑμῶν εἰς ὑμᾶς χωρεῖ ἡ εὐλογία.

– – – ″ | – – ‿ – – ‿ – ‿ – – ″ –

εὐχαριστῶ σοι, | πάτερ, ἐνέργεια τῶν δυνάμεών μου·
εὐχαριστῶ σοι, | θεέ, ⟨ – – – – – – – – – – – ⟩.

– – – ″ – | { / – / – / } – ‿ – – – – ‿ – ″ –

ταῦτα βοῶσαι | αἱ δυνάμεις αἱ ἐν ἐμοὶ
    τὸ σὸν θέλημα τελοῦσι·
τὸ πᾶν ὑμνοῦσαι | ⟨ – – – – – – – – ⟩
    σῇ βουλῇ ⟨ – – – – – ⟩[1]

{ / – / – / } – ″ – | – – ‿ – – – ″

{ – / – } – ‿ – – – – ″ –

ὁ σὸς λόγος ⟨ – – – | – – ⟩ δι' ἐμοῦ ὑμνεῖ σε·
λόγον γὰρ τὸν ἐμὸν | ποιμαίνεις σὺ ὁ νοῦς.
δι' ἐμοῦ ἀπὸ πάντων | δέξαι λογικὴν θυσίαν·
    τὸ πᾶν γὰρ ἀπὸ σοῦ, | καὶ ἐπὶ σὲ τὸ πᾶν.

– – ‿ – – ″ – | ‿ – – – ‿ ″ –

{ / – / – / } – – – ″ | – { / – / } – – – ″

τὸν νοῦν τὸν ἐν ἡμῖν | φώτιζε φῶς·
τὴν ψυχὴν ⟨ – – – ⟩[2] | σῶζε ζωή.

– { / – / } – – – ″ | ‿ – – – ″

ταῦτα βοᾷ ὁ σὸς παῖς
    διὰ τῶν σῶν κτισμάτων,
    ἀπὸ τοῦ σοῦ αἰῶνος
τὴν εὐλογίαν εὑρών.[3]

‿ – – – ‿ – – ″

– – – – ‿ – ″ –

– – – – ‿ – ″ –

– · – – ‿ – – ″

----

[1] ⟨ὑπηρετοῦσι⟩? [2] ⟨τὴν ἐμὴν⟩?
[3] In this quatrain the lines are arranged in the order *a b b a*. We might get
the more usual order *a b a b* by interchanging the third and fourth lines.

ὃ ζητῶ εἶδον·

⟨– – – – –⟩.[1]

βουλῇ ⟨– –⟩[2] τῇ σῇ | ἀναπέπαυμαι·

θελήματι τῷ σῷ | ⟨θεὸς γέγονα (?)⟩.

– ͜ – – – ͝ | – – – ͝ – –

In the hymn in *Corp.* I. 31, there is a passage in which similar rhythmical correspondence may be seen :

δέξαι λογικὰς θυσίας [ἁγνὰς]

ἀπὸ ψυχῆς καὶ καρδίας

πρός σε ἀνατεταμένης,

ἀνεκλάλητ', ἄρρητε,

σιωπῇ φωνούμενε.

$\left\{ \begin{matrix} ͜ \\ – \end{matrix} \right\}$ – – $\left\{ \begin{matrix} – \\ ͜ \end{matrix} \right\}$ – – ͝ – (*ter*)

– – – ͜ – ͝ – – (*bis*)

Syllabic and accentual correspondences of the same kind present themselves in some of the clauses of a document entitled στήλη ἀπόκρυφος, *Pap. mag. Par.* i. 1115–1166, and can be got in other clauses of it by slight alterations of the text. This document, as written in the Papyrus, was intended to be recited as a magic spell ; but it seems to have been made up by putting together three distinct hymns, or parts of hymns, which were originally meant for use in religious worship. The sorcerer by whom the magic document was compiled may very likely have got all three from one and the same hymn-book. These hymns must have been composed before A. D. 300. In respect of their form, they are rather like the hymns in *Corp.* XIII ; and they give support to the hypothesis that accentual metre, of the same character as that of the Byzantine hymns, was already in use in Egypt at the time when *Corp.* XIII was written. The text may be read as follows :

1115 A.[3] χαῖρε, τὸ πᾶν σύστημα

τοῦ ἀερίου πνεύματος.[4] * [5]

χαῖρε, τὸ πνεῦμα τὸ διῆκον ἀπὸ οὐρανοῦ ἐπὶ γῆν,[6] *

---

[1] Possibly ⟨οὗ ἐρῶ ἔχω⟩, or something of the sort.   [2] ⟨σωθεὶς⟩ ?

[3] A is a hymn to πνεῦμα, in the Stoic sense of that term.

[4] Exact syllabic correspondence might be got by writing

either { χαῖρε, τὸ πᾶν σύστημα / τοῦ αἰθρίου πνεύματος

or { χαῖρε, τὸ ὅλον σύστημα / τοῦ ἀερίου (αἰθερίου ?) πνεύματος.

[5] I have substituted asterisks for the *voces arcanae* (i. e. bits of gibberish, supposed to be magically potent,) which the sorcerer has inserted.

[6] Possibly, [χαῖρε τὸ πνεῦμα]

{ τὸ διῆκον ἀπὸ οὐρανοῦ / ⟨– – – – – –⟩ ἐπὶ γῆν.

$$\begin{cases} καὶ ἀπὸ γῆς τῆς ἐν μέσῳ κύτ⟨ε⟩ι [τοῦ κόσμου] \\ ἄχρι τῶν περάτων τῆς ἀβύσσου. * \end{cases}$$

1120

χαῖρε,

$$\begin{cases} τὸ εἰσερχόμενόν με \\ καὶ ἀντισπώμενόν μου \\ καὶ χωριζόμενόν μου \end{cases}$$

κατὰ θεοῦ βούλησιν

ἐν χρηστότητι πνεῦμα.[1] *

1125 B.[2]
$$\begin{cases} χαῖρε, ἀρχή ⟨τε⟩ καὶ τέλος τῆς ἀ⟨ει⟩κινήτου φύσεως· * \\ χαῖρε, στοιχ⟨ε⟩ίων ἀκοπιάτου λειτουργίας δ[ε]ίνησις. * \end{cases}$$

1130
$$\begin{cases} χαῖρε, ἡλιακῆς ἀκτῖνος ┃ ὑπηρετικὸν κόσμου[3] καταύ- \\ \quad γασμα· * \\ χαῖρε, νυκτιφαοῦς μήνης[4] ┃ ἀνισολαμπὴς κύκλος \\ \quad ⌜αἰώρημα.⌝[5] * \end{cases}$$

$$\begin{cases} χαίρετε,[6] πάντα ἀερίων εἰδώλων πνεύματα·[7] * \\ χαίρετε, οἷς τὸ χαίρειν[8] ἐν εὐλογίᾳ δίδοται[9] \end{cases}$$

1135

ἀδελφοῖς καὶ ἀδελφαῖς, ὁσίοις καὶ ὁσίαις.[10]

---

[1] The πνεῦμα ('life-breath') of an individual man is a detached portion of the cosmic πνεῦμα. It 'enters into' the man at his birth, 'clings to' him during his life, and 'departs from' him at his death. And birth and death alike are determined by God's will, and take place 'in goodness', that is, are ordered for man's good by God's beneficence.

ἐν χρηστότητι πνεῦμα agrees with the first three phrases both in the number of syllables and in the position of the last stress. Perhaps κατὰ θεοῦ βούλησιν, which contains the same number of syllables, but differs in accentual rhythm, ought to be bracketed.

[2] B is a hymn to the Kosmos.

[3] Perhaps ὑπηρετικὸν κόσμῳ, 'serviceable to the universe'.

[4] Exact correspondence could be got by writing either νυκτιφαοῦς σελήνης or νυκτιφαέος μήνης.

[5] Perhaps ἀνισολαμπὲς (or ἀνισολαμποῦς) κύκλου αἰώρημα.

[6] χαιρε τα Pap.

[7] 'Spirits of airy phantoms' may be taken to mean daemons, or disembodied souls. But it is a strange phrase; perhaps the original reading has been altered by the sorcerer.

This and the following line agree in the number of syllables and the position of the last stress. There is no close parallelism in the sense; but the inhabitants of the air appear to be paired with human worshippers on earth.

[8] χαιρειν Pap.: perhaps substituted by error for some other verb (possibly συμπνεῖν? The words συμπνεῖν ἐν εὐλογίᾳ might mean 'to sing praises in accord' with the airy πνεύματα).

[9] διδοτε Pap.: perhaps δέδοται.

[10] Perhaps ⟨ὦ⟩ ἀδελφοὶ καὶ ἀδελφαὶ ὅσιοι καὶ ὅσιαι, which would correspond metrically with the two preceding lines. Or possibly { ὦ ἀδελφοὶ ὅσιοι { καὶ ἀδελφαὶ ὅσιαι.

This mention of 'brethren and sisters' shows that the hymn in which it occurred was used in congregational worship by some religious community. But the three lines χαίρετε πάντα ... καὶ ὁσίαις have little connexion with the σχῆμα κόσμου, which is the thing spoken of in the rest of B; and it may be suspected that the sorcerer got them from another part of the hymn, or from another hymn.

ὦ μέγα [μέγιστον] ἐγκύκλιον ἀπερινόητον σχῆμα κόσμου,[1]

1140
{ οὐράνιον, * ⌜οὐράνιον⌝,[2] *
{ αἰθέριον, * ⌜ἐναιθέριον⌝, *

{ ὑδατῶδες, * γαιῶδες,[3] *
{ πυρῶδες, * ἀνεμῶδες, *

{ φωτοειδές, *
{ σκοτοειδέ(ς), *
1145 { ἀστροφεγγές,[4] *

ὑγρο⟨ξηρο⟩πυρινόψυχρον [πνεῦμα].[5]

C.[6] αἰνῶ σε,[7] ὁ θεὸς τῶν θεῶν

ὁ τὸν κόσμον καταρτισάμενος, *

ὁ τὴν ἄβυσσον θησαυρίσας[8] ⌜ἀοράτῳ θέσεως ἑδράσματι⌝[9] *

1150 ὁ διαστήσας οὐρανὸν καὶ γῆν,

καὶ τὸν μὲν οὐρανὸν πτέρυξιν χρύσεαις[10] ⌜αἰωνίαις⌝[11] σκεπάσας,[12]*

τὴν δὲ γῆν ἑδράσμασιν αἰωνίοις στηρίσας·[13] *

1155
{ ὁ τὸν αἰθέρα ἀνακρεμάσας | μετεώρῳ ὑψώματι,[14] *
{ ὁ τὸν ἀέρα διασκεδάσας | πνοαῖς αὐτοκινήτοις· *

---

[1] Possibly, ὦ σχῆμα κόσμου
{ μέγα ἐγκύκλιον
{ ἀπερινόητον.

[2] ουρανιον ενρωχεσυηλ | υ ουρανιον Pap. Perhaps,
{ οὐράνιον, ἰ⟨π⟩ουράνιον,
{ αἰθέριον, ἐναέριον.

If that were written, both pairs of epithets alike would refer to the contrast between heaven and the sublunar world.

[3] Perhaps γαιῶδες, ὑδατῶδες, which would make a still closer correspondence.

[4] Perhaps { φωτοειδές, σκοτοειδές,
{ ἀστροφεγγές, ⟨— — — –⟩ (e. g. νυκτηρεφές).

[5] πνεῦμα must be cut ont. Its insertion was probably suggested by hymn A, after A and B had been put together. The adjectives belong to σχῆμα κόσμου; they would not be applicable to πνεῦμα. The material universe is 'moist, (dry,) hot, and cold'; i. e. it is composed of elements that are respectively characterized by these four qualities. But perhaps this odd compound is to be attributed to the sorcerer; the original reading may have been { ὑγρόν, ξηρόν,
{ θερμόν, ψυχρόν.

[6] C is a hymn to God as maker of the world. In that respect it resembles the first part of the hymn of Hermes in *Corp.* XIII.

[7] εν ω σε Pap.

[8] A reminiscence of *Ps.* 32 (33). 7 : τιθεὶς ἐν θησαυροῖς ἀβύσσους.

[9] θέσεως is meaningless; and ἑδράσματι has probably come from ἑδράσμασιν below.

[10] χρυσιαις Pap.

[11] αἰωνίαις has come from αἰωνίοις in the following line.

[12] Cf. *Ps.* 16 (17). 8 : ἐν σκέπῃ τῶν πτερύγων σου σκεπάσεις με. *Ps.* 60 (61). 4 : σκεπασθήσομαι ἐν σκέπῃ τῶν πτερύγων σου. But what is meant by saying that God sheltered *heaven* under wings?

[13] Possibly, { τὸν μὲν πόλον (or τὰ μὲν ἄνω) πτέρυξιν | χρυσαυγέσι σκεπάσας,
{ τὴν δὲ γῆν ἑδράσμασιν | αἰωνίοις στηρίσας.

[14] Correspondence might be got by writing ὑψώματι μετεώρῳ, and counting the εω as one syllable.

$$\begin{cases} \dot{o} \ \tau\dot{o} \ \ddot{v}\delta\omega\rho \ \kappa\nu\kappa\lambda o\tau\epsilon\rho\dot{\epsilon}s \ \pi\epsilon\rho\iota\epsilon\nu\dot{\epsilon}\gamma\kappa as, \ * \\ \dot{o} \ \tau o\dot{v}s \ \pi\rho\eta\sigma\tau\hat{\eta}\rho as \ \langle - \ - \ - \ - \ -\rangle^1 \ \dot{a}\nu\dot{a}\gamma\omega\nu\cdot \ * \end{cases}$$

1160
$$\begin{cases} \dot{o} \ \beta\rho o\nu\tau\dot{a}\zeta\omega\nu, \ * \\ \dot{o} \ \dot{a}\sigma\tau\rho\dot{a}\pi\tau\omega\nu, \ * \end{cases}$$

$$\begin{cases} \dot{o} \ \beta\rho\dot{\epsilon}\chi\omega\nu, \ * \\ \dot{o} \ \sigma\langle\epsilon\rangle\dot{\iota}\omega\nu, \ * \end{cases}$$

$$\dot{o} \ \zeta\omega o\gamma o\nu\hat{\omega}\nu, * \ \dot{o} \ \theta\epsilon\dot{o}s \ \tau\hat{\omega}\nu \ a\dot{\iota}\dot{\omega}\nu\omega\nu.^2$$

$$\begin{cases} \mu\dot{\epsilon}\gamma as \ \epsilon\hat{\iota}, \ \kappa\dot{\nu}\rho\iota\epsilon \ \theta\epsilon\dot{\epsilon}, \\ \delta\dot{\epsilon}\sigma\pi o\tau a, \ \tau o\hat{v} \ \pi a\nu\tau\dot{o}s \ \dot{a}\rho\chi\dot{H}. \ *^3 \end{cases}$$

LIBELLVS XIV

Contents

All visible things have been made; there must therefore be a Maker of them. The Maker has not been made; he is prior and superior to all things made; and he can be seen in his works. §§ 2, 3.

The Maker is our Father. We may call him by three names,— God, Maker, and Father. § 4.

There are these two,—that which is made, and the Maker; and there is nothing beside. The two are correlative, and neither can exist without the other. §§ 5, 6.

All things are good when first made; but in course of time, evil grows on them, as rust forms on metal. God is not the author of evil; and since evil results from the duration of the things made, he has subjected terrestrial things to change (i.e. made them mortal), and so provided that the evil shall be purged away. § 7.

It is foolish and impious to deny that all things are made by God. If God is not the maker of all things, it must be because there are things which he either disdains to make, or is unable to make. But God is good, and therefore cannot be either disdainful or incapable. §§ 8, 9.

God makes things of different kinds; he makes immortal beings in heaven, and mortal beings on earth. There is life everywhere, and

---

[1] E. g. $\langle\dot{a}\pi\dot{o} \ \tau o\hat{v} \ \beta\nu\theta o\hat{v}\rangle$.

[2] Possibly, $\begin{cases} \dot{o} \ - - - - \ \overset{\cdot}{-} \ - \ (\text{e. g. } \dot{o} \ \tau\hat{\eta}s \ \zeta\omega\hat{\eta}s \ \gamma\epsilon\nu\nu\dot{\eta}\tau\omega\rho), \\ \dot{o} \ \theta\epsilon\dot{o}s \ \tau\hat{\omega}\nu \ a\dot{\iota}\dot{\omega}\nu\omega\nu. \end{cases}$

[3] $\tau o\nu \ \pi a\nu\tau os \ a\rho\chi\iota\zeta\omega \ | \ \nu\nu o\nu\theta\eta\nu \ \kappa.\tau.\lambda.$ Pap.

all life is made by God. There are these two then,—God, and the world made by him,—and there is nothing beside them. § 10.

Sources. God is spoken of as the Maker of the world both in the *Timaeus* and in *Genesis*; and a similar conception occurs in native Egyptian documents also. The Platonic notion of God the Maker, derived from the *Timaeus*, must have been known to the writer of *Corp.* XIV; whether any Jewish or Egyptian statement of the doctrine was also known to him, we cannot tell. But he aims at simplifying the teaching that has been handed down to him, and retaining only so much of it as he holds to be indispensable; and accordingly, he omits what was said by Platonists about ὕλη (the raw material out of which things are made), and about the νοητὰ εἴδη (the patterns in the likeness of which things are made).

We are told in § 1 that this *libellus* is a summary of doctrines more fully set forth in preceding discourses of Hermes to Tat. But it is at the same time a protest against the πολυλογία and ματαιολογία (§ 5) of certain teachers,—that is, against the doctrines of certain people who taught a more complicated theology, and recognized other entities besides God and the Kosmos. The writer's criticism would apply to some of the extant *Hermetica*, in which a Being intermediate between the supreme God and the Kosmos is spoken of. But doctrines such as he condemns were taught not only by Hermetists, but by other Platonists of the period also; and he may have had in mind the lectures or writings of some of these teachers. It is possible that some form of Christian theology, Catholic or Gnostic, was also known to him, and was included among the teachings which he contemptuously describes as 'idle chattering'. In his defence of the position that all things are made by God, he seems, like the author of *Corp.* XI. ii, to be contending especially against some one who taught that τὰ ἀθάνατα alone have been made by the supreme God, and that τὰ θνητά are the work of another and inferior Demiurgus (see § 10).

Date. It appears from § 1 that at the time when *Corp.* XIV was written, the διεξοδικοὶ λόγοι of Hermes to Tat were already in existence ; and as the διεξοδικοὶ λόγοι were probably later than the γενικοὶ λόγοι, it may be inferred that this document is one of the later *Hermetica*. There is also some reason to think that the author knew *Corp.* XI. ii, which is probably one of the later documents. Moreover, the complications of Platonic theology increased as time went on; and the later we place the date, the more reason there would be for such a protest against them as we find in *Corp*. XIV. This *libellus* then can hardly have been written before the second century A. D., and is more likely to have been written in the third century than in the second.

Title. The MSS. give two different headings, viz. Ἑρμοῦ τοῦ τρισμεγίστου Ἀσκληπιῷ εὖ φρονεῖν, and Ἑρμοῦ πρὸς Ἀσκληπιόν. The former is right; for this document is an epistle (ἐπιστεῖλαι, § 1), and not, like most of the *Hermetica*, a report of an oral discourse or dialogue. Hermes, in accordance with his character as a religious teacher, substitutes εὖ φρονεῖν ('I wish you health of mind, or wisdom') for the χαίρειν ('I wish you joy') or ἐρρῶσθαι ('I wish you health') commonly employed in letter-writing. Cf. Plato *Ep*. 3 *init*.: Πλάτων Διονυσίῳ χαίρειν ἐπιστείλας ἆρ' ὀρθῶς ἂν τυγχάνοιμι τῆς βελτίστης προσρήσεως; ἢ μᾶλλον κατὰ τὴν ἐμὴν συνήθειαν γράφων εὖ πράττειν; Seneca *Ep*. 15 *init*.: 'mos antiquis fuit, usque ad meam servatus aetatem, primis epistulae verbis adicere " si vales, bene est; ego valeo ". Recte nos dicimus " si philosopharis, bene est ". Valere autem hoc demum est: sine hoc aeger est animus.' Synesius *Ep*. 138: ἔρρωσο καὶ φιλοσόφει. Synes. *Ep*. 139: καὶ ὡς πρὸς τοιοῦτόν (to such a man as you) μοι τῆς ἐπιστολῆς τὸ πρόσρημα "πολλὰ φρονεῖν", οὐ "χαίρειν", οὐδὲ "εὖ πράττειν", τὸ μετριώτερον.

Cyril, quoting from *Corp*. XIV (see § 6), says γράφει . . . Ἑρμῆς ⟨ἐν τῷ ?⟩ περὶ τῆς τοῦ παντὸς φύσεως. Cyril probably found this description of the contents written as a heading in his copy; and it may have been suggested by the words of § 1 *init.*, τὴν τῶν ὄντων ἠθέλησε φύσιν μαθεῖν.

§ 1. ἐπεὶ ὁ υἱός μου . . . ἐπιστήμονι τῆς φύσεως. The situation described is this. Asclepius is the elder of the two pupils of Hermes, and has already learnt much from him. But he has for some time been parted from his master. In his absence, Hermes has been instructing Tat; and he wishes to confer a corresponding benefit on Asclepius. But in teaching Tat, who was a beginner, he found it necessary to give full and detailed explanations concerning every matter dealt with. It would be superfluous to repeat all this to Asclepius, who knew much that Tat did not know; Hermes therefore considers it enough to send to Asclepius a short summary of his discourses to Tat. Asclepius will be able to fill in the outlines and supply the explanations for himself.

This implies that the author of *Corp.* XIV had before him a series of discourses of Hermes to Tat, and wrote this document as an epitome of their contents, or rather, of those parts of their contents which he considered to be of primary importance (τὰ κυριώτατα κεφάλαια). And from the words in which he describes the discourses which he is summarizing (περὶ ἑνὸς ἑκάστου ἠναγκάσθην πλείονα εἰπεῖν κ.τ.λ.) it may be inferred that they were those entitled οἱ πρὸς Τὰτ διεξοδικοὶ λόγοι. Compare *Corp.* X (Hermes to Tat), which is described in the opening words (addressed to Asclepius) as an epitome of οἱ πρὸς Τὰτ γενικοὶ λόγοι.

Apart from some slight alterations of the text, this introductory section presents no difficulty ; and I see no reason to doubt that it was written by the author of *Corp.* XIV.

τὴν τῶν ὄντων . . . φύσιν μαθεῖν. Cf. *Corp.* XI. (i) 1 b, where Hermes asks Nous to instruct him περὶ τοῦ παντὸς καὶ τοῦ θεοῦ. *Corp.* I. 3 : μαθεῖν θέλω τὰ ὄντα καὶ νοῆσαι τὴν τούτων φύσιν, καὶ γνῶναι τὸν θεόν. ' Knowledge of nature ' (φυσική) is knowledge of the Kosmos (τὸ πᾶν) ; and in both those passages, knowledge of this kind is spoken of as a thing distinct from knowledge of God, though connected with that higher knowledge and leading up to it. The same distinction is probably implied in XIV. 1. The ' knowledge of nature' which Tat desired was knowledge of the Kosmos ; and to get this knowledge is the first stage on the way to *gnosis.* Asclepius has already traversed this preliminary stage ; there is therefore no need for Hermes to repeat to him the lessons in φυσική which he has given to Tat in the διεξοδικοὶ λόγοι ; the teacher is free to assume all this as known, and proceed at once to speak of God, the Maker of the Kosmos. Accordingly, we find that in this document the Kosmos is spoken of only under the collective term τὰ γινόμενα (or τὰ γεννητά), and is not described or explained in detail, as it is in some of the other *Hermetica* (e. g. *Corp.* XI. ii *init.*).

ὡς νεωτέρῳ καὶ ἄρτι παρελθόντι ἐπὶ τὴν γνῶσιν.—(ὡς υἱὸς καὶ νεώτερος ἄρτι παρελθὼν ἐπὶ τὴν γνῶσιν MSS.) The youth of a pupil, and the fact that he is a beginner, are reasons for explaining things fully to him ; but they are not reasons for his demanding to be taught without delay. These words must therefore be connected with what follows (περὶ ἑνὸς ἑκάστου ἠναγκάσθην πλείονα εἰπεῖν). But a transcriber preferred to connect them with what precedes (ὑπερθέσθαι . . . οὐκ ἐπέτρεπεν), and consequently altered the datives into nominatives. It was presumably the same person that inserted υἱός, which has no meaning except in connexion with οὐκ ἐπέτρεπεν, and even in that connexion, is hardly wanted after ὁ υἱός μου above. Its insertion was probably suggested by *Corp.* XIII. 3 (μὴ φθόνει μοι, πάτερ· γνήσιος υἱός εἰμι· διάφρασόν μοι κ.τ.λ.) ; and if so, this sentence may have been altered by the compiler of the *Corpus*, in order tớ make the introductory section of *Corp.* XIV appear to refer to *Corp.* XIII, with which it originally had nothing to do.

[μυστικώτερον αὐτὰ ἑρμηνεύσας]. This seems to mean 'expressing them in language which would be intelligible only to the initiated ', i. e. presenting them in an obscure and esoteric form. But there is nothing esoteric in the language of this *libellus*, which is rather distinguished from other *Hermetica* by its straightforward simplicity. In § 5, (if my explanation of that passage is right,) the writer declares himself opposed to hiding things away ἐν μυχῷ; and that phrase seems to mean much the same as μυστικῶς ἑρμηνεύειν. It is therefore probable that the words μυστικώτερον αὐτὰ ἑρμηνεύσας were not written by the author, but were inserted by some one else. The interpolator apparently failed to see that it is the omission of preliminary teaching about the Kosmos that makes the epistle suitable only for an advanced student, and therefore thought it necessary to allege another reason, namely, the obscurity of the language,—though as a matter of fact the language is not obscure.

§ 2. [τὰ δὲ γεννητὰ οὐχ ὑφ' ἑαυτοῦ ἀλλ' ὑφ' ἑτέρου γίνεται]. This appears to be a doublet of γίνεται δὲ ὑφ' ἑτέρου τὰ γινόμενα. The writer cannot have intended both these clauses to stand in the same sentence ; and it seems best to cut out the first of them. In place of ὑφ' ἑαυτοῦ, we should have expected ὑφ' ἑαυτῶν.

πολλὰ δὲ [   ] τὰ φαινόμενα, καὶ πάντα [τὰ] διάφορα καὶ οὐχ ὅμοια. Cf. τὴν ποικιλίαν τῶν γινομένων in § 7 *init.* The 'differences' with which the writer is chiefly concerned are the different degrees of goodness or badness, and especially, the difference between τὰ θνητά (terrestrial creatures) and τὰ ἀθάνατα (the heavenly bodies). See § 10.

This parenthesis rather awkwardly interrupts the argument; perhaps πολλὰ δὲ . . . οὐχ ὅμοια is wrongly placed.

§ 3. οὗτος δὲ ⟨⟨εἷς, καὶ⟩⟩ ⟨πάντων⟩ κρείττων, καὶ [[εἷς καὶ]] μόνος ὄντως σοφὸς τὰ πάντα. The point that there is but one Maker is emphasized in the parallel passage *Corp.* XI. ii. 8 b as emended : δεῖ οὖν τοιοῦτόν τινα εἶναι, καὶ τοῦτον πάντως ἕνα. The superiority of God in power and wisdom is regarded as following from the fact that he is 'older' (πρεσβύτερος) than all else. Cf. Synesius *De insomniis* 1, Migne Tom. 66 col. 1284 : καὶ Ὁμήρῳ δὲ ἄρα διὰ τοῦτο τῆς τοῦ Διὸς γνώμης ἐξῆπται τὰ τῶν θεῶν πράγματα, ὅτι " πρότερος γέγονεν, καὶ πλείονα οἶδεν ", αὐτῷ δήπου τῷ πρεσβύτερος εἶναι. . . . καὶ ὅστις οὖν θεὸς ὢν ἄρχειν ἀξιοῦται θεῶν, νοῦς ὤν, σοφίας περιουσίᾳ κρατεῖ.

ἄρχει γὰρ καὶ τοῦ πλήθους τῶν γινομένων τῷ μεγέθει, καὶ τῆς διαφορᾶς τῇ συνεχείᾳ τῆς ποιήσεως.—(ἄρχει γὰρ καὶ τῷ πλήθει καὶ τῷ μεγέθει καὶ τῇ διαφορᾷ τῶν γενομένων καὶ τῇ συνεχείᾳ τῆς ποιήσεως MSS.) It is clear that πλῆθος must be an attribute of τὰ γινόμενα, and μέγεθος an attribute of God. The words πλῆθος and διαφορά, used in connexion with τὰ γινόμενα, correspond to πολλὰ δὲ τὰ φαινόμενα καὶ πάντα διάφορα above. The 'many things' are subject to the one God, because he extends beyond them and encompasses them all by reason of his μέγεθος ; and their differences or variations are subject to him, because he is perpetually making things, that is, because his creative activity manifests itself afresh at every successive moment, and keeps pace with all variations in the things made. Perhaps it is implied, as in § 7 *fin.*, that when things change for the worse, God is always ready to replace them by other things, and so to 'purge away the evil'. As to τῇ συνεχείᾳ τῆς ποιήσεως (and ἀεὶ οὖν ποιῶν below), cf. *Corp.* XI. ii. 14 a : ἀεί ἐστιν ἐν τῷ ἔργῳ.

ἐπεὶ[τα] δὲ τὰ γεννητὰ ὁρώμενά ἐστι, κἀκεῖνος δὴ [ἀ]ὁρατός· διὰ τοῦτο γὰρ ποιεῖ, ἵνα [ἀ]ὁρατὸς ᾖ. ἀεὶ οὖν ποιῶν, ἀ(εὶ) ὁρατός [τοιγαροῦν] ἐστιν. The Hermetist cannot have said that God makes the universe in order to render himself *invisible* (ἵνα ἀόρατος ᾖ) ; he must have said that God makes it in order to render himself *visible*, i.e. in order to manifest himself in his works. It is therefore necessary to write ἵνα ὁρατὸς ᾖ ; and from this it follows that ὁρατός, and not ἀόρατος, must be the right word in the other places also. Cf. *Corp.* XI. ii. 22 a : δι' αὐτὸ τοῦτο πάντα πεποίηκεν, ἵνα διὰ πάντων αὐτὸν βλέπῃς. . . . ὁ θεὸς (ὁρᾶται) ἐν τῷ ποιεῖν. It is to be presumed that some reader, puzzled by the paradoxical statement that God is ὁρατός, altered the words with a view to making them express the orthodox doctrine of Platonism, that God is ἀόρατος, and so made nonsense of the passage. The word τοιγαροῦν, which is obviously out of place, is probably an alternative for the preceding οὖν.

§ 4. οὕτως ἄξιόν ἐστι νοῆσαι, καὶ νοήσαντα θαυμάσαι, καὶ θαυμάσαντα ἑαυτὸν μακαρίσαι ⟨ὡς⟩ τὸν πατέρα γνωρίσαντα. Cf. *Ev. sec. Hebraeos*, Clem. Alex. *Strom.* 2. 9. 45 : κἂν τῷ καθ' Ἑβραίους εὐαγγελίῳ " ὁ θαυμάσας βασιλεύσει" γέγραπται " καὶ ὁ βασιλεύσας ἀναπαήσεται ". Clem. *ib.* 5. 14. 97 : οὐ παύσεται ὁ ζητῶν ἕως ἂν εὕρῃ, εὑρὼν δὲ θαμβήσεται, θαμβηθεὶς δὲ βασιλεύσει, βασιλεύσας δὲ ἐπαναπαύσεται. *Logia Iesu,* Oxyrhynchus Pap. 654 (Klostermann, *Apocrypha* II, p. 17) : μὴ παυσάσθω ὁ ζη(τῶν τὸν πατέρα ἕως ἂν Swete) εὕρῃ· καὶ ὅταν εὕρῃ (θαμβηθήσεται, καὶ θαμ)βηθεὶς βασιλεύσει, κα(ὶ βασιλεύσας ἀναπα)ήσεται. The better form of the saying is that which is given in the *Logia* ; and the resemblance of this to the Hermetist's words (at least if we accept the conjectural supplement τὸν πατέρα in the *Logion*) seems too close to be accidental. But there is no need to assume direct borrowing on either side. The saying may have been widely known, and may have been ascribed by some to Jesus, by others to Hermes, and possibly to other teachers also.

τί γὰρ γλυκύτερον πατρὸς γνησίου ; Cf. *Ascl. Lat.* 41 b as emended : πατρικὴν εὔνοιαν καὶ στοργὴν καὶ φιλίαν, καὶ εἴ τις γλυκυτέρα, ἐνεργείᾳ ἐνεδείξω. In the *Timaeus,* the word πατήρ is employed, as a synonym for γεννητής, to describe the relation of God to the Kosmos which he has brought into being ; and when thus used, it did not carry with it any implication of fatherly affection towards men. But when the word had in this way come to be commonly accepted as a name of God, it was sometimes taken to connote also God's kindly care of his human children.[1] This change in the meaning of the term ' Father ' as applied to God by Pagans is parallel to, but not necessarily dependent on, that by which the Jewish conception of God as creator, law-giver, and judge developed into the Christian[2] conception of ' our Father who is in heaven '.

§ 5. τῆς πολυλογίας τε καὶ ματαιολογίας ἀπαλλαγέντας χρὴ νοεῖν δύο ταῦτα, τὸ γινόμενον καὶ τὸν ποιοῦντα· μέσον γὰρ τούτων οὐδέν. The

---

[1] Instances of this occur in Epictetus ; e. g. *Diss.* 1. 6. 40 : ὅ γε θεός, ... ὁ ἦν ἀγαθοῦ βασιλέως καὶ ταῖς ἀληθείαις πατρός, ἀκώλυτον τοῦτο ἔδωκεν κ.τ.λ. *Ib.* 1. 9. 7 : τὸ δὲ τὸν θεὸν ποιητὴν ἔχειν καὶ πατέρα καὶ κηδεμόνα κ.τ.λ. *Ib.* 3. 24. 15 : ᾔδει γὰρ (ὁ 'Ηρακλῆς) ὅτι οὐδείς ἐστιν ἄνθρωπος ὀρφανός, ἀλλὰ πάντων ἀεὶ καὶ διηνεκῶς [ὁ] πατήρ ἐστιν ὁ κηδόμενος. οὐ γὰρ μέχρι λόγου ἠκηκόει ὅτι πατήρ ἐστιν ὁ Ζεὺς τῶν ἀνθρώπων, ὅς γε καὶ αὐτοῦ πατέρα ᾤετο αὐτὸν καὶ ἐκάλει, καὶ πρὸς ἐκεῖνον ἀφορῶν ἔπραττεν ἃ ἔπραττεν.

[2] But in the Old Testament also, God is sometimes described as a loving father ; e. g. *Isaiah* 63. 16 : ' thou, O Lord, art our father ; our redeemer from everlasting is thy name.' *Jeremiah* 31. 9 : ' I will lead them ... ; for I am a father to Israel, and Ephraim is my first-born.' *Ps.* 103. 13 : ' like as a father pitieth his children, so the Lord pitieth them that fear him.'

Speaking of the early Christians, Harnack (*Hist. of Dogma,* Eng. tr. 1894, vol. i, p. 180) says that ' God is named the Father ' by them ' (1) in relation to the Son ... ; (2) as Father of the world ' (as in the *Timaeus*) ; ' (3) as the merciful one who has proved his goodness, declared his will, and called Christians to be his sons.' It is the third of these three senses that corresponds to the use of the word πατήρ in *Corp.* XIV. 4 and *Ascl. Lat.* 41 b.

writer of *Corp.* XIV aims at simplifying theology by rejecting all superfluities. He recognizes only God and the Kosmos, and refuses to admit the existence of any intermediate entity. But what are the particular theories which he has in mind, and against which this polemic is directed? He would condemn, as 'idle chattering', doctrines which are taught in several of the other *Hermetica*; e. g. he would reject the αἰών of *Corp.* XI. i; the τόπος-νοῦς of *Corp.* II; and the hypostatized λόγος, the 'second νοῦς', and the Archanthropos of *Corp.* I. But were those documents, or any of them, known to him? As he closely follows some parts of XI. ii, it is probable that he had read XI. i also, and was thinking, *inter alia*, of the hypostatized αἰών of XI. i. The 'second God' of Numenius, and Plotinus' triad (ἐν—ἀγαθόν, νοῦς, and ψυχή), would fall under the same condemnation. He would also reject, supposing that he had heard of them, the λόγος and δυνάμεις of Philo, the Christ of Paul and the fourth Gospel, and still more decidedly, the complicated systems of αἰῶνες or δυνάμεις constructed by Valentinus and other Christian Gnostics. But there is nothing to show whether it was some one or more of these doctrines, or others of like character, that he was specially opposing.

μηδὲν ἐν ἀπορίᾳ ⟨⟨ἢ ἐν μυχῷ⟩⟩ τιθέμενος. As to ἐν ἀπορίᾳ, cf. XI. ii. 16 b: μὴ εἰς ἀπορίαν τὸν λόγον περιστήσωμεν· οὐδὲν γὰρ ἄπορον περὶ τοῦ θεοῦ νοουμένοις. The words ἢ τῶν ἐν μυχῷ are clearly out of place where they stand in the MSS., and must in any case be cut out there; and their presence can be best accounted for by assuming that ἢ ἐν μυχῷ was accidentally shifted from the place where I have inserted it, and τῶν was afterwards added. The phrase ἐν μυχῷ τίθεσθαί τι may be taken to mean 'to hide a thing away in a dark corner', and so 'to make a mystery of it'. The writer objects to all obscure and esoteric doctrines.

ἑκάτερον (-ρος MSS.) γὰρ αὐτῶν αὐτὸ τοῦτό ἐστιν. 'Each of them is just this and nothing else'; that is, the essence of the Maker consists in his making things, and the essence of the things made consists in their being made. The phrase is obscure in itself, but is explained by what follows (ὁ ποιῶν ἄλλο οὐδέν ἐστιν ἢ τὸ ποιοῦν μόνον κ.τ.λ.).

οὐκ ἔστι τὸ ἕτερον τοῦ ἑτέρου χωρισθῆναι. Cf. *Corp.* XI. ii. 12 b: ἂν ἐκείνων καταργηθῇ, ὁ θεὸς . . . οὐκέτι ἐστὶ θεός. *Ib.* 14 a: εἰ γὰρ χωρισθείη αὐτοῦ, πάντα μὲν συμπεσεῖσθαι, πάντα δὲ τεθνήξεσθαι ἀνάγκη.

§ 6. [στερήσει τοῦ ἑτέρου.] This is a doublet of τοῦ ἑτέρου ἄνευ.

§ 7. μὴ διὰ τὴν ποικιλίαν τῶν γινομένων φυλάξῃ. The 'variety' of the things made means the fact that they are not all alike good, but are partly good and partly bad. Cf. *Ascl. Lat.* II. 15 : 'hoc est ergo totum qualitatis ⟨diversae, prout natura est⟩ materiae.' μὴ φυλάξῃ means 'do not be on your guard (against the doctrine that all things are made by God)', i. e. do not hesitate to accept it.

φοβούμενος μὴ ταπεινότητα καὶ ἀδοξίαν τῷ θεῷ περιάψῃς. It is implied that there are people who consider it beneath the dignity of God to make things of lower grade. According to the view against which the writer is contending, God may perhaps be the maker of celestial things (τὰ ἀθάνατα), but cannot be the maker of terrestrial things (τὰ θνητά), because all terrestrial things are more or less κακά and αἰσχρά.

μία γάρ ἐστιν αὐτῷ δόξα, τὸ ποιεῖν τὰ πάντα. This use of the word δόξα is rather Jewish than Hellenic.

τοῦτό ἐστι τοῦ θεοῦ ὥσπερ οὐσία (σῶμα MSS.), ἡ ποίησις. It would be possible to say that *the world which God has made* is God's body, though I do not think that any such phrase occurs in the extant *Hermetica*. But it is hardly possible to say that *the act of making things* is God's body. See *Corp.* IV. 1 b, where the MSS. give τοῦτο γάρ ἐστι τὸ σῶμα ἐκείνου.

ὥσπερ ὁ ἰὸς τῷ χαλκῷ. Cf. Plotinus 4. 3. 7 : οὐ γὰρ δὴ ἔξω που δραμοῦσα ἡ ψυχὴ σωφροσύνην καθορᾷ καὶ δικαιοσύνην, ἀλλ᾽ αὐτὴ παρ᾽ αὐτῇ, ἐν τῇ κατανοήσει ἑαυτῆς καὶ τοῦ ὃ πρότερον ἦν, ὥσπερ ἀγάλματα ἐν αὐτῇ ἱδρυμένα ὁρῶσα, οἷον ὑπὸ χρόνου ἰοῦ πεπληρωμένα καθαρὰ ποιησαμένη.

ἡ δὲ τῆς γενέσεως διαμονὴ καθάπερ ἐξανθεῖν ποιεῖ. Both here and in the following sentence, τῆς γενέσεως means τῶν γενητῶν. The subject of ἐξανθεῖν is τὴν κακίαν. Possibly αὐτὴν (*sc.* τὴν κακίαν) may have fallen out after ἐξανθεῖν. The διαμονή (or ἐπιδιαμονή) of terrestrial things is the fact that each of them, when once made, continues to exist (for a finite time). In this sense διαμονή is contrasted with ἀθανασία in *Corp.* XI. i. 2. Everything made by God is good when first made ; but in course of time, evil 'breaks out on it', like rust on metal, or an eruption on the skin. Compare the description of the gradual depravation of the incarnated soul in *Corp.* X. 15 b.

It is not clear how this attempt to explain the origin of evil is to be reconciled with the writer's view that God 'is always making things', which would seem to imply that God does not make a thing once for all and then leave it to itself, but that it is by his action that the thing is maintained in existence from moment to moment, and consequently, that its condition from first to last must be his work. Who, if not God, makes the 'rust'? The Platonic answer to that question would be 'it comes from the ἀταξία which is inherent in ὕλη, and which God cannot wholly overcome' (see *Ascl. Lat.* II); but the writer of *Corp.* XIV says nothing about ὕλη.

διὰ τοῦτο ἐποίησε τὴν μεταβολὴν ὁ θεός, ὥσπερ ἀνακάθαρσιν τῆς γενέσεως. Since the evil which 'breaks out on' things comes by lapse of time, and increases with lapse of time, evil can be kept within bounds only by limiting the time during which each several thing (in the sublunar world) continues to exist. For this reason God has instituted μεταβολή; that is, he has established the law by which every terrestrial organism sooner or later undergoes dissolution, and is replaced by another. The new organism starts on its career free from the rust of evil by which its predecessor was corrupted. Wicked old men die, and innocent children are born. In this way the total amount of evil is prevented from increasing.[1]

§ 8. τῷ μὲν αὐτῷ ζωγράφῳ ἔξεστι καὶ οὐρανὸν ποιῆσαι καὶ γῆν . . . ., τῷ δὲ θεῷ οὐ δυνατὸν πάντα ποιεῖν; This passage was evidently suggested by Pl. *Rep.* 10. 596 B, C : ἀλλ' ὅρα δὴ καὶ τόνδε τίνα καλεῖς τὸν δημιουργόν, . . . ὃς πάντα ποιεῖ . . .. ὁ αὐτὸς γὰρ οὗτος χειροτέχνης οὐ μόνον πάντα οἷός τε σκεύη ποιῆσαι, ἀλλὰ καὶ τὰ ἐκ τῆς γῆς φυόμενα ἅπαντα ποιεῖ, καὶ ζῷα πάντα ἐργάζεται, τά τε ἄλλα καὶ ἑαυτόν, καὶ πρὸς τούτοις γῆν καὶ οὐρανὸν καὶ θεοὺς καὶ πάντα τὰ ἐν οὐρανῷ καὶ τὰ [ἐν Ἅιδου] ὑπὸ γῆς ἅπαντα ἐργάζεται. . . . τῶν τοιούτων γάρ, οἶμαι, δημιουργῶν καὶ ὁ ζωγράφος ἐστίν. But the Hermetist, while imitating Plato's words, uses the instance of the painter for a different purpose. As employed in *Corp.* XIV, it takes the place of the comparison in *Corp.* XI. ii. 12 a : σοῦ τοσαῦτα ποιοῦντος· καὶ γὰρ βλέπεις καὶ λαλεῖς κ.τ.λ. Below, in § 10, the instance of a man sowing different seeds is used to illustrate the same point.

τὸν γὰρ θεὸν φάσκοντες εὐλογεῖν . . . τὰ μέγιστα εἰς αὐτὸν ἀσεβοῦσι. Cf. *Corp.* IX. 9 : ὑπὸ γὰρ δεισιδαιμονίας βλασφημοῦσι.

§ 10. ἴδε γεωργὸν σπέρμα καταβάλλοντα εἰς γῆν, ὅπου μὲν πυρόν, ὅπου δὲ κριθήν, ὅπου δὲ ἄλλο τι τῶν σπερμάτων. . . . οὕτω καὶ ὁ θεὸς ἐν μὲν οὐρανῷ ἀθανασίαν σπείρει, ἐν δὲ γῆ μεταβολήν. Cf Paul,

---

[1] Cf. Tennyson:

> 'The old order changeth, yielding place to new,
> And God fulfils Himself in many ways,
> Lest one good custom should corrupt the world.'

1 *Cor.* 15. 37 : ὃ σπείρεις, οὐ τὸ σῶμα τὸ γενησόμενον σπείρεις, ἀλλὰ
γυμνὸν κόκκον εἰ τύχοι σίτου ἤ τινος τῶν λοιπῶν· ὁ δὲ θεὸς δίδωσιν
. . . ἑκάστῳ τῶν σπερμάτων ἴδιον σῶμα. . . . καὶ σώματα ἐπουράνια,
καὶ σώματα ἐπίγεια. The two passages deal with different subjects ;
(Paul is speaking of the resurrection of the dead, and the Hermetist,
of the making of the Kosmos ;) yet there is a real resemblance
between them ; in both alike, we are told of a ' sowing ' from which
spring bodies of different kinds, and in particular, both heavenly
(i. e. immortal) and earthly (i. e. mortal) bodies. It is possible
therefore that the language used by the two writers is derived in part
from a common source.

In *Corp.* IX. 6, the Kosmos is described as growing successive
crops of living creatures ὥσπερ ἀγαθὸς [ζωῆς] γεωργός. In a magic
Papyrus (*Pap. mag. Berl.* i. 26), the Agathos Daimon is invoked
with the words ἧκέ μοι, ἀγαθὲ γεωργέ.

ἐν μὲν οὐρανῷ ἀθανασίαν σπείρει, ἐν δὲ γῇ μεταβολήν. Cf. *Corp.* XI.
i. 5 : ἀθανασίας καὶ μεταβολῆς ποιητής. XI. ii. 12 a : τί μέγα τῷ θεῷ
[ ] καὶ ἀθανασίαν καὶ μεταβολὴν ποιεῖν ; *Corp.* XII. ii. 22 : ὑπὸ τίνος
ἀθανατίζεται τὰ ἀθάνατα ; ὑπὸ τίνος μεταβάλλεται τὰ μεταβλητά ;

[ταῦτα δὲ οὐ πολλά ἐστιν, ἀλλ᾽ ὀλίγα καὶ εὐαρίθμητα· τὰ γὰρ πάντα
τέσσαρα.] The four things appear to be ἀθανασία, μεταβολή, ζωή,
and κίνησις. But these are not four distinct things ; for ἀθανασία
and μεταβολή are different modes of ζωή, and κίνησις is merely the
manifestation of ζωή. Nor is there any apparent motive for number-
ing them. And in what relation do these *four* things stand to the
two, (viz. ' the Maker, and what is made ',) in which, as we were told
before, all that exists is comprised, and to which the Hermetist
recurs in the following words (ὁ θεὸς καὶ ἡ γένεσις) ? It seems most
likely then that the sentence ταῦτα . . . τέσσαρα is a note inserted
by some reader.

LIBELLVS XVI

Contents

Preface, §§ 1, 2. In this treatise all the Hermetic teachings are
summed up. The doctrine set forth in it is at variance with the
opinions of the many.

The meaning of the Hermetic writings is clear to those who read
them in the right spirit ; but to others, these writings appear to be

obscure. Their apparent obscurity is increased, and their force impaired, when they are translated into Greek.

God and the universe, § 3. God is all things; but at the same time, God is one; for all things go to make up a single whole.

God, Sun, light, §§ 4–10 a and 12. The three grosser elements, viz. earth, water, and air, come from below, and are supplied by the Earth; but light, the life-giving element, comes from above, and is supplied by the Sun. §§ 4, 5.

The light of the Sun is the 'receptacle' (or vehicle) of incorporeal substance,—if there is such a substance. But whence that incorporeal substance comes, we know not. God is hidden from us; but the Sun we see with our eyes. He is stationed in the midst of the universe, and floods with his life-giving light both heaven above and earth below. He controls the movement of the heavens, as a charioteer controls his team. By the light which he sends forth upward, he maintains the everlasting life of the heavenly bodies; by the light which he sends downward, he maintains life in a perpetual succession of terrestrial organisms. §§ 6–10 a.[1]

The Sun then supplies ⟨the light⟩ by which the life of all things is maintained; ⟨and the Earth⟩ supplies the matter of which terrestrial organisms are composed, and receives ⟨this matter⟩ back into herself at their dissolution. § 12.

God, Sun, Planets, Daemons, §§ 13–16. ⟨The planet-gods are under the command of the Sun; and⟩ each of the planet-gods has under his command a separate corps of daemons. The daemons are partly beneficent, and partly maleficent. They have dominion over all things upon earth; and by their action are brought about the troubles which beset both communities and individual men. Daemons are seated in all parts of our bodies. At each man's birth, the particular corps of daemons which is under the orders of the planet ruling at that moment takes possession of him. If a man is illuminated by the light of God, the daemons have no power over him. But such men are few; and all others are driven by the passions which the daemons set working in them by means of the bodily organs.

---

[1] *Interpolated passage on daemons*, §§ 10 b, 11. There are numerous bands of daemons. They hold a position intermediate between immortals and mortals. Executing the commands of the gods, they superintend the affairs of men, and punish impiety by plagues inflicted on human communities. Impiety alone is punished by the gods; all other sins are pardoned.

Conclusion, (*God, Sun, Spheres, Daemons,*) §§ 17–19. Life-giving energy issues from God, and is transmitted from him, through the intelligible Kosmos, to the Sun. The eight spheres (viz. the sphere of fixed stars, the five spheres of the planet-stars, the moon-sphere, and the atmosphere) are dependent on the Sun; the daemons are dependent on the eight spheres (or in other words, are subject to the gods who preside over the eight spheres); and men are dependent on the daemons. Thus all things are dependent on God. §§ 17–18.

All things are made by God, and are parts of God. God then is all things; and in making things, he makes himself. And he will never cease from making things. § 19.

Sources. In his conception of the supreme and supracosmic God, the writer of *Corp.* XVI agrees with the Platonists. He has adopted the Platonic terms νοητὴ οὐσία and νοητὸς κόσμος; but he does not seem to have fully grasped the doctrine which these terms imply, and he speaks of things incorporeal with less confidence than of things corporeal. (See § 6, εἰ δέ τις ἔστι καὶ νοητὴ οὐσία, and στοχασμῷ βιαζομένων.) In § 15 (τὰ δύο ⟨ἄλογα⟩ μέρη τῆς ψυχῆς) the Platonic psychology is presupposed; and in § 16 (ἔρως) there is a reference to Pl. *Phaedrus* 238 B. The theory of daemons expounded in §§ 13–16 is partly based on the daemonology of the Platonists, but presents some peculiar features. I do not know from what source the writer got his notion of an army of daemons marshalled in battalions of which the several planets are the commanders. (Was any such notion current among the Mithraists?)

The theory of the elements in §§ 4–10 a shows traces of Stoic influence; but the writer has discarded πῦρ, the term used by the Stoics to denote the celestial and vitalizing element, and speaks of φῶς instead.

The view that the planets preside over men's births and determine their characters and actions (§ 15) is connected with the astrological beliefs commonly accepted in the time of the Roman empire. The use of the term εἱμαρμένη (§ 16 *fin.*) to denote the government of human life by the planets is of Stoic origin. The statement (§ 15 f.) that the 'illuminated' man is free from the dominion of 'gods and daemons' (i. e. of the planets and their emissaries) is a Platonic modification of the Stoic doctrine of Heimarmene.

Both in §§ 4–10 a and 12, and in §§ 13–16, the Sun is supreme within the Kosmos, and subordinate only to the supracosmic God.

This exaltation of the Sun-god is in accordance with a tendency which began before the Christian era, and prevailed more and more as time went on. A large part of the Egyptian religion, from the earliest times, consisted of Sun-worship; and under the later dynasties, almost all the more important gods of Egypt were identified with the Sun-god, or regarded as aspects of the Sun. In the religions of Syria also, Sun-worship was prominent. Among the Greeks, any Platonist who was disposed to Sun-worship would find warrant for it in Pl. *Rep.* 6. 508, where the Sun is spoken of as the offspring and visible image of τὸ ἀγαθόν. The Stoic Cleanthes (about 270 B. C.) placed the *hegemonikon* of the universe in the Sun (Arius Didymus, Diels *Doxogr.* p. 465), and not, as most of the Stoics, in the highest sphere of heaven. The Neo-Pythagoreans, from the Christian era onwards, were Sun-worshippers (see e. g. Philostratus *Vita Apollon. passim*), and identified Apollo, the god to whom Pythagoras was said to have been specially devoted, with the Sun. Plutarch (about A. D. 100), in his exposition of the Delphic religion (*De Ei apud Delph.* 21, 393 D), speaks of people who identify Apollo with the Sun, but himself prefers to identify him with the supracosmic deity of whom the Sun is the visible image. In the Mithraic cult, which spread to all parts of the Roman empire in the course of the second century A. D., the Sun-god was regarded sometimes as identical with Mithras, and sometimes as distinct from him,[1] but next to him in rank. The emperor Elagabalus (A. D. 218–222) was a devotee of the Syrian Sun-god; and from his time onward, the Syrian form of Sun-worship was firmly established in the West. By the end of the third century, *Sol invictus* had become the chief God of the Roman empire.[2] Thus

---

[1] Cumont, *Les Mystères de Mithra*, 1902, p. 102. In one of the documents out of which the Mithraic *Apathanatismos* or 'Mithrasliturgie' (*Pap. mag. Par.* i. 475–834) is made up, Helios is identified with Mithras, while in another of them he is distinguished from Mithras, and regarded as a mediator between Mithras and men. See Appendix on Rebirth.

[2] Cf. Firmicus Maternus (c. A.D. 337), *Math.* I. 10. 14: 'Sol optime maxime, qui mediam caeli possides partem, mens mundi atque temperies, dux omnium atque princeps, qui ceterarum stellarum ignes flammifera luminis tui moderatione perpetuas.' *Ib.* lib. 5 *praef.* 5: 'Sol optime maxime, qui omnia ⌈super omnia⌉ per dies singulos maiestatis tuae reconditae conponis, per quem cunctis animantibus inmortalis anima divina dispositione dividitur, qui solus ianuas aperis sedis supernae, ad cuius arbitrium fatorum ordo disponitur.' See also Julian (c. A.D. 360) *Or.* 4, *Ad regem solem*, passim: e. g. 137 C: ὁ περὶ γῆν τόπος ἐν τῷ γίνεσθαι τὸ εἶναι ἔχει. τίς οὖν ἐστιν ὁ τὴν ἀιδιότητα δωρούμενος αὐτῷ; ἆρ' οὐχ ὁ ταῦτα μέτροις ὡρισμένοις συνέχων; ἄπειρον μὲν γὰρ εἶναι φύσιν σώματος οὐχ οἷόν τ' ἦν. ... τὴν δὴ τοιαύτην φύσιν ὁ θεὸς ὅδε (sc. ὁ ἥλιος) μέτρῳ κινούμενος προσιὼν μὲν ὀρθοῖ καὶ ἐγείρει, πόρρω δὲ ἀπιὼν ἐλαττοῖ καὶ φθείρει. μᾶλλον δὲ αὐτὸς ἀεὶ ζωποιεῖ, κινῶν καὶ

the doctrine of *Corp.* XVI, that the Sun is 'second God' and cosmic Demiurgus, is in agreement with a conception of the Sun-god which gained more and more general acceptance among the Pagans of the Roman empire in each successive generation, down to the final defeat of Paganism by Christianity.

Date. The preface (§§ 1, 2) implies that a large body of Hermetic writings, including a collection of 'Discourses of Hermes to Asclepius', was already in existence. *Corp.* XVI must therefore be one of the later *Hermetica*; and it was most likely written in the third century A. D.

The Hermippus.

The writer of the dialogue entitled *Hermippus* (*Anonymi Christiani Hermippus, de astrologia dialogus*, ed. Kroll and Viereck, Teubner 1895) made use of *Corp.* XVI. I append the passages in which he has borrowed from it. Words and phrases taken from *Corp.* XVI are here printed in distinct type. *Hermippus* 1. 4. 24 : πρὸς δὲ τῷ **μέσῳ** [1] τῶν τοιούτων **σφαιρῶν**, ὃ δὴ καρδίᾳ τὸ ἀνάλογον ἂν ἔχειν δόξειεν, ὅτι πλεῖστον τῆς αὐτοῦ δυνάμεως συνεμφορήσας συνέθετο,[2] **φῶς ἀνάψας** αἰσθητόν, καὶ **ζωογόνον** [3] ἐμβαλὼν δύναμιν. (*Ib.* 1. 13. 78 : ὁ ἥλιος καὶ τὸ ἐν αὐτῷ θερμὸν τὴν **μέσην** χώραν ἐν ἅπασιν ἔσχηκεν.)

1. 10. 63 : τὰ ἐπὶ γῆς ἠρτῆσθαι μὲν πρῶτον τῆς φύσεως, αὐτὴν δὲ τῶν ἀστέρων, τούτους δὲ τοῦ δημιουργικοῦ νοῦ καὶ πρώτου.[4]

1. 16. 112–122 : ἐπανιτέον δέ, καὶ τὴν τοῦ ἡλίου ἐπεξεργαστέον εἰς τὰ γεννητὰ δύναμιν, ἐπειδὴ καὶ τὸ πᾶν σχεδὸν κῦρος οὗτος ἀνέζωσται. . . . οὗτος γὰρ (*sc.* ὁ ἥλιος) ἔχει μὲν ἐν ἑαυτῷ τὴν τῶν ὅλων οὐσίαν . . .· ἡγεμὼν δ' ἐστὶ τοῦ σύμπαντος κόσμου, καὶ πάντων γεννητικός· γεννῶν δὲ

ὀχετεύων αὐτῇ τὴν ζωήν· ἡ δὲ ἀπόλειψις αὐτοῦ καὶ ἡ πρὸς θάτερα μετάστασις αἰτία γίνεται φθορᾶς τοῖς φθίνουσιν. Ammianus Marcellinus (*c.* A.D. 380), 21. 1. 11 : 'sol, . . . ut aiunt physici, mens mundi, nostras mentes ex sese velut scintillas diffunditans.' Macrobius (*c.* A. D. 400), *Sat.* 1. 19. 9 : 'sol mundi mens est.' Proclus (*c.* A.D. 450), *Hymn* I, to Helios (Abel *Orphica* pp. 276–278).

Remnants of sun-worship persisted among Christians at least as late as the fifth century. Eusebius of Alexandria (fifth century) : πολλοὺς γὰρ οἶδα τοὺς προσκυνοῦντας καὶ εὐχομένους εἰς τὸν ἥλιον· ἤδη γὰρ ἀνατείλαντος τοῦ ἡλίου προσεύχονται καὶ λέγουσιν '' ἐλέησον ἡμᾶς''. καὶ οὐ μόνον ἡλιογνῶσται καὶ αἱρετικοὶ τοῦτο ποιοῦσιν, ἀλλὰ καὶ Χριστιανοί, καὶ ἀφέντες τὴν πίστιν τοῖς αἱρετικοῖς συναναμίγνυνται. (Quoted by Jung, *Psychology of the Unconscious*, Eng. tr., 1919, p. 114; he does not give the reference.) The author of *Corp.* XVI might be called a ἡλιογνώστης.

[1] *Sc.* the Sun. Cf. *Corp.* XVI. 7 (μέσος γὰρ ἵδρυται) and 17 (περὶ δὲ τὸν ἥλιον αἱ ὀκτώ εἰσι σφαῖραι).

[2] *Sc.* the Creator.

[3] Cf. *Corp.* XVI. 10 a : ἡ ζωογονία αὐτοῦ.

[4] Cf. *Corp.* XVI. 17. The function here assigned to φύσις corresponds to that of the 'daemons' in *Corp.* XVI.

αὖθις καὶ διαλύει καὶ πρὸς τὸν σπερματικὸν λόγον ἀναλαμβάνει, διδοὺς
μὲν τῇ ὕλῃ οὐσίαν σχεδὸν καὶ ζωήν, ἀνταπολαμβάνων δὲ τὴν ἄνωθεν
ὕπαρξιν.[1] μέσος γὰρ ἵδρυται, τὰ ἄκρα συνδέων, καὶ καθάπερ ἡνίοχος
ἀγαθὸς τὸ τοῦ κόσμου ἅρμα ἀσφαλῶς ἐλαύνων· εἰσὶ δὲ αἱ ἡνίαι ζωὴ καὶ
ψυχὴ καὶ πνεῦμα καὶ γένεσις[2] κατὰ τὴν ἑκάστου φύσιν τῶν γεννητῶν· καὶ
τῷ μὲν καταλαμβανομένῳ καὶ περιλάμποντι τὸ πᾶν ὕδατος καὶ γῆς καὶ
ἀέρος κύτος ζωογονεῖ, γένεσιν δὲ ἀνακινεῖ καὶ μεταβολὴν τῷ παντί·[3]
ἡγεμών τε καὶ τροφὸς παντὸς γένους ἐστί. καὶ ὥσπερ ὁ νοητὸς κόσμος,
τὸν αἰσθητὸν περιέχων, πληροῖ αὐτὸν ὄγκων ταῖς ποικίλαις καὶ παντομόρφοις ἰδέαις, ὡς δὲ καὶ ὁ ἥλιος ἐν τῷ κόσμῳ πάντα περιέχων ὄγκοῖ
πάντων τὰς γενέσεις καὶ ἰσχυροποιεῖ, καμόντων τε καὶ ῥυέντων ἀποδέχεται
τὰς συστάσεις.[4] καὶ χοροί τινων θειοτέρων οἶμαι δυνάμεων ἑστῶτες περὶ
αὐτὸν ἐφορῶσι τὰ τῶν ἀνθρώπων, στρατιᾷ τινι ἐοικότες·[5] ἕτεροι δ᾽ αὖ ὑπὸ
τὰς τῶν ἀστέρων πλινθίδας τεταγμένοι, ἑκάστῳ τούτων ἰσάριθμοι, ὑπηρε-
τοῦσι τὰ πρόσφορα. καὶ μετὰ τούτους ἑτέρα τις δύναμις δευτέρα καὶ
ὑφειμένη καὶ οἶον τὴν φύσιν μικτή. ὑποκάτω δὲ τούτων ἐξέπεσεν ὁ τῶν
ἐναερίων πνευμάτων ἑσμός· πολλοὶ δὲ οὗτοι καὶ παντοδαποὶ καὶ ποικίλοι,
οἳ δὴ δαίμονες κέκληνται, φύσιν ἔχοντες τὴν ἐνέργειαν.[6] οὗτοι, τὴν ξηρὰν
καὶ ὑγρὰν καὶ ἐναέριον λῆξιν διαλαχόντες, κυκῶσιν αὐτὴν καὶ ταράττουσιν·
ἑκάστου τε τῶν ἐπὶ γῆς πραγμάτων ἄρχειν ἰσχυριζόμενοι, καὶ ἄγειν οἷ
βούλοιντο, ποικίλους θορύβους καὶ ταραχὰς ἔν τε πόλεσι καὶ ἔθνεσιν ὅλοις
καὶ ἰδίᾳ ἑκάστῳ τῶν ἀνθρώπων ἐργάζονται.[7] . . . τὸ μέντοι τοῦ Δημοκρίτου
(οὐ) καλῶς ἂν ἔχοι παραλιπεῖν, ὃς εἴδωλα αὐτοὺς (sc. τοὺς δαίμονας)
ὀνομάζων μεστόν τε εἶναι τὸν ἀέρα τούτων φησί,[8] καὶ ⟨. . .⟩ νεύροις καὶ

---

[1] Cf. *Corp.* XVI. 4 : ἀνταπολαμβάνει δὲ (ἡ γῆ) τὴν ἄνωθεν ὕπαρξιν.

[2] Cf. *Corp.* XVI. 7. In *Hermippus*, καὶ ἀθανασία is omitted before καὶ γένεσις.

[3] Cf. *Corp.* XVI. 8.

[4] Cf. *Corp.* XVI. 12.

[5] Cf. *Corp.* XVI. 10 b. The writer of the *Hermippus* rightly makes § 12 a
continuation of §§ 4–10 a ; and he places the contents of the first daemon-passage
(§§ 10 b, 11) after § 12, so as to bring them into connexion with those of the
second daemon-passage (§§ 13–16). It is possible that in his copy of *Corp.* XVI
the sections stood in the order 4–10 a, 12, 10 b–11, 13 ff. ; but if he had them
before him in the order of our MSS., he found it necessary to change the order in
writing his summary of their contents. He contrives to combine §§ 10 b–11 with
§§ 13–16 by assuming that the former passage has to do with spirits of a different
kind from those spoken of in the latter.
The words τὴν φύσιν μικτή correspond to ἀγαθοὶ καὶ κακοὶ ὄντες τὰς φύσεις and
εἰσὶ δέ τινες αὐτῶν κεκραμένοι ἐξ ἀγαθοῦ καὶ κακοῦ in *Corp.* XVI. 13 ; the writer of
the *Hermippus* distinguishes these ' partly good and partly bad ' beings from the
' swarm of atmospheric spirits ', whom he regards as wholly bad. Being a
Christian, he is accustomed to use the word δαίμονες in the sense of ' devils ', and
consequently applies this word to the latter class alone.

[6] Cf. *Corp.* XVI. 13.

[7] Cf. *Corp.* XVI. 14.

[8] Cf. Cic. *Nat. deor.* I. 12. 29 : 'Democritus, qui tum imagines (i. e. εἴδωλα)
earumque circuitus in deorum numero refert' &c. *Ib.* 43. 120 : ' Tum enim censet

μυελοῖς ἐγκαθημένους ἀνεγείρειν καὶ ἀναπλάττειν τὰς ψυχὰς ἡμῶν εἰς αὐτούς, διά τε φλεβῶν καὶ ἀρτηριῶν καὶ αὐτοῦ τοῦ ἐγκεφάλου καὶ μέχρι τῶν σπλάγχνων διήκοντας·[1] τὴν ἀρχήν τε ἕκαστον γενόμενον καὶ ψυχωθέντα παραλαμβάνειν τοὺς κατ᾽ ἐκεῖνο τῆς γενέσεως ὑπηρέτας,[2] κἀντεῦθεν τὴν ἐπίγειον ταύτην διοίκησιν δι᾽ ὀργάνων τῶν ἡμετέρων σωμάτων διοικεῖν.[3]

The text of *Corp.* XVI which the writer of the *Hermippus* had before him differed little, if at all, from that given by our MSS.; where our text of the passages used by him is corrupt, his borrowings show the same corruptions. He has borrowed not only from *Corp.* XVI, but also from four at least of the other documents of the *Corpus.* He makes use of *Corp.* I. 5 b in *Hermipp.* 1. 6. 37; *Corp.* I. 6, in 1. 13. 97; *Corp.* IV. 10, in 1. 18. 135; *Corp.* X. 6, in 2. 20. 187; *Corp.* X. 13, in 1. 13. 96; *Corp.* X. 24 f. (probably), in 1. 6. 40; *Corp.* XIII. 6, in 2. 20. 186.[4] It is therefore most likely that he had in his hands a copy of the *Corpus* as a whole. The date of the *Hermippus* is unknown. Kroll (*Hermipp.* p. v) gives reasons for thinking that it cannot have been written much before A.D. 500. But there is no definite *terminus ad quem*, except the date of the earliest extant MS. of the *Hermippus* (A.D. 1322); and since the text of the *Corpus* as known to the author of the *Hermippus* seems to have been identical with the corrupt text of our MSS. of the *Corpus*, which are very likely derived from the copy used by Psellus, it may be conjectured with some probability that the *Hermippus* was written by a contemporary of Psellus (*c.* A.D. 1050), in connexion with the revival of Platonism which took place under his leadership (Krumbacher *Byz. Litt.* 1897, p. 433).

Corp. XVI, **Title.** The word ὅροι must be due to some mistake. It might mean ' definitions ' of philosophic terms (cf. the Platonic

(Democritus) imagines divinitate praeditas inesse in universitate rerum, tum principia mentis, quae sint in eodem universo, deos esse dicit, tum animantes imagines, quae vel prodesse nobis soleant vel nocere.' Sext. Emp. 9. 19: Δημόκριτος δὲ εἴδωλά τινά φησιν ἐμπελάζειν τοῖς ἀνθρώποις, καὶ τούτων τὰ μὲν εἶναι ἀγαθοποιά, τὰ δὲ κακοποιά. . . . εἶναι δὲ ταῦτα μεγάλα τε καὶ ὑπερμεγέθη, καὶ δύσφθαρτα μέν, οὐκ ἄφθαρτα δέ· προσημαίνειν τε τὰ μέλλοντα τοῖς ἀνθρώποις, θεωρούμενα καὶ φωνὰς ἀφιέντα. *Ib.* 42: εἴδωλα εἶναι ἐν τῷ περιέχοντι ὑπερφυῆ καὶ ἀνθρωποειδεῖς ἔχοντα μορφάς.

[1] Cf. *Corp.* XVI. 14. The author of the *Hermippus* must have known that he was borrowing this passage (νεύροις καὶ μυελοῖς . . . διήκοντας) from *Corp.* XVI, and cannot have ascribed it to Democritus; some words (such as ὁ δὲ Ἀσκληπιός φησι) must therefore have been lost before νεύροις καὶ μυελοῖς.

[2] Cf. *Corp.* XVI. 15.   [3] Cf. *Corp.* XVI. 16.

[4] Reitzenstein (*Poim.* p. 210) adds that he has copied some phrases in *Corp.* XVIII; but this seems more doubtful.

Ὅροι, ' *Incerti auctoris definitiones* ', printed in Stallbaum's *Plato*, 1873, p. 638 ff.) ; and perhaps it might also be used in the sense of ' aphorisms '. But *Corp.* XVI is neither a collection of definitions nor a collection of aphorisms.

The original heading must have been Ἀσκληπιοῦ πρὸς Ἄμμωνα βασιλέα. The document is an epistle addressed by a pupil of Hermes and associate of Tat (§ 1 b) to a king (§§ 1 a, 2) ; the persons meant are doubtless Asclepius and Ammon ; and as the author does not name them in the body of the epistle, he must have named them in the title. King Ammon is the god Amun euhemerized ; it is assumed that he was an ancient king of Egypt, and that the teachers Hermes and Asclepius (similarly evolved by euhemerism from the gods Thoth and Imhotep) lived in his reign.

Lactantius, *Div. inst.* 2. 15. 6 sq. (*Testim.*), says ' Asclepius quoque auditor eius (*sc.* Hermae) eandem sententiam latius explicavit in illo sermone perfecto quem scripsit ad regem.' The passage to which these words refer appears to be *Corp.* XVI. 15 sq.; and if so, it is implied that the title of *Corp.* XVI as known to Lactantius was Ἀσκληπιοῦ πρὸς (Ἄμμωνα) βασιλέα λόγος τέλειος. But λόγος τέλειος (*sermo perfectus*) is elsewhere used, by Lactantius and others, only as the distinctive title of *Ascl. Lat.* ; it seems therefore that Lactantius, if he wrote *perfecto* here, must have added the word by mistake. It may possibly have been suggested to him by the phrase πάντων τῶν ἄλλων ὥσπερ κορυφήν in *Corp.* XVI. 1 a.

[περὶ θεοῦ . . . κατ᾽ εἰκόνα ἀνθρώπου.] This is a very unsatisfactory description of the contents of the document. περὶ θεοῦ might perhaps be taken as referring to § 3 ; περὶ ὕλης, to § 4 ; [περὶ κακίας, to § 11 (?) ; περὶ εἱμαρμένης, to § 16 (?) ;] περὶ ἡλίου, to §§ 5–10 a ; περὶ νοητῆς οὐσίας (of which περὶ θείας οὐσίας may be a variant), to § 6 ; περὶ ἀνθρώπου, to §§ 14–16 (?) ; [περὶ οἰκονομίας, unintelligible ;] ⟨περὶ ?⟩ τοῦ πληρώματος, to § 3 ; περὶ τῶν ἑπτὰ ἀστέρων, to §§ 13 and 17 (though, if those sections are meant, it ought rather to be τῶν ἐξ ἀστέρων). But thé passages ' concerning daemons ' (§§ 10 b, 11, and 13–16) are ignored ; and on the other hand, there is nothing in the text that could possibly be described as περὶ τοῦ κατ᾽ εἰκόνα ἀνθρώπου, which must mean ' concerning the man created in the image of God ' (*Gen.* 1. 26). It seems probable therefore that this list of subjects was written as an index of the contents of a collection of *libelli* (of which *Corp.* XVI may have been one), and has been inserted here by error.

§ 1 a. ⟨τοῦτον⟩ τὸν λόγον . . . διεπεμψάμην. διεπεμψάμην is the 'epistolary past'. οὗτος ὁ λόγος is *Corp.* XVI, which Asclepius writes with the intention of sending it to King Ammon.

πάντων τῶν ἄλλων ὥσπερ κορυφὴν καὶ ὑπόμνημα. οἱ ἄλλοι (λόγοι) are other Hermetic documents; and the phrase implies that a considerable number of them were already in existence when *Corp.* XVI was written.

The writer says that this document contains the 'crowning' doctrine (κορυφή) in which the teaching of all the earlier *Hermetica* is summed up, and that it will remind the reader (ὑπόμνημα) of the truths set forth in them. Cf. Herm. *ap.* Stob. *Exc.* VI. 1 : ὁ κυριώτατος πάντων λόγος καὶ κορυφαιότατος οὗτος ἂν εἴη.

⌜φανήσεται γάρ σοι καὶ τοῖς ἐμοῖς ἐνίοις λόγοις ἀντίφωνος.⌝ This is unintelligible. It looks as if the writer meant to say that the doctrine of *Corp.* XVI will be (wrongly) thought to be inconsistent with that of some of the earlier *Hermetica*. But if so, he cannot have said it in these words. γάρ does not rightly give the connexion with what precedes; it ought to have been δέ. The word σοι is strange; Asclepius would hardly say that the man to whom he is writing will mistake the meaning of what he writes, though he might very well say that others will. ἐνίοις is probably a variant for ἐμοῖς. As to τοῖς ἐμοῖς λόγοις, cf. μου τοῖς βιβλίοις in § 1 b. But if the meaning is 'my previous teachings', we should rather have expected τοῖς προτέροις λόγοις. The word ἀντίφωνος commonly means 'sounding in response', and not 'discordant'.

§ 1 b. ⟨. . .⟩ Ἑρμῆς μὲν γάρ . . . πολλάκις μοι διαλεγόμενος καὶ ἰδίᾳ καὶ Τὰτ ἐνίοτε παρόντος. It may be inferred from this that the author knew numerous written dialogues in which Hermes was the teacher and Asclepius the pupil, and that in some of them Tat also was present. (In *Ascl. Lat. init.* Tat and Ammon are present as well as Asclepius; and Asclepius is present in *Corp.* X, in which Hermes addresses Tat.) But the saying of Hermes which is here quoted cannot have occurred ' many times ' in those dialogues; and perhaps it did not occur in any of them, but was invented by the author of *Corp.* XVI.

The gist of this passage is that the *Hermetica* will appear to some people to be *obscure*; γάρ therefore implies some previous mention of obscurity. But in the preceding clauses, Asclepius has spoken only of differences of doctrine or opinion, and not of the obscurity of the documents; something must therefore have been lost before Ἑρμῆς μὲν γάρ.

ἔλεγεν ὅτι δόξει τοῖς ⟨εὐσεβῶς ?⟩ ἐντυγχάνουσί μου τοῖς βιβλίοις κ.τ.λ. It may be doubted whether the saying of Hermes is reported in *oratio recta* or in *oratio obliqua*. In the former case, μου τοῖς βιβλίοις would mean books written by Hermes; in the latter, it would mean books written by Asclepius. The books spoken of are presumably οἱ Ἑρμοῦ πρὸς Ἀσκληπιὸν λόγοι; but by whom did the author of *Corp*. XVI suppose those books to have been written? Did he assume that Hermes, after talking to Asclepius, had himself set down the talk in writing? Or did he assume that these discussions had been written down by Asclepius, and that Hermes was speaking of the writings in which Asclepius had recorded them?

It is not quite clear how much of what follows is ascribed to Hermes, and at what point Asclepius begins to speak in his own person; but it seems best to make what 'Hermes said' end at λόγων ἔχουσα. Hermes said that some people would think the writings obscure; Asclepius adds that the apparent obscurity of the writings will be increased when they are translated.

τῶν Ἑλλήνων ὕστερον βουληθέντων τὴν ἡμετέραν διάλεκτον εἰς τὴν ἰδίαν μεθερμηνεῦσαι. The author adheres to the tradition that the *Hermetica* had been written in Egyptian in ancient times, and had but recently been translated from that language into Greek. He knew that this was not true in the case of the document which he was writing; but he may possibly have believed it to be true of some of the earlier *Hermetica*.

He must have been an Egyptian by race; and in spite of his Hellenic education, he is still strongly conscious of his Egyptian nationality. He speaks of the Greeks as foreigners, and regards them with contempt; he holds them unworthy to know the holy secrets (μυστήρια) of the true religion.

§ 2. τὸν λόγον διατήρησον ἀνερμήνευτον. Does τὸν λόγον mean the document which Asclepius is now writing, or 'the teaching', i. e. the whole body of *Hermetica*? Even if the former is meant, the arguments urged against the translation of this document would apply equally to all other Hermetic writings.

There is not the slightest reason to suppose that *Corp*. XVI is a translation from an Egyptian original; it was doubtless written in Greek from the first. Yet its author pretends that Asclepius wrote it in Egyptian, and wished to prevent its translation. What was his motive for making Asclepius express that wish? His assumption that Asclepius wrote in Egyptian is natural enough ; an ancient Egyptian teacher could not reasonably be supposed to have written in any other language. But why does the author, in the act of writing a religious treatise in Greek, make Asclepius say that Greek is an unsuitable language for that purpose? Probably he found it necessary to write in Greek, because most of those for whose instruction he was writing knew Greek, and did not know Egyptian ; but he regretted this necessity, and felt that he could have expressed himself with more effect in his native language.

ἡ τῶν Ἑλλήνων ⌜ὑπερήφανος⌝ φράσις καὶ ἐκλελυμένη καὶ ὥσπερ κε-καλλωπισμένη. The feeble elegance (ἐκλελ. καὶ ὥσπερ κεκαλλ.) of the Greek style is contrasted with the rugged strength of the Egyptian. κεκαλλωπισμένη might perhaps be rendered 'meretricious'. The rhetorical devices by which Greek writers seek to embellish their writings detract from the force and significance of their language. The epithet ὑπερήφανος ('arrogant' or 'disdainful') is not applicable to the style of Greek philosophic writings ; and there can be little doubt that the word is corrupt. It may possibly have come from a note written by some Greek reader who resented the contemptuous tone of the passage : 'this Egyptian speaks ὑπερηφάνως.'

As to the superiority of Egyptian to Greek as the language of religion, and the inadequacy of translations, cf. *Abammonis Responsum* 7. 4 sq. (an Egyptian priest is speaking) : ἀλλὰ διὰ τί τῶν σημαντικῶν τὰ βάρβαρα πρὸ τῶν ἑκάστῳ οἰκείων προτιμῶμεν ; ... τῶν ἱερῶν ἐθνῶν, ὥσπερ Αἰγυπτίων καὶ Ἀσσυρίων, οἱ θεοὶ τὴν ὅλην διάλεκτον ἱεροπρεπῆ κατέδειξαν. ... ἐκ δὴ τοῦδε καταφαίνεται ὡς εὐλόγως καὶ ἡ τῶν ἱερῶν ἐθνῶν προκέκριται φωνὴ πρὸ ⟨τῆς⟩ τῶν ἄλλων ἀνθρώπων· οὐδὲ γὰρ πάντως τὴν αὐτὴν διασώζει διάνοιαν μεθερμηνευόμενα τὰ ὀνόματα, ἀλλ᾽ ἔστι τινὰ καθ᾽ ἕκαστον ἔθνος ἰδιώματα, ἀδύνατα εἰς ἄλλο ἔθνος διὰ φωνῆς σημαίνε-σθαι. ἔπειτα κἂν εἰ οἷόν τε αὐτὰ μεθερμηνεύειν, ἀλλὰ τήν γε δύναμιν οὐκέτι φυλάττει τὴν αὐτήν. ἔχει δὲ καὶ τὰ βάρβαρα ὀνόματα πολλὴν μὲν ἔμφασιν πολλὴν δὲ συντομίαν, ἀμφιβολίας τε ἐλάττονος μετέσχηκε καὶ ποικιλίας ⌜καὶ τοῦ πλήθους⌝ τῶν λέξεων. διὰ πάντα δὴ οὖν ταῦτα συναρ-μόζει τοῖς κρείττοσιν. Clem. Alex. *Strom.* I. 143: αἱ δὲ πρῶται καὶ γενικαὶ διάλεκτοι βάρβαροι μέν, φύσει δὲ τὰ ὀνόματα ἔχουσιν· ἐπεὶ καὶ τὰς εὐχὰς ὁμολογοῦσιν οἱ ἄνθρωποι δυνατωτέρας εἶναι τὰς βαρβάρῳ φωνῇ λεγομένας. See also Orig. *c. Cels.* 5. 45 *sq.*

αὕτη ἐστὶν (ἡ) Ἑλλήνων φιλοσοφία, λόγων ψόφος. Cf. a letter of the Indian gymnosophist Calanus to Alexander, quoted by Philo *Quod omn. prob. liber* 14. 96, Cohn VI, p. 28 : Ἑλλήνων δὲ φιλοσόφοις οὐκ ἐξομοιούμεθα, ὅσοι αὐτῶν εἰς πανήγυριν λόγους ἐμελέτησαν, ἀλλὰ λόγοις ἔργα παρ' ἡμῖν ἀκόλουθα.

φωναῖς με[γι]σταῖς [τῶν] ἔργων. Cf. *Didache Apost.* 2. 5 : οὐκ ἔσται ὁ λόγος σου . . . κενός, ἀλλὰ μεμεστωμένος πράξει.

§ 3. [καὶ πάντα ὄντα] τὸν [ἕνα] καὶ ἕνα ὄντα ⟨καὶ⟩ τὰ πάντα. The text of the MSS. seems to be a conflation of two alternative readings, τὸν καὶ πάντα ὄντα καὶ ἕνα, and τὸν καὶ ἕνα ὄντα καὶ τὰ πάντα.

οὐ ⌜δευτεροῦντος⌝ τοῦ ἑνός, ἀλλ' ἀμφοτέρων ἑνὸς ὄντος. The writer probably meant to say that τὸ ἓν καὶ τὰ πάντα οὐ δύο εἰσίν, ἀλλ' ἀμφότερα (*sc.* τὸ ἓν and τὰ πάντα) ἕν ἐστι. 'The one' and 'all things' are not two distinct and separate things ; they are identical. But this meaning is not rightly expressed by οὐ δευτεροῦντος (or δευτερεύοντος or δευτέρου ὄντος) τοῦ ἑνός, which would rather signify 'the One does not take the second place'.

ἐκδεξάμενος τὴν τῶν πάντων προσηγορίαν ἐπὶ πλήθους, οὐκ ἐπὶ πληρώματος. τὰ πάντα must be thought of, not as a πλῆθος, i. e. a number of separate things, but as a πλήρωμα, i. e. as things which go to make up a whole, and without any one of which the whole would be incomplete. The whole which τὰ πάντα go to make up is God ; cf. § 19, μόρια τοῦ θεοῦ πάντα ἐστίν.

οὐδέποτε παύεται [ἓν] ὄντα. Cf. § 19 : οὐκ ἄν ποτε παύσαιτο ⟨πάντα ποιῶν ὁ θεός⟩.

§ 4. ἴδοις ἂν (*al.* ἰδὲ οὖν) ἐν τῇ γῇ πολλὰς πηγὰς ὑδάτων καὶ ἀέρος (πυρὸς MSS.) ἀναβρυούσας ἐν τοῖς μεσαιτάτοις μέρεσι. The opening is abrupt ; but it is hardly necessary to assume a lacuna before ἴδοις ἄν. After the preliminary invocation of the supreme God, and the remarks on the One and the All which that invocation suggested, the writer begins his exposition by speaking of the ὕλη of which terrestrial things consist ; and in doing so, he starts with an appeal to the evidence of the senses. Cf. *Corp.* XI. ii. 6 b, where the exposition begins with the words θέασαι δὴ τὸν κόσμον κ.τ.λ.

ὕλη here means gross matter, in contrast to φῶς. ὕλη is terrestrial ; φῶς is celestial. There are three kinds of ὕλη. Two of these are γῆ and ὕδωρ. The third, according to the MSS., is πῦρ ; but this must be a mistake. In § 8, the world of gross matter is called τὸ πᾶν ὕδατος καὶ γῆς καὶ ἀέρος κύτος ; and there can be no doubt that in § 4 the same three elements were spoken of, and that in place of πυρός we ought to read either ἀέρος, or πνος (i. e. πνεύματος) in the sense of ἀέρος. In proof that these three substances are closely interconnected, the writer points to the fact that springs of water and jets of air or πνεῦμα are seen to issue from the earth. (ἐν τῇ γῆ . . . ἐν τοῖς μεσαιτάτοις μέρεσι is apparently equivalent to ἐν τοῖς μεσαιτάτοις μέρεσι τῆς γῆς. The meaning intended would have been more exactly expressed by saying ἐκ τῶν μεσαιτάτων μερῶν τῆς γῆς, 'from the depths of the earth'.) For the notion that currents of air are emitted by the earth, cf. Seneca *Nat. quaest.* 5. 4 (probably from Posidonius): 'Quo modo ergo, inquis, fiunt venti . . .? Non uno modo; alias enim terra ipsa vim magnam aeris eicit et ex abdito spirat.' *Ib.* 14: 'Repetam nunc quod primo dixeram, edi e specu ventos recessuque interiore terrarum' &c. It could not be said that jets of *fire* are seen issuing from the earth, except in the case of a volcanic eruption; and the reader could hardly be told to observe that rare phenomenon with his own eyes.

The combination ἴδοις ἂν . . . ὁρωμένας is awkward; but it may be due merely to careless writing, and not to corruption.

ὅθεν καὶ ⟨ἡ γῆ⟩ πάσης ὕλης πεπίστευται εἶναι ταμιεῖον. 'The earth' here means the terrestrial globe, rather than the element earth. The writer probably held that the water and air which rise out of the earth are produced by transmutation from the element earth; but he does not expressly say so.

ἀναδίδωσι μὲν αὐτῆς (*sc.* τῆς ὕλης) τὴν χορηγίαν, ἀνταπολαμβάνει δὲ τὴν ἄνωθεν ὕπαρξιν. The terrestrial globe supplies out of itself the three elements (earth, water, and air) of which all earthly organisms are composed. But there is another substance, here called ἡ ἄνωθεν ὕπαρξις, which comes down from above, and enters into the organisms composed of terrestrial matter; and it is the operation in them of this 'substance from above' that makes them living beings. This celestial and life-conveying element corresponds to the πῦρ of the Stoics; but the writer of *Corp.* XVI calls it, not πῦρ, but φῶς, and identifies it with the sunlight. Cf. *Corp.* XI. ii. 7, φῶτος δὲ πάντα πλήρη κ.τ.λ., where it is said that the fire emitted by the Sun is changed into light in the course of its descent to earth.

The life-conveying light descends upon the surface of the earth, and enters into the organisms which are produced there; the Earth may therefore be said to 'receive it in exchange' for the gross elements which she gives forth.

§ 5. οὕτω γὰρ οὐρανὸν καὶ γῆν ⟨συν⟩ά⟨γ⟩ει ὁ δημιουργός, λέγω δὴ ὁ ἥλιος. This writer applies the term *Demiurgus* not to the supreme

God (who is called ὁ θεὸς ὁ τῶν ὅλων δεσπότης καὶ ποιητὴς καὶ πατήρ in § 3), but to the Sun, who is the 'second God', and works as agent or vicegerent of the supreme God. The Sun is the 'maker' (δημιουργός) of all living beings; that is, he puts life into them, and maintains life in them, by means of the light which he emits. Light, the vehicle of life, belongs to heaven; and in pouring it down upon earth, the Sun 'brings heaven and earth together'.

τὴν μὲν οὐσίαν κατάγων, τὴν δὲ ὕλην ἀνάγων. Life, or the light by which life is conveyed, is here called οὐσία, 'true being', in contrast to ὕλη, 'gross matter'. This use of οὐσία is intermediate between the Platonic use of the word to signify incorporeal substance, and the Stoic use of it to signify corporeal substance. The οὐσία here spoken of is light-and-life, (cf. φῶς καὶ ζωή in Corp. I,) regarded as a corporeal substance, but a substance of celestial origin, and of higher order than the terrestrial elements (earth, water, and air).

But what is meant by saying that the Sun τὴν ὕλην ἀνάγει? This phrase, taken together with the following words εἰς αὐτὸν ⌜τὰ πάντα⌝ ἕλκων, seems to imply something similar to the Stoic doctrine of the upward and downward movement of the elements. According to the Stoics, portions of earth and water are constantly ascending in the form of exhalations (ἀναθυμιάματα); as they ascend, they are successively transmuted into air and fire; and in the form of fire, they serve as nutriment to the heavenly bodies. On the other hand, fire is constantly emitted by the heavenly bodies, and is transmuted into the grosser elements as it descends. Chrysippus said that the Sun in particular is fed by exhalations from the sea. (Arnim, Stoic. vet. fr. II, p. 196 ff., §§ 650, 652, 659, 661, 662; Zeller, Stoics, Eng. tr. 1880, pp. 198, 205.) The language of Corp. XVI. 5 may therefore have been suggested in part by some Stoic authority. But the writer nowhere asserts that ὕλη (i. e. earth, water, and air) is transmuted into φῶς, or φῶς into ὕλη; and when he says that the Sun 'raises up ὕλη', perhaps he means, not that ὕλη rises up to heaven in the form of exhalations, but merely that the Sun draws forth from the mass of the earth the portions of ὕλη which are formed into living organisms on the earth's surface. If so, the most obvious instance of the process may be seen in the growth of plants under the influence of the sunlight. Cf. Julian Or. 5, 172 B: ἕλκει μὲν (ὁ ἥλιος) ἀπὸ τῆς γῆς πάντα καὶ προ[σ]καλεῖται καὶ βλαστάνειν ποιεῖ τῇ ζωπυρίδι καὶ θαυμαστῇ θέρμῃ, διακρίνων οἶμαι πρὸς ἄκραν λεπτότητα τὰ σώματα, καὶ τὰ φύσει φερόμενα κάτω κουφίζει.

καὶ περὶ αὐτὸν ⟨. . .⟩.   A verb in the present indicative, seems to have been lost here.   Cf. μέσος γὰρ ἵδρυται κ.τ.λ. in § 7.

καὶ εἰς αὐτὸν ⌐τὰ πάντα⌐ ἕλκων, καὶ ἀπὸ ἑαυτοῦ ⌐πάντα⌐ διδούς.   The author cannot have written this.   Even if we assume that he accepted the Stoic doctrine of ἀναθυμίασις, he could hardly say that the Sun draws 'all things' into himself; for the bulk of the ὕλη of which terrestrial organisms consist, if not the whole of it, remains below when they are dissolved, and is not drawn up into the Sun. Nor could it be said that the Sun gives forth 'all things' from himself; for we were told in § 4 that ὕλη issues from the Earth, and not from the Sun.   It is possible that τὰ πάντα has been transposed, and originally belonged to the clause περὶ αὐτὸν ⟨. . .⟩.   What the Sun 'gives forth from himself' is φῶς, the vehicle of life ; and if he 'draws' anything 'into himself', it must be the φῶς which he has emitted.   Indeed, some statement to that effect seems needed to complete the system ; for if the φῶς which the Sun emits did not in some way return to him, it is difficult to see how his supply of it could be maintained ; and on the other hand, there would be a constantly increasing accumulation of φῶς, and therefore of life, on earth.   The writer's probable meaning might be expressed by writing καὶ εἰς ἑαυτὸν τὸ φῶς (or τὴν ζωὴν) ἕλκων, καὶ ἀπὸ ἑαυτοῦ τὸ φῶς (or τῇ ζωὴν) διδούς.   The Sun is the source and reservoir of φῶς, or life-stuff, as the Earth is the source and reservoir of ὕλη. When an earthly organism is broken up, the ὕλη of which it consists goes back into the Earth ; and the writer probably held that the φῶς or life-stuff which has entered into it goes back into the Sun.

πᾶσι γὰρ (πᾶσι· καὶ MSS.) τὸ φῶς ἄφθονον χαρίζεται.   This clause comes in rather awkwardly here ; perhaps it has been misplaced.

ἀγαθαὶ ἐνέργειαι.   The workings of the Sun are ἀγαθαί, i. e. life-giving.   Cf. τοῦ ἀγαθοῦ in § 17.

ἀλλὰ καὶ ἐπὶ γῆς ⟨. . ., καὶ⟩ εἰς τὸν κατώτατον βυθὸν [καὶ ἄβυσσον] διήκουσιν.   A verb has been lost after ἐπὶ γῆς.   The workings of the Sun (operate) in heaven and on the surface of the earth, and penetrate even to the lowest depths (of earth or sea) ; for in all these regions there are living beings, and the life in all of them is due to the light emitted by the sun.   ἄβυσσον is an alternative for βυθόν.

§ 6. ⟨. . .⟩ ⟪ἔστιν ὁ τούτου ὄγκος·⟫ εἰ δέ τις ἔστι καὶ νοητὴ οὐσία, ταύτης [[   ]] ὑποδοχὴ ἂν εἴη τὸ τούτου φῶς.—(εἰ δέ τις ἔστι καὶ νοητὴ οὐσία, αὕτη ἐστὶν ὁ τούτου ὄγκος, ἧς ὑποδοχὴ ἂν εἴη τὸ τούτου φῶς

MSS.) According to the MSS., the ὄγκος (material mass) of the sun is said to be νοητὴ οὐσία (immaterial substance). But that is nonsense. The author's meaning must have been that the material light of the sun is the 'receptacle' or vehicle of immaterial substance (i. e. of life, regarded as an immaterial thing); and that meaning may be got by the changes I have made. Cf. Plut. *Is. et Os.* 51 : ἥλιον σῶμα τῆς τἀγαθοῦ δυνάμεως ὡς ὁρατὸν οὐσίας νοητῆς ⟨ἀπείκασμα ?⟩ ἡγούμενοι. The clause εἰ δέ τις ἔστι καὶ νοητὴ οὐσία implies a preceding mention of αἰσθητὴ οὐσία ; and the sense required might be expressed by writing ⟨τῆς γὰρ αἰσθητῆς τοῦ φωτὸς οὐσίας πηγή⟩ ἐστιν ὁ τούτου ὄγκος· εἰ δέ τις ἔστι καὶ νοητὴ κ.τ.λ.

The writer is acquainted with the Platonic term νοητὴ οὐσία (cf. ὁ νοητὸς κόσμος in §§ 12 and 17); but he finds it difficult to attach any definite meaning to it. On the assumption that life is an immaterial thing, the visible sunlight, he says, must be considered its ὑποδοχή, i. e. the matter in which it inheres. But he is half inclined to adopt the Stoic attitude, and identify life with its material vehicle.

πόθεν δὲ αὕτη (*sc.* ἡ νοητὴ οὐσία) συνίσταται ἢ ἐπιρρεῖ, αὐτὸς μόνος οἶδεν ⟨ὁ θεός⟩. Life, if it is an incorporeal entity distinguishable from the material sunlight, must come from the supreme God, and be by him infused into the body of the sun, and there incorporated in the visible light which the sun emits. But the nature of the incorporeal is incomprehensible to us ; whence comes that incorporeal life which the Sun receives and transmits, and of what it consists, 'God only knows'. Cf. § 17 : ὁ ἥλιος διὰ τοῦ νοητοῦ κόσμου τὴν ἐπιρροὴν ἀπὸ τοῦ θεοῦ χορηγεῖται τοῦ ἀγαθοῦ. The νοητὴ οὐσία of § 6 is the ἀγαθόν of § 17 ; and both terms, in this connexion, mean life, or life-giving energy.

The subject of μόνος οἶδεν must have been the supreme God, and not the Sun. Cf. *Corp.* XII. i. 1 as emended : καὶ ποιά τις οὖσα τυγχάνει (ἡ τοῦ θεοῦ οὐσία), αὐτὸς μόνος ἀκριβῶς οἶδεν.

⟨καὶ ὁ μὲν θεὸς ἀφανής,⟩ μὴ ὑφ' ἡμῶν ὁρώμενος, στοχασμῷ δὲ βιαζομένων νοούμενος (νοεῖν MSS.)· ἡ δὲ τούτου (*sc.* τοῦ ἡλίου) θέα οὐκ ἔστι στοχάζοντος, ἀλλ' αὐτῇ τῇ ὄψει (αὐτὴ ἡ ὄψις MSS.) ⟨ὁρᾶται⟩. In spite of the mutilation of the text, it is clear that the writer is here contrasting the Sun with the supreme God. The Sun is 'near to us in place', being within the Kosmos, whereas the supreme God, if localized at all, must be thought of as situated in extracosmic space ; and the Sun is 'near to us in nature', being corporeal, whereas the supreme God is incorporeal. The supreme God is nvisible, and our conceptions of him are based on mere conjecture; but we have sure knowledge of the Sun, for we see him with our eyes.

§ 7. μέσος γὰρ ἵδρυται, στεφανηφορῶν τὸν κόσμον. What was the writer's view as to the relative positions of the Sun and the other cosmic bodies? He says that the Sun ' is stationed in the middle ', and 'wears the Kosmos as a wreath'. Taken by itself, this statement might seem to imply a heliocentric system. The theory that the Sun is at the centre of the universe, and that the earth travels round it, had been put forward, at least as a hypothesis, by Aristarchus of Samos, ' the Copernicus of antiquity ', about 280 B. C., and maintained by Seleucus, about 200 B. C. (Plut. *De fac. in orbe lunae* 6. 3, p. 923; Plut. *Plat. quaest.* 8. 2, p. 1006). But that opinion was condemned as impious by Cleanthes ; it was suppressed by the authority of the Stoics, who adhered to the geocentric system ; and a Hermetist of the second or third century A. D. is not likely to have reverted to it. Besides, the Sun is here compared to a charioteer, and that comparison would be unintelligible if he were thought of as stationary. The words must therefore be explained in some other way.

Among the Greeks, the number of the planet-stars was fixed, and their movements determined, in the fourth century B. C. ;[1] and from that time onward, it was commonly held that the earth stands fast at the centre, that the seven planets (i. e. Sun, Moon, and five planet-stars) travel round the earth in approximately circular orbits, and that the sphere of the fixed stars is more distant from earth than the planets. But as to the relative positions of the Sun and the other planets, opinions differed.[2] (*a*) Plato,[3] Aristotle, and Chrysippus

---

[1] Probably by Eudoxus, *c.* 366 B.C. Sen. *Nat. quaest.* 7. 3: ' Nova haec caelestium observatio est, et nuper in Graeciam invecta. Democritus quoque (*c.* 400 B.C.) . . . suspicari se ait plures esse stellas quae currant, sed nec numerum illarum posuit nec nomina, nondum comprehensis quinque siderum cursibus. Eudoxus primus ab Aegypto hos motus in Graeciam transtulit.' The five planet-stars had been earlier recognized and named in Babylonia (Jastrow, *Religion in Babylonia and Assyria*, pp. 217 ff.) ; Egyptian astronomers learnt from Babylonians, and Eudoxus studied astronomy in Egypt.

Philolaus the Pythagorean, a contemporary of Democritus, is said to have spoken of five planet-stars (Aetius, Diels *Doxogr.* p. 337 : according to Philolaus, there are ' ten divine bodies ', viz. the sphere of fixed stars, the five planet-stars, Sun, Moon, Earth, Antichthon ; and the ten, placed in this order, circle round the central fire). But there is much doubt about the authenticity and date of the doctrines ascribed to Philolaus.

[2] Macrob. *Somn. Scip.* 1. 19 f. See Cic. *Nat. deor.* 2. 52, and J. B. Mayor's note *ad loc.*

[3] *Tim.* 38, *Rep.* 10. 616 (cf. *Epinomis* 986 f.). Of the five planet-stars, Plato

placed the planets as follows in order of distance from the earth, beginning with the nearest :—Moon, SUN, Venus, Mercury,[1] Mars, Jupiter, Saturn. (*b*) Archimedes (*c*. 230 B. C.), Geminus (*c*. 77 B. C.), Cleomedes (following Posidonius), and Ptolemaeus placed them thus :—Moon, Venus, Mercury, SUN, Mars, Jupiter, Saturn. (*c*) Heraclides Ponticus said that Venus and Mercury revolve round the Sun ; his order therefore was this :—Moon, SUN (with Mercury and Venus as satellites), Mars, Jupiter, Saturn.

If the writer of *Corp*. XVI adopted order (*b*), he might say that the Sun μέσος ἵδρυται, meaning that the Sun holds the middle place among the planets.[2] Philo calls the Sun μέσος in this sense, *Quis rer. div. heres* 45. 222 f., Wendland III, p. 50 : ὁ μέσος τῶν ἑπτά, ἥλιος. μέσον δ' αὐτὸν οὐ μόνον ἐπεὶ μέσην ἐπέχει χώραν, ὡς ἠξίωσάν τινες, καλῶ, ἀλλ' ὅτι καὶ θεραπεύεσθαι καὶ δορυφορεῖσθαι πρὸς ὑπασπιζόντων ἑκατέρωθεν . . . δίκαιος ἄλλως ἐστί. . . . ἄριστα δ' ἐμοὶ στοχάζεσθαι δοκοῦσιν οἱ τὴν μέσην ἀπονενεμηκότες ἡλίῳ τάξιν, τρεῖς μὲν ὑπὲρ αὐτὸν καὶ μετ' αὐτὸν τοὺς ἴσους εἶναι λέγοντες, ὑπὲρ αὐτὸν μὲν φαίνοντα (Saturn), φαέθοντα (Jupiter), πυρόεντα (Mars), εἶθ' ἥλιον, μετ' αὐτὸν δὲ στίλβοντα (Mercury), φωσφόρον (Venus) τὴν ἀέρος γείτονα σελήνην.

This interpretation of μέσος ἵδρυται would agree well with what is said in § 17 ; but it is difficult to reconcile it with § 8, where we are told that the Sun sends light *upward* to the heavenly bodies (τὰ ἀθάνατα μέρη τοῦ κόσμου), and *downward* to the terrestrial sphere (τὸ πᾶν ὕδατος καὶ γῆς καὶ ἀέρος κύτος). It can hardly be doubted that the moon and the planet-stars are included among 'the immortal parts of the Kosmos '; and if so, it follows that the Sun is lower (i. e. nearer to the earth) than the moon and the five planet-stars, and the meaning of μέσος ἵδρυται must be that the Sun holds a position intermediate between the heavens and the earth,—that is, the position which the Greeks in general assigned to the Moon. If this is the meaning of the passage, the writer of *Corp*. XVI rejected in this respect the teachings of Greek astronomy, and we must suppose that he was following some Oriental authority.

As to στεφανηφορῶν τὸν κόσμον, compare a magic invocation (*Pap*.

mentions by name only Ἐωσφόρος (Venus) and ὁ ἱερὸς Ἑρμοῦ (Mercury). All five are named in the *Epinomis*, written soon after Plato's death.

[1] On the question whether Plato placed Venus or Mercury nearer to the earth, authorities differ. There was much doubt about the relative positions of these two planets.

[2] Cf. Proclus *In Remp*. 69. 27 P. : εἰ δὲ δὴ κρατοίη τὸν μὲν ἥλιον ἐν τῷ μέσῳ τάττειν τῶν ἑπτά, καθάπερ οἱ θεουργικοὶ λόγοι (i. e. Juliani Theurgi *Hyphegetica*) καὶ οἱ θεοί (i. e. the *Oracula Chaldaica*) φασιν. (Kroll, *Orac. Chald.* p. 33.)

mag. Par. i. 959 *sqq.*, Reitzenstein *Poim.* p. 27) in which the Sun-god is addressed as ὁ ἐντὸς τῶν ἑπτὰ πόλων καθήμενος, ὁ ἔχων ἐπὶ τῆς κεφαλῆς στέφανον χρύσεον. The Sun-god was commonly depicted with a radiate wreath or crown upon his head ; and the writer takes this στέφανος to symbolize the system of heavenly bodies disposed above and around him. The following simile of the chariot-driver is inconsistent with the picturing of the Kosmos as a στέφανος, and cannot have formed part of the same sentence ; something must therefore have been lost before καθάπερ ἡνίοχος, and the misplaced words ἄφηκεν οὖν φέρεσθαι κ.τ.λ. supply what is wanted to fill the gap.

τὸ τοῦ κόσμου ἅρμα . . . ἀναδήσας εἰς ἑαυτόν, μή πως ἀτάκτως φέροιτο. In the Roman chariot-races, the driver looped the reins round his waist (Smith *Dict. Ant.* s. v. *Circus*) ; the horses might therefore be said to be ' bound to ' the man.

κόσμος seems here to mean the heavens, or the heavenly bodies, rather than the universe as a whole. The earth is motionless ; but the heavenly bodies ' are borne along together with the Sun' as he sweeps round the sky in his diurnal course ; and the writer holds that their movement is controlled and regulated by him. The Sun then is the charioteer, and the heavenly bodies are the team he drives. The notion that the team would run away if not held in may have been suggested by the story of Phaethon.

Cf. Philo *De Cherubim* 7. 24, Cohn I, p. 175 : God made the sphere of the fixed stars and the seven planet-spheres, καὶ καθάπερ ἔποχον ἐν ὀχήματι ἀστέρα ⟨ἕκαστον ?⟩ ἐν οἰκείῳ κύκλῳ θείς, τὰς ἡνίας ἐπίστευσε τῶν ἐπόχων οὐδενί, πλημμελῆ δείσας ἐπιστασίαν, ἀπάσας δ' ἐξήρτησεν ἑαυτοῦ, νομίσας ἐναρμόνιον τῆς κινήσεως μάλιστα οὕτως τάξιν γενήσεσθαι· τὸ γὰρ σὺν θεῷ πᾶν ἐπαινετόν, τὸ δ' ἄνευ θεοῦ ψεκτόν. This is a protest against the view that the planets are themselves the supreme ' drivers' or rulers of the Kosmos.

εἰσὶ δὲ αἱ ἡνίαι ⟨. . .⟩ [ζωὴ καὶ ψυχὴ καὶ πνεῦμα] [καὶ ἀθανασία καὶ γένεσις]. 'The reins', i. e. the things by means of which the Sun controls the heavenly bodies, and restrains them from disorderly movement, are certainly not 'life, soul, and vital spirit' ; nor are they 'immortality and birth'. They ought rather to be the rays of light which the Sun emits. ζωὴ καὶ ψυχή and ἀθανασία καὶ γένεσις are perhaps two fragments of a lost sentence which led on to what is said in §§ 8 and 9 concerning the distinction between the immortal life of the heavenly bodies and the mortal life of terrestrial organisms.

The Sun, by means of his light, maintains everlasting life in immortal ζῷα, and generates temporary life in mortal ζῷα. Cf. *Corp.* XI. i. 4 a as emended : ὁ αἰὼν κοσμεῖ τὴν ὕλην, ἀθανασίαν καὶ διαμονὴν (i. e. immortal life and mortal life) ἐνθεὶς τῇ ὕλῃ. *Ib.* 5 : ἀθανασίας καὶ μεταβολῆς ποιητής. XI. ii. 12 a : καὶ ἀθανασίαν καὶ μεταβολὴν ποιεῖν.

§ 8. ⟨⟨τὰ ἐν τούτοις τοῖς μέρεσι τοῦ κόσμου⟩⟩ ζωοποιῶν καὶ ἀνακινῶν ⟨εἰς⟩ γένεσιν, καὶ μεταβολαῖς [[ ]] ⟨τὰ⟩ ζῷα [ἕλικος τρόπον] μεταποιῶν καὶ μεταμορφῶν. Some such alterations as these are needed to make sense. μεταβολή means death, in contrast to γένεσις, birth. The organisms into which the Sun puts life in the terrestrial region perish, and are replaced by fresh organisms composed of the same matter; and this is what is meant by saying that they are ' remade and transformed '.

I can make nothing of ἕλικος τρόπον. The Sun himself might be said to move 'helically'; for as the points of sunrise and sunset shift from day to day, the apparent course of the Sun is not circular, but helical. Cf. Pl. *Tim.* 39 A : τοὺς κύκλους αὐτῶν στρέφουσα ἕλικα. But there is no sense in saying that the Sun remakes and transforms living beings ' in the manner of a helix '.

§ 9. ⌈εἰς ἄλληλα γένη γενῶν . . . ποιεῖ δημιουργῶν.⌉ This is hopelessly corrupt. εἰς ἄλληλα has probably been duplicated by error. The only things which could properly be said to be changed 'into one another' are the three terrestrial elements, or forms of ὕλη, viz. earth, water, and air (see § 4). A fairly satisfactory sense might be got by writing [εἰς ἄλληλα] [γένη γενῶν καὶ] εἴδη εἰδῶν ἀντικαταλλασσόμενος [[ ]]· καθάπερ καὶ ἐπὶ τῶν μεγάλων σωμάτων ποιεῖ, ⟨⟨τῇ εἰς ἄλληλα μεταβολῇ⟩⟩ ⟨καὶ ταῦτα⟩ δημιουργῶν. This would be intelligible, if we take τὰ μέγαλα σώματα to mean the three terrestrial elements, and assume that the writer held them to be subject to transmutation. The term τὰ μέγαλα σώματα might also mean the heavenly bodies; but it could not be said of the heavenly bodies that they are transmuted into one another.

τοῦ μὲν ἀθανάτου ἀδιάλυτος (*sc.* ἡ μεταβολή). Cf. Herm. *ap.* Stob. *Exc.* XI. 2. (2) : πᾶν σῶμα μεταβλητόν, οὐ πᾶν σῶμα διαλυτόν. The ἀθάνατα σώματα are the heavenly bodies. Though not subject to dissolution, they are subject to μεταβολή; for they are maintained in existence by a perpetual inflow of light, which issues from the Sun, and replaces the light perpetually emitted by them.

The writer probably held that the body of the Sun is perpetually renewed by light which returns to it after circulating through the

Kosmos (see note on εἰς αὐτὸν ⌜τὰ πάντα⌝ ἕλκων in § 5) ; and if so, the Sun itself, no less than the other heavenly bodies, is subject to μεταβολή.

§§ 10 b, 11. καὶ γὰρ δαιμόνων . . . δίκη ὑποπέπτωκε.   *Corp.* XVI contains two distinct and separate passages concerning daemons, viz. §§ 10 b, 11, and § 13 ff. In the second passage, the topic is introduced *de novo*, and in words closely resembling those used at the beginning of the first passage.

The functions assigned to the daemons are different in the two passages. In the first, their business is to punish sin by plagues inflicted on human communities collectively. In the second, they are the agents by whom all material processes are carried on ; and as to that part of their operation by which men are directly affected, there is indeed a brief mention of 'troubles to cities and nations ', but more is said about their action on individuals. It is evident that these two passages cannot have been written as parts of the same treatise ; one of the two must be an interpolation. The first of them (§§ 10 b, 11) interrupts the sequence of thought ; if we cut it out, § 12 falls into its right place as a continuation of §§ 5–10 a, in which the function of the Sun is dealt with. It seems probable therefore that 10 b, 11 was extracted from some other document, and inserted in the margin of *Corp.* XVI as a parallel or supplement to 13 ff.

§ 10 b. καὶ γὰρ δαιμόνων χοροὶ περὶ αὐτόν. In what follows, the daemons are spoken of as subject to ' the gods ' in general (τὰ ὑπὸ τῶν θεῶν ἐπιταττόμενα ἐνεργοῦσι), and not to the Sun-god. It may therefore be suspected that, in the document from which this paragraph was taken, the reading was περὶ αὐτούς (*sc.* τοὺς θεούς), and that after the passage had been inserted in *Corp.* XVI, αὐτούς was altered into αὐτόν, in order to make an apparent connexion with the preceding statements about the Sun.

⌜σύνοικοι καὶ τῶν ἀθανάτων οὐκ εἰσὶ πόρρω ἐνθένδε⌝. This is an unintelligible remnant of a passage which must have been to the effect that the daemons are intermediate between the immortal gods and mortal men, and are connected with both. For σύνοικοι, cf. *Ascl. Lat.* III. 33 b : '⟨in terra⟩ commorari nobiscum.'

μεταβολαῖς ἀέρος (πυρὸς MSS.). ' Changes of fire ' is meaningless. A satisfactory sense may be got by writing μεταβολαῖς ἀέρος, ' changes (i. e. corruptions) of the atmosphere '. Cf. *Ascl. Lat.* III. 25 *fin.* : ' aer ipse maesto torpore languescet.' Pestilences were thought to be caused by corruption of the air ; so that μεταβολαῖς ἀέρος would serve as a substitute for λοιμοῖς.

ἀμυνόμενοι τὴν ⟨⟨εἰς θεοὺς⟩⟩ ἀσέβειαν. The punishment of sin was commonly said to be the function of δίκη ; cf. Pl. *Laws* 716 A, τῷ δὲ (θεῷ) ἀεὶ ξυνέπεται δίκη, τῶν ἀπολειπομένων τοῦ θείου νόμου τιμωρός, and Herm. *ap*. Stob. *Exc*. VII. In *Corp*. XVI. 10 b, the daemons are the agents by whom δίκη is administered.

§ 11. αὕτη γὰρ (*sc*. ἡ ἀσέβεια) ἀνθρώποις [[ ]] ἡ μεγίστη κακία. Cf. Hermes *ap*. Lactant. *Div. inst*. 2. 15. 6 : τὸ γὰρ ἓν καὶ μόνον ἐν ἀνθρώποις ἐστὶν ἀγαθὸν εὐσέβεια.

[θεῶν μὲν γὰρ τὸ εὖ ποιεῖν, [ ] δαιμόνων δὲ τὸ ⟨τοῖς θεοῖς⟩ ἐπαμύνειν.] This sentence is an interruption. It may have been shifted from some other place, possibly from the corrupt passage in § 10 b *init*.

τὰ γὰρ ἄλλα τὰ ὑπ' ἀνθρώπων τολμώμενα ἢ πλάνη τολμᾶται (ἢ πλάνη ἢ τόλμη MSS.) ἢ ἀνάγκη [ ] ἢ ἀγνοίᾳ· ⟨καὶ⟩ ταῦτα πάντα παρὰ θεοῖς ἀνεύθυνα. A pious man may sometimes act amiss; but if he does, his wrongdoings are only such as are caused by error, compulsion, or ignorance ; and for actions thus caused, he is not held to be responsible. Cf. Ar. *Eth. Nic*. 3. 1, on involuntary actions : δοκεῖ δὲ ἀκούσια εἶναι τὰ βίᾳ (= ἀνάγκη) ἢ δι' ἄγνοιαν γινόμενα. All actions that are truly sinful result from impiety, and therefore impiety alone is punished by the gods.

§ 12. σωτὴρ δὴ (δὲ MSS.) καὶ τροφεύς ἐστι παντὸς γένους ὁ ἥλιος. This statement sums up the contents of §§ 8–10 a. πᾶν γένος means every race or kind of ζῷα, whether mortal or immortal.

ὥσπερ ὁ νοητὸς κόσμος, τὸν αἰσθητὸν (αἰσθητικὸν MSS.) κόσμον περιέχων, πληροῖ τὸν ὄγκον (πληροῖ αὐτὸν ὀγκῶν MSS.) [ταῖς] ποικίλαις καὶ παντομόρφοις ἰδέαις. The Platonists said that all individual beings are constituted by the imposition of ἰδέαι on ὕλη, and that the source of these ἰδέαι is the νοητὸς κόσμος. The writer accepts this Platonic dogma, and tries to bring it into connexion with his own doctrine that ζῷα are constituted by the influx of sunlight into gross matter. He finds an analogy between the ἰδέαι which stream into the universe from the Noetos Kosmos and the life-conveying rays of light emitted by the Sun. The comparison between the Noetos Kosmos and the Sun may have been suggested by the comparison between τὸ ἀγαθόν and the Sun in Pl. *Rep*. VI.

τὸν ὄγκον presumably means the mass of matter on which the ἰδέαι are imposed. The νοητὸς κόσμος is said to 'encompass' the αἰσθητὸς κόσμος, because it is imagined to be situated in extracosmic space.

οὕτω καὶ ὁ ἥλιος πάντα ⟨τὰ⟩ ἐν τῷ κόσμῳ [περιέχων] ⟨...⟩ ὀγκοῖ
⌜πάντων τὰς γενέσεις⌝ καὶ ἰσχυροποιεῖ. The reading of the MSS. is
meaningless. The Sun, being stationed 'in the middle', cannot be
said to 'encompass all things in the Kosmos'; and it is most likely
that the preceding περιέχων has been repeated here by error. πάντων
τὰς γενέσεις might perhaps be taken as equivalent to πάντα τὰ γιγνόμενα; but what could be meant by saying that the Sun 'gives bulk to
all things that are produced'? The Sun gives life to things, not
bulk; it is the Earth that gives material bulk to them, by supplying
ὕλη. It seems then that the verb of which ὁ ἥλιος was the subject
must have been lost, and that the subject of ὀγκοῖ and the following
verbs (ἰσχυροποιεῖ and ὑποδέχεται) must have been ἡ γῆ.

καμόντων δὲ καὶ ῥευσάντων ⟨...⟩ ὑποδέχεται. An accusative is
wanted. The writer most likely held that, when terrestrial organisms
are broken up, the ὕλη of which they were composed goes back into
the Earth, and the φῶς which entered into them and made them live
goes back into the Sun. Accordingly, if the subject of ὑποδέχεται
were ὁ ἥλιος, the object required would be τὸ φῶς; but if, as is more
probable, the subject is ἡ γῆ, the missing object must be τὴν ὕλην.

§ 13. ὑπὸ τούτῳ δὲ ἐτάγη ὁ τῶν δαιμόνων χορός. Down to this point,
we have been told that the Sun operates on things by means of the
light which he emits. But in the paragraph which here begins, we
are told that he operates on things through the agency of troops of
daemons commanded by the planets. These two doctrines are
independent of one another, and cannot easily be reconciled. It
seems that the author or compiler of Corp. XVI has put together two
distinct and inconsistent theories. In both of them, the Sun is
second God, and vicegerent of the supreme God. But according to
the first (§§ 4–10 a and 12), the Sun works by means of light;
according to the second (§§ 13 ff.), the Sun works (through his
subordinates, the planets,) by means of daemons. We must suppose
that the writer took the contents of these two parts of the document
from different sources; and he has made no attempt to fuse them
into a consistent whole.

ἑκάστῳ τούτων ἰσάριθμοι. This appears to mean ἑκάστῳ τῶν ἀστέρων
ἰσάριθμοί εἰσι χοροί; which might be taken to signify either 'each of
the ἀστέρες commands an equal number of χοροί', or 'each ἀστήρ
commands one χορός, and the several χοροί are composed of equal
numbers of daemons'. The writer has expressed himself obscurely;
but he probably meant the latter.

διατεταγμένοι οὖν ⟨κατὰ⟩ ⟨⟨πλινθίδας⟩⟩ ὑπηρετοῦσιν ἑκάστῳ τῶν ἀστέρων. It must be the daemons, and not the ἀστέρες, that are arranged in πλινθίδες; I have therefore shifted πλινθίδας. The word πλινθίς means a rectangular body. In this connexion, it must signify a body of troops drawn up in rectangular formation, and may be translated 'a column', 'a battalion', or 'a corps'. πλινθίον is used as a term of military tactics in Joseph. *Ant.* 13. 4. 4: τάξας τὴν στρατιὰν ἐν πλινθίῳ.

Each πλινθίς of daemons is commanded by one of the ἀστέρες; and οἱ ἀστέρες must here mean 'the planets', or more exactly, the five planet-stars and the moon; for the Sun, being commander-in-chief, has no one πλινθίς specially assigned to him. It might be inferred from this that there are six πλινθίδες of daemons. But in § 17, there appear to be eight, corresponding respectively to the sphere of fixed stars, the five planet-stars, the moon, and the atmosphere. It is not clear whether the χοροί are identical with the πλινθίδες or not; if not, each of the six (or eight) πλινθίδες must be made up of a number of χοροί, as a battalion is made up of a number of companies.

The planet-gods, working in subordination to the Sun, govern the material world; i. e. they collectively discharge the function of εἱμαρμένη. And each of them discharges his special part of this function through the agency of a particular corps of daemons subject to his orders.

ἀγαθοὶ καὶ κακοὶ ὄντες . . . τὰς ἐνεργείας. Some daemons are beneficent, others maleficent. Did the writer hold that some of the planets are beneficent and others maleficent, and that each corps of daemons takes its character from its commander? Or did he hold that each planet is partly beneficent and partly maleficent, and accordingly, that each corps includes both beneficent and maleficent daemons?

δαίμονος γὰρ οὐσία ἐνέργεια. The daemons are in this document the personal beings by whose action all physical processes in the terrestrial region are carried on (πάντων τῶν ἐπὶ γῆς πραγμάτων τὴν ἐξουσίαν κεκληρωμένοι, § 14); or in other words, they are the forces of nature, regarded as persons. And the writer holds that all natural processes result from the operation of the planets. Cf. Herm. *ap.* Stob. *Exc.* VI. 10, where we are told that the daemons have no independent existence as living beings, but are merely ἐνέργειαι of the Decani, who are the highest order of astral gods in the peculiar doctrine of that document.

The daemons are 'both good and bad'; that is, the forces which operate in the material world sometimes work good, and sometimes harm. But how does it come to pass that they sometimes work harm? The daemons are subject to the planet-gods, who are subject to the Sun, who is subject to the supreme God; hence, if the daemons are partly κακοὶ τὰς ἐνεργείας, it might be inferred that the supreme God is the author of evil as well as of good. But the writer ignores this inference. It would have been possible for him to evade it by saying that the evil passions wrought in a man by the daemons (i. e. by the physical forces which operate in his body) are inflicted on him as a punishment for his ἀσέβεια (cf. *Corp.* XII. i. 5–9), and that just punishment is in accordance with the right government of the universe; but he does not say this, and it seems that the difficulty did not occur to him.

§ 14. ποικίλην ταραχὴν ἐργάζονται καὶ κοινῇ ταῖς πόλεσι καὶ τοῖς ἔθνεσι καὶ ἰδίᾳ ἑκάστῳ. From this point to the end of § 16, the writer speaks only of the *harm* done to men by the daemons, and says nothing about the *good* done by them.

ἀναπλάττονται γὰρ καὶ ἀνθέλκουσι (ἀνεγείρουσι MSS.) τὰς ψυχὰς ἡμῶν εἰς ἑαυτούς. ἀνεγείρουσι εἰς ἑαυτούς is meaningless. For ἀνθέλκουσι, cf. Pl. *Rep.* 4. 439 B: εἴ ποτέ τι (τὴν ψυχὴν) ἀνθέλκει διψῶσαν. The daemons 'mould our souls into another shape', i. e. a shape other than that of the unembodied soul; and they 'drag our souls away (from God or from divine things) to themselves', i. e. to the material things in which they operate. Cf. στροβοῦσιν πρὸς τὴν ἰδίαν ἐνέργειαν below.

ἐγκαθήμενοι ἡμῶν νεύροις κ.τ.λ. Cf. Lydus *De mens.* 4. 32 (*Ascl. Lat.* III. 33 b): τοὺς μὲν τιμωροὺς τῶν δαιμόνων, ἐν αὐτῇ τῇ ὕλῃ παρόντας, τιμωρεῖσθαι τὸ ἀνθρώπειον κατ' ἀξίαν. See *Corp.* IX. 3, where it is said that evil νοήματα are bred in men by daemons.

The daemons spoken of in this passage are identical with the defiling or corrupting influences of the body on the soul, as commonly described by the Platonists, except that the writer conceives these influences as persons, and holds them to be emissaries of the planets.

[καὶ αὐτῷ τῷ ἐγκεφάλῳ.] This is an alternative for μέχρι καὶ αὐτῶν τῶν σπλάγχνων. Some said that the seat of the *hegemonikon* is the brain; others said that it is the σπλάγχνα, and more especially the heart. The question is discussed in Galen *De plac. Hippocr. et Plat.*

§ 15. γενόμενον γὰρ ἡμῶν ἔκαστον . . . παραλαμβάνουσι δαίμονες οἱ κατ᾽ ἐκείνην τὴν στιγμὴν τῆς γενέσεως ὑπηρέται. Cf. *Ascl. Lat.* III. 35 : 'inmutantur (formae) totiens, quot hora momenta habet circuli circumcurrentis.' No two men are alike in bodily constitution, (and consequently, no two men are alike in the πάθη which result from the action of the body on the soul,) because no two are born under the same astral influences. In the terms of *Corp.* XVI, this may be expressed by saying that no two men are influenced by the same daemons.

οὗτοι γὰρ κατὰ στιγμὴν ἐναλλάσσονται, οὐχ οἱ αὐτοὶ ἐπιμένοντες, ἀλλ᾽ ἀνακυκλούμενοι. οὗτοι probably means οἱ ἀστέρες, and not οἱ δαίμονες. The function of presiding over the births of men passes from planet to planet in rapid rotation. Consequently, if A is born a moment before B, A's body will throughout his life be under the control of a corps of daemons commanded by a certain planet, and B's body will be under the control of a different corps of daemons, commanded by another planet.

εἰς τὰ δύο ⟨ἄλογα⟩ μέρη τῆς ψυχῆς δύντες. 'The two irrational parts of the soul' are those distinguished by Plato, viz. τὸ θυμοειδές and τὸ ἐπιθυμητικόν, as opposed to τὸ λογικὸν μέρος τῆς ψυχῆς (= τὸ λογιστικόν in Pl. *Rep.*), which is mentioned in the following sentence. It seems necessary to insert ἄλογα, as τὰ δύο μέρη alone would hardly convey this meaning.

τὸ δὲ λογικὸν μέρος τῆς ψυχῆς ἀδέσποτον τῶν δαιμόνων ἕστηκεν. This might be otherwise expressed by saying that the man in whom νοῦς rules (i. e. the εὐσεβής, or he who has got *gnosis*) is free from the dominion of Heimarmene. This passage is referred to by Lactantius, *Div. inst.* 2. 15. 7. Cf. *Ascl. Lat.* III. 29 b *init.* (quoted by Lactantius *ib.*) : εὐσεβοῦς γὰρ ἀνθρώπου οὔτε δαίμων κακὸς οὔτε εἱμαρμένη κρατεῖ. *Corp.* XII. i. 9 as emended : οὐδὲν (τῷ νῷ) ἀδύνατον, οὔτε εἱμαρμένης ὑπεράνω θεῖναι ψυχὴν ἀνθρωπίνην κ.τ.λ. The εὐσεβὴς ἄνθρωπος is unaffected by the πάθη bred by the body.

§ 16. ⟨ὅ⟩τῳ οὖν ἐν τῷ λογικῷ ἀκτὶς ἐπιλάμπει ⟨ἀπὸ τοῦ θεοῦ⟩ [διὰ τοῦ ἡλίου], [[ ]] τούτῳ[ν] καταργοῦνται οἱ δαίμονες. The ἀκτίς is the ray of divine νοῦς by which the pious man is illuminated (φωτίζεται). It comes from the supreme and supracosmic God (cf. ἀκτῖνα τοῦ θεοῦ below) ; and in the phrase εἰς ὑποδοχὴν τοῦ θεοῦ, it is identified with God himself. The writer must have held that this ἀκτίς comes from God to men immediately and directly, and not that it is transmitted by the Sun ; διὰ τοῦ ἡλίου must therefore be cut out. The Sun is the source of our physical life, and conveys it to us by means of his light; but his light is φῶς αἰσθητόν, whereas the ἀκτίς here spoken of is φῶς νοητόν. The soul which is illuminated by the invisible and incorporeal 'light' of the divine νοῦς is thereby freed from the corrupting influences of the body, which are here personified as daemons.

οὔτε δαιμόνων οὔτε θεῶν. The θεοί are the planet-gods, whose commands are executed by the daemons.

ὁ λόγον οὐκ ἔχων ἔρως (ὁ λόγος οὐκ ἔρως MSS.) ⟨οὗτος?⟩ ἐστίν, ὁ πλανώμενος καὶ πλανῶν. The writer is thinking of the definition of the lower kind of ἔρως in Pl. *Phaedr.* 238 B: ἡ γὰρ ἄνευ λόγου δόξης ἐπὶ τὸ ὀρθὸν ὁρμώσης κρατήσασα ἐπιθυμία, πρὸς ἡδονὴν ἀχθεῖσα κάλλους,[1] καὶ ὑπ' αὖ τῶν ἑαυτῆς συγγενῶν[2] ἐπιθυμιῶν [ἐπὶ σωμάτων κάλλος] ἐρρωμένως ῥωσθεῖσα [νικήσασα ἀγωγῇ], ἀπ' αὐτῆς τῆς ῥώμης ἐπωνυμίαν λαβοῦσα, ἔρως ἐκλήθη. That passage is manifestly corrupt ; and the words ὁ πλανώμενος καὶ πλανῶν, used by the writer of *Corp.* XVI in referring to it, suggest a suspicion that, in the reading of it which was known to him, some form of πλανᾶσθαι occurred.[3] The existence of such a reading is made more probable by the fact that Maximus Tyrius, with the same sentence of the *Phaedrus* in his mind, writes thus (19. 2 Hobein) : τοῖς μὲν γὰρ ἄλλοις (i. e. to those who loved basely) ὁ ἔρως ἦν ὄνομα ἐπιθυμίας ἐν ἡδοναῖς ⌜πλανώμενον⌝ (πλανωμένης Reiske). *Ib.* 20. 5 : ἐπισπᾶται δὲ αὐτὸν (*sc.* τὸν ὑβριστὴν ἔρωτα) κάλλους ⌜φήμη⌝ (read ἡδονή) οἰστρούμενον, ὑπὸ δὲ τῆς ἀγνοίας πλανώμενον. Compare *Corp.* I. 19 *fin.*: ὁ δὲ ἀγαπήσας [[ ]] ἐκ πλάνης ἔρωτος ⟨⟨τὸ⟩⟩ σῶμα, οὗτος μένει ἐν τῷ σκότει πλανώμενος.

ταύτην δὲ τὴν διοίκησιν Ἑρμῆς εἱμαρμένην ἐκάλεσεν. This appears to be a reference to *Corp.* I. 9 : καὶ ἡ διοίκησις αὐτῶν (*sc.* of the seven planets) εἱμαρμένη καλεῖται. If so, the writer assumed the unnamed teacher who speaks in *Corp.* I to be Hermes, as did the

---

[1] Socrates has just said that ἔρως (of the lower kind) is one among many kinds of ἐπιθυμία, and that every ἐπιθυμία is a desire for some sort of ἡδονή, and as such, is to be distinguished from δόξα ἐφιεμένη τοῦ ἀρίστου (= δόξα ἐπὶ τὸ ὀρθὸν ὁρμῶσα). He gives as instances of ἐπιθυμίαι the desire for food and the desire for strong drink. The object of this kind of ἔρως then is ἡδονὴ (σωματικοῦ) κάλλους, as that of γαστριμαργία is ἡδονὴ ἐδωδῆς.

[2] The συγγενεῖς ἐπιθυμίαι must be the other desires (γαστριμαργία and the like) which are associated with ἔρως (lust), and intensify it by their presence beside it.

[3] Perhaps in connexion with ἐπὶ σώματος κάλλος (which appears to be a repetition of πρὸς ἡδονὴν ἀχθεῖσα κάλλους). For instance, it would be possible to write ⟨⟨ἐπὶ σώματος κάλλος⟩⟩ ⟨πλανηθεῖσα⟩, καὶ ὑπ' αὖ τῶν ἑαυτῆς συγγενῶν ἐπιθυμιῶν [[ ]] ἐρρωμένως ῥωσθεῖσα.

writer of *Corp.* XIII. But ταύτην . . . ἐκάλεσεν may have been
inserted by a later hand.

§§ 17-19. ἤρτηται οὖν . . . αὐτὸς ἄπαυστος. This concluding
paragraph is dependent partly on the contents of §§ 4–10 a and 12,
and partly on those of §§ 13–16, and presupposes both those
passages. § 17 (ἤρτηται οὖν ὁ νοητὸς κόσμος κ.τ.λ.) contains statements suggested by § 6 (πόθεν δὲ αὕτη—*sc.* ἡ νοητὴ οὐσία—ἐπιρρεῖ
κ.τ.λ.) and by § 12 (ὥσπερ ὁ νοητὸς κόσμος κ.τ.λ.); and δημιουργὸς
δὲ ὁ ἥλιος in § 18 is a repetition of ὁ δημιουργός, λέγω δὴ ὁ ἥλιος in § 5.
But on the other hand, §§ 17 and 18 adhere to the doctrine of
planets and daemons set forth in §§ 13–16, and ignore the doctrine
of φῶς set forth in §§ 4–10 a and 12. Moreover, § 19 is closely
related to § 3. It seems then that the construction of *Corp.* XVI
(apart from the preface, §§ 1 a-2,) may be best explained as
follows. The writer took from one source a theory of φῶς, and
from another source a theory of planets and daemons; he set down
these two theories side by side,—the one in §§ 4–10 a and 12, and
the other in §§ 13–16,—leaving them unreconciled; and he wrote
§ 3 as an introduction to the whole composed of these two parts,
and §§ 17–19 as a conclusion to it.

§ 17. ἤρτηται οὖν ὁ νοητὸς κόσμος τοῦ θεοῦ [ὁ δὲ αἰσθητὸς τοῦ νοητοῦ]
ὁ δὲ ἥλιος διὰ τοῦ νοητοῦ [καὶ αἰσθητοῦ] κόσμου κ.τ.λ. It is necessary
to cut out the mentions of the αἰσθητὸς κόσμος, which must have
been inserted by some unintelligent reader. According to the
doctrine of *Corp.* XVI, the Sun, as second God, presides over the
sensible universe; his life-giving power must therefore come to him
from a supracosmic source, and cannot be transmitted to him through
the αἰσθητὸς κόσμος, which is subordinate to him. The descending
series is ὁ θεός, ὁ νοητὸς κόσμος, ὁ ἥλιος; and the αἰσθητὸς κόσμος,
if spoken of at all, ought to be spoken of as the object or field of
the Sun's demiurgic activity, and not as the source of it.

διὰ τοῦ νοητοῦ [ ] κόσμου τὴν ἐπιρροὴν ἀπὸ τοῦ θεοῦ χορηγεῖται
τοῦ ἀγαθοῦ, τουτέστι τῆς δημιουργίας. This is an attempt to answer
the question which in § 6 was said to be unanswerable. 'The good'
issues from God, and is transmitted to the Sun through the Noetos
Kosmos. As to the meaning of τὸ ἀγαθόν here, cf. *Ascl. Lat.* III.
27 a: 'deus . . . dispensator . . . est bonorum, id est sensus, animae,
et vitae.' We might rather have expected τῆς ζωῆς in place of τῆς
δημιουργίας; but perhaps δημιουργίας may be allowed to stand, if we
take it to mean 'life-giving energy'.

περὶ δὲ τὸν ἥλιον αἱ ὀκτώ εἰσι σφαῖραι, τούτου ἠρτημέναι.　Cf. μέσος ἵδρυται in § 7. We found reason to think that in §§ 4–10 a the Sun is regarded as the nearest to earth of all the heavenly bodies. According to that view, the Sun would have above him seven of the eight spheres here enumerated, (viz. that of the fixed stars, those of the five planet-stars, and that of the moon,) and below him, one of them only (viz. ἡ περίγειος σφαῖρα, i. e. the atmosphere). But it is possible that the position assigned to the Sun in §§ 17–19 is different from that assigned to him in §§ 4–10 a, and that the arrangement here assumed is as follows :—fixed stars, Saturn, Jupiter, Mars, SUN, Mercury, Venus, Moon, atmosphere. In that case, the Sun would have four spheres above him, and four spheres below him.

It may be inferred from this passage that besides the six corps of daemons commanded by the six planet-gods (§ 13), there is a seventh corps, commanded by a god who presides over the sphere of the fixed stars, and an eighth, commanded by a god who presides over the atmosphere. Compare the list of οὐσιάρχαι in *Ascl. Lat.* III. 19 b.

τῶν δὲ δαιμόνων (ἤρτηνται) οἱ ἄνθρωποι. The few men who are 'illumined by God's light' must be excepted ; but that exception is not here mentioned. As far as their bodies are concerned, all men alike ' are dependent on the daemons '; but ' the illuminated ' are unaffected by bodily influences.

§ 18. διὸ πατὴρ μὲν πάντων ὁ θεός, δημιουργὸς δὲ ὁ ἥλιος· ὁ δὲ κόσμος ὄργανον τῆς δημιουργίας. According to the doctrine of §§ 4–10 a, the ὄργανον δημιουργίας (i. e. the instrument by means of which the Sun puts life into things) is the sunlight; according to that of §§ 13–16, the ὄργ. δημ. is the army of daemons commanded by the planets. On the assumption that the writer here had in mind the former doctrine, the words ὁ δὲ κόσμος ὄργανον τῆς δημιουργίας would be meaningless, and it would be necessary to write τὸ δὲ φῶς ὄ. τ. δ. instead. But in §§ 17, 18, the doctrine of φῶς is ignored, and that of planets and daemons only is recognized ; and that being so, it is possible to make sense of the words as they stand, if we take ὁ κόσμος to mean the system of spheres which has just been described. The Sun does his work as δημιουργός by means of the eight spheres ; i. e. he employs as his instruments or agents the god of the fixed stars, the gods of the five planet-stars and the moon, and the god of the atmosphere ; and these gods employ as their instruments or agents the daemons who are subject to them. Compare § 7, where ὁ κόσμος seems to mean the heavenly bodies regarded collectively.

καὶ ⌜οὐρανὸν μὲν ἡ νοητὴ οὐσία διοικεῖ, οὐρανὸς⌝ δὲ θεούς, δαίμονες δὲ θεοῖς ὑποτεταγμένοι ἀνθρώπους διοικοῦσιν. This is unintelligible. The θεοί to whom the daemons are subject must be the gods of the eight spheres. But according to §§ 13–16, these gods are subject, not to 'Heaven', but to the Sun ; and there remains no function which could be assigned to an entity called οὐρανός. If the passage was intended to agree with §§ 13–16 (as it probably was), it ought to have been written thus : καὶ ἥλιον μὲν ὁ θεὸς διὰ τῆς νοητῆς οὐσίας διοικεῖ, ἥλιος δὲ θεούς· δαίμονες δὲ κ.τ.λ. If it had been meant to agree with §§ 4–10 a, it would have been necessary to write something like this : καὶ ἥλιον μὲν ὁ θεὸς διὰ τῆς νοητῆς οὐσίας διοικεῖ, ἥλιος δὲ διὰ τοῦ φωτὸς πάντα δημιουργεῖ. The word οὐρανόν, which seems to have been wrongly substituted for ἥλιον, may possibly have arisen out of ὄργανον in the preceding line.

§ 19. πάντα οὖν ποιῶν ἑαυτὸν ποιεῖ. Cf. Corp. XI. ii. 14 a : ἀεί ἐστιν (ὁ θεὸς) ἐν τῷ ἔργῳ, αὐτὸς ὢν ὃ ποιεῖ.[1]

οὐκ ἄν ποτε παύσαιτο ⟨ποιῶν⟩. The Kosmos therefore will continue to exist for ever.

[καὶ ὥσπερ ὁ θεὸς . . . τέλος ἔχει.] This is merely a paraphrase of the preceding sentence. (But see note on Ascl. Lat. III. 29 c.)

LIBELLVS XVII

In the MSS., this passage (εἰ δὲ νοεῖς . . . ἑξῆς θεολογήσομεν) follows the last words of Corp. XVI (τέλος ἔχει) without a break, as if it formed part of the ' Epistle of Asclepius to King Ammon '. But it is evidently the conclusion of another libellus, of which

---

[1] Compare Joannes Scotus Erigena (ninth century), De divisione naturae I. 72, Migne Patr. Lat. CXXII. 517 D : ' Coaeternum igitur est Deo suum facere et coessentiale. . . . Non ergo aliud est Deo esse, et aliud facere, sed ei esse id ipsum est et facere. . . . Cum ergo audimus Deum omnia facere, nil aliud debemus intelligere, quam deum in omnibus esse, hoc est, essentiam omnium subsistere. Ipse enim solus per se vere est, et omne, quod vere in his quae sunt dicitur esse, ipse solus est. Nihil enim eorum quae sunt per se ipsum vere est ; quodcunque autem in eo vere intelligitur, participatione ipsius unius, qui solus per seipsum vere est, accipit.' Ib. 3. 1, Migne 621 B : God is ' principium omnium, et inseparabilis ab omni diversitate quam condidit. . . . In ipso enim immutabiliter et essentialiter sunt omnia, et ipse est divisio et collectio universalis creaturae '. Erigena derived this part of his doctrine from the Neoplatonists, chiefly through Dionysius Areopag.

all except the last few sentences has disappeared, presumably through the loss of some leaves of the archetype from which our MSS. are derived. (By a similar accident, the beginning of *Corp.* II has been lost, together with the *libellus* which originally preceded it, and of which the title alone remains.) It is possible that the lost leaves contained the end of *Corp.* XVI also, and that our text of that document is consequently incomplete; but this is uncertain, as § 19 serves very well as a conclusion of the Epistle of Asclepius, and it is not apparent from internal evidence that anything is missing after it.

Corp. XVII is a dialogue between Tat (son of Hermes) and a king, who is probably Ammon. The concluding words (τῇ δὲ ἐπιούσῃ περὶ τῶν ἑξῆς θεολογήσομεν) show that the dialogue as a whole came under the head of θεολογία, i. e. discussion of the gods or of God; and also, that its author intended to write one or more other dialogues of the same kind, in which other branches of the same subject were to be dealt with. If he carried out his intention, these other dialogues have perished.

As the argument ends with the injunction προσκύνει τὰ ἀγάλματα, the particular topic (or the last of the topics) discussed in *Corp.* XVII must have been the question whether men ought to worship statues of the gods. That is a question to which the Christian attacks on idolatry forced Pagans to give attention in the third century especially, though it was sometimes discussed in earlier times, e. g. by Dio Chrysostomus and Maximus Tyrius.

The writer is familiar with the Platonic contrast between σώματα and ἀσώματα, αἰσθητά and νοητά, and uses the Platonic term ὁ νοητὸς κόσμος.

In this dialogue, the teacher is Tat; this implies that Hermes has departed to heaven, and that his son and disciple Tat has succeeded him as 'prophet' upon earth. (Cf. *Kore Kosmu*, Stob. *Exc.* XXIII. 6 : Hermes ἀνέβαινεν εἰς ἄστρα. ἀλλ᾽ ἦν αὐτῷ διάδοχος ὁ Τάτ, υἱὸς ὁμοῦ ⟨τούτου⟩ καὶ παραλήπτωρ τῶν μαθημάτων.) This notion is not likely to have arisen until a large body of Hermetic writings, including a collection of 'Discourses of Hermes to Tat', was in existence. *Corp.* XVII must therefore be one of the later *Hermetica*; and we may conclude that it was probably written in the third century A. D.

εἰ δὲ νοεῖς, ἔστιν κ.τ.λ. 'If you give your attention to it, (you cannot but see that) there are' &c.

ἔστιν ... καὶ σωμάτων ⟨εἴδωλα⟩ ἀσώματα. ... Τὰ ἐν τοῖς ἐσόπτροις φαινόμενα κ.τ.λ. The reflections seen in mirrors are mentioned as instances of εἴδωλα in Pl. *Soph.* 239 D, where, in a discussion of the question ' what is meant by an εἴδωλον', Theaetetus says Δῆλον ὅτι φήσομεν τὰ ἐν τοῖς ὕδασι καὶ κατόπτροις εἴδωλα, ἔτι καὶ τὰ γεγραμμένα καὶ τὰ τετυπωμένα (i. e. pictures and sculptures) κ.τ.λ.

The word ἀσώματος is here applied both to the εἴδωλα which are seen in mirrors, and to the ἰδέαι which are seen in bodies ; and the writer makes use of the εἴδωλα ἀσώματα seen in mirrors to explain by analogy the meaning of the statement that the ἰδέαι are ἀσώματοι. Cf. *Corp.* XI. ii. 17 a (μὴ θαυμάσῃς εἰ ἔστι τις ἀσώματος ἰδέα κ.τ.λ.), where the instance of a picture (i. e. an εἴδωλον of another kind) is employed to illustrate the meaning of ἀσώματος.

[θείως νοεῖς.] The words ὁ βασιλεὺς εἶπεν could hardly be placed after the two distinct statements οὕτως ἔχει, ὦ Τάτ, and θείως νοεῖς. Besides, there is nothing specially ' divine' in the thought that the image seen in a mirror is not a body.

⟨. . .⟩ οὕτως ἀντανακλάσεις εἰσὶ τῶν ἀσωμάτων πρὸς τὰ σώματα. There is a want of sequence here. οὕτως was probably preceded by a clause beginning with ὥσπερ, and containing a statement about ἔσοπτρα and the εἴδωλα seen in them. As εἴδωλα are given off by bodies, and are seen in mirrors, so ἰδέαι are given off by τὰ νοητά (= τὰ ὄντως ὄντα, the entities of which the νοητὸς κόσμος is composed), and are seen in bodies. In other words, bodies are mirrors in which the νοητά are reflected. We cannot see the νοητά themselves ; but we can see reflections of them in material things.[1] It is these reflections, and not τὰ ὄντως ὄντα themselves, that in this passage are called ἰδέαι (= *formae visibiles*). They correspond to τὰ εἰσιόντα καὶ ἐξιόντα τῶν ὄντων ἀεὶ μιμήματα in Pl. *Tim.* 50 c. Cf. *Ascl. Lat.* III. 36 *fin.* : ' sunt enim (sol et luna) quasi speculorum nostrorum similes, imaginum similitudines aemulo splendore reddentium.'

In ἀντανακλάσεις τῶν ἀσωμάτων, the term ἀσώματα, which was previously applied (1) to the εἴδωλα, and (2) to the ἰδέαι, seems to denote neither εἴδωλα nor ἰδέαι, but the νοητά (= ὄντως ὄντα) from which the ἰδέαι come. In place of πρὸς τὰ σώματα, we might rather have expected ἐν τοῖς σώμασι (cf. αἱ ἰδέαι αἱ ἐν σώμασι φαινόμεναι above). What the writer probably meant might be expressed thus : ἰδέαι τῶν ἀσωμάτων ἀντανακλῶνται πρὸς τὰ σώματα. ' Forms

---

[1] Cf. Paul, I *Cor.* 13. 12 : βλέπομεν γὰρ ἄρτι δι' ἐσόπτρου ἐν αἰνίγματι.

460   CORPVS HERMETICVM

of (or derived from) the incorporeal νοητά are reflected *against* bodies', i.e. are projected on bodies, and reflected from them to our eyes, as the image of a thing is projected on a mirror and reflected from it.

[καὶ τῶν σωμάτων πρὸς τὰ ἀσώματα, τουτέστι τοῦ αἰσθητοῦ πρὸς τὸν νοητὸν κόσμον.] This is a meaningless addition. It could not be said that bodies are reflected in τὰ νοητά as in a mirror.

καὶ τοῦ νοητοῦ ⟨κόσμου⟩ πρὸς τὸν αἰσθητόν. The Aisthetos Kosmos (i. e. the whole made up of all σώματα) is a mirror in which the Noetos Kosmos (i. e. the whole made up of all νοητά or ὄντως ὄντα) is reflected.

διὸ προσκύνει τὰ ἀγάλματα, . . . ὡς καὶ αὐτὰ ἰδέας ἔχοντα ἀπὸ τοῦ ⟨νοητοῦ⟩ κόσμου. Here, the general principle laid down in the preceding sentences is brought to bear on the question whether statues of the gods ought to be worshipped. On this question, see *Ascl. Lat.* III. 24 a and 37. Perhaps it was in answer to Christian attacks on idol-worship that the author of *Corp.* XVII wrote in defence of the Pagan usage, as the passages on ' god-making ' in *Ascl. Lat.* III were certainly written in defence of the Pagan cults against the attacks of Christians.

A cult-statue is a σῶμα, and, like all σώματα, presents a ' reflection ' of a νοητόν. But the νοητόν which the statue ' reflects ' is a living being,—a νοητὸς θεός. Compare Philo's identification of the ἰδέαι or λόγοι with daemons or angels (Schürer, *Gesch. des Jud. Volkes* 1909, iii, p. 707).

As to the notion that cult-statues are mirrors in which νοητά are reflected, cf. Plut. *Is. et Os.* (Parthey) 77, on Egyptian animal-worship : εἴπερ οὖν οἱ δοκιμώτατοι τῶν φιλοσόφων οὐδ' ἐν ἀψύχοις καὶ ἀσωμάτοις πράγμασιν αἴνιγμα τοῦ θείου κατιδόντες ἠξίουν ἀμελεῖν οὐδὲν οὐδ' ἀτιμάζειν, ἔτι μᾶλλον οἴομαι τὰς ἐν αἰσθανομέναις καὶ ψυχὴν ἐχούσαις καὶ πάθος καὶ ἦθος φύσεσιν (i. e. animals) ⌐ἰδιότητας⌐ (ὁμοιό-τητας Squire) [κατὰ τὸ ἦθος] ⟨. . .⟩. ἀγαπητέον οὖν οὐ ταῦτα (sc. τὰ ζῷα) τιμῶντας, ἀλλὰ διὰ τούτων τὸ θεῖον, ὡς ἐναργεστέρων ἐσόπτρων, καὶ φύσει γεγονότων, ⌐ὡς ὄργανον ἢ τέχνην ἀεὶ τοῦ πάντα κοσμοῦντος θεοῦ νομίζειν.⌐ (Perhaps, καὶ φύσει γεγονότων [ὡς ὄργανον], ἢ⟨ν⟩ τέχνην δεῖ τοῦ πάντα κοσμοῦντος θεοῦ νομίζειν. Statues of the gods are τοῦ θείου ἔσοπτρα, made by human τέχνη ; the animals worshipped by the Egyptians are ἐναργέστερα τοῦ θείου ἔσοπτρα, made by φύσις, which is God's τέχνη.) Plotinus 4. 3. 11 : καί μοι δοκοῦσιν οἱ πάλαι σοφοί, ὅσοι ἐβουλήθησαν θεοὺς αὐτοῖς παρεῖναι, ἱερὰ καὶ ἀγάλματα ποιησάμενοι, εἰς τὴν τοῦ παντὸς φύσιν ἀπιδόντες ἐν νῷ λαβεῖν ὡς πανταχοῦ μὲν εὐάγωγον ψυχῆς φύσις, δέξασθαι γε μὴν ῥᾷστον ἂν εἴη ἁπάντων, εἴ τις προσπαθές τι τεκτήναιτο, ὑποδέξασθαι δυνάμενον μοῖράν τινα αὐτῆς. προσπαθὲς δὲ τὸ ὁπωσοῦν μιμηθέν, ὥσπερ κάτοπτρον ἁρπάσαι εἶδός τι δυνάμενον.

Ὥρα ἐστίν, ὦ προφῆτα, περὶ τὴν τῶν ξένων ἐπιμέλειαν γενέσθαι (γίνεσθαι MSS.). The time has come for the evening meal, at which the King must be present as host; the discussion must therefore be adjourned. Cf. the concluding words of Julian *Or.* II : ἀλλ' ὥρα λοιπὸν πρὸς ἔργον τρέπεσθαι.

Tat is here called προφήτης. The word may mean 'an inspired teacher'. But προφήτης was the title borne by Egyptian priests of a certain rank or grade; and it is possible that the writer intended to imply that Tat was a priest of the class denoted by this title.

LIBELLVS XVIII

This document has nothing to do with Hermes or any pupil of Hermes; and the only reason for calling it 'Hermetic' is that it is included in the *Corpus Hermeticum* in one of the two classes of MSS. in which the collection has come down to us, and in that respect stands on a par with *Corp.* XVI and *Corp.* XVII. It consists of two or three fragments of an epideictic oration 'in praise of kings'. Its author does not, like the Hermetists, put what he has to say into the mouth of a prehistoric teacher, but speaks in his own person. He appears to have been a *rhetor* by profession, and one who made high claims for the art which he professed. He says that musicians and other artists are inspired by God, and asserts that he himself, as an artist in speech-making, is likewise inspired.

The circumstances presupposed are these. The Roman empire is under the rule of two or more 'kings' who reign conjointly. The rulers have recently brought a formidable war, or series of wars, to a successful conclusion (ἐκ τῶν ἐκείνων τροπαίων ἡ τοῦ λόγου προθυμία, § 7 b ; αὐτοῖς τὰ τῆς νίκης πεπρυτάνευται, § 8 ; πᾶσαι αἱ νῖκαι, § 9 ; οἷς ἡ νίκη . . . πεπρυτάνευται κ.τ.λ., § 10 ;) and established peace (τοὺς τῆς κοινῆς ἀσφαλείας καὶ εἰρήνης πρυτάνεις, § 10 ; τοσούτης ἡμῖν εἰρήνης εὐετηρίαν ἁπλώσασι κ.τ.λ., § 16). Their success is celebrated at a festival held in some city of the empire;[1] and the orator does his part in the celebration by delivering this speech.

Who are the reigning ' kings ' ?   That part of the oration in which their actions were spoken of in detail has been lost; but the style and diction agree well with a date not far from A. D. 300.[2]   It is most likely then that Reitzenstein is right in his conclusion that the ' kings ' are Diocletian and his colleagues,—i. e. the two *Augusti*, Diocletian and Maximian, and the two *Caesares*, Galerius and Constantius,—who reigned jointly[3] from A. D. 293 to 305.   During the first five or six years of their joint rule, Maximian and Constantius re-established the imperial power and restored security in the West by a series of successful wars in Gaul, Britain, and Africa, while Diocletian and Galerius did the like in the eastern half of the empire. Galerius secured the Balkan peninsula against barbarian invasion by his campaigns on the Danube; Diocletian in person reconquered Egypt (295–296); and the war waged by Diocletian and Galerius against the Persians (296–297) was concluded by a treaty of peace, the terms of which were highly satisfactory to the Romans.   By the year 298, a situation such as is implied in *Corp.* XVIII had been attained ; a series of successful wars had ended in the establishment, throughout the empire, of peace and prosperity such as had long been unknown.[4]   It is probable then that the speech was composed in or about A. D. 300.

----

[1] Reitzenstein (*Poim.* p. 199) says that the oration is addressed to certain emperors 'who are present, or are supposed to be present'. But I can find no proof that the presence of the emperors, or any of them, is assumed. The βασιλεῖς are spoken of in the third person only. ὦ τιμιώτατοι, § 7 a, may very well have been addressed to the local dignitaries who presided at the festival, and not to the emperors themselves : and' αὐτοῖς τοῖς βασιλεῦσι φίλον, § 8, does not necessarily imply that the ' kings ' are present.

[2] Keil, in Reitz. *Poim.* pp. 371 ff., investigates the rhythm of the *clausulae* in *Corp.* XVIII, and seeks to show that the writer observed laws of accentual rhythm which were in force for artistic prose in the fourth century A. D., but not earlier ; and he infers from this that the speech ' cannot have been written before the end of the third century'.   This inference seems to me to be stated somewhat too positively.   In the first place, the rhythmical form of a large proportion of the *clausulae* is doubtful, because of the corruption of the text.   In the second place, it is not likely that all writers of artistic prose throughout the Roman empire adopted the new laws of accentual rhythm simultaneously ; and it would be difficult to prove that rules which were commonly observed in the fourth century were not observed by a few writers here and there before A. D. 300.   Still, Keil's argument gives support to the opinion that the speech was not written before the reign of Diocletian, which is probable for other reasons.

[3] 'Quattuor principes mundi . . . unum in rem publicam sentientes' (Vopiscus, *Hist. Aug.* 30. 18. 4).   Cf. the description of celestial concord in *Corp.* XVIII. 14 b.

[4] *Paneg. Lat.* VIII. (V.) 20. 2 (A. D. 298): 'Tenet uno pacis amplexu Romana respublica quidquid variis temporum vicibus fuit aliquando Romanum ; et illa, quae

There is nothing to show in what city the oration was delivered, or supposed to be delivered.[1] *Corp.* XVIII has come down to us in a collection of documents most of which were certainly written in Egypt; and this fact points to Alexandria. But the successes of the rulers must have been celebrated in every city of importance throughout the empire; speeches of this character were doubtless delivered at many different places,—e. g. at Antioch, and at Nicomedia (Diocletian's place of residence); and the compiler of the *Corpus* (or the man who added *Libellus* XVIII to the *Corpus*) may have used for his purpose any such oration, of which a copy chanced to have come into his hands.

Did he include the whole of the speech in his collection? If so, the loss of the greater part of it might be due either to accident or to deliberate excision. (A Christian transcriber would have a strong motive for omitting the praises of Diocletian and Galerius, of which it is to be presumed that the bulk of the speech consisted.) But it seems more likely that the compiler of the *Corpus* himself selected those parts of the speech in which religious thoughts occurred, and rejected the rest. He would be interested in the theory of inspiration which is set forth in the *prooemium* (§§ 1–7 a), the 'praises of God' with which the oration began and ended (§§ 7 b–9 and 11–14 a), and the passage in which the concord of the celestial gods is spoken of (§ 14 b); but he would see no reason to include in his collection of religious documents a description of the achievements of certain Roman emperors.

The probable character of the missing parts of the speech may be inferred from the rules which Menandros Rhetor (Περὶ ἐπιδεικτικῶν, Spengel *Rhetores Graeci*, vol. iii, pp. 368 ff.) lays down for the composition of an ἐγκώμιον βασιλέως, and from extant specimens of such

saepe veluti nimia diffluxerat mole, tandem solido cohaesit imperio. Nihil ex omni terrarum caelique regione non aut metu quietum est, aut armis domitum, aut pietate devinctum.' (The *Panegyrici Latini*, ed. G. Baehrens, Teubner 1911, are a series of orations spoken mostly in Gaul, and ranging in date from A.D. 291 to 391. See especially *Paneg.* VIII (V), delivered March 1, A.D. 298, addressed to Constantius, and dealing chiefly with his reconquest of Britain; and X and XI, addressed to Maximian.)—D. Cozza, *L' Imperatore dalmata* (*Diocletianus*), 1912, p. 68, says that 'after the Persian war, or, to speak more precisely, about A. D. 300, the Roman world was tranquil; the defence of the boundaries was by that time guaranteed, and peace was assured'. Diocletian's *Edictum de pretiis rerum venalium*, A.D. 301, begins thus: 'Fortunam rei publicae nostrae, cui iuxta immortales deos bellorum memoria, quae feliciter gessimus, gratulari licet, tranquillo orbis statu et in gremio altissimae quietis locato . . . .'

[1] We cannot be sure that it was really delivered; it may be a literary composition written in the form of an oration.

encomia, e. g. the anonymous Εἰς βασιλέα included in the works of
Aelius Aristides (*Or.* 35, vol. ii, p. 253 Keil), and Julian's panegyrics
of Constantius (*Or.* 1 and 2).

The traditional text of *Corp.* XVIII presents numerous passages
in which a phrase or statement is repeated in slightly different words.
The author of the oration cannot have thus repeated himself; how
then did these iterations arise? They might perhaps be accounted
for by the supposition that our text is not derived from the author's
manuscript, but that two or three men who heard the speech
delivered took notes of it in writing, and a written text was constructed by putting their notes together. Or possibly the text given
in the *Corpus* may have been transcribed from a rough copy or first
draft of the speech, in which the author wrote down alternative
phrases as they occurred to him, with the intention of subsequently
choosing between them, and working up this raw material into a
finished oration.

Contents.

Prooemium, §§ 1-9, ⟨⟨15⟩⟩, 10, ⟨⟨16⟩⟩. If the music goes amiss by
reason of a defect in the instrument, the blame must not be laid on
the musician. And so, if my speech goes amiss by reason of my
human weakness, you must not lay the blame on the inspiration
which comes to me from above. God is the great musician; he
makes music in all the universe; and I too am an instrument on
which he plays. If there is any failure, do not blame the divine
Musician,—for he cannot fail,—but lay the blame on the defects of
his human instrument. §§ 1–4.

But sometimes a musician, when his instrument has failed him,
has found the defect made good by help sent from above. And so
it is with me. I feel in me a God-given power which will make
good my deficiencies; and so I shall not fail. §§ 6, 7 a.

I am to speak in praise of kings. I will begin by praising God,
the supreme King. God reigns for ever; and from him all earthly
kings derive their power. §§ 7 b–9.

Having praised God, I will pass on to the praise of these our
kings on earth. In praising them, we shall be training ourselves to
praise God rightly. God has given them their sovereignty, and
grants them victory even before war begins. To them our thanks
are due for the boon of peace. To establish peace is the chief
function of a king. The very word 'king' suggests peace; and the
statue of a king is a safe refuge. §§ ⟨⟨15⟩⟩, 10, ⟨⟨16⟩⟩.

Praise of the reigning kings (missing, except this fragment) :
Among the celestial gods there is perfect concord ; ⟨and in like manner there is concord among our kings⟩. § ⟨⟨14 b⟩⟩.

Peroration, §§ 11–14 a :
I will end, as I began, by praising God. God is to us as the Sun is to the plants. He fosters the growth of our souls by pouring down on us the efflux of his wisdom ; and it is meet that we should use in praise of him the faculties which he has fostered in us. § 11.

God is to us as a father is to his infant children. His greatness transcends all that we can say ; but he pardons the inadequacy of our praise, and takes pleasure in our childish lispings. §§ 12, 13.

God is good, and infinitely great. He is eternal, and he makes the world endure for ever. § 14 a. (The rest is lost.)

Title. The original title is lost. Some late transcriber has inserted περὶ τῆς ὑπὸ τοῦ πάθους τοῦ σώματος ἐμποδιζομένης ψυχῆς before § 1, and περὶ εὐφημίας τοῦ κρείττονος, καὶ ἐγκώμιον βασιλέως before § 11. The first of these two headings is inappropriate, but must have been meant for an interpretation of what is said about the musician and his instrument in §§ 1–7 a.[1] The other is made up of two distinct headings. περὶ εὐφημίας τοῦ κρείττονος would be a suitable heading for §§ 11–14 a ; and ἐγκώμιον βασιλέων (not βασιλέως) would serve either as a heading for §§ 15–16, or as a title of the whole document.

§§ 1–5. τοῖς τῆς παμμούσου . . . ἐναρμόσασθαι λύραν. In this passage, the statement that the musician is not to be blamed for a failure caused by a defect in his instrument is repeated no less than five times. (§ 1 : ὁ μὲν γὰρ . . ., τῶν δὲ ⟨ὀργάνων⟩ τὸ ἀσθενὲς καταμέμφεται. —§ 2 : οὐ τῷ πνεύματι . . ., τῇ δὲ τοῦ ὀργάνου καταμέμφεται σαθρότητι. —§ 4 : μὴ εἰς αὐτὸν . . ., τῆς δὲ χορδῆς καταμεμφώμεθα τὴν ἀσθένειαν.— § 5 : τοῦ συμπτώματος περὶ τὸ ὄργανον γεγενημένου, οὐδείς ποτε τὸν μουσουργὸν ᾐτιάσατο.—*Ib.*: οὐκ ἔσχον [τὴν] κατ᾽ αὐτοῦ αἰτίασιν.) Seeing that the author was evidently trying to produce a masterpiece of style, and must have taken pains about his composition, it is impossible to believe that he can have been guilty of this purposeless iteration. Some of the phrases in which the thought is repeated may have been written as alternatives or substitutes ; and some of them may have been notes intended to explain the meaning of the text.

§ 1. ἡ τῶν ὀργάνων ἀναρμοστία. Properly speaking, it is the musician

---

[1] The man who inserted this heading must have taken ' the musician ' to mean the soul, and ' the instrument ' to mean the body.

that ἁρμόττεται (tunes) τὴν λύραν, i. e. adjusts the several strings so as to make them sound the notes of the particular scale (ἁρμονία) which he intends to use. But it may be supposed that there is some defect in the lyre which makes it impossible for the musician to tune it rightly, or causes it to go out of tune after he has tuned it rightly; e. g. a peg may be loose, and fail to keep the string at the right pitch.

[καταγέλαστον τὸ ἐπιχείρημα· τῶν γὰρ ὀργάνων ἐξασθενούντων πρὸς τὴν χρείαν, τὸν μουσουργὸν ἀνάγκη παρὰ τῶν θεωρῶν ἐπιτωθάζεσθαι.] The statement that, under the circumstances supposed, 'the musician is bound to be jeered at by the audience' contradicts a proposition which is asserted five times over in the text (οὐδείς ποτε τὸν μουσουργὸν ᾐτιάσατο, &c.); therefore it cannot have been written by the author, but must be a note appended by an objector. That being so, it seems best to take καταγέλαστον τὸ ἐπιχείρημα as part of the same note, and translate 'The writer's argument is absurd; for' &c. (ἐπιχείρημα, 'an attempted proof', is a technical term of logic.) The words καταγ. τὸ ἐπιχ. would not be suitable as an apodosis to εἰ . . . ἐμποδὼν . . . γένηται κ.τ.λ.; for though the *result produced* might be ridiculous, there would, according to the author's view, be nothing contemptible in the *enterprise* or *endeavour* (ἐπιχείρημα) of the musician.

[ὁ μὲν γὰρ (sc. μουσουργὸς) ἀκάματον [εὐγνωμόνως] ἀποδίδωσι τὴν τέχνην, τῶν δὲ (sc. ὀργάνων) τὸ ἀσθενὲς καταμέμφεται (ὁ ἀκροατής?).] For ἀκάματον, cf. ἀκάματός ἐστιν (ὁ θεός) below. εὐγνωμόνως is probably an alternative for ἀκάματον.

§ 2. [ἄρτι μὲν [καὶ] σαλπιγκτῶν . . . τὴν μολπὴν ἐπιτελούντων.] This seems to be a description of a concert in which four different kinds of instruments are used. The instruments are the trumpet (σάλπιγξ), the flute (αὐλός), the reed-pipe (κάλαμος),[1] and the lyre (implied by πλῆκτρον, the thing with which the lyre is struck). From the words ἄρτι μὲν . . . ἄρτι δέ it must be inferred that in the case supposed these different kinds of instruments are played, not simultaneously, but separately and in succession.

The passage is clearly out of place here; and I cannot find any place at which it would fit into the text.[2] Possibly it may have

---

[1] Does κάλαμος here mean an instrument made of a single reed, with holes at intervals,—a simpler kind of flute? Or does it mean a 'Pan-pipe' (σῦριγξ), i. e. a mouth-organ consisting of a number of reeds of different lengths fastened together?

[2] It might perhaps be made to follow the words τοῖς τῆς παμμούσου μελῳδίας τὴν ἁρμονίαν ἐπαγγελλομένοις, § 1 *init.*; but this would unduly lengthen out a sentence that is already long enough.

come from a sentence preceding § 1 ; the orator may have begun by describing a concert, and then gone on to put the case of defects occurring in the music. The opening of the oration might perhaps be accounted for by assuming that, at the festival at which it was delivered, the speech-making was preceded by a concert such as is here spoken of. An audience that had just been listening to a series of musical performances would be prepared to appreciate what the speaker says about musicians and instruments.

οὐ τῷ πνεύματι τοῦ μουσικοῦ τις ἀναπέμπεται τὴν αἰτίαν. πνεῦμα here means 'inspiration', in the sense of artistic impulse derived from a divine source. The writer assumes that the musician is 'inspired', as poets were commonly said to be. Cf. Pseudo-Pl. *Axiochus* 370 c (see note on *Corp.* XII. ii. 19). *Spiritus* (= πνεῦμα) is similarly used by Latin authors. Cic. *Arch.* 8. 18 : the poet is 'divino quodam spiritu inflatus'. Hor. *Sat.* 1. 4. 46 : 'quidam comoedia necne poema | esset quaesivere, quod acer spiritus ac vis ǀ nec verbis nec rebus inest.' *Od.* 2. 16. 38 : 'mihi spiritum Graiae tenuem Camenae Parca non mendax dedit.' *Od.* 4. 6. 29 : 'spiritum Phoebus mihi, Phoebus artem carminis nomenque dedit poetae.' Hence, 'to lay the blame on the musician's πνεῦμα' means, to say that the failure results from the inadequacy of the artistic impulse which comes to him from God.

[οὐ τῷ κρείττονί ⟨τι ἀναπέμπεται⟩ τὴν αἰτίαν, ἀλλὰ τῷ μὲν ἀποδίδωσι πρέπον τὸ σέβας.] This was evidently written as an alternative for οὐ τῷ πνεύματι τοῦ μουσικοῦ τις ἀναπέμπεται τὴν αἰτίαν.—τῷ μέν must mean τῷ κρείττονι (= τῷ θεῷ), and not τῷ μουσικῷ ; for σέβας (reverential awe) is too strong a term to describe the hearer's approval of a competent performer.

ἐμποδὼν κατέστη, . . . ⌜ἐμποδίσασ⟨α⟩⌝. ἐμποδίσασα has probably been substituted by error for some nearly equivalent word, e. g. ἐνοχλήσασα. But it is possible that the sentence originally ended at ἐμποδὼν κατέστη, and that τῷ μὲν . . . συλήσασα has been subsequently added.

§ 3. οὕτωσὶ δὲ καὶ ἡμῶν τῆς περὶ τὸ σῶμα ἀσθενείας χάριν μή τις τῶν θεωρῶν καταμέμψηται ⟨τὴν τέχνην⟩. καταμέμφεσθαι usually takes an accusative ; cf. τὸ ἀσθενὲς καταμέμφεται in § 1, and καταμεμφώμεθα τὴν ἀσθένειαν in § 4. (In § 2, it seems best to read τὴν σαθρότητα in place of τῇ σαθρότητι.) Menandros Rhetor Περὶ ἐπιδεικτικῶν, Spengel III, p. 374 : καταμέμφεσθαι τὴν θρασύτητα. Hence it is to be presumed that an accusative has been lost after καταμέμψηται ;

and τὴν τέχνην would serve the purpose.   In this connexion, ἡ τέχνη differs little in meaning from τὸ πνεῦμα.

At this point, the speaker brings to bear on his own case the principle which he has laid down in the instance of the musician and his instrument.   The orator's πνεῦμα or τέχνη (i. e. he himself, *qua* inspired artist) corresponds to the musician ; the orator's σῶμα (i. e. he himself, as subject to human weakness or error,) corresponds to the instrument. If his performance falls short of perfection, the hearers must ascribe the blame, not to his πνεῦμα or τέχνη (which comes from God, and partakes of God's infallibility), but to personal defects arising from the body in which his immortal soul is incarnated.   The thought might be expressed in terms familiar to Platonists by saying that the πνεῦμα or τέχνη of the human artist is one aspect of the divine νοῦς implanted in man, and that the divine νοῦς is infallible.   Perhaps the writer had in mind Pl. *Rep.* 1. 342 B, where Socrates maintains that an artist, *qua* artist, cannot err ; οὔτε γὰρ πονηρία οὔτε ἁμαρτία οὐδεμία οὐδεμιᾷ τέχνῃ πάρεστιν, . . . αὐτὴ δὲ ἀβλαβὴς καὶ ἀκέραιός ἐστιν κ.τ.λ.

ἀκάματον μὲν [ἐστι] ⟨τὸ⟩ πνεῦμα ⟨εἰσπνεῖ? or χορηγεῖ?⟩ ὁ θεὸς ⟨εἰς⟩ ⟨⟨τὸ ἡμέτερον γένος⟩⟩.   (Cf. ὁ μὲν γὰρ ἀκάματον [   ] ἀποδίδωσι τὴν τέχνην in § 1.)   This very doubtful restoration of the text is at least a possible way of expressing what must have been the sense intended, viz. that the orator who delivers this speech is inspired by God, as musicians, and artists in general, are inspired (cf. ἡμῖν τῆς ἐκείνου σοφίας τὴν ἀπόρροιαν δεξαμένοις in § 11), and that, in so far as he is inspired, he cannot fail.

For the notion that *orators* are inspired, cf. Seneca the elder, *Suas.* 3. 6 : ' memini una nos ab auditione Nicetis ad Messalam venisse. Nicetes suo impetu valde Graecis placuerat.   Quaerebat a Gallione Messala, quid illi visus esset Nicetes.   Gallio ait " plena deo ". Quotiens audierat aliquem ex his declamatoribus quos scholastici caldos vocant, statim dicebat " plena deo ".'

I have inserted after this sentence the misplaced fragment ὁ γάρ τοι . . . ἀκάματός ἐστιν, because the statement that ' God is ἀκάματος ' serves to explain and justify the assertion that ' the πνεῦμα which God gives is ἀκάματον '.

⟨⟨ὁ γάρ τοι ⟨⟨θεός⟩⟩, κατὰ φύσιν μουσικὸς [[   ]] ⟨ὑπάρχων⟩, καὶ [   ] ἁρμονίαν οὐ μόνον ⟨ἐν τῷ παντὶ⟩ ἐργαζόμενος, ἀλλὰ καὶ ἄχρι τῶν κατὰ μέρος [   ] τῆς οἰκείας μελῳδίας τὸν ῥυθμὸν παραπέμπων, κ.τ.λ.⟩⟩   God is a musician.   The universe is the instrument on which he plays, and the cosmic process is the music which he makes.   (Cf. ἔρως . . . μίαν ἐργαζόμενος ἁρμονίαν τῶν πάντων in § 14 b. The writer was thinking of 'the music of the spheres'.) But God plays on each thing severally, as well as on the sum of things collectively; and when he inspires an individual orator, that is merely one special instance of his universal music-making.

For the notion that God 'plays on' the man inspired by him, as a musician plays on his lyre, cf. Philo, *Quis rer. div. heres* 52. 259, Wendland III, p. 59: προφήτης γὰρ ἴδιον μὲν οὐδὲν ἀποφθέγγεται, ἀλλότρια δὲ πάντα, ὑπηχοῦντος ἑτέρου. . . . μόνῳ δὲ σοφῷ ταῦτ' ἐφαρμόττει, ἐπεὶ καὶ μόνος (ὁ σοφὸς) ὄργανον θεοῦ ἐστιν, ἠχεῖον κρουόμενον καὶ πληττόμενον ἀοράτως ὑπ' αὐτοῦ. *Ib.* 53. 265 f.: ἐξοικίζεται γὰρ ἐν ἡμῖν ὁ νοῦς (i. e. our merely human intellect quits us) κατὰ τὴν τοῦ θείου πνεύματος ἄφιξιν. . . . ὄντως γὰρ ὁ προφήτης, καὶ ὁπότε λέγειν δοκεῖ, πρὸς ἀλήθειαν ἡσυχάζει, καταχρῆται δὲ ἕτερος αὐτοῦ τοῖς φωνητηρίοις ὀργάνοις, στόματι καὶ γλώττῃ, πρὸς μήνυσιν ὧν ἂν θέλῃ· τέχνῃ δὲ ἀοράτῳ καὶ παμμούσῳ ταῦτα κρούων, εὔηχα καὶ παναρμόνια καὶ γέμοντα συμφωνίας τῆς πάσης ἀποτελεῖ. Reitzenstein compares Montanus (Epiphan. *Haer.* 48. 4): ἰδοὺ ὁ ἄνθρωπος ὡσεὶ λύρα, κἀγὼ ἐφίπταμαι ὡσεὶ πλῆκτρον.

The ordered sequence of things may be described as a 'rhythm'; the word ῥυθμόν may therefore be allowed to stand here, though it is inappropriate in § 4 *fin.* But it would be possible to cut out τῆς οἰκείας μελῳδίας τὸν ῥυθμόν, and take the preceding ἁρμονίαν as the object of both ἐργαζόμενος and παραπέμπων.

ἀκάματός ἐστιν. God, the supreme Musician, cannot fail or fall short in his art.

ἀεὶ [δὲ καὶ] ὡσαύτως ἔχων τῆς [οἰκείας] ἐπιστήμης. I take this to be an explanation or expansion of ἀκάματός ἐστιν.

[διηνεκὴς δὲ ταῖς εὐδαιμονίαις]. This seems to be a clumsily written alternative for the following words, εὐεργεσίαις δὲ ταῖς αὐταῖς διὰ παντὸς κεχρημένος. The εὐεργεσίαι of God, in this connexion, are his gifts of πνεῦμα (inspiration) to men.

§ 4. εἰ δὲ μάλιστα [τῷ Φειδίᾳ] τῷ δημιουργῷ οὐχ ὑπήκουσεν ἡ τῆς ὕλης χρεία πρὸς ἐντελῆ τὴν ποικιλίαν ⟨. . .⟩. Hitherto, the only art discussed (except that of the orator) has been the art of music; and there has been nothing to lead up to a mention of Phidias the sculptor. If we cut out τῷ Φειδίᾳ, and take τῷ δημιουργῷ to mean God, the sentence expresses one of the leading thoughts of the *Timaeus.* God, in his ordering of the universe, aims at the best; and if the result falls short of perfection, that is due to the resistance of the ὕλη on which God has to work. Perhaps a genitive,—τοῦ κόσμου or something of the sort,—may have been lost after τὴν ποικιλίαν. We may suppose that τῷ Φειδίᾳ was inserted by a reader who misunderstood the sentence, and took τῆς ὕλης to mean the block of marble which the sculptor shapes.

In the missing words which followed, the writer must have applied the general principle laid down in the *Timaeus* to the particular case of the inspired orator. In this instance also, God does his part without fail; and if there is any failure in the speech delivered, it must be caused by the intractability of the ὕλη with which God has to deal,—that is, in this instance, by the human deficiency (ἡ περὶ τὸ σῶμα ἀσθένεια) of the orator.

The same thought might be expressed in another way by saying that it is not the divine Musician, but the human instrument, that is to blame ; and if we retain the following passage, ⟨. . .⟩ διήρκεσε δὲ αὐτὸς ὁ μουσουργὸς κ.τ.λ., we must interpret it accordingly ; i. e. we must here take 'the musician' to mean God, and 'the string' to mean the orator. This one repetition of the statement in § 2 (οὐ τῷ πνεύματι τοῦ μουσικοῦ κ.τ.λ.) may perhaps be allowed to stand, —especially as the terms are to be understood differently in the second passage. In § 2, the words are used in their literal sense ; 'the musician' there means the lyre-player, and 'the instrument' means his lyre. But in § 4, (the analogy having been explained in the interval,) the words are to be taken metaphorically ; 'the musician' means God, and 'the string' means the man whom God inspires. It might, however, be argued against this interpretation that the limiting words κατὰ δύναμιν are more applicable to the human artist than to God ; and I am not sure that it would not be better to bracket διήρκεσε . . . ἠφάνισεν.

τῆς εὐμουσίας τὸν ⌜ῥυθμὸν⌝ ἠφάνισεν. ῥυθμός cannot here mean 'rhythm', in the sense in which that term is commonly used in speaking of music ; for the fact that a string is out of tune makes no difference to the rhythm. Even if every note were wrong in pitch, the rhythm might still be faultless. If the reading is sound, we must take τῆς εὐμουσίας τὸν ῥυθμόν to mean, not the keeping of right *time*, but the sounding of right *tones*. But this would be a strange use of the word ῥυθμός.

§ 5. [ἀλλὰ δὴ] [τοῦ συμπτώματος . . . τὸν μουσουργὸν ᾐτιάσατο κ.τ.λ.] The thought so many times repeated is here expressed in plain and simple language ; and as such language is out of keeping with the florid style of the oration, it is most likely that this passage is an

explanatory note appended by some reader. ἀλλὰ δή is perhaps
a doublet of the ἀλλὰ δή at the beginning of § 6.

⌜ὁπότε τῆς κρούσεως πολλάκις πρὸς τὸν τόνον ἐμπεσούσης⌝. These
words might perhaps be struck out with advantage ; but if we retain
them, we must suppose the writer's meaning to have been 'when the
musician strikes the string ⟨rightly, and yet the sound produced is
wrong⟩'.

[οὕτω καὶ ἡμεῖς, ὦ τιμιώτατοι.] This may be a misplaced duplication either of οὑτωσὶ δὲ καὶ ἡμῶν κ.τ.λ. in § 3 init., or of οὕτως
οὖν καὶ αὐτὸς . . ., ὦ τιμιώτατοι in § 7 a init.

§ 6. [ὥσπερ αὐτῷ πολλάκις ὀργάνῳ κεχρημένον (al. κεχρημένος).]
If we altered this into ⟨ὁ θεὸς⟩ αὐτῷ (sc. τῷ ἀνθρώπῳ) πολλάκις ⟨⟨ὥσπερ⟩⟩
ὀργάνῳ κεχρημένος, it would be intelligible as a fragment of a sentence
dealing with the subject of §§ 3, 4 (God plays on the man inspired
by him as a musician plays on his instrument) ; and it may
possibly have come from the lost passage after τὴν ποικιλίαν in § 4.

[καὶ τὴν τῆς νευρᾶς θεραπείαν.] This looks like a doublet of καὶ
τῆς νευρᾶς φυλάττειν τὴν χώραν below.

⟨τὴν λύραν⟩ δι' ἀπορρήτων ἐναρμοσάμενον. (Cf. τὴν οἰκείαν ἐναρμόσασθαι λύραν in § 5 fin.) The following story of the cicala is told
for the purpose of illustrating this statement. The orator ' puts
his lyre in tune by mysterious (or supernatural) means ', i. e. makes
up for his own deficiencies by means of πνεῦμα breathed into him by
God, as in the story the musician made the tune go right, in spite
of his broken string, by means of the cicala sent by Apollo. For
δι' ἀπορρήτων, cf. πληττόμενον ἀοράτως ὑπ' αὐτοῦ and τέχνῃ ἀοράτῳ
in Philo Quis rer. div. heres 52. 259 and 53. 265, quoted above.

[λέγεται μὲν δὴ κ.τ.λ.] In the traditional text, two differently
worded versions of the story have been intermixed.

(a) λέγεται μὲν δὴ ⟨ὡς⟩ καί
τινος τεχνίτου κιθαρῳδίαν διαγωνι-
ζομένου, τῆς νευρᾶς ῥαγείσης, [ὑπὸ
τοῦ κρείττονος] τὸ παρὰ τοῦ κρείττονος εὐμενὲς ⟨. . .

. . .⟩ τὴν νευρὰν ἀνεπλήρωσεν
αὐτῷ, καὶ τῆς εὐδοκιμήσεως παρέσχε
τὴν χάριν.

(b) λέγεται μὲν δή τινα τεχνίτην,
τὸν τῆς μουσουργίας ἔφορον θεὸν
ἔχοντα εὐμενῆ, ἐπειδὴ ἐναγώνιον
τὴν κιθαρῳδίαν ποιουμένῳ [ἢ] νευρὰ
ῥαγεῖσα πρὸς ἐμπόδιον τῆς ἀθλήσεως
αὐτῷ γεγένητο, ⟨. . .⟩. ἀντὶ μὲν
γὰρ τῆς νευρᾶς αὐτῷ τέττιγα κατὰ
πρόνοιαν τοῦ κρείττονος ἐφιζάνοντα
ἀναπληροῦν τὸ μέλος [ ], τὸν
κιθαρῳδὸν δὲ [ ] τῆς λύπης παυσά-
μενον τῆς νίκης ἐσχηκέναι τὴν
εὐδοκίμησιν.

ὑπὸ τοῦ κρείττονος is probably a doublet of τὸ παρὰ τοῦ κρείττονος. The cicala must have been mentioned in (a) as well as in (b); something corresponding to τέττιγα . . . ἐφιζάνοντα must therefore have occurred in (a) before τὴν νευρὰν ἀνεπλήρωσεν. In (a), the verbs ἀνεπλήρωσεν and παρέσχε are in the indicative, and must therefore have been preceded by ὡς or ὅτι; in (b), the corresponding verbs are in the infinitive, and the accusative τινα shows that the lost verb of the first sentence also must have been in the infinitive.

ἀντὶ (ἄρτι MSS.) μὲν γὰρ τῆς νευρᾶς αὐτῷ τέττιγα κ.τ.λ. This tale is told, on the authority of Timaeus (c. 264 B. C.), by Strabo, 6. 1. 9, p. 260 : ἐδείκνυτο δ᾽ ἀνδριὰς ἐν Λοκροῖς (Locri in South Italy) Εὐνόμου τοῦ κιθαρῳδοῦ, τέττιγα ἐπὶ τὴν κιθάραν καθήμενον ἔχων. φησὶ δὲ Τίμαιος Πυθίοις ποτὲ ἀγωνιζομένους τοῦτόν τε καὶ Ἀρίστωνα Ῥηγῖνον ἐρίσαι ⌈περὶ τοῦ κλήρου⌉. τὸν μὲν δὴ Ἀρίστωνα δεῖσθαι τῶν Δελφῶν ἑαυτῷ συμπράττειν· . . . τοῦ δ᾽ Εὐνόμου φήσαντος ἀρχὴν μηδὲ μετεῖναι ἐκείνοις αὐτοῖς (sc. the Rhegines) τῶν περὶ φωνὴν ἀγωνισμάτων, παρ᾽ οἷς καὶ οἱ τέττιγες εἶεν ἄφωνοι,[1] τὰ εὐφθογγότατα τῶν ζῴων, ὅμως εὐδοκιμεῖν μηδὲν ἧττον τὸν Ἀρίστωνα, καὶ ἐν ἐλπίδι τὴν νίκην ἔχειν· νικῆσαι μέντοι τὸν Εὔνομον, καὶ ἀναθεῖναι τὴν λεχθεῖσαν εἰκόνα ἐν τῇ πατρίδι, ἐπειδὴ κατὰ τὸν ἀγῶνα μιᾶς τῶν χορδῶν ῥαγείσης ἐπιστὰς[2] τέττιξ ἐκπληρώσειε τὸν φθόγγον.

Clem. Alex. *Protrept.* 1 : ἔχοιμ᾽ ἄν σοι καὶ ἄλλον τούτοις ἀδελφὸν[3] διηγήσασθαι μῦθον, ⌈καὶ ᾠδὸν⌉ Εὔνομον τὸν Λοκρὸν καὶ τέττιγα τὸν Πυθικόν. πανήγυρις Ἑλληνικὴ ἐπὶ νεκρῷ δράκοντι συνεκροτεῖτο Πυθοῖ, ἐπιτάφιον ἑρπετοῦ ᾄδοντος Εὐνόμου. . . . ἀγὼν δὲ ἦν, καὶ ἐκιθάριζεν ὥρᾳ καύματος Εὔνομος, ὁπηνίκα οἱ τέττιγες ὑπὸ τοῖς πετάλοις ᾖδον ἀνὰ τὰ ὄρη θερόμενοι ἡλίῳ. . . . ῥήγνυται χορδὴ τῷ Λοκρῷ. ἐφίπταται [ὁ] τέττιξ τῷ ζυγῷ· ἐτερέτιζεν ὡς ἐπὶ κλάδῳ τῷ ὀργάνῳ· καὶ τοῦ τέττιγος ⌈τῷ ᾄσματι ἁρμοσάμενος ὁ ᾠδὸς⌉ τὴν λείπουσαν ἀνεπλήρωσε χορδήν.[4] οὐκοῦν ᾠδῇ τῇ Εὐνόμου ἄγεται ὁ τέττιξ, ὡς ὁ μῦθος βούλεται. χαλκοῦν ⌈ἀναστήσας⌉[5] Πυθοῖ[6] τὸν Εὔνομον αὐτῇ τῇ κιθάρᾳ καὶ τὸν συναγωνιστὴν

---

[1] Strabo has just said that in the territory of Rhegium the cicalas are mute, whereas those across the border, in the territory of Locri, sing like the rest of their kind.

[2] Perhaps ἐπιπτὰς.

[3] I. e. similar to the tales told about Amphion, Arion, and Orpheus.

[4] Sense might be made by reading either τοῦ τέττιγος τὸ ᾆσμα [ ] τὴν λείπουσαν ἀνεπλήρωσε χορδήν, or τοῦ τέττιγος τῷ ᾄσματι ⟨τὴν κιθάραν⟩ ἁρμοσάμενος ὁ ᾠδὸς τὴν λ. ἀ. χ.

[5] Perhaps ἀνέστησαν. It could not be said that the μῦθος set up a statue.

[6] Strabo speaks of a statue at Locri; Clement speaks of a statue at Delphi. There must have been somewhere a statue of a musician with a cicala perched on his lyre ; and no doubt the story was invented to account for the statue.

τοῦ Λοκροῦ.[1] Clement ignores the point of the story ; for he uses it merely to show that, according to the mistaken belief of the Pagans, animals have sometimes been charmed by music.[2]

Pseudo-Julian *Ep.* 186 Bidez and Cumont, 421 d (a letter to Iamblichus, written by a *rhetor*, probably about A. D. 325) : ἤδη που . . . κιθαρῳδῷ τὸν ὄρθιον (*sc.* νόμον) ᾄδοντι πρὸς τὸ ἐλλεῖπον τῆς χορδῆς ὑπὸ τῷ τέττιγι τὸ ἴσον ὁ Πύθιος ἀντεφθέγξατο.

κατὰ πρόνοιαν τοῦ κρείττονος. τὸ κρεῖττον means τὸ θεῖον or ὁ θεός.

§ 7 a. οὕτως οὖν καὶ αὐτὸς αἰσθάνομαι πάσχειν. The orator's bodily organs, or merely human faculties, correspond to the strings of the musician's lyre. They are defective ; but the deficiency is made good by an influx of divine inspiration, just as in the story the broken string was replaced by the cicala. The orator himself, as distinguished from his organs or faculties, corresponds to the musician in the story.

The application of the analogy of music in this paragraph is different from that in §§ 3, 4, according to which God is the musician, and the orator is the instrument on which God plays. When God is the player, there is nothing that can be compared to the cicala which was sent to help the player.

ἄρτι μὲν γὰρ τὴν ἀσθένειαν καθωμολόγησα (καθομολογεῖν ἔοικα MSS.). This refers to τῆς περὶ τὸ σῶμα ἀσθενείας χάριν in § 3. The orator's ' body' is a lyre with a broken string. There would be no sense in saying '*it seems that* I am (or was) confessing', when it is an unquestionable fact that the speaker has confessed; I have therefore cut out ἔοικα here, and written ⟨⟨ἔοικα⟩⟩ μουσουργ⟨ήσ⟩ειν below.

πρὸ βραχέος ἀρρώστως διακεῖσθαι (καθωμολόγησα) is an alternative for ἄρτι . . . τὴν ἀσθένειαν καθωμολόγησα.

§ 7 b. τοιγάρτοι τὸ πέρας τῆς ⌐ὠφελείας⌐ ἐστ[α]ὶ βασιλέων εὔκλεια. Down to this point, the orator has been speaking of himself ; he has told his audience that he is a man inspired by God. He now proceeds to announce the subject of his oration ; it is to be a speech ' in praise of kings '. πέρας here means ' end ' in the sense of ' aim ' or ' object' (σκοπός). Cf. Lucian *Harmonides* 2 : ἐπὶ τὸ πέρας ἀφίξῃ τῆς εὐχῆς. *Ib.* 3: ἐπὶ πέρας ἥκειν με τῆς ἐλπίδος. It is impossible to make sense of ὠφελείας. The author may perhaps have written ἐπαγγελίας ; cf. τοῖς . . . ἐπαγγελλομένοις in § 1 *init.*

---

[1] I. e. τὸν τέττιγα. The cicala 'helped him in the contest'.
[2] *Ib.* § 2 : πῇ δὴ οὖν μύθοις κενοῖς πεπιστεύκατε, θέλγεσθαι μουσικῇ τὰ ζῷα ὑπολαμβάνοντες, κ.τ.λ.

474   CORPVS HERMETICVM

ἐκ τῶν (τῶν ἐξ MSS.) ἐκείνων τροπαίων ἡ τοῦ λόγου προθυμία. It is because of the victories which our kings (i. e. the reigning Augusti and Caesares) have won that I am eager to tell forth their praise. As to ἡ τοῦ λόγου προθυμία, one might compare *Ps.* 44 (45). 1 : ἐξηρεύξατο ἡ καρδία μου λόγον ἀγαθόν· λέγω ἐγὼ τὰ ἔργα μου τῷ βασιλεῖ.

ἄγε δὴ ἴωμεν· τοῦτο γὰρ [[ὁ μουσουργὸς]] ⟨ὁ θεὸς⟩ βούλεται. The μουσουργός spoken of in this section is the orator himself. The word cannot here mean God, the Musician who uses the orator as his instrument ; for it could hardly be said that God 'will make sweeter melody' (λιγυρώτερον μελῳδήσει) when he deals with a loftier theme. Cf. § 9 *init.*, where ὁ μουσουργός is spoken of as praising God, and therefore cannot be God, and must be the orator. But if ὁ μουσουργός means the orator, τοῦτο ὁ μουσουργὸς βούλεται would mean merely 'I wish this', which would be intolerably feeble and pointless ; I have therefore substituted ὁ θεός for ὁ μουσουργός in this clause.

[ἄγε δὴ σπεύσωμεν· τοῦτο γὰρ ὁ μουσουργὸς θέλει.] This is an alternative for ἄγε δὴ ἴωμεν . . . βούλεται.

[καὶ πρὸς τοῦτο τὴν λύραν ἥρμοσται.] I have bracketed these words, because they too closely resemble τὰ τῆς λύρας ἐνήρμοσται in § 8 *init.*

ὅσῳπερ τὰ τῆς ὑποθήκης μείζονα [τὴν ᾠδὴν] ἔχει. τὰ τῆς ὑποθήκης means τὴν ὑπόθεσιν, 'his theme'. The subject of ἔχει is ὁ μουσουργός ; but a reader took τὰ τῆς ὑποθ. to be the subject of the verb, and inserted τὴν ᾠδήν to serve as object.

§ 8. εἰς βασιλέας αὐτῷ μάλιστα τὰ τῆς λύρας ἐνήρμοσται, καὶ τῶν ἐγκωμίων τὸν τόνον ἔχει. The orator is prepared (1) to speak of *kings*, and (2) to speak in *praise* of them. But it may be suspected that the author wrote εἰς βασιλέων ἐγκώμιον αὐτῷ μάλιστα τὰ τῆς λύρας ἐνήρμοσται, and that καὶ . . . τόνον ἔχει is a subsequent addition. The following words, [καὶ τὸν σκοπὸν εἰς βασιλικοὺς ἐπαίνους], are mere repetition of this.

τοὺς κατ' εἰκόνα ἐκείνου τὴν σκηπτουχίαν ἔχοντας. Earthly kings are εἰκόνες of God, the supreme King. The thought is similar to that of Hor. *Od.* 3. 1. 5 : 'regum timendorum in proprios greges, reges in ipsos imperium est Iovis, clari giganteo triumpho, cuncta supercilio moventis.' (*Clari giganteo triumpho* corresponds to καλλίνικος πρῶτος in § 9.)

§ 9. ὃς ἀθάνατος μέν ἐστι [διὰ παντὸς] [ἀίδιός τε] καὶ ἐξ ἀιδίου τὸ κράτος ἔχων. An earthly king reigns for a little time ; but God lives and reigns from a past without beginning to a future without end. διὰ παντός is a meaningless addition to ἀθάνατος, which of itself implies ' living on through all time '. Perhaps ὃς ἀΐδιος μέν ἐστι καὶ ἐξ ἀιδίου τὸ κράτος ἔχων would be more satisfactory.

§ 15. ⟨⟨οὕτω μὲν δὴ τὸν θεὸν . . . ἡ πρὸς τοὺς βασιλέας εὐφημία.⟩⟩ In § 11, the speaker says ' I will now *end* my speech by praising God '. All that followed § 11 must therefore have had to do with God, and not with human kings. But §§ 15 and 16 have to do with human kings, and not with God. It is evident then that these two sections are out of place, and must have been shifted from an earlier position. § 15 fits in well after § 9, and § 16 after § 10.

δεῖ γὰρ [ἀπὸ τῶν βασιλέων ἀρξαμένους καὶ] ἀπὸ τούτων ἀσκουμένους. The speaker has said ' I will begin with God ' (§ 8), and has done so (§ 9). He would be contradicting himself if he then proceeded to say ' we must *begin* with human kings '. But he might very well say ' it is good to praise human kings, because the practice which we get in doing so will enable us to praise God better ',—especially as it is his intention, after speaking of human kings, to come back to the subject of God, and praise him again at greater length (§ 11 ff.).

§ 10. ἐπὶ ⟨τοὺς τούτων⟩ ἐπαίνους τοίνυν ἡμῖν καταβαίνει ὁ λόγος. This is almost a repetition of ἀλλὰ δὴ καταβαίνομεν καὶ ἐπὶ τοὺς δεξαμένους παρ' ἐκείνου τὰ σκῆπτρα in § 15. But perhaps καταβαίνει may have been substituted for some other verb.

οἷς [πάλαι] μάλιστα τὸ κῦρος ἀρὰ τοῦ κρείττονος [θεοῦ] κεκορύφωται. This looks like a reminiscence of Pindar *Ol.* 1. 182: ἐπ' ἄλλοισι δ' ἄλλοι μεγάλοι, τὸ δ' ἔσχατον κορυφοῦται βασιλεῦσι ('the topmost summit is for kings', Gildersleeve). πάλαι may have arisen out of a duplication of μάλιστα.

οἷς ἡ νίκη πρὸς τῆς ἐκείνου δεξιᾶς πεπρυτάνευται. τῆς ἐκείνου δεξιᾶς is probably a sign of Jewish influence. The ' right hand ' of God is often spoken of in the Old Testament; e. g. *Ps.* 117 (118). 15: δεξιὰ Κυρίου ἐποίησε δύναμιν, δεξιὰ Κυρίου ὕψωσέν με.

οἷς τὰ βραβεῖα καὶ πρὸ τῆς ἐν πολέμοις [ἀρρωστίας] ⟨ἀριστείας⟩ προευτρέπισται. This probably means that a mere threat of war is enough to make the enemy yield, so that there is no need for actual fighting. Perhaps the speaker alludes especially to the recently concluded treaty of peace with the Persians; for though battles were fought with them in 296 and 297, the Persian king recognized the superiority of the forces organized by Diocletian before they were fully brought into action, and the settlement with which the war ended was considered a triumph of Roman diplomacy rather than a conquest by force of arms. *Paneg.* X. 7. 5: ' . . . antequam

Diocletiano sponte se dederent regna Persarum. Verum hoc Iovis sui more nutu illo patrio, quo omnia contremescunt, et maiestate vestri nominis consecutus est.' *Ib.* 10. 6 : ' Rex ille Persarum, numquam se ante dignatus hominem confiteri, fratri tuo (i. e. Diocletiano) supplicat, totumque, si ingredi ille dignetur, regnum suum pandit ; . . . amicitiae nomen impetrare contentus promeretur obsequio.' *Paneg.* XI. 5. 4 : ' etiam illa quae armorum vestrorum terrore facta sunt velut armis gesta praetereo, Francos ad petendam pacem cum rege venientes, Parthumque vobis munerum miraculis blandientem.' Cf. *Paneg.* VIII (V). 13. 1 (of the recovery of Britain by Constantius) : ' Hoc igitur bellum . . . ita, Caesar, adgressus es, ut, statim atque illo infestum maiestatis fulmen intenderas, confectum omnibus videretur.'

[οἷς οὐ τὸ βασιλεύειν μόνον ἀλλὰ καὶ τὸ ἀριστεύειν συντέτακται.] This feeble clause is an a ticlimax after the more vigorous phrases which precede it ; and τὸ ἀριστεύειν is a repetition of ἀριστείας (ἀρρωστίας MSS.). It is very likely that one or two of the other parallel clauses also are interpolations. Perhaps the sentence originally ended at προευτρέπισται, and ὧν . . . ἵσταται and οὓς . . . τὸ βάρβαρον, as well as οἷς . . . συντέτακται, were subsequently added. (Note the rhythmical correspondence of κεκορύφωται, πεπρυτάνευται, and προευτρέπισται.)

§ 16. τοσαύτης (τοσαύτην ?) ἡμῖν εἰρήνης εὐετηρίαν ἁπλώσασι κ.τ.λ. The thought expressed by τοὺς τῆς κοινῆς ἀσφαλείας καὶ εἰρήνης πρυτάνεις in § 10 is carried on and amplified in what is said about εἰρήνη in § 16. εἰρήνης εὐετηρίαν is rather awkward ; it is possible that the original reading was τοσαύτην ἡμῖν εἰρήνην ἁπλώσασι, and that εὐετηρίαν was written as an alternative for εἰρήνην.

καὶ ⟨διὰ⟩ τοῦ λόγου [τοῦ εἰς εἰρήνην (al. καὶ τῆς εἰρήνης)] κρατεῖ. This must be intended for an explanation of βάσει λείᾳ ταῖς κορυφαῖς ἐπεμβαίνει. The true king gets the mastery by reason or persuasion (and not by force) ; his authority meets with no resistance ; and so he attains to the topmost height ' with smooth tread ', i. e. by peaceful means. But it may be suspected that the words καὶ ⟨διὰ⟩ τοῦ λόγου κρατεῖ were added by a later hand, and that the passage originally ran thus : βασιλεὺς γὰρ διὰ τοῦτο εἴρηται, ἐπειδὴ βάσει λείᾳ ταῖς κορυφαῖς ἐπεμβαίνει· ὥστε καὶ τοὔνομα σύμβολόν ἐστιν εἰρήνης.

[καὶ ὅτι γε ὑπερέχειν πέφυκε [τῆς βασιλείας] τῆς βαρβαρικῆς.] If we retain the traditional text, we get the statement that kings, as such, are necessarily victorious over certain kings. This absurdity can be avoided by cutting out τῆς βασιλείας, supplying γῆς with τῆς βαρβαρικῆς, and assuming that the writer applied the term βασιλεύς to the Roman emperors alone.

[τοιγάρτοι καὶ ἐπηγορία βασιλέως πολλάκις εὐθὺς τὸν πολέμιον ἀνέστειλεν (ἀναστέλλειν πέφυκεν MSS.)]. πέφυκεν can hardly be combined with πολλάκις; and it may very well be a mistaken repetition of πέφυκε above.

In this paragraph, the speaker is talking about the blessings of peace; it is therefore inappropriate here to speak of driving back the enemy in war. For the same reason I have bracketed ἐνήργησε τὴν νίκην καί below.

καὶ οἱ ἀνδριάντες οἱ τούτου τοῖς μάλιστα χειμαζομένοις ὅρμοι τυγχάνουσιν [εἰρήνης]. This probably refers to the practice of claiming ἀσυλία (ius asyli) by clinging to a statue of the emperor. Do the words ἤδη δὲ καὶ μόνη εἰκὼν φανεῖσα βασιλέως τὸ ἄτρομον προυξένησε refer to that same practice, or to incidents of some other kind?[1]

§ 14 b. ⟨⟨οὐκ ἔστιν οὖν ⟨τοῖς⟩ ἐκεῖσε . . . ἁρμονίαν τῶν πάντων.⟩⟩ ἐκεῖσε (= ἐκεῖ) means 'in heaven'; and οἱ ἐκεῖσε are the astral gods. In this passage the orator speaks of gods, but not of God; it cannot therefore have formed part of the peroration (§ 11 ff.), which consisted of 'praise of God'; and it is presumably a detached fragment of the lost 'praise of earthly kings' which preceded § 11. The unanimity of the celestial gods was doubtless spoken of as a type or pattern of the unanimity of the kings (Diocletian and his colleagues). Cf. Aelius Aristides Περὶ ὁμονοίας ταῖς πόλεσιν, 23. 76 f., vol. ii, p. 52 f. Keil: οὗτος (sc. concord) ὁ τῶν πόλεων κόσμος ἀληθινός . . . · ἐπεὶ καὶ τὸν πάντα οὐρανὸν καὶ κόσμον . . . μία δή που γνώμη καὶ φιλίας δύναμις διοικεῖ· καὶ μετὰ ταύτης ἥλιός τε πορεύεται τὴν αὑτοῦ χώραν φυλάττων δι' αἰῶνος, καὶ σελήνης φάσματα καὶ ἀστέρων φορὰ χωρεῖ, . . . καὶ τάξεις ἑκάστων πρὸς ἄλληλα . . . φυλάττονται, νικώσης τῆς ὁμολογίας, διαφορᾶς δὲ οὐδεμίας ἐνούσης οὐδὲ ἐγγιγνομένης, ἀλλὰ τῷ θεσμῷ πάντων συγκεχωρηκότων, καὶ μιᾷ γνώμῃ περὶ παντὸς τοῦ προσ-

---

[1] Schiller, Gesch. der röm. Kaizerzeit II, p. 34 : ' in the third century, the images of the emperors played an important part, and one of the first cares of a new government is to set up such images, and to send them to the provinces. From the time of Maxentius onward, we can see more exactly what was meant by sending them. When Maxentius got the sovereignty, he caused his image to be carried about in Africa, and thereby publicly proclaimed his rule. This practice had developed out of a custom of the camps. The image of the reigning emperor stood in the shrine of the camp, and received divine worship there; the fall of an emperor caused this image to be thrown down, and when a new emperor was appointed, his image was at once set up.' Paneg. Lat. VIII (V). 15. 6 : ' Demens qui nesciebat, quacunque fugeret, ubique vim vestrae divinitatis esse, ubi vultus vestri, ubi signa (statuae) colerentur.'

ἥκοντος χρωμένων· ὥστ᾽ εἰ τὸ μιμεῖσθαι τοὺς κρείττους εὖ φρονούντων ἐστίν, εὖ φρονούντων ἂν εἴη καὶ τὸ ὡς οἷόν τε μάλιστα ἕν τι τοὺς σύμπαντας αὐτοὺς ἡγεῖσθαι. ὑπάρχει δ᾽ ὑμῖν καὶ τῶν ἀνθρωπείων παράδειγμα ἐν ὀφθαλμοῖς τὸ μέγιστον, οἱ πάντα ἄριστοι βασιλεῖς (M. Aurelius and L. Verus, A. D. 161–169), οἷς πολλῶν καὶ μεγάλων ὑπαρχόντων κάλλιστον εἶναι δοκεῖ ἡ πρὸς ἀλλήλους ὁμόνοια καὶ σπουδή. . . . καὶ μὴν βασιλεῖς μὲν ἄριστ᾽ ἂν ἄγοιεν τὰ τῶν ἀνθρώπων πράγματα τοῖς τῶν ὅλων κυρίοις ὁμοιοῦντες ἑαυτοὺς τοῖς θεοῖς, πόλεις δ᾽ ἄριστ᾽ ἂν ἄγοιντο ἐγγυτάτω τῆς τῶν ἀρχόντων γνώμης ἰοῦσαι. Paneg. VIII (V). 4. 1 : ' Illa Iovis et Herculis cognata maiestas in Iovio Herculioque principibus (i. e. Diocletian and Maximian) totius mundi caelestiumque rerum similitudinem requirebat. Quippe isto numinis vestri numero (i. e. the number four) summa omnia nituntur et gaudent : elementa quattuor, . . . et duobus caeli luminibus (i. e sun and moon) adiuncti Vesper et Lucifer.' Paneg. X. 10. 1 (to Maximian) : ' Vos vero, qui imperium non terrae, sed caeli regionibus terminatis, tantam vim, tantam potestatem mutuo vobis impartire divinae profecto immortalisque fiduciae est, quam cupiditas nulla perturbet.' . . . 11. 1 : ' Vestra hoc concordia facit, invictissimi principes, ut vobis tanta aequalitate successuum etiam fortuna respondeat. Rempublicam enim una mente regitis ; neque vobis tanta locorum diversitas obest quominus etiam velut iunctis dexteris gubernetis. Ita, quamvis maiestatem regiam geminato numine augeatis, utilitatem imperii singularis consentiendo retinetis.' Paneg. XI. 6. 3 (to Maximian) : ' Quanta vosmet invicem pietate colitis ! Quae enim umquam videre saecula talem in summa potestate concordiam ? Qui germani geminive fratres indiviso patrimonio tam aequabiliter utuntur quam vos orbe Romano ? Ex quo profecto manifestum est . . . animas esse . . . vestras . . . caelestes et sempiternas.'

[μία δὲ πάντων πρόγνωσις.] The star-gods foresee and collectively predict the future. This seems to be an allusion to astrology ; but if so, it is irrelevant here.

εἰς αὐτοῖς νοῦς [ ], μία αἴσθησις. The writer of *Corp.* IX speaks of the νόησις and αἴσθησις of the Kosmos, and the νόησις and αἴσθησις of God.

[δι᾽ αὐτῶν ἐργαζομένη.] ἐργαζομένη has come by duplication from ἐργαζόμενος below.

τὸ ⟨γὰρ⟩ εἰς ἀλλήλους φίλτρον ἔρως ὁ αὐτός. That which unites them to one another (as if by a magic charm), and makes peace and harmony among them, is their ἔρως (τοῦ καλοῦ, or τοῦ θεοῦ), which

is the same in each and all of them. The word ἔρως here carries
with it its Platonic associations. For φίλτρον, cf. Plut. *Numa* 16 :
τὴν γεωργίαν . . . οἶον εἰρήνης φίλτρον ἐμμίξας τοῖς πολίταις.

§ 11. ἀλλὰ σπεύδει ὁ ⌜λόγος⌝ . . . περατῶσαι τὸν λόγον. ὁ λόγος
has been substituted by error for some term meaning ' the
speaker '.

This is the beginning of the peroration. The whole of the
discourse in praise of the reigning ' kings ', which must have followed
§§ 1–10 ⟨⟨16⟩⟩, and preceded § 11, has been lost, with the exception
of the misplaced fragment 14 b.

[ἔπειτα δὲ καὶ τῶν θειοτάτων βασιλέων τῶν εἰρήνην ἡμῖν βραβευόντων.]
There ought to be no mention of kings here. The meaning must
have been that the orator, having been employed in praising earthly
kings throughout the main body of his speech, will now end by
praising God, as he began by doing so (§§ 8, 9). The simile which
follows (ὥσπερ ὁ ἥλιος κ.τ.λ.) supplies a reason for praising God, but
not for praising kings. The words ἔπειτα . . . βραβευόντων must
have been added after §§ 15, 16, in which earthly kings are spoken
of, had been shifted from their original position to the end of
the text.

[ὥσπερ γὰρ ἐκ τοῦ κρείττονος [καὶ τῆς ἄνω δυνάμεως] ἠρξάμεθα, οὕτως
εἰς αὐτὸ πάλιν τὸ κρεῖττον ἀντανακλάσομεν τὸ πέρας.] This is a
paraphrase of the preceding sentence, and was most likely written
as an explanatory note on it. The words εἰς . . . τὸ κρεῖττον
ἀντανακλάσομεν τὸ πέρας directly contradict ἔπειτα δὲ καὶ τῶν θειοτάτων
βασιλέων κ.τ.λ. If the speaker said that he was going to *end* his
oration by talking about God, he could not say that he was going
to pass on *afterwards* to human kings.

τῆς ἄνω δυνάμεως is a correct but superfluous explanation of τοῦ
κρείττονος.

ὥσπερ ὁ ἥλιος . . . τὴν βλάστην ἅπασαν κ.τ.λ. The Sun fosters the
growth of plants by pouring down his light and heat upon them ;
and when they have grown and flowered, he draws out their fragrance,
and takes it to himself as the firstfruits of the produce.   Thus the
sweet scents which rise from the plants are a payment which the
Sun receives from them in return for what he has done for them.—
God is to us as the Sun is to the plants. He fosters the growth of
our souls (i. e. develops our faculties) by pouring down on us ' the
efflux of his wisdom ' ; and it is our duty to use in his worship the
powers which he has made to grow up in us. We ought then to

send up our songs of praise to God, to whose fostering we owe it
that we have power to sing, as the plants give forth their fragrance
to the Sun, to whose fostering they owe it that they have power to
give forth fragrance.

[πρῶτος (πρῶτον ?) ἀνασχών.] There is no reason to speak of the
sunrise here. It is not 'on his first rising' only, but throughout
the day, that the Sun both fosters the growth of plants and draws
out their fragrance.

τῶν καρπῶν τὰς ἀπαρχάς. The scent of the flowers is regarded as
the 'firstlings' of the produce which the plants will yield when the
fruit has ripened. The heat of the sun makes the flowers give
forth their scent; and this is what is meant by saying that the
Sun ' plucks the sweet odours of the plants with his rays '.

χερσὶ μεγίσταις [   ] ταῖς ἀκτῖσι. This is repeated in the words
[καὶ χεῖρες αὐτῷ αἱ ἀκτῖνες]. The notion might be illustrated by the
carvings of Ikhnaton, the heretic king of Egypt, in which the sun-
disk is depicted sending forth rays, each of which terminates in
a hand.

[ἀπὸ τοῦ κρείττονος ἀρξαμένοις καί.] This has nothing to do with
the simile of the Sun. The interpolation was suggested by ἐκ τοῦ
κρείττονος . . . ἠρξάμεθα in the preceding sentence.

τὰ [ἡμέτερα] τῶν ψυχῶν [ὑπερ]ουράνια φυτά. This is a reminiscence
of Pl. *Tim.* 90 A : πρὸς δὲ τὴν ἐν οὐρανῷ ξυγγένειαν . . . ἡμᾶς αἴρειν, ὡς
ὄντας φυτὸν οὐκ ἐγγεῖον ἀλλὰ οὐράνιον. See note on *Ascl. Lat.* I. 6 b,
'desuper deorsum radices pervenientes.'

καταχρωμένοις πάλιν εἰς αὐτὸ(ν) [   ] [   ] τὴν βλάστην ἅπασαν. ἡ
βλάστη ἅπασα is that in us which corresponds to πάντα τὰ βλαστήματα
in the case of the plants nurtured by the Sun; that is, it means the
faculties which God has developed in us by means of the ἀπόρροια
τῆς ἐκείνου σοφίας which he has poured down on us. We must
apply these faculties to the worship of Him from whom we have
received them.

[γυμναστέον τὰ τῆς εὐφημίας]. The verb γυμνάζειν is meaningless
in this context; it must have come from § 15, where γυμνασία is
spoken of. But γυμναστέον may have taken the place of some other
verbal in -τέον; and we might get a satisfactory construction for
the sentence by writing ἀνοιστέον τὰ τῆς εὐφημίας (cf. τὴν εὐφημίαν
ἀναφέρεσθαι πρέπει in § 12), and placing these words before
καταχρωμένοις. The praise which we send up to God corresponds
to the scent which the sun's heat draws forth from the flowers.

[ἧς αὐτὸς ἡμῖν ἐπομβρήσει.] ἐπομβρεῖν τί τινι means 'to rain down something on something'. ἐπομβρίζειν is sometimes used in the same sense, but occurs also in the sense 'to water (something) with rain'. If we write ἦν αὐτὸς ἡμῖν ἐπώμβρισεν, and put this after τὴν βλάστην ἅπασαν, we get a possible meaning: 'all the growth (of faculties within us) which God has watered (with the ἀπόρροια of his wisdom)', i. e. which God has fostered by showering down his wisdom on us. A mention of rain seems inappropriate in a sentence in which God is compared to the Sun; but perhaps the Sun, as lord of heaven, might be considered to send down rain upon the plants as well as light and heat.

A man speaking in Egypt would not be likely to mention 'rain' in this connexion; it may therefore be thought probable that this phrase at least, if not the whole oration, was written elsewhere than in Egypt. But the word ἐπομβρίζειν might perhaps be applied to irrigation also.

§ 12. τῷ πατρὶ τῶν ἡμετέρων ψυχῶν. In this paragraph the simile of the Sun is dropped, and the relation between God and men is described by a different figure; 'we are God's infant children'.

κᾶν εἰ μὴ [τὸ] πρὸς ἀξίαν ἔστιν εἰπεῖν. Cf. Pseudo-Aristides Εἰς βασιλέα, 35. 3 f., vol. ii, p. 254 Keil: ὅμως δὲ οὐκ ἀποδειλιατέον, ἀλλ' ὅση δύναμις πειρατέον εἰπεῖν. οὐδὲ γὰρ ἂν θύωμεν τοῖς θεοῖς, τὸ πρὸς ἀξίαν, οἶμαι, ⌜ὁρῶντες⌝ (ὁρῶντες ?) τοῦτο ποιοῦμεν, ἀλλ' ὅσον δυνατὸν ἡμῖν χάριν αὐτοῖς ταύτην ἀποτίνομεν.

[καὶ συγγνώμην ἔχουσιν.] This unduly anticipates αἰτητέον δὲ τὰ τῆς συγγνώμης κ.τ.λ. in § 13; and it is not wanted here, as the word πρεπόντως sufficiently implies that all is well when the children do the best they can.

τὸ μείζονα αὐτὸν εἶναι ⟨τοῦ⟩ τῶν ἑαυτοῦ γεννημάτων ⟨ἐπαίνου⟩. It would be absurd to say that 'the fact that God is greater than his offspring' redounds to his glory; it is small glory to a father that he is taller and stronger than his infant children. The thing which redounds to God's glory must be this,—that the utmost that men can say is too little to describe his greatness. Cf. Corp. I. 31: ἅγιος εἶ, ὁ κρείττων ⟨πάν⟩των ἐπαίνων.

τὸ ὁμολογεῖν τὸν πατέρα ἀπειροδύναμον ⟨εἶναι⟩ καὶ ⌜ἀπειροτέρμονα⌝. God's power and (goodness?) are infinite; (and we, being finite, are incapable of describing what is infinite.) All that we can say in praise of God amounts to no more than acknowledging this.

ἀπειροτέρμων does not occur elsewhere. It ought to signify 'having infinite boundaries or limits'; but that, if it means anything at all, can only mean what would be more clearly expressed by ἄπειρος or ἀτέρμων.

§ 13. [φύσει γὰρ ἡμῖν τοῖς ἀνθρώποις, ὥσπερ ἐκγόνοις [ἀπ'] ἐκείνου τυγχάνουσι, τὰ τῆς εὐφημίας ἔνεστιν.] The sentence interrupts the sequence of thought. It is probably part of an explanatory note on the paragraph.

⟨⟨καὶ⟩⟩ ὥσπερ [[καὶ]] τοὺς [ ] ἀρτιγενεῖς . . . χαίρειν ἐπὶ τῆς ἐπιγνώσεως, οὕτω[σι δὲ] καὶ ⟨ἡμᾶς . . .⟩. In the preceding sentence, it was said that God pardons us for the inadequacy of our praise. In this sentence, the speaker goes further, and says that God not only pardons us, but takes pleasure in our praise, inadequate though it be. For χαίρειν ἐπὶ τῆς ἐπιγνώσεως, cf. Corp. I. 31 : ἅγιος ὁ θεός, ὃς γνωσθῆναι βούλεται.

⌜καὶ τὴν εἰς θεὸν εὐφημίαν ἣν ἡμῖν ἐδωρήσατο⌝. The subject of ἐδωρήσατο must be God ; and its object cannot be τὴν εὐφημίαν, but might be τὴν τῆς εὐφημίας δύναμιν, 'our power to praise him'. Perhaps the original may have been something like (ὁ θεὸς) τὴν τῆς εὐφημίας δύναμιν ἡμῖν ἐδωρήσατο ; and it is possible that this may have come from a note on the simile of the Sun in § 11. It is fitting that we should praise God, because it is from him that we have received our power to praise.

§ 14 a. ἐν ⟨ἑ⟩αυτῷ [ ] τῆς οἰκείας ἀριπρεπείας (ἀειπρεπείας MSS.) ἔχων τὸ πέρας. God's pre-eminence is limited by himself alone, i. e. by nothing external to him. This seems to be a roundabout way of saying that God's greatness is infinite. God is αὐτοπερίγραφος, and therefore ἀπερίγραφος. Compare the use of αὐτογέννητος as an equivalent for ἀγέννητος.

ἀθάνατος δὲ ὤν, καὶ [ἐν ἑαυτῷ] τὴν ἀτελεύτητον λῆξιν [περιέχων] [ ] [ ] ἀπὸ τῆς [ ] ⟨⟨ἀεν[ν]άου⟩⟩ ἐνεργείας καὶ εἰς τόνδε τὸν κόσμον παρέχων. ἐν ἑαυτῷ has been repeated by error ; and περιέχων is a doublet of παρέχων.—τὴν ἀτελεύτητον λῆξιν must be taken to mean τὴν τῆς ἀτελευτησίας λῆξιν, 'its appointed lot of endless existence'. God, being himself immortal (or eternal), bestows everlasting duration on the Kosmos. Cf. Pl. Tim. 39 D and 41 B; Corp. VIII. 2 as emended : ὁ δὴ κόσμος ὑπὸ τοῦ πατρὸς ἀιδίου ὄντος ἀθάνατος γέγονε.

⌜τὴν ἐπαγγελίαν εἰς διασωστικὴν εὐφημίαν⌝. The sentence ends with these meaningless words ; and the rest of the 'praise of God' with which the oration concluded has been lost.

PRINTED IN ENGLAND
AT THE OXFORD UNIVERSITY PRESS

$20.00